CAN "THE WHOLE WORLD" BE WRONG?

Lethal Journalism, Antisemitism, and Global Jihad

Antisemitism in America
Series Editor: Eunice Pollack (University of North Texas, Denton, Texas)

CAN "THE WHOLE WORLD" BE WRONG?

Lethal Journalism, Antisemitism, and Global Jihad

RICHARD LANDES

BOSTON
2022

Library of Congress Cataloging-in-Publication Data

Names: Landes, Richard, 1949- author.
Title: Can "the whole world" be wrong? : lethal journalism, antisemitism, and global jihad / Richard Landes.
Description: Boston : Academic Studies Press, 2022. | Series: Antisemitism in America | Includes bibliographical references and index.
Identifiers: LCCN 2022024877 (print) | LCCN 2022024878 (ebook) | ISBN 9781644696408 (hardback) | ISBN 9781644699942 (paperback) | ISBN 9781644696415 (adobe pdf) | ISBN 9781644696422 (epub)
Subjects: LCSH: Antisemitism--United States--History--21st century. | Muslims--United States--Attitudes. | Islam--Relations--Judaism--History--21st century. | Religious right--United States--History--21st century. | United States--Ethnic relations--History--21st century.
Classification: LCC DS146.U6 L36 2022 (print) | LCC DS146.U6 (ebook) | DDC 305.892/4073--dc23/eng/20220610
LC record available at https://lccn.loc.gov/2022024877
LC ebook record available at https://lccn.loc.gov/2022024878

ISBN 9781644696408 (hardback)
ISBN 9781644699942 (paperback)
ISBN 9781644696415 (adobe pdf)
ISBN 9781644696422 (epub)

Book design by Lapiz Digital Services.
Cover design by Ivan Grave.

Published by Academic Studies Press.
1577 Beacon Street
Brookline, MA 02446, USA
press@academicstudiespress.com
www.academicstudiespress.com

Is it possible that everybody can be wrong, and the Jews be right?

—*Ahad Ha'am*, 1892 (on the gentile response to Jews denying
the blood libel)

I don't think the whole world, including the friends of the Israeli people and government, can be wrong.

—*Kofi Anan*, 2002 (in response to IDF operation in Jenin)

You will never convince anyone that the Palestinians are the aggressors.

—*Jacques Chirac* to Ehud Barak, October 4, 2000.

Stupidity is a more dangerous enemy of the good than malice. One may protest against evil; it can be exposed and, if need be, prevented by use of force. Evil always carries within itself the germ of its own subversion in that it leaves behind in human beings at least a sense of unease. Against stupidity we are defenseless. Neither protests nor the use of force accomplish anything here; reasons fall on deaf ears; facts that contradict one's prejudgment simply need not be believed—in such moments the stupid person even becomes critical—and when facts are irrefutable they are just pushed aside as inconsequential, as incidental. In all this the stupid person, in contrast to the malicious one, is utterly self-satisfied and, being easily irritated, becomes dangerous by going on the attack. For that reason, greater caution is called for when dealing with a stupid person than with a malicious one. Never again will we try to persuade the stupid person with reasons, for it is senseless and dangerous.

—*Dietrich Bonhoeffer*, Letters and Papers from Prison

If I were a Muslim, I'd take the stupidity of Westerners as a sign from Allah that I should join Global Jihad.

— Richard Landes

To all those who have been
shunned
stigmatized
canceled
made pariahs
for resisting the wave of folly this book chronicles.

Contents

Acknowledgments

It's hard to remember everyone who has helped me in this more-than-a-decade project. I hope anyone I forget will forgive me.

Thanks to Charles Jacobs for encouraging me to write this book, although the final product is nothing like what he initially imagined. In addition to those scholars whose works I cite favorably in my notes, I add the following personal friends whose conversations helped me clarify my thoughts.

Above all, my friend Steve Antler (may his memory be a blessing) who did not live long enough to see this book to its conclusion and to Noam Yavor, my tolerant friend and talented video editor, to Charles Jacobs and Avi Goldwasser, Jacob Meskin, Nidra Poller, Mark Spero, Brenda Brasher and Stephen O'Leary, Gerard Rabinovitch, Phyllis Chesler, Lauri Regan, Asaf Romirowsky, Philip Salzman, Donna Divine, Richard Cravatts, Andrew Pessin, Jeffrey Woolf, Yitzhak Sokoloff, Pedro Zuquete, Lazar Berman, Stuart Green, Arnold Roth, Elihu Stone, Jonathan Hoffman, Liel Liebowitz, Cary Nelson, Yossi Kuperwasser, Ellen Horowitz, David and Ariel Resnikoff, Jonathan Hoffman, Damian Thompson, Daniel Eilon, my children, Aliza, Noa, and Hannah, who came into their own in its shadow, and my beloved wife Esther who has put up with it for far too long.

I also want to thank my editor Eunice Pollack, whose encouragement and fine eye have saved me from many a howler. Any that remain are my own fault. I also thank Academic Studies Press for their courage in publishing a book that others feared might cause them too much trouble.

Warning to the Reader

If I'm Right, We're in Deep Trouble

This book is not for everyone. First, it's not for people who hate democracy and want to replace it with a theocracy that re-invents inquisitorial, totalitarian efforts to police thought, and resurrects holy war (religious or secular) to eliminate designated enemies. Secondly, it's not addressed to those who think that their race, or tribe, or super-tribe, or cause gives them the right to dominate others.

It *is* addressed to people who have liberal and progressive values, especially those capable of acknowledging that, for all its flaws, Western democracy constitutes a significant and perhaps unique step in the direction of freedom and human dignity. It is addressed to those who wish to preserve and improve that record rather than go all or nothing (perfection or destruction). It is for people who can't understand why the West seems to be falling apart, torn by a culture war that pits left against right in a winner-take-all struggle that, it seems with every news cycle, has been reaching ever-more terrifying extremes.

This book is something of a take it or leave it. You're free to walk away from this analysis and write it off as the rantings of an "Israel-firster," a Zionist propagandist. And from some points of view, that's an obvious and easy way to deal with my argument. Easy, that is, as long as you're right that I'm wrong. On the other hand, if I'm right, then you, liberal, progressive, democratic, lover of human dignity and freedom, engage in very high-risk behavior by ignoring what I have to say.

As far as I can make out, some the great ironies of the twenty-first century—and there are many candidates—are:

- Since the 9–11 assault by devout Muslims, many more Muslims proudly wear hijabs in the West, and many fewer Jews, out of fear, wear kippahs in public.
- The Jewish people are the only people who are the standing targets of state-sanctioned incitement to hate and genocide, but also the only people who are themselves accused of being genocidal.
- The same people who make heroic efforts to ban hate speech that might offend others, have immense tolerance for hate speech directed at themselves and at their Jewish co-citizens.
- The postmoderns, whose philosophy was to renounce both the illusion of objectivity and grand narratives, have produced a political movement that, in the name of progressive values and peace, has adopted a war-mongering premodern grand narrative, and use "science" and "facts" to promote their cause.
- Vast numbers of people around the world want to emigrate to societies whose own elites have come to consider them the embodiment of evil.
- Western democracies, who had convinced themselves and their Jews that they had renounced Jew-hatred after the Holocaust, may be destroyed by a medieval apocalyptic movement that exploits their unacknowledged Jew-hatred.

This book tests readers' ability to think differently about what they thought they knew. Although the book is about the fate of the democratic modern world, under assault by a medieval religious movement, it focuses much of its attention on Israel's dilemma and the Western world's response to it. It cuts against the grain of much of the current public discourse about Israel, a country readily associated in the public sphere today with violence and oppression. In that sense, my take fits directly into the image, so readily and contemptuously dismissed as "Zionist propaganda," by precisely those people this book criticizes for their unthinking and foolish adoption of far more lethal propaganda from Palestinian, and beyond that, Caliphator cognitive-war factories. And one of the more striking abuses of both language and values is the way Palestinians accuse Israel of being the "new Nazis" and present themselves as the new "victims of genocide."

A major step in mainstreaming this previously marginal belief in the West was taken by Nobel-Prize winning author Jose Saramago, denouncing the state of Israel in April of 2002, at the very height of the first-ever jihadi suicide-terror campaign against a democratic nation (chapters 1, 3).

> Intoxicated mentally by the messianic dream of Greater Israel which will finally achieve the expansionist dreams of the most radical Zionism [that is, Greater Israel, from the river to the sea]; contaminated by the monstrous and rooted "certitude": that in this catastrophic and absurd world there exists a people chosen by God and that, consequently, all the actions of an obsessive, psychological and pathologically exclusivist racism are justified; educated and trained in the idea that any suffering that has been inflicted, or will be inflicted on everyone else, especially the Palestinians, will always be inferior to that which they themselves suffered in the Holocaust, the Jews endlessly scratch their own wound to keep it bleeding, to make it incurable, and they show it to the world as if it were a banner. Israeli seizes hold of the terrible words of God in Deuteronomy: "Vengeance is mine, and I will be repaid." Israel wants all of us to feel guilty, directly or indirectly, for the horrors of the Holocaust; Israel wants us to renounce the most elemental critical judgment and for us to transform ourselves into a docile echo of its will; Israel wants us to recognize de jure what, in its eyes, is a de facto reality: absolute impunity. From the point of view of the Jews, Israel cannot ever be brought to judgment, because it was tortured, gassed and incinerated in Auschwitz.[1]

This rant contains all the elements of what would become "woke" attitudes of the late teens early '20s towards those they deemed morally inferior: indignation, condemnation, scorn, and certainty.

Now replace Israel in this text with those who declare her their enemy:

---

1 Jose Saramago, "De las piedras de David a los tanques de Goliat,". *El Pais*, April 21, 2002, https://elpais.com/diario/2002/04/21/opinion/1019340007_850215.html; discussed in Paul Berman, *Terror and Liberalism* (New York: W.W. Norton, 2003), 139–44. This text is a response to reports of an Israeli "massacre" at Jenin (below, chap. 3).

Intoxicated mentally by the messianic dream of a **global Caliphate [i.e., Islam from ocean to ocean**], which will finally achieve the expansionist dreams of the most radical **Muslims**; contaminated by the monstrous and rooted "certitude" that in this catastrophic and absurd world there exists a people chosen by **Allah** and that, consequently, all the actions of an obsessive, psychological and pathologically exclusivist **religious triumphalism** are justified; educated and trained in the idea that any suffering that has been inflicted, or will be inflicted on everyone else, especially on the **Jews**, will always be inferior to that which they themselves suffered in the **Nakba, the Palestinians** endlessly scratch their own wound to keep it bleeding, to make it incurable, and they show it to the world as if it were a banner. **Jihadis** seize hold of the terrible words of **Allah in the Quran (8:12): "I will cast terror into the hearts of those who disbelieve. Therefore, strike off their heads and strike off every fingertip of them."** Palestinians want all of us to feel guilty, directly or indirectly, for the horrors of the **Nakba; Caliphators** want us to renounce the most elemental critical judgment and for us to transform ourselves into a docile echo of their will; **Caliphators** want us to recognize de jure what, in their eyes, is a de facto reality: absolute **Muslim** impunity. From the point of view of the **Muslims, Islam** cannot ever be brought to judgment, because the **infidel** has humiliated it, and because **Allah** is on their side.

What we have in these two paragraphs is the double inversion so characteristic of twenty-first century public discourse. On the one hand, while both these statements are true of *some* Jews and *some* Palestinians/Muslims, the ugly attitudes depicted permeate the mainstream of the Muslim public sphere to a far greater degree, whereas the ones Saramago attributes to Jews, when not outright wrong, inhabit the very margins of the Jewish/Israeli public sphere.

Indeed, at the core of Saramago's passage lies its inversion of reality. On the one hand, Saramago misreads the Biblical passage—"Vengeance is mine, says the Lord"—and accuses the Jews of *his* misreading.[2] On the other hand,

---

2 Indeed, shortly before Saramago's piece, an orthodox rabbi voiced exactly the opposite opinion: "The Orthodox Jewish viewpoint, across the board, with rare exceptions, is that vengeance is God's alone. . . . Throughout two millennia of exile and suffering, the Jewish people have never

multiple Qur'anic passages explicitly call on the faithful to exercise violence on Allah's behalf; and the number of jihadis who believe they are the agents of Allah's divine wrath and the tools of his vengeance, outnumber several times over, all the Jews on the planet.

This empirical imbalance in accuracy gets further inverted when it comes to prominent Western thought leaders willing to denounce these two forms of zealotry. Curiously enough, as eagerly as many like Saramago view Israeli Jews negatively, as unthinkingly as they project onto them deliberate malice, as easily as they turn a fringe Jewish phenomenon into the symbol of Jewish being, that's how few dare to say anything remotely similar about Islam and Muslims. On the contrary, much intellectual effort in the twenty-first century has gone into insisting the jihadi narrative is marginal to Islam, that Muhammad is a "Prophet of Peace,"[3] and "moderate, peaceful Muslims," are the "vast majority," when not "99.9%" of the billion plus Muslims on the planet.[4] As a result, few will utter anything resembling the (largely accurate) paragraph above about Muslim triumphalism, while many feel free to shout the (deeply inaccurate) paragraph about Israelis from the rooftops of Western publications. And in so doing, these Western "thought leaders" have transformed themselves into a "docile echo of their [enemy's] will."

In 1897, Ahad Ha'am (Asher Ginsburg) wrote about the blood libels circulating in Europe at the time. Echoing an oft-heard rejoinder to Jewish claims that the stories were libels, he quoted a common dismissal from the gentiles: "Is it possible that the whole world is wrong and the Jews are right?" In 2002, a century later, UN Secretary General, Kofi Annan, expressed a similar astonishment at Israel's denial of massacre allegations at Jenin: "I don't think the whole world, including the friends of the Israeli people and government, can be wrong."[5] And yet, the answer to the question: "Could the "the whole world," including the self-professed friends of Israel, be wrong to side with jihadis against Israel, as at Jenin?" is "Yes."

---

encouraged the exercise of vengeance by human beings." Charles Radin, "Israel mourns as 10 fall to lone Palestinian sniper," *Boston Globe*, March 4, 2002.

3 Juan Cole, *Muhammad: Prophet of Peace Amid the Clash of Empires* (New York: Nation Books, 2018). Critique: Andrew Harrod, "Juan Cole Invents a Peaceful Islam," *The American Spectator*, December 10, 2018.

4 The quote is from President Obama: Ian Schwartz, "Obama: This 'Medieval Interpretation Of Islam' is Rejected by '99.9%' of Muslims, Not a 'Religious War,'" *Real Clear Politics*, February 1, 2015.

5 Joel Brinkley, "Israel Starts Leaving Areas, but Will Continue Drive," *New York Times*, April 8, 2002.

The challenge to you, critical reader of a critical author, is to undergo the following mental exercise: what if ... you (and the "entire international community" as journalists like to call it)[6] are wrong about Israel, indeed, wrong about the challenges that face the democratic world in the twenty-first century? What if, in trying to escape from the imaginary frying pan of too much "Jewish control" (they invented propaganda you know), you have leapt headlong into the very real fires of a jihad you do not, will not, acknowledge?

Scholars of millennial movements must imitate Odysseus, tied to the mast in order to listen to the sirens' song without getting mesmerized ... fatally. The German government sent Hitler to investigate the Thule Society and its populist front, the German Worker's Party) in 1919, and he ended up converting to their millennial message, and crashing all Europe onto the rocky shores of a millennial war that, for casualties, dwarfed the just completed "War to End all Wars."[7] The millennial scholar dealing with Caliphators must navigate a double danger, between on the one hand, the Scylla of such horror at the monstrosity of it all, that we become the mirror opposite—violent haters of our enemies—and on the other, the Charybdis of such fear of it, that, as a protective measure, we adopt their hatreds against our own societies. It turns out, that's no easy task.

To meet the challenge, however, you must board the ship and enter the straits of Messina. If you feel up to the task ... turn the page. If not, just sit in your tub tweeting about white, racist privilege, while you bleed out.

---

6 Richard Landes, "Everybody Agrees: The BBC and CNN on UNSC Resolution #2334 and Kerry's Speech," *Al Durah Project*, uploaded February 18, 2017, interview, 20:54, https://vimeo.com/256281399.

7 Richard Landes, *Heaven on Earth: The Varieties of the Millennial Experience* (Oxford: Oxford University Press, 2011), chapter 12.

Introduction

Reflections of a Heretical Medievalist

―――――――

On History, Values, and Astounding Stupidity

As the reader will rapidly understand, this book expresses astonishment at a collective folly that I see at this troubling dawn of the new millennium. As a result of it, value judgments, including judgments on the stupidity of given utterances, permeate the book's look at an epoch-defining, disastrous configuration that crystallized in the Western public sphere two decades ago, at the turn of the millennium. This book is much more judgmental than the normal professional historical fare, even though I claim to be an historian and to write a reliably accurate history (of the present).

So, in order to make clear on what basis I make these judgments, I lay out some of the key values that inform this work. If you disagree with these values, the book may not have much to offer (except reaffirmation that your anti-democratic side is winning); but if you agree with them, then *stupidity matters*, if only because stupidity is a negative indicator for longevity.

Let me phrase the issue of values in terms of a set of choices between two poles of behavior. Overall, the issue concerns a choice between invidious zero-sum relations and generous positive-sum ones. Throughout the book, I refer to the values delineated in the second column as "demotic," from the Greek word for people (demos), in that I think they are values that empower all the people, including commoners, at once to dismantle the "Prime Divider" that privileges honor-driven aristocrats over stigmatized commoners, and instead, to create dignity cultures of egalitarianism and freedom, ones in which the whole people (commoners and elites) share the same rights and opportunities. Demotic values make mutual freedom possible.[1] They don't solve every problem; life is messy and sometimes bitter. But they unquestionably make life much sweeter for everyone, even those whose domineering wings are clipped by their demands.

Domineering	Demotic
zero-sum: for me to win, you must lose	positive-sum: for me to win you must win
Manual labor stigmatized; honor to those who don't work, contempt for laborers	Dignity of manual labor, unearned wealth is shameful
Honor: peer-group granted status	Dignity: integrity-based (self-)esteem
Social order from coercive imposition, hierarchy	order from voluntary association, (social) contract
rule or be ruled	reciprocally granting freedom to each other
disciplining/dominating/controlling others	mutual self-discipline, self-control
resolving disputes through violence	resolving through a discourse of fairness
blaming/scapegoating the other	self-criticism
tribal solidarity: *my side right or wrong*	justice: *whoever's right my side or not*
hostility to the "other"	empathy for the other
authority from caste, class, connections	authority from merit
destructive envy	constructive competition
self-aggrandizing by belittling others	respecting dignity and success of others
war as a first resort (sport of kings)	war as a last resort
censorship to protect honor	freedom of speech to get at truth

1   Landes, *Heaven on Earth*, chapter 8.

The value judgments in this book are addressed to those who share a principled preference for the demotic choices outlined in the right-hand column, and yet who (knowingly or not) deal on a regular basis with people who, in the name of those principles, undermine those values repeatedly. This book tries to identify these *demopathic* attacks that, even as they invoke generosity and empathy, actually undermine (the historically rare) societies that favor demotic choices. I believe that dedication to these principles, despite the powerful gravitational (natural/hard-wired/limbic) pull of the left-hand column, has created modern, (relatively) free, and (remarkably) productive societies. So let me make clear again at the outset: this book is addressed to genuine liberals and progressives, people who cherish these demotic values.

Demotic societies (largely Western so far) are hardly free of faults, and, given the immense technological empowerment these principles have provided, some of those faults are potentially catastrophic (WMDs, global warming). But whatever these shortcomings, demotic cultures offer vast improvements in freedom for commoners, freedom to speak, freedom from hunger and pain, and freedom to correct the (inevitable) abuses of both the society and its governing officials and public authorities. No earlier Prime Divider society has ever provided so vast a number of its members with so many wondrous advantages.

The economist Carlo Cipolla defined stupidity as "creating damages for others even when it does not advantage you."[2] In game theory terms, Cipolla's stupid person plays a gratuitously self-defeating zero-sum game in which, without winning, he nonetheless damages others, who might otherwise be favorable. In this book, I define *astoundingly stupid* as "those who create advantages for those who want to hurt them," those who, in the name of positive-sum principles, fall dupe to the hard, zero-sum strategies of their self-declared, demopathic enemies. And they do this repeatedly, with no apparent inkling of where the road paved with their "good" intentions leads. Fool me once, shame on you; fool me dozens of times ... ?

Overwhelming Odds against What Happened

My medieval history professor at Princeton, Patrick Geary, began his lecture on Europe in the eleventh century, with the following paradox: If one looks at the world in the year 1000, the most successful civilizations, the "first world" of the day, was made up of Song China and Abassid Arabia. The European West would be down at the bottom of the third world—vulnerable to waves of

---

2   Carlo Cipolla, *The Basic Laws of Human Stupidity* (Milan: il Mulino, 2011).

raiders invading from all sides, exporters of primary goods, including human beings.[3] And if one looked to the West for any small success stories, it would be the German Ottonians, then led by their third Otto, *mirabile mundi*, renovator of Rome. At the bottom of the pile of Western prospects, one would probably put the future hexagon of France, where an excommunicated king, leader of a new and failing dynasty, "ruled" over a countryside increasingly riven by castle-protected warlords who plundered the peasantry at will.

And yet, when one looks back from the end of that same century, France is the powerhouse of Europe, and Europe the new power on the globe. In that eleventh century, France became the font of an exceptionally vigorous and expansive new culture: pilgrimage, church architecture, urban and rural communes, markets and fairs, university learning, legal thought, religious reform movements, "heresies" and new ecclesiastical orders, lay literature, chivalry, troubadour poetry, crusading knights. The Arabs who met the crusaders in the late 1090s, in their *deeds-of-God-through-us* phase, referred to all Western Europeans as "Franks." Indeed, this new Europe had shifted quite suddenly from victim of invasion to aggressive conqueror, poised with its new and constantly developing technology, for encounters with the rest of the world that would result in global mastery over the rest of the millennium.[4]

Had this lecture taken place shortly after Superbowl 2017, where the New England Patriots overcame 99.8% odds, my professor might have used it to illustrate the problem: looking at Europe in 1000, one would have given Europe very low odds in becoming the leading force on the planet in the coming centuries, and one would have certainly considered Y1K *France* the least likely to become Europe's leader in this transformation (unless you had your eye on the Peace of God).[5]

Let's do a thought experiment on the year 2000. Go back two decades ago, say to January 2000, and look ahead into the new century: who would be the winners and losers in the coming century, the coming millennium? With the Y2K computer "bug" safely passed, it was full steam ahead for global civil society and the internet that created so many dazzling new possibilities. The big winners in the

---

3   Our word "slave" coming from the Slavs that Europe exported to the Muslim world.

4   For a medieval take: Robert Bartlett, *The Making of Europe: Conquest, Colonization and Cultural Change, 950–1350* (Princeton: Princeton University Press, 1994). Within the framework of modernity: David Landes, *The Wealth and Poverty of Nations: Why Some Are so Rich and Some so Poor* (New York: W. W. Norton & Company, 1999) estimates that by 1500 the West was decisively superior to the rest of the world in technology and cultural expansion.

5   Richard Landes, *Relics, Apocalypse and the Deceits of History: Ademar of Chabannes, 989–1033* (Cambridge, MA: Harvard University Press, 1995).

new, the global, millennium? The Western societies that produced these agents and technologies of globalization: those who could innovate, navigate the open currents of cyberspace, the world without borders, the world of cooperation and hybridization. Not tribal cultures bent on war. Certainly, that's how the promoters of the European Union felt at the launch of the Euro (1999–2002).

One might argue finer points—Europe vs US, China, India, vs the West, maybe even a peaceful *New Middle East* from Lebanon and Syria, via Israel, Palestine and Jordan to Egypt and beyond (!). But at the bottom of the list of possibilities for success in the new century, was a tiny millenarian Muslim movement, based largely in the caves of Afghanistan that wanted to spread *Dar al Islam* to the entire world in this generation, the *Caliphators*.

Where would the odds-makers in January of 2000, put the chances of a Caliphator takeover of even one Western democracy in the twenty-first century, however brief? Less than 0.2%? Anyone who took them more seriously, whether Samuel Huntington or Daniel Pipes or Steven Emerson, got dismissed as belligerents who sought to create the clash about which they warned. If most people, still in the 2020s, think Caliphator success is a complete impossibility, imagine how incredulous people were before 9–11 and its successor attacks. Of course, the danger here arises in that, precisely what the observer dismisses as impossible, acts as a summons for the doer of impossible things. "By declaring war on the United States from a cave in Afghanistan, bin Laden assumed the role of an uncorrupted, indomitable primitive standing against the awesome power of the secular, scientific, technological Goliath; he was fighting modernity itself."[6]

And in that mistake, one risks a bruising battle with one of the most painful laws of apocalyptic dynamics: "Wrong does not mean inconsequential" ... especially in the case of active cataclysmic movements.[7] Hitler was wrong about his *Tausendjähriger Reich* by 988 years, but that's small consolation to the tens of millions whom he killed while trying during those first twelve.

And yet, as this book seeks to elucidate, at the end of the year 2000, and over the course of the following three years, the winds suddenly shifted out of the Western sails. David Brooks, writing in 2017, looked back with bewilderment at the sudden collapse:

> Starting decades ago, many people, especially in the universities,
> lost faith in the Western civilization narrative. They stopped

---

6 Laurence Wright, *The Looming Tower: Al-Qaeda and the Road to 9/11* (New York: Vintage, 2006), 426.

7 Landes, *Heaven on Earth*, chapter 2.

teaching it, and the great cultural transmission belt broke. Now many students, if they encounter it, are taught that Western civilization is a history of oppression. It is as if a prevailing wind, which powered all the ships at sea, had suddenly ceased to blow.[8]

Actually, no. It was the prevailing wind that powered *Western*, modern, ships that ceased to blow. But the winds in the sails of the Caliphators grew mighty. In 2000, Global Jihad became the strong horse ... a realization so difficult for Westerners to even contemplate that, when Bin Laden claimed it after 9–11, they thought it was nothing but posturing. We infidels, it turns out, were doing the posturing in pretending it was nonsense.

In a sense, this book should not have had to be written, and I should be able to work on the origins of modern Western civilization in the demotic millennialism of eleventh-century France to my heart's content.[9] If we had done a good job of teaching each generation about what modernity had accomplished, if we had kept an eye on just what it was about medieval attitudes and practices that we had knowingly, willingly, and with great difficulty, renounced—like the pervasive notions that women and manual laborers should belong to men of honor, to be sold and given over along with property, or that religious authorities had the right to torture and execute people whom they felt mis-interpreted "their" sacred scriptures, or that rulers should go to war annually to "plunder and distribute," or that for the sake of honor, one had to shed blood—then the reappearance of such traits would not pose such a problem of recognition. But something has happened, and we seem to sleepwalk past avatars of medieval monsters without even noticing them; we dismiss them as figments of our imagination, as monsters in the closet. Or worse, some imagine that they are teddy bears we can hug; and that the folks warning us against them are just racist xenophobes.[10]

And yet, I will argue in this book, the paradox that faces us runs as follows: Indeed, it is absurd for Caliphators to believe they can take over the West; the chasm between ability and desire is so great that it justifiably elicits Western infidel derision. But that's not their feeling: in the intensity of their passionate desire, they ignore the very "realities" that so reassure us. In matters apocalyptic, undertaking a wildly asymmetric war against vastly more powerful forces *reassures* believers that they fight on the *right, the just,* on *God's,* side. And

---

8   David Brooks, "The Crisis of Western Civ," *New York Times*, April 21, 2017.
9   Richard Landes, *While God Tarried: Disappointed Millennialism from Jesus to the Peace of God,* 33–1033. Forthcoming.
10 On Steven Spielberg's contribution to this attitude vis-à-vis ETs, see Landes, *Heaven on Earth,* 404–5.

they fight tirelessly with all their might. The degree to which we ignore the phenomenon, misread the demands of Caliphators as either nonsense, or as exaggerated-but-legitimate claims for the kinds of rights we have created for our citizens, the *less* seriously we take them *at their word* ... that is the degree to which we enable their impossible dream.

The history of misreading apocalyptic phenomena constitutes a core issue in the volatile and difficult field of Millennial Studies.[11] A vast gap in mentality divides the apocalyptic "roosters" crowing the day of the Lord has dawned and their chroniclers and analysts, anti-apocalyptic "owls." The beliefs seem so ludicrous retrospectively that scholars have difficulty taking these ideas seriously: "nonsense is nonsense, but the history of nonsense is scholarship," quipped one historian introducing a scholar of messianic movements.

The mental gap is doubled by a historical fact: every past apocalyptic movement predicted by roosters has *failed* (the End/Millennium still has not come). That tends to skew the documentary record and shape retrospective attitudes: in the period of apocalyptic disappointment, where the roosters prove wrong and the owls prove right, an extensive retelling of events occurs about the period before failure, after people knew who was wrong and who right (*ex post defectu*). Lost in this process are the social dynamics that prevailed when the apocalyptic roosters dominated the scene, and their storm drowned out the warnings of skeptical owls. As a result, one gets a documentary configuration somewhat like an iceberg, where the small top pushes above the surface, the written (documentary) waterline, while a whole world of discourse teems under the surface, an oral world, mostly invisible to the observer unschooled in apocalyptic phenomena.

It is one thing for medieval historians to dramatically misread the apocalyptic impact of the year 1000 on European culture (or, for that matter, the impact of the year 6000 Annus Mundi on the Coronation of Charlemagne).[12] Confident that any traces of apocalypticism in the textual record constitute mere flotsam

---

11 Landes, "On Millennial Studies, Vesperian Scholars, and the Millennial Clashes of the Twenty-First Century," in *Beyond the End: The Future of Millennial Studies*, ed. Joshua Searle and Kenneth C. G. Newport (Sheffield: Sheffield Phoenix Press, 2012), vii-xxii.

12 Landes, "On the Dangers of Ignoring Apocalyptic Icebergs, Y1K and Y2K," *Groniek: Historisch Tijdschrift* (February 2015): 387–409. In 2014 I gave a talk in Paris at a conference on "Charlemagne after Charlemagne," and asked the audience who knew that Charlemagne was crowned on the first day of the year 6000 from the Creation of the World? Virtually no one had, twenty years after major articles in English, Spanish and German had been published on the subject. Not only did they not know about their own millennial past, but they had no clue to the active cataclysmic movement in their midst, which would rear its ugly head only a few weeks later on July 13, 2014 when a crowd of Muslims, furious at the news reported of Israeli strikes in Gaza, went from shouting "Death to the Jews" in Place de la Bastille to attacking a synagogue filled with Jews on rue de la Roquette. Veronique Chemla, "Des 'Blacks, Blancs,

and jetsam, medievalists can sail their ships of historiographical reconstruction into the hidden icebergs of apocalyptic discourse without noticing when they hit them, or when their ship has sunk. As long as no contemporary can naysay them, as long as their fellow historians agree, a strong academic consensus can take a tendentious written record at face value. No one can *prove* that this narrative vessel sank on an unseen iceberg, that this picture of the past misses a key part of the story.[13] It's not the end of the world if we got the origins of our remarkably productive civilization wrong.

On the other hand, if we make the same errors in appraising apocalyptic Islam at the dawn of the first global millennium (third millennium CE), then we run serious risks. When our exegetical schemes hit an *extant* iceberg of violent apocalyptic discourse, whose magnitude we dramatically underestimate, whole civilizations can sink. Would one not want to serve one's generation better, than to partake of a particularly dangerous act of collective denial, a Broadway production of the Emperor's New Clothes writ large, but this time following an icon of hatred rather than a vain and foolish emperor? Hans Christian Andersen does not tell us in the end whether, when people openly acknowledged that the emperor was naked, they laughed or they cried. In this case, apart from those who have silently changed sides, there is no question what our response when the shingles eventually fall from our eyes. Would it not be a tragic irony if future historians wrote the history of the West in terms of two unnoticed millennial movements, one at its origins in Y1K and one at its demise in the wake of Y2K? Especially ironic, when one considers that some of the demotic lessons of the turn of Y1K might have helped deal with the crises of Y2K.

* * *

Part One of this book considers four key moments in the onset of our collective folly that continues now, twenty years later, if anything strengthened and metastasized. It describes the crystallization among many thought leaders of Western culture, of an attitude that could not suit their enemy's agenda more ideally: *when jihadis attack a democracy, blame the democracy.* It traces the powerful impact this mindset (which I call Y2KMind based on the year it took hold), on the course of the millennial war between Caliphators and Westerners in the opening years of the new millennium. These four chapters examine key

---

Beurs' antisémites attaquent les Juifs à Paris," July 15, 2014. The attacks on Charlie Hebdo and the Bataclan followed rapidly in 2015.

13 See Landes, *Heaven on Earth*, chapter 3.

inflection points in the process: two chapters concern Israel, a major battlefield in this global war, and two concern the West, one US, one Europe.

- Chapter 1 treats the outbreak of the **first jihadi attack on a democracy** in late September 2000, the launching of the first blood libel of the twenty-first century, and the blaming of the democracy attacked.
- Chapter 2 discusses **9–11** (2001), and the blaming of the US for that attack.
- Chapter 3 discusses an exceptional case of lethal journalism, the **"Jenin Massacre"** (April 2002), which inspired Western progressives to protest a democracy defending itself from jihadi attacks—even, to show their solidarity, wearing mock suicide belts, the very weapons soon to be turned on them.
- Chapter 4 considers the **Danish Cartoon Scandal** of 2005–6, in which Caliphators picked a fight with the West, and the West backed down, accepting a de facto extension of Muslim blasphemy laws to Dar al Harb.

I know there are other, equally important moments to which I only give brief attention—Durban 2001; the "anti-war" demonstrations of 2003; the 7–7 attacks on London; the French suburban riots of 2005. I am confident that a closer look at any of these and a host of other events will only further prove and illustrate the points I make here. This opening part makes no claim to scope, only to analytic precision.

Part two examines the key players in this millennial war:

- **Shame-honor warriors** who play by the hard-zero-sum game of *rule or be ruled* and the impact their mindset has on the problem of peace-making in the Middle East.
- **Caliphators**, members of an active cataclysmic apocalyptic millennial movement seeking world conquest in *this* generation, by some combination of jihad (kinetic war) and da'wa (cognitive war).
- **Western liberals** committed to noncoercive, positive-sum relations, with their fateful tendency to project their own refined mentality on others, however inappropriate.
- **Western progressives**, believers in an active, transformative, apocalyptic millennial movement seeking a global community of equality, diversity, tolerance, and dignity for all.
- **Lethal journalists** who report the war propaganda of one side as news, in this case that of the Palestinian jihadis fighting Israel. Unbeknownst to them, they were reporting their own enemy's war propaganda as news—**own-goal war journalism**.

- **Jews-against-themselves**, those who side with their people's declared enemies in order to prove their good will and commitment to progressive values.

Part three reviews the behavior of these key actors over the last two decades: the course of the Caliphator war on the West and the role of Y2KMind in systemically weakening the targeted West. It then discusses the flip side of the Y2K coin, preemptive dhimmitude, wherein "progressive" and "liberal" leaders of infidel communities, to ward off Islamic dominance, enforce the primary law of submission: *Do not offend Muslims!* The inevitable cognitive and moral dissonance of their sincere pretense has produced a politics of outrage that fills "the worst . . . with passionate intensity," and produces a radically disoriented West under attack.

I should have written this book quickly over a decade ago after I began it, and in some sense, the record of my thinking shows up in my blog, the *Augean Stables*, started in late 2005. Instead, it became a meditation on apocalyptic time, millennial wars, and the deceits of cognitive warfare. Each chapter raised more issues, led down more dark corridors. So, in the end, I went back to where I thought it all took so dreadful a turn for the worse—late 2000.

But it has not been easy, either to capture this apocalyptic time in a book of words, nor to find the right words to penetrate the thick walls that protect the foolish from the uncomfortable reality I describe. That it has taken me this long is partly my own procrastinating fault, partly that of a generation that has consistently opted for aggressive timidity, for pretensions to moral grandeur married to craven appeasement, for anger at those who do not appease, rather than courageous confrontation with the medieval aggressors. To paraphrase a Renaissance thinker, this book is a report from one of the rafts navigating the white water where the big ship of fools founders and breaks apart. Read it to your benefit, dismiss it at risk of your harm.

We all, at some level, have *onēidophobia* (fear of public shame). None of us likes to realize we've been publicly wrong. How hard it is to look in the mirror and see reflected back, our public folly. And yet, if I were a Muslim today, especially a young alpha male, I would take the stupidity of Westerners as a sign from Allah that I should join the Caliphator jihad and shout at the author of this book: "Shut the f*ck up, you white supremacist, privileged, Nazi-Zionist-racist, Islamophobe![14] Don't even try and tell me that the whole world can be wrong and Israel right."

---

14 "Lewandowsky, Jew, Psychologist! Shut the fuck up you Nazi Zionist Kike!"—From the author's inbox; Stephan Lewandowsky, "In Whose Hands the Future?" in *Conspiracy Theories and the People Who Believe Them*, ed. Joseph Uscinski (New York: Oxford University Press, 2018), 149.

Part One

SELECTIVE HISTORY OF THE DISASTROUS EARLY AUGHTS (2000–2003)

1. **Al Durah: Spreading a Jihadi Blood Libel (2000)**
    We need not have been
    Mouths open, inhaling, when
    The sh*t hit the fan.

2. **9–11: Taking the World by Storm (2001)**
    How many ways can
    A nation under fire, get
    It so very wrong?

3. **Jenin: Cheering on the Jihadi Suicide Terror (2002)**
    Fooled by news that made
    Nazis of Jews, they
    Cheered on their worst enemy

4. **Danoongate: The Muslim Street Extends Dar al Islam (2005–6)**
    Did those mean Danes hurt
    Your feelings? Please, don't hate us too.
    We're so progressive.

1

Al Durah: Spreading a Jihadi Blood Libel (2000)

We need not have been
Mouths open, inhaling, when
The sh*t hit the fan.

On September 30, 2000, a nuclear explosion went off in the global public sphere. That evening, Charles Enderlin, senior Middle East Correspondent for France2, and former member of the IDF spokesman's unit, broadcast footage from his Palestinian cameraman, Talal abu Rahma, accompanied by the cameraman's "eyewitness" narrative.[1] The news report affirmed that abu Rahma had captured, on-camera, the killing of a defenseless twelve-year-old Palestinian boy, Muhammad al Durah, in the arms of his father, despite their pleas. . . . Enderlin announced that they were the "target of fire coming from the Israeli position."

The footage and its accompanying narrative immediately went viral, then mythical. The footage was spectacular, as emotionally powerful as the dogs attacking Black protesters in Birmingham (1963), and the terrified Vietnamese girl running down the road naked, aflame with napalm (1972) ... one of those *images choc* that can so profoundly mark a television-shaped public.[2] Despite extensive problems with the footage itself, with its cornucopia of anomalies that

---

1 *The Al Durah Project*, http://www.aldurah.com; Landes "The Al Durah Dossier," *Augean Stables*, 2008, http://www.theaugeanstables.com/al-durah-affair-the-dossier/; Nidra Poller, *Al Dura: Long-Range Ballistic Myth* (Paris: authorship intl, 2014).

2 Vickie Goldberg, *The Power of Photography: How Photographs Changed Our Lives* (NY, 1993). Tamar Liebes and Anat First "Framing the Palestinian Israeli Conflict," in *Framing Terrorism: The News Media, the Government and the Public*, ed. Norris, Kern and Just (NY, 2003), chapter 4.

either did not corroborate, or directly contradicted, the news report, journalists piled on the story. The cameraman helped the process by claiming, *under oath* to a notary of a Palestinian "human rights" group, that the IDF had gunned down the boy "in cold blood."[3] The image of a terrified boy under merciless fire from the Israelis rapidly mutated from sensational news scoop to that of a mythical icon, which, in turn, swept through both the Muslim world and the West. It became *the* icon of hatred for the twenty-first century.[4]

One cannot overestimate its impact.[5]

Al Durah and Lethal Journalism: At the Heart of a Professional Failure

But what did viewers of Enderlin's broadcast and its host of epigones at all the major news outlets really see? Did they see footage of the Israelis shooting a boy down in cold blood, as narrated by the cameraman and reported by the journalist? Given the mythical proportions this *icon of hatred* has taken on in the unhappy twenty-first century, few stories would have been more important for journalists to "get right," according to their professional commitments to accuracy.

And yet, purely in terms of journalistic procedures, this episode constitutes one of the most monumental failures of professional journalism in the long and volatile history of war journalism. These failures operated at every level of the journalistic profession, starting with the cameraman (if one holds Palestinians to professional standards), a master of Pallywood techniques, employed for over a decade by both CNN and France2, to whom add his eagerly duped Western boss, a journalist of great prestige, who packaged the story so effectively *as news,* eventually extending to the entire profession of 21st century journalists. The first major case of (still uncorrected) "fake news" in the new century.[6]

---

3 Tala abu Rahma "Notarized Statement," PCHR, October 3, 2000, https://tinyurl.com/avk6mmvu.

4 Richard Landes, Icon of Hatred, October 2005, https://vimeo.com/67058931.

5 Barbie Zelizer, *About to Die: How News Images Move the Public* (New York: Oxford University Press, 2010), who places the discussion of al Durah in her chapter on "Certain Deaths" despite her awareness of the questionable nature of the footage, 197–203.

6 On the matter of "objectivity in journalism, see Stephen Ward, *The Invention of Journalism Ethics: The Path to Objectivity and Beyond* (Montreal: McGill-Queens University Press, 2006). Despite the date of publication, the author nowhere deals with the Middle East conflict, nor does he cite Goldberg's book on media bias.

So extensive are the contradictions that the original footage raises about the lethal narrative—the direction of the bullets, the lack of blood (especially for a fatal stomach wound), the movements of the father and son allegedly injured/ dead, the sudden absence of other cameramen at the scene to film extraordinary events, the positioning of the two victims with the boy in take 1 kneeling and in take 4 (after being hit) on his stomach over the same spot, the lack of footage to back up a claim of an ambulance shot up and a driver killed—that only true believers could insist that Abu Rahma's and Enderlin's original narrative was accurate. To the contrary, of the five possible reconstructions of what Abu Rahma's footage (before Enderlin's editing)[7] indicates—1) Israelis, by accident, 2) on purpose; 3) Palestinians by accident, 4) on purpose; and 5) staged—by far the most likely is that this scene, like so many others shot that day by abu Rahma and other Palestinian cameramen working for Western news agencies, was staged.[8]

And yet, in late 2000, the journalistic "community" of foreign correspondents in Israel all—without exception—behaved like true believers.

The indictment goes far beyond Enderlin himself, and the pack of correspondents that he stampeded to follow suit. It includes an entire generation of "investigative journalists" who failed to do the research or state the obvious. Only eight journalists across the world had the courage to investigate further and state even the most obvious truth: the Israelis did not kill him.[9] But even among these brave souls, two refused to venture any further in their investigation— Esther Schapira initially, and James Fallows consistently. Fallows, who acknowledged that the Israelis did not shoot the boy, would not even *speculate* about the obvious next question: "What *did* happen?" Repeatedly, to this day, journalists ask the wrong question: "Who killed the boy?"

In comparison with the rest of the mainstream news profession, however, Schapira and Fallows stood out for courage and integrity. While tenacious investigative journalists either got marginalized as "Jewish" and therefore "Israel-firsters"—including non-Jews, like the scholar Pierre André Taguieff and

---

7   On the footage Enderlin supplied the court, and which he admitted he had cut, see "Raw Footage Presented to French Court," YouTube, https://www.youtube.com/watch?v=fUz55tLLXUg; on the edits: "Gambling with a Lie: Enderlin pulls a Rosemary Mary Woods" *Augean Stables*, November 14, 2007.

8   The staged hypothesis was literally "unthinkable" for most Westerners: only a tiny minority of people, when presented with the first four options could even imagine the fifth. On staging, see *Pallywood*, 2005, https://vimeo.com/65294892.

9   Stephan Juffa and Amnon Lord in Israel, Nidra Poller, Luc Rosenzweig, Clement Weill-Raynal in France, Esther Schapira in Germany, and James Fallows in the USA. In France three major figures were not journalists: Gerard Huber, Pierre-André Taguieff, Philippe Karsenty.

Esther Schapira[10] —the rest of the profession (including the Israeli press) clung tenaciously to the original narrative, no matter how flawed. When I spoke to a renowned Israeli journalist in 2003 about the case, he responded, "100% Israel did it." When, in 2007, a French court rejected Enderlin's petition that critics had "damaged his honor," and defended the rights of citizens to criticize his work, hundreds of major "professional" journalists, signed a petition that called the French court's decision "a blow to freedom of the press." In fact, the court's decision constituted a) a defense of freedom to criticize the press, and hence, b) a blow to the license of the press to say anything they want no matter how inaccurate.[11]

And finally, the indictment concerns the entire profession of journalists. The clock on this ticks longer every day. For over twenty years now, we have journalistic denial, an across-the-boards failure to investigate, reconsider, and correct this tragic episode. (At this point, the typical off-the-record response is, "We know it was a mistake. But what's the point? It's history.") In 2014, when the Israeli government's Kuperwasser Commission came out with its report, the coverage *even in* Israel was minimal, the number of people who bothered to follow up on the implications of the findings, nearly nonexistent.[12] If we define stupidity as the absence of critical thought in matters of import, then the stupidity involved in this ongoing journalistic failure is monumental and ongoing.

But all these investigative details aside, the key to the news report's disastrous consequences lies in the most crucial and lethal statement uttered by Enderlin in the original broadcast: "the target of fire coming from the Israeli position." In it lies the key aspect of the blood libel, elaborated under oath by the cameraman Talal abu Rahma for the Arab world: it was a deliberate killing, a cold-blooded murder of a defenseless child, shot in his father's lap. And yet, nothing in the footage supports

---

10 Schapira had a Jewish father. Taguieff is not at all Jewish, despite Tariq Ramadan's including him in a list of six "*communautaristes juifs*" whom he denounced for abandoning their universal values to defend Israel (Berman, *Flight of the Intellectuals*, 157f).

11 "Affaire al-Doura: une pétition pour Charles Enderlin," *Nouvel Obs*, June 6, 2008; fisked by R. Landes, "What Checks and Balances to the Fourth Estate: Appeal for Charles Enderlin Poses the Question," *Augean Stables*, June 6, 2008. See Ivan Rioufol, "Les médias, pouvoir intouchable ?" *Figaro*, June 13, 2008; Anne-Elisabeth Moutet's follow-up with people who signed: "*L'Affaire Enderlin*: Being a French Journalist Means Never Having to Say you're Sorry," *The Weekly Standard*, July 7 2008.

12 "The France 2 Al-Durrah Report, its Consequences and Implications: Report of the Government Review Committee," Ministry of International Affairs and Strategy, State of Israel, May 19, 2013, https://www.scribd.com/doc/142658793/Kuperwasser-Report. The only serious exception, Shmuel Rosner, "Revisiting the Alleged Killing of a Palestinian Boy by Israeli Forces," *New York Times*, May 22, 2013.

that assertion and, upon closer examination, virtually every detail contradicts it. Some viewers suspected staging the moment they saw the film. Starting with Nahum Shahaf, an Israeli physicist, a small group investigated the matter in detail, and convinced at least three journalists—Stefan Juffa, Esther Schapira, and James Fallows—to follow up.[13] Among their major findings was a ballistic analysis that made it clear that the bullets did *not* come from the IDF's position.[14]

Indeed, every case of a bullet striking the wall on camera clearly came from the same direction, not the Israeli position at a 30 degree angle, but from 90 degrees, from behind the cameraman. Fifteen bullet holes, all head on, adorn a wall that, according to Talal, had been the object of heavy gunfire (bullets like rain), for twenty minutes. None of the holes show signs of a 30 degree angle entry that would indicate fire from the Israeli position. In one case, an Israeli bullet would have had to take a 90 degree right turn in order to enter the wall as it did. Nor did any bullet hole involve the splatter of blood on the wall behind, despite claims that the father and boy were hit over a dozen times.

Even some of Enderlin's sympathizers agreed that he had overstepped his role as a professional journalist—especially since he was not an eyewitness to the events he recounted.[15] Asked respectfully by a sympathetic Israeli journalist whether he might not have been "too hasty" in using the phrase "the target of fire coming from the Israeli position," Enderlin responded:

> I don't think so. If I hadn't said that the child and father were victims of shooting coming from the direction of the IDF position, they'd say in Gaza "How come Enderlin does not say it's the IDF?"[16]

What can this answer mean? Was Enderlin somehow obligated to promote Palestinian lethal narratives about the IDF *deliberately* killing Palestinian children? Unthinkingly, did he give us a glimpse of how in this case, he was a (apparently willing) tool of Palestinian propaganda.[17] *Haaretz*, perhaps aware

---

13 For the work of Stephan Juffa, see MENA, http://www.menapress.org/index.php?searchwo rd=al+dura&option=com_search&Itemid=; Esther Schapira, *Three Bullets and a Dead Child* (2002); James Fallows, "Who Shot Muhammad al Dura?" *Atlantic Monthly*, June 2003.

14 Jean Claude Schlinger, Affair Al Doura: Examen technique et balistique, *The Augean Stables*, December 7, 2021.

15 Elisabeth Schemla, "Un entretien exclusif avec Charles Enderlin, deux ans après la mort en direct de Mohamed Al-Dura à Gaza," *Proches Orient Infos*, October 1, 2002.

16 Adi Schwartz, "בואו נראה את זה שוב" [Come, let us look at this again], *Haaretz*, November 1, 2007.

17 For a discussion of how widespread this approach by Western journalists, see chapter 9.

of the embarrassing nature of Enderlin's response, removed the passage from its English translation.[18]

And yet that specific detail—the targeting of the innocent, defenseless boy—lay at the heart of the mythical accusation. Veteran lethal journalists took the lead. Robert Fisk wrote: "When I read the word 'crossfire,' I reach for my pen. In the Middle East, it almost always means that the Israelis have killed an innocent person."[19] ABC's Gillian Findlay asserted unequivocally that the Israelis had fired the shots.[20] The *Guardian*'s Susanne Goldberg gave her considered ballistics analysis:

> The result of that salvo is visible on the cinderblock wall. Aside from the circle of bullet holes—most of them below waist level—the expanse of wall is largely unscarred. This appeared to suggest that the Israeli fire was targeted at the father and son.[21]

And with such prose, she promoted the most lethal version of the narrative. Apparently, the Palestinian witness can speak of bullets like rain, and the journalist can detect in the few bullet holes, evidence that Israelis targeted the boy.[22]

And the rest followed suit. CNN's Mike Hanna, who had just begun as Jerusalem Bureau chief in August, turned down the footage the day before, but was now under pressure from his staff to get on the story.[23] Human interest stories told the tale of the last day of Muhammad al Durah's sad life as a refugee, and his tragic death "at the hand of the Jews," as Osama bin Laden put it. There was consensus among virtually *all* the legacy news media, despite how problematic and volatile a story it was, that the Israelis killed this boy. If there were doubts, they expressed themselves in a reluctance of some news outlets and journalists to pay too much attention to the story, not in contradiction. For nearly two

---

18 Noted by CAMERA, "In the footsteps of the al Durah controversy"; Arnold Roth: "If we knew then what we discovered today about how France2's correspondent decided the IDF killed a child in Gaza 13 years ago," *This Ongoing War*, May 23, 2013. In 2010, Enderlin favors Talal's testimony to evidence he denies: *Un enfant est mort: Netzarim, 30 septembre 2000* (Paris: Don Quichotte éditions, 2010), 5.

19 Fisk, "Where 'caught in the crossfire' can leave no room for doubt," *Independent*, October 2, 2000.

20 Joshua Muravchik, *Covering the Intifada: How the Media Reported the Palestinian Uprising* (Washington: The Washington Institute for Near East Policy, 2003), 15.

21 Susanne Goldenberg, "Making of a Martyr," *Guardian*, October 2, 2000 [italics mine].

22 On the bullet holes, see Landes, *Al Durah: Making of an Icon* 5:53–6:15, https://vimeo.com/67060204.

23 Izzy Lemberg, CNN field editor, personal testimony.

decades, there has been little dissent, only a few investigators, all of whom either saved their careers by dropping the story (Fallows, Daniel Leconte, and Denis Jeambar) or were rapidly dismissed as conspiracy theorists. This "lethal narrative," designed to create hatred and inspire violence, the product of both Palestinian malevolence and one Western journalist's professional malfeasance, elicited no critical thinking. It entered the global public sphere as unchallenged news,[24] and once there, only the most despicable people would try to defend Israel and "blame the victim." And, as the Palestinians and other jihadis like Bin Laden never tire of saying, "The whole world saw it."

And what did they see? In order for the tale to operate at the mythical levels at which, alas, it has grown and penetrated both Muslim and Western cultures, Israel *had* to have *deliberately* murdered an innocent defenseless child who died in the arms of his father . . . on camera. Were it not intentional, merciless, and murderous, the deed could not have exercised its immense symbolic role.[25] And on that particular point, all the ballistics and forensics aside, Enderlin did the bidding of the Palestinians and betrayed his profession.

The Muslim Al Durah Myth: Blood Libel, Summons to Jihad

Abu Rahma's lethal tale of cold-blooded murder was pure war propaganda, designed to prove from this single case that he actually "caught on film," the truth of all those myriad Palestinian accusations that the Israelis deliberately killed their children. Indeed, two days later, when a Tanzim Palestinian shot his baby daughter in the head while cleaning his gun, Palestinian spokespeople accused an Israeli settler of shooting them while on the way to the hospital (they even shot up a car as proof), and the media went to town. *Paris Match* dedicated half an issue to the story, replete with bloody pictures.[26] When the journalists encourage their readers to think that Israelis target children—which, like eating

---

24 E.g., Charles Enderlin, "Making an Icon: The Al-Dura Conspiracy," in *Reporting the Middle East: The Practice of News in the Twenty-first Century*, ed. Zahera Harb (London, 2017), 163–78.

25 Poller, *Al Dura*, chapter 1.

26 "Cette guerre qui tue les enfants," *Paris Match*, #2681, Octobre 2000. On the actual events, see Laetitia Enriquez, "Enquête: Qui a tué la petite palestinienne?" *Actualité Juive*, November 2, 2000. Madeleine Albright had the CIA investigate; even PA police told him the father accidentally killed the child. Alain Genestar, director general of Paris Match responded: "Un grand reporter de Paris-Match est à mes yeux plus crédible qu'un agent secret de la CIA."

blood is strictly forbidden—conspiratorial supersessionists of all stripes read: proof of Jewish malevolence.[27]

Palestinian poet Mahmoud Darwish wrote a poem that works from Talal abu Rahma's (later retracted) lethal testimony, deploring the inhuman cruelty of the cold-blooded shooter, describing scenes "on camera" that do not exist, invoking "baby Jesus."[28] Bin Laden immediately seized upon this blood libel's meaning: "It is as if Israel—and those backing it in America—have killed all the children in the world."[29] And that reasoning, straight out of the annals of European paranoia—that Jews deliberately kill gentile children as part of a program of enslaving the goyim—allowed Bin Laden to justify killing enemy children in revenge, a fateful turn in the course of Caliphator jihad up to that point that justified their great new weapon—suicide terror.

This is the blood libel, that entered into the mainstream of the Arab and Muslim public sphere. And it had similar impact there as had blood libels had at the turn of the previous century in Europe.[30] Riots, where possible, attacks on Jews, paranoid rumors of cosmic conspiracies, calls to holy war and genocide. Here, contrary to the comparison so common among contemporary observers—twenty-first-century Islamophobia = twentieth-century antisemitism—we find twenty-first-century Muslim anti-Zionism closely paralleling the dynamics of European antisemitism in the twentieth. And the allegedly modern, professional Western press, consistently fed that hatred with its errors and resolute refusals to correct itself, even after both the truth, and the damage the false report had caused, became abundantly clear. Looking back over two decades littered with other such costly failures, the Fourth Estate's treatment of the al Durah material at the dawn of the century still stands out for its reckless disregard for both its profession and the public it serves.

What was previously an experiment in Western-style news coverage, Al Jazeera, rode to the heights of popularity throughout the Arab and Muslim world, saturating the public sphere with this icon of hatred.

> Al-Jazeera ran repeatedly the clip of the boy being shot, and for several days the *picture of his dying became the network's emblem* of the Intifada. This had a *deeply galvanizing effect on the wider*

---

27 On supersessionism and its adepts, see the case of Tom Paulin (n69), more generally, chapter 8.

28 Mahmoud Darwish, "Muhammad," *Revue d'études palestiniennes* 78 (Winter 2001), https://mronline.org/2006/09/30/darwish300906-html/.

29 *Messages to the World: The Statements of Osama Bin Laden*, ed. Bruce Lawrence (London: Verso, 2005), 147f.

30 Pierre-André Taguieff, *Criminaliser les Juifs: Le mythe du "meurtre rituel" et ses avatars (antijudaïsme, antisémitisme, antisionisme)* (Paris : Hermann, 2020), 281–92.

Arab public. Arabs everywhere became desperate for bulletins from the Occupied Territories, but state-run Arab news providers were slow to give good coverage . . . from the very start Al-Jazeera's live coverage from the front line far outstripped any other network's coverage.[31]

Within Palestinian culture, it was probably the worst. The footage appeared endlessly, slow motion, to the blare of martial music, 24/7. It not only galvanized Arabs in the "Occupied Territories," but within Israel. For three days, in absolutely unprecedented fashion, Israeli Arabs rioted throughout the country. Some journalists openly anticipated the collapse of the Green Line (i.e., the reignition of hopes for a "Palestine from the river to the sea").[32] PA TV's editors, who played the al Durah footage endlessly, further weaponized it by splicing into the footage a clip of an IDF soldier aiming his (rubber bullet) rifle at Israeli Arabs rioting *because* of the footage. The result: the Palestinian viewer saw an Israeli soldier deliberately targeting and murdering the boy.[33]

As soon as the pictures appeared, they provoked outrage. The very next day, October 1, 2000, Arabs began to riot not only in the Palestinian territories but also in Israel—Nazareth, Sahknin, Ramleh, Jaffa. Reported the Or Commission of investigation:

> The opinion shared by most of them [leaders of the Arab minority heard by the Commission] was that *the pictures of Mohamed Al-Durah, that were broadcast by the media, constituted one of the elements that led people of the Arab sector to violence* in the streets on 1 October 2000. Concordantly, police sources and other security sources considered that *the presentation of the images had a considerable weight, as a factor in the outbreak of the events.*[34]

---

31 Hugh Miles, *Al-Jazeera: The Inside Story of the Arab News Channel That is Challenging the West* (New York, 2006), 73–4. Fouad Ajami, similarly noted "the image's ceaseless repetition signaled the arrival of a new, sensational breed of Arab journalism," Ajami, "What the Muslim World is Watching," *New York Times Magazine*, November 18, 2001. Ironically and forebodingly, French news did the same (see n51).

32 Graham Usher, "Uprising wipes off Green Line," *Al Ahram*, October 12–18, 2000.

33 Clip from Schapira, "Three Bullets and a Dead Child," https://vimeo.com/661738105.

34 Ohr Commission Investigation Report into the Clashes between Security Forces and Israeli Citizens in October 2000, conclusion, 172, http://elyon1.court.gov.il/heb/veadot/or/inside_index.htm; translation adapted from Juffa's article (next note); the official English summary does not mention al Durah, https://www.jewishvirtuallibrary.org/the-official-summation-of-the-or-commission-report-september-2003.

As Dr. Sabikh, an Israeli Arab, explained to Stephan Juffa of the Metula News Agency:

> You understand, Steph, when we saw these pictures [of Mohamed al-Durah], we said that there was a radical change in the way Jews considered us. We had never seen or imagined Israeli soldiers shooting a child to kill him, and for forty minutes. In the towns and villages, at Sakhnin, Nazareth, Rameh, we thought that if you had no pity for Arab children, you were going to massacre us all! So it was urgent to go out into the streets and show you that we were not about to give up and it would cost you dearly.[35]

The logic may be questionable (normally people don't riot in front of soldiers who have just proven that they kill children in cold blood), but the role of al Durah as incitement is clear, and if the damage was less than the old European pogroms, it's only because the Israelis could defend themselves as the Jews of Kishinev could not.

The fury this image inspired among Palestinians can be gauged by events eleven days later. Ramallah police had taken two Israeli reservists into custody, but enraged men soon overran the police station and beat the Israelis to death, throwing one body out the window, mutilating it, parading it through the street as a trophy. Any Homeric warrior would recognize this behavior, but it terrified Mark Seager, a veteran world reporter who thought he had seen it all.

> They were dragging the dead man around the street like a cat toying with a mouse. It was the most horrible thing that I have ever seen, and I have reported from Congo, Kosovo, many bad places. In Kosovo, I saw Serbs beating an Albanian, but it wasn't like this. There was such hatred, such unbelievable hatred and anger distorting their faces.[36]

---

35 Stéphane Juffa, "France 2's report on Al-Dura at the Origin of the Riots of October," MENA, September 23, 2001, http://www.theaugeanstables.com/2018/10/10/stephane-juffa-on-france2s-al-dura-report-at-the-origin-of-the-riots-of-october-2000/.

36 Mark Seager, "'I'll have nightmares for the rest of my life," *The Daily Telegraph*, October 15, 2000, http://rotter.net/israel/mark.htm. Seager had several reasons to regret the article and it is no longer available at the *Telegraph*, hence the alternative url. For more on Seager and intimidation/advocacy, see below 325f, 341f.

And all day, as they shouted their delight in the slaughter and desecration of these two Israelis, they proclaimed "Revenge for the blood of Muhammad al Durah."[37]

As Bin Laden insisted, the only possible response to this unbearable outrage at infidels murdering innocent Muslims—at the hand of the Jews!—was revenge at any and all costs. Within months of the alleged "murder," Bin Laden came out with a recruiting video for Global Jihad, and at the heart of its appeal stood Muhammad al Durah.[38] It damned every Arab leader for their cowardice in not avenging the boy's death and challenged every self-respecting Muslim to stand up for "justice."

Al Durah justified all the apocalyptic hatred of the Jews and the *kuffâr* that Hamas and other jihadi preachers had been promoting all along. Public opinion overwhelmingly favored striking back, and rejoiced in the use of the forbidden suicide terror: from 25% support before, to 80% support.[39] Those who dominated the public sphere praised the piety of those who blew themselves up to kill infidel children: *Istishahadiyya*, the "martyrdom operations" of the heroic *Shuhada*, the martyrs who blow themselves up killing Israeli civilians. The first suicide bombers featured al Durah in the videos they left behind. The twenty-first century's first *icon of hatred* justified targeting Israeli civilians . . . right down to infants in their mother's arms (Shalhevet Pass, a sniper's "poetic" payback), and religious kids eating pizza after school.

Thus did the double Islamic blasphemy of suicide terror—killing oneself, killing civilians—become a great and blessed deed, martyrdom, Shahada. Initially, 2000–2005, this wide Muslim consensus formed around Israel and Jews, the Al Aqsa Jihad's legitimate targets of vengeance. Even people Westerners considered moderate, warmly endorsed Hamas and their suicide attacks.

As the author of an apocalyptic pamphlet, inspired by the "Intifadha of Rajab," and published online on 9–11, 2001, described the impact of al Durah:

> Israeli brutality that shocks even her most loyal friends, disturbs
> her secret friends, and drives those who previously had wavered

---

37 Stéphane Juffa, "France 2's report on Al-Dura."

38 On the video, see Richard Bulliett and Fawaz Gerges, "A Recruiting Tape of Osama bin Laden: Excerpts and Analyses," *Columbia International Affairs Online*, October 2001; Julia Magnet, "His Grasp of Spin is Chilling," *Daily Telegraph*, November 16, 2001. For the section on Al Durah, see "Bin Laden on Al Durah," https://vimeo.com/463485002.

39 See the statistics on support for suicide terrorism at Jerusalem Media and Communications Center over the period from 1997–2002, http://www.jmcc.org/polls.aspx.

into the camp of her open enemies. An unprecedented Muslim consensus that the only solution is jihad, these are the words of leaders, scholars, thinkers, strategists, populists, preachers, the illiterate masses, men, women, children.... *Everyone agrees* with these words which no sooner enter the ear and settle into the depths of the heart, then new questions arise: how?...

A government-appointed scholar of the Azhar declares on the most widely viewed satellite television channel (Al Jazeera) that the only way to deal with the Jews is with the principle: "Slay them wherever you find them." The interviewer asks, "But Shaykh, do you mean actual killing?" (That is, "Do you understand what you are saying?") "Does the Azhar agree with you?" And the answer is unequivocally: "Yes." Tremendous anger everywhere...[40]

This passage on the al Durah footage (by far the most shockingly brutal thing attributed to the IDF), represented a (deeply ominous) mutation in jihadi practices and beliefs, from a more passive to a much more active participation in the coming cataclysm. One finds a similar mutation in the Old French tale of Roland's "martyrdom" (ca. 1100), which radically reinterpreted the classic Christian conception of martyrdom (pacifist self-sacrifice), into dying in a heap of the enemies the "martyr" has slain in an orgy of blood.[41]

At the same time that the al Durah blood libel, seen in astonishment and accepted in indignation by "the whole world," became a symbol of the Jews' murderous nature, it also justified precisely that murderous nature among triumphalist Muslims the world over. Certainly, among Arab Muslims living in proximity to Israel, the hadith of the trees and the rocks, a genocidal meme about the Jews attributed to the Prophet, went viral. Preachers in mosques invoked the apocalyptic promise and TV shows spread their words far and wide: "The prophet, prayer and peace be upon him, said: "The [End]time will not come until Muslims will fight the Jews (and kill them); until the Jews hide behind rocks and trees, which will cry: O Muslim! there is a Jew hiding behind me, come on and kill him!"[42] In their 1988/1408 Charter, Hamas introduced this hadith

---

40 Safar ibn abd al-Rahman Hawali, "The Day of Wrath – Is the Intifadha of Rajab only the beginning?" posted on September 11, 2001, https://english.religion.info/wp-content/uploads/2016/08/2001_The-Day-of-Wrath.pdf, 4.

41 Landes, "Roland, Suicide Bomber, October 2000," *Augean Stables*, September 6, 2011.

42 On the hadith, see Sahih Muslim, *Portents of the Last Hour*, 41:6981–85.

with the comment: "The Hamas has been looking forward to implement[ing] Allah's promise whatever time it might take." Still a pious if ominous hope.

After al Durah, the End Times had come, and Global Jihad engaged, here in the land between the River and the Sea, between jihadis eager to slaughter enemy civilians, and the upstart sovereign Jews, who kill Muslims mercilessly: hence the wave of suicide terror—the ultimate in sacrificing the self in order to kill the enemy. The *Ummah's* public sphere so strongly approved this radical new form of jihad against Israeli "cruelty and oppression," that the scholars and theologians and judges had to back away from traditional prohibitions against both suicide and targeting civilians. Noted Noah Feldman:

> Given that embracing Palestinian suicide bombing had become a widespread social norm, it would have been essentially unthinkable for an important Muslim scholar to condemn the practice without losing his standing among Muslims worldwide. In the Islamic world, as in the US Supreme Court, the legal authorities cannot get too far away from their public constituency without paying a price.[43]

This exceptional victory of the most vicious and powerful of all jihadi "weapons" bears witness both to the strength and impotence of Muslim triumphalism at that moment—dying to kill!—as well as to the power of outrage generated by the lurid coverage of the "Second Intifada." On the one hand, powerless to fight Israel on the battlefield, Palestinians of all stripes, not just jihadis, embraced suicide terror as their deliverance. "Finally, after 50 years, we've reached a balance of power, a balance, your F-16 versus our suicide bomber," a Palestinian psychiatrist crowed to a stunned Israeli intelligence chief in early 2002.[44] And whereas the good Palestinian doctor may have only seen a means to "balance power" with Israel, the Global Jihadi saw the ultimate weapon in the asymmetrical war for a global Caliphate.[45]

---

43 Noah Feldman, "Islam, Terror and the Second Nuclear Age." *The New York Times Magazine*, October 29, 2006. The comparison with the US Supreme Court responding to progressive public opinion and al Ahram responding to vengeful bloodlust sounds a bit like humanitarian racism: Manfred Gerstenfeld, "Beware the Humanitarian Racist," *Ynet*, January 23, 2010.
44 Iyad Saraj, Palestinian psychiatrist to Ami Ayalon, 2002. *Gatekeepers* 2012. Discussed below, 407f.
45 Patrick Cockburn, *The Age of Jihad: Islamic State and the Great War for the Middle East* (London: Verso Books, 2016).

Most journalists had no idea of this apocalyptic dimension to jihad and were hardly curious. It did not sit well with their narrative frame. When I told one reporter about the apocalyptic hadith, he promptly corrected me: "That's not apocalyptic—you hear it all the time!" Apparently, he thought apocalyptic meant on the fringe, thus missing the most dangerous possible case, where apocalyptic tropes go mainstream and you hear them "all the time." He was apparently not interested in the notion that, as far as those fighting Israel with every fiber of their being are concerned, these are genocidal battles in an apocalyptic process, that the suicide terror that struck Israel laid the groundwork for subsequent attacks on democratic states and the advent of a global Caliphate. Given the dominant forms of analysis at that time (freedom fighters versus colonialists), this would seem ridiculously paranoid.

And the result of this Western inability to conceive of Muslim apocalyptic fervor, resulted in a systematic misinformation and ignorance among the Western consumers of this (unknown to them) pack journalism, the first collapse of information "professionalism" in the twenty-first century. The price: not understanding how suicide terror and the slaughter of the Jews is a prelude to world conquest. At the height of the Jenin operation (below, chapter 3) PATV ran the following sermon:

> We believe in this Hadith [of the Rocks]. We are convinced also that this Hadith heralds the spread of Islam and its rule over all the lands. . . . Oh Allah, annihilate the Jews and their supporters. . . . Oh Allah, raise the flag of jihad across the earth. . . . Oh beloved, look to the East of the earth, find Japan and the ocean; look to the West of the earth, find the country and the ocean. Be assured that these will be owned by the Muslim nation, as the Hadith says, "from the ocean to the ocean."[46]

One might reasonably expect Middle East journalists to disseminate widely and discuss at length such a startling development. If "never again [the Holocaust]," means anything, it means that when some group preaches genocide from the pulpits,[47] and these genocidal sermons are then broadcast to the public by the authorities and taken up by mass murderers, that's *news*, relevant and accurate.

---

46 "Friday Sermon on Palestinian Authority TV," MEMRI, Special Dispatch, No. 370, April 17, 2002. See chapters 3 and 6. Twenty years later: Imam Yousef Makharzah, "We Shall Shatter the Heads of America and the Infidels, Conquer Rome," *MEMRI*, May 28, 2021.

47 Something that German pastors and priests did not do even at the height of the Nazi Holocaust and the admiration of *Deutsche Christen* for Hitler; see Landes, *Heaven on Earth*, chapter 12.

Indeed, such awareness might sensitize journalists to how their coverage affected Muslims globally, raising awareness of the toxic perception of Islam under attack, summoning jihadis everywhere to a genocidal apocalyptic campaign against *al Yahud.* At such a juncture, it was time for journalists, the "witnesses to their time," to speak up.

But no. Yet another of the mainstream news media's massive miscarriages of their vocational aspirations as information professionals came with the systematic failure of the journalists operating in the Middle East to discuss, or even to reveal, the presence of this extensive genocidal discourse in the Palestinian public sphere.[48] Viewers of the news during the intifada, readers of the daily weekly statistics of disproportionately Palestinian casualties, had no idea that Hamas suicide terror arose from a genocidal apocalyptic ideology,[49] nor that that murderous hatred targeted anyone—Americans included—the jihadis deemed "in the same trench" with Israel. Westerners on the outside thought that suicide terror was resistance to Israeli occupation and war crimes—al Durah!—against Palestinian humanity, not jihadi genocidal war propaganda, at once delivered and concealed by their own journalists.[50]

The Progressive Al Durah Myth: Replacement Theology and Legitimate Jew-Hatred

If the al Durah narrative had a violent mythical impact on Muslim discourse, it had no less a mythical impact on the Western world. The Al Durah icon of hatred was a sensation, especially in France. As with Al Jazeera, daily news reports at French TV began with this *image choc de l'intifada.*[51] Magazines and journals elaborated the tale with heart-breaking details of human interest. Abu Rahma won prestigious Western awards for his journalism.[52] "Le petit Mohamed" was on all lips, and it was, in every case, a reproach: "What did your people do to

---

48 On the behavior of William Orme of the *New York Times,* see chapter 9.

49 Anne Marie Oliver and Paul F. Steinberg, *The Road to Martyrs' Square: A Journey into the World of the Suicide Bomber* (Oxford: Oxford University Press, 2006).

50 Robert Pape, *Dying to Win: The Strategic Logic of Suicide Bombers* (New York: Random House, 2006).

51 One French Jew put it: "the image that French news fed us till it was coming out our ears (*à en baver*)." *L'Express* referred to it as "L'image choc de l'Intifadah," Landes, "Kafka in Wonderland: *L'Express* weighs in," *The Augean Stables,* October 19, 2006.

52 Talal received numerous awards including the "Festival Scoop 2000" in France; the "Mujahid Shield" from the President of Iran in 2001; the Best Picture award for 2000 of the Italian newspaper Republica, and the *Rory Peck Award* in England.

that poor boy?" asked French gentiles of their Jewish co-workers, neighbors, and classmates the following Monday.

In the Western public sphere, Israel suddenly became the whipping boy. Four days after Enderlin's broadcast, as the leaders gathered in Paris to try and stop the violence, Chirac humiliated Israel globally for "killing children," thus giving the upper hand to the same Arafat who was unleashing the hounds of jihad.[53] Parisian dinner-table conversations became occasions for people to engage in extensive verbal abuse towards Israel and respond to anyone who came to Israel's defense with: "I didn't know you were Jewish."[54] In 2006, the Jewish French consul to New England, asked if this reply reflected broader attitudes in France, replied, "Of course people assume that if you defend Israel, you're Jewish. Who else would defend Israel?"[55]

But Al Durah took the French, the Europeans, and more broadly, the Global Progressive Left, beyond mere revulsion with Israel's behavior, into mythical realms, where this story had the power to displace the most powerful icon of the postwar era. Shortly after its appearance, the news anchor Catherine Nay commented: "With the symbolic power of this photo, the death of Mohammed nullifies, erases that of the boy, hands up in front of the SS in the Warsaw Ghetto."[56]

The statement qualifies for both criteria of an *astounding stupidity*: it is both morally and empirically ludicrous on the one hand, and the "vast majority" of French nodded in agreement when they heard it. First the moral problem: a picture of a boy killed in a crossfire started by his own side firing at the Israelis from behind him, in a conflict that in seventy years has killed a few tens of thousands, "replaces, erases" a picture that symbolizes 1.5 million Jewish children, sought out in their homes and industrially murdered, all in the course of four years?

Apparently, yes: Nay really meant it, and so did those who nodded emphatically when they heard her pronouncement. Emmanuel Brenner laid out

---

53 On Chirac's remarks, see 309. On a later comment by the ranking French diplomat in London, see 68f.

54 Landes, "On the hidden costs of Media Error: Muhammed al Durah and the French Intifada," *The Augean Stables*, November 15, 2005.

55 At a meeting with the American Jewish Committee. See below for a similar response from London Times reporter Janine di Giovanni when confronted with Martin Himmel's questioning her savaging of Israel over Jenin, 107–12.

56 "Avec la charge symbolique de cette photo, la mort de Mohammed annule, efface celle de l'enfant juif, les mains en l'air devant les SS, dans le Ghetto de Varsovie." Catherine Nay, Anchor for Europe1 News. The statement appears in the film *Decryptage* by Bensoussan and Tarnero, 2003; cited, among many, by Pierre-André Taguieff, *La Judéophobie des Modernes: Des Lumières au Jihad Mondial* (Paris: Odile, 2008), 300f. Nay responded to her appearance in *Decryptage* in *Marianne* #301 (January 2, 2003); republished *France42 Blogspot*, November 8, 2007; see 58n34.

the reasoning: "Really, 'these people' [the Jews] behave as badly as we do. The shame of the Holocaust no longer exists! The death of Muhammad had wiped out the boy in the ghetto."[57] The Jews of France (and their rare friends) could protest all day long, their complaint fell on deaf ears: it was just the whining of *communautaristes*.[58] The comparison's power to liberate those who felt guilty for the Nazi murder of Jews, was nearly irresistible. It offered the perfect "exonerating projection."[59]

No more Holocaust guilt, or rather, no more Holocaust shame. Now the Jews, the autonomous Jews who, once in power (in Israel), were no better than the Nazis, now *they* bore the shame before the "whole world." Indeed, they were worse than the Nazis, because they should have known better. As the Israeli-born Gilad Atzmon wrote in the pages of an Arab publication: "We have to admit that Israel is the ultimate evil rather than Nazi Germany."[60]

Only this unseemly desire to flee from Holocaust shame—of which there was apparently a good deal in France—could mobilize such a colossal moral failure. As Leon Wieseltier characterized the Israel = Nazi comparison: "It is not only spectacularly wrong, it is also spectacularly unintelligent [where "unintelligent" is a clumsy euphemism for stupid]."[61] Only the most wanton inflation of moral equivalence could compare the two images, much less have Al Durah trump the boy in the ghetto. One must be awfully eager to throw out the old icon in order to seriously, with a straight face, argue that that symbol of human evil has been erased and replaced, in the moral pantheon of "crimes against humanity," by this dubious footage of one boy's "death."

Holocaust Guilt Versus Holocaust Shame: The Dynamics of Moral Disorientation

The widely endorsed narrative of the Israeli Goliath (Nazi) and the Palestinian David (Jew) inverts both moral and empirical reality: the Jews are .02% of the world population and right now control less than .02% of the Arab world. The

---

57 Emmanuel Brenner, quoted at "Comment les médias français contribuent à entretenir l'Irénisme en France," *Naibed*, January 31, 2007.

58 Pascal Boniface, *Est-il permis de critiquer Israël* (Paris: Robert Laffont, 2003); Dominique Vidal, *Le mal-être juif. Entre repli, assimilation & manipulations* (Paris: Agone, 2003).

59 The phrase is Dan Diner's, quoted by Hans Kundnani, "Günter Grass and changing German attitudes towards Israel," *Guardian*, April 5, 2012.

60 Gilad Atzmon, "Beyond comparison," *Al-Jazeera*, August 12, 2006. On Jewish anti-Zionism see chapter 10.

61 Leon Wieseltier in "Tutor," *New Republic*, December 30, 2002.

very word *intifada*—the shrugging of a great beast to chase off a fly—tells us what the Palestinians think of the Israelis. Whereas the Israelis, the Jews, try hard to spare civilians (indeed they have quietly become the standard to learn from in urban warfare),[62] the Palestinians and other jihadis do what they can to target civilians and use their own civilians as shields for protection. Who, properly informed by their information professionals, would believe Israel was the genocidal force in this conflict?

Unless, of course, that folly were induced by a new, gratifying replacement theology, in which the Jews are as bad as or worse than the Nazis, and the Palestinians, as innocent as the Jews whom those Nazis murdered. Then Europeans can eagerly claim that this *icon of hatred* "annuls, erases," the shame they feel about the Holocaust. But really, alas, it was mostly about being freed from a sense of obligation to the Jews, a chance to take up again the Jew-baiting so long denied Europeans by a politically correct post-Holocaust sobriety. Al Durah became the symbolic *proof* that that secular replacement narrative so treasured by the Global Progressive Left was true. Never mind that in so thinking, they scattered empirical and moral understanding to winds that brought hatred and war. Never mind that in order to place "Moral Europe" at the cutting edge of global moral progress they had to see their moral rivals as Nazis, and their mortal enemies as innocent victims.[63]

At work here is a failure on a civilizational scale, based on a confusion of Holocaust shame and Holocaust guilt.[64] A sense of guilt would mean genuine regret at one's people's past deeds, whether acts of commission or omission, and a corresponding intention not to repeat: *Nie Wieder!* Never again would those who felt guilt for the Holocaust allow the kinds of genocidal hatreds that seized Europe and inspired the Arab world in the 1930s/1350s to return, to arise again, unopposed . . . much less endorsed and encouraged.[65]

Holocaust *shame*, on the other hand, like most shame, is not about doing the evil deed, but about getting caught, not about having sinned or committed an odious crime, but about the public perception that one is as bad, as criminal, as the world considered the Nazis in the aftermath of the Holocaust. If that sense

62 Richard Kemp notes how European countries, whose diplomats, politicians, scholars and journalists regularly pillory Israel, send their military to Israel to learn the most humane techniques for fighting jihad, "Israel as a Strategic Asset of the West," *Jewish Political Studies Review*, November 17, 2017.

63 For further analysis of "progessive supersessionism" see 271–75, 288–95.

64 Landes, "Europe's Destructive Holocaust Shame," *Tablet*, September 5, 2017.

65 Joseph Spoerl, "Parallels between Nazi and Islamist Antisemitism," *Jewish Political Studies Review*, 31 (2020).

of shame is stronger than a sense of guilt for having done the deed, then doing something to change the public's attitude, something to "save face," will matter more than serious contrition. To seize upon "Le petit Mohamed" in order to displace moral outrage onto Israel, to make that country the new "Holocaust bad guy"—that is an attempt to avoid shame, not rectify guilt.

It seems strange that a shabbily staged scene of the IDF "killing" a boy could actually move Europeans to think they no longer bore the responsibility to prevent another outbreak of genocidal Jew-hatred. It may help, however, to think of what this new, secular, replacement narrative meant to Europeans, especially progressives. Here we find a third player: in addition to the Nazi Israelis and the innocent (if base/childish) Palestinians, we find the moral leaders of the emerging global community, the "Global Progressive Left," who towered over both of them. In one fell swoop, Europeans who embraced the cause of "le petit Mohamed" forsook their guilt by shifting the shame they refused to bear any longer, onto those they had so badly injured, and on behalf of others, who most ardently wished to "finish Hitler's job."[66]

For many on the Global Progressive Left, including progressives whose own nations bore minimal Holocaust guilt, like England, US, and Australia, Israel still *had* to be new Nazi, and the al Durah icon of hatred *needed* to be true. "Well, the Jews have been asking for it, and now, thank God, we can say what we think at last," noted one Brit.[67] When James Fallows noted that the Arab/Muslim world would probably never acknowledge the deceptions of the al Durah lethal narrative, he did not perhaps realize that the Western progressives would prove similarly impervious to the evidence, so insatiably did they hunger for stories about Jews behaving badly.

Thus, we can understand the British enthusiasm for the virulent new anti-Zionism. Unlike the French, for example, they did not have collaboration (with the really nasty Nazi occupiers) on their conscience; on the contrary, they could claim highest honors in resisting. And yet they welcomed, elaborated, and disseminated the new narrative of Israeli child killers with at least as much energy as the French. Indeed, some observers deemed England the central diffusion zone of global antisemitic discourse, at once the jihadi variety and the

---

66 Klaus-Michael Mallmann and Martin Cüppers, *Nazi Palestine: The Plans for the Extermination of the Jews in Palestine* (New York: Enigma Books, 2010); more currently, "Admiration of Hitler and Nazism," *PMW*, https://www.palwatch.org/main.aspx?fi=655; Bernard Harrison, *Blaming the Jews: Politics and Delusion* (Bloomington: Indiana University Press, 2020), 15–29.

67 Petronella Wyatt, "Poisonous Prejudice," *Spectator*, December 8, 2001. Further discussion, 68n68.

Global Progressive Left version.[68] Tom Paulin's poem about al Durah, which itself played off Fisk's lethal formula, *when you hear crossfire, you know the IDF is murdering civilians*, gives some interesting insight into the phenomenon.

> We're fed this inert
> this lying phrase
> like comfort food
> as another little Palestinian boy
> in trainers jeans and a white tee-shirt
> is gunned down by the Zionist SS
> whose initials we should
> —but we don't—dumb goys—
> clock in that weasel word crossfire.[69]

Unpacked, this means: the Israelis are the Nazis, who cover their murder of Palestinian children with media-relayed terms like "crossfire," and while "some 'dumb goys' might be fooled, some of us are not. We know the Israelis are the Nazis."

Perhaps the supreme irony of this poem is how dumb a goy Paulin is. Not only did he get the story wrong, he also got the identity of the "Nazi" player wrong. Indeed, the jihadis, whose discourse is a terrifyingly faithful continuation of Nazis genocidal paranoia, are completely absent from his imagination (as are blood libels from his list of antisemitic acts he abhors). So, in the name of *not* being fooled by those evil devious Jews, he plunges, supremely confident, into the folly of swallowing jihadi war propaganda hook line and sinker. Shades of those German people who devoured Hitler's antisemitic delirium in the late 1930s and brought megadeath upon the continent.[70]

In this poisonous matrix of jihadi apocalyptic hysteria about the Jewish Dajjal, Global Progressive Left supersessionism about the Israeli Nazi, fevered conspiracy theory viruses emanating from the Petri dish of the internet, and the failure of the mainstream news media, a new antisemitism took hold, first and most pervasively in France, but rapidly throughout progressive circles around the world. The replication of antisemitic tropes in a new, anti-Zionist idiom

---

68 Anthony Julius, *Trials of the Diaspora: A History of Anti-Semitism in England* (Oxford: Oxford University Press, 2010).

69 Tom Paulin, "Killed in a Crossfire," *Observer*, February 17, 2001.

70 Julius points out how it this idea of stupid goyim whom the crafty Jews dupe comes straight from the *Protocols of the Elders of Zion* (*Trials of the Diaspora*, 236–40). Winston Pickett, "Nasty or Nazi? The use of antisemitic topoi in the left-liberal media," *Engage Journal*, 2 (2006).

somehow made all the indulgences of moral *Schadenfreude*—the pleasure one takes in the moral failure of others—at the expense of the Jews permissible. Like French pastries, stories of Jews behaving badly begged to be consumed, and a European public, starved of the joy of Jew-baiting for over half a century, went on a major binge.

And of course, those who binge, do not want to hear dietary advice. In this case, the last thing that moral *Schadenfreude* addicts wanted to hear was information that either undermined the role of Israel as villain or the Palestinian role as victim. Thus, the moral and empirical inversion at the heart of the Al Durah lethal narrative—Israel is the genocidal maniac, Palestinians are the innocent victims—had to be maintained at all costs. Irwin Cotler provides the definitive formulation of this twenty-first-century phenomenon: "It is not only that the Jewish people are the only people who are the standing targets of state-sanctioned incitement to hate and genocide [Iran], but they are the only people who are themselves accused of being genocidal."[71] *Nothing* about this industry of incitement to genocide that prevails in the Palestinian public sphere, and spills out from there throughout triumphalist circles, and through lethal journalists to the West, made it into the mainstream news media's coverage of the Israeli-Palestinian conflict.[72] Instead, a wide range of Holocaust inversions and reversals "took" in Western discourse.[73]

Own-Goal War Journalism I: The Rise of the Muslim Street

If we define war journalism as running war propaganda as news, most of it has involved journalists doing the dirty work for their own side: *patriotic war journalism*. It is not strictly professional, but it happens ... a lot.[74] But when journalists run war propaganda from their *enemy* as news, we've stepped through the looking glass, and entered the bizarro realm of *own-goal war journalism*.

---

71 Irwin Cotler, "Debate on the Rise in Antisemitism," February 24, 2015, https://irwincotler.
   liberal.ca/blog/takenote-debate-rise-antisemitism/.

72 See chapter 9.

73 See chapter 8.

74 Robert Jackall, ed., *Propaganda* (New York: New York University Press, 1995), 105–73. Much
   of the literature in the West is highly critical of Western journalists for "falling in with the state,"
   S. A. Nohrstedt et al., "From the Persian Gulf to Kosovo: War Journalism and Propaganda,"
   European Journal of Communication 15:3 (2000): 383–404. For a good example of Israeli
   self-criticism, see Avshalom Ginosar and Inbar Cohen, "Patriotic journalism: An appeal to
   emotion and cognition," *Media, War & Conflict* (2017): 1–16.

By constantly showing the image of al Durah on TV, even as Europeans thought to banish their Holocaust shame, they were waving the flag of jihad in front of their restive Muslim populations, who began their assault on French society by assaulting French Jews—their neighbors, their teachers.[75] Late 2000 marks the definitive break between Jewish communities in France, most of whom came from North Africa, and the more recent Muslim arrivals from back home with whom they shared their neighborhoods. From October 2000 onwards, France was the site of repeated Muslim attacks on Jews and Jewish property.

And when these outraged diaspora Arabs attacked European Jews for media-reported Israeli crimes, progressives shrugged.[76] When they were not formally denying the new and disturbing outbreak of antisemitism in their midst, French intellectuals reiterated the very *amalgame* they forbid anyone from applying to Muslims: "What do you expect, look at what your fellow Jews are doing to their cousins?"[77] In other words, they had no problem with a terrible *amalgame* born of the very stuff of blood libel: Jews everywhere share the guilt for what some of them are accused of doing.[78]

In any case, the Pattern described by David Deutsch was restored: Aggression against Diaspora Jews because of Israel's (reported) deeds was now legitimate—just as suicide terror was "freedom-fighting resistance," attacks on Jews were justifiable indignation.[79] And just as this approach had no problem lumping Jews and Israelis in the same *amalgame*, it had insuperable problems even considering a *link* between jihadis and the "vast majority of peaceful, moderate Muslims." Imagine democracies telling their Muslim citizens who get beat up by vigilantes: "What do you expect, look at what your fellow Muslims do to our fellow countrymen."

The results were catastrophic: the "lost territories of the republic" began to multiply at an alarming rate. The first signs of the new and powerful "Muslim Street" in France came with the anti-Israel demonstrations that broke out all over Europe in late 2000, but with special intensity in France, to cheer on the

---

75 See 148.

76 See 26–28.

77 Shmuel Trigano, "Le 'repli communautaire' dans les hebdomadaires français?" *Le conflict israélo-palestinen: Les medias français sont-ils objectifs?* (2002), 145–49. On this amalgame and its one-way application, see the case of Tim Wilcox: Nick Cohen, "The BBC: Blaming the Jews for attacks on Jews," January 12, 2015.

78 See Bernard Harrison, *The Resurgence of Anti-Semitism: Jews, Israel and Liberal Opinion* (Lanham, MD: Rowman & Littlefield, 2006), 68–78; Julius, *Trials of the Diaspora*, 474–99.

79 On "The Pattern," see 474f.

Intifada.[80] Nothing better illustrates the combination of lethal journalism and leftist militancy that opened up the public sphere to Caliphator hatreds than these demonstrations, organized the world over, on Saturday, October 6, 2000, to protest the IDF's murder of Muhammad al Durah.

The one in Paris, Place de la Republique, was attended by a large group of "beurs" (slang for Arabs) and a wide range of "left" groups, "some sixty organizations—political parties, trade unions, anti-racist groups, pro-Palestinian groups"—gathered to protest against Israel. The *beurs* took control of the center of the Place, climbing up on the monument, and draping a huge banner that had Star of David = Nazi Swastika = Picture of the Al Durahs under fire, with the legend: "They also kill children."

FIGURE 1. Place de la Republique, Paris, October 6, 2000.

Despite the presence of groups like the League for the Rights of Man and the Movement against Racism and for Friendship among Peoples (MRAP), cries of

---

80 On the Muslim street in France, Nidra Poller, "The Death of France's 'Multiculturalism,'" *Front Page Magazine*, March 30, 2005; Hussey, *The French Intifada*, who covers the long history but deals with the "intifada des banlieues" really only from the 2005 riots onwards.

"Death to the Jews!" "Jews Murderers!" "Death to Israel!" rang out in the streets of Paris, the first call to genocide of the Jews (or anyone) heard in the streets of a European capital since Hitler's day.[81] One particularly paradoxical placard, held aloft by a woman in a hijab, read: "Stop Hitlerian Terrorism! 1 Dead Palestinian = 1000 inhuman [Jewish] lives." Carefully read, it embodies the Nazi inversion in a terrifying fashion.

These gatherings gave Arab demonstrators permission, even encouraged them to act out the first public expressions of the new and violent hatred of Israel. Attacks on Jews in Europe became common, and rarely punished.[82] A new and aggressive tone seized the voice of the radical left, now closely linked to the Caliphators in their midst. The "Muslim Street" in Europe—a twenty-first-century phenomenon of major significance[83]—takes root in this moment of anti-Zionist frenzy. What the French did not realize, indeed denied, was that the *intifada* for which al Durah was the "image choc"—was the first round of a global war that also targeted them. And so, they played it day after day.[84] In so indulging their moral *Schadenfreude* over Jews behaving badly, and displacing their Holocaust shame on their Zionist scapegoat, they were waving the flag of jihad in front of their restive Muslim population.

Either they thoughtlessly presumed that their sympathy for "le petit Mohamed" and their support of the Palestinian cause would protect them from the hatred of the Caliphators, or they did not care. At the time, the al Durah image was apparently so comforting to French/ European/ Progressive identity, and the victims of Caliphator violence so overwhelmingly Jewish, that it did not seem to matter. Certainly, talking with the French about these issues went nowhere. "Faits divers [local items]," said one when I showed her the evidence about "le petit Mohammed."

In mid-2005, a journalist asked some hard questions of a Muslim Brotherhood activist from one of the "lost territories of the Republic," about the antisemitism in a recent speech by an outside preacher from the Brotherhood:

---

81 Brenner, "France's Scarlet Letter" *Vanity Fair*, June 2003; Paul Giniewski, "The Jews of France Tormented by the 'Intifada of the Suburbs,'" *Nativ*, 5 (2004).

82 *Les anti-feujs: Le livre blanc des violences antisémites en France depuis septembre 2000* (Paris: Calmann-Lévy, 2002); Trigano, *Observatoire du monde juif* (2000-), http://obs.monde.juif. free.fr/.

83 Ömer Taşpınar, "Europe's Muslim Street," *Brookings Institute*, March 1, 2003.

84 As Jacques Tarnero's documentary *Decryptage* (2003) pointed out, from 2000–2002 more people were killed in Islamist violence in Algeria—a place where France had a major historical involvement and current concerns—than in the Israeli conflict. But French news media gave it only a fraction of the coverage they gave Israel.

"He said nothing unusual," Mr. Amriou said with a shrug. He clicked on his cellphone, bringing up a picture of a Palestinian boy allegedly killed by Israeli troops [Muhammed al Durah]. He showed it to the [other Muslim] men and they nodded in agreement, anger crossing their faces. The preacher's questionable remarks were forgotten.[85]

Later that year, the suburbs throughout France exploded in rioting for over three weeks.[86]

Of course, the problem for the gentile infidels was that the jihad to which Talal's icon beckoned targeted much more than the Jews. Like so many apocalyptic movements, the jihadis see the world in white and black, those who are with us and those who are against us . . . there is no in-between. For jihadis, the enemies list is mind-boggling—the Israelis, the Jews, the Americans, Europeans, any non-dhimmi infidels, heretics like the Shi'is, and eventually (or is it first of all?) the lax or westernized Muslim Kufrs (apostates) who probably all have Jewish friends. What the French—and most of our "interpreting classes"—did from 2000 on was to ignore any evidence that, from the perspective of Global Jihad, all infidels were also the objects of the hatred aroused by this icon.

The Dynamics of Civilizational Suicide: The Collapse of the Cultural Maginot Line

In the month of October, 2000, the cultural defenses of French democracy began to collapse before an onslaught of virulent hatred for which they were not prepared and to which they had no effective response. At the time, the only people to notice were the Jews on the front line, the teachers in the schools in the *banlieues*, the *"zones urbaines sensibles"* en route to becoming lost territories. For some decades now, the *République's* writ ran with great difficulty in these schools, and when al Durah hit, it triggered widespread violence against the Jews, both verbal and physical. In the historical scale of things, the physical was relatively limited, a handful of attacks on Jews, some desecration of cemeteries

---

85 Johnson and Carreyrou, "As Muslims Call Europe Home." *Wall Street Journal*, July 11, 2005.
86 On these riots and the determined effort by politicians and the commentariat to deny that they had anything to do with Islam, see 143–51.

and synagogues.[87] And yet, these attacks occurred in a democratic state that remained silent about them.

Far more extensive, however, was the verbal assault on Jews, that took place everywhere—dinner table conversations, seminar rooms, radio talk shows, progressive NGO meetings—but nowhere so extensively and damagingly as the high schools. In 2002, just months before Taguieff published the first post-millennial study of the new antisemitism in France, Georges Bensoussan (under the pseudonym of Emmanuel Brenner) put together a collection of testimonies of teachers in the French school system. They independently and collectively described a massive onslaught of verbal and physical bullying by Muslims of Jewish students, Jewish teachers (especially women), and anyone who tried to defend them.[88]

Here in the schools, the Maginot line collapsed first and (a good liberal might argue) most ominously. There was no pushback, not from the teachers who were terrified (and only gave testimony anonymously), not from administrators (who dutifully gave diplomas to students who threatened their professors), not from the state (which denied anything of the sort was happening), and not from the press (who assaulted Brenner for his "Islamophobic pack of lies").

The result: French Jews fled the public schools, teachers either retired, or submitted to the demands of their aggressive Muslim students and parents, who would have no truck with subjects like the Dreyfus Affair or the Holocaust, and the public school system in some areas (designated simultaneously ZEP [*zones d'éducation prioritaires*] and ZUS [*zones urbaines sensibles*]) became a case study in everything that a civil society tries to discourage: bullying, misogyny, racism, verbal and physical abuse, newspeak educational curricula (no Holocaust, which offends), failure to teach and to learn.

And the response of the French public sphere to the book? Dismissal, denial, silence.[89] As one of the few teachers who gave his real name for the book commented:

---

87 This was not limited to France. Patrick Goodenough reported a knife attack on October 16 in London on an Orthodox Jewish student, "Radical Islam: The Enemy in our Midst," *CNS Commentary*, October 18, 2000. Similar reports from Belgium literally the day after the airing of the al Durah report.

88 Pierre-André Taguieff, *La nouvelle judéophobie* (Paris: Mille et Une Nuits, 2002); Emmanuel Brenner, *Les territoires perdus de la République: Antisemitisme, racisme et sexisme en milieu scolaire* (Paris: Mille et Une Nuits, 2002). Almost all the testimony and the worst excesses date after September 2000.

89 See, e.g., Dominique Vidal's short dismissal, "Revue," *Le Monde diplomatique*, May 2003, which ends with a misreading of a claimed misreading. Vidal had documented the right-wing "*communautarisme*" of the French Jews and blamed much of the violence on it, *Le mal-être juif,*

In my class, the students will not obey a woman. One child yelled at a woman whose name was Rabin, "Jew! Jew!" I live with these children during the day, and when I tell my family about it, they are frightened. But when I talk to some journalists, they say, "That can't be true," [and] "You are only seeing antisemitism because you are a Jew."[90]

When, three years later, these same "lost territories" erupted in violence all over France, not only were most French observers shocked, but they then hastily and pervasively insisted that the rioting had nothing to do with Islam.[91] By decade's end, the schools in these ZUS became the site of extensive anti-white (anti-French) racism. Absent the Jews, the favored targets are not only the French students and teachers, but also insufficiently devout Muslims.[92]

Lethal Journalism and the "Terror" Label

It had become fashionable, already in the late 1990s, not to call Palestinians "terrorists." George Carlin, in a famous rant on euphemisms in 1997, managed to demonstrate just how little he understood the words he mocked: "Israeli murderers are called commandos and Arab commandos are called terrorists."[93] Using the "terror" label was okay, however, if it allowed you *also* to accuse the Israelis of terrorism. In the wake of the media's lethal reports of the "Jenin Massacre," Ted Turner, owner of CNN, opined:

> The Palestinians are fighting with human suicide bombers, that's all they have.[94] The Israelis . . . they've got one of the most

---

Paris, 2003). See also Alain Gresh, "Les nouveaux habits du racisme," *Le monde diplomatique*, April 2004, which considers Brenner's thesis *"inane"* and ultimately racist against the Arabs. Gresh is still at it, confirming Amnesty International's accusation of Israel Apartheid: "Amnesty International dissèque l'apartheid d'Israël," *Orient XXI*, February 1, 2022.

90 Quoted in Marie Brenner, "France's Scarlet Letter." A Muslim convert to Judaism in the USA told me that when she tried to tell her new fellow Jews in a liberal, Reform Temple that she was raised to hate Jews from an early age, they responded, "We don't believe you."

91 See chapter 4.

92 Tarik Yildiz, *Le racisme anti-blanc—Ne pas en parler: un déni de réalité* (Paris: Puits de Roulle, 2010).

93 "George Carlin on Soft Language," 1997, https://www.youtube.com/watch?v=o25I2fzFGoY &feature=youtu.be.

94 Note the echoes of a common meme discussed at the beginning of chapter 3: "What choice do they have?"

powerful military machines in the world. The Palestinians have nothing. So, who are the terrorists? I would make a case that both sides are involved in terrorism.[95]

The *Guardian*'s headline made it clear who was the target of this "even-handed" condemnation: "CNN Chief Accuses Israel of Terror."[96] And of course, both Turner and his audience assumed that the war—which witnessed this new weapon of blowing oneself up amidst enemy civilians—was a war of liberation against Israeli oppression, not a jihad against *Dar al Harb*.

At first, only some journalists and news agencies refused to use the term "terrorist" to describe Palestinian attacks that targeted Israeli civilians,[97] but after the outbreak of the suicide terror campaign that began on January 1, 2001, the practice spread across the boards. Professional Western journalists refused to use "terror" in describing Palestinian leaders, organizations, ideology, and deeds. Rather, they increasingly followed a protocol that scrupulously treated both terrorists and their victims "equally."[98] Given guidelines for only identifying terrorism when "innocents" are targeted, NPR reporters, in what ends up as a parody of journalism, almost to the man and woman, chose not to use the term "terror" for Palestinians attacking (apparently guilty) Israeli civilians, even as they used the terror-term freely for other conflicts.[99]

Some explicitly, and contemptuously, exempted the Israeli-Palestinian conflict from any use of the word terrorism: MSNBC's "reporters and producers have been instructed not to use [the term "terrorism"] in news reports on the Israeli-Palestinian conflict except in direct quotations."[100] Indeed, to most foreign correspondents reporting from Israel, no conflict better illustrated the dictum, "One person's terrorist is another's freedom fighter," than the one involving Israelis and Palestinians. "What we [MSNBC] don't do (and this is what irks 'HonestReporting') is throw the T-word [terrorism] around at every Palestinian

---

95 Oliver Burkeman and Peter Beaumont, "CNN Chief Accuses Israel of Terror," *Guardian*, June 18, 2002.

96 On the Jenin media fiasco, and CNN's Andrea Koppel's participation in it, see 104–6.

97 CAMERA criticized *The Economist* for using "terrorist" to describe the IRA, Kurds, Basques, and Peruvians, but "militant" and "guerilla" for Hamas's suicide attacks, "The *Economist*'s Descent," September 30, 1996.

98 The BBC covered the Sbarro Pizza bombing without mentioning either terror or agency except in citations (from Israelis), "Israel stunned by Jerusalem blast," *BBC*, August 9, 2001. For further discussion, see 34.

99 Alex Safian, "NPR's Terrorism Problem," *National Review Online*, June 10, 2000. More broadly, see Kenneth Lasson, "Betraying Truth: The Abuse of Journalistic Ethics in Middle East Reporting," *Express* (2009).

100 "Misreporting Terror," *Honest Reporting*, March 22, 2002.

who opposes the Israeli occupation of the West Bank and Gaza Strip."[101] What they really meant was the opposite: "We don't use it for any Palestinian, even those targeting civilians." Ironically, the most dishonest slogan of the allegedly pacifist "Palestinian Solidarity Movement"—*Resistance is not Terror!*—a non sequitur if there ever was one, became the creed of the Western mainstream news media.

In so doing, journalists, who loudly and proudly refused to comply with Israeli demands that they describe attacks on civilians as "terrorism," actually complied with Palestinian demands.[102] When Colin Powell, who apparently had not yet gotten the memo by early 2001, told Arafat to "take action against the terrorists [Hamas] and stop the violence," Marwan Barghouti denounced him in Arabic. For Barghouti, killing Israeli civilians was an act of resistance, of bravery, of glory.[103] Twenty years later, Palestinians still consider killing mothers a "right."[104]

The Western media rapidly followed suit. The US administration would soon catch up even before the Obama administration. When, in 2018, US Ambassador to the UN, Nikki Haley, proposed a resolution condemning Hamas for terrorism, then Fatah Movement Central Committee member, now prime minister, Mohammad Shtayyeh responded:

> From this podium we condemn this resolution, because under no circumstances will we agree to any Palestinian organization being defined as a terrorist organization. We will not agree! Because today it is Hamas, tomorrow [Islamic] jihad, two days from now Fatah, and so on. We know the story. Our disagreement [with Hamas] is internal, but under no circumstances will we agree to Hamas being condemned.[105]

---

101 "Moran's Public Whining," *Honest Reporting,* June 14, 2002.

102 See a similar dynamic among feminists and patriarchal Muslim men, 419–28.

103 Uri Dan, "Powell warns Arafat, demands attacks end after Israeli outburst," *NY Post,* October 6, 2001; Barghouti response, *Al-Quds,* Feb. 25, 2001. Barghouti, later imprisoned for targeting Israeli civilians, would make the op-ed pages of the *New York Times* from that prison, presented as a "political prisoner," an error later, reluctantly, rectified. See Conor Friedersdorf, "The Journalistic Implications of Ian Buruma's Resignation," *Atlantic,* September 25, 2018. In 2016, Archbishop Desmond Tutu nominated Barghouti for the Nobel Peace Prize, "Desmond Tutu nominates jailed Palestinian for Nobel Peace Prize 2017," *AfricaNews,* August 6, 2016.

104 Lauren Marcus, "Killing Jews is 'our right,' says brutal murderer who 'hopes for 'peace,'" *World Israel News,* January 26, 2022.

105 Official Fatah Facebook page, Dec. 2, 2018, http://palwatch.org/main. aspx?fi=157&doc_id=26805.

Unpacked, this means, "By the Western definition (targeting civilians) we are all terrorists, so even though we're enemies, we'll protect Hamas from the accusation."

The outbreak of the Al Aqsa Intifada/Oslo Jihad marks a key turning point, in which, by refusing to identify terrorists as such, journalists could violate every journalistic principle concerning coverage of terrorism without being regarded as doing so. The Israelis were the first on the planet to suffer from this shift. Families of victims of terror, interviewed by the Western news media outlets, gave testimony to their pain and loss, only to discover that the interview was matched with, in some cases eclipsed by, an equally sympathetic interview with the family of the suicidal terrorist.[106]

As Seth and Sherri Mandell, one set of parents whose fourteen-year-old son and friend were butchered, lamented:

> In a stunning and painful development, many American newspapers, including the *New York Times* and the *Washington Post*, have bought the Palestinian propaganda line that murderers who kill innocent Israelis like Koby are not terrorists trying to instill fear and demoralize a civilian population, but rather "militants" who are engaged in a campaign of warfare against a repressive government.[107]

When an eighteen-year-old Palestinian girl recruited by the PA-sponsored Al Aqsa brigade blew herself up at an Israeli shopping mall, killing, among her five victims, an Israeli girl of the same age, *Newsweek* magazine ran a cover story with the two sharing the front cover, and covering their stories.

---

106 Arnold Roth, "ABC Producer: 'It will be difficult to proceed without appearing *unbalanced*,'" *Malki Foundation*, September, 2003. The question here is: "appearing unbalanced to whom?"
107 Seth and Sherri Mandell, "The 'good' terrorist," *Jerusalem Post*, November, 13 2001.

FIGURE 2. *Newsweek* cover, April 15, 2002, in response to the Afula Mall bombing of May 19, 2003.

Same-same. Arsonists, Victims, Firefighters. Such matching profiles did not appear in any cases of terror not involving Palestinians and Israelis.

Of course, behind this alleged impartial, non-emotive, objectivity, was a massive shift towards the side of the jihadi terrorists and their supporters. The journalists covering events in the land between the river and the sea and their editors back home consistently represented Palestinian attacks on Israeli civilians as "resistance," and—reflecting their unthinking ingestion of the Al Durah blood libel—tacitly assumed that Israeli civilians somehow deserved this whereas other infidels did not.[108] As one Israeli journalist who worked for CNN at this time told me about Western journalists covering the dozens of suicide terror attacks

---

108 On the tacit logic here, see Cherie Blair: "As long as young people feel they have got no hope but to blow themselves up you are never going to make progress." Cherie Blair at a charity event after Jerusalem suicide terror attack, June 19, 2002 (Michael White, "Cherie Blair apologises for remarks," *Guardian*, June 19, 2002); and Jenny Tonge: "I think if I had to live in that situation—and I say that advisedly—I might just consider becoming one myself," ("Tonge sacked over suicide comment" [*BBC*, January 23, 2004]).

on Israelis in the early aughts: "The most striking thing was the complete lack of empathy for the victims."[109] Why? Because, alas, they silently thought they deserved it. Lethal journalists and moral *Schadenfreude* are fellow travelers.

As a result, the press systematically removed the negative descriptors from Palestinian actions against Israel, used passives in characterizing their attacks, and focused on Israeli reactions rather than Palestinian deeds, no matter how merciless, no matter how deliberately the Palestinians targeted helpless civilians, including children, babies, old folks . . . precisely what in their brief moments of lucidity, they described as "terrorism" and "absolutely unacceptable."[110]

But those moments of lucidity concern others, not Israel. In response to the suicide bombing of a Sbarro Pizza parlor filled with children and mothers, CNN's headline read: "Israel hits back after deadly bombing."[111] And the Spanish newspaper, La Razon's headline blared: *Bush alarmed: Sharon Prepares the annihilation of the Palestinian people.*

FIGURE 3. Cover of *La Razon*, Madrid, in response to Sbarro Bombing of August 9, 2001, Jerusalem.

---

109 Conversation with Izzy Lemberg.
110 Octavia Nasr, "Inside al Qaeda," *CNN*, June 13, 2006.
111 "Israel hits back after deadly bombing," *CNN*, August 8, 2001.

Eventually, AP coined the term "revenge bombings" to describe the desperate Palestinians responding to Israeli aggression.[112]

So much did Western journalists believe the Israelis were not innocent, but justified targets of Palestinian, "freedom-fighting," resistance attempting to get a state in Gaza and the West Bank,[113] that, as the non-Jewish infidel dead piled up around the world in the succeeding years, information professionals issued lists of terror-victims the world over that did not include Israel.[114] In their eyes, at least sub-consciously, Israel was *guilty* of oppression and the Palestinians were *not guilty* of terrorism. As we will see in the next chapter, after 9–11, these morally wanton practices came to haunt the West.

The Pathetic Folly of It All: Pallywood and Lethal Journalism

One of my most shocking and transformative experiences occurred in late October 2003, when I had the opportunity to see the raw footage that the Palestinian cameraman Abu Rahma had filmed three years earlier at Netzarim Junction on September 30, 2000 which concluded with the 59 seconds of footage of al Durah under fire. I was viewing "raw footage," unedited by journalists preparing it for the public—a peek, as it were, behind the curtain, at what a Palestinian cameraman filmed on a day of riots that reportedly killed many in the Gaza Strip. For the viewing, I sat with the employer of this cameraman, senior French-Israeli journalist and France2 chief correspondent, Charles Enderlin on my left, and on my right, an Israeli cameraman working for France2, who had been with Enderlin in Ramallah the day of the filming.

What I saw astonished me. In scene after scene, Palestinians staged scenes of battle, injury, ambulance evacuation, panicked flight, which the cameraman

---

112 "AP calls terrorists 'revenge bombers,'" *CAMERA*, September 23, 2003.

113 Ricki Hollander, "Reuters: News Agency or Political Advocacy Group?" *CAMERA*, September 3, 2003.

114 Martin Peretz, "Why Won't Obama List Israelis Among the Victims of Terrorism?" *New Republic*, September 8, 2011. Robert Spencer, "UN lists acts of terrorism, leaves out all mention of Israeli victims of 'Palestinian' stabbing attacks," *JihadWatch*, March 4, 2016; Simon Plosker, "Which Country is Missing From AP's Vehicular Terror List?" *HonestReporting*, March 23, 2017. Wikipedia's "List of Islamist Terror Attacks" mentions only two attacks on Israelis (1989 and 2015); in the interactive chart of "Terrorism" at *Our World in Data*, adding Israel to the graph gives a flat line. For "Terror attacks in 2016," Wikipedia's entry makes no mention of any of the 1,415 attacks in Israel compiled by *CAMERA*: "BBC News coverage of terrorism in Israel – December 2016 and year summary," *CAMERA*, March 27, 2017.

deliberately filmed. There were even signs of makeup men, producers, and directors at work. To judge by Abu Rahma's 21 minutes of film, and a Reuters cameraman's two hours (obtained by Nahum Shahaf), Netzarim Junction that September day was the site of multiple makeshift stages upon which cameramen, most Palestinian, some foreign, filmed "action sequences," performed by everyone from military men with guns to teenagers and kids standing by.

The basic sequence: fake a dramatic injury, have people gather around you, pick you up (few stretchers) and rush you to an ambulance, helpers eagerly joining the group in order to get on camera. Those carrying the wounded throw him in the back of the ambulance, slam shut the doors, and the driver takes off, sirens blaring. That evening, everyone goes home to see how often they made the news.

At one point in our viewing, a very large, fat man grabbed his leg and began to limp badly. Perhaps he had not faked his injury convincingly enough, perhaps his size discouraged anyone from picking him up. In any case, only children gathered around, whom he shooed away, and, after looking to see if someone were coming to help him, walked away without a limp.

The Israeli France2 cameraman snorted. "Why do you laugh?" I asked. "It's so obviously fake," he responded. "I know," I said, turning to Enderlin, "this all seems fake." "Oh," the senior correspondent replied, "they do that all the time. It's a cultural thing." "But," I responded, thinking of a particularly grave case of potential faking, "why couldn't they have done it with Al Durah?" "They're not good enough," he responded. "They can't fool me."[115]

The other shoe had dropped. In earlier sessions with Nahum Shahaf, the first serious investigator of the al Durah affair, I had seen over an hour of footage from Netzarim Junction that day, filmed by a Palestinian cameraman working for Reuters, and I was familiar with the Palestinian practice of staging scenes.[116] I understood that Palestinians faked footage to make war propaganda; what I now also understood was that the mainstream news media had accepted it as a normal practice, and used the fakes to tell the "real" story. Modern journalists in their own democracies, scruple so about this issue that even staging B-roll can

---

115 Landes, "On Seeing the France2 Rushes from September 30, 2000, *Augean Stables*, September 24, 2007. Note that when the French court demanded that Enderlin give them the rushes to examine, he cut the passage described above. Landes, "Gambling with a Lie: Enderlin pulls a Rose Mary Woods," *Augean Stables*, November 14, 2007. He got away with it, but even the remaining footage was so damaging the court found against him: "Karsenty Court of Appeals Decision (English), May 21, 2008," *Augean Stables*.

116 The footage, acquired by Nahum Shahaf, is available at the Second Draft, first used by Stephan Juffa. http://www.seconddraft.org/index.php?option=com_content&view=articl e&id=58&Itemid=63.

be considered unethical.[117] But in the Middle East, war correspondents whose first imperative as serious information professionals was to filter out such war propaganda, apparently had no problem even with Palestinian-staged A-roll, and they used their staged B-roll extensively.

For anyone familiar with the Arab/Muslim attitude towards "journalism," the staging should not come as a surprise. The Arab world is quite explicit on the (premodern) values that govern their journalistic ethos:

> To combat Zionism and its colonialist policy of creating settlements as well as its ruthless suppression of the Palestinian people ... Islamic Media-Men should censor all material that is either broadcast or published, in order to protect the Ummah from influences that are harmful to Islamic character and values, and in order to forestall all dangers.... The Arab media should care about Arab solidarity in all material that is presented to the public opinion inside and outside—it should contribute with all its capacity in supporting understanding and cooperation between the Arab countries. It should avoid what might harm Arab solidarity and restrain from personal campaigns.[118]

Indeed, as one honest Jordanian editor noted, "fake news has a long and distinguished pedigree in the Arab world."[119] And when this self-censorship fails and Muslims criticize their own, the "honor-brigade" steps in to save Muslim face.[120]

---

117 Daniel Viola, "The Ethics of Staging," *Ryerson Review of Journalism*, May 1, 2012.

118 The first two quotes come from the *Islamic Mass Media Charter* (Jakarta, 1980); the last from the *Arab Information Charter of Honour* (Cairo, 1978). Imagine the following:
>   To combat Islamic imperialism and its colonialist policy of trying to spread Dar al Islam, as well as its ruthless terrorism against civilians ... Israeli Media-Men should censor all material that is either broadcast or published, in order to protect the Jewish people from influences that are harmful to Jewish character and values, and in order to forestall all dangers ... etc.
>   ... followed by a denial of any significant difference between Western and Jewish journalistic ethics: Kai Hafez "Journalism Ethics Revisited: A Comparison of Ethics Codes in Europe, North Africa, the Middle East, and Muslim Asia," *Political Communication*, 19:2 (2002): 225–250.

119 Rana Sabbagh "Fake News Took Over the Arab World Long Ago, but Investigative Journalism Might Save It," *Global Investigative Journalism Initiative*, December 1, 2017.

120 Asra Nomani, "Meet the honor brigade, an organized campaign to silence debate on Islam," *Washington Post*, January 16, 2015.

Only a Western cognitive egocentric could not imagine a Palestinian cameraman based in Gaza who considered himself a warrior for the cause, whose bread and butter was staged scenes. Consider Talal himself: He openly films fakes. He lies readily to the press and smiles charmingly when caught.[121] He makes deadly accusations against the IDF under oath and then denies them in unannounced faxes.[122] He proudly proclaims his participation in the struggle for Palestine and his determination to "continue to fight with my camera."[123] I certainly had no problem imagining Talal's role.

But this meeting with Enderlin was the first time that I got the response of a *Western* journalist to this rather obvious acting: "Oh, they do it all the time. It's a cultural thing." A few months later, when the same footage was viewed in Paris with three "independent" journalists from the French legacy news media, they too remarked on the extensive fakery, and they got a similar response: "Yes Monsieur, but, you know, it's always like that," said Didier Eppelbaum, Enderlin's boss. One of the outside journalists responded indignantly, "You may know that, but the public doesn't."[124] This public secret so pervaded French journalistic circles, that one commentator actually invoked it to dismiss Enderlin's most vocal critic:

> Karsenty is so shocked that fake images were used and edited in
> Gaza, but this happens all the time everywhere on television, and
> no TV journalist in the field or a film editor would be shocked.[125]

Both Enderlin and his boss will admit, off-record, to this highly unprofessional behavior done "all the time." But on record, they state precisely the opposite. "Talal abu Rahma, Enderlin assured Esther Schapira in 2007, "is a journalist like

---

121 See interview with Esther Schapira in her *Three Bullets*, https://vimeo.com/65561799.

122 Notarized statement under oath to the Palestinian NGO PCHR claiming Israel deliberately killed the boy "in cold blood," see 4n3., versus a fax of September 2, 2002 to France2, denying having claimed anything of the sort, http://www.theaugeanstables.com/al-durah-affair-the-dossier/al-durah-chronology/.

123 Talal abu Rahma, Arab Media Awards gala ceremony, Dubai, September 2001, http://seconddraft.org/article_pr.php?id=253.

124 "Interview avec Jeambar et Leconte," *Radio de la Communauté Juive (RJC)*, February 1, 2005, http://acmedias.free.fr/q436.wma; English translation/transcription, "Background on the Rushes: Interview with Jeambar and Leconte," *Augean Stables*, September 18, 2007. Despite this candid interview, neither Leconte nor Jeambar followed up, reportedly on instructions from Jacques Attali, a prominent Jewish political figure.

125 Brett Kline, "The Al Durah Controversy Lives on," *JTA*, September 12, 2007, quoting Clement Weill-Raynal, who probably meant it sarcastically. Either way, it's evidence that a veteran journalist had seen plenty of staging.

me; he's a prima facie witness. He told me what happened. I've no reason not to believe him."[126] Three years later, in his self-justifying book, he elaborated: "Never failing in his professionalism, Talal is a most credible source, and has been employed by France2 since 1988."[127]

In other words, the insiders in the TV news media shared a public secret that viewers did not: Palestinians faked scenes and journalists regularly edited that footage, taking small, believable soundbites, stringing them together, to present the Palestinian narrative of victimization by the Israeli Goliath. When Esther Schapira asked the PA TV editor who spliced in the shot of an Israeli "targeting" al Durah, why he did so, he responded:

> These are forms of artistic expression, but all of this serves to convey the truth. ... We never forget our higher journalistic principles to which we are committed of relating the truth and nothing but the truth.[128]

How revealing the vast gap that (in principle) separates Western modern professional journalistic attitudes towards "truth," and Palestinian, premodern, attitudes in which manipulating evidence to make accusations of murder, is loyalty to a "higher truth"! It is the distinction between a premodern world in which journalists repeated blood libels and conspiracy theories abounded, and a modern one, in which professional commitments to accuracy supposedly weed out such lethal stuff.

And yet, more than one Western commentator adopted the same argument "from higher truth."

> In other words, above and beyond "historical" truths of what actually happens in particular "singular" events, there are "philosophical" truths of what "probably or necessarily" happens "universally" in certain types of events ... it [the fake] is an authentic symbol of the Israeli occupation."[129]

---

126 Charles Enderlin, Interview with Esther Schapira, 2007, https://vimeo.com/89803797.

127 Enderlin, *A Child is Dead*, 2010, 4.

128 "PATV Official Explains Doctoring al Durah Footage," from Esther Schapira, *Three Bullets* (2002), https://www.youtube.com/watch?v=E2xHB35umcU.

129 Adam Rose, "The Truth of Mohammed al-Dura: A Response to James Fallows," *Support Sanity*, 2003. See discussion in Jeff Weintraub, "'The Truth of Mohammed al-Dura'—If iconic imagery makes for powerful propaganda, should we treat questions of historical truth or falsehood as irrelevant?" *Commentaries and Controversies*, May 20, 2013, https://jeffweintraub.blogspot.com/2013/05/the-truth-of-mohammed-al-dura-if-iconic.html.

Or, as the *New York Times* headline ran in defense of Dan Rather's forged letter from George Bush's commander in the National Guard, released just before the 2004 election, "Memos on Bush Are Fake, But Accurate, Typist Says."[130] When the "higher truth" is more attractive, mundane facts and professional commitments cede to the narrative.[131]

And so it was with Pallywood, whose higher truth was the Israeli-Goliath and Palestinian-David. Thus, talented, respected journalists like Enderlin, perhaps unaware, perhaps unconcerned, perhaps grateful to have the material, could offer stories of clashes between Palestinian children throwing rocks and Israelis soldiers armed to the teeth, shooting rifles, peppered with high casualty figures for the Palestinian victims, all to the background footage of injury and evacuation. In other words, B-roll for Palestinian lethal narratives. And as far as Enderlin was concerned, the Al Durah story was believable precisely because it "corresponded to the situation in the West Bank and Gaza Strip at the time."[132] In other words, the issue is not that PA journalist-warriors were not good enough to fool him, but that either he was so stupid that even their rubbish fooled him, or he was so venal, that it didn't matter.

I left the building still stunned by Enderlin's response—he had been using the cameraman for twelve years—thinking about the deep symbiosis of Palestinian staging and Western news reports. "It's an industry," I thought, "a 'national' industry, like Hollywood, or Bollywood . . . it's *Pallywood*."

Had Enderlin had the courage to respond to Abu Rahma's al Durah lethal propaganda by firing him, and running a sensational piece on how his own Palestinian cameraman had tried to trick him into running a staged scene of what could easily have become an explosive blood libel . . . had he warned his fellow journalists of the danger to their professional integrity in running Palestinian-filmed footage without checking carefully . . . the course of the Oslo Jihad, and with it, the fate of civil society in the twenty-first century, might have been very different.

---

130 Maureen Balleza and Kate Zernike, "The National Guard Memos on Bush are Fake but Accurate," *New York Times*, September 15, 2004.

131 Sunny Hostin (ABC *The View*) says even though Justice Sotomayor was wrong on the facts (100,000 children seriously ill with COVID vs. 3,500 actually hospitalized), she was still right: "That's a real thing and those are real numbers." Tweet, January 10, 2022, https://twitter.com/CalebHowe/status/1480607195410706435?ref_src.

132 ". . . pour moi, l'image correspondait à la réalité de la situation non seulement à Gaza, mais aussi en Cisjordanie," Charles Enderlin, "Non à la censure à la source", *Le Figaro*, January 27, 2005.

Al Durah, Patron Saint of the UN Conference against Racism, Durban 2001

Few incidents illustrate the noxious impact of the Al Durah myth on the progressive agenda as clearly as the icon's role at the Durban conference, a year later. Here, at this massive global gathering, al Durah was a star, the center of attention, especially in the NGO section (separate from the more formal UN proceedings) at Kingsmead Stadium, a magnificent cricket pitch for 25,000 fans.

The body of Muhammad al Durah was paraded in effigy through processions of thousands of angry demonstrators voicing their hatred of Israel. Arafat flew Muhammad's father, Jamal al Durah, into the conference on his jet, to bear witness to Israel's deliberate murder of his son. Everywhere, all the time, the cry was "Free, Free Palestine!"[133]

FIGURE 4. Palestine's Images of Hate: Al Durah carried in effigy (centre below), Durban, South Africa, August to September 2000.

Here participants were issued an official t-shirt (with UN logo fraudulently added), featuring a picture of Muhammad al Durah and his father under fire: above, the text reads: "Racism can, will and must be defeated. Apartheid is real," and below the picture: "Killed on September 30, 2000, for being Palestinian.

---

133 Joëlle Fiss, *Durban Diaries: What really happened at the UN Conference against Racism in Durban (2001)* (New York: AJC, 2008).

Since then, over 532 persons killed, a third children." On the back of the t-shirt: "Occupation = Colonialism = Racism. End Israeli apartheid." Another flyer, with a picture of Adolf Hitler, read: "What would have happened if I had won? The Good things. There would have been no Israel and no Palestinian's bloodshed." When Israeli activists came up with an alternative t-shirt urging: "Fight Racism not Jews," the crowds beat them up.[134]

Here, a well-prepared war campaign took place that blindsided real human rights activists with a narrative of collective redemption that joined postcolonial and jihadi themes together about the two great Satans: the USA and Israel. Hijacking the conference, the NGO forum obsessed over the crimes of the United States and Zionism, the one for past slavery and twenty-first-century imperialism, the other for their racist, genocidal, colonialism against the Palestinians.[135] Calls for restitution in the name of racial justice rang out.

Israel, the current *active*, global villain, was committing genocide against the poor defenseless Palestinians. Angry demonstrations, virulent speeches, indignant resolutions pounded away at a Manichaean message: Israel was the incarnation of evil. Indeed, a medievalist, well acquainted with the workings of relic cults and mass assemblies, might opine that al Durah was the "patron saint" of Durban, the presiding cathartic presence that gave the proceedings their emotional power to bind together activists from all over the world.

And so, the Global Progressive Left, in the form of "human rights NGOs" developed a program for a systematic "soft power" (i.e., cognitive) war aimed at rendering Israel a global pariah, and destroying her legitimacy. The final NGO's declaration called for

> a policy of complete and total isolation of Israel as an apartheid state ... the imposition of mandatory and comprehensive sanctions and embargoes, the full cessation of all links (diplomatic, economic, social, aid, military cooperation and training) between all states and Israel ... [and condemned] those states who are supporting, aiding and abetting the Israeli apartheid state and its perpetration of racist crimes against humanity including ethnic cleansing, acts of genocide.[136]

---

134 David Kramer, "Why I was almost Lynched for the T-Shirt I Wore," *Times of Israel*, June 16, 2015.

135 See the background to the conference in Harris O. Schoenberg, "Demonization in Durban: The World Conference Against Racism," *American Jewish Yearbook*, 2002.

136 NGO Declaration, Durban, September 3, 2001, par. 425.

Reportedly, the East European NGOs refused to sign on because they knew totalitarian language when they saw it.[137] The tragedy was that Western "human rights" giants like HRW and Amnesty International were major players in the moral and empirical catastrophe, even though, in the end, they also did not sign.[138]

Bernard-Henri Lévy deconstructed the meaning of "anti-imperialism" at Durban:

> If you replace the word America with the word Israel, and put Zionism in place of imperialism (even though the two are indissolubly mixed because the people in Durban ... never insult Israel without also letting it be understood, or even coming out and saying, just to beat a dead horse, that it was only the plaything, the marionette, of the United States, and never mention the crimes and misdemeanors of the United States without also referring, usually very quickly, to the even more monstrous "American-Zionist Axis" and, therefore, to the diabolical Israel), you see the same kind of vise, the same kind of trap, the same discursive structure, that underlies the concept of Empire—and for which Durban was simply the giant laboratory.[139]

---

137 David Matas, "Durban Conference: Civil Society Smashes Up," *Zionism-Israel*, December 31, 2002.

138 Gerald Steinberg, "The Centrality of Human Rights NGOs in the Durban Strategy," *NGO Monitor*, July 11, 2006

139 Bernard-Henri Levy, *Left in Dark Times: A Stand against the New Barbarism* (New York: Random House, 2008), 139.

FIGURE 5. The Progressive Antichrist: Sign held up at Bay Area Protests against War in Iraq, February 2003. Credit: Zombietime.

Before the conference took place, it was already clear to some, what this Durban hijacking of human rights portended for the global struggle against racism. As the old adage goes, "what starts with the Jews does not end with them." Durban caused immense collateral damage to victims of human rights violations the world over—in particular in the Muslim world—whose woes were eclipsed by the enthusiastic adoption by the "human rights community" of the jihadi death cult of the boy martyr.

Standing in Kingsmead Cricket Pitch in Durban, where chants to destroy Israel mingled with cries of Muhammad al Durah, Bernard-Henri Levy commented bitterly on how the obsession with evil Israel literally smothered the voices of real victims the world over:

> I thought about—and I still think about, every time I think about that great moment of shame, contempt, and moral failure—about all the activists for all the just causes who had arrived [at Durban] full of hope, persuaded that they finally had a stage upon which to express themselves, and who ended up reduced to silence by the screaming activism of those who wanted, in Durban's Kingsmead Stadium, to see a single face, that of the little boy Muhammad al-Durrah—and only wanted to hear a single slogan: "Free, free Palestine."[140]

Those angry violent demonstrations, led by Muslims, at Durban represent a real, live case of an Emperor's New Clothes parade. But instead of courtiers following a vain emperor making fools of himself and them, it was alleged proponents of human rights, following in the train of an icon of Palestinian hatred, at a conference allegedly dedicated to fighting hatred.

Durban 2001 marks a critical turning point in the dynamics of the global community. It "became the tipping point for the coalescence of a new, virulent globalizing anti-Jewishness reminiscent of the atmospherics that pervaded Europe in the 1930s," noted Canadian jurist Irwin Cotler.[141] The NGOs who signed Durban's final document denouncing Israel mark a decisive victory of Y2KMind, the victory of Caliphator demopaths and their progressive dupes.

---

140 Levy, *Left in Dark Times*, part three, chapter 4.

141 Irwin Cotler, cited in Wistrich, *A Lethal Obsession: Anti-Semitism from Antiquity to Global Jihad* (New York: Random House, 2010), 486n81; see also Anne F. Bayefsky, "Terrorism and Racism: The Aftermath of Durban," *Jerusalem Center for Public Affairs, Letter/Viewpoints* #468, Dec. 16, 2001.

From Durban to 9–11: A Matter of Days

Only days after the conclusion of the Durban conference, Bin Laden took the new form of global jihadi warfare—suicide terror—to a whole new level: *offensive* jihad against a nation in *Dar al Harb,* with which Muslims were not, at that time, openly at war. On the contrary, the US had just recently intervened in the Balkans on the side of Muslims and helped Bin Laden himself in his fight against the Russians in Afghanistan. But Bin Laden did not play by the semi-old rules about defensive jihad and the necessity of a Caliph to permit offensive jihad, much less feel beholden to Western infidels, playing by the Realpolitik rules where "my enemy [USSR]'s enemy [al Qaeda] is my [USA's] friend."[142]

Not at all. The apocalyptic call of a world conquest demanded a blasphemously daring blow against America, the greatest of the enemies that Global Jihad sought to bring low. Most Muslims, especially the cowardly leaders who had some kind of détente with the West, might try to placate the US with denunciations of these acts. But in apocalyptic time, "my enemy's enemy is my enemy,"[143] and the blasphemous attack of 9–11 was a brilliant transgression, well worth the prize.

And its spectacular success, seen the world over in real time, washed away any concerns. The "Magnificent 19" had changed the world by changing the jihadi paradigm. Civilians *everywhere*—not just in Israel—were legitimate targets in a jihad waged, on the one hand, to avenge the killing of Muslims; on the other, to conquer the world for Islam. Al Durah became the signature of a new, open, suicidal, hatred of *kuffār.* Khalid Sheikh Mohammed, the al Qaeda operative who planned 9–11, executed *Wall Street Journal* reporter Daniel Pearl, *as a Jew,* for the murder, by his people (Israel), of Muhammad al Durah. His videographers edited into their footage of Pearl's beheading, the footage of the crime for which he atoned: the cold-blooded murder of Muhammad al Durah. It was the first political snuff film uploaded in the new century, with its millions of downloads, to be followed with Nicholas Berg and a whole industry of snuff videos, whose roots reached back to the Algerian jihad of the 1990s.[144]

The twenty-first-century phase of the Global Jihad first launched in 1400/1979, began on September 30, 2000, with this explosive, lethal, cheap

---

142 "Defensive jihad" comes into the Islamic legal discussion after two centuries of constant offensive jihad and Islamic expansion. See Ephraim Karsh, *Islamic Imperialism: A History* (New Haven: Yale University Press, 2010), 62–83.

143 Landes, *Heaven on Earth,* chapter 2.

144 Jean Pierre Lledo, *Algerie: Histoire à ne pas dire* (2008); contemporary scene: Ariel Koch, "Beheading Videos and Their Non-Jihadi Echoes," *Homeland Security,* August 16, 2018.

fake. It was the first blood libel of the twenty-first century, the first major Muslim blood libel, the first blood libel circulated by a self-identified ("good") Jew, the first blood libel to carry conviction the world over. Its poison still circulates in the information systems of the global public sphere,[145] a key component of the hatred of Israel that has penetrated the most mainstream elements of liberal and progressive, not to mention neo-Nazi, discourse: Israel targets the innocent!. If today, two decades later, people with good progressive credentials can speak of Zionism as if it were a crime, it's thanks to the Muhammad al Durah blood libel and the tsunami of hatred it brought in its wake.

We are all – Muslims above all – impoverished by its predatory grip on our imaginations.

---

145 See the comparisons between al Durah and the death of a paraplegic Palestinian activist: Nasser Atta, ABC Middle East Newsproducer tweeted that Palestinians believe this "will be the beginning of the start of a third intifada, they compare [Thuraya] to Mohammed al-Dura," Rachel Roberts, "Ibrahim Abu Thuraya: Disabled Palestinian activist shot dead by Israeli troops in Jerusalem protest," *Independent*, December 16, 2017. Closer examination (much of the evidence not available because the Palestinian authorities would not release it), showed no proof that he had been killed by Israel other than the default belief that any Palestinian killed was by Israelis: Tal Raphael, "The Death of Abu Thuraya: What Really Happened?" *CAMERA*, June 22, 2018.

Astoundingly Stupid Statements Discussed in This Chapter

... the target of fire coming from the Israeli position. [*... le cible de tirs venu de la position israelienne.*] (Charles Enderlin, September 30, 2000, France2).

This appeared to suggest that the Israeli fire was targeted at the father and son. (Susanne Goldenberg, the *Guardian*, on the Al Durah affair, October 3, 2000).

When I read the word "crossfire," I reach for my pen. In the Middle East, it almost always means that the Israelis have killed an innocent person. Robert Fisk, "Where 'caught in the crossfire' can leave no room for doubt," the *Independent*, October 2, 2000.

This death erases replaces the image of the boy in the Warsaw Ghetto. Catherine Nay on Muhammad al Durah.

Oh, they do that all the time. It's a cultural thing. Charles Enderlin, October 31, 2003, responding to the observation that most of the footage his Palestinian cameraman, Talal abu Rahma, provided from Netzarim on September 30, 2000 was staged.

They're not good enough. They can't fool me. Charles Enderlin rejecting any possibility that his cameraman had duped him into running an explosive story, Oct 31, 2003.

He is a journalist like me; he's a prima facie witness. He told me what happened. I've no reason not to believe him. .... Never failing in his professionalism, Talal is a most credible source, and has been employed by France2 since 1988. Charles Enderlin on his cameraman Talal abu Rahma; 2007 interview with Esther Schapira in *A Child is Dead* (2010).

The court's decision is a blow against the freedom of the press. Jean Daniel, "Petition en support de Charles Enderlin," *Nouvel Obs*, 2007.

That's not apocalyptic, you hear it all the time. Reporter about the genocidal hadith of the rocks and trees.

2

9–11: Taking the World by Storm (2001)

How many ways can
people under fire get
it so very wrong?

Did the global triumph of demopathic hatred targeting the US and Israel at Durban have anything to do with 9–11?

Not causally. The triple attack plan had been afoot for years. But given the atmosphere at Durban, Osama had every reason to expect that his spectacular deed would resonate both inside and beyond the Muslim world: in his mind, an act of world conversion. When he gave the green light, he took the hate-fest of Durban to new levels, aligning the Muslim and the Progressive narrative of world redemption as a fight against the twin Western evils, the "Big and Little Satans," the US and Israel. Just as Arafat basked in the eager approval of the world press, so Bin Laden had good reason to expect he too would gain widespread approval.

At the time of 9–11, very few people had ever heard of Bin Laden or Al Qaeda. Those who paid attention reached few people with their warnings, and struck many as alarmist fear-mongers. When Fiamma Nirenstein told her editor at *La Stampa* that the demonstrators at Durban held pictures of Bin Laden aloft, he told her to leave the camel-herder alone.[1] Indeed, almost anyone in the 1990s warning about Global Jihad was treated, as was Samuel Huntington "with his poisonous theories," as warmongers, who created the very clash of civilizations

---

1 Conversation with Fiamma Nirenstein, September 2021.

they warned about.[2] In retrospect, the authors of the 9–11 Commission report admitted that it did not occur to US Intelligence to anticipate suicide-hijackers, even though Muslim suicide-bombers had attacked the US in 1998 and been attacking Israel for almost a year.[3] So, when the jihadis hit New York and Washington, DC, ripples of horror and astonishment tore through Western society. Who were they?

The responses to 9–11 among Westerners (including Western Muslims) ranged widely, even within the breast of a single individual. This chapter focuses on four responses that were especially enduring and especially mistaken, or put differently, self-destructive (at least where the West is concerned). Arguably, these responses still dominate the discourse in the public sphere today, certainly in circles that consider themselves "woke." Of all the extensive archive of responses to 9–11 that qualify as astoundingly stupid, four take pride of place and will serve as the subjects of this chapter:

- "Islam is a religion of peace."
- "Rejoice at 9–11!"
- "Bush did it."
- "One man's terrorist is another's freedom fighter."

George Bush's Response to 9–11: Islam is a Religion of Peace

Let's begin with the statement, pronounced at the Islamic Center in DC, on September 17, 2001 by then-President George Bush, less than a week after the event:

> Like the good folks standing with me, the American people were appalled and outraged at last Tuesday's attacks. And so were Muslims all across the world. Both Americans and **Muslim friends and citizens, tax-paying citizens, and Muslims in nations were just appalled** and could not believe what we saw on our TV screens. **These acts of violence against innocents**

---

2 Seumas Milne, "They can't see why they are hated: Americans cannot ignore what their government does abroad," *Guardian*, September 13, 2001. See also, 71.

3 National Commission on Terrorist Attacks upon the United States, *The 9/11 Commission Report* (New York: July, 2004), 339–45; Joel Fishman, "The Need for Imagination in International Affairs," *Israel Journal of Foreign Affairs*, 3:3 (2009), 101f; Kobrin, "The Death Pilots of September 11," in *Banality of Suicide Terrorism*, 35–50.

violate the fundamental tenets of the Islamic faith. And it's important for my fellow Americans to understand that. The English translation is not as eloquent as the original Arabic, but let me quote from the Koran, itself: "In the long run, evil in the extreme will be the end of those who do evil. For that they rejected the signs of Allah and held them up to ridicule." The face of terror is not the true faith of Islam. That's not what Islam is all about. **Islam is peace.** These terrorists don't represent peace. They represent evil and war.[4]

It would be difficult to fit more folly into so confined a statement; indeed, when properly understood, it constitutes a combination of systematic disinformation for *kuffār* (i.e., for American citizens) and a summons to jihad for Muslims, all delivered by the leader of the most powerful nation in *Dar al Harb*, just after a massive jihadi assault on his nation. Given both the content and the wooden delivery, one suspects that this was not written by George Bush or his speech writers, but by, or with strong assistance from, a Muslim triumphalist.[5]

Bush assures us:

> Like the good folks standing with me, the American people were appalled and outraged at last Tuesday's attacks. And so were Muslims all across the world. Both Americans and Muslim friends and citizens, tax-paying citizens, and Muslims in nations were just appalled and could not believe what we saw on our TV screens.

Among the good folks standing next to him was Nihad Awad, a member of CAIR and a vocal supporter of Hamas, and, when it came to Israel *at least*, a fully committed terrorist (targeting civilians as a right of "resistance").[6] If Amir,

---

4   "'Islam is Peace,' Says President: Remarks by the President at Islamic Center of Washington, DC," September 17, 2001.

5   Michael Gerson, "Bush, Obama set pattern—condemning Islam is wrong course," *Desert News Opinion*, February 10, 2015; Napp Nazworth, "Should Presidents Call Islam a 'Religion of Peace'?: Two George W. Bush Officials Debate," *Christian Post*, Nov 21, 2014. For a belated revelation of how much Muslim Brotherhood affiliated Caliphators had penetrated the White House, see Ryan Mauro, "Bush was to Meet Muslim Brotherhood Affiliates on 9/11," *Clarion Project*, April 2, 2005.

6   The career of Nihad Awad offers a fine example of a "moderate" Caliphator, executive director of CAIR, whose sympathies lie with Hamas and Hizballah: "We do not and will not condemn any liberation movement inside Palestine or Lebanon," *Investigative Project Profile*.

the fictional, fully-assimilated, secular, American Muslim in Ayad Akhtar's play *Disgraced*, felt a tug of pride at 9–11, imagine how he felt at the sight of the Twin Towers coming down?[7] Did he see that as a civic tragedy? Or payback to the United States for all the indignities its prominence showered on triumphalist Muslims?

As for "Muslims all across the world," the number who celebrated wildly was not small, and included not just Palestinians[8] and other Arab Muslims, but even non-Muslim Arabs, like Lebanese Christians. An Italian journalist who happened to be in Beirut that day was stunned that "90% of Arabs thought America had it coming," a response heard anecdotally from the celebrators and soon confirmed by an Egyptian poll that put that number at 91%.[9] Even as the party-run press in Egypt toed Mubarak's pro-American line, the opposition papers exulted: "Rejoicing is a national and religious obligation."[10] The Syrian, Arab Writers Association Chairman wrote: "I felt like someone delivered from the grave; my lungs filled with air and I breathed in relief, as I'd never breathed before."[11] Saudi doctors, trained in America (often by Jewish doctors), and their patients receiving Western medical care, clapped spontaneously at the sight on their TVs of the Twin Towers collapsing.[12]

Alas, 9–11 was a source of unalloyed joy to anti-Americans the world over, *a fortiori* to anti-American Muslims, no matter what expressions of sympathy came from diplomatic voices including the Iranian ayatollahs.[13] Only the most fantastic, egocentric, reading of reality could believe that Muslims around the world were "as appalled" as Americans about 9–11. And yet, that is precisely what the jihadis wanted the *kuffār* to believe, and that is what President Bush assured his people was true. It was also what so many of us, good citizens, wanted to believe: **"i think 99% of arab people because they are human beings would**

---

7   Ayad Akhtar, *Disgraced: A Play* (New York: Little Brown, 2013).

8   See 84.

9   On Christian Arabs in Beirut, see Elisabetta Burba, "An eyewitness to Arab 9/11 celebrations in Beirut," *Wall Street Journal*, September 22, 2001; on NY-trained Saudi doctors' joy, see Qanta Ahmed, *In the Land of Invisible Women: A Female Doctor's Journey in the Saudi Kingdom.* (Naperville, IL: Sourcebooks Inc., 2008), 395–411. Muslim responses: Tantor, "Muslims celebrated 9–11," *BlackFive*, September 10, 2012. In the famous "Dinner Party Tape" (released December 13, 2001) one of Osama's men described an Egyptian family exploding with joy at the footage, like their team won at soccer: http://edition.cnn.com/2001/US/12/13/tape.transcript/.

10   "Terror in America (8)," *MEMRI*, Special Dispatch 274, September 25, 2001.

11   *Ibid.* (9).

12   Ahmed, "9–11 in Saudi Arabia," *In the Land of Invisible Women*, chapter 37.

13   For a list of the dutifully sympathetic *diplomatic* statements, see "Reactions to 9–11: Muslim World and Middle East," *Wikipedia*.

be totally against what happened," wrote one person–a perfect formula for calling anyone who disagrees a racist, and a classic liberal conflation of human and humane.[14]

On one level, good for us, that we think that way! Yitzhak Katznelson could exclaim about those who went through the Holocaust, "Blessed are we that we could not believe it!"[15] But we who come after, alas, no longer have the luxury of being unable to imagine collective murderous malice.

Which brings us to the second fantasy propounded by Bush in this speech. "These acts of violence against innocents violate the fundamental tenets of the Islamic faith. And it's important for my fellow Americans to understand that." In fact, genuine Muslim sources—Qur'an, Hadith, Sharia, and commentaries—take positions that directly contradict Bush's claims. In the more belligerent versions of this triumphalist discourse, Qur'anic verses and subsequent literature call for violence against *kuffār* (infidels).[16] According to one not unpopular opinion among triumphalist Muslims, there is no such thing as an innocent infidel: *kuffār* by definition "are guilty of not believing in God," literally (and deliberately) "covering-up" the truth of the Prophet's message.[17] That is to say, some Islamic thinking doesn't even recognize the status "innocent infidel civilian."

No one gains more from these obfuscations than the very Caliphators who have undertaken this outrageous asymmetrical war, and still need cover while their war is in the covert stage. Westerners may think badly of Bin Laden, but every other Muslim, whether "of good will" or deep admirers of Bin Laden, must not be blamed. Twenty-first-century French talking heads have a favorite expression: *"pas d'amalgames"*—no lumping. Normally, they use this to mean you can't lump the violent extremists with the "vast majority of moderate peaceful Muslims," who should not be tarred with suspicion that they share

---

14 Comment on Burba's article in the *Wall Street Journal* (see n9). Shades of my student who thought Daniel Goldhagen "dehumanized" those German policemen who exterminated Jews because he portrayed them as sadistic, thereby confusing human and humane: Daniel Goldhagen, *Hitler's Willing Executioners* (New York: Vintage, 1997).

15 "We could not believe it because of the Image of God that is in us.... We did not believe it could happen because we are human beings" Yithak Katznelson, *Vittel Diary* (Tel-Aviv: HaKibbutz HaMeuchad, 1972), 83–84.

16 David Cook, *Understanding Jihad* (Los Angeles: University of California Press, 2005), 5–31; David Bukay, "Islam's Hatred of the Non-Muslim," *Middle East Quarterly* (Summer 2013): 11–20.

17 Steven Sackur and Anjem Choudhary, *HardTalk*, August 8, 2005, video and transcript: https://keeptonyblairforpm.wordpress.com/2008/09/09/transcript-anjem-choudary-hardtalk-interview-77-london-bombings/.

the radical beliefs of the jihadis.[18] Ironically, Bush—and the many people who continued this approach—made a massive *amalgame* of all Muslims (aside from the mad zealots) and presented them and their beliefs as mirror images of modern Christianity. Everybody knows that *"no faith teaches people to massacre innocents."*[19]

Mousab Hassan Youssef, the former Muslim, son of one of the founders of Hamas, remarked ominously: "When the leader of the free world says Islam is a religion of peace, he creates a perfect climate for terrorism,"[20] by which he meant that jihadis who prepare their terror campaigns operate most effectively among an infidel population that believes Muslims are peaceful by *religious* principle.

President Bush then read out a passage from the Qur'an to prove his radically misleading previous statement about the fundamental tenets of the Muslim faith:

> The English translation is not as eloquent as the original Arabic, but let me quote from the Koran, itself: "In the long run, evil in the extreme will be the end of those who do evil. For that they rejected the signs of Allah and held them up to ridicule" [Qur'an 30:10]. The face of terror is not the true faith of Islam. That's not what Islam is all about. Islam is peace. These terrorists don't represent peace. They represent evil and war.

This transition from quote to conclusion is puzzling. First, Bush reads, as proof that Islam is a "religion of peace," a passage from the Qur'an that says nothing about peace, but rather focuses on the punishment, the "evil that will, eventually, befall those who do evil."[21] And what evil is this that will be punished so badly? That act that Muslim triumphalists find most unbearably offensive: people who "reject the signs of Allah and mock them."

In other words, this passage, selected for the president's recital, might give us insight into the response of people like Nihad Awad to 9–11. It was just deserts

---

18 On the common use of the amalgam to lump diaspora Jews with the "crimes" of Israel, see 24.

19 President Obama, "Transcript: President Obama's remarks on the execution of journalist James Foley by Islamic State," Washington Post, August 20, 2014.

20 Speech to Jerusalem Post conference, NYC, May 23, 2016, http://www.israelvideonetwork.com/the-son-of-a-top-hamas-leader-just-said-something-that-will-completely-shock-you/, at 07:28.

21 Note that three days earlier at the national prayer service in the Washington Cathedral, Muzammil Siddiqi expressed similar sentiments: "but those that lay the plots of evil, for them is a penalty terrible, and the plotting of such shall not abide," https://youtu.be/p86BmTdXQ1E?t=1m14s.

for American arrogance, or, as the good Reverend Wright put it in his own burst of *Schadenfreude*, "America's chickens coming home to roost!"[22] As a Saudi doctor explained to a visitng American-trained Muslim doctor: "It's time you realized: America's been doing this to people all over the planet. Murder. It was their turn. They deserved this."[23]

This verse, chosen to prove "Islam is peace" has nothing to do with peace, but rather with punishment. The Sura comes, according to the traditional Muslim chronology, at the end of Muhammad's initial preaching in Mecca (621 CE? = -1 AH), on the cusp of the shift from the Qur'an's more peaceful (earlier, Meccan) verses to the (Medinan) verses of the sword. The surah is named *al rum* (Rome) because it begins with prophecies about the fates of the two great empires of the day, Rome (Byzantines) and Persia (Sassanids). In contemporary Caliphator apocalyptic narrative, the US is the second 'Ad, the arrogant survivor of the destruction of the great Eastern Empire, the USSR, which fell in 1991, shortly after Bin Laden's jihad had chased them from Afghanistan in 1989.[24] It promises that *kuffār*, especially those who ridicule triumphalist Muslims, will eventually get the punishment they deserve. If this "eloquent verse" has any meaning in the context of 9-11, it is that the attack was a harbinger of those wars of revenge and dominion to come.

So, if the logic of the Qur'anic verse has nothing to do with peace, why bring it up as a proof of Islam's peaceful nature? Because the Muslim advisors of the speech offered it up, and no one had the presence of mind to point out the problem? And if the logic here is so transparent, why have so many people, left and right, for so long, quoted the speech as if it were a great contribution to progressive principles? Indeed, almost a decade later, when Global Jihad was far stronger than in 2001/1422, the *New York Times* ran an op-ed by Samuel Freedman, praising Bush for this speech—one of the few good things he had said during his time in office.[25] Columnist E. J. Dionne wrote fondly of this "remarkable speech" in which Bush "stood up for the rights of American Muslims when doing so was essential."[26] And in response to Trump's blunt talk

---

22 Jeremiah Wright, "The real sermon given by Pastor Wright," September 16, 2001, https://youtu.be/FqPUXjFYh38?t=191; Daniel Pipes, "America's Chickens are Coming Home to Roost," *Lion's Den*, Mar 13, 2008.

23 Ahmed, *In the Land of Invisible Women*, 400.

24 David Cook, *Contemporary Muslim Apocalyptic Literature* (Syracuse: Syracuse University Press, 2005), chapter 7.

25 Samuel Freedman, "Six Days after 9–11," *New York Times*, September 8, 2012.

26 E. J. Dionne, *Why the Right Went Wrong: Conservatism—From Goldwater to the Tea Party and Beyond* (Simon and Schuster, 2016), 199.

about the problems with Islam, Bush's daughter retweeted her father's remark as a rebuke.[27]

One of President Bush's speechwriters explained why he (and others) thought the response was so apt at the moment—itself a classic formulation of Y2KMind. Presidential statements about Islam as a peaceful religion are not only appropriate but "theologically sophisticated," because presidents should promote the cause of those who hold values consistent with democratic governance.

> *Every* religious tradition has forces of tribalism and violence in its history, background and theology; and, every religious tradition has sources of respect for the other. And you emphasize, as a political leader, one at the expense of the other in the cause of democracy. That is a great American tradition that we have done with every religious tradition that comes to the United States— include them as part of a natural enterprise and praise them for their strongly held religious views, and emphasize those portions that are most compatible with those ideals.[28]

The logic clearly strikes Michael Gerson as inescapable: if you want people to be peaceful, treat them peacefully, include them, praise them, and emphasize what you [think you] share in common.

But this is therapeutic rhetoric, designed to draw people into the Western positive-sum world of democracy and a free public sphere, not a realistic description of either triumphalist Islam or many of the reactions in the Muslim community, including Muslims in America. For example, at a rally held at Lafayette Park, Washington, DC, less than a year before 9–11, an advisor to President Clinton on Muslim Affairs, Abdurahman Alamoudi, who was later found guilty of raising funds for terrorist organizations, asked the assembled if, like him, they support Hamas (the creators of Islamic suicide terror). They shouted their agreement, while Mahdi Bray, a black American convert to Islam and major player in the future "anti-war movement," fist-pumped his approval. Alamoudi then cried out for *takbir*—the call to acknowledge the faith—to which the crowd responded "Allahu Akhbar."[29] While the 9–11 Commission

---

27 Leo Shvedsky, "Jenna Bush Tweets Dad's Own Words on Islam to Shame Trump," *Good*, February 1, 2017.

28 Nazworth, "Should Presidents Call Islam a 'Religion of Peace'?"

29 Mahdi Bray, Lafayette Park Rally 10/28/2000, *The IPT*, https://www.youtube.com/watch?time_continue=44&v. On Hamas' creation of the theology of Muslim suicide terror, see Oliver and Steinberg, *Martyr's Square*.

admits that US intelligence did not see suicide terror coming, American Muslim leaders, Caliphators, had publicly promoted Muslim suicide terror targeting infidel (Israeli) civilians for years.

In London, on November 18, 2001 (five weeks after 9–11), tens of thousands gathered to protest the coming war in Afghanistan. Later, one of the Muslim participants recalled how the "climate of recognition and acceptance was epitomized ... when the *adhaan* (call to prayer)—it was Ramadan—was announced over a packed and silent Trafalgar Square to resound in the heart of empire, and so, inscribing another line in the post-colonial history of Britain."[30] Does that mean that in his mind, the respect that infidels paid that day, publicly, in the heart of the (former) empire, prefigured Islam's integration as another civil religion that has renounced its triumphalist imperialism and any resort to coercion and violence? Or that it prefigures the former empire's fall to those imperialists now responding to that call to devotion to Allah?

The therapeutic rhetoric about Islam as a religion of peace and the "vast majority of Muslims" as "moderate," deliberately ignores the possibility that their strongly held religious views, for which we praise them by projecting our civic mindset onto them, are not so friendly. It ignores how tribal elements are more strongly at play in current Islam—triumphalism, supersessionism, imperialism—than in any other major religion to which democracies have extended the right to enjoy its bounteous (and, historically, extremely rare) public sphere of freedom of religion.

How Muslims interpret the Qur'anic command *al-Walā' wal-Barā'*—love good and hate evil—for example, should matter to infidels.[31] Most Westerners, even alleged experts, do not know or do not like to dwell on how often the exegesis of that phrase is tribal, zero-sum: love the good (all your fellow Muslims), hate the evil (unbelievers, all). This interpretation reflects the basic premodern notion of justice, my side right or wrong.[32] As a religious claim,

---

30 Andrew Murray and Lindsey German, *Stop the War: The story of Britain's biggest mass movement* (London, Bookmarks Publications, 2005), 59. For some clips of speeches and comments from participants, see "Anti-War Protest, London, November 2001," David Wheeler Films.

31 Raymond Ibrahim, "When Muslims Betray Non-Muslim Friends and Neighbors: Why Islamic treachery in the Middle East should concern Americans," *FrontPage*, July 9, 2015. On the doctrine of *al-Walā' wal-Barā'*, see Bukay, "Islam's Hatred of the Non-Muslim"; Harold Rhode, "The Concept of Brotherhood in Islam: How Muslims View Each Other and How They View Non-Muslims," *Gatestone*, November 9, 2011; Mohamed bin Ali, "The Islamic Doctrine of Al-Wala' wal Bara' (Loyalty and Disavowal) in Modern Salafism" (PhD diss., University of Exeter, 2012), especially chapter 5.

32 See chapter 6.

it is both supersessionist and triumphalist, and interacts badly with civic monotheism; indeed, it destroys any growth of civic monotheism by treating "lax" Muslims as apostates, deserving death.

The blanket extension of the status of "moderate, peaceful Muslims" to all but the most violent jihadis and their open supporters, ignores the possibility that some (how many?) Muslims are opposed to a public sphere in which people—*kuffār!*—can say things that offend Muslims, rather than show respect, as they must, for Muslim honor. It ignores the possibility that such hostile Muslims (again, how many?) will systematically exploit our good will to their imperialist ends, and that the first victim of their power challenges and grabs, will be the weak among their own people, especially Muslim women. They have no protection from the Caliphators in Muslim majority countries, and certainly not from Western progressives, especially feminists, who trip over themselves not to offend those claiming to speak for "the vast majority of Muslims."[33] This ignorance constitutes a kind of aggressive naïveté built on a profound denial of even the possibility of bad news about Muslims.

It's a real-life parody of the cold-war joke: in this updated one, a liberal is bragging to a Muslim about how free democracies are. "Why, I could stand on the White House lawn and say the president of the United States is an idiot, and I could teach from the pulpits of theology schools that the Bible is an historical document, written not by God or his prophets, but many centuries later by political hacks." And the Muslim responds, "So could I." When this joke is on you, when you are ready to take that answer as a legitimate defense of Islam, then no matter how smart you are, you cannot identify those triumphalist Muslims who target you even as they abuse their communities, their women, and their children.[34] Indeed, those so incapable, end up declaring that calling a progressive POTUS an idiot is an offense worthy of firing.[35]

---

33 On the issue of feminism and Caliphators, see 419–28.

34 The deliberate abuse of Palestinian children for the war on Israel was so unbelievable to Catherine Nay that she attributed her admittedly hasty "Warsaw ghetto comparison" to her outrage at Sharon's making that accusation (above, 18). (At the time she made her comparison, Sharon was not yet prime minister and this is most likely a retrospective memory.) See, however, Justus Reid Weiner, "The Use of Palestinian Children in the Al-Aqsa Intifada," *JCPA*, #441 (1 November 2000); idem, "The Recruitment of Children in Current Palestinian Strategy," *Jerusalem Issue Brief*, 2:8 (1 October 2002). For an empathic look at the dilemma of Palestinian mothers, see Flore de Prineuf, "The Children's War," *Salon*, October 18, 2000. For a more recent report, see Itamar Marcus, "The Palestinian Authority's child soldier strategy," *Jerusalem Post*, February 6, 2022.

35 David Huber, "Principal allegedly fired for posting conservative memes on social media," *College Fix*, November 28, 2020.

And yet, that is precisely the problem that faced Americans (and, although they didn't know it, Western infidels all over), in the wake of 9–11. As Zuhdi Jasser, a civic American Muslim, discovered when he tried to rally public Muslim support for the United States, that rare place in the world where all Muslims could freely practice their devotion to Islam in peace (certainly not in the Muslim world), he discovered that much of the leadership in the Islamic community, both religious and lay, not only refused to join, but actively opposed him.[36] And by and large, the media favored and gave far more attention to these radical opponents of an open society.

The problem goes well beyond a simple contradiction: for example, the fact that the Qur'anic verse about punishment offers nothing remotely like proof of the assertion that Islam is a religion of peace. The real problem concerns whose reading becomes dominant: Bush's speech makes perfect sense as a strategic demand of *da'wa* ("summons," proselytizing) operating as an adjunct to *jihad*: it asks the infidel to deny that the violence has anything to do with Islam, a "religion of peace" and compassion, even as one makes clear to "*mocking kuffār*" that "if you want peace, then please Allah and do not offend Muslims." That's how to avoid being the target of jihadi violence.

So the president of the United States, the most powerful nation on earth, embodiment of the success of modernity, hegemon of a post-World-War II period of exceptional peace and productivity, center of a vigorous culture that, via technological revolutions in transportation and communications, filled the whole world with its presence, had just responded to a spectacular attack in its heartland by giving a speech that systematically misinformed the *kuffār*—his fellow Americans—and waved the flag of jihad before triumphalist Muslims the world over.

For statements that literally inverted both reality and the balance of forces between an open and tolerant society (whatever its flaws) on the one hand, and a vindictive and oppressive society (overflowing with flaws) on the other, at least by progressive standards, this speech, written for, and delivered by, George Bush on September 16, 2001, at the Islamic Center of DC, ranks among the most damaging. This was a massive cognitive-war victory for Islam, literally while the smoke was still billowing at ground zero, and a correspondingly damaging loss for the West. One might be tempted to view it as a *Nakba* for civil global culture, a collapse of democratic culture's Maginot line. Well intentioned, no doubt; but one should not promote virtuous behavior with such crucial inaccuracies.

---

36 Zuhdi Jasser, *A Battle for the Soul of Islam: An American Muslim Patriot's Fight to Save His Faith* (New York: Threshold Editions, 2013), chapter 6.

Scholars who had learned about Islam in the academy before Said's *postcolonial effect* (1980s on), might have responded to Bush's speech with a loud guffaw, knowing as they did Islam's long bloody history of both *jihad* (Muslims killing infidels) and *fitna* (Muslims killing Muslims), that go back to the prophet's life and immediately following his death.[37] Had they done a minimum of Religious Studies, they would know that Islam's sustained, imperialist warfare over its first centuries surpassed that of any other monotheistic faith.[38] They also would have known about the impact those violent hostilities towards infidels and heretics had on the very language of the Qur'an, on its exegesis, and on the shape of the bloody Sun'ni-Shi'i split that re-emerges in unthinkable violence today from Yemen to Al-Shams (Levant) and, since Obama's deal with the Shi'is in Iran, has driven Saudi Arabia towards Israel (!).

Granted, we all wanted, for the sake of the civil society we prize, that our leader calm the waters of vigilante violence against American Muslims, against this small minority, who were *not* guilty of this terrible act. So, one can approve of the speech as therapeutic rhetoric, perhaps, but not a description of empirical reality. One would have expected our information professionals, who knew better, to host a national conversation in which infidels learned about Muslim triumphalism, the worldview of those Muslims who did attack us, and tried to understand why so many cheered, openly and privately, at such a mighty blow against the *kuffār*, especially against the most powerful *kuffār*, the "USA." One would expect, minimally, that after 9–11, American nonbelievers would learn, from their teachers, their professors, their journalists, their public intellectuals, about *Dar al Islam, Dar al Harb*, military *jihad*, various interpretations of *al-Walā' wal-Barā'*, and the laws of the *dhimma*.

Not at all.[39] On the contrary, both academics and journalists, strove mightily to promote Bush's speech. Even—especially—in the depiction of the attackers in the 9–11 memorial.[40] And everywhere, from the school curricula to the nonreciprocal dialogue groups, to the strictures of Homeland Security intelligence, one finds the effects of this bizarre assertion that Islam means peace and nothing else. Any violence involved? Can't be Islam. As Brian Paddick said in

---

37 David Cook, *Understanding Jihad*; Michael Bonner, *Jihad in Islamic History: Doctrines and Practice* (Princeton: Princeton University Press, 2006).

38 Karsh, *Islamic Imperialism*.

39 These terms often get single, passing mentions, if at all, in the abundant literature for Westerners about Islam after 9–11. E.g., "academic" John Esposito's *What Everyone Needs to Know about Islam* (New York: Oxford University Press, 2002); more recently, Cole, *Muhammad*.

40 Sharon Otterman, "Film at 9/11 Museum Sets off Clash over Reference to Islam," *New York Times*, April 23, 2014.

the name of the London Police force after the 7–7 2005 attacks: **"As far as I am concerned, Islām and terrorists are two words that do not go together."**[41]

The same trope thus moved from high diplomatic rhetoric on global TV (i.e., face-saving discourse), to security intelligence (i.e., self-defense). What a cogwar victory for Caliphators! Enough to inspire some to believe, that this crazy idea of Islamic global supremacy just might have a chance. One might be forgiven for taking Bin Laden seriously when he claimed to be the strong horse. Of course, if one said so out loud, one ran the risk of accusations of paranoid Islamophobia for suggesting that both the jihadi message had great resonance within the Umma, and the response of those eager to minimize it, served the Caliphators' ends.

And sure enough, Americans twice elected to office a president who took Bush's "policy" on Islam still further, arguing that Islam is by definition a peaceful religion and that any violence coming from Muslims has nothing to do with Islam and its teachings, and to say so, is to insult the vast majority—"99.9%" (!)—of moderate Muslims who reject "this medieval interpretation of Islam."[42] This led to some grimly comic moments in Congressional hearings, where administration officials sounded like automatons programmed not to think, but to repeat newspeak.[43] Indeed, in the acceptable public discourse anyone talking about various aspects of Muslim triumphalism—Islamism, Sharia, jihad, al-Walā' wal-Barā'—was automatically relegated to the margins of the public sphere; they were *Islamophobes*, bent on making things worse, hate-mongers encouraging people to dislike Muslims and Islam. They won't make it into mainstream publications, and so they publish it where "good people" don't read.

Some mainstream news agencies systematically filtered out any awareness of belligerent Islamic teachings and attitudes. The BBC seemed to implement the policy of keeping terrorism and Islam apart. Thus, when the BBC's *HardTalk* host, Stephen Sackur, interviewed radical Islamist Anjem Choudhary in the wake of the 7–7 (2005) London transport bombings, he first found out that

---

41 British deputy commissioner of the Metropolitan Police, Brian Paddick, 7-7-2005. Melanie Phillips, *Londonistan: How Britain Is Creating a Terror State Within* (London: Gibson Square, 2006), 101. See Ken Livingstone's similar remarks on Yussuf al Qaradawi as a moderate: "Livingstone invites cleric back," *BBC*, July 12, 2004; Daniel Pipes, "[The Islamist-Leftist] Allied Menace," *National Review* July 14, 2008.

42 Michael Oren, "How Obama Opened His Heart to the "Muslim World,'" *Foreign Affairs*, June 19, 2015. On Obama's use of "99.9% of Muslims" see above, xv.

43 Attorney General Eric Holder and Republican Representative Lamar Smith, May 13, 2010, YouTube; Assistant Defense Secretary for Homeland Security, Paul Stockton and Republican Representative Dan Lundgren, December 13, 2011, YouTube. Analyzed by Daniel Pipes, "Denying Islam's Role in Terror: Explaining the Denial," *Middle East Quarterly*, Spring 2013.

according to some Muslims, no non-Muslim was innocent; that infidels were, by definition, guilty of rejecting Islam.[44] Sackur was stunned. "You mean, when Huzb-ut-Tahrir leader Omar Bakri condemns the killing of innocents in the 7–7 attacks, he's only talking about Muslims?" Precisely.

Well into the teens of the new century, when I spoke to audiences, whether public, academic, or even members of Homeland Security, most people still did not know what *Dar al Islam* and the other key triumphalist terms mean.[45] What more could Caliphator Da'is hope for than *kuffār* leaders who disinform their own people about the enemy they face? This self-imposed ban on discussion of "radical Islam" inflicted a critical blindness among Western policymakers and intelligence gatherers; it produced the cognitive disorientation embodied in the meaningless term "war on terror." It accordingly strengthened the Caliphators and weakened more civil (less aggressive) Muslims whom they targeted as lax if not apostate. This approach continues to generate an ongoing catastrophe in which Western progressives validate the victimizers as (resisting) victims (e.g., Palestinian jihadis) and abandon dissident religious minorities in the Middle East—Jews, Druze, Bedouin, Maronites, Christians, Zoroastrians, Yazidis, Berbers—to the tender mercies of these predatory triumphalists.[46] Israel alone has successfully resisted . . . provoking moral hysteria in some corners of the West.

Whence this critical, possibly fatal ignorance about an enemy that has openly declared war on Western society?

There are many answers, most involving some acknowledgment of fear of offending triumphalist Muslims (below, chapter 13), most prominent in the media's refusal to use the word terror for jihadis who attack civilians (see below). First, I will examine two explanations for the self-weakening attitudes towards Islam that illustrate less the push of the jihadis, than the pull of a peculiar Western folly that Caliphators systematically exploit to assault the West.

---

44 "Justifying acts of terror?" BBC, August 10, 2005 (above, 17). On Choudhary, Omar Bakri and the circle of radical Muslims in England, see Jon Ronson, *Them: Adventures with Extremists* (New York: Simon and Schuster, 2002), chapter 1.

45 Peter Townsend, *Arabic for Unbelievers* (2014); Nancy Kobrin, *The Jihadi Dictionary: The Essential Intel Tool for Military, Law Enforcement, Government and the Concerned Public* (Mamaroneck, NY: MultiEducator, 2016).

46 For an understanding of what awaits minorities in Muslim-majority lands who, unlike the Zionists, cannot defend themselves, see Raymond Ibrahim, *Crucified Again: Exposing Islam's New War on Christians* (New York: Regnery Publishing, 2013).

Baudrillard and the Marriage of Postmodern Masochism and Premodern Sadism

The day after 9–11, all around the Western world, the shock was palpable, and the sympathy for the victims—some 3000 dead Americans, among them Muslims—was widespread, at least in diplomatic circles. Expressions of condolence and sympathy poured in, even from Iran, even from Yasser Arafat (who, to compensate for his people's embarrassing celebrations, faked giving blood to help victims who had been pulverized in the attack), only to be scorned by the Arab press for failing to stand with his people, and making a show of himself.[47] The notoriously anti-American *Le Monde* anticipated the later hashtag of #WeAreAll [fill in blank with latest terror victims], with an editorial entitled, "*Today, We Are All Americans*." In it, in addition to the obligatory digs at the US for giving birth to this devil (Bin Laden), the editorial noted that any attempt to justify this attack as war on behalf of the poor third world was to

> credit the authors of this murderous madness with "good intentions" or of some project where they must avenge oppressed peoples against their unique oppressor, America. It would permit them to claim the mantle of "poverty"—an offense, an injury to genuinely impoverished people the world over! What a monstrous hypocrisy. None of those who contributed to this operation can pretend to want the good of humanity. They do not want a better, more just world. They just want to erase ours from the map.[48]

Empirically accurate, exactly right level of "us" solidarity (Western democracies), morally acute, in limpid prose. Most decidedly not stupidly pro-jihad. And given *Le Monde*'s deeply embedded anti-Americanism, quite impressive in its generosity of spirit. When they want to, the French can think and write clearly.

And yet, two weeks later, the same *Le Monde* ran a piece by Jean Baudrillard, a major sociologist and philosopher (two French terms for critical theorists

---

47 *Al-Wafd*, the daily of Egypt's largest opposition party, was revolted by Arafat's obsequiousness: *Al-Wafd* (Egypt), September 14, 2001, cited in "Egypt's Opposition Press: Rejoicing is a National and Religious Obligation," *MEMRI*, Special Dispatch 274, September 25, 2001. On the fake blood donation—Arafat abhors needles—for victims (who had been incinerated and did not need blood?), see Joel Pollak, "Enderlin: Arafat faked 9/11 blood donation," *Guide to the Perplexed*, 17 January 2008.

48 "Nous sommes tous américains," *Le Monde*, September 13, 2001.

at the cutting edge of academic discourse), in which he articulated precisely the sentiments the editors had dismissed as "monstrous hypocrisy" only days before.

> All the verbiage and commentaries betray a gigantic abreaction to the very event and the fascination it exercises. Moral condemnation and the sacred union against terrorism match the prodigious jubilation engendered by witnessing this global superpower being destroyed [sic]; better, by seeing it more or less self-destroying, even suiciding spectacularly. **Though it is she [the US] that has, through its intolerable power, engendered all that violence brewing around the world, and therefore this terrorist imagination that—unknowingly— inhabits us all.**
>
> **That we have dreamed of this event, that everybody without exception has dreamt of it, because everybody must dream of the destruction of any power hegemonic to that degree—this is unacceptable for Western moral conscience, but it is still a fact,** and one which is justly measured by the pathetic violence of all those discourses which attempt to erase it.[49]

Here the moral clarity of the editors becomes a monstrous hypocrisy of *Schadenfreude* at America's suffering, dressed up as a universal sense of moral offense at the American colossus.[50] (It does have a certain refreshing honesty, though: "everybody rejoiced, don't buy into the hypocritical pieties of those who express their sympathies.") At the same time, Baudrillard did precisely what *Le Monde*'s editors had just warned against: he glorified "freedom-fighting" jihadis who struck a mortal [sic] blow at the suffocating American hegemon ("intolerable power" or what Said referred to as the "frighteningly global reach of the last remaining superpower"[51]). As aberrant as it may strike some sensibilities (empathy and value of human life), this became a defining approach on the left: One French socialist opined a month after 9–11: "Islam is, after all, the poor.

---

49 Jean Baudrillard, "L'esprit du terrorisme," *Le Monde*, November 2, 2001.

50 For the German response, see Clemens Heni, *Schadenfreude: Islamforschung und Antisemitismus in Deutschland nach 9/11* (Berlin: Edition Critic, 2011).

51 Said, *Humanism and Democratic Criticism* (New York: Columbia University Press, 2003), 47.

And it pisses [us brave socialists] off (*ça fait chier*) to [see the US] beat up the poor."[52]

It takes a special kind of "malignant desire," to use Baudrillard's own term, for someone to be so struck with envy and resentment at the success of another (in this case a historical, civilizational ally/rival in the creation of democratic societies, one that twice within living memory had saved Europeans from their own madness), that one rejoices in an attack like 9–11. To cheer the blow to Americans even when that "hegemon" has been far more beneficent and far less authoritarian toward weaker nations or peoples than any earlier hegemon in history over whom it had a massive military advantage, reflects a staggering self-absorption in which American superiority to France/Europe is more unbearable than massive assaults on "innocent" infidels. An act of *mauvaise foi* (bad faith) worthy of Sartre's pen at the height of his useful idiocy ... the beginning of a genuine *huis clos* (no exit).[53]

It seems hard to conceive of such a reaction, when the force (jihad) that struck the blow against one's civilizational peer (US), also seeks vengeance against your own nation (France), known for its heartless massacres of Muslim civilians in Algeria,[54] a force that hates progressive iconoclasts more than anyone but Jews. Who attacks one's friends and supports one's enemies? The answer, in the world of shame-honor dynamics, is: "the weak." How does one shield oneself from that awareness? In adopting the foolish syllogism: "Courage is attacking the strongest, and America is strongest."[55]

In England, people like Seumas Milne in the *Guardian* asserted the real "lesson" of 9–11: that Americans, thick-headed fools that they are, can't understand why they're hated, why this attack represented "reaping the dragons' teeth harvest they themselves had sown," among other things by siding with Israel against the poor Palestinians.[56] His whole article is wrapped in a serene

52 Cited by Rénaud Dely, "Les socialistes malmenés par leur base: l'anti-américanisme perdure chez les militants," *Libération*, October 16, 2001, 10; similar sentiments from Alain Gresh of *Le monde diplomatique*, "Les enjeux d'un dialogue. Entretien avec Alain Gresh", *Regards* 73 (November 2001), 20. Both cited in Pierre André Taguieff, *La nouvelle judéophobie*, 100n157.

53 Sartre, *Huis clos* (*No Exit*) in which hell is being eternally stuck dealing with others of bad faith; on Sartre's bad faith, see Tony Judt, *Past Imperfect: French Intellectuals, 1944–1956* (Los Angeles: University of California Press, 1994), 153–86.

54 Manfred Halpern, "The Algerian Uprising of 1945," *Middle East Journal* 2:2 (1946): 191–202.

55 French journalists in conversation, February 2003, Landes, "Chiraq-Iraq: Sailing Full Speed in Iceberg-Laden Waters," Paris, March 5–16, 2003, *The Augean Stables*.

56 Seumas Milne, "They can't see why they are hated." *The Guardian*, September 13, 2001. On Milne's letter as reflective of widespread "liberal" opinion and the powerful echoes in the more "intellectual" *London Review of Books*, see Andrew Anthony, *The Fallout: How a guilty liberal lost his innocence* (London: Random House, 2007) 10–16. For a review of "the universal and

certainty that this is the only viable reading of world events. Yet another way the Palestinian cause locked the Left into a politics of odium.

And many Americans, especially on the left, agreed. Susan Sontag immediately Westsplained the attack as if its motives should be obvious to all:

> Where is the acknowledgment that this was not a "cowardly" attack on "civilization" or "liberty" or "humanity" or "the free world" but an attack on the world's self-proclaimed superpower, undertaken as a consequence of specific American alliances and actions? How many citizens are aware of the ongoing American bombing of Iraq? . . . In the matter of courage (a morally neutral virtue): whatever may be said of the perpetrators of Tuesday's slaughter, they were not cowards.[57]

Judith Butler described 9–11 as a "dislocation from first-world privilege, however temporary,"[58] where "first-world privilege" and "intolerable power" described the same grand-narrative villain. Long-time progressive thinker, Michael Walzer, meditating on the guilt engendered by enjoying the privileges of living in America, listed the emotions that arise in response—"festering resentment, ingrown anger, and self-hate" and then concluded:

> Certainly, all those emotions were plain to see in the left's reaction to September 11, in the failure to register the horror of the attack or to acknowledge the human pain it caused, in the *Schadenfreude* of so many of the first responses, the barely concealed glee that the imperial state had finally gotten what it deserved.[59]

sound rejection" of Huntington's thesis, Ervand Abrahamian, "The US Media, Huntington, and 9–11," *Third World Quarterly*, 24.3 (2003): 529–544. For Milne as a representative of the anti-imperialism of fools that Said so effectively established, see 292n115.

57 Susan Sontag, "New Yorker Writers Respond to 9–11," *New Yorker*, September 24, 2001. Response by Charles Krauthammer, specifically addressing the "we're still bombing Iraq" comment: "Voices of Moral Obtuseness," *Washington Post*, September 21, 2001. More broadly, Andrew Anthony, *The Fallout*, esp. 3–19.

58 Judith Butler, *Precarious Life: The Powers of Mourning and Violence* (NY, 2004), xii.

59 Michael Walzer, "Can There Be a Decent Left?" *Dissent*, Spring 2002. For an extensive discussion of the manichaean left and its response to 9–11, see Michael Bérubé, *The Left at War* (New York: New York University Press, 2009).

Reasonably, Walzer feared that when we indulge these emotions, it "makes it impossible to sustain a decent (intelligent, responsible, morally nuanced) politics." Salmon Rushdie expressed similar concerns: the US faces "an ideological enemy that may turn out to be harder to defeat than militant Islam: that is to say, anti-Americanism, which already then was taking the world by storm."[60]

Given the choice between the moral clarity and grounded empiricism of the initial reaction of *Le Monde's* editors on the one hand, and the compulsive, self-destructive, moralizing, *Schadenfreude* of Baudrillard, on the other, French culture shifted decisively against the US and towards the joys of watching a rival get battered. Noted a French researcher into anti-Americanism:

> The fury of the responses testified to a profound horror at the
> very idea that one could call oneself "American" and thus annul,
> if only during a crisis, the long work of differentiation between
> "us" and "them" that has mobilized for over a century, a good
> portion of French intellectual energies.[61]

French intellectuals had their own "tribal," "us-them" instincts, invidious ones, which they indulged to the fullest.

Nidra Poller described the sudden shift after Bin Laden's attack: if Al Durah sounded the death knell for Zionism in French public discourse, then 9–11 sounded it for the US. Returning to Paris from the US only weeks after 9–11, Poller could cut the anti-Americanism in Parisian society with a knife.[62] Dinner-table conversations, seminar rooms, street demonstrations ... *le tout Paris* indulged in a collective celebration of *Schadenfreude* over America's misfortune. Baudrillard, like Catherine Nay, spoke for many when he claimed that we *all* rejoice when we see so suffocating a hegemon receive such a painful blow. America deserved it.

In 2002, Philippe Roger published a history of Europe's centuries-long unhappy relationship with America, something he had been working on for many years. He declined to comment on 9–11: "The collection of idiocies (*le sottisier*) of French reactions remains to be made, but I lack the heart."[63] Jean Francois Revel, in a book conceived in 2000, but written after 9/11 has a chapter,

---

60 Salmon Rushdie, "Anti-Americanism takes the world by storm," *Guardian*, February 5, 2002.
61 Roger, *L'ennemi américain*, 578.
62 On Poller's reflections on the early years of the new century, see *Troubled Dawn of a New Century* (Paris, 2017).
63 Roger, *L'ennemi américain*, 578.

"Why so much hate? And why so many errors?" in which he criticizes narcissistic journalists who, to feed their indulgence "in dreams of a factitious superiority," therefore betray their publics by so dramatically misinforming them about so important a topic as the United States.[64] In 2004, Paul Hollander published a collection of essays on anti-Americanism globally, with a heavy emphasis on the delirium that characterized its post-9/11 behavior.[65] Andre Markovits's *Uncouth Nation* tells the sad tale of the early aughts in gory detail.[66]

European discourse was thick with *Schadenfreude*, fueled by widely believed conspiracy theories about how George Bush and the US government had planned and executed the attack to justify a war against Islam. This hostility to the US in the name of "peace and justice" became emblematic of both European elites and of the movement that called itself the "global progressive left." For them, American hegemony, the dominance of an (ironically termed) "Eurocentric" worldview, became the great foe of freedom and justice. The postcolonial paradigm, articulated at great length by Hardt and Negri in their book *Empire* (2000), dominated academic discourse. In this reading of global history, Western imperialism in its global capitalist form is the worst, most intrusive force ever, and the US, the most stifling of hegemons.[67]

In England, perhaps a bit behind France's trailblazing anti-Americanism, 9–11 prompted a wave of antisemitism [!]. Petronella Wyatt, a highly placed London journalist noted in December of 2001 that, "Since September 11, antisemitism and its open expression has become respectable at London dinner tables," with a *Guardian*-reading peer remarking: "Well, the Jews have been asking for it, and now, thank God, we can say what we think at last."[68] As if to prove Wyatt's comment true, three weeks later, at one of those dinner tables, French diplomat, Daniel Bernard referred to Israel, as that "shitty little country"

---

64 "... ils [les erreurs] gonflent sans doute ceux qui s'y adonnent d'une illusion de revanche et de la jouissance onirique d'une supériorité factice." Jean-François Revel, *L'obsession anti-américaine : Son fonctionnement, ses causes, ses conséquences* (Paris : Plon, 2002), 99–140, citation p. 101.

65 Hollander, *Understanding Anti-Americanism: Its Origins and Impact at Home and Abroad*. See, for example, Adam Garfinkle's "The Peace Movement and the Adversary Culture," 301–21.

66 Markovits, *Uncouth Nation: Why Europe Dislikes America* (Princeton, NJ: Princeton University Press, 2007).

67 Hardt and Negri, *Empire* (Cambridge, MA: Harvard University Press, 2000). Favorable review: Slavoj Zizek "Have Michael Hardt and Antonio Negri Rewritten the Communist Manifesto For the Twenty-First Century?" *Rethinking Marxism*, 13:3/4 (2001); critical: Mitchell Cohen, "Un empire de la langue de bois: Hardt, Negri, et la théorie politique postmoderne," *Controverses*, 1 (2006). See further discussion chapter 8.

68 Petronella Wyatt, "Poisonous Prejudice," *Spectator*, December 8, 2001.

which was leading the world into World War III.[69] Jonathan Sacks, then Britain's chief rabbi, admitted that he had dismissed the concerns about a coming wave of antisemitism that I had shared with him in a meeting in 1999; but that after 9–11 he thought, "Landes was right."[70] In an article about the third wave of antisemitism in 2002 (next chapter), Michel Gurfinkiel observed two previous spikes: after the al Durah affair and again after 9–11.[71]

Markovits, in researching his *Uncouth Nation*, discovered that European anti-Americanism and anti-Zionism were not, as he thought, "kissing cousins," but rather "twins."[72] And one of their (many) common aspects concerns the virulent—in the twenty-first century the near-hysterical—reaction among Europeans when either of those two countries exercises military force. The crescendo of this open hostility to both Israel and the USA came in 2003, with the anti-war demonstrations that, literally, swept the world.

> One plus two plus three: From the extreme Left to the extreme Right, everyone in French politics—simple activists, members of parliament, trade unionists, cabinet ministers, and the head of state in unison—is raving against the intervention in Iraq: "***Bush equals Sharon equals murderers***" is the chant from the street. "Sharon equals Bush equals disregard for international law" is the pronouncement from the salons. The rise of antisemitism is really not a result of the Intifada, but rather a twin brother of the wave of anti-Americanism that has sloshed up onto the coasts of Europe since September 11 and flooded the continent since the Iraq war.[73]

I would differ with this astute description only on its chronology. Focusing on America, Markovits missed the prelude to the madness that he, and most of us, only first noticed with the delirious responses to 9/11. But already, since the outbreak of the intifada in the fall of 2000, the Europeans had been engaged in virulent anti-Zionist invective, from the streets to the highest levels of

---

69 Tom Gross, "A Shitty Little Country: Prejudice & Abuse in Paris & London," *National Review*, January 10, 2002.
70 Jonathan Sacks, "Making the Case for my People," *Standpoint*, September 2009.
71 Gurfinkiel, "France's Jewish Problem," *Commentary*, June 2002.
72 Markovits, *Uncouth Nation*, chapter 5.
73 Markovits, *Uncouth Nation*, 150.

state—Israel had become a pariah state in the minds of many for almost a year before 9/11.[74] And of course, the USA was Israel's major (only) supporter.

The madness, having already started on September 30, 2000, struck the major structures of the cultural Maginot Line that defends democratic societies; civic values had already crumbled in France, leaving an ever-widening stain of territories lost to the Republic—neighborhoods, suburbs, schools.[75] It became a consensus among global progressives at Durban in August-September 2001: there "human rights" NGOs excoriated the US and Israel for racism and slavery in chorus with nations and peoples who still practiced slavery and exuded racist hatreds. The global progressives had adopted the jihadi apocalyptic narrative: US and Israel were the two Satans. This response—blame the US and Israel, side with Muslims, even the jihadis—stood at the heart of the collapse that first started in 2000 and, over the next years and decades, continued to scale the heights of folly.

Alongside Baudrillard, for example, on the same pages of *Le Monde*, Jacques Derrida, the father of postmodern deconstruction, co-indicted the West as terrorist. ***"If we can prevent human suffering and don't, is that not terrorism?"***[76] The simple answer to that rhetorical question is, "No, that would be an abuse of an important term." What Derrida describes as terrorism is failure to live up to the highest (messianic) human aspirations of lovingkindness for all people, a remarkably high standard, unprecedented in the history of mankind. It's not *targeting* civilians.

The American, Noam Chomsky, took Y2KMind one step further. America is not *as bad as* the 9–11 jihadis, but worse!

---

74 Robin Shepherd, *State Beyond the Pale: Europe's Problem with Israel* (London: Orion, 2009).

75 See *Atlas des Zones urbaines sensibles* (ZUS), https://sig.ville.gouv.fr/Atlas/ZUS/. After the attacks on the Bataclan in November of 2015, the controversy heated up about ZUS as "no-go zones," or "Sharia-zones." Some had insisted on their pervasiveness (Soeren Kern, "European 'No-Go' Zones for Non-Muslims Proliferating: 'Occupation Without Tanks or Soldiers,'" *Gatestone Institute*, August 22, 2011, while others denied their existence (Catherine Thompson, "How Did The Muslim 'No-Go Zones' Myth Get Started Anyway?" *Talking Points Memo*, January 21, 2015). Five year later, undercover cop Noam Anouar published a book about these neglected and denied no-go zones: *La France doit savoir: Un flic chargé de la surveillance des Islamistes raconte* (Paris: Plon, 2020). Predictions of a future explosion much worse than 2005: Milliere, "France's No-Go Zones: The Riots Return," *Gatestone*, May 10, 2020. Death threats to journalists and residents who expose the sharia zones: Henry Samuel, "French Left-wing 'abandon' journalist who received death threats over radical Islam," *Telegraph*, February 2, 2022.

76 On Derrida's essay, see 268.

The [9–11] terrorist attacks were major atrocities. In scale, they may not reach the level of many others, for example, the bombing of the Sudan with no credible pretext, destroying half its pharmaceutical supplies and killing unknown numbers of people (no one knows, because the US blocked an inquiry at the U.N. and no one cares to pursue it).

Chomsky estimated over tens of thousands of deaths, based on a calculus of who *may have* died from lack of medication that the factory *would* have produced (since only one person actually died in the bombing).[77] Chomsky insisted that this accusation of Americans wantonly killing tens of thousands of Muslims did not justify Bin Laden's attack. Bin Laden, on the other hand, had no hesitation drawing that conclusion, as did Reverend Wright in his sermon where he cited the bombing of the plant in Sudan, along with his own projected embellishment that "we killed hundreds of hard working people mothers and fathers who left home to go that day, not knowing that they'd never come home."[78] This is not history, it is weaponized fake news.

Chomsky was not alone even among Americans. Indeed, he was widely echoed, either explicitly or implicitly especially in academia. Phyllis Chesler describes her exchange with a feminist professor at an American college: "after what we did in Guatemala and all our other dirty doings in South America, you can't say we don't deserve having this thrown back at us on 9–11. You *do* understand that America deserves being hated everywhere, don't you?"[79] Indeed, the "Why do they [justifiably] hate us?" meme was widespread, especially in postmodern, postcolonial, and liberal Christian circles.[80] The axis of evil here replicated precisely what Iranian theocrats had insisted since 1400 AH: the great and little Satan, in secular lingo, American imperialism and Israeli colonialism. For these thinkers, the question: "Why do they hate us?" was rhetorical. "Why would they *not* hate us? [We do.]"

---

77 Chomsky, "On the Afghanistan War, American Terrorism, and the Role of Intellectuals," *Salon*, January 16, 2002. Christopher Hitchens, "A Rejoinder to Noam Chomsky," in *Love, Poverty, and War: Journeys and Essays* (New York: Nation Books, 2004), 421–29. On Chomsky's presence in Caliphator reading materials, see below n102.

78 Reverend Wright, "The real sermon given by Pastor Wright," 04:37.

79 Phyllis Chesler, *The Death of Feminism* (London: Palgrave Macmillan, 2005), 21.

80 See also Joyce Davis, "A Minister's Question: What Have We Done That They Hate Us So?" *Martyrs: Innocence, Vengeance, and Despair in the Middle East* (New York: St. Martin's Press, 2003), chapter 1; Peter Ford, "Why do they hate us?," *Christian Science Monitor*, September 27, 2001; approvingly cited by Abrahamian: they hate the US because of its support for Israel, "US Media, Huntington and 9–11." For a survey of the more outlandish responses to 9–11, see John Leo, "Learning to love terrorists," *US News and World Report*, Oct. 1, 2001.

Two days after 9–11, some German intellectuals held a public forum at the Academy of Arts in Berlin to discuss the meaning of events. At one point, a woman in the audience intervened with an extensive critique of the USA for, among other things, "creat[ing] hunger all over the world."

> György Konrad, the President of the Academy of Arts, interrupts her: "And 10,000 people have to be killed because of that? Is that what you're saying?" The woman responds that they don't have to be: "I'm not at all for killing people. But children are starving all over the world and I know where the people are to be found who are responsible for that." The audience apparently knows too and shows its approval with applause.[81]

To paraphrase Derrida on 9–11: If we can't live up to messianic expectations, we're moral failures; if we reduce hunger at rates no society (much less the entire globe) has seen in human history,[82] that's not enough; on the contrary, it's criminal. The West—especially the US—is the world's misfortune. QED.

Bush (or Sharon) Did It: 9–11 Truthers and the Psychology of Conspiracy

And then, of course, there are the conspiracy theories—9–11 Truthers—who took Chomsky one step further. "Not only did America do worse than 9–11 to others, but the Bush administration *did* 9–11 to its own people!" Starting instantly in the Muslim world where it rapidly commanded an overwhelming majority of opinion, taking off in France with Thierry Meyson, whose *L'effroyable imposture* sold like hot-cross buns, and moving to Canada, it eventually invaded the USA.[83] Within a few years, up to a third of Americans believed that their own government had committed these attacks. Somehow it not only seemed

---

81 Henryk Broder, "The Americans are to Blame," from *Kein Krieg, nirgends* [No War, Nowhere] (Berlin: Berlin Verlag, 2002), translation by John Rosenthal, http://www.theaugeanstables. com/2022/01/03/8156/. Note that Academy President Konrad does not challenge her ludicrous assertion about hunger.

82 "In 1820, 94% of the world's population lived in extreme poverty. In 1990, 34.8%, and in 2015, just 9.6%." Alexander Hammond, "The World's Poorest People Are Getting Richer Faster," *Foundation for Economic Education*, October 27, 2017.

83 60 Minutes, "The Big Lie: Find Out Why Many Muslims Think Bin Laden Is Innocent," *CBS*, September 4, 2002. Thierry Meysson, *11 septembre, 2001: L'effroyable imposture* (Chatou: Carnot, 2002).

appropriate to declare the US guilty of attacking itself, but also, as a corollary, exonerate al Qaeda.

In addition, there were the anti-Zionists chiming in. For the most conspiracy-minded, it was actually the Mossad that planned and executed 9-11, a belief that dominated the public sphere in the Muslim world. For others, however, it was the Israelis who were responsible for the hostility to the US, a kind of contact contagion. Tony Judt, soon to become one of the most important Jewish anti-Israel voices among progressives, asserted that "the Israel-Palestine conflict and America's association with Israel are the greatest single source of contemporary anti-US sentiment."[84] In the Jewish-American community, the fear of being associated with the 9-11 attacks was so great, that leaders rebuffed my efforts to tackle the al Durah affair, lest it draw attention to how the accusation inspired Bin Laden—understandably.

Conspiracy theories explain catastrophes that have already occurred, or soon threaten to, as the work of men who claim to be beneficent, but secretly conspire to bring about those catastrophes. They assume the worst of these men, whom they imagine so consumed by the desire to dominate others that they will stop at nothing—including the most dastardly deeds—to achieve their goal. They posit a small group of conspirators, manipulating the public's perception to a) carry out a nefarious deed of great damage to the public, and b) have the public blame the wrong agents.

Most conspiracy theories work on the principle of "*cui bono?*" (to whom the good?), and identify those who benefit from catastrophe as guilty of creating it. A Nietzschean cynic might call it a loser's narrative: by the very fact that we are the innocent victims, we are the good guys; and anyone who does well, is guilty. The rationale becomes a cognitive and emotional booby prize: "Now we know why we're screwed, and it's not our fault." Notes Chip Berlet, "Conspiracism is a particular narrative form of scapegoating that frames demonized enemies as part of a vast insidious plot against the common good, while it valorizes the scape-goater as a hero for sounding the alarm."[85]

Conspiracy theories work on several psychological levels. Cognitively, they offer a gratifying world view that explains everything. All details cohere, unnoticed or unexplained facts fit into place, everything connects, gains shape

---

84 Tony Judt, "America and the War," *New York Review of Books*, November 15, 2001; see Benjamin Balint, "Future Imperfect: Tony Judt Blushes for the Jewish State," in *The Jewish Divide over Israel*, chapter 5. See Seumas Milne, n56.

85 Chip Berlet and Matthew Lyons, *Right-Wing Populism in America: Too Close for Comfort* (New York: Guilford Press, 2000), 9.

and color. There is no loose change.[86] To the believer, now semiotically aroused with his new hermeneutic, the troubling world makes sense. Like Gnostic belief, itself profoundly conspiracist, Conspiracy theories offer powerful hidden knowledge about the cosmos, available only to the initiated, attractive, even true, *by the very virtue of its being proscribed.*[87]

And it's now all someone else's fault: conspiracy theories systematically project bad faith onto the conspirators. They embody the cognitive egocentrism of bad faith.[88] The articulators and believers in conspiracy theories live in a universe where everyone is driven by *libido dominandi,* everyone wants to dominate and, as Eli Sagan so eloquently puts it describing the basic political axiom of the premodern world, we function on a *rule or be ruled* basis.[89] The only motivation possible among the conspiring "enemy" is a ruthless lust for power.

The emotional blandishments of conspiracy theory are at least as attractive as the cognitive rewards. They offer above all freedom from any responsibility: failures, setbacks and sufferings, are not the victim's fault; they are the work of the conspirators. The dualistic moral universe of "us" and "them" that conspiracy theory provides shows up in stark and simple contrasts with no grey areas. Conspiracy theories are a quintessential expression of what, combining Nietzsche and James Scott, we might call a hidden transcript of *ressentiment.* It also thrives in apocalyptic time.

At the same time as a conspiracy theory may ease one's conscience, it also liberates it. That is, "there are no limits on what 'we' must do in order to defend ourselves against so evil an enemy." The more dire the conspiracy, the more liberated the violence of the response: anything is permitted when struggling for one's very existence against such an evil agent. Conspiracy theories are narratives that justify aggressive action; the worse the conspiracy, the more aggressive the justifiable action. At their worst, they are "warrants for genocide."[90]

---

86 *Loose Change 9/11* (2005), illustrates this thinking: a myriad of loose details, all of which cohere if one accepts the conspiracy theory. There is no random, no stupid, no incompetent . . . all is *a priori* malevolent design.

87 Michael Barkun, "Conspiracy Theories as Stigmatized Knowledge: The Basis for a New Age Racism?" in *Nation and Race: The Developing Euro-American Racist Subculture,* ed. Jeffrey Kaplan and Tore Bjorgo (Boston: Northeastern University Press, 1998), 58–72.

88 See chapter 7, Liberal Cognitive Egocentrism. On the conspiracy at the heart of Gnosticism, see Paul Zweig, *The Heresy of Self-Love* (New York: Basic Books, 1980), chapter 1.

89 Eli Sagan, *The Honey and the Hemlock: Democracy and Paranoia in Ancient Athens and Modern America* (New York: Basic Books,1991).

90 Norman Cohn's book on the *Protocols of the Elders of Zion* was entitled, *Warrant for Genocide* (New York: Harper and Row, 1969).

The Dynamics of 9–11 Truthing

The hostility between "liberals" and "conservatives" in the US, a reflection of the larger "culture wars" that plague every "modern" (democratic) culture to some extent in the 21st century, feeds conspiracy theory by making the people on both sides eager to believe the worst of their opponents. In the case of how Bush handled 9–11, the role of personal animus plays a significant role. This is true both of Europeans across the political spectrum who have deep contempt not only for Bush but Americans, as well as of people on the American and Canadian "left."[91]

This animosity is critical in imagining a president capable of, at worst, plotting to destroy three of the most important American sites, kill thousands, if not tens of thousands of Americans, all based on motives that range from sagging polls, a desire to avenge his father in Iraq, to guaranteeing Halliburton contracts in war-torn Iraq and Afghanistan, and plans for a new fascist world order. The degree of widespread bad faith that these conspiracies accept as "assumed" in the logic of the argument—that thousands of people in the government would stay silent about the conspiracy—says a great deal about how they view their fellow Americans. This belief in the malevolence of the American political elite and middle-level bureaucrats is all the stronger in Europe, à la Baudrillard.

People who believe in a 9–11 conspiracy consider our elites every bit as unprincipled and predatory as earlier aristocracies who would, indeed, sacrifice commoners' lives with little hesitation.[92] One might even argue that this particular conspiracy, when attributed to an American president, represents one of the most terrible of all such theories, far worse in its moral implication than the one about Roosevelt allowing the Pearl Harbor attack in order to have a reason to go to war. As 9–11 Truther David Ray Griffin writes: "It is very difficult for Americans to face the possibility that their own government may have caused or deliberately allowed such a heinous event."[93]

Griffin and others feel no need to explain how our government could get involved in such morally aberrant behavior and everyone succeeded in keeping quiet about the entire 9–11 conspiracy theory. *No one leaked it.* It goes without

---

91 For a survey of conspiratorial responses to 9–11, Michael Barkun, *Culture of Conspiracy: Apocalyptic Visions in Contemporary America* (Los Angeles: University of California Press, 2003), 161–69.

92 See remarks on prime divider societies, chapter 5.

93 David Ray Griffin, *The New Pearl Harbor: Disturbing Questions about the Bush Administration and 9/11* (Northampton MA: Interlink Publishing Group, 2008), forward by Richard Falk. Argument: we couldn't be this dumb; it must be intentional.

saying for Griffin and other truthers, however, that this kind of thing can and does happen.[94] As Michael Prell summarizes:

> [T]he US government somehow staged the 9/11 hijackings, intercepted the hijacked aircraft, removed all passengers, transferred them to new planes, impersonated their voices in fake phone calls back to their families, then flew them to their deaths in the Atlantic Ocean while taking the original planes and flying those, via remote-control, into their targets where the government had, over the previous months, tunneled through the interior walls of the World Trade Center buildings—without any of the office workers noticing—and planted thousands of pounds of explosives so they could be detonated to bring the Twin Towers down (which, if true, would make the whole airplane hijacking plot a bit unnecessary).[95]

Like all conspiracy theories, this one assumes that *all* people in power are naturally evil or easily corruptible and willing to look the other way no matter how heinous the deeds.

The proliferation of conspiracy theories about 9–11 represents a relatively new stage in Western conspiracy theorizing. In the Arab and Muslim world, conspiracy theories were already mainstream long before 2000, and became even more virulent afterwards. In the West, however, they were marginal, especially after the Holocaust, when Nazis in the throes of a particularly malevolent conspiracy theory, the *Protocols of the Elders of Zion*, tried to exterminate ten million people.[96] Indeed, as we have just seen in the case of Muhammad al Durah, accusations of "conspiracy theory" became a mark of opprobrium against the one peddling such nonsense.

9–11 conspiracy theories, however, rapidly invaded the public sphere—the coffee houses, taverns, dinner table conversations—and soon knocked at the gates of published discourse and elected officials. US Mainstream media refused to give these conspiracy theories any credibility, but just under the surface these ideas simmered. In 2003, when I spoke with a journalist from ABC about al Durah, he asked me at the end of the conversation what I thought of these

---

94 For a review of Griffin, see Robert Baer, "Dangerous Liaisons," *Nation*, September 9, 2004.

95 Michael J. Prell, *Underdogma: How America's Enemies Use Our Love for the Underdog to Trash American Power* (Dallas: BenBella Books, 2011), 161.

96 Cohn, *Warrant for Genocide*; Daniel Pipes, *Conspiracy: How the Paranoid Style Flourishes and Where It Comes From* (New York: Touchstone, 1999), 215–43.

rumors that Mossad knew about the bombing beforehand, suggesting that in his circles, the idea circulating was considered plausible, at the very least.[97] In 2006, I asked my students how many had heard the conspiracy theories about Bush's involvement, and two-thirds reported hearing them from at least one source who considered the hypothesis likely. When the first conference "documenting" a 9-11 conspiracy took place in Chicago in 2006, the New York Times's article about it topped its list of "most emailed."[98] By then, one poll found 36% of Americans considered it either very or somewhat likely that the US government was involved in 9-11.[99]

These conspiracy theories about Bush show all the signs of serving the normal functions of Conspiracy Theory: demonizing and scapegoating the accused while exculpating major sources of the problem.[100] In other words, far more than a real battle of "facts," these conspiracy theories represent a major piece in a chess game of culture wars, in which one sees the near-enemy—here, the Republican administration—as far worse than the far enemy—in this case Global Jihad. Notes Barkun: "for believers in secret knowledge, the breadth of support for the Al Qaeda explanation made it prima facie suspect."[101]

Indeed, recognizing this impending evil (future American fascism) enables us to deny the very existence of the far-enemy, already in an advanced stage of fascism (the jihadis). Bush used the 9-11 *he* caused to launch a *false* war on terror. *We have met the enemy and he is us.* As for those Muslim fellows out there who rant and scream about wanting to massacre us, they are products of our imperial arrogance. When we stop oppressing them, they will stop wanting to kill us. Osama Bin Laden had Griffin's 9-11 Conspiracy book on his bookshelf, doubtless as comic relief.[102]

---

97 *Unraveling Antisemitic 9/11 Conspiracy Theories* (ADL, 2003).

98 Alan Feuer, "500 Conspiracy Buffs Meet to Seek the Truth of 9-11," *New York Times*, June 5, 2006.

99 Carl Stempel et al., "Media Use, Social Structure, and Belief in 9/11 Conspiracy Theories," *Journalism & Mass Communication Quarterly*, June 2007; "Why the 9/11 Conspiracy Theories Won't Go Away," *Time magazine*, September 3, 2006.

100 For a good discussion of the psychological stakes involved, see Prell, *Underdogma.*

101 Barkun, *Culture of Conspiracy*, 161.

102 Bin Laden's Bookshelf, Office of the Director of National Intelligence, March 1, 2016. So was Chomsky, so was Robert Fisk, whom Bin Laden urged Westerners to read (*Al Qaeda Reader*, ed. Raymond Ibrahim [New York: Doubleday, 2007], 216). Speaking of the reading list compiled by the Muslim Brotherhood's outreach to young Muslims in America, Feoktistov notes: "Some of the books on the 'must-read' list have nothing to do with Islam, such as several books written by Howard Zinn, Noam Chomsky, and Michael Moore. Having young Muslims read books by far-left atheists of Jewish and Christian backgrounds shows that the goal of Tarbiya (MB outreach) is not just to develop a Muslim's spirituality, but also to develop within him a deep animosity to Western democracy" (Feoktistov, *Terror in the*

These three intertwining responses to 9–11

- the "Islam, Religion of Peace" meme promoted by Bush and Da'wa Caliphators,
- "America, the intolerable, suffocating hegemon" which richly deserved the hatred it inspired, and
- "America, the evil conspirator" against all that is good and decent

first appeared as marginal. When Susan Sontag admired the courage of the jihadis, or principled journalists refused to call them "terrorists," strong voices objected. But together they embody the disorientations and disarray of the West faced with the challenge of Global Jihad; and over time they came to dominate. Whether through forbidding a discussion of the dangers of triumphalist Muslims and their war on the progressive West, or through a systematic vilification of the US and either a corresponding glorification of triumphalist Muslim hostility, or its complete denial, the response of progressive Western information professionals across the boards, undermined Western democracies in the aughts of the new century.

All these responses to 9–11, that is, responses to the spectacular declaration of jihad against the West at the dawn of the twenty-first century, represented major propaganda victories for triumphalist Muslims with ambitions for global dominion. Either they didn't do it (conspiracy theory), or they did it and the US deserved it. In either case, it has nothing to do with Islam. And yet, none of these responses could be more self-destructive, especially from the perspective of progressive values that cherish *humane* attitudes towards others, tolerance, mutual respect, dignity.

"One Man's Terrorist . . .": Editorial Compliance with Jihadi Demands

Among its many effects, 9–11 revealed an issue in journalism that had remained hidden from most news consumers, but which became a major topic of discussion and journalistic opinion in the subsequent years. For some years already, Western news agencies had adopted an increasingly formal rejection of the word "terrorism/terrorist." It was, they argued, "too emotive" and

---

Cradle of Liberty: How Boston Became a Center for Islamic Extremism (New York: Encounter, 2019), 244.

notoriously difficult to define.[103] Its use in describing persons or acts unfairly prejudiced the news consumer against those so designated. After all, **"One man's terrorist is another's freedom fighter."**

With this practice, news agencies aligned themselves with a position staked out in academia by the new and advocacy-driven "field" of Peace and Conflict Studies, and by the Said-dominated "Middle East Studies Association."[104] Martin Kramer, serious critic of the postcolonial academy, noted the absence of "terrorism" in the MESA statement on 9–11 and its hefty program of talks at its conference that year:

> For years the academics' response to terrorism has been to act as amplifiers for the "grievances" behind it. For the professors, terrorism was a kind of political protest—and since they sympathized with its supposed motives, they expelled the word "terrorism" from their lexicon. This weekend's [MESA] conference demonstrates the neglect: With the exception of a hastily announced special panel, nothing in the program deals with terrorism.[105]

In other words, mainstream news media had become practitioners of "peace journalism," lining up with a postcolonial paradigm weaponized against the victims of the jihadi attack. Given how "peace journalism" had disoriented the Israelis at the approach of the Al Aqsa Intifada,[106] it was a highly dubious direction in which to move.

Few expressions better qualify as an astoundingly stupid statement than "One man's terrorist . . .," not because there are no cases where one man's terrorist is another's freedom fighter, not because it is absurd (just a false dichotomy[107]),

---

103 I use "terrorism" to designate deliberate targeting of civilians in order to terrify the larger population.

104 See below, 276–84.

105 Martin Kramer, "Terrorism? What Terrorism," *Wall Street Journal*, November 15, 2001 (with rejoinder by Said).

106 See chapter 5.

107 1) False dichotomy: fighting for freedom doesn't mean one can't also be a terrorist (i.e. deliberately attack civilians). 2) False identity: terrorists rarely end up freedom fighters. Menachem Begin's participation in the Israeli democratic process, for twenty-eight years in the opposition, constitutes the exception that proves the (opposite) rule: terrorists rarely bring freedom: see Anna Geifman, "When Terrorists become State Leaders," *Death Orders: The Vanguard of Modern Terrorism in Revolutionary Russia* (Santa Barbara, CA: Praeger, 2010), 122–38. See also Gerard Rabinovitch, *Terrorisme/Résistance: D'une confusion lexicale à l'époque des sociétés de masse* (Paris: Le Bord de L'eau, 2014).

but because in this case editors applied it to exactly the wrong situation. A great deal here hangs on what one means by "freedom." In some cases, "resistance" and its attendant terror comes not from fighting for independence and autonomy, but for dominion. So anyone claiming that an imperialist movement that repeatedly attacks civilian populations marked for subjection should not be called "terrorists," because they might be "freedom fighters," shows little respect for either language or empirical reality. Here, the "enlightened" Western mind meets triumphalist religiosity in the raw and cannot see it for what it is. For the Caliphate is not about freedom; it is literally about "submission"—*Dar al Islam*.

Reuters Refuses to Use Terrorism Label for 9–11: One Man's Terrorist . . .

And yet, no matter how wildly inappropriate the use of this meme by journalists to avoid calling jihadis terrorists, many people in the twenty-first century sagely nodded their heads. While initially a flippant remark meant to *épater les bourgeois*, the proverb became increasingly adopted as an axiomatic principle in journalism. As we have seen, the first place it was systematically applied was in Western coverage of the Middle East conflict between Palestinians and Israelis in the 1990s, the Oslo years.[108] Then on the morrow of 9–11, Americans discovered that their attackers might also be freedom fighters. In an in-house memo, Reuters chief editor Stephen Jukes instructed those responsible for news production not to use the terror word to describe 9–11. If someone else used the word, one could quote the person, but for its own journalists, Reuters deemed "terrorism" an inappropriate term:

> **We all know** [sic] **that one man's terrorist is another man's freedom fighter** and that Reuters upholds the principle that we do not use the word terrorist. . . . To be frank, it adds little to call the attack on the World Trade Center a terrorist attack.[109]

Jukes issued a FAQ in October of 2001, which elaborated the argument behind the policy:

---

108 See chapter 1.

109 A Reuters's employee forwarded it to columnist Howard Kurtz, "The T Word," *Washington Post*, September 24, 2001; link broken. For a general discussion of the problem, see Susan Moeller, *Packaging Terrorism: Coopting the News for Politics and Profit* (Oxford: Blackwell, 2009), chapter 1.

> As part of a long-standing policy *to avoid the use of emotive words,* we do not use terms like "terrorist" and "freedom fighter" unless they are in a direct quote or are otherwise attributable to a third party. We do not characterize the subjects of news stories, but instead report their actions, identity and background so that readers can make their own decisions based on the facts.[110]

For the first time, this principle that so galled Israelis—they called it an inability to distinguish between arsonist and fire-fighter—was applied on a major scale in the United States. Not accidentally, the first agency to formally insist on not using the "terrorist" designations for those "freedom fighters" whom admirers called the "Magnificent 19," was European—Reuters... quickly followed by the BBC, whose Chief Deputy Editor Mark Damazer explained:

> However appalling and disgusting it was, there will nevertheless be a constituency of your listeners who don't regard it as terrorism. Describing it as such could downgrade your status as an impartial and independent broadcaster.[111]

In other words, out of deference to those of our viewers who don't think of the attacks on the US as terrorism, we will avoid using the term, lest this constituency (who apparently could not care less about impartial and independent broadcasting), think badly of the BBC.

Among American journalists, for whom such "dispassion" would alienate all but the most "universalist" of their audiences, the practice aroused indignation and mockery.[112] But in the coming years, Reuters's position became the industry standard, formally adopted by the top US papers: the *Washington Post,* the *New York Times,* the *Boston Globe* (below). When home-grown jihadis hit London on July 7, 2005, the BBC, the *Guardian,* and Reuters all initially used the word terror to describe the attacks, but quickly "recovered." The BBC issued a memo formally discouraging the use of "terrorism" to describe the attacks on the

---

110 Updated, Stephen Jukes, October 2000. No longer online. For the formal statement of policy see *Reuters Handbook of Journalism* (April 2008); Tom Gross, "The Case of Reuters: A news agency that will not call a terrorist a terrorist," *National Interest,* July 26, 2004.

111 Matt Wells, "[BBC] World Service will not call US attacks terrorism," *Guardian,* November 15, 2001.

112 Michael Kinsley, "Defining Terrorism," *Washington Post,* October 5, 2001.

London subway by Muslims born and raised in England, and quietly tried to change previous headlines so as to hide their initial "error."[113]

This may seem like an academic game of little serious import beyond the hurt feelings of (in this case) Americans, who feel themselves the object of an atrocious attack on working men and women and find "activist" and "militant" far too bland to describe the perpetrators. When Jukes noted frankly that "it adds little to call the attack on the World Trade Center a terrorist attack," he appeals to the obvious—*everyone* knew it was. But, again as the Israelis had already complained, this terminological policy brought with it more problematic practices, including humanizing the terrorists, and framing their deeds as resistance against oppression and a struggle for freedom.[114] And sure enough, the doctrine of not using "terrorist" became so deeply engrained among some journalists that some even cleaned up the language of independent sources as well.[115]

Among the many things this high-minded journalistic discourse obscured (I think, intentionally) was how ferociously the terrorists (jihadis) themselves, and especially their defenders/apologists (*da-is*), objected to the use of the term "terrorists" to designate them. Indeed, they apparently felt so strongly about the terminology, that they were willing to kill journalists who called them terrorists, a phenomenon war correspondents in Lebanon knew as early as the 1970s.[116] Just in case they needed reminding, Reuters's Gaza correspondent Nidal al-Mughrabi issued a travel advisory for journalists, cautioning his colleagues: "Never use the word 'terrorist' or 'terrorism' in describing Palestinian gunmen and militants" lest offence be given to locals who consider them "heroes of the conflict, and ideals." From the perspective of Da'wa Caliphators, the problem was not the crime (terrorism), but how it gave jihadis a negative image, one that reflected badly on their own emphasis on an exclusively "moderate, peaceful" Islam.

Of course, those who find any public criticism insulting tend to consider them offenses that demand violent retaliation. "Call my jihadis 'terrorists,'

---

113 Tom Gross, "The BBC Discovers 'Terrorism,' Briefly," *Jerusalem Post*, July 12, 2005; Meryl Yourish, "The T-Word," *Yourish.com*, July 9, 2005.

114 Shahid Alam, professor of economics at Northeastern University compared the 9–11 attackers to the Minutemen at Lexington: "America and Islam: Seeking Parallels," *Scoop Media*, January 1, 2005.

115 Daniel Pipes, "Calling a Terrorist a Terrorist," *Blog*, April 27, 2004. For an example of a rogue editor at the Minneapolis Star "cleaning up" a *New York Times* story, see chapter 115n77.

116 Zev Chafets, *Double Vision: How the Press Distorts America's View of the Middle East* (New York: Morrow, 1985), 127–54.

and I'll savage you, even if you're the Foreign Minister of France."[117] "Call our religion violent and we'll riot and kill both infidels and Muslims in protest."[118] Playing the enforcer for the jihadis, the Muslim Street that rioted so often in the mid-aughts, insisted that the terrorist label *not* be applied to their co-religionists.

It mattered not that the accusation of terrorism was true, in a form rarely this unalloyed—deliberately targeting civilians for political advantage. For the Caliphators, the purpose was to remove a deep moral stain (in the eyes of the targeted enemy), to forbid them to express effective disapproval of Muslim terrorists. The media complied, using "emotive" as a neutral term to submit to the jihadi demand: Muslims *felt* very strongly about journalists depicting jihadi acts as terrorism. The media avoided the term not to remain "impartial" and "non-emotive" but in order not to emotionally provoke the terrorists and their supporters.

Thus, behind the Western language of peace, impartiality and understanding lay a different set of reasons for avoiding the term "terrorism," especially when it came to Muslim attacks on infidel civilians: the fear of retaliation. Behind the principled neutral language and the rather problematic insistence on "leveling the playing field" lurked something more disturbing and more shameful for journalists to admit: fear and intimidation. "*We don't want to jeopardize the safety of our staff,*" the head of Reuters explains to the inquiring journalist. "Our people are on the front lines, in Gaza, the West Bank and Afghanistan [NB: all Muslim lands]. The minute we seem to be siding with one side or another [sic], they're in danger." In the real world, however, journalists are only in danger if their publications seem to be siding with jihadi targets; they are not in danger if they are seen to be siding with the jihadis. In other words, "if we call jihadis who attack civilians 'terrorists,' our journalists are in danger from those very terrorists who, closely following how we cover their behavior, will attack us for violating their demands for coverage."

Apparently—who knew?—"jihadis care what the West thinks of them."[119] So much so, they are ready to use violence against journalists to get the coverage they want. So what motivated the Western media's widely accepted

---

117 "During a trip to Israel, FM Lionel Jospin called Hizballah actions "terrorist." At Bir Zeit, his car was nearly turned over; he was spit on and hit in the head by a stone. Paul Giniewski, "Jews of France Tormented by 'Intifada of the Suburbs,'", and Pierre Haski, "Quand Lionel Jospin qualifie Hezbollah de "terroriste"," *Le Nouvel Observateur*, May 23, 2013. See similar incident concerning Colin Powell and Marwan Barghouti, above, 31n103.

118 On the riots provoked by the pope's Regensburg speech, see 178f.

119 Bin Laden complained that Muslims like him are called terrorists by the worst terrorists (US): "Transcript of Osama Bin Ladin Interview by Peter Arnett," CNN, March 1997. Apparently he read the Chomsky he had on his shelves (above, n102.).

policy on "terrorism": principles or intimidation? And what were the cognitive consequences of that policy? Over the subsequent years, a distinct pattern emerged: more and more news editors adopted the Reuters principles and rationale for not using the term "terrorism" to refer to jihadis, even as the evidence for intimidation became ever more abundant.

Palestinians Celebrate 9–11 and Intimidate Media into Not Reporting

The intimidation of Western news media by terrorists concerned with their "image" came to the fore in the Palestinian territories in the wake of 9–11. Western film crews based in Israel filmed Palestinians celebrating the event, and openly praising Bin Laden for his blow against the US. This reaction would come as no surprise to anyone who followed the Palestinian media, where the US is only second to the Israelis as a target of hatred, and the celebration of massacred enemy civilians was an act of high culture.[120] But, in the immediate aftermath of 9–11, with widespread expressions of sympathy for the US coming even from Muslim countries that were openly hostile to the US like Iran, with the POTUS, directed by Muslim advisors, assuring the American people that Muslims around the world were appalled by the attacks of 9–11, these celebrations made the Palestinians look bad. Arafat, sensitive to image as always, shut down the demonstrations and staged a photo-op of him supposedly donating blood to the pulverized victims.[121]

As for the footage, Palestinian authorities, including the Tanzim, the military arm of the PA, did everything they could to prevent its circulation. They stopped camera crews at the site from filming; they called the camera crews who had filmed the celebrations into the PA offices and informed them that they would be held personally responsible if they showed this footage. Ahmed Abdel Rahman, Arafat's Cabinet secretary, said the Palestinian Authority "cannot guarantee the life" of any member of the camera crew, if they broadcast the footage. AP,

---

120 For the footage of celebrations, https://www.youtube.com/watch?v=P9yK0u-XH1M. In response to a claim that the footage was fake, David Mikkelson, "Palestinians Dancing in the Street: Did CNN Fake Footage of 'Palestinians dancing in the Street' after the Terrorist Attack on the USA?" *Snopes*, March 9, 2008. On Schadenfreude as a feature of Palestinian culture, Ian Fischer, "An Exhibit On Campus Celebrates Grisly Deed," *New York Times*, September 26, 2001.

121 Pollack, "Enderlin: Arafat faked 9/11 blood donation."

pressured both by the PA and their own cameramen, decided not to show the footage.

Publicly, AP Chief of Bureau Dan Perry protested somewhat entreatingly: "I ask the assurances of the Palestinian Authority that you will protect our journalists from threats and attempts at intimidation and that no harm would come to our freelance cameraman from distribution of the film.[122] Privately, he admitted to an inquiring journalist that the AP had to fold: "We are acting to assure the safety of our staff. The safety of our staff is paramount. At this point, we believe there to be a serious threat to our staff if the video is released and we have protested this to the PA."[123]

The incident confirmed what the events of the previous October in Ramallah had already illuminated: the *al Shabab* and PA officials play tough-cop/nice-cop, to control the news media and make sure that any news that might harm the Palestinian "image" in the West does not get out. Here, on the topic of 9-11, the AP's cautious response of pulling the footage resembles the behavior of journalists covering the Palestinians the previous year: Compliance with Palestinian demands, with a whimper of protest.[124]

And on the backs of this MSNM [mainstream news media] compliance, George Bush, five days later, could assure the American people that "Muslims all across the world were as appalled and outraged as you at last Tuesday's attacks." Lethal journalism's silence permitted triumphalist Muslims to hide their malevolent *Schadenfreude* at this blow to the US even as they asserted their innocence. Indeed, they could accuse as racist and Islamophobic anyone who brought up this disturbing behavior, as blaming the victim (Islam and the vast majority of moderate Muslims) for deeds that have nothing to do with the "Religion of Peace."

The "Responsible" Mainstream Media Adopt Reuters' Policy on the T-Word

While the Europeans had fewer problems, at least right after 9-11, with avoiding the T-word, both in the case of al Qaeda and Hamas, US papers tended to adhere

---

122 "AP Protests Threats to Cameraman," *The Associated Press.* September 12, 2001; cited in Aaron Lerner, "Interview: AP Bureau Chief on Palestinian death threats," *IMRA*, September 13, 2001.

123 *Ibid.* For more on Perry, see 303n37; 306n46.

124 In the specific case of the Ramallah Lynch 12r. see the behavior of journalists William Orme and Riccardo Cristiano, discussed 319-29.

to peace-journalism's dogma when dealing with Israel, but deploring al-Qaeda's attack on the US, as terrorist. After 9–11, the number of suicide attacks on Israeli civilians multiplied at an unprecedented rate, killing and wounding almost ten thousand Israelis, the proportional equivalent in the US of almost half a million people, almost 80% of whom were civilians. After calling Bin Laden and his jihadis terrorists, US papers now faced accusations of hypocrisy, especially from angry pro-Israel readers, for refusing to call this growing, devastating storm that engulfed Israel, "terrorism."

In September 2003, on the second anniversary of 9–11, the ombudsperson for the *Boston Globe*, Christine Chinlund wrote her reflections on the problem. Noting the clear negative connotations of the word, she expressed concerns that, "especially after 9–11 . . . the terrorist tag effectively banishes its holder from the political arena. More than ever, it condemns rather than describes." Invoking a false dichotomy whereby a word cannot both accurately describe and, thereby, condemn a group—the very essence of "terrorism" in civil discourse—she argued it was *inappropriate* to use the term with a group like Hamas:

> To tag Hamas, for example, as a terrorist organization is to ignore its far more complex role in the Middle East drama. The word reflects not only a simplification, but a bias that runs counter to good journalism. To label any group in the Middle East as terrorist is to take sides, or at least appear to, and that is not acceptable. The same holds true in covering other far-flung conflicts. One person's terrorist is another's freedom fighter; it's not for journalists to judge.[125]

How does the provision of "some social service functions" by Hamas "complicate" the argument that they are terrorists? What does one have to do with the other? Nazis had *lots* of social service functions for their own people, even as they exterminated others, and Bolsheviks had a lot of services for their own people, even as they starved ten million Ukrainians.

Like Jukes at Reuters, Chinlund considers not even "appearing" [to the jihadis] "to take sides," as a highest priority. Like Jukes, she cites as an unquestioned consensus the slogan "**One man's terrorist is another's freedom fighter.**" And like Jukes, she misapplies it. For like Al Qaeda, Hamas not only *are* terrorists, but they are decidedly *not* "freedom fighters." According to abundant evidence

---

125 Christine Chinlund, "Who should wear the 'terrorist' label?" *Boston Globe*, September 8, 2003.

journalists studiously keep from their audiences, it's not Palestine they want to build, but Israel they want to destroy; not Palestinians they want to free, but Jews they want to subjugate (at best), or preferably exterminate.[126]

Two weeks after Chinlund's *Boston Globe* piece, the *Washington Post*'s ombudsman, Michael Getler, contributed his paper's take on the "terrorist" issue, elaborating on Chinlund's distinction in order to legitimate calling al Qaeda terrorist, but not Hamas. After going over the delicacy of the issue of the T-word, Getler distinguishes:

> Hamas conducts terrorism but also has territorial ambitions, is a nationalist movement and conducts some social work. As far as we know, al Qaeda exists only as a terrorist network. It is composed of radicals from several Islamic countries. The Palestinian resistance is indigenous. Al Qaeda launched a devastating surprise attack on the United States. Israelis and Palestinians have been at war for a long time. Palestinians have been resisting a substantial and, to Palestinians, humiliating, Israeli occupation of the West Bank and Gaza since they were seized in the 1967 war. That resistance has now bred suicide bombers. These are terrorist acts, not to be condoned. But the contexts of the struggle against al Qaeda and the Israeli-Palestinian conflict are different. News organizations should not back away from the word terrorism when it is the proper term. But as a rule, strong, descriptive, factual reporting is better than labels.[127]

Of course, Hamas does not limit its territorial ambition to the West Bank and Gaza Strip, but to every last inch of the land between the river and the sea, a goal that existed long before the "occupation resulting from the '67 war." Indeed, if one listens, their ambitions extend to the entire world.[128] Their "social work" involves recruiting for "martyrdom operations"; their "education" involves brainwashing children with genocidal hatred; and their charter eagerly looks

---

126 See the extensive collection of material at Palestinian Media Watch.

127 Ombudsman Michael Getler, "The Language of Terrorism," *Washington Post*, September 21, 2003. For a rebuttal, Eric Rozenman, "Balancing Coverage of the Middle East" *CAMERA*, September 27, 2003.

128 See chapter 6.

forward to an apocalyptic slaughter of Jews.[129] And yet, their victim narrative, wherein their attacks should be viewed as resistance to a humiliating occupation, now permits American papers to continue to stick it to Israel by not calling her enemies who attack her civilians "terrorists," even as they get to complain about jihadi terrorists attacking their American homeland.[130] On such considered reasoning did the *Boston Globe* and the *Washington Post* justify their selective use of the T-word for Al Qaeda, but not Hamas.[131]

Caliphator Intimidation and the T-Word

Claiming the high moral ground, neither Chinlund nor Getler allude to the fear factor. On the contrary, they discuss all this in terms of the highest-minded independence: Getler quotes his paper's foreign editor David Hoffman, "We should always strive to satisfy our own standards and not let others set standards for us." In the shuffle, one might miss the key detail: the standards that "others" try to set for them and that they reject here are Israel's (call terrorists terrorists); the standards they adopt as their own, are those of Hamas (don't you dare). The WMSNM, in adopting their "principled" stand against the T-word, effectively took the side of jihadis who were the ones objecting to infidel journalists calling them terrorists.

The issue of fear of terrorists as the motivation for not so calling them, emerged clearly in a controversy that broke out the following year. The (conservative) news chain, *CanWest*, began to substitute the word "terrorist" for "militants, insurgents, activists," when they published pieces taken from the feed of larger, more politically correct, news agencies. On September 14, 2003 they added the descriptor "terrorist group" to a discussion of the Al Aqsa Martyrs Brigade, the PLO's brigades fighting the Oslo Jihad with suicide attacks on civilians. Despite the dead give-away of their name—warriors fighting for Jerusalem's holiest site (Al Aqsa), committing suicide to kill Israeli civilians (martyrs)—the

---

129 Itamar Marcus and Nan Zilbedik, "PA pays salaries to terrorists and not social aid to families," *PalWatch*, April 10, 2013; "Promoting Violence for Children," *PalWatch*, http://palwatch.org/main.aspx?fi=844; "Hamas's Genocidal Ideology," *PalWatch*, http://palwatch.org/main.aspx?fi=584.

130 On the lack of meaningful distinction between Caliphator jihadis from the infidel point of view, see 229.

131 For a response to the *Washington Post* editorial, Rozenman, "Balancing."

mainstream of information professionals presented the group as largely secular, insurgent, freedom fighters.[132]

Alerted to CanWest's actions, Reuters tried to stop them. In so doing, they claimed, *CanWest* was "taking sides" (the Israeli side, a "right-wing" thing to do), by describing the Al Aqsa Martyrs' Brigade as terrorists. A spokesman for the AP, the other major international Anglophone news agency, rejected any change like this because it would "make an AP report unbalanced, unfair or inaccurate."[133] In other words, "We, the major news outlets, are the authoritative voice offering balanced, fair, and accurate coverage, while you, CanWest, by bringing in emotive words, are guilty of taking sides and fanning the flames of war."

CanWest fought back:

> Terrorism is a technical term . . . a tactic: the deliberate targeting of civilians in pursuit of a political goal. Those who bombed the nightclub in Bali were terrorists. Suicide bombers who strap explosives to their bodies and blow up people eating in a pizza parlour are terrorists. The men and women who took a school full of hostages in Beslan, Russia, and shot some of the children in the back as they tried to flee to safety were terrorists. We as journalists do not violate our impartiality by describing them as such. Ironically, it is supposedly neutral terms like "militant" that betray a bias, insofar as they have a sanitizing effect. Activists for various political causes can be "militant," but they don't take children hostage.[134]

In other words, they countered, when the press uses euphemisms for "terror" (and "jihad"), they fail to properly inform their public, and make "unbalanced, unfair and inaccurate" reports that in fact take the side of the terrorists.

Reuters's global managing editor David Schlesinger responded with the standard talking point: **"Our editorial policy is that we don't use emotive words when labeling someone.** If they [CamWest] want to put their own judgment into it, they're free to do that. But then they shouldn't say that it's by

---

132 The allegedly neutral *Wikipedia* describes "Al Aqsa Martyrs Brigade," as "a secular coalition of Palestinian armed groups in the West Bank."

133 Ian Austen, "Reuters Asks a Chain to Remove Its Bylines," *New York Times*, September 20, 2004.

134 Arthur Weinreb "CanWest, Reuters and the 't' word," *Canada Free Press*, September 27, 2004, http://canadafreepress.com/2004/media092704.htm.

a Reuters reporter." CanWest responded: "If you're couching your language in order to protect certain people, are you telling the truth? And if they're terrorists, aren't you putting us all in danger by mislabeling them as they demand? And if so, why do it?"

The answer became clearer as a result of some follow-up by Ian Austen at the (still serious) *New York Times*.[135] Schlesinger explained Reuters's concerns to him about any "confusion that might endanger its reporters in volatile areas or situations." In other words, to spare our journalists retaliation from terrorists who do not want us to call them that, we cannot be associated with the use of the T-word. Shades and echoes of Riccardo Cristiano pointing his finger at Mediaset to Arafat: "Please, oh you dear friends whose reprisals we fear, don't *misunderstand, we here at Reuters* don't describe you as terrorists. It's the CanWest folk."[136]

No wonder Reuters editors above all wanted anonymity. They were ducking. Never mind that, by covering themselves from the fire of those objecting to their self-censorship, "in the name of objectivity and non-emotivity," they were "perversely hid[ing] a defensible concern for the safety of their reporters behind an idiotic moral relativism."[137] Never mind that, in effect, this policy, adopted by many other information professionals, provided a soporific that continued to stupefy the West as things got worse.

To complete his scorn for the public's intelligence—fully justified given that so few even bothered to object—Schlesinger uttered his notable oxymoron: **My goal is to protect our reporters and protect our editorial integrity.** In fact, he was protecting his reporters *at the cost* of his editorial integrity. Rephrased, Schlesinger was saying: "our media do not call a terrorist group 'terrorist' because the terrorists threaten our journalists with violence, and that determines our unprincipled editorial policy." And yet, despite these public secrets being widely known among journalists, neither the *New York Times* reporter, nor most of the journalistic profession (aside from the "right wing" editors at CamWest and critics like Michael Kinsley and Daniel Pipes) bothered to challenge this counterfactual rationalization.

Nor was the ban on the T-word limited to the news media: it pervaded the information professions even unto Western (infidel) intelligence services. Melanie Phillips argued that the mentality that lay behind this combination of political correctness and self-censorship, had completely blinded MI5 to

---

135 Austen, "Reuters asks a chain to remove its bylines."
136 See below, 326–29.
137 Kinsley, "Defining Terrorism."

the homegrown radicalism that eventually produced both Al Qaeda as an international jihadi network, and the 7–7 attacks themselves. And yet, if we cannot, should not, hurt the feelings of violent zealots who target civilians with that "emotive word," then whose feelings should we offend? Why should we defer to the people who complain violently when we insult them, and dismiss the complaints of their victims as efforts to silence criticism?[138]

A decade later, the response of the New York Times to criticism that it was the only important US paper in January 2015 not to show the Charlie Hebdo cover with a depiction of the Prophet, revealed the extent to which intimidation lay behind the legacy media's principled self-censorship, especially in the international news agencies. Mark Cooper, a journalism professor at the University of Southern California, criticized the Times harshly on his Facebook page for its failure to publish a picture of the Charlie Hebdo cover:

> Exactly how many people have to be shot in cold blood before your paper rules that you can show us what provoked the killers? Apparently 23 shot including 11 dead is not enough. What absolute cowardice. These MSM managers act is if they are running insurance companies, not news organizations.

Dean Baquet, the executive editor of the New York Times, pugnaciously defended his paper's decision not to publish, calling Cooper an "asshole" [!] for claiming it was fear of reprisal,[139] and insisting that his paper declined showing the publication purely out of concern for the feelings of Muslim readers who might take offense: "But let's not forget the Muslim family in Brooklyn who read us and is offended by any depiction of what he sees as his prophet. I don't give a damn about the head of ISIS but I do care about that family and it is arrogant to ignore them."[140] Note here the combination of noble concern for the feelings of the hypothetical (and presumably moderate and even patriotic) Muslim family in Brooklyn, bravado about any threats from ISIS, and contemptuous response to the "asshole" critic.

---

138 Chinlund acknowledged that the policy of not designating Palestinian attacks on Israeli civilians as terrorism, "infuriated" Israel supporters ("Who should wear the 'terrorist' label?"), but apparently the journalists didn't feel threatened by them, didn't mind triggering their "emotivity." On the role of fear of retaliation (or its lack) in shaping the way "progressives" treated Israel vs the Palestinians, see Dave Brown's cartoon, 125–30.

139 Dylan Byers, "Dean Baquet calls N.Y. Times critic 'a—hole,'" On Media, January 9, 2015.

140 Dylan Byers, "Dean Baquet addresses NYT's republication of antisemitic cartoons," Politico, January 8, 2015. See also Margaret Sullivan, the New York Times's public editor, "A Close Call on Publication of Charlie Hebdo Cartoons," New York Times January 8, 2015.

A week later, however, in a follow-up article at the *Huffington Post*, a former chief editor of the *New York Times*, Bill Keller, belied such bravado by letting slip the real reason why the *Times* had censored what everyone else showed.

> An editor running a large, high profile, global news organization has to consider the potential consequences for reporters, photographers, translators and other staff. It's easy for an editor in New York or Washington to take a stand (or strike a pose) but the dangers fall on journalists in the field. If you've had a few of your people murdered, as *The Times* has, this is not a concern you take lightly.[141]

And apparently, it's easy for the executive editor of the *New York Times* to strike a pose of indifference to jihadi threats and abiding concern for local Muslims when the journalists "investigating" are so lacking in curiosity.

On the contrary, Keller's frank remark confirmed Cooper's wry (and apparently painful) dig about the *New York Times* acting like an insurance company. It offers an important key to many controversies over coverage of triumphalist Islam, including the one between Reuters and CamWest: the newspapers hide behind claims of objectivity to concede to the demands of (to side with) the terrorists. And Baquet's obscenity aimed at Cooper for stating the obvious is a classic response of the honor-driven in the face of accurate criticism.[142] In all matters of honor, loud and energetic denial is a norm.

The big news agencies, the ones with overwhelming influence on the news we in the free world get, are also the most vulnerable to threats. They are the ones with journalists in unsafe places and hence most likely to bend to threats. Caliphators win, and their useful infidels, trying to justify their compliance, pull the wool over our eyes with their chatter about objectivity, not "taking sides," and not letting "others" (namely those fighting Caliphators) set their policies.

One person's coward is another's "principled" journalist. And, as this pseudo-ethics permeated the profession, one person's journalist was another's propagandist.[143]

---

141 Michael Calderone, "NY Times Only Top US Newspaper not to Publish Charlie Hebdo Cover," *Huffington Post*, January 15, 2015.

142 Kenneth Greenberg, *Honor and Slavery* (Princeton: Princeton University Press, 1998), 20–22.

143 After the attack on the Capitol on January 6, 2021, CNN had no problem redefining terrorism in the most expansive way and using it to describe what happened: "This was terrorism. The definition of terrorism is violence in pursuit of a political goal. This was domestic terrorism."

Stupidities Featured in This Chapter

Islam is peace. POTUS George Bush, speech at Islamic Center of Washington, September 17, 2001.

i think 99% of arab people because they are human beings would be totally against what happened. blog comment.

They [Al Qaeda] did it [9–11], we wanted it. French sociologist, Jean Baudrillard November 2, 2001.

If we can prevent human suffering and don't, is that not terrorism? Derrida on 9–11.

True courage is fighting the strongest, and America is the strongest. French journalist, February 2003.

As far as I am concerned, Islam and terrorists are two words that do not go together. Brian Paddick, deputy assistant commissioner of the (British) Metropolitan Police, July 7, 2005.

One man's terrorist is another's freedom fighter. (Reuters, BBC News, AP, the *Boston Globe*, the *Washington Post*, etc., etc., ad nauseam.)

Our editorial policy is that we don't use emotive words when labeling someone. David Schlesinger, Reuters global managing editor, September 2004.

My goal is to protect our reporters and protect our editorial integrity. David Schlesinger, Reuters global managing editor, September 2004.

Josh Campbell, former FBI Special Agent. Wolf Blitzer found this term's use worthy of repetition (*The Trump Insurrection*, 17:14). Note the expansive definition of "terrorism" as any violence for political ends. Suddenly, it need not even target civilians.

3

Jenin: Cheering on the Jihadi Suicide Terror (2002)

> Fooled by news that made
> Nazis of Jews,
> They cheered their worst enemy

The battle fought in the Jenin refugee camp between the IDF and Hamas was the first full-fledged battle between a Western infidel army and Caliphator jihadis who used suicide terror as their main weapon, in their apocalyptic war against infidels who resist subjection. There have been many pitched battles between infidels and jihadis since, and there will be more in the future; yet, given how difficult it is to stop someone who wants to die, the power of suicide attacks constitutes a particularly devastating weapon.[1] The manner in which the Western nations, who will have to fight these battles, responded to Jenin—cheering on the "martyrs"—represents one of the greater acts of folly of the new century. And to this day, almost two decades later, few people, and certainly not those primarily responsible for that misbegotten response, namely the purveyors of the "Jenin Massacre" meme, have realized what they did, much less apologized to their Western audiences for it. In fact, they continue to pursue the folly.

---

1   "The demons released by this age of chaos and war in the Middle East [suicide bombing] have become an unstoppable force." Patrick Cockburn, *Age of Jihad*, final sentence.

What Choice Do They Have?

In the winter of 2002, a colleague in my History department asked why I looked so troubled. "Well, it's these suicide bombings," I said, referring to the wave of suicide terror attacks in Israel that had sent Arab Muslim youth—girls and boys—to blow themselves up among the most vulnerable Israelis: school kids, shoppers, diners, travelers, night-club goers. This particular week, there had been three such murderous attacks. "Yes," he sighed, "what choice do they have?"

At the time, I was angry and hurt. "Ever hear of Camp David?"

"Oh," he replied. "That is a point." Conversation over. No discussion of how unfair and wide of the mark his initial observation.[2] In retrospect, his remark, coming from one of my more open-minded and thoughtful colleagues, strikes me as among the most ominous of those I would hear in the years that followed.

What was so terrifying was not only the staggering cognitive and moral folly my colleague's remark expressed, but its banality. He did not come up with this zinger on his own. His field was far from the Middle East, and he had previously shown little knowledge of, nor interest in, what went on there. No, he had just repeated something he had heard others say, something that was apparently commonly accepted in his circles.[3] So why not repeat it?

The astonishing stupidity: **What choice do they have?** Those five words contain four major and many minor idiocies.

- Above all, it makes light of some of the ugliest, most morally depraved human behavior—a new low in the annals of human hatred.[4] Suicide terror involves leadership instilling, and also implementing, murderous teachings in its own people, sacrificing its young for the sake of blowing up those they hate. And since the main weapon of Global Jihad in the twenty-first century is suicide terror, such moral levity about a weapon that would soon target him (indeed already had on 9–11), was nothing short of self-destructive folly.

- My colleague's statement also reflected the presumption that Arab Muslims have no moral agency—no capacity to deal with frustration, no choice but to lash out. If Ariel Sharon visits the Temple Mount, *of course* Palestinian Muslims respond with a murderous intifada, where

---

2 "'What Choice do they Have?': Meditations on Liberal Folly, Jenin 2002," *Augean Stables*, April 15, 2017.

3 One can hear the sentiment in Ted Turner's remark: "The Palestinians are fighting with human suicide bombers, that's all they have," Shuman, "CNN Chief Accuses Israel of Terror."

4 For the pre-Islamic history of suicide terrorism the late 19th century, see Geifman, *Death Orders*.

snipers kill babies in their mother's arms. If the pope calls Islam violent, *of course* Muslims riot in the street. "What choice do they have?" rather than "*Of course* they have a choice. And this is what they choose."

- And why do they have no choice? Because the Jews must be treating the Palestinians terribly; after all, why else would they hate Israel so? If the suicidal campaign of mass murder is a matter of desperation, then it must be Israel's fault—not the product of an internally driven campaign of genocidal hatred, but of Israeli abuse to which the Palestinians have no alternative. Rather than an aspiration to commit genocide that was frustrated by Israeli determination to survive, it becomes a frustrated desire to be free, exacerbated by Israeli refusal to grant the Palestinians the freedom (Western liberals were so sure) they wanted. Noted Paul Berman: "each new act of murder and suicide testified to how oppressive were the Israelis. Palestinian terror, in this view, was the measure of Israeli guilt. The more grotesque the terror, the deeper the guilt.[5]

- Finally, as I pointed out in my initial response, these presumptions completely ignored the dynamics of the Oslo Peace Process and the Camp David offer made by Israel the previous summer, as if the Palestinians *had* to say no, and *had* to start a vicious war they could only lose. The only way one can read this behavior as even remotely "rational" is to, again, blame Israel.[6]

The following contraries to the previous statements are true:

- Suicide terror is the act of people so desperate to strike at an enemy that they will sacrifice their own children just to do damage. It constitutes a ghastly combination of human (child!) sacrifice and a genocidal death cult—not exactly the kind of behavior any serious moral thinker waves off with banal rhetorical questions.

- Not to hold Muslims to moral standards is a form of "humanitarian racism," in which white privileged people show utter moral contempt for "people of color." "Of course, they behave like savages, what do you expect? Self-restraint?" Whether born of moral disdain or fear of rebuking those whom one fears, this approach encourages the worst behavior among those so treated, and, in this case, accepts the legitimacy of suicide terror, the bane of twenty-first-century global society. It also

---

5   Berman, *Liberalism and Terror*, 154.
6   See 210f.

ignores a toxic Jew-hatred that not only rivals but surpasses the Nazis in its openly genocidal rage. (No German preacher called for genocide from the pulpit, a quotidian occurrence among Imams.)

- In the history of "occupations," Israel has treated the Palestinians remarkably well, and Palestinian quality of life measurements, including economic and educational growth since 1967 are remarkably high, even in comparison with "non-occupied" Arab populations in the surrounding areas. Indeed, in a supreme irony, Israel treats Palestinians better than Palestinian—or any other Arab—leaders treat their people.[7]

- The Palestinian leadership took the concessions Israel made at Oslo—allowing the PLO to return—as a chance to bring in a Trojan Horse, which exploded in the first campaign of Global Jihad in the twenty-first century in the fall of 2000.[8] Now, using the rhetorical stupidity "What choice do they have?" outside observers, especially on the "left," blamed Israel fully for Oslo's failure.

Neither my colleague (who voted for Ralph Nader in 2000), nor his circle of interlocutors on the progressive left, had any idea what they were doing. And yet, with the condescending folly of "What choice do they have?" they were justifying and approving a movement of exterminationist antisemitism only fifty-five years after the Holocaust—and giving a seal of approval to the most potent weapon in the arsenal of jihad's insurgency against their own societies. Two decades later, journalists who occupy the middle ground in the MSNM (CNN, NBC, *Time*, the *Atlantic*) and the left (MSNBC, *The New Republic, The Nation, VICE*) repeat the same nonsense, despite extensive evidence to the contrary:

> **Sulome Anderson** @SulomeAnderson May 14
> Imagine the desperation it takes to walk into live gunfire from the Middle East's most powerful fighting force, armed with nothing more than rocks & the occasional Molotov or grenade. Try to conceive of the circumstances that could drive so many human beings to such an act. #Gaza[9]

---

7   For a recent example of the growing awareness of this in the surrounding areas, currently melting down under the blows of tribal and sectarian warfare, see, Maayan Groisman, "Lebanese journalist: 'Aleppo would have been safe like the Golan were it annexed by Israel,'" *Jerusalem Post*, May 1, 2016.

8   Landes, "Oslo Disaster; and below, chapter 5.

9   Sulome Anderson, tweet, May 14, 2018, https://twitter.com/SulomeAnderson/status/996015215538995201.

It has to be desperation, couldn't be aspiration.[10]

* * *

In the cognitive theater of war of the twenty-first century, 2002 represents a spectacular year of success for Global Jihad. In Israel, jihadis pursued a wave of suicide attacks on civilians from January 2001 into the spring of 2002. It was the period when sane voices both in the West and the Muslim world should have come out boldly in condemnation of so portentous and morally revolting a development and apologized to Israel for urging them to arm and empower the leaders of this attack. From the perspective of the 2020s/1440s, where this suicide terror has metastasized globally, and has since killed and continues to kill *far more* Muslims and even Westerners than Israelis, the failure to oppose it then, stands out as one of the most pregnant failures of the "moral left."

Instead of Westerners expressing concern for this catastrophic failure of Muslim jurisprudence to hold the line on humane *versus* genocidal warfare at the dawn of the new global century, there was a giddy, even elated, enthusiasm among the Global Progressive Left for Palestinian suicide terror. And as with the Muslim world, this enthusiasm expressed itself with particular vigor when the target was Israelis. In 2002, the global public mobilized major anti-war demonstrations against Israel's reported "massacre" in Jenin. In their outrage at Israelis' (mis)reported deeds, protesters wore suicide belts to show their solidarity with the Palestinian "resistance."

Given that 9–11 had already happened only months earlier, and that these jihadi attacks would soon target infidels and Muslims the world over (Bali was four months, Barcelona two years, London three years later), these demonstrators effectively mimicked the movie *Independence Day*, in which enthusiastic crowds of "new-agers" gather on high-rise rooftops to greet the aliens with peace and love, just before getting pulverized by those they so warmly welcomed.[11] At least these celluloid demonstrators had no knowledge of the folks they enthusiastically embraced; in 2002, the demonstrators knew full well whom they cheered on—they wore mock explosive belts—and somehow,

---

10 Itamar Marcus and Barbara Crook, "Aspiration not Desperation," *Jerusalem Post*, January 29, 2004.

11 *Independence Day* (1989). On the efforts of some filmmakers, like Steven Spielberg to ease the paranoid attitude of earthlings towards ETs, see Landes, *Heaven on Earth*, 401–5.

there was no sense of a moral problem. On the contrary, being "pro-Palestinian" became a "litmus test" of being a liberal.[12] Life tragically mimics parody.[13]

Israel in the first years of the century bore the full brunt of jihadi suicide-terror's ravages. For sixteen months Israel endured them without their allegedly hot-headed, brutal prime minister, Ariel Sharon, making a move against the centers of those attacks in Oslo-ceded territory. Over 600 civilians were killed, and three times as many were wounded, in many cases crippled for life by the deliberate and careful packing of ball bearings and other shrapnel to spread the damage as far and wide as possible.[14] And there was no mistake about the target of this "resistance": the vast majority—4/5—of Israeli victims were civilians, especially children.[15] The murderous assault on the Park Hotel, filled with families celebrating Passover Seders in Netanya on March 27, 2002, finally tipped the scales and Israel struck back, invading Area A, especially the Jenin refugee camp, where this suicide terror campaign had set up its operations base.[16]

The Jenin "Massacre": Israel Loses the Moral High Ground

Then began the Jenin episode, perhaps the most remarkable example of own-goal lethal journalism in the history of news-reporting. In what will go down in the annals of war as the most lawful and careful military campaign to strike an enemy embedded in an urban civilian population, on April 1, 2002, the Israelis attacked a five-block area within the Jenin refugee camp. Even though NATO troops had bombed Kosovo from the air only three years earlier and suffered no

---

12 Ian Buruma, "How to Talk about Israel," *New York Times*, August 31, 2003.

13 For a fine example of how Western "progressives" reacted, see Edward Said's two essays during the operation, *From Oslo to Iraq and the Road Map* (New York: Vintage, 2005), chaps. 27–28.

14 Elihu Richter, "Response to Giacaman: Terror toll before Jenin," *European Journal of Public Health*, 15:1, February 1, 2005.

15 Don Radlauer demonstrated statistically that Palestinians targeted civilians: "An Engineered Tragedy: Statistical Analysis of Casualties in the Palestinian—Israeli Conflict, September 2000—September 2002," *Institute for the Study of Asymmetric Conflict*. On children as a deliberate target, see Ahlam Tamimi specifically choosing the site of a pizzeria to kill children, "Female Palestinian terrorist does not regret murder of 15 civilians at Sbarro pizza shop that she planned," *Palestinian Media Watch*.

16 Even PA officials referred to the Jenin Refugee camp as "the capital of the suicide martyrs": "Letter from Fatah members in Jenin to Marwan Barghouti," Yagil Henkin, "Urban Warfare and the Lessons of Jenin," *Azure* (Summer 2003): 53.

casualties as a result, the IDF chose not to evacuate and bomb the camp, but to go in house to house, in order to limit civilian casualties.[17]

When it was over, Israel had killed 52 to 56 Palestinians, about 40 of whom were combatants, and lost 23 soldiers, many in an ambush forced on them by their commander's insistence on going door to door.[18] Indeed, these IDF soldiers were most scrupulous about not "stealing" the food in the houses where they took refuge, and in general behaved in exemplary ways.[19] In the world annals of urban warfare, little compares to the self-sacrifice and care with which the IDF treated enemy civilians; no example can come close the ratio of 5 combatants to 2 civilians for an urban battle lasting weeks. On the contrary, up until the end of World War II, much urban warfare *targeted* civilians. Even afterwards, *good*, humane ratios in urban warfare were generally 3 civilians killed to 1 combatant. Jenin represents a high point in modern military ethics, in the extensive effort to avoid civilian casualties and the extraordinary risks soldiers took towards that end.[20]

The outside world heard a different story, however, from their journalists working in Israel. For two weeks, while the house-to-house fighting took place, the IDF kept out reporters. During that time, the media gave maximal credibility to Palestinian claims, run indiscriminately in their news media, that Israelis were massacring civilian populations ... mass executions and mass graves, inviting comparisons with German Police Battalions exterminating Jews and Hutus slaughtering Tutsis.[21] Saeb Erakat, one of the more "moderate" of Palestinian politicians on the scene (a "lead negotiator" for Oslo), elaborated on unsubstantiated claims to the news media, which readily repeated them as credible. Not even the switch from 3,000 massacred (Abd Rabbo) to "only" 523

---

17 Benjamin Lambeth, *NATO's Air War for Kosovo: A Strategic and Operational Assessment* (Washington DC: Rand, 2001).

18 Report of the Secretary-General prepared pursuant to General Assembly resolution ES-10/10, August 1, 2002. Amnesty International, using their own peculiar definitions, estimated that 22 were civilians. That's still fewer than the Israeli soldiers who lost their lives in an effort to limit damage to Palestinian civilians. On the joy of Palestinian "militants" at Israel walking into their death trap, see Rehov, *La route de Jenin*, 09:48.

19 See Brett Goldberg's descriptions of the campaign from the perspective of Israeli soldiers, and the deadly risks they took to maintain their "purity of arms": *Psalm in Jenin* (Israel, Modan Publishing, 2003).

20 Henkin, "Urban Warfare," compares Jenin operation with other late twentieth-century military operations in urban warfare.

21 One Greek cartoon, published only days into the operation, depicted two IDF soldiers with Nazi-like uniforms, stabbing two helpless Arabs to death: "Don't worry brother. We were in Auschwitz and Dachau not to suffer but to learn." *Ethos*, April 7; cited in Manfred Gerstenfeld, *Holocaust Inversion: The Portraying of Israel and Jews as Nazis*, JCPA, 2007, 24.

(Erakat) aroused suspicion. On the contrary, on April 11, *Libération* spoke of a bloodbath. *Time* cited an Iranian estimate (how did *they* know?) of 16,000![22]

"Human Rights" NGOs, enjoying credibility from their "halo effect," followed the Durban Strategy of stigmatizing Israel. They amplified the accusations and strengthened Palestinian claims.[23] Reporters, even European politicians, picked up the "massacre" meme.[24] A. N. Wilson accused Israel of "massacre, and a cover-up, of genocide," in the pages of the self-consciously high-brow *Evening Standard*.[25] How tempting it was in those days to debase Israel, that "shitty little country," without even knowing if the accusations were true.[26]

The news was so convincing that even Jews accepted the comparisons with the Nazis. In the preface to a book published the following year, Daniel Boyarin wrote of Israel and her Jewish supporters' "total disdain for any but Jewish lives and bodies," (despite the sacrifice of 23 soldiers to spare Palestinian civilians; and with no reference to the murderous ideology of those Israel fought): "It has been said by many Christians that Christianity died at Auschwitz, Treblinka, and Sobibor. I fear—G-d forbid—that my Judaism may be dying at Nablus, Daheishe, Beteen (Beth El), and al Khalil (Hebron.)"[27] Holocaust inversion is a cognitive disorientation that knows no borders.

So committed were the journalists to their narrative of Israelis massacring innocent Palestinians that, even after they made it into the stricken area after the battle, some did not change their minds. Faced with the cognitive dissonance of finding no evidence to support the claims of "massacre"—au contraire—they soldiered on.[28] *"Jenin 'massacre evidence growing'"* blared the next day's BBC

---

22 Cited by Giniewski, *Guerre des hommes-bombes: Israël, 2000–2006* (Paris: Cheminements, 2006), 186.

23 Gerald Steinberg, "The Role of NGOs in the Palestinian Political War Against Israel," *JCPA*; Margarete Wente, "Call it Sham-nesty International, an apologist for terror," *Globe and Mail*, May 9, 2002.

24 Tom Gross, "Jeningrad: What the British media said," *National Review*, May 13, 2002.

25 A. N. Wilson, "A demo we can't afford to ignore," *Evening Standard*, April 15, 2002. Winston Pickett, "Nasty or Nazi? The use of antisemitic topoi in the left-liberal media," *Engage Journal*, 2 (2006).

26 Tom Gross, "A Shitty Little Country."

27 Daniel Boyarin, "Interrogate my Love," in *Wrestling with Zion: Progressive Jewish-American Responses to the Israeli-Palestinian Conflict*, ed. Tony Kushner and Alisa Solomon (New York: Grove Press, 2003), 198–205.

28 As Jack Schwartz noted about the Guardian's editorial ("The battle for the truth: What really happened in Jenin camp?" *The Guardian*, April 17, 2002): "One would have to believe from the intemperate tone of this article that the editors would be disappointed if a massacre HADN'T taken place," "Old habits die hard: The renewed antisemitism in historical context," *Mideast Dispatch*, June 3, 2002.

headline, citing HRW operative, Derrick Pounder, as a viable analyst who explained the empty hospitals:

> Normally [i.e., in the case of indiscriminate urban warfare], one would have expected to find three people severely injured for everyone killed. Even if one accepts the Israeli claim that "only" 40 Palestinians died, there ought to be another 120 lying badly wounded, in hospital. But they are nowhere to be found.... We draw the conclusion that they were allowed to die where they were.[29]

In other words, faced with empty hospitals, very few corpses in and out of morgues, and no mass graves, Pounder assumed that after three weeks of fighting 1) the Israelis fought not according to the rules laid down by their exceedingly demanding code (and the Geneva Conventions), but by the "normal rules" of urban warfare with its high levels of collateral damage; and 2) the Israelis, with their exceptional medical ethics,[30] left people to die *in situ* (and then buried/hid their bodies). And, of course, plenty of reporters lined up to assure their readers that, despite only 16 bodies in the morgue, many more lay beneath the treads of Israeli tanks.[31]

Phil Reeves of the UK *Independent*, on the morrow of gaining access to the camp, also reported according to his expectations:

> A monstrous war crime that Israel has tried to cover up for a fortnight has finally been exposed. Its troops have caused devastation in the centre of the Jenin refugee camp, reached yesterday by *The Independent*.... Rubble has been shoveled by bulldozers into 30ft piles. The sweet and ghastly reek of rotting

---

29 Pounder's speculation prompted the BBC headline: "Jenin 'massacre evidence growing,'" BBC, April 18, 2002.

30 For a visiting American's protest at how strictly impartial Israeli hospitals' were in their treatment of Israeli victims and Palestinian attackers (and their Arab Israeli sympathizers also getting medical treatment) during the Al Aqsa Jihad, see Larry Miller, "It gets hard when they cheer," *Weekly Standard*, August 19, 2002. Today, especially under Corona conditions, Israeli hospitals represent one of the most successful venues of a civil, merit-based coexistence between Muslims and infidels on the planet.

31 Suzanne Goldenberg, "Disaster zone hides final death toll: Just 16 bodies recovered at Jenin camp but hundreds more may lie under wreckage," *The Guardian*, April 17, 2002. See the full complement of Guardian writers sustaining the myth *after* they gained entry to the site of the alleged "massacre": Myrrh, "Ten Years Since Something That Never Happened: A Learning Moment for the Guardian [not]," *Harry's Place*, April 14, 2012.

human bodies is everywhere, evidence that it is a human tomb. The people, who spent days hiding in basements crowded into single rooms as the rockets pounded in [sic], say there are hundreds of corpses, entombed beneath the dust, under a field of debris, crisscrossed with tank and bulldozer treadmarks. A quiet, sad-looking young man called Kamal Anis led us across the wasteland, littered now with detritus of what were once households, foam rubber, torn clothes, shoes, tin cans, children's toys. He suddenly stopped. This was a mass grave, he said, pointing. We stared at a mound of debris. Here, he said, he saw the Israeli soldiers pile 30 bodies beneath a half-wrecked house. When the pile was complete, they bulldozed the building, bringing its ruins down on the corpses. Then they flattened the area with a tank. We could not see the bodies. But we could smell them.[32]

Only in August, after the UN reported on 50 dead did he apologize.[33]

Forced by the evidence to renounce the "massacre" meme, Terje-Roed Larsen, the UN official on the scene and one of the main proponents of the Oslo Process, hammered home the message of wanton destruction. "What we are seeing here is horrifying, horrifying scenes of human suffering... ***Israel has lost all moral ground in this conflict.***"[34] Reporters cited him in articles that beat the drum of IDF war crimes.[35] In France, such images, like those of al Durah, and unlike those of Palestinians celebrating 9–11,

> were immediately turned into a symbol of the "martyred Palestinian people" because they confirmed and reinforced the negative stereotypes used by anti-Israelis, participating

---

32 Phil Reeves, "Amid the ruins of Jenin, the grisly evidence of a war crime," *Independent*, April 16, 2002.

33 Phil Reeves, "Even journalists have to admit sometimes they're wrong," *Independent*, August, 2002. This article is not available at the *Independent*'s online site. I have tried to contact the author for a copy without success.

34 John Lancaster, "U.N. Envoy Calls Camp 'Horrifying,'" *Washington Post*, April 19, 2002.

35 *Ibid.*; Peter Beaumont, "Not a massacre, but a brutal breach of war's rules," *Guardian Weekly*, 25 April 2002. In France, among many (see n37), Amnon Kapeliouk, "Jénine, enquête sur un crime de guerre", *Le Monde diplomatique*, no 578, May 2002, 16–17; at Harvard, student columnist Nadr al Hassan, '02 excoriated the American media for not reporting the massacre: "What Massacre?" *Harvard Crimson*, May 1, 2002. Notes Taguieff, "despite its extravagance (*démesure*), these claims were taken up as Gospel Truth by the [French] media, with few exceptions," Pierre-André Taguieff, *La nouvelle propagande antijuive: Du symbole Al-Dura aux rumeurs de Gaza* (Paris: Presses universitaires de France, 2010), 274f.

in the intellectual teachings (*"doxa intellectuelle"*), shared by journalists and intellectuals and politicians, a *doxa* become transnational.[36]

Even in the USA, where coverage was, comparatively speaking, more accurate and professional, there were journalists who kept alive the postcolonial narrative of Israel, brutalizing the Palestinians well after the propaganda libel was proven false.[37]

Egocentric Journalists Helpless before Palestinian Disinformation

That Palestinians might not have been telling their eager audiences the truth—or worse, that they were engaged in war propaganda designed to alienate support from the enemy and arouse rage among their own—seems never to have occurred to these journalists.[38] On the contrary, widespread credulity, almost a principled credulity prevailed, despite the long and consistent record of Arab and Palestinian lying about Israel.

In the abundant thesaurus of astonishingly stupid statements made in the early twenty-first century, Andrea Koppel's remarks about Jenin hold a special place.[39] Koppel had just arrived in Israel; no journalist had yet been in the Jenin Camp at the time of her conversation. Nonetheless, while still in Tel Aviv, she responded to an Israeli complaining about the media's use of moral equivalence.

> Andrea Koppel: "So when Israeli soldiers slaughter civilians in Jenin, that is not equivalent?"
> Adam Ruskin: "What are your sources? Were you in Jenin? How exactly do you know there was a slaughter?"

---

36 Taguieff, *La nouvelle propagande antijuive*, 97.

37 On the difference between European (primarily British) and American coverage, see the British journalist Tom Gross, "Jeningrad." On the American coverage, see Muravchik, *Covering the Intifada*, 101–10. On the French coverage of the Jenin "massacre," see Taguieff, *Nouvelle propagande anti-juive*, 273–76; Catherine Leuchter, "Etats des lieux au 31 mai 2002: Qu'avons-nous appris des médias?" *Le conflict israélo-palestinen: Les medias français sont-ils objectifs?* (2002), 8–50; Giniewski, *Guerre des hommes bombes*, 186–97.

38 For documentation of the systematic lying involved both by Palestinian spokespeople, medical officials, and people on the street, see Landes, *Pallywood* (2005), https://vimeo.com/65294892.

39 Diana Lynne, "Pro-Palestinian Bias among CNN Ranks?" *WorldNetDaily*, April 23, 2002. The conversation took place on April 14, at which point no journalists had access to the camp.

AK: "I just spoke with my colleagues who were there, and they told me of the slaughter."

AR: "Did they actually see the shooting, the bodies?"

AK: "Palestinians told us about the slaughter."

AR: "And you believe them without evidence. Could they possibly be lying and distorting facts?"

AK: **"Oh, so now they are all just lying?"**

Phrasing it as a rhetorical question in which the only way not to look like a racist was to say, "no, they're not all liars," she literally boxed herself and her interlocutors *out* of reality. When it comes to Palestinian spokespeople "informing" Western journalists about Israeli "war crimes," the rhetorical question should be: "Oh, so now they're all scrupulously honest?"

And repeatedly, the real story turned out to be the opposite of what Palestinians told anyone who would listen. Abo Gali, the head of the hospital in Jenin, told everyone that the Israelis had targeted the hospital with eleven tank shells that destroyed one wing, and subsequently did their best to keep the wounded from being treated in the hospital, including by blocking food supplies.[40] On the contrary: the IDF had gone out of its way to protect the hospital, guarantee its continuing supply of food and medicine, and ensure the treatment of wounded Palestinian combatants, all while combatants used ambulances to ferry suicide belts to the battlefield. As for the strike on the hospital, when Pierre Rehov asked to see the damage, all Gali could do was show him some bullet marks.

Similarly, an old man, Ali Youssef, testified to how an Israeli sniper shot him in the foot and the hand, when in fact the Israeli medical team not only treated him for injuries (not bullets), but also sent him to an Israeli hospital to treat his undiagnosed congestive heart failure.[41] One must see these interviews with documentary-makers like Omar Bakri, Pierre Rehov and Martin Himmel to realize how easily and convincingly these Palestinian "witnesses" lied ... repeatedly.[42]

For a serious journalist like Koppel, trained to be suspicious of third-hand eyewitness accounts, and double-check them, her principled credulity bespoke a dramatic collapse of professional standards, precisely where and when they were

---

40 Bakri, *Jenin, Jenin*, 14:17–15:49; 35:30–38:50; Rehov, *Road to Jenin*, 28:40–32:40. Similar claims to Himmel in *Jenin: Massacring the Truth*. Note that in the al Durah affair, the rejection of the possibility of a conspiracy relies heavily on the notion that at the very least, the doctors in the hospital would not take part in such a lie, Enderlin, *Un enfant est mort*, chapter 5.

41 Bakri, *Jenin, Jenin* 05:29–06:20; 29:47–31:50. Rehov, *Road*, 39:00–40:54; Himmel, *Jenin*.

42 Phyllis Chesler, *The New Antisemitism* (Jerusalem: Gefen Publishing House, 2015), 65–69.

most needed.[43] Instead, she opted for the Saidian Zeitgeist in which any unflattering observation about Arab culture is racist Orientalism.[44] Nor was she the only one. CBS's correspondent Mark Phillips, indignant at Israel's "destruction of the peace process," explained that one should evaluate what happened at Jenin depending on whom one believed (that is, he preferred the Palestinian narrative). Joshua Muravchik commented wryly that Phillips "sounded like a modern-day literary critic approaching a "text" of which all constructions were equally subjective, thus equally valid."[45] A Human Rights Watch activist gave the poor journalist's version of narrative equivalence. Giving a small nod to the evidence, he explained to the *Washington Post*'s John Lancaster that "the final tally will probably be somewhere in the middle [between Israeli and Palestinian claims]."

It wasn't anywhere near: the final tally fell not *between* Palestinian claims (of thousands dead) vs Israeli estimates (a hundred). Rather, the final tally came to *half* the IDF estimates.[46] The Jenin affair represents one of the most extraordinary episodes in the battle for the soul of twenty-first-century journalism: narrative *versus* accuracy. Here, accuracy undermined the apparently enormously exciting narrative that Israel was massacring Palestinians. For many, that narrative was too good to pass up.

When confronted by questions about why they described Israeli behavior as "war crimes," but Palestinian suicide bombing as a "violation of international humanitarian law," Human Rights Watch spokeswoman Urmi Shah walked an unusual line:

> One of the key factors in deciding whether a violation amounts to a war crime is whether it was intentionally done so. . . . Clear example from the situation in the Jenin refugee camp would be the shooting of a Palestinian civilian who was under direct control of Israeli forces. That is a summary execution. That is a war crime.[47]

Of course, this is anything but a "clear case." Not having been in the camp at the time, HRW "observers" were in no position to judge whether the shooting of a

---

43 Koppel denied making these remarks, despite the independent testimony of three witnesses. This is typical of astounding stupidities: in one context they're self-evident, and everyone nods (e.g. among journalists), in another, they become deeply embarrassing, to be categorically denied.

44 See 276–84.

45 Muravchik, *Covering the Intifada*, 107.

46 General Yossi Kuperwasser: around a hundred.

47 Himmel, "The Human Rights NGOs," *Jenin*; transcript at NGO Monitor.

civilian was a "summary execution" or "collateral damage." Yet when it comes to suicide terror, the deliberation is clear, from the pre-operation video, to the location of the detonation, to the ideology of "pink mist" (i.e., mingling the "Shahid's" blood with the blood of their victims).

So how did Shah handle the contradiction to her principle of deliberation? With a smile, a new technical distinction.

> Urmi Shah: One of the other things is, it's militant groups. It is not a state force, in the case of Palestinians.
> Martin Himel: Are militias or militants not held at the same accountability as military organizations?
> Umri Shah: Sure, but unfortunately—there's a difference between a state sanctioned if you like, or state-controlled individuals, groups, militant groups unfortunately are not—the Palestinian authorities are not able to control them.

Leaving aside the issues of whether the PA "controlled" Palestinian suicide bombers, encouraged them, made no effort to control them, or, in the case of the Al Aqsa Martyrs Brigade, *sponsored* them, this technicality seems morally dubious—if one cannot pin the attack on state power, then deliberately killing Israeli civilians is not a war crime? HRW does not hold Palestinian terrorists who have declared war on Israel to the legal standards they hold the Israelis because they are not a state? Apparently, HRW agrees with radical groups (International Solidarity Movement) who insist that "Resistance is not terrorism;" indeed, terror, in this upside-down moral universe, can only come from the state.[48]

Profiles in Lethal Journalism: Janine di Giovanni, She Who Cannot Err

When the UN came out with its report of fifty plus dead, some papers and individual journalists, like Phil Reeves, ran apologies for the errors of their

---

48 HRW's later study called suicide bombing a "crime against humanity" no matter who commits it: "Erased in a Moment: Suicide Bombing Attacks against Israeli Civilians," October 15, 2002. Shah's comments to Himmel were made after the report's issue, which apparently had no impact on the HRW party line. See Gerald Steinberg's review: "Human Rights Watch's Report: Erased in a Moment: Suicide Bombing Attacks Against Israeli Civilians, *NGO Monitor,* January 17, 2003.

coverage.[49] Others, often the most egregious offenders, like the *Guardian*, refused outright to acknowledge the error, even a decade later.[50] Martin Himmel, with one of the soldiers from Jenin, tried to track down some of the British press's most lethal journalists, and found themselves either refused audience, or, when granted interviews, dismissed with more misinformation.[51]

David Blair of the *Daily Telegraph*, one of the few to agree to an interview, had, in the days after journalists had access to the camp, described how in "Jenin town [sic] . . . all but a few of the streets [sic] have been blown apart," and used the destruction to predict that Palestinian claims of hundreds would prove more accurate than Israeli estimates of dozens.[52] When confronted with his lack of coverage of the Israeli efforts to prevent civilian casualties, including sacrificing soldiers, he replied with the dishonest memory that "when I was writing those articles and others were, the Israelis weren't telling us anything. If you would have told us this, I would have reported it."

Of course, the Israelis were telling their side to everyone they could, taking reporters on tours of the camp at the very time Blair wrote his pieces. As one IDF general put it: "We had stacks of material for the journalists. They wouldn't take it."[53] It would just get in the way of the lethal journalism's modus operandi in Israel: *Report Palestinian claims as true; dismiss Israeli claims as state propaganda; and when it turns out the opposite, fall silent on the past and move on to the next accusation.*

But the prize for dishonest response to being caught engaging in lethal journalism goes to Janine di Giovanni, whose claim to fame was writing in the London *Times* (possibly Britain's most high-minded paper), **"*Rarely in more than a decade of war reporting from Bosnia, Chechnya, Sierra Leone, Kosovo, have I seen such deliberate destruction, such disrespect for human life.*"**[54] Given the massive and savage destruction of Bosnia, Chechnya et al., where massacres of civilians and mass rape of women ran into the thousands and tens of thousands, where whole cities were devastated, as compared to five square blocks of an evacuated, booby-trapped, refugee camp, it is hard to imagine a more dishonest, personal "testimony."

Note, however, that both remarks involve attributing (malevolent) motive: "*deliberate* destruction . . . *disrespect* for human life." Apparently for this journalist,

---

49 See n33.

50 "Truth-Seeking in Jenin," *Guardian*, August 2, 2002; on the ten-year retrospective, see note 31.

51 Himmel, "Challenging the British Media," *Jenin: Massacring the Truth*.

52 David Blair, "Horror stories from the siege of Jenin," *The Telegraph*, April 15, 2002.

53 Conversation with (rtd) General Yossi Kuperwasser, 2006.

54 Janine di Giovanni, "Inside the Camp of the Dead," *London Times*, April 16, 2002.

bad motive is more important than any empirical reality of actual destruction. The traces of the blood-libel abound—Jewish soldiers intentionally destroy, treat gentile life with contempt. And, of course, as the propaganda behind the lethal journalism intends, those of her readers who wanted to put Israel, that nation of sovereign Jews, in the gutter of Nazi-like behavior, could readily avail themselves of her false "witness" as a journalist.

Unlike A. N. Wilson of "genocide" fame at the *Evening Standard,*[55] and the *Guardian's* team (Susanne Goldenberg, Peter Beaumont, Seumas Milne, Brian Whitaker, and Chris McGreal), all of whom declined to be interviewed by Himmel, di Giovanni, completely unrepentant, had the immodesty to think she could defend herself. In so doing, she gives us a striking profile of a lethal journalist—how such a one thinks about her work, her subjects, her critics, even herself. . . . None of it is attractive, much is very damaging, to a profession with alleged ethical standards.

"We're not naïve," Di Giovanni insists, not realizing that the alternative to naïve in this case, is maliciously dishonest. "Well into 15 years of covering war, we [I and my colleagues like the *Guardian* gang] were horrified, really horrified. The level of destruction was quite unnecessary, to level it, to make it look like a football pitch was shocking," she explained, as if she knew the military issues that made the IDF's choices "unnecessary," and as if so tightly contained an area of destruction were worse than the vast, indiscriminate, urban destruction she had been seeing for 15 years. "They were hiding something," she asserts confidently, clinging to the massacre-meme that the Israelis had buried the bodies of those they had executed.[56] "What happened at Jenin was an outrage and a violation of all human rights," she asserts, though she does admit that the Israelis had not committed a massacre.

Asked if she might apologize for her coverage, she responds authoritatively, "I would never do that. I stand completely by what I write." Whether this is meant as a normative statement (my impression), or specifically about Jenin, it bespeaks a remarkable attitude toward self-criticism on the part of an alleged journalist. Not only is it obvious to her that she has done nothing wrong, it is equally obvious that Israel has committed heinous war crimes. For her, the only significant difference between the Serbs, the Hutus, and the Israelis is that when it came to the first two, war criminals were condemned, but "the Israelis never are," as if *everyone knows* they're guilty but they always get away with it.

---

55 See n25.

56 A theme that recurs in Palestinian testimony over and again in *Jenin, Jenin* (see below).

Asked to explain how 56 dead in three weeks of urban warfare can be worse than Chechnya and Bosnia, where a third of a million, primarily civilians, died, Di Giovanni first takes refuge behind her personal experience—"Have you been to Chechnya?"—then philosophizes:

> Was it [my comparison] disproportionate? Well I've been to all those places, and I've been to Jenin, and I don't ... *I still really believe that one human life is one human life ...* so I think in a sense ... [discusses the thousands and thousands massacred by the Hutu] ... *horror is horror, injustice is injustice, human rights abuse is human rights abuse.*[57]

This is not the seasoned voice of a serious war correspondent, who understands the terrible truth of triage, who "bears [honest] witness" to her time. Rather, it is the sophomoric voice of the "every life is precious" meme, of the most empathic of progressives living in a civil society bubble of nonviolence and safe-spaces. Having thus undermined her repeatedly invoked "I've been around and let me tell you..." claim, Di Giovanni then switches to a "ridiculous" moral equivalence, in which painfully avoided collateral damage is equated with deliberate genocide—because in both cases, people died. As Martin Sieff comments to Himmel, "Where were these people coming from? What did they see and what did they imagine they were seeing?" Legacy Media meet Y2K Journalism.

Di Giovanni has seen a war crime in Jenin. No evidence could dissuade her:

> Time and time again Sharon has been excused for massive human rights violations ... I could go on and on, and it's not just that they're excused from it, but it's very rarely accurately reported ... in America, in North America ... [where] the Zionist Lobby is much stronger than in Europe.

Consider this double imprint of the lethal journalist's attitude. First, the target has been chosen: Sharon and the IDF are *a priori* guilty, as bad as the worst, and need to be brought to justice. Therefore, as a journalist, she is completely justified in comparing the IDF to the Hutus and Serbs, in order to right that standing "injustice" of Sharon going unpunished. Second, like those who attack the press for being too pro-Zionist,[58] she complains that not enough Palestinian

---

57 Himmel, *Jenin*, "Comparing Jenin with other Conflicts."
58 See 299–301.

claims get passed on as news, and that American journalists, less willing to be lethal journalists and turn on Israel, are less free to speak.[59] How can we get Sharon and the IDF punished for their crimes, if not enough of these "massive human rights violations" get reported?[60]

But perhaps her most telling attitude was towards the Israeli soldier who had come with Himmel. Asked to address her self-justification to the soldier before her, she responded, "I don't want to talk to him. In fact, I don't even want him in the room when I'm talking." Then turning to Himmel, she asks, "Are you Israeli? Are you Jewish?" In other words, the "human rights" advocacy journalist has so completely bought the Palestinian narrative that she will not even consider interacting with an Israeli "war criminal." As she insists, there is no way that she might be wrong and he might be right.

In this, she sheds light on David Blair's false memory that he would have reported it, had the Israelis made their case, and Kuperwasser's observation that these journalists were not listening to Israelis (unless they confirmed their beliefs). They always already considered Israeli claims as "beyond the pale."[61] When she asks Himmel about being Jewish, it reflects the widespread attitude that "only a Jew would defend Israel."[62] Her contemptuous treatment of another human, one making a sophisticated and civil moral challenge, would qualify as racism were any other minority involved.[63]

None of this hurt Di Giovanni's career. She went on to positions in *Newsweek* and *Vogue,* where she has repeated her self-justification about Jenin.[64] She even gave a talk in which she advised aspiring journalists on how to do the job professionally.[65] Here the lethal journalist has cleaned up her act (aside from

---

59 This is the complaint not only of the academics who defend the lethal journalists (Falk and Philo), but of the Palestinians themselves: Abo Gali complains to Rehov that the (mis) information does not flow as it should.

60 For an example of excoriating the US press for failing to report the massacre as luridly as the European press, see above, Harvard student al Hassan, "What Massacre?"

61 For an in-depth analysis of this syndrome, see Shepherd, *State Beyond the Pale.*

62 See French consul's remark to me, 18.

63 See Richard Ingrams, a columnist for the Observer, who refuses to read letters from Jews about the Middle East, and wants Jewish journalists to declare their "racial" origins when writing on Israel. Julie Burchill, "Good, Bad and Ugly," *Guardian,* November 29, 2003.

64 Antonina Jedrzejczak "In Love and War: Four Questions for Reporter and Writer Janine di Giovanni," *Vogue,* July 27, 2011; critiqued, Andrea Levin, "Bias in Vogue," CAMERA, May 1, 2007.

65 Janine di Giovanni, On Research, Responsibility, and Narrative Nonfiction," *Power of the Pen Fiction Nonfiction,* [no date], https://www.youtube.com/watch?time_continue=22&v=huEit1qPQb0.

warmly recommending Amnesty International and Human Rights Watch as reliable sources).

> You have to be extremely careful and check stories, especially of massacres.... The reader will always be able to tell if you have bias ... footage is often not reliable.... Be very careful when interviewing ... you have to maintain distance without giving witnesses impression you don't trust them ... you need to be objective. I try not to be for one side of the other, but sometimes it's very hard when someone is the victim of state terror.... There's no need to exaggerate, just tell the story.... You're not a prosecutor ... [but] an objective writer, above, trying to tell it.

The only hint of her Jenin prosecutorial, lethal journalism is the semi-admission of bias: "it's very hard when someone is the victim of state terror." In other words, in Jenin, she sided against Israel which was, in her and Human Rights Watch's victimology book, committing "state terror," the worst kind of terror of all.[66] Today she's a professor of journalism at Yale, and continues to practice lethal journalism.[67] And so even those who found the refusal to use terrorism to designate 9–11 revolting, got fed a narrative by someone who had no trouble blaming the democracy.

Global Impact of Lethal Journalism

In the Arab world, where no one publicly doubted it, this massacre meme had immense resonance. Angry demonstrations around the Arab and Muslim world mobilized fundamental Caliphator apocalyptic war memes: evil Jews exterminating innocent Muslims, while the infidel nations stand by approvingly. Osama Bin Laden called for Muslims to slaughter infidels, especially Jews and Americans:

> I call for a revolt against the heretics [Muslims in favor of a peace settlement with Israel]. They must be killed. I call for the

---

66 On Urmi Shah at HRW, see n47.

67 Tamar Sternthal, "Janine Di Giovanni: Veteran Correspondent Has Bias Despite Experience," *CAMERA*, January 26, 2022.

murder of all Americans, all Jews, by bullets, by knife, or even by stoning.[68]

It inspired a particularly expansive call to Global Jihad from a Hamas preacher who not only called for the extermination of the Jews, but also of their allies (especially Americans), as a prelude for Islamic rule from sea to shining sea. "Oh Allah, raise the flag of jihad across the earth.... Be assured that these will be owned by the Muslim nation, as the *Hadith* says, 'from the ocean to the ocean.'"[69] Nothing could have suited the Caliphator agenda more completely than an accusation of an IDF massacre of innocent Muslims that they could claim was true—because even the West reported it.

Nor did the Caliphators' victory occur primarily in the Arab-Muslim world, where it greatly enhanced their emotional power; it also took place in the West where, unlike Israel's armed and trained Jews, *unarmed* Jews—*committed civilians*—were easier targets. In the democracies, the "Jenin massacre" meme, weaponized by Caliphators, inspired a new round of Muslim attacks on Jews.[70]

At the same time, just as with the al Durah story, Muslims increasingly dominated public "anti-war" rallies. The Muslim Association of Britain, for example, made its first public appearance that spring, by organizing in partnership with the "progressives," a Saturday march against Israel, in London on April 13, 2002. According to a participating socialist group:

> The Trafalgar Square rally started with long readings from the Koran. Although speakers such as Labour left MP Jeremy Corbyn and Tony Benn were on the platform, their speeches were punctuated by chants—led by an Imam who used the stage microphone—of "Allah-o-Akbar" ("God is great")....
> The organisers, marshalling the crowd at the start of the march, attempted to segregate the march along male-female lines. If the march had not been so large, and consequently so difficult for those stewards to organise, the demonstration might well

---

68 Frédéric Vézard, "Sur Internet, Ben Laden menace à nouveau l'Amérique," *Le parisien*, June 3, 2002.

69 "Friday Sermon on Palestinian Authority TV," MEMRI, Special Dispatch, No. 370, April 17, 2002. On the genocidal hadith, see 225–27, on Caliphators. For full quote, chapter 1 n46.

70 "[A] wave of antisemitic attacks that have flared up since Israel launched its military offensive in the West Bank," "New antisemitic attack in France," CNN, April 13, 2002; Jim Bitterman, "France facing antisemitic attacks," CNN, April 4, 2002. For a broader tally, see Gabriel Schoenfeld, "Israel and the Antisemites," *Commentary*, June 1, 2002.

have set off with men at the front, and women at the back. . . . Leafleters freely gave out Islamist literature which called for "Putting the Jews to the sword." . . . Dominant on the march were banners equating Sharon to Hitler, Zionism to Nazism, and the Star of David to the swastika. . . . "Death to Israel" and "From the river to the sea."[71]

A. N. Wilson was there, and dutifully and indignantly reported the accusations in the *Evening Standard*: "Massacre, cover up, genocide." If, as Robert Wistrich wrote about the 2003 rally of over a million people, "the Marxist-Islamist axis achieved its first mass expression," then this rally was a major warm-up.[72]

In Washington DC, International A. N. S. W. E. R. held a rally which began with a series of speakers identifying themselves as Palestinians, then calling on the crowd to cry out, "I am Palestinian!" and "Free Palestine."[73] In France, demonstrations featured "Islamists" shouting, "Jews to the ovens. . . . Death to Israel, death to the Jews."[74] In Madrid, fashion models demonstrated in suicide-belt bikinis out of solidarity with people who would happily gut their bodies.[75] In those days, life imitated parody: European progressives cheered on the jihadis who would, in short order, target them. At a rally outside the "Jewish-owned" department store Marks & Spenser in October 2003,

> an elegantly dressed businessman next to me, who seemed normal except for the fury in his eyes . . . said, "*I love and revere the suicide bombers.* Every time I hear of a suicide bomb going off I wish it had been eighty or ninety Jews instead of a pitiful handful."[76]

Fewer than two years later, the jihadi suicide bombers he so loved and revered would strike his city, his people.

---

71 AWL, "Solidarity with the Palestinians—but don't line up behind Hamas!" April 13, 2002, https://www.workersliberty.org/story/2009/02/23/we-were-saying-muslim-association-britains-first-public-appearance-april-2002.

72 Wistrich, *A Lethal Obsession*, 415. On the later rally, see 135–39.

73 International A. N. S. W. E. R. Rally, April 20, 2002.

74 *Libération*, April 29, 2002; described by Brenner, *Les territoires perdus de la République*, 216–17. This began with al Durah (24), reappeared in 2003 (136), and became widespread by 2014: Robert Wistrich, "Summer in Paris," *Mosaic Magazine*, October 5, 2014.

75 Madrid, April 7, 2002. Noted in Berman, *Terror and Liberalism*, 143.

76 Carrol Gould, "I Wish 80 or 90 Jews Would Die," *Israel National News*, October 22, 2003.

Caliphators could do this because the West, especially Western Europe, got this powerful dose of lethal pack journalism about Jenin that swept up even normally sober newspapers in its wake.[77] This reporting failure—narrative inverting reality—had an electrifying effect on the Western public sphere. Armed with the lethal narratives their journalists offered up as reliable, professional *news*, angry anti-war demonstrators hit the streets of Europe and the West. They brought some of that tribal energy from Durban to the world. Israel, the new "Nazis," committing genocide against the Palestinian "Jews." In response to the siege of the Bethlehem church, where jihadis had fled from the Israelis and systematically desecrated the church, the Italian *La Serra* published a cartoon of baby Jesus surrounded by Israeli tanks, asking "Are they going to do this to me again?"[78]

Moved to speak out, Oriana Fallaci published a furious denunciation of the grotesque and shameful spectacle of rampant, public, Jew-hatred.

> I find it shameful that in Italy there should be a procession of individuals dressed as suicide bombers who spew vile abuse at Israel, hold up photographs of Israeli leaders on whose foreheads they have drawn the swastika, incite people to hate the Jews. . . . I find it shameful that the Catholic Church should permit a bishop, one with lodgings in the Vatican no less, a saintly man who was found in Jerusalem with an arsenal of arms and explosives hidden in the secret compartments of his sacred Mercedes, to participate in that procession and plant himself in front of a microphone to thank in the name of God the suicide bombers who massacre the Jews in pizzerias and supermarkets. To call them "martyrs who go to their deaths as to a party." . . . I find it shameful that in France, the France of Liberty-Equality-Fraternity, they burn synagogues, terrorize Jews, profane their cemeteries. I find it shameful that the youth of Holland and Germany and Denmark flaunt the keffiyeh just as Mussolini's avantgarde used to flaunt the club and the fascist badge. I find it shameful that in nearly all the universities of Europe, Palestinian students sponsor and nurture antisemitism. . . . I find it shameful

---

77 See the apologies offered by the Minneapolis Star for the professional failings of one its editors: "Minn Star Tribune Admits Errors in Coverage of Alleged Massacre in Jenin," *Israel Resource Review*, June 15, 2002. Note how the same (unnamed but faulted) editor who buried the acknowledgement that there was no massacre (from headline to ¶21), also rigorously erased any use of the T-word (even from a quote taken from the *New York Times*).

78 On the siege of the Church of the Nativity, Giniewski, *Guerre des hommes bombes*, 84–87.

... that state-run television stations contribute to the resurgent antisemitism, crying only over Palestinian deaths while playing down Israeli deaths, glossing over them in unwilling tones ... that in their debates they host with much deference the scoundrels with turban or keffiyeh who yesterday sang hymns to the slaughter at New York and today sing hymns to the slaughters at Jerusalem, at Haifa, at Netanya, at Tel Aviv. . . . I find it shameful that the Roman Observer, the newspaper of the Pope . . . accuses of extermination a people who were exterminated in the millions by Christians. By Europeans.[79]

The rant did more to damage her reputation than that of the global progressives who were, at this point, working-up a full head of steam.

Losing the Moral High Ground: Moral Schadenfreude *and the Postcolonial Replacement Narrative*

The reference of UN official and major Oslo "Peace Process" activist Roed-Larsen to losing the "high moral ground" was a widespread meme early in this century.[80] I remember attending a yearly conference that extended over the late '90s and early aughts, and every year, from 2001 on, one of my closer intellectual interlocutors kept repeating, *"This time, Israel has lost the moral high ground."* I couldn't figure out how anyone can lose the moral high ground to people who teach their children to so hate another people that they want to blow themselves up amid that people's children, and sow as much pain as possible. Then I realized: in his mind, Israel had lost the moral high ground not to the Palestinians, but to progressives like himself. Now, he (and Roed-Larsen, and others) could unreservedly dump on Israel from imagined moral heights.[81]

That's when I first recognized the phenomenon of moral *Schadenfreude*, that is, the pleasure one takes in seeing another's discomfiture when their moral failures are revealed to public opprobrium. Part of the reason that progressives so credulously welcomed Palestinian lethal narratives about Israel was that it permitted them to look down on this irritating people who had a moral claim

---

79 Oriana Fallaci, "On Jew Hatred," *Panorama magazine*, April 17, 2002, http://www.imra.org.il/story.php3?id=11611.
80 See above, n34.
81 See chapter 8.

on them. The eagerness with which people on the left embraced language that compared Israel to the Nazis had nothing to do with empirical reality, nor even much to do with the worst of the lethal journalism. Even the most extravagant claim of 3,000 dead at Jenin was a slow day at Babi Yar (34,000 killed in a week)— one might even call that accusation an insult to a country with overwhelming military superiority and three weeks in which to work! Had they wanted, they could have killed hundreds of thousands of Palestinians effortlessly.

Rather, comparisons to the Nazis and South African racist apartheid were not descriptions of reality, but contemptuous insults, degradations, acts of shaming and humiliating Israel where it mattered most, blackening her moral face.[82] The loss of the "high moral ground" at Jenin replicated Nay's comment about al Durah replacing the Warsaw Ghetto youth: it freed Europeans from their (sense of) moral debt to Jews and Israel, and permitted them to indulge in the old, venerable, Christian (and Muslim) practice of Jew-baiting. This was not about guilt or repentance, but about fleeing shame by blaming those whom one has wronged: as Benjamin Weinthal paraphrases the German Israeli psychiatrist Tzvi Rix, *Europe will never forgive Israel for the Holocaust.*[83]

No wonder that those who indulged in this Jew-baiting to the point that they believed their demeaning rhetoric actually reflected reality, ended up fatally disoriented, both morally and empirically, dancing in the streets in mock-suicide belts.

In such a kangaroo court of public opinion, where whatever the evidence, Israeli guilt was assumed, indeed pounced upon, it was apparently easy to get the story very wrong. Meanwhile, the fake news reports of Jews killing Muslim children not only enraged Muslims around the world, but outraged Westerners, progressives, Jews, even Zionists, who couldn't believe what they were seeing, but couldn't imagine that the MSNM (full of Jewish reporters and editors) would tell so terrible a collective lie. A massive consensus grew among the cultural elites that Israel was the terrible aggressor, and the Palestinians the innocent victims of their malice, when it was actually a fight between members of a civil society defending themselves from a death cult that ultimately threatened everyone.[84] This upside-down universe led to one of the most remarkable statements of the young twenty-first century, the very stuff of jokes, when Kofi Annan, then

---

82 See n100.

83 Benjamin Weinthal, "Europe will never forgive Israel for the Holocaust" *Jewish Press*, June 30, 2010; Landes, "Europe's Destructive Holocaust Shame," *Tablet*, September 25, 2017.

84 Citing an editorial from *The Sun* ("The Jewish Faith is not an Evil Religion," April 15, 2002), Robert Wistrich commented "Some of the tabloids ... have a better understanding and more empathy for Israel's predicament than the so-called quality press." *Lethal Obsession*, 1016, n.109.

secretary-general of the UN, referring to Israel's refusal to immediately stop their "murderous" military operation against the first base camp of suicide-terrorist jihadis in the twenty-first century, noted rhetorically: "I don't think the whole world, including the friends of the Israeli people and government, can be wrong."[85]

Seen from the perspective of a "whole world" that prizes diversity and tolerance over uniformity and violent intolerance, Israel was right to fight back against this Hamas death cult that targeted its children, that was part of a larger movement of Global Jihad that targeted the rest of the "whole world." Had they better understood the players and the stakes, Western observers would have been encouraging Israel to stop this plague before it metastasized. Instead, they paraded in the streets of Europe to show their solidarity with jihadis who target *kuffār* civilians like themselves.

What would the next two decades have looked like, had they challenged the atrocious logic of death cult promoters and apologists who repeated idiotic memes to wide assent—***Resistance is not terrorism ... One man's terrorist is another's freedom fighter ... What choice do they have***? And certainly, from the point of view of an investigation into what actually happened at Jenin—the tiny number of dead, the even tinier number of civilian dead, the exceptional self-sacrifice of the IDF—Annan and world opinion were wrong. In any fair judgment contrasting what the "whole world" thought about Jenin—the journalists' lethal narratives—and what Israel said had happened, again, overwhelmingly, the "whole world was wrong," and Israel was right.[86]

Not only was Israel right, but the whole world was wrong precisely from the point of view of the nations of the world that Annan represented. Understood from the perspective of a peaceful and tolerant world, in which different peoples and religions and ethnicities live side by side in peace, it's a no-brainer, both empirically and morally: Israel was fighting for everything the UN stood for in principle; the suicide-terror jihadis, everything a sane world should have opposed.

---

85 Joel Brinkley, "Israel Starts Leaving 2 Areas, but Will Continue Drive," *New York Times*, April 9, 2002.

86 For a good example of rejecting the evidence of the UN commission which counted only 56 dead, see Peter Cave, "UN Report on Jenin Massacre [sic] Flawed," *Australian Broadcasting Company*, August 4, 2002.

FIGURE 6. "Non-Violence," by Carl Fredrik Reuterswärd. Sculpture at the UN.

In a telling irony, moreover, this particular phrasing of Kofi Annan—*the whole world cannot be wrong (and Israel be right)?*—unwittingly replicated and updated a verbal formula already in play at the turn of the twentieth century in Europe. The pogroms that spread through Eastern Europe at that time did so on the wings of blood libels about Jews killing Christian children and making matzah with their blood. So widespread was the credulity about these accusations that when Jews protested that they did nothing of the sort, that eating blood was specifically forbidden to them, the reply came: "Is it possible that everybody can be wrong and the Jews are right?"[87]

That dynamic of credulous malice dominated the public sphere at the turn of the twentieth century in its hostility to Jews and, *mutatis mutandis*, at the turn of the millennium in its hostility to *Israelis*. So remarkable a linguistic replication alerts us to common forces at work, suggesting that behind the repeated Western credulity about Jewish evil, human emotions were at work that do not come from the better angels of our nature. Certainly, they indict modern, allegedly professional journalists, as *false* witnesses to their time, at the very least when it came to Israel's conflict with Arab Muslim triumphalism. Sadly, from the 2020s, looking back, it turns out that Israel was only patient-, or rather, victim-zero, of a rising tide of advocacy, narrative-driven, fake news.[88]

---

87 Ahad Ha'am, (1892), *Selected Essays*, tr. Leon Simon (Philadelphia: Jewish Publication Society, 1912), 203.
88 Matti Friedman, "You're All Israel Now." *Tablet*, July 27, 2020.

Pallywood Documentaries: A New Art Form

Palestinian film maker Omar Bakri came to Jenin weeks after the fighting and made a movie about the massacre, a mockumentary that told the "Palestinian Truth." In his film, *Jenin, Jenin,* he perfected the techniques of Pallywood—of transforming footage of "performative narrativity" into the lethal narratives of "Palestinian suffering" and Israeli *malevolence,* to be shown, discussed and rendered into poetry by purveyors of this jihadi death cult. Bakri interviewed victims of Israel who detailed the cruel manner in which they had been treated, and interspersed their comments with images that gave the sense of immediacy that seemed to document the accusations: the tanks crushing massacred bodies . . . the shelling of a hospital wing in the night. . . . Like Talal abu Rahma's footage of Al Durah, the film won multiple prizes at European film festivals, and received great support from the European press.

As they already had to reporters, Palestinians lied repeatedly, not by exaggerating reality but by inverting it. One of the stars of *Jenin, Jenin* was the elderly man the Israelis had gone out of their way to treat, not only for slight wounds, but for an undiagnosed and potentially fatal ailment. He told Bakri tales of suffering from deliberate, gratuitous Israeli sniper attacks on his hands and feet. Others accused the Israelis of being inhuman, committing genocide, executing civilians. The Palestinians presented themselves as innocent victims who had done nothing to deserve the attack. And they had a willing audience, especially among the left, including the clan's aspiring Israeli members.

Apparently unaware that it was dishonest propaganda, the Jerusalem Cinematheque premiered *Jenin, Jenin,* and invited an Israeli doctor and IDF reservist David Zangen, who was chief medical officer at Jenin during the operation, and who had treated the elderly liar. He was shocked both by the film's "distortion of reality" and by the standing applause from the audience of Israelis, who had apparently come to hear how badly their own army had behaved. Zangen tried to criticize the film's numerous inaccuracies, but was shouted down by his fellow citizens, who, in order to show their magnanimous solidarity with their enemy, called *him* a "war criminal."[89]

The Israeli battalion Bakri had so systematically libeled sued in an Israeli court, primarily to challenge his widely admired dishonesty. The Israeli court, concerned about (Israel's reputation for) upholding freedom of speech, turned down the suit on a technicality (no one was libeled by name), despite acknowledging the extent of the libel involved. For global progressives, *Jenin Jenin*

---

89 David Zangen, "Seven Lies About Jenin."

is Truth—dogma, *doxa*. If they acknowledge the misinformation, it is merely to reassert a higher "fake but accurate" Truth. Palestinian victim discourse has epistemological priority. Israel had to be evil.

Postscript to Jenin, Jenin

On January 11, 2021, the regional court in Lod condemned Mohammad Bakri for the libels in his movie, *Jenin, Jenin*, forbade its screening in Israel and fined him for slander.[90] The response was as predictable as it was disheartening. Many Israelis and their supporters approved of the case, rejecting the multitude of lies Palestinians told Bakri and he reported.[91] Even *Haaretz* ran a somewhat sympathetic article about the key IDF soldier involved in this round of legislation.[92] In response to the profile, filmmaker Nadav Lapid set up the conflict in terms of the Israeli (right-wing) propaganda versus the Palestinian (left-wing) truth, citing every high casualty figure he could find for the broader campaign, but never mentioning the 50+ killed at Jenin.[93] Bakri complained that he was being persecuted for not being pro-Israeli; and the *Israeli* Film Association sided with him.[94]

England: First Efforts to Implement BDS

In this toxic reversal of both moral and empirical reality, the Boycott Divestment and Sanctions Movement (BDS) was born, implementing the cognitive war goals of Durban: according to the promoters of a postcolonial narrative, Israel was the pariah, the outcast from among nations. Her scholars should be shunned to show solidarity with those who blow themselves up killing her people; after all, everyone knows that anti-Zionism has nothing to do with antisemitism. Suddenly a wave of prominent figures, many until that point "invisible" Jews (i.e., not publicly identified as such), came out the closet, "as a Jew," to denounce

---

90 Court ruling (Hebrew) https://bit.ly/3qCMjHR.

91 E.g., Amotz Asa-El, "'Jenin, Jenin': A modern day blood libel," *Jerusalem Post*, January 14, 2021.

92 Doron Koren, "The Israelis 'Fighting till the Last Drop of Blood' against Palestinian Documentary," *Haaretz*, August 8, 2020.

93 Nadav Lapid, "'Jenin, Jenin' article is propaganda clothed as journalism," *Haaretz*, August 11, 2020.

94 Mohammad Bakri, "'Good' Arabs Tell the Israeli Story," *Haaretz*, January 15, 2021; Post [Hebrew] at Facebook page of the *Association of Filmmakers*, January 19, 2002, https://www.facebook.com/directorsegud/posts/5320347104672016.

Israel. They took up the relay from the journalists, taking the "factual" narratives of Israeli war crimes and turning them into a moral indictment of Israel as the "new Nazis."[95]

Feeling the heat of an *amalgame* that no one would dream of applying to Muslim "moderates," Diaspora Jews, especially in Europe, found themselves blamed and attacked for the behavior of the Israelis. Their cry went up: "Israel is endangering *us!*" Judt lamented about how "[t]oday, non-Israeli Jews feel themselves once again exposed to criticism and vulnerable to attack for things they didn't do.... The [alleged] behavior of a self-described Jewish state affects the way everyone else looks at Jews." It apparently never occurred to the historian that the Israelis also didn't do those things, nor that he would never accept such an *amalgame* when applied to the Muslim community. Instead he wrote the classic postcolonial attack on Israel.[96] British "Finkler" Jews led the pack. Wrote Anthony Lerman, founder of *Independent Jewish Voices*: "[B]y provoking outrage, which is then used to target Jews, Israel bears responsibility for that anti-Jewish hostility."[97] It would never cross his mind to accuse the BBC and the *Guardian* and the *Independent* (Robert Fisk's paper) of dishonestly provoking outrage, much less those who manifested that anti-Jewish hostility of a racist *amalgame* that made diaspora Jews guilty of the [media-reported] deeds of Israelis.

Much of the worst vitriol against Israel came from Jews. In France, *alter-juifs* like the Sociologist Edgar Morin tripped over themselves to denounce not only Israelis, but also fellow Jews as arrogant and cruel practitioners of their status as "chosen people."[98] In England, figures like Harold Pinter, Michael Neumann, and Jacqueline Rose, "appalled by what the Israeli state perpetrates on a daily basis in the name of the Jewish people," felt no compunction about comparing the Jewish state to the Third Reich engaged in genocide, decrying its moral depravity, and circulating calls for its elimination.

---

95 In short order, Tony Kushner and Alisa Solomon put together a collection of essays by Jews assaulting Israel: *Wrestling with Zion* (2003).

96 Judt, "Israel: The Alternative," *New York Review of Books*, October 23, 2003. Discussed below, 371–76.

97 Anthony Lerman, "Must Jews always see themselves as victims?" *Independent*, March 7, 2009. Why not just victimize themselves?

98 Edgar Morin, Sami Naïr and Danièle Sallenave, "Israel-Palestine: le cancer," *Le Monde*, June 4, 2002. Morin was found guilty of defaming the Jews with this remark: Jon Henley, "Le Monde Editor 'Defamed Jews,'" *Guardian*, June 4, 2005. On Edgar Morin (né Nahoum) as an *alterjuif*, see Catherine Leuchter, "Edgar Morin: le penseur de la 'complexité' en flagrant délit de simplisme," *Les alterjuifs, Controverses*, 4 (February 2007): 154–212; discussion of the passage cited above, 155–57. Strong parallels with Tony Judt in the stark contrast between their subtle scholarly work and their moral panic about Israel (discussed below, 371–76).

These days saw a wave of attacks on European Jews, and the first round of academic petitions and calls to boycott Israel, especially in England.[99] They combined Holocaust inversion with moral *Schadenfreude*. As a professor of pathology at Oxford University, Andrew Wilkie, explained to an Israeli student, whose application he had rejected on the basis of the student's nationality: "I have a huge problem with the way that Israelis take the moral high ground from their appalling treatment in the Holocaust, and then inflict gross human rights abuses on the Palestinians."[100] Moral high ground asserted.

In an address to the Harvard University community, Lawrence Summers noted: "There have been synagogue burnings, physical assaults on Jews, or the painting of swastikas on Jewish memorials in every country in Europe. Observers in many countries have pointed to the worst outbreak of attacks against the Jews since the Second World War." Given the correlation between the verbal violence against Israel and the physical violence against Jews, Summers concluded that hypercritics of Israel "were antisemitic in effect, if not in intent."[101] He didn't even get around to pointing out the way in which that promoted jihadi goals.

Judith Butler responded indignantly (and at great length), that Summers was in effect, if not in intention, suppressing academic freedom.[102] For someone who was against the very existence of Israel, who allied with notorious Judeophobes like Hatem Bazian, founder of the increasingly fascist SJP (Students for Just Us in Palestine), who had signed the earliest petition calling for divestment from Israel, and who recycled every Palestinian lethal narrative about Israel, and responded to any criticism with cries of "Islamophobia," this was a masterpiece of aggressive naiveté. Butler spoke as if her existential attacks on Israel were nothing more than "legitimate criticism," which Summers was trying to smother with his accusations of encouraging antisemitism. Why, there was a whole crew of "post-Zionist," "good" Israelis who supported these "criticisms of Israel."[103] Like Enderlin, she demanded the freedom to slander *without pushback*.[104]

---

99 Michel Gurfinkiel, "France's Jewish Problem," *Commentary*, July 2002; Suzanne Goldenberg and Will Woodward, "Israel boycott divides academics," *Guardian*, July 8, 2002.

100 Robin Shepherd, "Blind Hatred," *Jerusalem Post*, September 29, 2004.

101 Lawrence Summers, "Address at Memorial Church, Harvard University," September 17, 2002.

102 Judith Butler, "No it's not antisemitism," *London Review of Books*, August 21, 2003.

103 "... Adi Ophir and Anat Biletzki ... Uri Ram ... Avraham Oz and the poet Yitzhak Laor. Are we to say that Israelis who are critical of Israeli policy are self-hating Jews, or insensitive to the ways in which criticism may fan the flames of antisemitism?" Yes, according to Alvin Rosenfeld, *"Progressive" Jewish Thought and the New Anti-Semitism* (New York: American Jewish Committee, 2006) and Edward Alexander, *Jews Against Themselves* (New Brunswick, NJ: Transaction Publishers, 2015), 63f. See chapter 10.

104 David Hirsh discusses Butler's response to Summers as an early example of the Livingstone Formulation: "Accusations of malicious intent in debates about the Palestine-Israel conflict

Indeed, the two memes, co-sponsored by Butler and Bazian constitute one of the more stupefying platitudes of the twenty-first century:

- ***Islamophobia is the new antisemitism*** (old hate, new targets), and
- ***Cries of antisemitism are just ways of silencing criticism of Israel*** (Livingstone Formulation).

Inversely, the following contraries to this are true:

- Anti-Zionism is the new, "legitimate" avatar of antisemitism in the twenty-first century (old hate, same, modified target),[105] and
- Islamophobia is a term systematically used to silence criticism of Islam.

Islamophobia as it is defined (let's take the work of Hatem Bazian) constitutes an elaborate structure for silencing any voice that warns about Caliphators. Using both Saidian rhetoric and the apologetic doctrine adopted by multiple US administrations that Islam is peace and anything violent is not Islam, Bazian and his cohorts attacked any effort to link jihadi violence with Islam.[106]

But denunciation was not sufficient for Bazian: Islamophobia should be criminalized, banned. Despite extensive data indicating that Jews are much more likely to be victims of hate crimes than are Muslims (and most often at the hands of Muslims), both in the USA and Europe, advocates insisted that banning "Islamophobia" would preserve peace.[107] Muslim states that systematically oppress their own religious minorities with increasing ferocity, insist that Islamophobia be banned in the name of tolerance and peace.

The contrast then, between the virulence of Muslim discourse about Jews and other *kuffār* on the one hand, and hypersensitivity to criticism of Muslims, actually reverses the *rapports de force*. In fact, most Zionists are willing to tolerate and even encourage remarkable levels of criticism before they hit the limits of what they find offensive and Jew-hating—i.e., comparisons with Nazis,

---

and about antisemitism: The Livingstone Formulation," *Transversal*, 1 (2010): 61–63. Seumas Milne uses the Livingstone Formulation to defend the *Guardian's* Jenin coverage, "This slur of antisemitism is used to defend repression," *Guardian*, May 9, 2002; cited in Wistrich, *Lethal Obsession*, 392.

105 Note that antisemitism, in the late nineteenth century was the new, legitimate, scientifically based term for traditional, religious, Jew-hatred. (Hard to hate Jews for killing God when you don't believe in such a thing.)

106 Hatem Bazian, Decolonial Islamic Thinker, http://www.hatembazian.com/.

107 "2019 Hate Crimes Statistics," *FBI*; "Hate against Jews: data gaps hide true picture," *FRA*, September 10, 2020.

accusations of organ-stealing, of targeting children, of committing (a very slow) genocide. On the contrary, self-appointed spokespeople for Muslims find the slightest criticism unacceptable.[108] Most of these "spokespeople" are covert triumphalists, doing the work of the jihadis in blinding their targets (Western *kuffār*) to the danger they face. In Bazian's case, he not only fully supports of Hamas suicide terror as "resistance," and may well have cited approvingly the genocidal apocalyptic hadith of "the rocks and the trees," but he also calls for an intifada in the United States.[109]

In combining anti-Zionism with anti-Islamophobia, these militants rearticulate the secular "replacement theology," whereby Israelis (the new Nazis) embody evil and anything one does ("resistance") or says ("calls to genocide") in opposition to Israel is legitimate. By these lights, attacking Israel as essentially racist—"apartheid"—and genocidal is fine. By contrast, even pointing to the historical generalization—rendered all the more accurate and pertinent by the developments set in motion by the "Arab Spring"—that Muslim societies "trend towards despotism and away from progress," or that some (how many?) Muslims in the West support jihadi terror and want to impose Sharia on their host countries, is pure, ugly, racist, Islamophobia.

Prologue to the Danoongate: Independent Bullies and Fear of Islam

In the wake of Jenin and the assassination of Israel's character by the "progressive mainstream media," the *Independent* ran a cartoon by Dave Brown in January 2003, on Holocaust Remembrance Day. He used Goya's *Chronos Devouring His Children* to depict Israeli Prime Minister Ariel Sharon eating a baby.

---

108 The key here concerns attitudes towards any link between "True Islam" (religion of peace) and jihadi ideology. The denunciation of Maajid Nawaz by the SPLC as an Islamophobe shows how far the accusation can go. Moderate Muslims who admit their religion has problems are, in the eyes of the accusers, Islamophobes: Maajid Nawaz, "I'm being smeared by angry white liberals as an 'anti-Muslim extremist,'" *Independent*, October 29, 2016.

109 "Profiles in Hate: Hatem Bazian," *Fight Hatred*, November 5, 2011.

FIGURE 7. Dave Brown cartoon published in the *Independent*, January 27, 2003.

Some Jews found this highly offensive (obviously not all; the editor in chief of the *Independent* was a Jew), arguing that it revived in the most grotesque way the blood libels of yore, that it would have found a familiar niche on the pages of Streicher's *Der Stürmer*, and that it brought into the Western public sphere the themes of the most vicious Arab propaganda. After all, what child could Sharon be eating but a Palestinian one, given the background of [what the press imagined] had happened at Jenin? Certainly, one easily found this blood libel of Sharon eating Palestinian babies in the Arab press, teeming with the most *Der Stürmer*-esque cartoons, even before Jenin, precisely at a time when the Shahids targeted Israeli babies.[110]

---

110 Joel Kotek, *Cartoons and Extremism: Israel and the Jews in Arab and Western Media* (Portland, OR: Valentine Mitchell, 2008).

FIGURE 8. "Al Quds" (Palestinian), May 17, 2001.

Anthony Julius lodged a formal complaint with the British press complaints commission on behalf of Sharon, describing the cartoon as "antisemitic, in a fantastically irresponsible way, at a particularly volatile time."[111] In trouble, Brown, completely oblivious to how others might "read" the cartoon insisted that he had not meant anything antisemitic:

> Do I believe, or was I trying to suggest, that Sharon actually eats babies? Of course not—one of the other benefits of the borrowed image was that it was sited squarely in the field of allegory. My cartoon was intended as a caricature of a specific person, Sharon, in the guise of a figure from classical myth who, I hoped, couldn't be farther from any Jewish stereotype.

---

111 Anthony Julius, "Mishcon de Reya, on behalf of Ariel Sharon and the Israeli Embassy," 2003, http://www.pcc.org.uk/cases/adjudicated.html?article. See Julius's discussion in *Trials of the Diaspora*, 527–29.

The *Independent*'s editor, Simon Kelner, claimed that having based the image on Goya's Saturn, who was eating his own children, the baby in the image was an Israeli representing the Israeli electorate, and hence not an echo of the blood libel of Jews drinking the blood of gentile children. "As a Jew," he claimed he was well-qualified to judge whether it was antisemitic, and it was not.[112] And yet, Tim Benson, the head of the Political Cartoon Society that gave this cartoon the prize for the best of the year, admitted three years later what everyone knew at the time: it depicted "Ariel Sharon eating a Palestinian baby."[113]

The Press commission, however, agreed with Kelner's obscurantist sophism, and found there was "nothing inherently antisemitic about the Goya image or about the myth of Saturn devouring his children, which has been used to satirize other politicians accused of sacrificing their own "children" for political purposes. While the cartoon "had caused great offence to a significant number of people," the commission wrote:

> It's unreasonable to expect editors to take into account all possible interpretations of material that they intend to publish ... that would be to interpret the code in a manner that would impose burdens on newspapers that would arguably interfere with their rights to freedom of expression."[114]

As if the reaction of the Jews who took offense were not predictable ... as if, in two years, when Muslims complained about the Muhammad Cartoons, the *Independent* (along with every other British paper) did not scramble to accommodate their hurt feelings and *not* publish the offending cartoons.[115] Apparently, according to the complaint commission's decisions, elderly women and Muslims deserve consideration for their hurt feelings, but Jews do not

---

112 Julius, *Trials*, 527.

113 In an article written in response to the Danish Cartoon scandal (next chapter), Tim Benson, "The Twice-Promised Land: A Cartoonist's Perspective," *Political Cartoon Society* [n.d.].

114 Adjudication, PCC, May 22, 2003. For coverage, see Ciar Byrne, "Independent Cartoon cleared of antisemitism," *Guardian*, May 22, 2003. Julius sets the decision in the context of widespread denial that anti-Zionism had anything to do with antisemitism.

115 See chapter 4 on Danish Cartoons. Julius notes that despite insisting that the Commission's "Code does not cover complaints about alleged discrimination against groups of people," in an earlier decision (1997), the PCC had decided in favor of the elderly women and those with mental problems who were offended by a(n intendedly) humorous piece, *Trials*, 769n538.

... and certainly not when recognizing those feelings would get in the way of criticizing Israel.[116]

To pile on the insults, the cartoon, now cleared of antisemitism, won the award of "Cartoon of the Year" from the British Political Cartoon Society. Reveling in the attention his drawing elicited, both from enthusiasts, but even more so from the cries of pain emanating from the Jewish community, Brown "thanked the Israeli Embassy for its angry reaction to the cartoon, which he said had contributed greatly to its publicity." Tim Benson, head of the awarding society, explained to Martin Himmel: "I believe it was chosen by our members, largely because of the impact it had initially ... we have had a hysterical response from all over the world. Our website, the day after the awards got 73,000 hits; we've been receiving over 400 hate mails a day." In other words, we awarded it because, on the one hand, it excited a lot of people, and, on the other, it infuriated the Jews, who, in their self-imposed impotence, would only object verbally.

When asked why there are no cartoons of Arafat eating babies, Benson responded with a disconcerting and sustained smile:

> Maybe [because] Jews don't issue fatwas ... if you offend a Muslim or Islamic group, as you know, fatwas can be issued by ayatollahs and such like, and maybe it's at the back of each cartoonist's mind that they could be in trouble if they do so ... if they depict an Arab leader in the same manner ... they could suffer death, couldn't they? Which is rather different.[117]

In a nutshell, Benson's breezy response illustrates the madness of Europe: on the one hand, it is open season on the Jews, who don't threaten violence or practice terrorism—indeed, the more hysterically Jews squeal in pain, the merrier (including when you accuse them of terrorism);[118] on the other, one must avoid offending Muslims at all costs, including accusing them of terrorism. So, don't expect to see British cartoonists do anything with this photo of a Hamas and an Egyptian Muslim Brotherhood politician kissing a dead baby, killed not by Israel, but by their own rockets.

---

116 As Clare Short, the Labour MP who awarded the prize to Brown noted, applying the Livingstone Formulation: "Israelis often fall into the trap of mistaking criticism for antisemitism." Benson, "The Twice-Promised Land.

117 Himmel, *Jenin*, 53:47–57:15. Note that Brown refused to be interviewed (see above on the other lethal journalists who refused to be interviewed, 109), https://youtu.be/qy0tvGq-icU.

118 Landes, "The Hidden Costs of Jew-Baiting in England," *Journal for the Study of Antisemitism*, 2 (2010): 413–17.

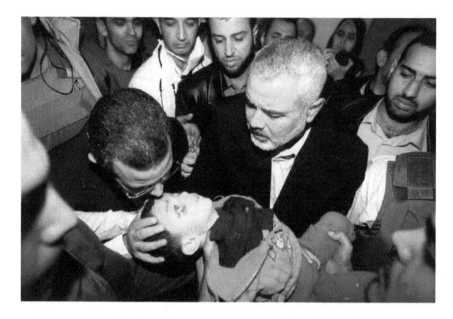

FIGURE 9. Hamas leader Ismail Haniya and the Egyptian (Muslim Brotherhood) foreign minister Amr Kandil make pious photo op of kissing a child that Hamas had killed (2012).

What's wrong? You never seen politicians kissing dead babies?

In the process, these journalists and commentators corrupt institutions that should guarantee fairness; they hide their cowardice behind the false bravado of "speaking truth to power;" and they dig their own grave. Lemmings going over the cliff while gnawing on their moral *Schadenfreude*.[119] The full implications of this aggressive cowardice will become clearer in the next chapter on the Danish Cartoon scandal.

* * *

2002 CE: Not a good year for the progressive principles of fairness and freedom in the world. European progressive elites led the way down. Own-goal lethal journalism dominated coverage of the Arab-Israeli conflict, provoking Muslim attacks on European Jews, and the spread of the poison of antisemitism throughout the public sphere, under the guise of "criticism of Israel." Political

---

119 On the link between resurgent antisemitism and the appeasement/surrender to Muslim aggression, see Wistrich, "Eurabia," in *A Lethal Obsession*, chapter 13. On the dead child above (Mahmoud Sadallah), see Harry's Place, "Hamas dead baby horror stunts get free pass in the West's press," *Adloyada*, November 119, 2012; https://adloyada.typepad.com/adloyada/2012/11/hamas-dead-baby-horror-stunts-get-free-pass-in-the-wests-press.html.

elites in the West either denied antisemitism or blamed it on Israel. Global progressives, under influence of own-goal war journalism, gave Muslim triumphalists a major foothold in the public sphere as allies in a global anti-imperial struggle.

1423 AH: A great year for Caliphators, especially in their Da'wa campaign against the West: full cooperation of Western media and extensive cooperation of Western academia in disseminating jihadi propaganda designed to arouse hatred of Israel; Jews essentially prevented from defending themselves in the public sphere (dhimmis must not bear witness against Muslims); Israelis shamed and greatly impeded from resisting jihad; Muslim Street and its permanent shadow, jihadi violence, make strides in Europe primarily by targeting Jews and Israel, but also any editor foolish enough to offend the most zealous of Muslims; Europeans publicly endorse Muslim suicide terror against infidels (thinking: "that's not about us").

Astoundingly Stupid Statements Appearing in This Chapter

What choice do they have? In reference to Palestinian suicide terror campaign, 2001-

Resistance is not terrorism. "Pacifist" NGO International Solidarity Movement slogan during Palestinian suicide terror campaign.

What we are seeing here is horrifying, horrifying scenes of human suffering, . . . Israel has lost all moral ground in this conflict. Terje Roed-Larsen about Jenin, April 18, 2002.

Normally, we would have expected to find three people severely injured for everyone killed. Even if one accepts the Israeli claim that "only" 40 Palestinians died, there ought to be another 120 lying badly wounded, in hospital. But they are nowhere to be found. . . . We draw the conclusion that they were allowed to die where they were. Prof. Derrick Pounder, Amnesty International researcher, about Jenin (April 23, 2002).

Oh, so now they are all just lying?? Andrea Koppel to Israeli who challenged her assertion, based on Palestinian claims, that Israel had committed a massacre at Jenin, Sunday, April 14, 2002.

Rarely in more than a decade of war reporting from Bosnia, Chechnya, Sierra Leone, Kosovo, have I seen such deliberate destruction, such disrespect for human life. Janine di Giovanni, "Inside the Camp of the Dead," the *Times*, April 16, 2002.

I still really believe that one human life is one human life . . . horror is horror, injustice is injustice, human rights abuse is human rights abuse. Janine di Giovanni justifying her comparison of Jenin to Bosnia et al. to Martin Himmel, *Jenin: Massacring the Truth.*

I don't think the whole world, including the friends of the Israeli people and government, can be wrong. Kofi Anan about Israel withdrawing from Jenin.

If I were a Palestinian I'd be a terrorist too. Israeli Prime Minister Ehud Barak.

It's poverty, lack of opportunity, lack of independence that makes them so desperate.

I love and revere the suicide bombers. British demonstrator, London, 2003.

4

Danoongate: The Muslim Street Extends Dar al Islam (2005–6)

Did those mean Danes hurt
Your feelings? Please don't hate us,
We're *good* infidels.

At the end of the last chapter, I discussed the case of Dave Brown's cartoon of Ariel Sharon as Chronos devouring a Palestinian baby as an electoral gambit, and the disturbing way that Tim Benson casually explained how cartoonists decide whom to insult, and whom to reward for those insults. Since Jews do not issue fatwas, it is open season on them, with prizes for those who elicit the loudest cries of pain from Jews. Muslims do, however, issue fatwas, which means one had best be very careful about anything that might offend them. In this chapter, we look at another cartoon controversy that hit the European scene, this time provoked by the people who *do* issue fatwas.

In response to a Danish newspaper's publication in 2005 of twelve cartoons depicting Muhammad the Prophet, Caliphators, using three additional and genuinely blasphemous cartoons that they themselves had created, attacked. They accused Western infidels of wantonly blaspheming against deeply felt Muslim beliefs, demonstrating Islamophobic hatred. In response to this staged emergency of violent outrage, Western leaders—from opinion leaders, to information professionals, to elected and appointed officials—made error upon error, a collective folly splendidly displayed on an international stage. In the end, the joke that should have been on the Caliphator leadership—you riot to protest being called violent?—became a joke on radically disoriented Western infidels.

Although it means skipping over crucial developments in the dynamic of Caliphator attacks (Bali 2002 and Madrid 2004, to name two) and only briefly surveying key Western losses to cogwarrior Da-īs (anti-war rallies of 2003, London attack of 7-7-05, French riots of 2005), there has been one incident that fully illustrates how they're so smart because we're so stupid. That was Danoongate, and it therefore serves as the closing chapter of my review of the disastrous beginning of the first global millennium.

Build-up to Danoongate

To fully understand the magnitude of the folly in the international response to the Danish Cartoons Scandal, one must consider several incidents that occurred between 2002 (last chapter) and the early months of 2006 (this chapter), each of which deserves a chapter of its own. They concern two prongs of the Caliphator assault on the West—jihadi terror attacks and Da'wa cogwar campaigns. These two approaches attest to the growth of an increasingly aggressive and independent "Muslim Street" in the West, which, like the Arab Street in the Middle East, frightened decision-makers into self-destructive choices.

Anti-War Demonstrations of 2003: The Muslim Street Ascendant

In the first years of the new century, especially at the first Durban Conference against Racism (August–September, 2001), progressives took global activism to new levels, most evident in the coordinated mass action around the world.[1] Literally days after 9–11, the key drivers in the anti-war movement in the USA created International A. N. S. W. E. R., with a sister organization in Britain, the "Stop the War Coalition."[2] Both had a small cadre of key players whose association with Trotskyite and other hard left groups was extensive.[3] It was through them that so many of the self-destructive follies chronicled in this book went from the margins to the center, from the "anti-imperialism of fools" and its compulsive

---

1   Paul Berman, *The Flight of the Intellectuals* (Brooklyn, NY: Melville House, 2010), 157–204.
2   Camila Bassi, "'The Anti-Imperialism of Fools': A Cautionary Story on the Revolutionary Socialist Vanguard of England's Post-9:11 Anti-War Movement," *ACME: An International E-Journal for Critical Geographies*, 2010, 9 (2): 113–137.
3   On the alphabet soup of such organizations, including the SWP (England) and the WWP (USA), see Kevin Coogan, "The International Action Center: 'Peace Activists' With A Secret Agenda?" *The Hit List* (November/December 2001).

hatred of American "imperialist" democracy to the hatred of Israel, the unstinting support of "liberationist" terror, and the alliance with radical Islam.[4]

The earliest rallies organized by the anti-war movements were in response to the belligerent attitude of the US responding to 9-11. These rallies, organized primarily by radical Marxist groups, had a significant presence of American Muslims, who enthusiastically supported Hamas and Hizballah, including one in the spring of 2002 that protested Israel's "massacre" at Jenin.[5] But by far, the most dramatic mobilization took place on February 15, 2003, in response to George Bush's plans to invade Iraq. It had unprecedented reach. Global progressives mobilized "anti-war" public opinion, and millions poured into the streets of cities the world over to protest. But, as some honest observers managed to note, it was not an anti-war rally; rather, it was a rally to defend one of the worst dictators and mass murderers on the planet.[6] Indeed, led as it was by Labour Party parliamentarians George Galloway and Jeremy Corbyn and London mayor Ken Livingstone, it was a celebration of anti-Americanism and pro-jihad, disguised as anti-war.

The "anti-war" progressives, however, claimed that the world opinion they mobilized and represented constituted, in the words of a *New York Times* journalist, one of the "two superpowers on the planet: on the one side, the United States, and on the other, world public opinion."[7] Or as Jonathan Schell put it in *The Nation*, it was a "miraculous time in history . . . for "never before in the history of the world has there been a global, visible, public, viable, open dialogue and conversation about the very legitimacy of war." This was what it looked like . . . to be "waging peace." It was "a miracle." Shock and awe had found its riposte in courage and wonder.[8] Could this massive display of public opinion be wrong?

---

4 On the bizarre career of Ramsey Clark, the founder and "respectable" (front) leader of International A. N. S. W. E. R., see left-wing critiques both before and after 2000: Ian Williams, "Ramsey Clark, the war criminal's best friend," *Salon*, June 21, 1999; David Corn, "Behind the Placard," *LA Weekly*, October 30, 2002; Marc Cooper, "Our Peace Movement—Not Theirs," *LA Weekly*, December 11, 2002.

5 John Vidal, "Another coalition stands up to be counted," *Guardian*, November 19, 2001; Amir Taheri, "The London Streets, Who are these anti-Bush people?" *National Review*, November 18, 2003. For lists of the anti-war rallies after 9-11, starting on September 29, 2001, see "Protests against the War in Afghanistan," Wikipedia, https://en.wikipedia.org/wiki/ Protests_against_the_war_in_Afghanistan#2001.

6 Nick Cohen, *What's Left: How Liberals Lost their Way* (London: Harper Perennial, 2007), chapter 7; Ian McEwan, *Saturday* (New York: Anchor, 2005).

7 Patrick Tyler, "A New Power in the Streets," *New York Times*, February 16, 2003. Tyler later wrote a book about the Middle East conflict: *Fortress Israel: The Inside Story of the Military Elite Who Run the Country—and Why They Can't Make Peace* (New York: Farrar, Strauss, Giroux, 2012). A classic case of humanitarian racism.

8 Jonathan Schell, "The Other Superpower," *Nation*, April 14, 2003. See the film and website "We Are Many: the story of the largest global protest that would change the world,"

Tragically, though the anti-war movement may have been right about the advisability of the war in Iraq, it was wrong about everything to do with peace. On the one hand, Bush was wrong: there were no WMDs in Iraq, and no democracy on its way, much less a domino effect on the whole Arab world. Rather, the years following the war saw more terrorism and more radicalization, endless war and its psychic cost. On the other hand, the rallies were not *anti-war*, but *anti-US war*—the significance being that the activists welcomed belligerent elements of the Caliphator movement, carrying signs glorifying Saddam Hussein and Yasser Arafat, along with other placards demonizing George W. Bush, Tony Blair, and Ariel Sharon. Not incidentally, some wore headbands proclaiming, "Death to Jews."[9] While these dreamers sought to stop one war, they fed another, and in this one, the Caliphators targeted *them*. Waging peace, own-goal style.

Nothing better illustrates the folly of the messianic "peace movement" than the discussion of the "Muslim Mobilisation" in Andrew Murray and Lindsey German's breathlessly self-aggrandizing account of "Britain's biggest mass movement."[10] Acknowledging that "no aspect of the movement had been more subject to misunderstanding and even abuse," they heralded its "unprecedented scope and intensity"—without the slightest trace of irony—as "one of the most important and novel elements of the anti-war movement, and one that may have enduring repercussions for British politics and society." Insisting that British Muslims had already mobilized politically against racism and fascism [sic], they noted that "[t]he idea of Muslim people playing a leading part in a peace movement had apparently not occurred to anyone"—possibly for good reason. (Actually, as we have seen, the process had already begun in the wake of 9–11 with the active participation of the Muslim community.)

Overall, with a tone of supreme self-confidence, and contemptuous dismissal of dissenting voices concerned about fundamentalist Islam, the authors celebrate the inclusion of the Muslim Association of Britain as a group entirely different from, and opposed to, the tiny, more radical jihadi groups. They asserted this, despite MAB's behavior only the previous year, calling for "the sword."[11] Indeed, they heralded MAB's inclusion as essential for the creation of a "genuine *mass*

---

http://wearemany.com/; and Andrew Murray and Lindsey German, *Stop the War: The story of Britain's biggest mass movement* (London, Bookmarks Publication Society, 2005); Ian Sinclair, *The march that shook Blair: An oral history of 15 February 2003* (London: Peace News Press, 2013). On the role of peace ideology in the twenty-first century, see 284–88.

9   On the dark side of these demonstrations, see Cohen, *What's Left*, chapter 7; Adam Garfinkle, "The Peace Movement and the Adversary Culture," cited above, 68n65.

10 Murray and German, *Stop the War*, 57–63.

11 Above, 114n71.

movement." For that to happen, certain compromises had to be made: calls to prayer in the middle of a rally, segregated seating for women,[12] and a devil. Israel. As Eric Hoffer put it, "Mass movements can rise and spread without belief in a God, but never without belief in a devil."[13]

Above all, we find a classic demopathic discourse (articulated, apparently, by dupes) in which the fight against racism and Islamophobia and the defense of civil liberties became the occasion for including (scarcely disguised) Caliphators in the "peace" movement.[14] If you ever wondered how Superman could fool everyone just by putting on glasses and dressing like a reporter, here is a real-life example: the Muslim Association of Britain (MAB) as moderate, peace-loving Muslims, who, underneath it all, were really a Muslim Brotherhood Front. Their genuine platform made them avid promoters, along with their spiritual guide, Youssef al Qaradawi, of female genital mutilation, of takfir (death to apostates), of "martyrdom operations" that targeted Israeli and Iraqi Shi'ite civilians, and of an Islamic conquest of Europe and America.[15]

As a result, these "anti-war" demonstrations drew millions of well-meaning people who really wanted to end war, and who opposed the deposition of one of the most murderous dictators and violators of his own people's human rights in the world, even as they simultaneously opened the gates of legitimacy and public participation to pro-war Arabs and Muslims carrying pictures of Yasser Arafat, leader of the murderous intifada against Israel, and Saddam Hussein, the killer of over a million Iraqi Muslims of all denominations and ethnicities.[16] It was an alliance of the well-meaning Western peace camp and the triumphalist Muslims—worthy to surpass Durban in both its stunning global presence and its spectacular betrayal of progressive values. In Paris, a Muslim "anti-war" contingent chased a contingent of Jewish pacifists from the demonstration, and

---

12 This had been attempted in the Hyde Park March of December 9, 2001, and attempted in the April 2002 march without success. It became a regular feature of many marches, which increasingly partnered with openly radical Muslim groups.

13 Eric Hoffer, *The True Believer: Thoughts on the Nature of Mass Movements* (New York, Harper, 1951), 91.

14 On Azzam Tamimi, the Palestinian-born spokesman for Muslim Association of Britain, see n36.

15 On the movement's view of the alliance with the MAB, specifically in solidarity with their Palestinian advocacy, see Murray and Lewis, *Stop the War*, 81–95. For a leftist denunciation of the role of the MAB the previous year's anti-Israel demonstration, see "As we were saying: the Muslim Association of Britain's first public appearance, April 2002," *Association of Workers' Liberty*, pamphlet posted February 23, 2009.

16 See Nick Cohen's indictment of this demonstration, *What's Left*, chapter 10.

savagely beat them up.[17] The French news media, which had shocking footage of the attack, reported the incident only with great reluctance.[18]

At the same time, anti-Americanism dominated European discourse. The French of all political registers, even snarky leftist intellectuals, glowed with patriotic pride when their ("right-wing") foreign minister, Dominique de Villepin, publicly attacked the US at the UN, to the near universal approval of a global audience, including the jihadis. The whole world agreed: Bush was a monstrous idiot and whatever went wrong was his fault. In a conversation with French journalists, after we had all seen *Decryptage*, one informed me, "**True courage is opposing the strongest, and America is the strongest.**"[19] The others nodded in agreement.

Courage is actually fighting those who violate basic principles of humanity (Saddam far more than Blair or Bush), and who, when challenged, will retaliate violently against you for opposing them.[20] Posturing as courageous by attacking America (and Israel)—who will not retaliate, who do not issue fatwas, and who tolerate exceptionally high levels of public criticism—was self-delusion. Shades of Tim Benson and the Sharon cartoon controversy.

And it certainly did not fool the triumphalist enemy, who, firmly ensconced in its zero-sum world, saw (accurately) this "courageous" posturing as a sign of cowardice. A friend wrote to me from Morocco at the time of the great "anti-war" demonstrations: "The Arabs see the French as weak because they side with their enemies and attack their friends." Indeed, after the French veto of American war planes in the UN, French "beurs" (slang for Arabs) proudly shouted, "*Le veto, c'est nous!*"

But such analysis could not penetrate the excitement that permeated progressive circles, especially in Europe. Michael Moore's *Fahrenheit 9–11*, was a documentary that Christopher Hitchens called "a spectacle of abject political cowardice masking itself as a demonstration of 'dissenting' bravery," not as bad as *Jenin, Jenin*, but almost.[21] The "documentary" is filled with contradictions,

---

17 Phillip Carmel, "War in Iraq As Anti-War Fever Roils France, Jews Suffer Anti-semitic Attacks," March 27, 2003; Sarah Wildman, "Iraq assault triggers antisemitic backlash in France," *The Christian Science Monitor*, April 4, 2003.

18 Marc Perelman, "Wave of Antisemitic Crime Continues to Rise in France," *Forward*, April 4, 2003.

19 Above, 65n55.

20 "The Dixie Chicks are free to speak their mind. They can say what they want to say ... that's what so great about America." Text of Brokaw's Interview with Bush, *New York Times*, April 25, 2002.

21 Christopher Hitchens, "On Michael Moore's 'Fahrenheit 9/1,'" *History Network*, June 22, 2004.

misrepresentations and falsehoods, an "utterly propagandistic" pro-Saddam, anti-American collection that even "al Jazeera, on a bad day, would not have put together." And yet, the movie was greeted in Europe with standing ovations from movie-goers.[22] One of the most telling indictments of European intelligentsia in the twenty-first century is how much its members admire Michael Moore. Another is that they consider Noam Chomsky one of the great American intellectuals.[23] Apparently resentful envy in those early heady days of the new century could fully substitute for serious thought.

Warnings about Eurabia **Versus** *European Triumphalism*

In the mid-aughts of the twenty-first century (ca. 2005/1425), two sets of books hit the market. One set announced an imminent peril to Western civilization, and especially to Europe. The other announced the triumph of the European Union as the moral, noncoercive, soft-superpower of the new century.

On the one hand, *Why Europe Will Run the 21st Century* by Mark Leonard,[24] trumpeted the mood. *The United States of Europe: The New Superpower and the End of American Supremacy*, by T. R. Reid, laid out the displacement narrative.[25] *The European Dream: How Europe's Vision of the Future Is Quietly Eclipsing the American Dream*, by American Jeremy Rifkin, explained the liberal cognitive egocentric's vision of the future: voluntary, positive-sum, contractual agreements will replace the predatory world of the power-abusing elites of yore.[26] The European Union, being the highest accomplishment of that liberal, contractual political arc, will exercise the greatest power/influence/quiet hegemony—the new global world, ruled by soft power, with positive-sum Europeans in the lead. Fukuyama's melancholy "last man" had, in the minds of happy Hegelians, become the telos of the civic dialectic.[27]

---

22 In addition to winning the *Palme d'or* at Cannes (the first documentary since Jacques Cousteau in 1959 to win that prize), the film got a 15–20 minute standing ovation, the longest in memory, Gregg Kilday, "'Fahrenheit' lights fire in Cannes début," *Hollywood Reporter*, May 18, 2004.

23 Duncan Campbell, "Chomsky voted world's top public intellectual," *Guardian*, October 18, 2005.

24 Mark Leonard, *Why Europe Will Run the 21st Century* (London: Fourth Estate, 2006); reviewed favorably by Stanley Hoffman, *Foreign Affairs*, May–June 2005.

25 New York, Penguin, 2004.

26 New York: Penguin, 2004.

27 Francis Fukuyama, *The End of History and the Last Man* (New York: Free Press, 1992).

On the other hand, the mid-aughts also gave birth to the first warnings about the fall of that great new soft power. Bat Ye'or's *Eurabia* laid out the contours of a civilizational war that confident Europeans not only did not see coming, but, in their ignorance, had strengthened their enemies.[28] Mark Steyn's *America Alone* identified Europe as the weakest of the Western democracies under attack, with a disastrous combination of demographic trends—high Muslim immigration and birthrate versus high European emigration and low birthrate.[29] Melanie Phillips's *Londonistan* described England as a particularly egregious case of own-goal policies empowering Muslim radicals and marginalizing real moderates. And Bruce Bawer's *While Europe Slept* described the classic apocalyptic pattern of catastrophic failure, in which people move insensibly from euphoric dream to nightmare.[30] "Sweet as honey in your mouth, but sour in your stomach!" (*Revelation* 10:9).

Given the choice between dire warnings of decline and narcissistic assurances of greatness, the near-universal response of the European intelligentsia—what Bat Ye'or calls the thought-police—was to treat the warnings as ridiculous, Islamophobic, conspiracy theories, and embrace the imminent victory of EU moral soft-power.[31]

7–7: Home-Grown Suicide Terror Hits London[istan]

In the midst of this dialogue of the deaf, the first jihadi, mass suicide-terror attack in Europe took place in London, on July 7, 2005.[32] "7–7" quickly took its place alongside 9–11 in the annals of the Caliphator war. The attack on England broke with all the assumptions that the British (and other Europeans), had

---

28 Bat-Ye'or, *Eurabia: The Euro-Arab Axis* (Philadelphia, Fairleigh Dickinson University Press, 2005).

29 Mark Steyn, *America Alone: The End of the World as We Know it* (Washington, DC: Regnery, 2006).

30 "Peu à peu, un changement se faisait à l'intérieur des âmes, comme celui qui, la nuit, transforme insensiblement un songe en cauchemar." Marguerite Yourcenar, describing the experience of the Anabaptists under siege at Münster in 1533–35: *L'Oeuvre au Noir* (Paris: Gallimard, 1968). Bruce Bawer, *While Europe Slept: How Radical Islam is Destroying the West from Within* (New York: Broadway Books, 2006).

31 See Danios, "Bat Ye'or: Anti-Muslim Loon with a Crazy Conspiracy Theory Named 'Eurabia,'" *Loonwatch*, September 10, 2009. In her recently published memoirs, Bat-Ye'or discusses her pariah status after publication of *Eurabia*: even people who used her work avoided mentioning her, Bat Ye'or, "L'étoile jaune," *Les provincials*, 2018. Exceptions: [Wistrich, "Eurabia," in *A Lethal Obsession*, chapter 13; Douglas Murray, *The Strange Death of Europe: Immigration, Identity, Islam* (London: Bloomsbury Continuum, 2017)].

32 The earlier, devastating attack on Madrid rush-hour commuters that killed almost 200, was not a suicide attack; but it did express how grateful jihadis were for the support of the Madrid models two years earlier.

about suicide terror. Up to that point, most victims had been Israelis, Americans, Russians, Spanish—all, imperialist oppressors or their toadies (somehow Balinese didn't register). Just as Muslim theologians made an exception for Israel to the rule against targeting civilians, so had many Europeans, sincerely believing that a) Israelis deserved the terror for what [the journalists told them] the IDF did to the Palestinians; b) European civilians were innocent, so jihadis would not attack them [already disproven in Spain]; and c) that such attacks would certainly not come from their own Muslims. After all, if these "terrorists" were really "freedom fighters," why should Europeans worry?[33]

7–7, on the other hand, made it clear to anyone paying attention that a) the terrorists involved had previously been successful, assimilated British-born Muslims; b) they had deliberately attacked British civilians: and c) as far as jihadis were concerned, there were no innocent infidels, no "civilians."[34] This of course, created a crisis between British infidels and the Muslims in their midst. Any Muslim organization that wanted the label "moderate" had to condemn the 7–7 bombings. The Muslim Association of Britain's Azzam Tamimi, in his condemnation, played directly to British self-image, distinguishing between British civilians, illegitimate targets of suicide terror, and Israelis who deserved it.[35] In response to further criticism for supporting suicide terror at all, he clarified his understanding of the problem with misdirection. "Martyrdom," he explained solemnly, "is dying for justice and peace … not blowing oneself up killing innocent people."[36] Deciphered, he actually meant: "martyrdom is killing infidels to attain justice (revenge) and peace (Dar al Islam)."

But to absorb the ominous lessons of 7–7, one needed to think clearly, pay attention—"grasp its message if we dare listen and are able to endure"—and use appropriate terminology when discussing it. That is when the BBC stepped in. Naturally in response to this heinous act of terror, the British press, even the BBC and the *Guardian* had included (as had the American press) the terms "terrorist" and "terrorism" when describing this act that targeted British civilians. Did this lead the BBC and other high-minded progressives to have more empathy for Americans and Israelis, and reconsider the ban on using "terrorism" to describe jihadi attacks on infidel civilians?

---

33 For a good example of Westsplaining Muslim terrorism and blaming Israel, see the former Labour government advisor David Clark, "This terror will continue until we take Arab grievances seriously," *Guardian*, July 9, 2005. Bin Laden much appreciated Westsplainers like Robert Fisk (see 177, n102).

34 See Anjem Choudary explaining the issue to a stunned Stephen Sackur, above 61f.

35 "Newsnight: Muslim Response to London bombing," BBC, July 15, 2005.

36 Azzam Tamimi, "Martyrdom misunderstood," *Guardian*, August 25, 2006.

Not at all. The BBC's editorial board immediately circulated a memo insisting on *not* using the word "terrorist" to describe the British Muslims who had strapped on bomb vests and blown themselves up in the London public transport, amid their fellow citizens. Ran the memo:

> We must report acts of terror quickly, accurately, fully and responsibly. Terrorism is a difficult and emotive subject with significant political overtones and care is required in the use of language that carries value judgements. We try to avoid the use of the term "terrorist" without attribution. When we do use the term, we should strive to do so with consistency in the stories we report across all our services and *in a way that does not undermine our reputation for objectivity and accuracy*.
>
> The word "terrorist" itself can be a barrier rather than an aid to understanding. We should convey to our audience the full consequences of the act by describing what happened. We should use words which specifically describe the perpetrator such as "bomber," "attacker," "gunman," "kidnapper," "insurgent," and "militant." We should not adopt other people's language as our own [?]; our responsibility is to remain objective and report in ways that enable our audiences to make their own assessments about who is doing what to whom.[37]

And this self-imposed ban on using the word "terrorism" worked its stealth jihadi magic. Not only did it protect terrorist groups from well-deserved opprobrium, but it also disguised the problem of triumphalist Muslims who sympathized with and supported these terrorists. Britain's orientation after 7–7, reflected this high-minded, self-inflicted blindness: *Londonistan* sought alliances with radical triumphalists to help them with the community, while the triumphalists shielded the jihadis and discredited the true moderates.[38]

Those were the glory days of the new *Respect Party*, the political arm of the anti-war movement spearheaded by George Monbiot and Salma Yaqoob, whose main politician, George Galloway proudly announced at a rally a year after the attacks: **Hezbollah has never been a terrorist organization. I am here, I am here, to glorify the Lebanese resistance, Hezbollah, and I am here to glorify the resistance leader, Hassan Nasrallah."**[39] Anti-war had graduated to full-fledged

---

37 "Language when reporting terrorism," *BBC Editorial Guidelines*.
38 Phillips, *Londonistan*.
39 London Anti-war rally, July 22, 2006. Nick Cohen, *What's Left?*, 293f.

own-goal war. The tough cop (jihadi terrorist), nice cop (Da'ī cogwarrior) routine worked to perfection on a whole range of willing (self-)executioners.

The French Riots of October to November 2005/Ramadan to Shawwal 1426

On October 27, 2005, in the largely Muslim suburb of Clichy-sous-bois, three boys, running from the police, took refuge in a high voltage zone and two of them died of electrocution. On the wings of a lethal narrative about malevolent policemen deliberately killing them, riots "spontaneously erupted." Within the week, burning cars, attacking civilians, destroying buildings and pillaging stores spread throughout the *"Zones urbaines sensibles"* of the Paris suburbs, and from there, throughout France.

FIGURE 10. Map of riots in France, October to November 2005 (*Le Parisien*).[40]

---

40 "Emeutes de 2005, dix ans après," *Le Parisien.*

By November 8, 2005, President Chirac declared a national emergency. Rioters, some shouting *Allahu Akhbar* and *Na'al abouk la France!* [Fuck France!"], competed with each other for the damage they could do, using cell phones to send out their competitive results. Not until November 16 did the violence begin to subside.

The French press was divided in two over the riots: there were those who blamed the rioters and those who blamed French society.[41] But virtually everyone who was anyone agreed that "Islam had nothing to do with the riots." Determined to ignore any aspect of the growing Caliphator movement and its gang Islam, analysts delivered remarkable displays of liberal cognitive egocentrism: "They're just like us, and it's their frustration at not being able to integrate, to become equal citizens in the French republic that makes them so hostile."[42] Emmanuel Todd explained:

> But I do not see anything in the events themselves which radically separates the children of immigrants from the remainder of French society. I see the opposite exactly there. I interpret the events like a refusal of marginalization. All of that could not have occurred if these children of immigrants had not interiorized some of the fundamental values of French society, of which, for example, the couple freedom-equality.[43]

Or, as political scientist Riva Kastoryano assured her readers, "This time, the 'youth of the banlieues' wanted stubbornly to be heard, to be seen, and to be accepted."[44] Evidence that contradicted this egocentric narrative went unexamined, or worse, proscribed as racist. Noted Alain Finkielkraut: "The looters do not demand more schools, more day-nurseries ... more buses: they burn them." His French interview mistranslated into Hebrew by *Haaretz*, and then back to French, elicited outraged accusations of racism.[45]

---

41 Stéfanie Peeters, "La couverture médiatique de la "crise des banlieues": métaphores, représentations et l'apport indispensable du cotexte", *CORELA—RJC Cotexte, contexte, situation*, January 2012.

42 On the "diagnostic error" involved, see Alexandre Devecchio, *Les nouveaux enfants du siècle: Djihadistes, identitaires, réacs. Enquête sur une génération fracturée* (Paris: Du Cerf, 2016).

43 "Emmanuel Todd, "Rien ne sépare les enfants d'immigrés du reste de la société", *Le Monde*, October 29, 2005; translation at *Daily Kos*, November 13, 2005.

44 Riva Kastoryano, "Territories of Identities in France," *The Riots in France*, SSRC.

45 Alexis Lacroix, "Alain Finkielkraut: 'L'illégitimité de la haine,'" *Le Figaro*, November 15, 2005; for the convoluted details, see Alain Finkielkraut, "L'interview dans le journal Haaretz," *Wikipédia*.

Of course, the end result of this analysis comes out in the realm of Masochistic Omnipotence Syndrome (MOS). The French pundits were, in effect, saying: is all "our fault"—French racism, cop brutality, Sarkozy's insults all aggravated, and even caused the riots. The Sarkozy "contribution" was especially amusing: according to the accepted wisdom, his calling them *racaille* (riffraff) deeply wounded the rioters, and provoked their (otherwise manageable?) rage.[46] "Such inflammatory words only served to increase anger in the banlieues—it was clearly the language of war."[47] Much more likely, the rioters were amused by his words (*racaille* being a mild term for what they thought of themselves), and laughed at the infidel dupes who deplored that their leaders allegedly hurt the rioters' feelings. The spectacle of French elites using this nonsense to tear each other apart publicly could not have been more encouraging.[48]

The racism, brutality, and insulting language of the rioters?[49] "*N'en parlons pas....*" They were widely depicted as the victims, and as such, necessarily innocent. Whether they made it personal or not, the preponderance of the reporters and pundits gave the rioters Western motivations for revolt, and pointed the finger at the systemic failures of French society, a veritable orgy of *pénitence tyrannique*.[50] Yet, somehow, for all their self-flagellation, the French did not like the way outsiders, especially the Anglophone press reported the riots—"greatly exaggerating their impact," an "unattractive *démesure*" in the opinion of Jacques Chirac and his prime minister, de Villepin, who explained how the riots had not been nearly as bad as the Rodney King riots in 1992 in Los Angeles. This was no occasion for outsiders to engage in "*le french-bashing*," and certainly not to bring up Islam.[51]

---

46 NB: Sarkozy was responding to an Arab woman in the neighborhood who asked him when he'd get rid of this "racaille" that was making all their lives miserable.

47 Andrew Hussey, "The French Intifada: How the Arab banlieues are fighting the French state," *Guardian*, February 23, 2014.

48 See for parallel case, Ed Husain and Hassan Butt's comments (223f).

49 On the racism and hostility to anything French, white, infidel, see Colin Nickerson, "Youths' poverty, despair fuel violent unrest in France," *Boston Globe*, November 6, 2005; on hatred: the vicious discourse of French Muslim rappers prompted some ministers ("right wing," of course), to demand they be prosecuted: "Plus de 200 élus demandent des poursuites contre sept groupes de rap," *AFP*, 23 November 2005. On the demopathic accusation by Muslim racists of French "white" racism, see Léon Sann, "Violence Urbaines: Le cercle vicieux de la falsification des préférences," *Controverses* 1 (Paris, 2006), 147–73.

50 Pascal Bruckner, *Tyranny of Guilt: An Essay on Western Masochism* (Princeton: Princeton University Press, 2010). See chapter 8.

51 Théo Chapuis, "Émeutes de 2005: les critiques de la presse étrangère, miroir déformant du malaise français", *Konbini*, 2015.

For those who warned about Muslim triumphalism, these riots were clearly another phase in the invasion of Europe, a new and disturbing expression of the clash of civilizations.[52] The rioters did not protest being refused the chance to assimilate and join the majoritarian society. Rather, they saw the situation as an opportunity to further consolidate control of the "zones urbaines sensibles," and create no-go zones, to further the split between the unassimilated Arab Muslim community and the larger culture.[53] In Bat Ye-or's framework, the ruling elite of the "français de souche" were discovering that the Eurabia they imagined when they made the deal to bring in this worker population was not the Eurabia their immigrants' descendants seemed to have in mind.

Others, like Finkielkraut, argued that this was, in effect, a French intifada: an uprising by French Muslims against the state. Blaming an official policy of segregation was wide of the mark. These rioting French Muslims wanted to be segregated. The ghettoes were a way of ensuring a separate existence, eliminating the humiliating need to assimilate into French society.[54]

No, came the response. Islam has *nothing* to do with these riots. The *Independent's* John Lichfield explained:

> Talk of an intifada is absurdly misleading. Firstly, the rioters are far from being all Muslim (although more than half are from Islamic backgrounds). Second, they have no sense of political or religious identity and no political demands. Their allegiance is to their quartier and their gang.... The wider significance is therefore not politico-religious, but a warning of what happens if problems of deprivation and violence are allowed to fester.[55]

"More than half..."? "No sense of political or religious identity ..."? As if, by November 7 (not yet halfway through the episode), all this were clear as a bell.[56]

---

52 Steyn, *America Alone*; Phillips, *Londonistan*, more recently, Gilles Kepel who sees the riots as pivotal in the spread of a militant Islam: *Terror in France: The Rise of Jihad in the West* (Princeton: Princeton University Press, 2017), 11–33.

53 Fred Siegel, "The Lebanonization of Europe," *New York Sun*, 23 February 2006.

54 Melanie Phillips, "Ghettoes, Race Riots and the Lessons for us all," *Daily Mail*, November 7, 2005.

55 John Lichfield, "No intifada, no cause, just poor kids defending their territory," *Independent*, November 7, 2005.

56 The "not all the rioters were Muslim" meme was widespread, despite the obvious majority of Muslims rioting and their role in setting the tone and agenda ("Allahu akhbar" being a favorite battle cry.)

In so assuring his audience, Lichfield was conforming to a widespread discourse among information professionals.[57] Even the head of French Intelligence, Pascal Maihos, insisted that "[t]he role of radical Islamists in the riots was zero (*nulle*).[58] The presence of radical Islamists became a taboo subject. Patrick Poivre d'Arvor of TF1, interviewed Dominique de Villepin on the eve of the declaration of the state of emergency (November 7), and asked: "Is there a problem of religion here? Because no one is talking about it, as though it were politically incorrect."[59]

Jocelyn Cesari made perhaps the most revealing argument:

> Indeed, neither Islam nor religious concerns were motivating factors in the riots. The proof, as reported by Xavier Ternisien in the November 9, 2005 edition of *Le Monde*, is that attempts by the heads of the UOIF (the Union of French Islamic Associations) to communicate with the young rioters and bring them back to reason and calm met with little success.[60]

Despite the apparent "proof" provided here, we have what appears to be further evidence of the difficulty information professionals and analysts have in thinking clearly about triumphalist Islam. The very fact that French authorities had recourse to the imams (whom they had only recently offended with the ban on veils) reveals the subtext at work: everyone knew this was a Muslim problem. As for the lack of impact of the elders' appeal, it merely proves that the upcoming generation of Caliphators were not responsive to more traditional forms of (semi-assimilated) Islam. As Ed Husain described English Caliphators: "we shared a common ideology and veneration for Mawdudi and Qutb and we all despised traditional Islam."[61] It would be akin to arguing that Bin Laden's attack had nothing to do with Islam because conventional Islamic authorities forbade his kind of offensive jihad . . . in fact, a common argument at that time.

---

57 Stephane Dufois lists *thirteen* possible ways to frame the problem; not one mentions religion, much less Islam, "More Than Riots: A Question of Spheres," *Riots in France*, December 2, 2005.

58 Piotr Smolar, "L'antitérrorisme selon le patron des Renseignements généraux", *Le Monde*, October 23, 2008.

59 Tristan Mattelart, "French TV Confronts the Riots," *Global Media and Communication*, 2:2 (2006): 266.

60 Jocelyne Cesari, "Ethnicity, Islam, and les banlieues: Confusing the Issues," *Items: Insights from the Social Sciences*, November 30, 2005.

61 Ed Husain, *The Islamist: Why I Became an Islamic Fundamentalist, What I Saw Inside, and Why I Left* (London: Penguin, 2007), 53.

This removal of Islam from the equation meant that a whole series of issues, many directly supportive of the Eurabian thesis, were systematically eliminated from the discussion:

- The collapse of the school systems in these suburbs, the virulent anti-Jewish and anti-French discourse that had flourished since 2000, despite the fact that a study had come out deploring the situation of Islamicization of French schools, a few months earlier.[62]
- The publication at the end of 2004 of a major call to global Caliphators by al Qaeda strategist Abu Musaf al Suri, to mobilize badly assimilated and rebellious Muslim youth in the West, only needing the proper indoctrination and training to create a civil war in Europe. "This is the way the final dislocation of the West will lead to the global triumph of Islam."[63]
- The spread of radical Islam in these neighborhoods by Muslim Brotherhood "identity entrepreneurs" spreading Caliphator anger, hatred (including but not limited to antisemitism), and dreams of victory of infidel Europe in the lost territories.[64]
- The existence of a "gang, neo-Islam," which combined a new Muslim identity for those born in exile (*dar al Harb*), shifting the core message from the traditional identities rooted in particular communities to a collective identity shaped by internet-propagated radical Islam.[65] In the context of the shame-honor, gang-driven, and decidedly brutal communities of the "jeunes," this nonpious, but highly aggressive and triumphalist Islam failed to even register on the screens of most French Islam experts.

---

62 No article I have read brought up the accounts of the radical hatreds and violence against both Jews and the "République," in Emmanuel Brenner's *Territoires perdus de la République*; discussed, 28n88.

63 See Kepel, *Terror in France*, p, 23. Those Westerners who virtually paraphrase this goal are considered "right-wing Zionists and European neo-fascists," who express a "dangerous Islamophobic fantasy." Matt Carr, "You are now entering Eurabia," *Race and Class*, 48:1 (2006): 1–22.

64 Johnson and Carreyrou, "As Muslims Call Europe Home". For the role of Al Durah in that teaching, see chapter 1 n85. For a broad survey of the problem that came out literally days before the 7-7 London bombing and months before the French riots, see Robert Leikand, "Europe's Angry Muslims," *Foreign Affairs*, July–August, 2005. On identity entrepreneurs, see 228n61.

65 Kepel, *Terror in France*, 23.

So when Olivier Roy, one of France's major experts on Islam, analyzed what in modern media culture inspired violence among the youth, he discounted religious motives while fingering "the fascination for sudden suicidal violence as illustrated by the paradigm of random shootings in schools (the 'Columbine syndrome')," as if these French Muslim youth were watching Michael Moore documentaries, and not the wall-to-wall coverage of the Palestinian intifada.[66] Denial was everywhere: no Islam, no antisemitism, no no-go zones, and as for the foreign media, they were just malicious about French woes. In his book on the *French Intifada*, Andrew Hussey wrote:

> There was broad agreement that the riots had little or nothing to do with Islam or the historical French presence in parts of the Islamic world. Leftist intellectuals, in the pages of *Le Monde* or *Libération*, fell over themselves to distance the riots from any connection with the same anger that radicalised Islamists. According to these journalists, the riots were caused by a "*fracture sociale*" and lack of "*justice sociale*." In this way the riots of 2005 were domesticated and made part of a traditionally French form of protest. There was an almost complete denial that what was happening might be a new form of politics that was a direct challenge to the French state.[67]

By the anniversary of the riots, many wished to forget they had ever happened, their memory "covered in a veil of ignorance."[68]

Perhaps most striking of all the paradoxes of French coverage of the riots was their intuitive understanding of the dynamics of televised media. On one level, this was a French "al Durah" affair: the initial trigger, the death of two boys who took shelter from police in high voltage zone and were electrocuted was immediately turned into a lethal narrative of deliberate murder and assaults by the police—as was, three days later, the tear-gassing of a mosque filled with

66 Olivier Roy, "Al Qaeda in the West as a Youth Movement: The Power of a Narrative," *Center for European Policy Studies Policy Brief #168*, August 2008. Arun Kundani cites this analysis approvingly to minimize religion as a motive in Muslim violence, "Radicalisation: The journey of a concept," *Race & Class*, 54:2 (2012), 21. On the differences between France's two leading experts on French Muslims, Roy and Keppel, see Marc Weitzman, "France's Great Debate Over the Sources and Meaning of Muslim Terror," *Tablet*, May 25, 2021.

67 Andrew Hussey, "The French Intifada."

68 Sebastian Roché, "Des émeutes en 2005, quelles émeutes?", *Le Figaro*, October 28, 2006.

Ramadan worshipers.[69] To paraphrase Fisk on Al Durah, "When immigrant Muslim activists hear 'accidental ...,' they knows the cops have deliberately targeted the faithful." Second, the police response was deliberately low key—which may have contributed to why the riots went on so long.[70] The decision may be rooted in the fear that were a picture of a Muslim youth shot by the cops to circulate, it could lead to the spread of suicide terror to France as al Durah's image had in Israel.

All these parallels, however, operated below the surface of consciousness. French analysts did not have their news media's behavior during the Palestinian intifada in mind, even as they applied its lessons to the scenes at hand. All of a sudden, the French news media realized that excessive and credulous coverage inflames rather than helps control the violence. "Do we send teams of journalists because cars are burning or are the cars burning because we sent teams of journalists?" asked Patrique Lecocq, editor in chief of France 2.[71]

So, unlike its coverage of the Palestinian intifada, where the more journalists, the merrier, French news providers handled the sudden outbreak of Muslim rioting much as they handled the outbreak of French Muslim antisemitism after 2000—self-censoring Omertà. "Politics in France is heading to the right and I don't want rightwing politicians back in second [a reference to Marine Le Pen's shocking second place in the 2002 presidential elections], or even first place, because we showed burning cars on television," said Jean-Claude Dassier, owner of France1 TV.[72] In the end, the French media handled their domestic problems exactly opposite to the way they handled Israeli ones. With regard to the events in Israel, the French media were pyromaniacs, running repeatedly the most inflammatory footage and lethal narratives, encouraging the most "hard-line" reactions all around. For the French events, however, they self-censored extensively, in order to prevent viewers "from going to the right."

Ironically, both kinds of coverage—obsessing over Israel's victimization of Palestinians and censoring French Muslim's destructive rampages—had the same effect: facilitating Caliphator advances. In the end, the elaborate self-accusing and self-censoring approach of the French (and other) analysts,

---

69 "It was the tear-gassing of the Mosque of Bilal that provided the trigger for the events and their astonishing spread throughout the country," Kepel, *Terror in France*, 13.

70 Catherine Schneider, "Police Power and Race Riots in Paris," *Politics & Society*, 36:1 (March 2008): 133–159.

71 Claire Cozens, "French TV boss admits to censoring riot coverage," *Guardian*, November 10, 2005.

72 Ibid.

may well have come less from a genuine tendency to self-criticize, than from a disguising of their unwillingness or inability to defend their own civilization from so primitive an attack. "Heaven forbid the Islamophobic critics of Eurabia might be right!"

Extending the Reach of Sharia to Infidels in Dar al Islam: The Muhammad Cartoons Affair, February 2006/ Muharram 1427

On September 30, 2005, Flemming Rose, the cultural editor at the *Jyllands-Posten*, the prominent Danish newspaper, published twelve cartoons supposedly of Muhammad. Rose's project, conceived months earlier, addressed a worrisome trend in Europe. Since the assassination in the streets of Amsterdam of Theo Van Gogh for his blasphemy against Islam, a fear of offending touchy, fanatic Muslims became widespread among the "information professionals" of the West. The problem came to Rose's attention because Kare Bluitgen could not find an illustrator for her (very sympathetic) children's book on the life of the Prophet. Why? Because some zealous Sunni Muslims insisted on their tradition's iconoclastic prohibition of depicting the Prophet, and so threatened even non-Muslims for transgressions. Rose saw the exercise as one in which Danish cartoonists could address some of the more outlandish aspects of this coercive effort to tell non-Muslims—secular Europeans!—what they could and could not say about Islam.

If he hoped for some penetrating insights, Rose must have been disappointed. Some cartoonists actually avoided depicting Muhammad entirely. One depicted himself drawing the prophet, sweating in fear and trembling. One has a schoolboy called Muhammad pointing to a passage in Persian on the blackboard that reads: "The editorial team of *Jyllands-Posten* is a bunch of reactionary provocateurs." Some were more critical of Muslims: the most famous, by Kurt Westergaard, depicted an Ottoman (clearly not the historical Muhammad) in a turban with a bomb in it, thus associating Muslim terror with the anarchist terrorists of the turn of the previous century.

FIGURE 11. Kurt Westergaard (*Aftenpost*).

Frank Füchsel depicted Muhammad as Saladin, showing the ego-strength not to go ballistic with every challenge to his honor.

FIGURE 12. *Jyllands Posten* (Denmark), September 30, 2005.

Rasmus Sand Hoyer linked Muslim misogyny to blind and violent religious zealotry, by depicting two women in black burqas with only an open strip for their eyes, and an angry turbaned man with a scimitar and a strip of black across his eyes.

FIGURE 13. *Jyllands Posten* (Denmark), September 30, 2005.

Granted, these cartoons were not very flattering, but their primary target, radical Muslims, certainly deserved the criticism, and, according to the then prevalent politically correct discourse, these radicals "had nothing to do with true Islam." If the British Political Cartoon Society could give an award to a depiction of Sharon as Goya's Chronos devouring a (Palestinian) child, because, apparently, it accurately lampooned his political and military career, then nothing among the Muhammad cartoons comes anywhere near that level of raw hostility.[73]

Indeed, nothing was either so removed from reality (say, depicting Muhammad as a coward or effeminate), or so gratuitous (Muhammad as a pig) that it went

---

73 Cf. Tariq Modood: "They are all unfriendly to Islam and Muslims and the most notorious implicate the Prophet with terrorism ... that the Prophet of Islam was a terrorist," Modood et al., "The Danish Cartoon Affair: Free Speech, Racism, Islamism, and Integration?" *International Migration*, 44:5 (2006). Political cartoons are not supposed to be friendly.

anywhere near the limits of Western political cartooning, one of democracy's liveliest forms of social and political criticism.[74] On the contrary, these three critical cartoons in particular, had serious things to say about a Muslim tendency to touchy honor, violent rage, and aggressiveness towards the weak (e.g., women). Art Spiegelman, grand man of the graphic novel, after piously hoping he was not adding fuel to the fire, admitted that he found them "banal and inoffensive," before rating each cartoon with a "fatwa meter" of 1–4 bombs. He hoped to measure the "gulf in understanding," involved in a controversy that had, by then, killed about fifty people, almost all Muslims, by rampaging Muslims.

To many it was a tempest in a teapot. Non-Caliphator Muslims found the "Muslim" claims quite extraordinary. As a Muslim member of the Danish Parliament noted:

> My impression from different Arabic media is that the dominant position—perhaps surprising for some—can be summarised as follows: We cannot as Muslims dictate that non-Muslims comply with the allegedly prohibited depiction of the prophet.[75]

Indeed, they were right. Historically, the ban on images of Muhammad was the product of a specific school of Sunni thought, aimed at preventing Muslims from falling prey to the idolatry of worshipping the images. There was no reason to apply it to infidels who were in no danger of such idolatry. After an initial peaceful protest in Denmark, and some inconclusive legal action, the controversy momentarily died down. That's when a designated group of more radical Imams took the necessary steps to make this a Caliphator initiative, not about feelings or religious doctrines, but about infidel obedience to Sharia.

And for that, these Imams needed a more violent reaction. So, they went on tour of the Muslim majority world, armed with a dossier designed to arouse indignation and action, to stage a global "emergency."[76] But in order to do so,

---

74 Charles Press, *The Political Cartoon* (Philadelphia: Fairleigh Dickinson University Press, 1981).

75 Naser Khader, Member of Danish Parliament, cited at Wikipedia, "Opinions on the Jyllands-Posten Muhammad Cartoons controversy." On the "anodine" nature of the Danish cartoons and the blasphemous quality of the fakes, see Mohamed Sifaoui, *L'affaire des caricatures: Dessins et manipulations* (Paris: Editions Privé, 2006), 74–83.

76 Ashley Thorne, "Staged Emergencies: How Colleges React to Bias Incidents," *National Association of Scholars*, 2014. Among the groups he met with and shared his incendiary fake cartoons, were Hamas and Hizballah: Ateist, "Ahmed Akkari's Departure from Islamism," *Danish Muhammad Cartoons*, May 3, 2014, https://bibelen.blogspot.com/2014/05/akkari-my-departure-from-islamism-in-my.html.

they had to weaponize the dossier so that the *Umma* would come together and roar. As a result, they added three more cartoons to the initial dossier, including one of Muhammad as a pig [!], which they took from a picture of a pig-squealing contest in France, a diabolic Muhammad pedophile [!], and a dog, buggering Muhammad while he prayed [!]. Now all of these are, on Art Spiegelman's 1–4 fatwa meter, a 10.[77] In many Muslim societies, past and present, the mere rumor that a dhimmi had compared Muhammad to a pig or suggested that a dog had mounted him while he prayed, launched lynch mobs. Today, any such blasphemy can expect outrage and violence. It's a red flag for most, one might even be tempted to say, the "vast majority" of Muslims (and most anyone else for that matter). And there are few people, myself included, who would excuse such gross and gratuitous insults to others, even hostile others.

The men who identified these images as images of the Prophet, as pig, pedophile and dog-buggered, were the very imams who wanted to incite the hatred they felt, in the hearts of their fellow Muslims. Here was a lethal narrative, designed to provoke outrage, to sever ties, to intensify hatred, to unleash the dogs of war. These self-proclaimed champions of Muslim piety had done the most impious of things, they had debased the Prophet most blasphemously for political gain.

And yet, in the Arab world, that blasphemy worked. It inflamed the global Ummah to paroxysms of indignation. It inspired Muslim Brotherhood theologian and TV star, Yussuf al Qaradawi to call for a day of rage.

> The *ummah* must rage in anger. It is told that Imam al-Shafi'i said: "Whoever was angered and did not rage is a jackass." We are not a nation of jackasses for riding, but lions that roar. We are lions that zealously protect their dens and avenge affronts to their sanctities. We are not a nation of jackasses. We are a nation that should rage for the sake of Allah, His Prophet and his book. We are the nation of Muhammad, and we must never accept the degradation of our religion.[78]

---

77 "The extra pictures might not have made much difference [sic] ... but it shows how rapidly propaganda can add fuel to the fire." Reynolds, "Clash of Rights," BBC, February 6, 2006. The BBC's coverage failed to mention the fakes and then showed one (without identifying its provenance), in a photo of the Imams' tour of the Muslim world: Jytte Klausen, *The Cartoons that Shook the World* (New Haven: Yale University Press, 2009), 50–52. Flemming only mentions these fakes in passing in his account: *The Tyranny of Silence* (Washington DC: Cato Institute, 2014).

78 "Sheikh Al-Qaradhawi Responds to Cartoons of Prophet Muhammad: Whoever Is Angered and Does Not Rage in Anger is a Jackass—We are Not a Nation of Jackasses," February 3, Al Jazeera broadcast, *MEMRI*.

The violence and indignation that the West saw in the Muslim Street was not about what the Danes had done, but—unknowingly—what imams determined to subject infidels to (their interpretation of) Sharia had themselves done. Even the BBC got caught in the net of deception, informing their Arab language viewership that the pig image had run in the Danish paper.[79] A major fake news success in breaching the enemy's mainstream press.

What could justify such staggering levels of hypocrisy among devoted Muslims. An imam "making" an image of Muhammad as a pig? Whether dupe, or knowing participant in the theater of staged emergency, al Qaradawi saw these cartoons as too valuable for his purposes to give up their power in order to denounce his fellow Muslims as the real blasphemers. Apparently, the blasphemy can be forgiven a Caliphator, if these images can make the global *Ummah* roar like a lion and spread the fear of Allah in the hearts of *kuffār*, nations of jackasses, everywhere. In any case, the failure of the Western infidels to denounce the fakes, made Qaradawi's moves much easier.

At this point, the zero-sum game of honor-shame was afoot. The goal of the imams was to depict a world of hatred of Muslims—Islamophobia—every bit as feverish as the world of hatred of infidels and sectarian Muslims in which Muslims increasingly lived. The thinking ran roughly so: "We must destroy them before they destroy us. No lie, no deception was too low, too blasphemous, if it advanced that war." It was the triumphalist version of the honor-shame: "Call me a liar and I'll kill you, *especially* when I'm lying."[80]

At this point the West should have countered this cognitive attack by tracking down the fakes, and exposing or threatening to expose the true blasphemers. Every diplomatic meeting at which Muslims voiced their indignation at Western offenses should have included those fake cartoons, on the table before the ambassadors from the OIC.[81] Instead, when Javier Solana met with Muslim diplomats, he capitulated to the OIC's narrative:

---

79 Alex Thompson, "More Mohammed Cartoon Fun," *Drinking from Home*, January 30, 2006. The ignorance of the BBC journalists suggest that they hadn't even seen the original 12, and their casual repetition of war propaganda as news suggests at best laziness, since the fakes had already been revealed a month before. Nor did the BBC correct itself. Instead, they interviewed a Muslim activist explaining how offensive the 12 cartoons: narrative above all.

80 On the role of lying in shame-honor cultures, see Landes, "Primary Honour Codes in Tribal and Aristocratic Cultures."

81 Prompted by reader feedback, one BBC journalist noted: "Western diplomats appear to have missed this entirely, and seem to have made no attempt to counter some of the arguments in the pamphlet or to distinguish between the various portrayals." Reynolds, "Clash of Rights."

We understand the deep hurt and widespread indignation felt in the Muslim world. The freedom of the press, which entails responsibility and discretion, should respect the beliefs and tenets of all religions.[82]

Everyone, on both sides, understood that "all religions" meant Islam.

By and large, most people—Westerners and Muslims—did not see the cartoons, and therefore knew neither how mild the original ones were, nor how outrageous the imam-supplied lethal fakes were. Spiegelman admits his surprise at realizing how few of his friends had seen the cartoons. And when Steven Sackur quoted Afghan President Hamid Karzai claiming that Rose had insulted a billion Muslims, Flemming Rose suggested that Karzai himself might not have seen them (just as Khomeini had not read *Satanic Verses*). With finely-honed cognitive egocentrism, Sackur responded (talking over Rose), "I'm sure he's seen the cartoons. The internet allows everyone to see the cartoons, as you know."[83]

When asked about the three fake cartoons, Akkar explained them away as an effort to "give an insight into how hateful the atmosphere in Denmark is towards Muslims."[84] How could a news media, already deep in the Augean Stables, respond to this "fake but true" claim? Had they not already heard without objection Charles Enderlin's excuse that he reported that the IDF killed al Durah, even if he had not witnessed it, because it corresponded to what [he knew] was going on everywhere else? Had not the *New York Times* defended the George W. Bush National Guard forgeries as "false but accurate"? Not surprisingly, the same twenty-first century news media let the lethal forgers off the hook and empowered them to continue their cogwar campaign. Score one (more) for incendiary fake news, for own-goal journalism in the legacy media.

The Apology: Moebius Strip of Cognitive Egocentrism at Work

The victory of the Muslim victim narrative laid out the battle lines from the start, in which the cartoonists targeted for violent suppression became agents

---

82 United Nations Secretary General, "Joint UN, European Union, Islamic Conference Statement Shares 'Anguish' of Muslim World at Mohammed Caricatures, but Condemns Violent Response," news release, February 7, 2006.

83 *Hardtalk*, Stephen Sackur with Rose Flemming and Ahmed abu Laban, BBC, February 8, 2006.

84 Hjörtur J. Guðmundsson, "Scandinavian Update: Israeli Boycott, Muslim Cartoons," *Brussels Journal*, January 14, 2006.

provocateurs who are "asking for it. The West was therefore required to apologize for its aggression against Islam. The *Jyllands-Posten* was inundated by such requests from the start, and almost all diplomatic discussions centered on getting apologies from various players, from the editors of the newspaper to the prime minister of Denmark. Most Western public figures took these discussions seriously. They believed that Muslims had indeed been deeply offended by the cartoons—what Klausen calls "an emotional grievance," and that an apology could (and should) resolve the matter. Tariq Modood insisted: "From the Muslim side, the underlying causes of their current anger are a deep sense that they are not respected, that they and their most cherished feelings are 'fair game.'"[85] Klausen explains: "The grievance was about feelings and the demands for redress focused on restoration through symbolic action."[86]

The well-intentioned infidel here considered that the insult was indeed what Muslim spokesmen claimed: a terrible blow to their feelings of self-esteem and disturbing testimony to the hostility of their non-Muslim neighbors, proof of Islamophobia. And most liberal Westerners, when they thought of the "vast majority of Muslims," imagined them as people like us, perhaps a bit more fragile, but whose sincere feelings should be visibly respected. They favored a Western, non-Muslim, *gesture of respect*, of self-restraint, of self-criticism—if necessary, of self-censorship. Muslim Professor of Politics and Women's Studies at York University, Hileh Avshar, responding to criticism of judging Muslim feelings by a separate hypersensitive standard, demanded special treatment. "You can't expect Muslims to behave exactly like Westerners do. If the Muslims feel as a matter of their faith that they do not like to have the picture of their prophet, then that view should be respected."[87]

In the Western public sphere, respecting the feelings of Muslims—won as well. The Da'wa demopaths took the offensive, using the entire barrage of Western egalitarian human rights language to attack the West for its Islamophobia, xenophobia, and racism. In the language consecrated at Durban in 2001, the OIC set the powerful tone of reproach with a systematic projection of malice:

> It is evident that the intention of *Jyllands-Posten* was motivated
> to incite hatred and violence against Muslims. By exposing the
> level of understanding of Islamic religion and its symbols the

---

85 Modood et al., "The Danish Cartoon Affair."
86 Klausen, *Cartoons*, 47.
87 Reynolds, "Clash of Rights."

dailies have seriously damaged their credibility in the eyes of Muslim world and harmed democracy, freedom of the press, violated decency and civilized norms.[88]

Eleven ambassadors, from nations that execute blasphemers of Islam, wrote an indignant letter to the Danish prime minister, posing as defenders of good liberal values. They insisted on curbing "the Danish press and public representatives" who "should not be allowed to abuse Islam in the name of democracy, freedom of expression and human rights, the values that we all share."[89] What satisfaction it must have provided, for triumphalists to use this language against the very people—*kuffār*—who had previously tried to shame *them* for their "primitive" behavior (killing blasphemers). By flipping the accusation and emptying the moral language of all substance, the demopaths achieved a double victory: "if the *kuffār* act as if our claims were just, we win twice—they're so stupid, and they grovel at our tongue-lashing."

And indeed, the jihadis won the battle in the Western public sphere. Progressives picked up their cudgels and went after anyone who had the temerity to defend the Danes. Jytte Klausen, comfortably embedded in the progressive academic scene in Cambridge, suddenly found herself called to explain "how the 'good Danes' had turned into hate-filled racists with no respect for human rights."[90] International organizations like the UNHRC denounced the racism and xenophobia of the Danes and their supporters.[91] Even people who tried to be nuanced, conceded that at least *some* of the defenders of *Jyllands-Posten* had essentialized Islam, making them potentially racist and, if not racist, clearly anti-Islamic.[92]

Bruce Bawer, with his characteristically sharp eye, notes:

> [R]anged against [the editors of the *Jyllands-Posten* and the Danish prime minister] was virtually the entire international political establishment, including top United Nations and European Union brass—several of whom invoked the possibility

---

88 "OIC condemns publication of cartoons of Prophet Muhammad," *Islamic Republic News Agency*, February 5, 2006.
89 Statement of 11 Ambassadors. Bruce Bawer took special offense at that last line: *Surrender*, 43.
90 Klausen, *Cartoons*, Introduction.
91 Doudou Diène, "Report of the Special Rapporteur on contemporary forms of racism (E/CN.4/2006/17)," *UNCHR*, 13 February 2006.
92 Erik Bleich and Randall Hanson, "The Danish Cartoon Affair," *International Migration*, S. 44: 5 (2006): 3.

of taking official action against offensive speech. Just as the Dutch cultural elite had responded to van Gogh's murder by saying that he'd brought it on himself with his "vulgarity" and "insensitivity," so now *Jyllands-Posten* was blamed for getting itself in hot water by being—yes— vulgar and insensitive.[93]

Publishing and republishing the cartoons, according to EU Commissioner Peter Mandelson, "pours petrol on the flames."[94] BBC's Stephen Sackur asked Flemming Rose if he would "publish a picture of a Jewish rabbi dressed as Hitler in response to Jewish violence against Palestinians."[95] Ironically, not only was Sackur's analogy ridiculously wide of the mark (even Westergaard's cartoon came nowhere near such deliberate degradation), but his hypothetical cartoon regularly appears among Muslim cartoonists depicting Israel and the Jews as Nazis.

Explaining Muslim Ire: Liberal Cognitive Egocentrism in Overdrive

The BBC had no problem Westsplaining Muslim ire: "**It is the satirical intent of the cartoonists, and the association of the Prophet with terrorism, that is so offensive to the *vast majority* of Muslims.**"[96] And yet, nothing could be *less* clear. Muslims, observant and not, who appreciate the quiet religiosity of secular society did not take offense. They were more likely to read the "worst"— that is, the most offensive—cartoon the way its author, Kurt Westegaard, says he meant it:

> The general impression among [vocal] Muslims is that it is about Islam as a whole. It is not. It is about certain fundamentalist aspects that of course are not shared by everyone. But the fuel for the terrorists' acts stem from interpretations of Islam ... if parts of a religion develop in a totalitarian and aggressive direction, then I think you have to protest. We did so under the other "isms."

93 Bruce Bawer, *Surrender: Appeasing Islam, Sacrificing Freedom* (New York: Anchor, 2009), 44.
94 "UK Muslims voice Cartoons concern," BBC, February 2, 2006.
95 *Hardtalk*, Stephen Sackur with Flemming Rose and Ahmed abu Laban, BBC, February 8, 2006, https://www.youtube.com/watch?v=CKa66ryX830.
96 Abdelhadi, Magdi, "Cartoon row highlights deep divisions," BBC, 4 February 2006.

In other words, Westegaard targeted not Islam, but a violent form of triumphalist Islam with disturbing resemblance to the totalitarian movements of the twentieth century. For some Muslims to get upset at the criticism is perhaps understandable, but hardly justifiable, and certainly not when they conflate a legitimate criticism of one's radical fellow-religionists, with a critique of Islam ... unless, of course, this violent radical Islam *is indeed* Islam and you're looking for a fight. Who is doing the lumping here? Western critics like Westegaard? or Muslim critics like al-Qaradawi and those who appease his demands?

When someone on "the Muslim Street" says "There's one cartoon of the Prophet with a bomb on his head and this intimates that he is the root of terror, that Islam is terrorism, which is very insulting,"[97] is he insulted by the infidel who observes, or by the jihadis who are inspired by, the connection of Islam with terror? If jihadis see Muhammad specifically as the inspiration for their terrorism (which they do), and if the "Muslim Street" is more insulted by infidels allegedly making that connection, than by jihadis openly acting on it, whence this objection to Westergaard's drawing? It is not, as the dupes would have it, an insult to Islam, but rather, as the demopaths would admit privately, an accurate—and therefore unwelcome—revelation to Westerners of Caliphator intentions in the West.

Christopher Hitchens noted in characteristic accuracy and disgust:

> [N]obody in authority can be found to state the obvious and the necessary—that we stand with the Danes against this defamation and blackmail and sabotage. Instead, all compassion and concern is apparently to be expended upon those who lit the powder trail, and who yell and scream for joy as the embassies of democracies are put to the torch in the capital cities of miserable, flyblown dictatorships. Let's be sure we haven't hurt the vandals' feelings.[98]

And indeed so it was. What the Westsplainers perceived as a wrong done to (the "vast majority" of "moderate") Muslims and to Islam (the religion of Peace), was in fact a massive aggression of triumphalist Muslims against democratic and liberal principles and practices. They picked the fight (much like at Sharon's visit

---

97 Andrew Alderson, Nina Goswami, James Orr and Chris Hastings, "Unchallenged, a man poses as a suicide bomber," *Telegraph*, February 6, 2006.

98 Christopher Hitchens, "Stand up for Denmark! Why are we not defending our ally?" *Slate*, February 21, 2006; also *WSJ* editorial, "Clash of Civilization: The dictators behind those Muslim cartoon protests," February 11, 2006.

to Haram al Sharif), put together a Molotov cocktail of fake lethal narratives, war propaganda, and deliberate misinterpretation to whip up the Muslim Street (much like the Al Durah footage), and threatened infidels with death for offending them. They were not the victims here, but the belligerents and yet they managed to force the West, by leading with their glass jaw of ready and deep offense taken, to back down. Triumphalist demopaths accused the West of victimizing Muslims, and Western dupes beat their breasts in atonement. The marriage of premodern sadism and postmodern masochism renewed its vows.

The official Western explanation about why Muslims around the world were so angry is that they were deeply offended by the blasphemy (just as the French rioters were angry at not being allowed to become French, and the Palestinians angry at not being allowed independence). Our journalists did not tell us that the raging Muslims had been fed blasphemous war propaganda by radical imams determined to create a war between the West and Muslims. Nor did they note that apologizing for the offense actually empowered those Caliphators. On the contrary, the good people, like those at the UN, blamed Islamophobia for the war.

Put bluntly: "the proper response to triumphalist Muslim aggression is for Westerners to crack down on their negative feelings about Islam and Muslims. Don't p*ss us off."

Note the great irony here. The media is not telling us what the radical imams were really thinking, namely that "this is war and we're duping the infidel into submitting to Sharia law (no images, no criticism) even in Dar al Harb," but rather, they told us what these very imams wanted us to think, "that they're deeply hurt by the blasphemy [which they exploited]." We have here a case of Western journalism engaged in pure own-goal war journalism: they are the delivery system for propagating enemy demopathic lethal narratives—here, "Westerners hate Islam, and we Muslims justifiably hate Westerners for it"—specifically designed for our consumption and destruction.

By February 2006, the crisis had reached the level of a global struggle. The gauntlet was thrown, and the reactions publicly available. Either, stand with the Danes for freedom and publish the cartoons, or submit to the angry Muslim Street (and the jihadis who drive them to frenzies) and don't publish. The final totals make it clear who won. Of the couple of hundred newspapers that republished, very few were major publications which, as we have seen, felt particularly vulnerable to threats against their far-flung staff.[99] The "vast majority"

---

99 On not calling terrorism "terrorism," see above, pp29–35, 88–92.

fell silent.[100] American publications, backed by administration officials and the State Department, with troops in two Muslim countries, were especially notable for the lack of support they gave the Europeans, insisting on their desire to avoid giving "gratuitous" offense.[101] And of course, four years later, Yale University Press decided not to publish the cartoons in Klausen's book, lest they endanger their employees. Echoing Steven Sackur, they noted that anyone can view them online, anyway.

Victim Studies: Islamophobia Versus Antisemitism

The key to the Western capitulation was in identifying the Muslims as the victims. By accepting the astonishingly stupid idea that "these were racist, Islamophobic images, and deeply offended Muslim sensibilities," when these same Muslim sensibilities were shaped and developed in a far more ferocious public sphere where vicious hate-mongering operated at incomparably higher levels,[102] Westerners allowed the imams to frame the narrative. Muslim victimhood vs Western guilt. David vs Goliath.

Klausen, for example, unhesitatingly compared the most critical cartoons to antisemitic ones:

> Incomprehension and ignorance about Muslim feelings with respect to the Prophet aside, the editors also failed to notice that *several of the cartoons were malignant representations of stereotypes in the manner of European antisemitism.*

In so doing, she echoed Bill Clinton in Doha, who called the cartoons "appalling" and "completely outrageous," and compared them to European antisemitism before the Holocaust.[103] As recently as 2020, the *New York Times*'s former Paris correspondent, Adam Nossiter, then posted in Kabul, in the course of a broadcast on *France Culture* on Nov. 24, 2020, stated that "the caricatures of the Prophet

---

100 "List of Newspapers that reprinted *Jyllands-Posten*'s Muhammad Cartoons," *Wikipedia*.

101 Joel Brinkley and Ian Fischer, "US says it also finds Muhammad Cartoons Offensive," *New York Times*, February 4, 2006.

102 Kopek, *Cartoons and Extremism*.

103 "Clinton warns of rising anti-Islamic feeling," *AFP*, January 30, 2006. NB: facile comparisons to antisemitism.

Muhammad published in *Charlie Hebdo* reminded him of the exhibition titled "The Jew in France" held in Paris in 1941–42 under the German occupation."[104]

This is just absurd. What sane observer can compare the Danish cartoons (not the fakes) to the malignant stereotypes of European antisemitism, or, for that matter, *Muslim* antisemitic stereotypes.

FIGURE 14. The US and Israel eating from two sides of "the Arab states." *Al-Watan* (Qatar), May 13, 2003.

FIGURE 15. Borrowing (and updating) of *Protocols*-inspired twentieth-century antisemitic cartoons. (Algerian American cartoonist Bendib).

---

104 Cited by Pascal Bruckner, "France's Sins and Yours," *Tablet*, January 5, 2021.

It is hard to imagine what Klausen—and many others—felt was the kinship between these two worlds of cartooning. The only plausible explanation is that she imagined Muslims so insecure, so touchy, so violent, that *anything* that would bother them would *seem to them* as awful as the antisemitic ones *might* make Jews feel, and that by adopting that point of view, she had successfully "understood" the problem. In other words, she had taken a major step towards adopting the Da'wa narrative.[105]

In support of that narrative, Klausen then discussed Muslim comparisons to the Dreyfus affair, an early and famous case of modern antisemitism, where a French Jewish colonel was framed for treason by his superiors and sent to prison on Devil's Island. When the hoax came to light as the result of exceptional displays of investigative integrity, major cultural forces rallied against recognizing his innocence, lest the two pillars of society, the Army and the Church, suffer a crippling loss of honor. Only at the end of a two decades-long ordeal, in which the word "intellectual" was coined to describe someone capable of changing one's mind based on the empirical evidence, was Dreyfus "cleared and . . . his rank restored."

> Analogously, Muslims argued that the cartoons revealed the presence of entrenched Islamophobic sentiments in European societies (not just Denmark) and called for a wider recognition that antisemitism and Islamophobia are similar expressions of religious hate. It is conceivable that the "cartoon affair" may one day end with some symbolic act of restitution to Muslims and a new recognition of religious pluralism in European states.[106]

It is hard to understate the bizarre nature of this analogy: no false Western Islamophobic accusation of a Muslim crime of treason, no court handing down a harsh, unjust sentence, no investigative journalism to clear the falsely accused. On the contrary, the analogy is, if at all relevant, the opposite. European Muslims trump up charges, based on fakes, to accuse a Western newspaper of blaspheming the Prophet and the honor of Islam, and journalists prove loathe to investigate, while pundits excoriate the hate-mongering West.

But instead of critiquing the Muslim analogy, Klausen adopts it, and, in her own voice, supports an apology to the *false* accusers, as part of a therapeutic resolution: as if Dreyfus and the Jews should have apologized to the Church and to the army for tarnishing their institutional honor. The real Dreyfus affair here

---

105 She later attacked Ayaan Hirsi Ali as an "Islamophobe," below 421–24.
106 Klausen. *Cartoons That Shook the World*, 5.

would have been for Muslims to enter the modern world, as did intellectuals and French justice, by valuing truth and self-criticism over false claims and honor, acknowledging that their own blasphemous imams had unjustly accused non-Muslims of blasphemy, and apologizing. *Whoever is right, my side or not.* Indeed, belatedly, but extensively, Akkari repented and apologized.[107]

By presenting the analogy as she does, Klausen replicates the replacement narrative, whereby Muslims in the twenty-first century are the victims of the same European prejudices as Jews had suffered in the twentieth. Indeed, this was one of the Muslim's major arguments during the controversy, supported by Westerners like Roland Boer:

> In fact, some have pointed out that the rising tide of Islamophobia, where it is acceptable to publish and proclaim material that denigrates Muslims, where one can say and do things against Muslims purely because of their religious beliefs and ethnic background, is comparable to the rise of antisemitism in nineteenth and twentieth-century Europe.[108]

And presumably, it also sees Muslims as the victims of the same regressive forces that targeted Dreyfus, the same fascist willingness to sacrifice innocent scapegoats for the sake of collective cohesion and protection. In fact these coercive forces of "honor" in nineteenth-century France can be found most amply among the main aggressors in this affair, the imams and the audience of triumphalist Muslims they so successfully enraged.[109]

Jihad Triumphant in the Western Public Sphere

The peak moment for this wave of triumphalist spirit came in London, outside the Danish embassy on February 6, 2006. Here gathered the most shockingly

---

107 "Ahmad Akkari, Danish Muslim: I was wrong to damn Muhammad cartoons," *Guardian*, August 9, 2013.

108 Roland Boer, "On Free Speech: Some Reflections on Religion, Politics and Twelve [sic] Cartoons," January 17, 2008. For a more recent example of this equation, see the Mayor of Paris and presidential candidate Anne Hidalgo in December 2021: https://www.youtube.com/watch?v=_bnlpQaEsCQ.

109 "The whole culture was moulded by the continual emphasis upon the spectacular, and by the pride of the male ethos," Gregory Starrett, "Cartoon Violence and a Clash of Civilization," *Anthropology News*, March 2006. Cf. Robert Nye, *Masculinity and Male Codes of Honor in Modern France* (Los Angeles: University of California Press, 1998).

public display of jihadi animosity to the infidel nations yet. A crowd of every Brit's worst nightmare came out to demonstrate. Their signs—written by one source, possibly Anjem Choudhaury—all spoke with one voice: unbounded hatred of the kuffār, and unlimited violence in expiating that hatred.

FIGURE 16. Demonstration outside Danish Embassy, London, February 6, 2006.

Only months after 7–7, a man stood wearing a mock suicide belt.[110] Not only did the police not arrest him, but they prevented observers from photographing him. The rally took place in the full protection of a free Western public sphere.[111] A jihadi led the crowd in frenzied, shame-honor, triumphalism:

> Usama and Zawahiri are men.
> They will bomb you and Allah will be with them.
> We will take revenge on you.
> May they bomb Denmark so we can invade their country.
> And take their wives as war booty.[112]

---

110 This happened the following day in a follow-up demonstration (above, n97).

111 Phillips, *Londonistan*, 243–45.

112 "Violent Muslim Protest Outside the Danish Embassy in London," February 3, 2006, YouTube, https://www.youtube.com/watch?v=qoMeUcC_M20.

When I first heard this line about Danish women as war booty, I thought, "What a crazy (and terrible) fantasy world they live in. How medieval." Little did I realize that the rape jihad, already launched in the 1990s, was in full swing in England (e.g., Rotherham) and elsewhere, unopposed by Western authorities, unreported by Western journalists, who all feared accusations of Islamophobia.[113] Thus did Westerners turn a blind eye to the sexual enslavement of their own daughters.

What triumphalist Muslim wouldn't feel bullish that day in front of the Danish Embassy in London? They had paralyzed the West. Under the protection of an infidel police force that prevented other infidels from taking pictures of the outrageous events, they shouted their desires from the rooftops, and, at most, got a slap on the wrist.

There were people who understood what was at stake. One striking example had twelve major public intellectuals (seven born Muslims), all sounding an alarm in a civilizational war against Islamic totalitarianism on March 1, 2006:

> **MANIFESTO: Together facing the new totalitarianism**
> After having overcome fascism, Nazism, and Stalinism, the world now faces a new totalitarian global threat: Islamism. We, writers, journalists, intellectuals, call for resistance to religious totalitarianism and for the promotion of freedom, equal opportunity and secular values for all. The recent events, which occurred after the publication of drawings of Muhammed in European newspapers, have revealed the necessity of the struggle for these universal values. This struggle will not be won by arms, but in the ideological field. It is not a clash of civilizations nor an antagonism of West and East that we are witnessing, but a global struggle that confronts democrats and theocrats. Like all totalitarianisms, Islamism is nurtured by fears and frustrations. The hate preachers bet on these feelings in order to form battalions destined to impose a liberticidal and inegalitarian world. But we clearly and firmly state: nothing, not even despair, justifies the choice of obscurantism, totalitarianism and hatred.[114]
> Islamism is a reactionary ideology which kills equality, freedom

---

113 Peter McLoughlin, *Easy Meat: Inside Britain's Grooming Gang Scandal* (London: New English Review Press, 2016).

114 Note that the Europeans were at this point swimming against the currents they had so enthusiastically cheered on in 2002 by celebrating Palestinian jihadis' "acts of despair."

and secularism wherever it is present. Its success can only lead to a world of domination: man's domination of woman, the Islamists' domination of all the others. To counter this, we must assure universal rights to oppressed or discriminated people. We reject "cultural relativism," which consists in accepting that men and women of Muslim culture should be deprived of the right to equality, freedom and secular values in the name of respect for cultures and traditions. We refuse to renounce our critical spirit out of fear of being accused of "Islamophobia," an unfortunate concept which confuses criticism of Islam as a religion with stigmatization of its believers. We plead for the universality of freedom of expression, so that a critical spirit may be exercised on all continents, against all abuses and all dogmas. We appeal to democrats and free spirits of all countries that our century should be one of Enlightenment, not of obscurantism.

Ayaan Hirsi Ali, Chahla Chafiq, Caroline Fourest, Bernard-Henri Lévy, Irshad Manji, Mehdi Mozaffari, Maryam Namazie, Taslima Nasreen, Salman Rushdie, Antoine Sfeir, Philippe Val, Ibn Warraq.[115]

One gets the sense that the composers were well aware of Bat Ye'or's *Eurabia*, although they use here a secular language more appropriate to the twentieth century. They do not speak of jihad or Caliphate or dhimmi, and explicitly distance themselves from a "clash of civilizations," even as they fight it ... with the conceptual weapons of the last war against totalitarianism in the mid-twentieth century. And their protest failed to carry the day. Moral indignation ceded to "respectful" appeasement.

The Jihadi Cogwar View of the Danish Cartoon Controversy

When one views the controversy from the perspective of the Caliphator cogwar—Da'wa—this is a brilliant campaign, planned and carried out in order to extend the reach of the law of capital punishment for blasphemy into Dar al Harb, without even having to invade. In this sense, the Muslim demands around

---

115 "The Manifesto of 12: Together facing the new totalitarianism," March 6, 2006

the cartoons took their resounding victory of 1989 with Salman Rushdie, to new heights.[116] Bernard Lewis noted:

> The big difference between our case and the Rushdie affair is that Rushdie is perceived as an apostate by the Muslims while, in our case, Muslims were insisting on applying Islamic law to what non-Muslims are doing in non-Muslim countries ... a unique case that might indicate that Europe is perceived as some kind of intermediate state between the Muslim world and the non-Muslim world.[117]

Indeed, as noted above, non-Caliphator Muslims found the "Muslim" claims quite extraordinary. Why would sharia apply to infidels? What Muslims impose upon each other in Dar al Islam, is one thing. But the idea that Muslims should impose Sharia on infidels outside of Dar al Islam? To those Muslims who think the whole world should be subject to sharia, the answer is obvious.

The moderate position, the one that the imagined "vast majority of peaceful Muslims" would presumably embrace as people who want to enjoy the same religious freedoms as everyone else, would have denounced the incitement based on shameful fakes and dismissed the complaints as a misapplication of Sharia to non-Muslims. If this were the case, then, we would have had a remarkable inversion: some Muslim journalists and the vast majority of moderate Muslims in 2005 differing from the Caliphators, while most Western talking heads were busy repeating Muslim triumphalist claims. Londonistan writ large.

Of course, the triumphalist, still in his zero-sum world, sees this from a different angle. Imposing sharia on *Muslims* in the West—starting with the vaunted and denied Sharia Zones, reinforced by shame-murders targeting Muslim women who assimilate[118]—was only the first step towards the global Caliphate. For them, this was a war on both apostasy (i.e., Muslim dissent) and blasphemy (i.e., *kuffār* dissent). Terror, whether mass (Israel, 9-11, Barcelona, London) or individual (Theo van Gogh, Hitoshi Igarashi, Daniel Pearl, Luigi Padovese) was the weapon of intimidation. Westerners, in the minds of the triumphalists, were stupid not to understand that they did not have the right to

---

116 Daniel Pipes, *The Rushdie Affair: The Novel, the Ayatollah, and the West* (New York: Birch Lane, 1990).

117 Bernard Lewis in conversation with Flemming Rose, cited in "Naser Khader and Flemming Rose: Reflections on the Danish Cartoon Controversy," *Middle East Quarterly*, Fall 2007.

118 Unni Wikan, *Generous Betrayal Politics of Culture in the New Europe* (Chicago: The University of Chicago Press, 2002).

insult Islam. As Hlayhel, one of the drivers of the affair, put it: "When you see what happened in Holland [Theo van Gogh] and then still print the cartoons, that's quite stupid."[119] In other words, "Don't you *kuffār* get it yet? You cross us; we kill you." Here violence has clear and compelling meaning.

In this sense, Hlayhel's use of "stupid" is exactly the opposite of mine. For him, infidels who won't submit and behave like good dhimmi are stupid, whereas for me, infidels are stupid when they submit, thinking they are being considerate and generous. And our stupidity in being "smart" by their standards (i.e., appeasing their tantrums), reinforces their ambitions. As the French say, *l'appétit vient en mangeant* . . . how much the more true, when your ambitions are global and insatiable.

In the wake of the cartoon debacle, Bernard Lewis reaffirmed a dire prophecy he had already made two years earlier, to the major German paper, *Die Welt*: if current trends continue, Europe will be Islamic. Noting the new levels of aggression, he acknowledged the growing power, visible in the handling of the cartoon affair of an Islamicization of Europe trumping a Europeanization of Islam. And not just Europe was vulnerable, but, although somewhat less, the USA as well.[120]

Rather than call out the radicals for their blasphemous manipulation of pious Muslims, the West placated these very manipulators, allowing them to stage their moral emergency.[121] Rather than point out with sobriety and dignity that this prohibition is only incumbent on *some* Muslims, indeed bearing the clear signs of the most radical interpretations of Islam that the vast majority of moderates do not share, that cartoons about infidels in Muslim papers can be shockingly brutal, and above all, that by far the most blasphemous cartoons had been made and circulated by the Imams themselves! . . . instead of appealing to the "vast majority" of moderate, peace-loving Muslims they assured us were out there, with arguments designed to win them over to civic maturity, Western "moral" leaders hastened to appease the troublemakers' wrath.

As a result, the jihadi cogwarriors illustrated the claim of Muslim Brotherhood, global media star, Yussuf al Qaradawi made a decade earlier: "Europe and the USA will be conquered not by Jihad but by Da'wa." Actually, it was a combination: the winning one-two punch of jihadi terrorists striking fear

---

119 Paul Marshall and Nina Shea, *Silenced: How Apostasy and Blasphemy Codes Are Choking Freedom Worldwide* (New York: Oxford University Press, 2011), 186. NB: one of the jihadis leading the rally in London also invoked this principle, see n112.

120 Bernard Lewis, "Europa wird islamisch," *Die Welt*, April 19, 2006.

121 See Ashley Thorne, "Staged Emergencies," and the deployment of these techniques in the Pessin affair, *Salem on the Thames*, chapter 4.

in the hearts of the infidel, and Da'is pointing out to these terrified people just what proper behavior would avoid violent retribution. In this case, the required behavior was: "Don't publish the cartoons."

Like all triumphalist struggles, this was about honor in dominion and shame in submission. Triumphalist Muslims picked the fight by crying out in pain and rage at their wounded honor. Their prophet, *they claimed*, had been slandered and humiliated. They responded, as do all who want to protect their honor, with violence. In this they played the shame-honor script, but not honestly, for their outrage was deliberately manufactured, ginned up with propaganda—indeed with fake news. After the Muhammad as pig cartoon passed for an infidel production, what self-respecting Muslim would not find the whole affair deeply insulting.

Certainly, for the Caliphators, the stakes went well beyond the sentimental notion of "denigration." For them, this was a *kuffār* effort to resist their own dhimmification. The apology they wanted was not to assuage their allegedly hurt feelings, but as a sign of submission to restore their honor. For them, the decision not to publish was not a sign of Westerners' "consideration for Muslim feelings." On the contrary, it was a singular act of dhimmitude. It was a classic playing out of the Arab honor challenge: "exploiting possibilities . . . deftly and expeditiously to convert shame into honor on their own account, and vice versa for their opponents."[122]

International organizations—UN Bodies, human rights NGOs, public intellectuals and figures of stature—almost universally criticized the cartoons' *Islamophobic derision of Muslims and their faith.*[123] The story well illustrates how Huntington's clash of civilizations became internalized on both sides, leading to a victory of the jihadis on the Muslim side and of the preemptive dhimmi on the Western side. While Caliphators, using forged propaganda, declared war on Western civilization's principles of freedom of speech and dissent, the West took the strategic decision to avoid any confrontation that might make it even look like a clash of civilizations. Reynolds explained,

> The last thing these governments want is another confrontation in which Islam is seen to be pitted against the West. The strategy, therefore, is to try to prevent this from becoming a "clash of civilizations."[124]

---

122 David Pryce-Jones, *The Closed Circle: An Interpretation of the Arabs* (Chicago: Ivan R. Dee, 2009), 41.

123 Klausen. *Cartoons*, 41.

124 Reynolds, "A Clash of Rights."

As if it were not already, as if this decision did not mark the Caliphator cogwar victory of convincing the stronger side not to fight back. Fake news won again, and the Caliphators got to wage war on the West, while the West, in an effort to deny that war, waged war against themselves and surrendered massive cultural capital to Caliphator demands.

Thus, figures like Western progressive Javier Solana and the Muslim OIC Secretary General Ekmeleddin Ihsanoglu agreed fully on reproving the Danish newspaper and assuaging the feelings of Muslims the world over who had been outraged and insulted by these [sic] drawings. For both men, the goals were a Western apology and promise not to do it again on the one hand, and, on the other, an end to the growing violence by the angry Muslim Street, which had already taken more than 200 (mostly Muslim) lives the world over. The jihadis, claimed victim status for the "vast majority of Muslims everywhere," and the West concurred.

Klausen replicates the approach, assuming that the appropriate move was then, and presumably still is, to self-denigrate, to apologize. To do so showed consideration and would make friends. She did not consider the massive overlap between their generous behavior and a less glorious surrender to triumphalist Muslim demands. Thus, when someone like Ibn Warraq wrote

> Unless, we show some solidarity, unashamed, noisy, public solidarity with the Danish cartoonists, then the forces that are trying to impose on the Free West a totalitarian ideology will have won; the Islamization of Europe will have begun in earnest. Do not apologize.[125]

... all the appeasers could do was cringe at the thought that "Muslims read the newspapers' decision to reprint the by-now-ubiquitous cartoons as a coordinated campaign of denigration."[126] It was a classic case of crossed wires: thinking they were being considerate of moderate Muslims, their apologies encouraged Caliphators.

Klausen is quick to see Muslims favorably. When some of the key Muslim players in the cartoon crisis expressed regrets to Klausen about things "getting out of hand" (like the London demonstrations) she accepted them as sincere (and hence reassuring). But from the Caliphate perspective, it is supposed to work that way: violence engenders compliance, compliance makes the

---

125 Ibn Warraq, "Cartoon Democracy," *WritersRep.*, February 4, 2006.
126 Klausen, *Cartoons*, 48.

demopathic work of the Da'i Caliphators—tell the infidel how to behave—all the easier. When you can threaten the West with Muslims roaring like lions on the global street, then the Muslim Street gets to *designate what is blasphemy.* When dealing with infidels like a Danish professor at a Jewish university, the Caliphator demopath will gladly express regrets to his dupe and expect her to repeat them earnestly.

Similarly, Klausen sympathizes with those who took offense, and is quick to absolve key radicals of any intention to provoke violence. After describing how Qaradawi had issued a fatwa and called for a day of rage, the omniscient narrator explains: "His anger was genuine, but he hardly intended the consequences."[127] She tries hard to distinguish between violent and nonviolent Muslims, generally considering the latter "moderates." She warns her readers that just because someone is a Salafi, that does not make him an enemy of the West, a jihadi.

> Today many Salafists regard the Saudi kingdom with skepticism or worse and regard politics and power as sources of corruption. Opposition takes two routes: one that recognizes a distinction between sacred and secular power in the current age and advocates that Muslims focus on living righteous lives and observe the laws of the countries where they reside, and another revolutionary opposition that aims to re-create a new and pious caliphate and considers, in the manner of the Taliban and Al-Qaeda, democracy as forbidden for Muslims because it substitutes man-made laws for God's laws.[128]

After this hopeful description of how even the most radical and zealous of Muslims can be good citizens, Klausen then asserts categorically:

> Like the Salafists, the jihadists seek to restore Islam to a state of purity. But *there the similarities end.* The jihadis advocate the use of violence to bring about the Islamic state and claim it is an obligation to wage jihad against Christians, apostates, and the sitting Islamic governments.[129]

---

127 Ibid., 41.
128 Ibid., 85–88.
129 Ibid., 85.

For her, like for Hillary Clinton and the US Intelligence community in the early (heady) days of the "**Arab Spring**" describing the Muslim Brotherhood as a "moderate" and "largely secular organization,"[130] Klausen here took nonviolence as the litmus test of moderation: as long as they are not terrorists, they are moderates who understand and accept a secular government. Thus, she believes, and wants us to believe, that the *vast majority of Muslims are moderate*, including many Salafis. But actually, her analysis errs. Here the similarities do not end; on the contrary, the *only* dissimilarity is in the matter of using violence *for the moment*. All the rest is Caliphator territory.[131]

And that apocalyptic reality is considerably more fluid and dynamic than Klausen's model of good citizenship, which only holds as long as nothing can be done about our "current secular age." Most triumphalist Muslims in 2000, especially in the West, recognized their inferiority and, no matter how much they resented it, accepted a passive stance. As James Scott would put it, they kept their "transcript" hidden. As they have become true believers in the Caliphator vision that the "current age" is passing away, indeed that they can effectively contribute to that process of passing away, the more apocalyptic calls to violence grow stronger. And neither Klausen nor any of her academic friends, do anything to stop that process. On the contrary, the more foolish they are, the more they throw sand in the eyes of their readers, then the more attractive to Muslims becomes the very option she tacitly denies. *If I were a Muslim, I'd take the stupidity of Westerners as a sign from Allah . . .*

The Cartoon War was a great atavistic call to Muslim triumphalists, to supersessionist dominion. "Islam will dominate the world," may be the message of the extremists so prominently displayed in London, but it appeals to all Muslims who believe that the millennial goal of world dominion is the true destiny of their faith. The question, really, is when will it happen? The Danish imams who drove it hardest—Akkari and Hlayhel—were hard-core triumphalists. They wanted Islam to rule Europe, and they chose the "relatively"

---

130 James Clapper, "Testimony before House Intelligence Committee," *CSPAN*, (February 10, 2011). https://www.youtube.com/watch?v=POwd44zH9GA; A. Mohammed, "U.S. shifts to closer contact with Egypt Islamists," *Reuters*, June 30, 2011. Clapper also signed on to the (inaccurate) dismissal of the Hunter Biden laptop as Russian disinformation: Nolan Finley, "Hunter Biden's laptop finally gets some attention," *Boston Herald*, March 24, 2022.

131 Raymond Ibrahim's discussion of Sheikh Yassir al-Burhami, an Egyptian Salafi: "How Circumstance Dictates Islamic Behavior: Preach Peace when Weak, Wage War when Strong," *Middle East Forum*, January 8, 2012. See further discussion, chapter 6.

nonviolent, demopathic form of exploiting Western democratic values to advance that end.[132]

During Danoongate, however, Caliphator radio stations and mosques pumped out the new hatred to their European Muslim audiences: Jews were "sons of pigs and monkeys," "killers of innocent children," evil to be "exterminated."[133] When Swedish Jews complained about the teachings of the Stockholm Grand mosque at this time, the Swedish Chancellor of Justice, Goran Lambertz, ruled that these forms of speech should be judged differently and allowed "**because they are used by one side in a continuing profound conflict, where battle cries and invectives are part of everyday occurrences in the rhetoric that surround the conflict.**" Hence, it did *not* qualify as "incitement against an ethnic group according to Swedish law."[134] Result: the investigation into a jihadi Caliphator operation in the heart of Sweden's capital, got canceled. So rather than note the connection between this delirious Jew-hatred on the one hand, and both jihad and the exaltation of suicide bombing on the other, the Swedes gave Caliphators a green light to attack Jews at the very moment that they were being attacked with these same hatreds.[135]

The Muslims around the world, incensed by fake news, and starting with the OIC ambassadors, then Qaradawi and the preachers, finally climaxing in mob violence on the global Muslim Street, all expressed their hatred of the West. That it became more violent as it passed from diplomatic circles to TV appeals, to the mobs, hardly diminishes the common link. "Westerners must obey the rules of sharia, starting with the criminalization of blasphemy as defined by Muslims." And, in Sweden for example, Western authorities behaved just as their triumphalist foes wanted.

In their own eyes, global progressives, information professionals, ministers of justice, stood on the moral heights of generosity and good will towards

---

132 "Akkari was secretly filmed by a French TV crew suggesting to the delegation's head, Sheikh Raed Hlayhel, that Naser Khader—a moderate, integrationist Muslim and member of the Danish parliament—be bombed." Randall Hanson, "The Danish Cartoon Controversy: A Defense of Liberal Freedom," *European Union Studies Association*, 19:2, Spring 2006.

133 Known as the "Yassin Tapes," after Hamas ideologue Ahmed Yassin: Inti Chavez Perez and Nedjma Boucheloukh, "Moské säljer judefientligt material," *Ekot*, November 27, 2005. For the theme of Jews as descended from pigs and apes, see Neil Kressel, *"The Sons of Apes and Pigs": Muslim Antisemitism and the Conspiracy of Silence* (Washington, DC: Potomac Books, 2012).

134 Raphael Israeli, *The Islamic Challenge to Europe* (New York: Transaction, 2008), 163–66 (with translation of Lambertz decision); Landes, "If it's Anti-Israel, It's not Racism," *Augean Stables*, April 5, 2006.

135 Over a decade later, the problem continues to eat away at the public sphere: Judith Bergman, "Sweden: Hate Speech Just for Imams," *Gatestone*, February 22, 2017.

all—except, of course, those Jews the triumphalists hate, and those Westerners who "enrage" the Muslims with their criticism. From the triumphalist Muslim perspective, these progressives were cowardly fools who sided with their enemies and turned on their friends ... in other words, highly useful infidels. "The more Scandinavians apologize and show a smiling face, the more they are considered as powerless, spineless and ripe for capture and subjugation."[136]

The pattern of appeasement, the prime directive of the aughts—"don't piss them off," was firmly established here. Western authorities may defend the right of the *Jyllands-Posten* to their (deplorable) behavior, but it's understood, it shouldn't happen again. Those who obeyed were good liberals and progressives; those who resisted—and thereby angered them—were right-wing warmongers. As Caliphators of all stripes like to insist: *the Islamophobes are the cause of the terror.*[137]

Of course, behind the elaborate deference that progressives showed to Muslim sensibilities lay the same ugly confluence of cowardice masquerading as high-mindedness and moral contempt for Muslims that fueled the determination not to use the "terrorism label."[138] This was classic "humanitarian racism" at work: Muslims were a force of nature. Frans Groenedeijk noted:

> Those who really believe that drawing cartoons that ridicule Mohammedan extremists is like using a lighter in a powder magazine, actively dismiss the people who consider themselves Muslims, including those in the West, as barrels of gunpowder and as extraordinarily primitive.[139]

Make moral demands on Muslims? On the Umma? On Muslim leaders? Only very gingerly ("sorry, but our rules do not permit us to shut down the newspapers that publish cartoons even if we wish we could ... hope you understand").

Westerners adopted a language in which Caliphator propaganda circulated avidly: *Islamophobia* is the cause of the violence, Western racism and hostility must be suppressed, blasphemy is inexcusably offensive. While Western liberals thought they were somehow distancing themselves from the racists among

---

136 Israeli, *Islamic Challenge*, 162.
137 Tariq Ali, *Rough Music: Blair, Bombs, Baghdad and London Terror* (London: Verso, 2005). For a more academic version, see Tarek Younis, "Counter-Radicalization: A Critical Look into a Racist New Industry," *Yaqeen Institute*, March 21, 2019.
138 See chapters 1, 2, and 9.
139 Frans Groenendijk, *Islamophobia, Defying the Battle Cry* (Self-Published, 2012), Kindle location 625.

them (invariably to be found on the "right"), the Da'wa narrative was a bit more openly prejudiced: "The *West* hates Islam, democracy seeks to destroy Islam, Muslims cannot trust infidels, and must fight any who slander the Prophet (Peace Be Upon Him). Islam's destiny is to dominate the world, and we will do so by demanding infidel submission—by Jihad or by Da'wa." So while Klausen asserts: "There is one point on which everybody agrees: none of the protagonists think they won,"[140] in reality, this aggressive paranoid Caliphator message was the great winner of Danoongate in the Muslim world and in the West. In the triumphalist Muslim narrative, *they* were a nation of lions (as they claim); and the Westerners were the jackasses. And so, the jackasses threw under the bus the very Muslims, like Naser Khader, who wanted to live in a secular state and those fellow liberals who wanted to protect the practice of noncoercive religion. Everyone, infidel and Muslim, who was sensible and mature lost. The rabble-rousing Caliphators and their Da'ī colleagues won . . . big.

The Next Staged Emergency: "We riot and kill because you call us violent."

And that victory became the starting point behind the next "staged emergency" of the mid-aughts, the controversy about Pope Benedict's "Regensburg Lecture" (September–October 2006), in which, *intra muros*, he cited a passage from a fourteenth-century Byzantine emperor, that Islam was inherently violent. Certainly, at the time that Michael Psellus made that observation, it was consistent with eight centuries of direct Christian experience with their Muslim neighbors. And yet, despite the fact that the pope brought up this quotation up *in order to disagree* with it, the global Muslim Street once again raged.[141]

All the cogwar strategies of Danoongate reappeared here, and all the self-defeating Western appeasement kicked in. As with the Cartoons, the "insult" was invented to stage the moral outrage (the Muslim world was told that the Pope had espoused these sentiments). It was a violent staged global moral emergency (panic?) that cut right along the moebius strip: on one side, the jihadis who agreed completely with the description of Islam as a warrior religion, and who

---

140 Klausen, *Cartoons*, p. 9.

141 "This address is one of the world's most penetrating analyses ever made of intelligence and the consequences of the willful refusal to face its truth. If really taken to heart, Regensburg at one point may have been the touchstone for a more truthful world—and still might be, a decade later," James Day, "Benedict the Brave: The Regensburg Address Ten Years Later," *Catholic World*, September 12, 2016.

seized upon the occasion to promise the Pope and the West the very violence to which the Pope had alluded; and on the other side, the Westerners, eager not to fuel a religious war. And joining the two strips, were the demopathic Da'īs who performed their outrage, who publicly took offense at a dishonest description they privately agreed with, and manipulated their infidel dupes into not saying what any honest Caliphator would tell you was true.

Both the violence and the verbal outrage were not directed at restoring respect in Western eyes after the pope had disrespected them. Rather, it targeted the West's ability to criticize Islam, it demanded compliance. Caliphators did not stage their emergency because what the pope said was a false, demeaning libel; they did so to stop Western infidels from even discussing the violent dimension of Islam. Call me a liar and I'll kill you, especially if I'm lying.[142]

The sweetness of this victory over the pope and his Western critics, was how deftly the Caliphators managed to turn a joke on themselves—Muslims riot to protest being called violent—to one on infidels. The pope mumbles an apology insisting he did not really apologize, and the West begs the Muslims to calm down. And Rabelais's laugh did not ring out in the streets of Europe. No, the winner was Umberto Eco's inquisitor, who wanted to murder laughter.

2005: Mid-aughts. Caliphators, the very strong horse; Western progressives, the (unconscious) grooms; Western democrats, liberals, genuine progressives, in deep disarray. When those violently wielding power laugh, and those they bully bite their tongues, it is a dark day for freedom.

---

142 See above, n80.

Astounding Stupidities Included in This Chapter

1. *Why Europe Will Run the Twenty-First Century*, by Mark Leonard, 2005.

2. *The United States of Europe: The New Superpower and the End of American Supremacy*, by T. R. Reid.

3. *[S]everal of the Muhammad cartoons were malignant representations of stereotypes in the manner of European antisemitism.* Jytte Klausen, *Cartoons.*

4. *These riots have nothing to do with Islam.* French director of Intelligence, 2005.

5. *Islamophobia is the new antisemitism.*

6. *It is conceivable that the "cartoon affair" may one day end with some symbolic act of restitution to Muslims and a new recognition of religious pluralism in European states.* Klausen, *Cartoons.*

7. **Islamic genocidal hate speech is not covered by hate speech laws,** *"because they are used by one side in a continuing profound conflict, where battle cries and invectives are part of everyday occurrences in the rhetoric that surround the conflict."* Swedish Chancellor of Justice, Goran Lambertz, 200

Part Two

KEY PLAYERS

The previous section examined patterns of behavior that "took" in the early twenty-first century (third millennium for medievalists), patterns that empowered a medieval millennial movement and paralyzed the modern and postmodern West. In this section, I survey the key players in this theater of war, some witting, some unwitting. The **first two chapters** examine the key players among the attackers: "men of honor" and "Caliphators." **Chapter 7** focuses on the core of Western modernity, "liberals" and their fatal tendency to imagine that everyone shares their (actually quite rare) attitudes towards humanity. **Chapter 8** considers a radical variant on liberalism, the postmodern, postcolonial, woke progressive left, with their soft power millennialism. **Chapter 9** analyzes lethal journalists and their news agencies, who report the war propaganda of one side as "news" in what they think is a far-away war, without realizing that they're actually engaged in "own-goal war journalism"—reporting the war propaganda of their own society's enemy as news. Finally, **chapter 10** probes the unique phenomenon of Jews against themselves (JATs), anti-Zionist Jews who, imagining themselves paragons of virtue, ally with their own people's most remorseless enemies.

5. **The Premodern Mindset–Zero-Sum Honor**
Solidarity—
salvific limbic prison.
Blood—bleach of shamed soul.

6. **Caliphators: A Fifteenth-Century Millennial Movement**
I'm right about God.
So, I must rule, lest others
dare question my truth.

7. **Liberal Cognitive Egocentrics and Their Demopathic Kryptonite**
Imagining our
values universal, we
can't see just how rare.

8. **The Global Progressive Left (GPL) in the Twenty-First Century**
My side always right?
No! I embrace the "other"
Their side can't be wrong!

9. **Compliant, Lethal, Own-Goal War Journalism: The Bane of the West in the Twenty-First Century**
Running Jihadi
war propaganda as news . . .
How could that go wrong?

10. **Anti-Zionist Jews: The Pathologies of Self-Criticism**
Have ever before
lambs denounced lambs who refuse
to lie with lions?
An antisemite is one who takes seriously a tenth of the
jokes Jews tell about themselves.
An antizionist is one who takes seriously a tenth of the
criticism Jews tell about Israel.

5

The Premodern Mindset—
Zero-Sum Honor

Solidarity—
salvific limbic prison.
Blood—bleach of shamed soul.[1]

The Premodern Mindset—Zero-Sum Honor

Perhaps the most difficult thing for Westerners, raised in a positive-sum culture (especially since the 60s), to understand, are the dynamics of cultures that embrace zero-sum values. I begin with two "stories" that illustrate the two worlds. Over the course of the next four chapters, I'll outline how these two worlds operate and interact in the twenty-first century: the first two chapters, on Zero-Sum; the next two, on Positive-Sum. Although zero-sum and positive-sum are terms developed by mathematicians, and often appear in mathematical discussions that emphasize the rational-irrational dichotomy, both attitudes reflect some fundamental emotional stances that can neither be quantified nor located on a continuum between rational and irrational since, in their "home" environments, they make sense. In order to illustrate these intangible but very powerful tendencies, I offer two stories: a joke and one of Chaucer's Tales.

---

1   This chapter, written as a separate article many years ago, has benefitted from conversations with Doyle Quiggle, who, among other things, first introduced me to the expression "blood, bleach of the soul." For a more ample and footnoted version of the discussion of shame-honor, see "Primary Honor Codes in Tribal and Aristocratic Cultures," in *Honor and Shame in Western History*, ed. Jörg Wettlaufer, David Nash, and Jan Hatlen (London: Routledge, 2022).

Zero-Sum: *The Peasant and the Genie*

A peasant plowing his fields turned up a lamp. As he rubbed off the dirt, a genie appeared, thanked him for liberating him, and offered him one wish, on the condition that his neighbor got twice what he asked for. After a brief consideration, the wily peasant said, "poke out one of my eyes."

For those trained in civil society's world of generosity, such an answer shocks. Why not wish for wealth? So what if the neighbor has more? The obvious positive-sum answer: everybody wins. But the peasant lives in a zero-sum world, divided into "us and hostile them," where the neighbor's gain is my loss, where the interpersonal model is what Eli Sagan called the "paranoid imperative"— *rule or be ruled*. If his neighbor gets double, that makes him twice as powerful, and our peasant is left with concerns for his future. In a zero-sum world, one cannot win without the other losing. Granting his neighbor twice his windfall considerably increases the likelihood that in this exchange, he will be the loser. Will the man's neighbor use his new-found power in acts of gratitude, or to diminish his weaker neighbor, and eventually subject him? The peasant's choice to sacrifice an eye affirms the safe position—suspect; do not count on good will.

Envy—the peasant's, his neighbor's—plays a key role. How can I enjoy my wealth when my neighbor has twice as much? How can I win unless he loses? How can I give my neighbor the satisfaction of looking down on me. Clearly, a positive-sum wish for this peasant was, both in terms of emotions and security—counter-indicated.

But there is more to this choice than mere acquiescence to a bleak world of zero- and negative-sum choices where almost everybody loses. Were it a chess move (the most purely zero-sum game of all), our lucky peasant gets "!!" For not only has he rendered his neighbor blind, but made himself king, according to the proverb. His self-mutilation has given him decisive power over his neighbor. An eyeball is a small price to pay for such a promotion. (The demotic position, accordingly, would argue that all earthly kingship is built on self-mutilation.)

(The modern version of this joke is the prospect of one's ex getting three times as much [here envy and desire to punish the other roar back into consideration]. "Give me a little heart-attack." My favorite, and it's connected to Chaucer's "The Wife of Bath's Tale" (below), is: "give me one good wife.")

Positive-Sum: *"The Wife of Bath's Tale": What Do Women Want Most?*

After giving her remarkably lively and self-aware introduction to herself, Chaucer's pilgrim, the Wife of Bath, proceeds to tell a tale about a young knight who raped a maiden (we are not told her rank) and the king condemns him to death.[2] The Queen intervenes and asks that the youth be judged by her "court of love." Given jurisdiction, the Queen sentences the man to a quest: a year and a day to return to the court and accurately answer the question: "what do women want most?" If he fails, the king's judgment will be administered.

At the end of a long year in which he got many unconvincing responses, he heads home to execution. At the last river he must ford, however, he comes upon an old crone, who tells him she knows what he needs to know, and that she'll tell him, on one condition ... that if she's right and he lives, he will fulfill any wish of hers in his power to grant. He agrees, and when he appears at court, tells the queen that what women want most is "sovereignty." This answer finds instant favor with the court, and the knight is praised and welcomed.

At this point, the old crone makes her claim: "Marry me." Since her wish is clearly in his power to grant, he must agree. But then, what of the marriage bed? He curls up in a corner of the bed, unmanned. She says: "I'll give you a choice. I am actually a fairy and can change my shape. You may have me young and beautiful and spend the rest of your life worrying that you're being cuckolded, or ugly and loyal. Choose."

Note how the proffered choice is zero-sum: each choice has advantages and disadvantages, mutually exclusive wins and losses. But the knight applies his newly learned lesson about what women want and dissolves the mutual exclusion of zero-sum. He tells her that *she* can chose. And so she grants him both. On the positive-sum chessboard, this gets !!!.

This story has all the elements of a positive-sum orientation, from turning a harsh punishment into a test and potential learning experience, to granting the "other" freedom, to trusting reciprocity ... all the exact opposites of the zero-sum world. Generosity, renunciation of dominion, trusting and being trustworthy. Perhaps most critical to the story and to positive-sum interactions, is the centrality of voluntary behavior: the crone beauty is not forced or manipulated to grant the knight what he wants. On the contrary, he gives her sovereignty over her own life, and she exercises it as she will.

The spectacular win at the end of this tale, where everyone greatly benefits, reflects the exceptionally creative resolutions to what appear to be zero-sum choices that such levels of emotional generosity, vulnerability, and self-abnegation allow: in interpersonal relations, intimacy; in economic relations, prosperity; in political issues, freedom.

---

2 Geoffrey Chaucer, *Canterbury Tales*, 3.1, https://chaucer.fas.harvard.edu/pages/wife-baths-prologue-and-tale-0.

Navigating the Strait of Messina

The human condition, however, is constantly caught between the two options, the two orientations. Every culture, every society, every clan, every individual, navigates between this Scylla and Charybdis. No one (but a saint) can maintain these high levels of egolessness with everybody, all the time. And no matter how much we try, the appeal of the zero-sum, the thrill of "getting it all," the *Schadenfreude* of seeing someone *else* hurt, exert an enduring pull ... As one alpha kindergarten girl replied to her teacher when told she can't use the devastating line "you can't play" with her fellow students, "It will be fairer, but how are we going to have any fun?"[3]

So no human group, from state/institution to clans and associations will ever get rid of either of these polar approaches to human relations. It's all in the navigation. The focus of this chapter and the next is on cultures in which the zero-sum ethos dominates the thinking and feeling of key players, especially alpha males. This divides roughly into the socio-psychological dynamics of shame-honor, and the socio-political dynamics of prime divider societies.

Take, for example, the problem of the in-group and the out-group, us-them. In contemporary public discourse, thinking in terms of "us-them" constitutes unacceptable tribalism, xenophobia, and even racism. And yet, in earlier periods of human history, and for millennia longer than any modern cosmopolitan experiment, the basic structure of social reality (i.e., survival) revolved around a sharp dichotomy between us (band, clan, village, tribe), on whom we depend, and others (strangers), whom we, on principle, mistrust, oppose, even plunder, to survive.

In other words, what some of us today dismiss contemptuously as a *xenophobia*, has been the overriding and necessary *norm* for most of the 150 millennia of human experience: "moral tribalism."[4] Similarly, whereas today we consider anger management, conflict-aversion, and deference to women's concerns, praiseworthy, in a different environment, it was a matter of survival for societies to produce warriors, men who would police all insults to their or their clan's honor, lest the insulter get the idea he could add the injury of rustling livestock and women to an unpunished insult. All of this looks not only foreign to moderns, but morally objectionable.

---

3 Vivian Gussin Paley, *You Can't Say You Can't Play* (Cambridge MA: Harvard University Press, 1994).
4 Edward Banfield, *The Moral Basis of a Backward Society* (New York: Free Press, 1958); Joshua Greene, *Moral Tribes: Emotion, Reason, and the Gap Between Us and Them* (New York: Penguin, 2013).

In the fourteenth century CE (eighth AH), however, the North African social historian ibn Khaldun argued just the opposite: that this group solidarity—*asabiyya*—was the most important moral value that Allah gave to man.[5] Societies follow cycles from the desert to the town, from the egalitarian warriors with their tribal solidarity and Spartan life-style to "civilized" urban empire dwellers who share opulent space with outsiders and strangers and therefore lack the overriding commitment to kin and tribe necessary to survive over time. According to his reckoning, in four generations societies go from battle-hardened men with life and death commitments to each other, who successfully invade and conquer cities, to indulgent weaklings, incapable of defending themselves from the next invading wave of hungry, privation-disciplined, desert-dwellers.

Contemporary Westerners show every sign of Khaldun's later, decadent stages. But of course, secular Jeremiads on the imminent fall of the modern world have become a staple of the West at least since Gibbon (1776), and for reasons still uncertain, the West has continued to flourish. The West then, is not another iteration of ibn Khaldun's four generations, but rather a sustained, civilization-wide effort that has been building for at least the last millennium. That sustained and cumulative effort has mastered the more violent aspects of tribal warrior culture: its passion for public glory (*megalothymia*)—roaring like a lion—and its horror of public humiliation (*onēidophobia*)—looking like a jackass. Rather than reiterate us-them *asabiyya*, the progressive West has pursued a respect for the "other," and developed inclusive social bodies, that have made the rudiments of a sustained civil polity possible. In that space (until now largely created by constitutional democracies) and in an unprecedented manner, so many aspects of life—abundance, lack of violence, freedom of choice and speech—are available to so many.

It turns out to be quite difficult to institute such societies. The principle of "my side right or wrong," does not easily cede to "whoever is right, my side or not." It took a millennium for the West to reach the levels that it has (no matter how deficient one might consider those accomplishments so far). We should not then, as do many Westerners, assume that our modern civil polity is the domestic norm for human societies everywhere, even as we blame ourselves for not being sufficiently progressive and egalitarian. We use the term "senseless violence" as a tautology (all violence is ultimately senseless), whereas in

---

5   Ibn Khaldun, *The Muqaddimah: An Introduction to History* (Princeton: Princeton University Press, 1987).

other—historically, many—cultures, all violence, even the most seemingly gratuitous, is deeply meaningful.[6]

Violence, Honor, Justice

The man of honor owes overriding loyalty to his clan. If someone kills his kin, whether intentionally or not, he must retaliate in blood.[7] The earliest written Germanic law codes identify the wergild (man-money), the price of all the various groups within society—men, women, high-born, king's companion, warrior, commoner, slave, German, Roman. They do not replace, but provide an escape valve for the basic system: clan retributive justice, feud. For if the warrior upon whom the burden of vengeance falls, accepts blood-money (wergild) without first "giving his lance blood to drink," he brings everlasting shame upon himself and his clan.

This loss of honor has terrible consequences. For the warrior, it can be fatal: blood in the water to his fellow sharks. As the Arabic expression goes, *when the cow falls, the knives come out.* A man without honor is a sterile woman, contemptible, despised, useless. The Bedouin who has lost his honor only approaches the oasis last, after the women have washed off their menses.[8] He cannot speak in public for no one will heed his words; no one will defend him or his family when hostile forces gather. To avoid shame's living death, a warrior's woman will urge her husband to defend his (their) honor, even in the face of certain death. Sooner be the widow of an honorable man than the wife of a cowardly "woman."

Warrior alpha males and their honor-code dominate social dynamics in these cultures. For them, bravery, indomitability and the readiness to avenge insults or injuries stand out as the greatest of traits.[9] Such codes *accept, expect, even require, that the man shed blood for the sake of honor.* This blood could be that of a foe, a neighbor, a family member, or—all else failing—one's own. These are evolutionary developments adapted to environments of scarcity—food, women, resources—that have governed most human life for hundreds of

---

6   For an example of random murder as a sign of manly honor, see Patrick Meney's account of such a murder in Beirut to instill fear (Pryce-Jones, *The Closed Circle*, 38).

7   Charles Griswold, "The Nature and Ethics of Vengeful Anger," *Nomos*, 53 (2013), 77–124.

8   Suzanne Stetkevych, *The Mute Immortals Speak: Pre-Islamic Poetry and Poetics of Ritual* (Ithaca, NY: Cornell University Press, 1993), 174f.

9   James Bowman, *Honor: A History* (New York: Encounter Books, 2006), chapter 2.

thousands of years.[10] As the Yanomamö say: "the fierce men have the most wives and children."[11]

Whereas for the Western progressive, the expression "senseless violence" approaches the status of a tautology—all violence is irrational if not senseless; for the warrior, "senseless violence" is an oxymoron—all violence is meaningful.[12] The mafia expression "he made his bones," refers specifically to establishing "credibility" (seriousness), by killing someone: people, especially those afraid of dying, fear those who kill and those who kill have contempt for those afraid of dying.[13] And alongside "respect" from other lethal males, comes access to nubile females:

> Conflicts over the possession of nubile females have probably been the main reason for fights and killings throughout most of human history: the original human societal rules emerged, in all probability, to regulate male access to females and prevent the social chaos attendant on fighting over women.[14]

The remorseless nature of this honor-violence, locked into a hard zero-sum cycle, finds stark expression in a pre-Islamic Arabic poem:

> Then we, no doubt, are meat for the sword
> > And, doubtless, sometimes
> > > we feed it meat.
> By foe bent on vengeance, we are attacked,
> > Our fall his cure; or we, vengeance-bent,
> > > Attack the foe.
> Thus have we divided time in two,
> > Between us and our foe,
> > > Till not a day goes by but we're
> > > In one half or the other.[15]

---

10 K. Bennett, "Environment of Evolutionary Adaptedness (EEA)," *Encyclopedia of Personality and Individual Differences*, ed. Zeigler-Hill and Shackelford (Cham: Springer, 2018).

11 Napoleon Chagnon, *Yanomamö: The Fierce People* (New York: Holt McDougal, 1984).

12 Anton Blok, *Honour and Violence* (Oxford: Polity Press, 2001).

13 Mario Puzzi introduced this expression in his novel *The Godfather*. Chagnon noted that the *unokais* (i.e. those participating in killing expeditions), had three times as many offspring as those men who did not. See 235.

14 Napoleon Chagnon, *Noble Savages: My Life Among Two Dangerous Tribes—the Yanomamö and the Anthropologists* (New York: Simon & Schuster, 2014), 316.

15 Stetkovych, *Mute Immortals*, 63.

"A third of people die from war, a third from disease, and a third from the evil eye."
—North African proverb

Zero-sum attitudes have a close relationship to envy: if someone's success necessarily diminishes others in the eyes of the public, then any success will elicit envy, and, in many cases, mobilize forces to bring down the haughty ones. Envy, like shame and vengeance, may be peculiarly human, and play a key role in our evolution. As an individual phenomenon, it is hard to track since, being an admission of inadequacy in relationship to the person envied, few people want to admit to feeling envy.[16] As a social phenomenon—that is, collective envy—it may play an important role in distribution of wealth by forcing those with a great deal to share. In some tribes, hunter-gatherers hide food and eat it alone at night in order not to lose the "lion's share" to envious neighbors who demand theirs. This is the world of the one-eyed peasant-king.

Envy is a pervasive element of the human psyche and of human societies.[17] The expression "crabs in the basket" refers to the way if one crab tries to escape the basket, the others will pull it down, hence, the tendency of people in poverty to show hostility to someone who, by dint of effort, rises above the collective condition and, by implication, sheds an unflattering light on those he or she leaves behind. Envy is not always negative; it can serve as a strong anti-monarchical force, a contribution to egalitarian, even "democratic" culture.[18]

Hans Schoeck argues that cultures that accept destructive envy as an inevitable and pervasive part of their lives produce societies of "limited good," and by contrast, cultures that resist envy, even in relatively small but significant amounts, become wealth producing nations.[19] When envy dominates a culture, its members mobilize against success.

If in tribal conditions this envy prevents the emergence of kings, in civil societies, it hamstrings economic growth. When people can tolerate the success of others without wishing them ill, conditions favor enterprise. As Edmund Burke put it, "a law against property is a law against industry."[20] In the case of marriage, although monogamy can be painful for alpha males who want to (are genetically programmed to?) spread their seed, it eliminates many of the terrible conflicts of envy between multiple wives, not only for their own status, but for the status of their children. Polygamy gives full range to both the alpha male's

---

16 Hellmut Schoeck, *Envy: A Theory of Social Behavior* (Indianapolis: Liberty Fund, 1987), 1–15.
17 Ibid., 33–56.
18 Salzman, *Culture and Conflict in the Middle East* (New York: Humanity Books, 2008), 199–202.
19 Schoeck, *Envy*, 57–76.
20 Edmund Burke, *Tract on the Popery Laws*; cited in David Landes, *Wealth and Poverty*, 32.

power, and to a "family life" brimming with ferocious competitions at every level. The best answer to the genie's offer is: Give me one good wife.

The notion of the evil eye, the idea that a malevolent gaze can harm the object, appears, developed to various degrees, in most cultures.[21] Where the belief prevails, the members of the society take a wide variety of actions to ward off the evil eye, some magical (talismans), some preventive measures (hiding wealth, disguising good fortune, avoiding any public display of success). Much "black magic" aims at harming others invisibly, and the notion that some people can cast an "evil eye" on another and thereby curse them, is widespread.

The dynamics of avoiding shame and gaining honor are part of the human experience. Mystics can claim that "shame and fame are all the same,"[22] and one can experience moments where it is true. But, as with the Jewish notion of the "evil inclination," shame and honor are crucial sources of life and sociability: no society could exist in which such selfish drives are absent.[23] The key variable is not its presence or absence in a culture, but how that culture handles the hard edge of zero-sum emotions like the desire for personal fame.

The Arab Opposition to Israel as a Case Study in Honor-Shame[24]

No conflict has suffered more from a critical lack of honor-shame analysis in the last quarter of a century, than the Arab-Israeli conflict. As the result of a confluence of intellectual trends (postmodernism, postcolonialism, anti-Orientalism, peace anthropology) the role of honor-shame motivations in key decision-making in this conflict since the Oslo Accords has been systematically ignored. Indeed, the entire "Peace Process" was predicated on the rational, positive-sum assumption that, offered the right deal, Palestinians will say yes. As a result, scholars and policy makers alike have ignored abundant evidence of a limbic captivity to honor concerns among Arab patriarchal elites, so convinced

---

21 E. E. Evans-Pritchard, *Witchcraft, Oracles and Magic among the Azande* (Oxford: Clarendon Press, 1976); George Aquaro, *Death by Envy: The Evil Eye and Envy in the Christian Tradition* (Bloomington, IN: iUniverse, 2004).

22 Ram Dass, *Be Here and Now* (San Cristobal, NM: Lama Foundation, 1971), 107.

23 See the Talmudic tale of getting rid of the yetzer hara (evil inclination) and the chickens don't lay eggs (*Yoma*, 69b), https://www.sefaria.org/Yoma.69b.9?lang=en.

24 A more complete version in Landes, "Oslo's Misreading of an Honor-Shame Culture." *Israel Journal of Foreign Affairs* 13, no. 2 (2019), https://www.academia.edu/41012401/Oslos_Misreading_of_an_Honor-Shame_Culture.

were these Western analysts that their Peace and Conflict Studies formulas would work.

And yet, the affair turned into a fiasco of immeasurable proportions. As one observer who was in favor of the deal wrote in its aftermath:

> It has long been obvious to all but the incurably or willfully blind that the 1993 agreement signed in Oslo between the government of Israel and the Palestine Liberation Organization was a horrendous blunder on Israel's part. Rarely in history has a country so foolishly opened its gates to a Trojan horse as Israel did when it welcomed Yasir Arafat and his PLO brigades, handed over to them most of the Gaza Strip and much of the West Bank, and gave them the arms to impose their rule on the local inhabitants. How could such a mistake have been made by experienced political and military leaders, statesmen and generals whose careers had spanned a half-century of managing Israel's bitter conflict with the Arabs?[25]

In order to understand the role of hard zero-sum, shame-honor concerns in the attitude of Arabs toward Israel, one must first understand the traditional role of the Jew in the Muslim Arab honor-group. For the 13 centuries before Zionism, Jews had been subject to a political status in Muslim lands specifically designed around issues of honor (to Muslims) and shame (to Jews). Jews were *dhimmi*, "protected" from Muslim violence by their acceptance of daily public degradation and legal inferiority.[26]

Noted Chateaubriand in the nineteenth century:

> Special target of all [Muslim and Christian] contempt, the Jews lower their heads without complaint; they suffer all insults without demanding justice; they let themselves be crushed by blows.... Penetrate the dwellings of these people, you will find them in frightful poverty.[27]

---

25 Hillel Halkin, "Review of *The Oslo Syndrome* by Kenneth Levin," *Commentary* September 2005.

26 On dhimmi, see Bat Ye'or, *Islam and Dhimmitude: Where Civilizations Collide* (Philadelphhia: Farleigh Dickinson University Press, 2001), reviewed by Robert Irwin, *Middle Eastern Studies* 38.4 (2002): 213–215.

27 Chateaubriand, *Itinéraire de Paris à Jérusalem* (Lille, 1869) 275f; in English translation "Chateaubriand on the Oppression of Jews at Jerusalem," *Zion Blogspot*, June 26, 2005.

For more than a millennium, Arab and Muslim honor resided, among other places, in their domination and humiliation of their *dhimmi*—and when the occasional reformer equalized their legal status, he struck a heavy blow to Muslim honor. John Bowring, a British envoy to Egypt in the early nineteenth century noted the impact of Muhammad Ali's modernizing reforms which eliminated the *dhimma*:

> The Mussulmans ... deeply deplore the loss of that sort of superiority which they all & individually exercised over & against the other sects. . . . A Mussulman . . . believes and maintains that a Christian—& still more a Jew—is an inferior being to himself.[28]

Similar sentiments appeared among Southerners in the US, after the loss of slavery.[29]

For the honor-driven Arab and Muslim political player, in the twentieth century as in the tenth century, the very prospect of an autonomous Jewish political entity in Dar al Islam constitutes a blasphemy against Islam, and an insult to Arab virility. This is *not* to say that every period and place of Muslim rule involved deliberate humiliation of *dhimmi*. Nor is it to say that *all Arabs* think like this. Triumphalist religiosity, even when dominant, has no monopoly on Islamic practice, and some Muslims prefer demotic religiosity with its dignity and cooperation.

Rather, this kind of testosterone-fueled, authoritarian discourse where Muslims must visibly dominate, periodically imposes its interpretation of "honor" on the entire community, often violently. Thus, while the Arab leadership and "Street" agreed that for the sake of Arab honor, Israel must be destroyed, some Arabs in 1948 Palestine viewed the prospect of Jewish sovereignty as a valuable opportunity, if only for their own independence as well.[30] Triumphalists, however, viewed them as traitors to the Arab cause.[31]

---

28 Quoted in William R Polk, *The Opening of South Lebanon, 1788–1840* (Cambridge, MA, 1963), 138. Other nineteenth-century Western observers noted the same Arab-Muslim Judeophobia: Saul S. Friedman, *Land of Dust* (Washington, DC, 1982), 136.

29 Greenberg, *Honor and Slavery*.

30 Cohen, *Army of Shadows: Palestinian Collaboration with Zionism, 1917–1948* (Los Angeles: University of California Press, 2009).

31 Nashashibi vs Husseini clans discussed in Cohen, *Army of Shadows*, chapter 2 ("Who is a Traitor"). For a modern update, see the response of Palestinian leaders to Palestinians who either help Israelis hit by terror attacks ("Palestinian who saved Jewish kids after terror attack gets Israeli residency," *Times of Israel*, August 7, 2019) or attend the Bahrain conference on

For the honor-driven Arabs, however, the situation in Palestine was infinitely worse than the "normal" honor-challenges: the Zionist threat did not come from an historically *worthy* foe, like the Western Christians, fellow warriors. It came from Jews, traditionally the most passive, abject, and cowardly of the populations over which Muslims ruled. As the Athenians explained to the Melians in the fifth century BCE:

> One is not so much frightened of being conquered by a power
> which rules over others, as Sparta does, as of what would happen
> if a ruling power is attacked and defeated by its own subjects.[32]

So, the prospect of an independent state of should-be dhimmis struck Arab leaders as more than humiliating. In their minds it literally endangered Islam. Thus, Rahman Azzam Pasha, the head of the newly formed Arab League, spoke for his "honor group" when in an interview with an Egyptian journalist, he threatened that "if the Zionists dare establish a state, the massacres we would unleash would dwarf anything which Genghis Khan and Hitler perpetrated."[33] As the Armenians had discovered a generation earlier, the mere suspicion of rebellion could engender Muslim genocide.[34]

The military loss in 1948, therefore, constituted the most catastrophic possible outcome for this honor-group: seven Arab armies, representing the honor of hundreds of millions of Arabs (and Muslims), were defeated by fewer than a million Jews, the surviving remnant of the most devastating and efficient genocidal effort in history. Nothing could be more shattering than to fall to people so low on the scale that it was *dishonorable* even to fight them.[35] And this humiliating event occurred on center stage of the new postwar global community. In the history of a global public, never has any single and so large

---

economic development (Khaled Abu Toameh and Yassir Okbi, "After Threat from US, PA Frees Businessman Who Attended Bahrain Summit," July 1, 2019).

32 Thucydides, *History of the Peloponnesian War*, 5.89.

33 The quote has been problematized by some scholars (Benny Morris, "Revisionism on the West Bank," *National Interest*, June 28, 2010). Barnett and Karsh argue for its validity: "Azzam's genocidal threat," *Middle East Quarterly* (Fall 2011), 85–88.

34 Benny Morris and Dror Ze'evi, *The Thirty-Year Genocide: Turkey's Destruction of Its Christian Minorities, 1894–1924* (Cambridge MA: Harvard University Press, 2019); Mark Krikorian, "The Jihad-Genocide of the Armenians," *National Review*, April 24, 2015.

35 On the dishonor of even competing with a foe without honor, see Pierre Bourdieu, "The Sentiment of Honour in Kabyle Society," in *Honour and Shame the Values of Mediterranean Society*, ed. John Peristiany (Chicago: University of Chicago Press, 1974), 191–94.

a group suffered so much dishonor and shame in the eyes of so great—so global—an audience.[36]

Thus, alongside the physical *nakba* (catastrophe) that struck hundreds of thousands of the Arab inhabitants of the former British Mandate Palestine as a result of the war of 1948, we find yet another, much greater, psychological catastrophe that struck the entire Arab world, and especially its leaders, a humiliation so immense that Arab political culture and discourse could not digest it, and from which it has yet to recover, even today. Initially, the refugees used the term *nakba* to reproach the Arab leaders who started and lost the war that so damaged their lives and as a reproach to themselves, for listening to those leaders. One of the synonyms for *nakba* was *"ammā sharnā wa-tla'nā* ("when we blackened our faces and left"), i.e., when we followed the instructions of our leaders to disaster.[37] Initially, *nakba* meant: "when we Arabs did it to ourselves."

Constantine Zureiq, the first author to document and name the Nakba of 1948, laid the blame directly at the feet of the impotent blowhards who started the war of 1948 and lost it.

> Seven Arab states declare war on Zionism in Palestine, stop, impotent before it, and turn on their heels. The representatives of the Arabs deliver fiery speeches in the highest government forums, warning what the Arab states and peoples will do if this or that decision be enacted. Declarations fall like bombs from the mouths of officials at the meetings of the Arab League, but when action becomes necessary, the fire is still and quiet, and steel and iron are rusted and twisted, quick to bend and disintegrate.[38]

In a culture more open to self-criticism—what Zureiq was calling for—such observations might have led to the replacement of the honor-driven political elites with leaders more inclined to move ahead with positive-sum relations of the global politics of the world after World War II, the world of the United Nations, the Marshall Plan, the Geneva Conventions. But when appearances matter above all, any public criticism shames the nation, the people, and especially the leaders.

---

36 Richard Rubenstein, "Defeat, Rage, and Jew-Hatred," *Journal of Antisemitism*, 1:1 (2009): 95–138.

37 Ahmad H. Sa'di and Lila Abu-Lughod, *Nakba: Palestine, 1948, and the Claims of Memory* (New York: Columbia University Press, 2007), 253f.

38 Constantine Zurayk, *The Meaning of the Disaster* (1948 [Arabic], 1956), https://archive.org/details/zurayk-nakba.

So, instead, in a state of intense humiliation and impotence on the world stage, the Arab leadership chose denial—the Jews *did* not, *could* not, *have* not won. The war was not—could never—be over until Arab-Muslim victory. If the refugees from this Zionist aggression disappeared, absorbed by their brethren in the lands to which they fled, this would acknowledge the intolerable: that Israel *had* won and was here to stay. And so, driven by rage at, and denial of, this global public shame, the Arab honor group redoubled the catastrophe of its own refugees. They made them suffer in camps, frozen in time at the moment of the humiliation, waiting and fighting to reverse that Zionist victory.[39] The continued suffering of these sacrificial victims on the altar of Arab pride called out to the Arab world for vengeance against the Jews.[40] In the meantime, in many places where Muslims held power, they drove their Jews out: both the number of refugees and the amount of confiscated and lost wealth exceeding substantially the damage to Arab refugees from the area now called Israel.[41]

The Arab leadership's interpretation of honor had them responding to the loss of their own hard zero-sum game—*we*'re going to massacre *them*—by adopting a negative-sum strategy. Damaging the Israeli "other" became paramount, no matter how much that effort might hurt Arabs, especially Palestinians. When another several million Arabs fell under Israeli control in 1967—the *Naksa* or "setback, or defeat"—the strategy remained the same, "No recognition, no negotiations, no peace . . ."—eventually, no Israel.[42] Sooner leave millions of Muslims under Jewish rule than negotiate a solution. Sooner die than live humiliated, sooner live in misery than live in equality. As one Arab told the Peel Commission in 1939 why he had rioted against the Jews when their arrival had so greatly improved conditions for everyone: "*Better a mat of my own than a shared house.*" In 1948 that became "better refugee camps than two states between the river and the sea."

---

39 Mahmoud Darwish perpetuates this suspension in time: "an extended present that promises to continue in the future," "Not to begin at the end," *Al Ahram Weekly On-line*, May 10–16, 2001; English translation, Zahi Damuni, *Al Awdah*. On refugee camps as a weapon of war and the erosion of Western resistance, Asaf Romirowsky and Alex Joffe, *Religion, Politics, and the Origins of Palestine Refugee Relief* (New York: Palgrave, 2013).

40 Asaf Romirowsky and Louise Ellman, "UNRWA & the Right of Return," *The Henry Jackson Society*, June 18, 2012.

41 *Forgotten Millions: The Modern Jewish Exodus from Arab Lands*, ed. Malka Hillel Shulewitz (London, 1999). Most wealthy Palestinian Arabs left early with their wealth.

42 The three no's of Khartoum. Yoram Meital tries to downplay Arab rejectionism: "The Khartoum Conference and Egyptian Policy after the 1967 War: A Reexamination," *Middle East Journal*, 54:1 (Winter, 2000): 64–82.

To positive-sum players this negative sum approach seems like the height of irrationality, but it proves a surprisingly durable choice among human game-players.[43] The zero sum joke becomes negative-sum—"poke out both of my eyes if only I can damage one of my enemy's." And alas, the Palestinians were "blessed" with "friends" who approved. Thus, their negative-sum leaders had willing allies among European powers who, behind the scenes, were happy to leave the Arab world stewing in its revenge fantasies, and the state of the Jews in a permanent state of angst.[44]

By the late twentieth century, in the hands of the genocidal apocalyptic cult of Hamas, the negative-sum formula became, "sooner commit suicide to kill Jews than make peace with them."[45] As one Palestinian put it to an Israeli at the height of the Oslo terror war: "For us, victory is seeing you suffer. That's all we want. The more we suffer, the more you'll suffer."[46] A Hamas leader, in the early, glorious years of the Oslo Jihad, combined fantasies of omnipotence with the necessity of humiliating Israel:

> Tomorrow, our nation [Islam *not* Palestine] will sit on the throne of the world. . . . Tomorrow we will lead the world, Allah willing. Apologize today [you infidels], before remorse will do you no good. Our nation is moving forwards, and it is in your interest to respect a victorious nation. . . . Allah willing, before they die, Israel will experience humiliation and degradation every day.[47]

Even among the most Westernized Arabs, the wound of Israel's existence cuts deep, as does the instinct to scapegoat Israel for Arab failures. Ahmed Sheikh, editor in chief of Al Jazeera, consummate professional with children in the best international schools, blamed Israel for the lack of democracy in the Arab world:

---

43 For a good example of the way "Right of Return" for Palestinian refugees struck Westerners as irrational, but made perfect sense from the perspective of zero-sum logic, see Adi Schwartz and Einat Wilf, *The War of Return: How Western Indulgence of the Palestinian Dream Has Obstructed the Path to Peace* (New York: St. Martin's Press, 2020).

44 David Pryce-Jones, *Betrayal: France, the Arabs and the Jews* (New York: Encounter, 2006); John Loftus and Mark Arens, *The Secret War against the Jews* (New York: St Martin's Press, 1994), 125–324.

45 See Oliver and Steinberg, *Martyrs' Square.*

46 Ami Ayalon and Iyad Saraj, discussed 407f.

47 Khaled Mash'al, "The Nation of Islam Will Sit at the Throne of the World and the West Will Be Full of Remorse when it is too Late," *MEMRI*, February 3, 2006.

> The day when Israel was founded created the basis for our problems.... It's because we always lose to Israel. It gnaws at the people in the Middle East that such a small country as Israel, with only about 7 million inhabitants, can defeat the Arab nation with its 350 million. That hurts our collective ego. The Palestinian problem is in the genes of every Arab. The West's problem is that it does not understand this.[48]

Based on his blaming Israel for the Arab failure, Sheikh (who is a Palestinian, and may, therefore, exaggerate the extent to which his own people's complexes permeates the entire Arab world), comes to the conclusion that the way to democracy lies not in ending the irredentist fight with Israel and dealing constructively with the blow to the Arab ego of "always losing" to (modern) Jews, but rather in the Arabs' defeating Israel, and *then* they'll build democracies.

His thinking nicely illustrates a lack of understanding of the kind of demotic values and self-critical learning curves necessary to build democracies. But at least on one point, Sheikh is right: The West's problem is that, in their deep and unshakeable cognitive egocentrism, they don't understand this honor-driven *onēidophobia* in the Arab world when it comes to Israel. As a result, they make catastrophic miscalculations.

Land for Peace: The Positive-Sum Formula

The Oslo "Peace Process" illustrates how ignorance of (or ignoring) the shame-honor dynamics mislead Westerners trying to navigate the political cultures of the Middle East. The entire project based its logic on the positive-sum principle of an exchange of "land for peace": Israel cedes land to the Palestinians (most if not all the West Bank and Gaza) to create an independent state, while the Palestinians bury the hatchet of total war to destroy Israel, since they're getting the state they want, without the need for war. The logic placed particular urgency on Israel creating a Palestinian state lest they become demographically overrun by Arabs, and either stay democratic and lose control, or create an "apartheid" state.

---

48 Pierre Heumann, "An Interview With Al-Jazeera Editor-in-Chief Ahmed Sheikh," *World Politics Review*, December 7, 2006; analysis, Landes, "Why Israel's existence prevents Arab Democracy," *Augean Stables* December 8, 2006.

The accords banked on a Palestinian shift from their charter-defined commitment to regaining Arab and Muslim honor by wiping out the shame that is Israel, to a readiness to accept Israel's legitimate existence, and a commitment to Western values such as responsible and transparent government: two democracies living in peace side by side. Such a shift depended on their understanding that this promised concession to Israel would bring what Palestinians "yearn for," namely "the freedom to govern themselves in peace and dignity," a nation-state.[49] A win-win solution so obvious, that, as the BBC's Gavin Esler opined, "it could be solved with an email."[50]

William Quandt, one of the school of "liberal internationalists," insisted on both the readiness of the Arab world for democracy and the linkage between that development and peace in the Middle East.[51] Imagining anything else— like an Arab political culture fundamentally at odds with democracy—would be Orientalist warmongering and racism.[52] The underlying assumptions here, shared by many Western analysts including Israelis, even when they disagreed with Quandt on details, reflected one of the most pervasive and deep-seated forms of Western cognitive egocentrism, the cornerstone of (constructivist) Political "Science."

These political "scientists" might admit that Western categories, like nations, individuals, rule of law, human rights, don't carry the same weight in Arab culture; they might even tell you of Sadat's quip: that the only Arab nation was his Egypt, and the rest were "tribes with flags." But they still thought that under the

---

49 "Reiterat[ed] its vision of a region where two democratic States, Israel and Palestine, live side by side in peace within secure and recognized borders," UN Security Council Resolution 2334 (December 12, 2016). In the aftermath of the Sbarro Pizza bombing of July 2001, Clyde Haberman described the Israeli response (seizure of Orient House) as a "direct blow to the heart of Palestinian nationalism" the "government house" a symbol of "their yearnings for a state," "Israelis Grieve and Strike Back," *New York Times*, August 11, 2001; cited in Jerold Auerbach, *Print to Fit: The New York Times, Zionism and Israel, 1896–2016* (Boston: Academic Studies Press, 2019), 176.

50 Gavin Esler, BBC Dateline London, https://www.youtube.com/watch?v=uVLLylL-Nuo&feature=youtu.be. On the logic of Oslo, see Ofira Seliktar, *Doomed to Failure?: The Politics and Intelligence of the Oslo Peace Process* (Santa Barbara: ABC/CLIO, 2009), 7–49; Karsh, *Arafat's War*, chapter 7. On the role of progressive Peace and Conflict Studies in formulating this plan, see Steinberg, "Postcolonial Theory and the Ideology of Peace Studies," in *Post-Colonial Theory and the Arab-Israeli Conflict*, 115–18.

51 William B. Quandt, "The Urge for Democracy," *Foreign Affairs*, 73:4 (July–August 1994): 2–7; "After the Gulf Crisis: Challenges for American Policy," *Arab American Affairs* 35 (Winter 1990–91): 11–19.

52 Kenneth Levin, *The Oslo Syndrome: Delusions of a People under Siege* (Hanover, NH: Smith and Kraus, 2005), 344–57. For a typical example of the racist accusation (from an Israeli), see David Grossman, "Fictions Embraced by an Israel at War," *NYR*, October 1, 2002.

right circumstances, the Arab world is ready to make the shift. That is, however much they might see the cultural problem, they are so deeply committed to the democratic, positive-sum notions that underlie their culture, that they assume that, given the right conditions to accede to "our way of doing things," these other people will assent and shift. Avraham Shalom, who ran the Shabak from 1980–86, commented that when the Oslo Accords emerged:

> The Shin Bet looked for people to talk to, to understand what motivated the Palestinians. For the first time, some Jews raised the idea of a Palestinian state. I loved the idea, so I went to the Territories with people who dealt with the Palestinians.[53]

And once the process was engaged, a wide range of people, militating for peace, refused to acknowledge any evidence that these assumptions about Palestinian willingness to give up the grudge might be wide of the mark.[54] Liberal cognitive egocentrism had become a foreign policy doctrine, and, as we shall see with its abject failure in the summer and fall of 2000, it became a dogmatic assertion. As Edward Alexander notes:

> Peres' recent book shows his inability to imagine that the Arabs are motivated by anything apart from improving their economic condition. He imputes Arab fundamentalism to poverty—"In frustration ... these people have turned to mysticism and otherworldliness."[55]

Even the hard-headed, security-minded, Israelis, like Prime Minister Rabin and the highest people in Intelligence accepted the claim that the PLO had changed direction:

> If we ever want a serious chance at solving the Palestinian-Israeli problem, the time is now, and the partner is the PLO, which rid itself of the principles that I despised them for. The signing of the Oslo Accords between Israel and the Palestinians marked the first time that the PLO officially announced that it had

---

53 Dror Moreh, *The Gatekeepers* (2012).
54 Levin, *Oslo Syndrome*, 343–92.
55 Edward Alexander, *Jewish Wars* (New York: Routledge, 2011), 173; Shimon Peres, *The New Middle East*, 183. Peres's book is a compendium of liberal cognitive egocentrism; and Alexander a systematic critique of the problem.

abandoned terror and violence and recognized Israel's right to
exist in peace and security.[56]

And the Palestinians chosen for negotiation, some of them committed to peace
as well, were sufficiently engaged in the process, even Arafat, to give the Israelis,
eager to believe, reason to trust their good intentions.[57]

What the Oslo architects and their Western supporters completely
underestimated was the hold that Arafat's native honor-world and its triumphalist
religiosity had over him and his associates, how unready the Palestinians were
for this deal.[58] This not only dominated thinking in Western circles, *not* put at
direct risk by such a gamble, but even Israelis who had much more to lose in case
of misreading. Raphael Israeli puts his finger on the mindset:

> From the outset, the ill-coached Israeli negotiators [almost
> completely ignorant of Islamic religious beliefs among their
> interlocutors, including Arafat], believed that if their intentions
> were good and their means candid, their Palestinian counterparts
> would behave similarly.[59]

This (messianic) confidence in the power of doing good, even pervaded
intelligence circles:

> [I]t is clear that it was not only Israel's political leadership that
> was held hostage by the chimerical conception that an era of
> peace with the Palestinian Authority had begun: M[ilitary]
> I[ntelligence] and the Shin Bet security service had trouble
> liberating themselves from the same feeling. The intelligence
> officials were not always willing to let facts disturb a rosy
> perception of reality.[60]

---

56 Yaacov Peri, head of Shin Bet, 1988–94, explaining Rabin's thought at the outset of the Oslo
Process. *The Gatekeepers*, script.

57 Connie Bruck, "The Wounds of Peace," *The New Yorker*, October 14, 1996, gives a good sense
of the apparent emotional connections even between Arafat and Rabin.

58 Adi Schwartz and Eytan Gilboa, "False Readiness: Expanding the Concept of Readiness in
Conflict Resolution Theory," *International Studies Review* (2021), 1–21.

59 Raphael Israeli, *The Oslo Idea: The Euphoria of Failure* (New Brunswick: Transaction
Publishers, 2012), 58.

60 Yossi Melman, "Don't Confuse Us with Facts," *Haaretz* (Tel Aviv), Aug. 16, 2002; Levin, *The
Oslo Syndrome*, 343–57; see also Levin's discussion of Ari Shavit's awakening in late 1997,
403–5.

Just because Western and Israeli analysts failed to pay attention, however, does not mean the laws of honor-shame and triumphalist religiosity ceased to operate.

Honor-Shame Discourse: What Was Taken by Force Must Be Taken Back by Force

After the ceremonious signing of the deal on the White House lawn, PLO Chairman Yasser Arafat found himself the target of immense hostility from his Arab and Muslim honor-group for having brought shame upon himself, his people, upon all Arabs and all Muslims. In cultures where, for honor's sake, "what was taken by force much be retaken by force," any negotiations are shameful and cowardly.[61] When Arafat arrived in Gaza in July 1994, Hamas denounced him roundly: "His visit is shameful and humiliating, as it occurs in the shadow of occupation and in the shadow of Arafat's humiliating submission before the enemy government and its will. It is impossible to present a defeat as victory."[62]

Nor was it "merely" the apocalyptic religious fanatics who talked so. Edward Said, proud, secular, ecumenical, postmodern, who claimed to reject any kind of primitive tribalism,[63] who protested loudly that he opposed "the insouciant nativism and militant militarism of the [Palestinian] nationalist consensus,"[64] echoed the language of Hamas: the compromises involved a "degrading . . . act of obeisance . . . a capitulation" that produced a state of "supine abjectness . . . submitting shamefully to Israel."[65] Thus did the Ur-"postcolonial" intellectual speak the zero-sum, tribal language of Arab and Muslim honor-shame, attacking negotiation as dishonorable.[66] And Westerners dared not point out the problem of an "Oriental" Said, lest they be accused of being racists and "Orientalizing the Orient."

---

61 The slogan has been attributed to Nasser, specifically in reference to destroying Israel. It appears on the wall behind Muhammad al Durah in the footage shot of his alleged murder. It is commonly invoked in reference to Israel, as in "Jordanian Friday Sermon: The Jews Have No Right to Palestine, Which Will Be Regained Only by Force, *MEMRI*, March 20, 2017.

62 Stephen J. Sosebee, "Yasser Arafat's Return: New Beginning for Palestine," *Washington Report on Middle East Affairs*, Sept./Oct. 1994.

63 See p272, 277–84.

64 Appendix to the 1994 edition of Edward Said, *Orientalism* (New York: Vintage, 1979), 338.

65 Said, "The Morning After," *London Review of Books*, Oct. 21, 1993.

66 "Compromise is understood as humiliation, which is why political agreements between Muslims and other Muslims or non-Muslims are so difficult to reach. That is also why one almost never encounters Middle Eastern leaders who are prepared to compromise. From their perspective, compromise means you have given in, i.e., someone else has dominated you, a fate you must avoid at all costs. Honor goes only to the winner." Harold Rhode, *Modern Islamic Warfare: An Ancient Doctrine Marches On* (Washington: Center for Security Policy, 2017), 10.

This was, then, in Arab eyes, a "peace of cowards." The mood was captured in the poem by one of the Arab world's most famous poets, Nizar Qabbani, which became an overnight sensation.

Al Muharjiwuud [Those who scurry]
Al-Hayat, London, October 1995

The last walls of embarrassment have fallen
We were delighted
And we danced
And we blessed ourselves
For signing the peace of the coward
Nothing frightens us anymore
Nothing shames us anymore
The veins of pride in us have dried up.

We stood in columns like sheep before slaughter
We ran, breathless
We scrambled to kiss
The shoes of the killers . . .

Oh we dreamed of a green peace
And a white crescent
And a blue sea.
Now we find ourselves
On a dung heap.

Who could ask the rulers
About the peace of the cowards
About the peace of selling in installments
And renting in installments
About the peace of the merchants
And the exploiters?
Who could ask them
About the peace of the dead?
They have silenced the street
And murdered all the questions
And those who question . . .

Palestine saw its picture
Carried on the airwaves,
She saw her tears
Crossing the waves of the ocean
Toward Chicago, New Jersey, Miami.

Like a wounded bird
Palestine shouted:
This wedding is not my wedding!
This dress is not my dress!
This shame is not my shame! (Ajami, 1997, 256–58)

"Kissing the shoes of the killers. . ." is a defeat worse than death to those who should, themselves, be the killers whose feet the enemy kisses. The "dreamed of . . . green peace" has no room for those we tried so hard to kill.[67] Wedded to our zero-sum vision we will refuse any positive-sum offer and deny any responsibility for what we have done and continue to do.[68]

Nor was this attitude restricted to the Arab world. Muslims the world over wanted to know what Arafat meant by this volt-face vis-à-vis "the Zionist entity," his betrayal of the very cause he was to champion—the utter destruction of the enemy state. When he went to Johannesburg for the inauguration of Nelson Mandela in 1994, he visited the main mosque, where indignant Muslims (largely from the Indian subcontinent) demanded an explanation. Arafat responded (assuming this was off the record), by dropping any pretense to the "peace of the brave" that featured so prominently in his English pronouncements,[69] and instead invoked Muhammad's Treaty of Hudaybiyyah:

This agreement [the Oslo Accords], I am not considering it more than the agreement which had been signed between our Prophet Muhammad and Quraysh, and you remember the Caliph Omar had refused this agreement and considered it Sulha Dania [a despicable truce, just as you, my audience, view my behavior].

---

67 On the importance of perceptions of fairness in making peace negotiations acceptable, see Philippe Assouline and Robert Trager, "Concessions for Concessions Sake: Injustice, Indignation and the Construction of Intractable Conflict in Israel-Palestine," *Journal of Conflict Resolution*. March 2021.

68 Khaled abu Toameh, "Palestinians: No to Normalization with the 'Zionist entity,'" *Gatestone*, February 3, 2021.

69 Yasser Arafat, "Nobel Lecture," 1994, *Nobelprize.org*.

> But Muhammad had accepted it [until he felt strong enough to break it], and we are accepting now this [Oslo] peace accord.[70]

Those attacking Arafat were like Caliph Omar, men of honor—good men, but wrong. Arafat, like Muhammad, understood the situation and devised a deceptive plan for honorable war later.[71]

This highlights the key honor difference between Fatah (PA) and Hamas at the time: the latter maintained its honor by refusing to deal with Israel and openly declaring the desire to exterminate the Zionist entity; the former agreed to adopt a seemingly humiliating compromise with the enemy, but only insofar as it was a prelude to destroying it.[72] Were Arafat, through negotiations, to accept the West Bank back and stop there (the Oslo "Peace"), it would be a betrayal of the principle of honor through force. If he got back the West Bank and used it to attack Israel (Oslo Jihad), *that* might be honorable: if he failed, at least he went down fighting. Thus, from the Palestinian zero-sum perspective, the "peace plan" is actually a war plan, a deceit by those not powerful enough to "do what they will," in order to take back what they must . . . for their honor's sake. *Land for War.*

To the extent that Arabs and the Muslim "Street" were sold on the Oslo process, then, it was as a Trojan horse, not as fairly negotiated concessions to be made for the sake of freedom and peace (good liberal priorities, Clinton's priorities); rather, as a humiliating but temporary weakness that, if the trick works, will lead to a full and violent victory for the "Palestinian cause."[73] A *fortiori* this rule of violence applies where not only tribal honor, but the *Umma*'s honor is at stake. Thus, within the *Umma*, the debate concerned whether one supported the shameful deception in order to get what one could not get otherwise, or proudly rejected it.

To anyone paying attention, Arafat's speech provided a striking insight into the workings of the *Umma* in the late twentieth century CE/early fifteenth century AH. Muslims from the Indian subcontinent, not even Arabs, could only be reassured—if then—by the promise that this should *not* result in an

---

70 Audio recording of Arafat speech in Johannesburg, "Arafat compares Oslo Accords to Muhammad's Hudaybiyyah peace treaty, which led to defeat of the peace partners," *Palwatch*, May 10, 1994.

71 For a serious discussion of the Hudaybiyyah Treaty as a key to Arafat's thinking, and speeches in Arabic, see Israeli, *The Oslo Idea*, 62–69; Efraim Karsh, *Arafat's War: The Man and his Battle for Israeli Conquest* (New York: Grove Press, 2003), 178–214.

72 Jonathan Shanzer, *Fatah vs. Hamas: The Struggle for Palestine* (New York: Palgrave, 2008), 37–49.

73 See Abbas Zaki, below, n75.

ignominious Oslo Peace, that the *Umma* would *not* accept an autonomous state of Jews in Dar al Islam.[74] The Prime Directive: "From the river to the sea, Palestine will be Muslim." And everyone, certainly every Palestinian, knew it and knows it today: the elimination of Israel, one way or another, was a unifying, defining axiom.

> The agreement is based on the borders of June 4 [1967]. While the agreement is on the borders of June 4, the President [Mahmoud Abbas] understands, we understand, and *everyone knows* that it is impossible to realize the inspiring idea, or the great goal [from the river to the sea], in one stroke. If Israel withdraws from Jerusalem, if Israel uproots the settlements, 650,000 settlers, if Israel removes the fence—what will be with Israel? Israel will come to an end. If I say that I want to remove it from existence, this will be great, great, [but] it is hard. This is not a [stated] policy. You can't say it to the world. You can say it to yourself.[75]

No Palestinian professed faith in compromise publicly in Arabic; only in the languages of the infidels, to liberals, whether they were Western gentiles, Jews, or Westernized Muslims.[76] Rabin and Peres may have signed the Oslo *Peace* Accords, but Arafat signed the Oslo *Jihad* Accord.

And yet, despite the lessons to learn, by and large Western journalists and policymakers, including the "peace camp" in Israel, and even their intelligence services, ignored Arafat's invocations of Hudaybiyyah.[77] Advocates of peace viewed them as antics designed to appease Muslim public opinion (itself a phenomenon worth pondering); and remained confident that, in the end, the more mature call of the international community would sway Arafat to the side of positive-sum reason. Raymond Ibrahim remarks: "Whereas many of the world's Muslims make the connection and appreciate the continuity of

---

74 Faisal Husseini, *al-Arabi* (Cairo), June 24, 2001, in Special Dispatch No. 236, Middle East Media Research Institute (MEMRI), July 6, 2001.

75 Fatah Central Committee member Abbas Zaki, "Goal is end of Israel, but 'you can't say that to the world,'" Al-Jazeera, September 23, 2011.

76 This is a seemingly permanent feature of Palestinian demopathy and Western dupedom: Landes, "The Demopath's Lexicon: A Guide to Western Journalism between the River and the Sea," *Israel Affairs*, 26:3 (2020): 311–329.

77 Melman, "Don't Confuse Us with Facts"; idem, "Wild Card," *Haaretz*, Aug. 9, 2002. Arafat was consistent and clear in Arabic and to Muslim audiences about where he stood, literally from before the signing of the Accords in Washington, Levin, *Oslo Syndrome*, 343–57.

the words and deeds of their politically active coreligionists, the West remains oblivious."[78]

In his 800-page memoir on the Oslo failure, for example, Dennis Ross, the US Middle East envoy most deeply involved in negotiations with the Palestinian leadership, has not a word to say about the Hudaybiyyah controversy, despite how consistent it was with his own assessment of Arafat's most problematic behavior, his "failure to prepare his people for the compromises necessary for peace."[79] For Ross, this was more of an oversight, missed by the quixotic Arafat. It was actually much worse than that. Arafat's sin was not of omission, but of commission: he *prepared* his people for war right under the noses of the Israelis and the well-meaning West.[80] While the Israelis in the peace camp congratulated themselves on Arafat's visit to Rabin's widow, Leah—only years earlier imagining such a deed on Arafat's part would have been dismissed as "pure fiction"[81]—the Palestinian war camp prepared its 30,000 "police" and its youth for a war of extermination.

It apparently did not occur to the Israeli negotiators or Western liberals (or if it did, they immediately banished the thought), that even though Arafat might have violated a taboo by meeting publicly with Israelis, even—shudder—signing public accords with them, he nonetheless *never* renounced either the desire to destroy Israel, nor his limbic captivity to the shame involved in every meeting. Unquestionably, the accords that let Arafat back in (a huge concession from the Israeli perspective), proved disappointing to Arafat, who probably had not read them. He, in his childish way, seems to have expected Israel to commit suicide, and could not understand—and where possible ignored—the restrictions Israel imposed on his access to full sovereignty ... his own army and open borders with his Arab neighbors. Palestinians, well versed in demopathic discourse, complained bitterly of Israelis humiliating them gratuitously, for example, over borders, as if there were no reason for Israelis to worry.

The Hudaybiyyah episode also shed light on the international game at play in the Oslo Peace Process. When American commentators discussed the Hudaybiyyah speech (European presses tended not even to mention it; in the

78 Raymond Ibrahim, *Sword and Scimitar: Fourteen Centuries of War between Islam and the West* (New York: De Capo, 2018), xiv.

79 Dennis Ross, *The Missing Peace: Inside Story of the Fight for Middle East Peace* (New York: Farrar Straus and Giroux, 2004), 767–69, 776; Charles Enderlin, *Shattered Dreams: The Failure of the Peace Process in the Middle East*, trans. Susan Fairfield (New York: Other Press, 2002), 5–41; and Cheryl Rubenberg, *The Palestinians in Search of a Just Peace* (London: Lynne Reiner, 2003).

80 Karsh, *Arafat's War*, 151–64.

81 Bruck, "Wounds of Peace," 79.

US, only the "right-wing" press raised it), they immediately aroused the ire of Caliphator Da'is. Daniel Pipes wrote repeatedly about the meaning of the Treaty of Hudaybiyyah, and the trouble any Westerner who mentioned it quickly encountered when they brought up the subject. Despite being studiously fair to the Muslim prophet on historical grounds, citing as plausible the Muslim apologetic version that the Meccans broke the treaty, and Muhammad never meant a deliberate deception, Pipes provoked furious condemnation and some of the earliest accusations of "Islamophobia" from the Council on American-Islamic Relations (CAIR), a Muslim "civil rights" organization with ties to the same Muslim Brotherhood of which Hamas is a branch.[82]

The Muslim outcry essentially forbade infidel critics from examining evidence relevant to their pressing concerns, a pattern that replicated itself in academia, with Daniel Pipes' work being banned by some professors as "Islamophobic." Instead, peace enthusiasts viewed Arafat and the Palestinian leadership, as they themselves insisted they were while speaking English: full-fledged modern players who yearned for their own nation and freedom, and whom one could trust to keep commitments to the "peace of the brave." When the opportunity presented itself, they believed, Arafat would choose the imperfect, positive-sum, win-win, over the zero-sum, all-or-nothing, win-lose (which they would lose). They "believed" in the Palestinian leadership's ability to change, and rejected indignantly—even as racist!—anyone who dared to suggest the Palestinian leadership was still captive to their need to bleach their blackened face in blood.

Western journalists and policy experts not only failed (and continue to fail) to challenge such claims, but they ignored the long and troubling list of Palestinian violations of the accords, and pressured Israel to stop harping on the negative, lest they "queer" the peace process.[83] In discussing the Hudaybiyyah speeches, the New Yorker journalist, Connie Bruck notes:

---

82 Daniel Pipes, "Lessons from the Prophet Muhammad's Diplomacy," Middle East Quarterly, Sept. 1999; idem, "Arafat and the Treaty of Hudaybiya," Sept. 10, 1999; idem, "How Dare You Defame Islam?" Commentary, November 1999; idem, "Do I Win a British 'Islamophobia' Award?" Lion's Den, June 26, 2004. Pipes was more generous than Arafat, who, only weeks later, specified that the "treaty with the infidels was torn down two years later" (Karsh, Arafat's War, 149).

83 Ehud Barak's office prepared a white paper on Palestinian violations of the accord, released November 24, 2000: "Palestinian Authority and P.L.O. Non-Compliance with signed agreements and commitments: A record of bad faith and misconduct," United Jerusalem. Although published two months after Arafat had opened the Oslo Trojan Horse, it met with much derision both within Israel and especially abroad: Aluf Benn, "White Paper Tiger Unleashed," Haaretz, November 29, 2000.

The speeches were violations of the spirit, if not the letter, of the accords, and, although the Rabin-Peres Labor government rarely acknowledged it publicly, there were many other violations as well. . . . "We had books and books filled with violations," this person told me, and added, "I saw Rabin and Peres so angry at what they had to eat from the Palestinians."[84]

But of course, this was the price of peace . . . letting them violate the agreement without complaining, lest those who so complain, ruin the chances for peace.[85] Indeed, it was during the Oslo years that the Israeli peace camp first developed the techniques so fatal to the West after 2000, which I describe below as "cultural auto-immune dysfunction": they attacked those who warned of the coming jihad as "enemies of peace."[86]

Thus, even as Jerusalem and Washington prepared for a grand finale to the peace process at Camp David in the summer of 2000, even as Israel's media prepared their people for peace by dismissing the Hudaybiyyah talk and emphasizing the positive, Arafat's media prepared Palestinians for war. Palestinian TV featured staged footage of Israeli troops murdering Palestinian children and raping their women—the full panoply of lethal narratives with which the PA incited its people to war.[87] And none of the key decision-makers outside the Arab world paid any attention.

The Arab Muslim dynamics of maintaining honor (by fighting Israel) and avoiding shame (by not compromising with Israel), doomed the "delusional peace process" of Oslo to failure from the start.[88] As for the people involved, who thought that they were "so close . . . within reach . . ." and that if only Israel had given more, it would have worked, they got played over and over.[89] When, at Taba, in January 2001, Saeb Erakat said, "as long as Israel insists on Israeli sovereignty over the Wailing Wall, the Mount of Olives and the Jewish Quarter, there is nothing to talk about," Israeli negotiator Hirschfeld notes in pain: "From

84 Bruck, "Wounds of Peace."
85 Bruck's source fingers the fear of public humiliation that drove Peres and Rabin not to admit they were wrong about Arafat. Add to that the enormous (messianic) pressure to get the peace to succeed. See Golan Lahat's "The Sacrifices for Peace," *The Messianic Temptation: The Rise and Fall of the Israeli Left*. [Hebrew] (Tel Aviv: Am Oved, 2004), 96–115.
86 Levin, *Oslo Syndrome*, 361–86.
87 Itamar Marcus, "Rape, Murder, Violence, and War for Allah against the Jews: Summer 2000 on Palestinian Television," Palestinian Media Watch, Jerusalem, Sept. 11, 2000.
88 Levin, *Oslo Syndrome*, ix–xxi.
89 Gilead Sher, *The Israeli-Palestinian Peace Negotiations, 1999–2001: Within Reach* (London: Routledge, 2006).

the Israeli point of view, this was equal to saying that there was no place for an agreement."[90] Precisely. And that's how Erakat felt from the start.[91]

Instead of allowing themselves to understand, a determined school of "peace journalists," an outgrowth of "Peace and Conflict Studies" that was especially strong in Israel, did everything it could to downplay any Palestinian behavior that might arouse opposition to the "peace process," while emphasizing as much as possible their contributions—like misreporting the 1996 "amendment of the PLO charter" which never took place.[92] For the Palestinian decision-makers, on the other hand, it was never close: the best those pursuing the negotiations could do was apologetically claim to their people that it was the first stage of the "inspiring idea," the conquest of every inch of land from the river to the sea, and complain to outsiders about settlements—when for them, Tel Aviv was a settlement.

Why did Western strategists not consider that a "successful" deal would have led to more war? After all, according to zero-sum logic, the better the deal for the Palestinians—i.e., the "weaker" the Israelis—the more aggression would accompany its implementation.[93] "What will be with Israel? Israel will come to an end." Those are the only conditions whereby a current Arab leader can still maintain honor in the Arab public sphere, while engaged in the shameful (weak, womanly) behavior of negotiating with Israel: that is, by negotiating Israel's destruction.

Thus, in the summer of 2000, while "peace journalism" had Israelis and Westerners feeling they were "so close" to a final resolution to the Arab-Israeli

---

90 Yair Hirschfeld, *Track-Two Diplomacy toward an Israeli-Palestinian Solution, 1978–2014* (Baltimore: Johns Hopkins University Press, 2014), 251. The tendency of Israelis to blame themselves for the failure are extraordinary: in an entire book on how Israeli-Arab peace negotiations can be spoiled, where the overwhelming focus is on Israeli spoilers, the only "spoiling" behavior attributed to Erakat was his taking a nap: *Spoiling and Coping with Spoilers: Israeli-Arab Negotiations*, ed. Galia Golan and Gilead Sher (Bloomington, 2019), 19.

91 See his interview on Al Jazeera on March 27, 2009, in which he makes it clear that the Palestinians—neither Arafat in 2000, nor Abbas in 2009—would nor could make any concession on getting back "every single stone" of East Jerusalem, and getting back to '67 borders was only "this generation's goal": "Chief Palestinian Negotiator Saeb Erekat: 'Abbas Rejected Israel's Proposal at Annapolis Like Arafat Rejected the Camp David 2000 Proposal,'" *MEMRI*, April 14, 2009.

92 Wolfsfeld, *Media and the Path to Peace*, only indirectly mentions this matter. In his discussion of the 1996 elections he makes no mention, despite its role in Netanyahu's victory (pp. 104–36), and then in a retrospect on the elections, he mentions Netanyahu's use of the Palestinian refusal as an illustration of Netanyahu's demagoguery (183). Hirschfeld does not mention it at all (!). Karsh dedicates a chapter to the debacle: *Arafat's War*, chapter 4.

93 Joel Fishman, "The Delusions of Oslo in the Service of Disengagement," *Makor Rishon*, Aug. 20, 2004; Seliktar, *Doomed to Failure?*; Israeli, *The Oslo Idea*.

conflict, "war journalism" in Palestinian circles primed the culture to welcome Arafat returning from saying "no" at Camp David as a hero, and to cheer on the war against Israel as a valorous and necessary move against an enemy that rapes Palestinian women and targets children for death.[94] And the peace camp in Israel, America and Europe prepared Western democracies for Y2KMind: when the jihadis attacked in 2000, they blamed the democracy.

---

94 John Burns, "Hero's Welcome for Arafat, From Those Who Showed Up," *New York Times*, July 27, 2000.

6

Caliphators: A Fifteenth-Century Millennial Movement

I'm right about God.
So, I must rule, lest others
dare question my truth.

Caliphator: one who believes that in our day, in this generation, Islam will triumph over all other religions and establish a global Caliphate, i.e., a participant in an apocalyptic millennial movement.

Caliphators believe that now is the time for Islam to fulfill its disrupted destiny, and where there was *Dar al Harb* (realm of war, of free/unsubjected *kuffār*/infidels), there shall be *Dar al Islam* (realm of submission to Allah and his servants, of *dhimmi kuffār*). With this global victory, Caliphators believe, Islam will redeem humanity. Among the many currently active apocalyptic movements on the planet, few, if any, have had the success of Caliphators in promoting their rhetoric and mobilizing action in pursuit of their millennial goal.

The apocalyptic belief that the time has now come when this millennial dream will be realized, when Islam will rule not merely in Muslim majority nations, but the world over, distinguishes *Caliphators* from a broad range of "normal" Muslims who practice the faith. Apocalyptic time is warp speed; it can intensify some elements of normative Islam and burn up others. Major legal impediments are jettisoned, like bans on deliberate suicide and targeting children. Muslims who had lived in the West for a while did not, at first, recognize this latest avatar, and honestly told their infidel co-citizens, "this is not the Islam we learned from our elders." And, in a sense, they are right. This is not normative Islam, it's apocalyptic Islam. And yet, whether they know it or not, normative Muslims are, in the Caliphator's eyes, suspected of *murtadd* (apostasy).

1400 AH (1979–80 CE): The Mujaddid Launches Global Jihad

Caliphators first caught the attention of non-Muslims with the advent of the *mujaddid*/renewal at the Muslim century mark in 1400—most notably in Khomeini's stunning Shi'i takeover of Iran. For those paying closer attention, there was a good deal more than that. At the century-mark, a group of Sunni jihadis, following a self-declared Mahdi, took the Grand Mosque in Mecca, Islam's holiest site.[1] In that year, the Maitatsine ("he who damns") movement, forerunners of Boko Haram, appeared in Nigeria.[2] In Lebanon and Libya, a potential hidden Imam stirred emotions that gave birth to Hizballah some three years later.[3] And least spectacular, but perhaps most important, in that year Muslim Brotherhood exiles from Arab countries held a meeting in Switzerland, where they outlined plans for invading and conquering the West by Da'wa.[4]

Writing ten years after the passage of the century mark in 1410/1990, Muslim Brotherhood preacher Yussuf al Qaradawi characterized the *Mujaddid* of 1400 as an ongoing, generations-long process.

> This is what I prefer in understanding this noble hadith [*mujaddid*] and its implementation in our century, which we parted from [the fourteenth Hijri century which ended in 1980] in order to receive a new century; in which we ask Allah to make our today better than our yesterday, and our tomorrow better than our today.[5]

---

1 Yaroslav Trofimov, *Siege of Mecca: The Siege of Mecca: The Forgotten Uprising in Islam's Holiest Shrine and the Birth of al-Qaeda* (New York: Doubleday, 2007).

2 Rosalind Hackett, "Theorizing Radical Islam in Northern Nigeria," in *War in Heaven/Heaven on Earth: Theories of the Apocalyptic*, ed. O'Leary and McGhee (London: Routledge, 2014), 143–62; Abimbola O. Adesoji, "Between Maitatsine and Boko Haram: Islamic Fundamentalism and the Response of the Nigerian State," *Africa Today* 57:4 (2011): 98–119.

3 Fouad Ajami, *The Vanished Imam: Musa al Sadr and the Shia of Lebanon* (Ithaca, New York: Cornell University Press, 1986).

4 Sylvain Besson, *La conquête de l'Occident: Le projet secret des Islamistes* (Paris: Seuil, 2005), 35–37; The "Project" document available in Arabic and English at *The Investigative Project*.

5 Yusuf al-Qaradawi, *The preferences of the Islamic movement in the next stage* [Arabic] (Cairo, 1990), 13–14. NB: the text was composed a decade after the passage of 1400/1979. Besson considers al Qaradawi "the spiritual father," *La conquête de l'Occident*, 75–93.

Five years later, al Qaradawi made it clear what this "better tomorrow" would look like: "*Da'wa,*" he declared to a gathering of Muslim youth in the USA, "conquers the Crusaders in their own lands."[6]

How would that happen? In a section entitled "Understanding the role of the Muslim Brother in North America," their document laid out the plan:

> The process of settlement is a "Civilization-Jihadist Process" with all the word means. The Brotherhood must understand that their work in America is a kind of grand jihad in eliminating and destroying the Western civilization from within and "sabotaging" its miserable house by their hands and the hands of the believers so that it is eliminated, and God's religion is made victorious over all other religions.[7]

For Louis 'Atiyatallah, praising the 9–11 attacks, Bin Laden was the Mujaddid.[8] From the perspective of several decades since, the Caliphator energy released by the advent of 1400 has had a long impact on the 15th century AH.[9]

Like many other millennial movements, Caliphators view the current state of the world as irredeemably evil and corrupt: it must pass away to make way for the coming redeemed world. Among their apocalyptic signs of growing corruption and evil, are key Western cultural tendencies and values: women's liberation, freedom of speech and press, equal rights for all (including LGBTs, atheists, Jews, other infidels), freedom of assembly, friendships between Muslims and kuffār.[10] For Caliphators, the permissiveness of democracies has corrupted morals (sexual freedom, especially for women) and equality of Muslims and infidels has undermined social structures (patriarchy/triumphalist religiosity).[11] Indeed, for them, the West's scholarship, with its critical analysis

---

6   Yusuf al-Qaradawi speaking in 1995 to a gathering of the Muslim Arab Youth Association (MAYA) in Toledo, Ohio; exerpts at *The Investigative Project*; online, https://www.youtube.com/watch?v=jzh2mJf2ot4. Below, n23.

7   "An Explanatory Memorandum: On the General Strategic Goal of the Group [Muslim Brotherhood] in North America," May 22, 1991; text available at *The Investigative Project*, p. 21.

8   Cited by Cook, *Contemporary Muslim Apocalyptic*, 179, n12.

9   Jean-Pierre Filiu, *Apocalypse in Islam* (Los Angeles, 2011), chapter 4; Landes, *Heaven on Earth*, 445–51.

10   Bronislav Ostřanský, "The Lesser Signs of the Hour: A Reconstruction of the Islamic Apocalyptic Overture," *Oriental Empire* 81 (2013): 235–84, https://benjamins.com/catalog/ao.81.2.07ost.

11   Landes, "Triumphalist Religiosity: The Unanticipated Problem of the 21st Century," *Tablet*, February 10, 2016.

of holy documents, blasphemes against the one true faith, Islam. *Slay those who insult Islam!*

Like other millennial movements, this one recruits from a generation of seekers, of young people who face an uncertain and troubling future, who have lost faith in the sincerity of their own (traditional) leaders, and seek a true teaching that will mobilize and give direction to their entire being. Seekers are fervent and gravitate towards radical reorientations for spiritual guidance and discipline, for occasions to test one's faith, to grow stronger in the faith. Seekers have an affinity for apocalyptic communities who promise collective redemption in the coming messianic times. And like many other such movements, Caliphators use new technologies to recruit: neo-Islamic online jihad has immense power to capture the minds of young people, men and women, Muslim and infidel.[12]

On the *millennial* question of what this coming "heaven on earth," this world of *Dar al Islam*, of Islam triumphant, will look like, Caliphators remain vague, just as Marx and communists were vague about the workers' paradise.[13] The vaguer, the more people can be drawn into the apocalyptic excitement. Actual attempts to realize it, like ISIS, may disappoint, but, as with communists, they don't dissuade.[14]

Where Caliphators Disagree

Once inside apocalyptic time, Caliphators disagree on three major questions: 1) How fast will the redemption occur? 2) Where are we in the process? 3) How much of what is to come is due to the active work of the faithful, and what actions do the times demand? The answers give us a wide range of potential groupings within the movement. At the two extremes stand:

Jihad: *Active cataclysmic apocalyptic:* The global Caliphate will happen rapidly *because of* the faithful. By destroying evil (the unjust world that now prevails) *they* will bring on Allah's promised redemption. Thus, *mujahideen* (jihadis) are Allah's soldiers on earth to destroy evil and pave the way for the Caliphate. Tribal jihad has had remarkable success in the twenty-first century, especially

---

12 Reuven Paz, "Hotwiring the Apocalypse: Apocalyptic Elements of Global Jihadi Doctrines," in *Suicide Bombers: The Psychological, Religious and Other Imperatives*, ed. Mary Sharpe (Amsterdam, IOS Press, 2008), 103–18.

13 Cook, *Contemporary Muslim Apocalyptic*, 145–49.

14 On Marx's response to disappointment after 1848, see Landes, *Heaven on Earth*, chapter 10. To this very day, believers in that millennial dream still say, "communism has never really been tried."

in the Muslim world, where whole regions have melted down into states of chronic war, dislocating tens of millions of refugees—a veritable Nakba.[15] And as with the Palestinians confined to refugee camps, the jihadis use these camps to recruit and indoctrinate.[16] They have also penetrated Western societies with dramatic acts of suicide terror. In the opinion of one close observer, "The demons [especially suicide attacks] released by this age of chaos and war in the Middle East have become an unstoppable force."[17]

Da'wa: *Active transformative apocalyptic:* At the other end of the range are Caliphators who believe the process will happen more gradually, through persuasion rather than force. *Da'wa*—summons to the faith—they insist, is how Islam should spread: the faithful summon the infidels; and if they do not become Muslims, they will become *preemptive dhimmi* (accept subjection to Islam *before* conquest). The global Caliphate might come now, but it could also take another generation, it may even take till the end of this century, so auspiciously begun in 1400 (1979) and destined to conclude with a global Caliphate in 1500 (2076).[18]

As much as Westerners want to see meaningful signs of moderation and nonviolence in this difference, among Caliphators they constitute two fronts of the same war. Whereas for their Wahhabi forebears, Da'wa was a preliminary to jihad, a chance for infidels to convert and avoid the pains of military conquest,[19] today's Caliphators believe that with the judicious alternation between *Jihad* (terror) and *Da'wa* (directing the terrorized), Caliphators can successfully convert infidels the world over.

As far as Caliphators are concerned, infidels now have three options: become Muslim, become *dhimmi*, or die. Those waging both Jihad and *Da'wa* agree that the supreme goal, for which it is an honor to sacrifice one's life, is the dominion of Islam over the whole earth. In Caliphator circles, however, it is the Jihadis who have bragging rights to honor; they are martyrs and conquerors even in death. Da'īs do the less glamorous, even shameful, work of condemning

---

15 On tribal jihad, see Laurent Murawiec, *The Mind of Jihad* (New York: Oxford University Press, 2008), chapter 4.

16 Raymond Ibrahim, "Indoctrinated in Hate: 'This Is the Start of the New Caliphate,'" *Gatestone*, April 6, 2021.

17 Patrick Cockburn, *Age of Jihad*.

18 "The Time When the Mahdi will Emerge," http://www.geocities.ws/muslimapocalyptic/time_when_the_mahdi_will_emerge.htm.

19 See Natana DeLong's post-Orientalist treatment of Da'wa among the Wahhabis: "a more positive and inclusive approach of dialogue and discussion geared toward reconciliation and cooperation whenever possible," *Wahhabi Islam: From Revival and Reform to Global Jihad* (New York: Oxford University Press, 2004), 201.

fellow Muslims to please infidels (and thereby gain influence, protecting the Jihadis)[20]—anything to speed up the process, even enduring shame.

As with all such movements, the scenarios with which one enters apocalyptic time never pan out, and all believers end up having to negotiate the inevitable disappointments of apocalyptic time without losing that thrilling sense of living on the edge of cosmic finality. The genuinely zealous rarely give up: they shift scenarios in order to maintain their apocalyptic hopium. As they feel the need, they move back and forth from violence to pacifism, from Da'wa to Jihad. In apocalyptic time, categories are fluid, continually reconfiguring. The military fall of Al Qaeda or ISIS in no way signals the end of Caliphator creativity in generating combinations of *Da'wa* and Jihad. This is a generational struggle.[21]

Caliphator War on Infidels: Aims, Targets, Strategies

For Caliphators, *Occidens delendus est*: everything that the West prides itself on, and every technical advantage that it has over Muslims and Islam, must be seized or destroyed. Indeed, for some Caliphators, Western technologies prepare their way; globalization, the internet, modern forms of transportation, open borders, are all salvific vehicles for *their* victory, their messiah's donkey. Just as Eusebius argued that the Roman Empire served as a *praeparatio evangelica* in which the Roman empire laid the groundwork for the spread of the Gospels, so is globalization in the twenty-first century, a *praeparatio caliphatae*.

This may strike Western infidels (as it did Roman pagans) as a crazy ambition, based on the millennialists wildly overvaluing their capabilities. But for people moved by "outrageous hope," nothing is impossible. And, alas, even if they end up being wrong, like the Taiping and other violent messianic movements before them, Caliphators can do immense damage in the process of failing.[22]

Ironically, this Western incredulity at their ambitions has worked greatly to the Caliphators' advantage. Westerners hearing of Caliphator goals in the later twentieth century—Queen of England in a burkah, Green Flag of Islam flying from the White House—could not take the movement seriously.[23] Anyone

---

20 See above on the Muslim Association of Britain (MAB), p. 137 note 15.

21 Thomas Jocelyn, "What a New Report Tells Us About Al-Qaeda and ISIS," *The Dispatch*, January 12, 2022.

22 On Taiping and the killing of tens of millions of Chinese, see Landes, *Heaven on Earth*, chapter 7.

23 New York Imam Ahmad Dwidar: "In 1995, I Heard Sermons Calling on Muslims to March on the White House and Turn it into the Muslim House," June 9, 2005, Clip No. 730. Note the

who drew attention to the problem, was told to stop the bad joke; those who persisted became "Islamophobes."

For Caliphators, the two crucial global targets in the battle for world dominion are Israel, the invader of *Dar al Islam*, and the West, the most powerful civilization of *Dar al Harb*, especially its most powerful state, the USA. Both constitute successful autonomous infidel entities, therefore, insults to Muslim triumphalism. Caliphators consider those who dwell therein, inhabitants of the realm of the sword: *harbi'un*, those destined to the sword. Israel is especially unbearable: autonomous Jews invading the heart of Dar al Islam.[24] Indeed Jews play a central role in the apocalyptic literature of the fifteenth century AH (1979–2076), Israel is the heartland of evil from which the *Dajjal* (Antichrist) will appear.[25] Depending on the Caliphator, either Israel or the US is the "Great Satan."

Asymmetrical Warfare's Cognitive Campaigns: Caliphator Da'wa

Under modern conditions, however, an open war with the West, even with Israel, seems impossible. So, like all asymmetrical wars, the early stages take place largely on the cognitive battlefield: convince your more powerful foes not to use their superior force, while mobilizing yours by promising violence later.[26] But unlike more traditional combinations of guerrilla and cogwar that want to chase out a more powerful enemy (e.g., the Vietnamese versus American troops), Caliphators want to invade. And so, they face the far more difficult task of convincing their enemy to stand down and not resist their invasion. Thus, while violent *Mujahideen* attract the most attention and do terrible damage where they cannot be controlled (from Afghanistan across the Middle East to Nigeria), and spectacular damage in their surprise attacks in the West, by far the most active arm of the Caliphator movement in the West wages cognitive war (*Da'wa*).[27]

---

incredulity of the Western interviewer at the jihadi option before 9–11. This probably refers to the gathering at which al-Qaradawi gave his "Da'wa will conquer the West" speech (above, n6).

24 Landes, "The Emotional Nakba," *Tablet*, June 24, 2014.

25 Cook, *Contemporary Muslim Apocalyptic*, chapter 5; Filiu, *Muslim Apocalyptic*, chapter 5.

26 Stuart Green, "Cognitive Warfare," Thesis presented to Joint Military Intelligence College, Washington DC, 2008; Ron Schleifer, *Psychological Warfare in the Intifada* (Portland OR, 2006); Landes, "The Final Battle," *Tablet*, August 3, 2011.

27 *Global Insurgency and the Future of Armed Conflict: Debating Fourth-generation Warfare*, ed. T. Terriff, A. Karp and R. Karp (New York: Routledge, 2007).

Da'wa Caliphators living in *Dar al Harb* (e.g., the West), however, need to disguise their real goals, since people (even postmodern westerners) tend to resist when they know they're being invaded. Thus, the primary Caliphator concerns while operating in enemy territory are, by their very nature, deceptive: to hide their intentions from the people they target; to spread dissension in their enemy's ranks; and to leverage jihadi attacks into concessions, even as they publicly condemn the jihadis. To do so, Da'īs must find allies within target cultures, culture leaders who (like dhimmi leaders throughout the history of Islamic rule) suppress criticism of Islam among their people, attacking fellow infidels who draw attention to the behavior of the Caliphators.[28]

In early 2000 the likelihood of a global Caliphate seemed, even to many wannabe Caliphators, like an awfully tall order: impossible militarily, ridiculously quixotic as a cultural war. After all, Westerners weren't that stupid. . . . Only the most fervent of true believers could think that, even with Allah's help, the global Caliphate was possible.

So, as with all asymmetrical wars that pit tiny insurgencies against powerful foes, the early stages largely took place on the cognitive battlefield, not the kinetic one. Da'īs "summon" the infidels to convert to the one true faith. Their demotic message of universal liberation and equality can even sound kind and uplifting.[29] Of course, the freedom and equality are only for Muslims. Infidels who hear the kind message and refuse to convert, even when asked nicely, become another matter, especially if they criticize Muslims.[30]

At the heart of the Caliphator challenge to the contemporary power holders in the Muslim world, stands the reproach that they do too little to advance the Caliphate at home and abroad . . . they are weak Muslims, even apostates. When the "Mahdi" Mohammed Abdullah al-Qahtani and his followers attacked the Saudi Monarchy in 1400 AH (1979), at the heart or their call to arms was the Saud's failure to cleave to the path of jihad and to show sufficient hostility to the USA—worse, for allowing infidel troops to station in the kingdom.[31] In response, the Saudi royals bought domestic rule (permission from their theologians to violate the sanctuary of the Ka'ba and violently put down the revolt), in

---

28 See Bat-Ye'or on both the Muslim identification of criticism with blasphemy, and a mimicry complex in which the dhimmi adopt the beliefs of their masters in order to ingratiate themselves, Bat Ye'or, *Islam and Dhimmitude: Where Civilizations Collide*. Tr. Miriam Kochan and David Littman (Madison, NJ: Fairleigh Dickinson University Press, 2003), 106–10.

29 Dwidar articulates a more demotic message of the transformative Caliphator scenarios leading to Islam's ultimate victory (see n23).

30 An almost identical dynamic produced much of the Christian hostility to Jews: refusal to convert was taken as an intolerable insult.

31 Trofimov, *Siege of Mecca*, 45–75.

exchange for lavishly funding the most radical Wahhabi-Caliphator Da'wa in the West, to flood the West, via diaspora Imams, with the Caliphator message.[32] In that sense, 1400 in the Sunni world produced an almost instantaneous failure of jihad (the repressed takeover attempt), which nevertheless led to a massive intensification of cogwar against the West, systematically radicalizing mosques, neighborhoods, and colleges in *Dar al Harb*.[33]

Apocalyptic believers follow a consistent pattern in their relations with the "apocalyptic other." Often in the early stages of belief in an imminent apocalyptic finale, they are friendly, even passionate in pursuing good relations with those who have yet to hear "the good news." Only after disappointment, do those believers who remain grow testy, even hostile, to those who rejected their all-consuming offer. Especially where believers have taken the levers of power, one finds an oft-repeating pattern: what begins in generosity, turns, in frustration, to coercive purity.[34]

This pattern certainly marked the origins of Islam and is embedded in the range of divine instruction given in the Qur'an, notable in the difference between the early Meccan and later Medinan suras. Caliphator Da'is, to emphasize their good intentions and respect for the "other," like to cite the Qur'an to prove that Islam prohibits coercion in matters of religion (2:256). They omit mention that this verse was *abrogated* by later verses of instruction that call for war and terror as motivators for conversion.[35] The doctrine of abrogation locks in place that apocalyptic dynamic; later violence and triumphalism legally trump earlier expansive religiosity.

Are there Muslims who escape the ever-tightening (limbic) noose of tribal Manichaeism? Fortunately, there are, but who knows how numerous they are,

---

32 Harold Rhode, *Modern Islamic Warfare*, chapter 2; Dore Gold, *Hatred's Kingdom: How Saudi Arabia Supports the New Global Terrorism* (New York: Regnery, 2003), 106–55. The widespread use of Saudi teaching materials in American mosques, see Coughlin, *Catastrophic Failure: Blindfolding America in the Face of Jihad* (Washington, DC: Center for Security Policy Press, 2015), Part VI.

33 For a wide-ranging description of this Da'wa strategy for taking over America, see Daniel Pipes, *Radical Islam Reaches America* (New York: W.W. Norton, 2002). For the success of this strategy in radicalizing Muslims, see the twin memoirs of Ed Husain and Majeed Nawaz (below), and Coughlin, *Catastrophic Failure*, Part VII.

34 Lee Quinby, "Coercive Purity: The Dangerous Promise of Apocalyptic Masculinity," in *The Year 2000: Essays on the End*, ed. C. Strozier and M. Flynn (New York: New York University Press, 1997), 154–165. Analysis of the French Terror in these terms, Landes, *Heaven on Earth*, chapter 9.

35 On the doctrine of Abrogation, whereby earlier verses are rendered null by later contradictory ones, see *Approaches to the History of the Interpretation of the Qur'an*, ed. Andrew Rippin (Oxford, 1988), 130–1; David Bukay, "Peace or Jihad? Abrogation in Islam," *Middle East Quarterly* (Fall 2007): 3–11.

or how complete their escape? What happens then? Do they become stronger (if non-conformist) faithful? Agnostic? Atheist? Do they convert to other religions? Do they maintain a demotic curiosity and openness, a sense of self-deprecating humor? We infidels who do not want either to convert or to submit to Islam must ask ourselves two sets of questions: On the one hand: Why are so many Muslim seekers drawn to the most testosteronic, violent apocalyptic dreams? Why does a deeply destructive pathology have so much drawing-power among Muslim seekers? And on the other: Where are the demotic movements in Islam? It is our loss as a civilization, that we do not seek out such valuable allies, but rather, following the lead of triumphalist Muslims, shun them as ineffective, even inauthentic Muslims. The fact that we have no idea of their numbers, neither the demotic nor the Caliphators, testifies to our inadequate thinking (and indirectly to the power of Westsplaining)—to our ignorance of the culture/religion whose worst aspects we turn away from contemplating, even as it assaults us.

The Da'ī's Prayer in 2000

What we can know, even without leaving our armchairs, is that *Da'wa* Caliphators living in *Dar al Harb* need to disguise their real goals. They were, after all, trying to break into a scene that had, for decades, been dominated by radical demotic voices in which Caliphator ideas about women and infidels, if openly espoused, would be considered regressive to say the least. Tell infidels what *al-Walā' wal-Barā'* means to triumphalist Muslims, and it would go over like a lead balloon among folks for whom "tribal" was an insult. Who among those so targeted would give these invaders a platform? Who would endorse their ideas and cover-up their real intentions? Presumably no one ... well maybe some fringe neo-Trotskyites still stewing in their revolutionary hatreds, or neo-Nazis who, like Hitler, admired Islam's fighting spirit. But what weight could they carry?

Let us return to early 2000. Shortly after the Y2K bug had passed without incident, with the West leading the global community into a new millennium of civil society, the likelihood of a global Caliphate seemed like an awfully tall order, even to wannabe Caliphators: impossible militarily, ridiculously quixotic as a cogwar plan. "The West would never be stupid enough to let us invade," they might respond to al Qaeda's call to Jihad.

And this was probably the attitude of most Muslims at that time: even if they wanted a global Caliphate, the odds against were so great that only fools would openly embrace that dream, dedicate their lives to its realization, risk the terrible retribution such an open declaration of war might unleash. Like most millennial dreams before the advent of apocalyptic time, they were still largely private transcripts, and when they surfaced, they elicited resistance. Only the most fervent of true believers could think that the global Caliphate was possible, was worth sacrificing their lives.

So, imagine such a one, say, a disciple of Yussuf al Qaradawi—avid reader of the Caliphator writings of Maududi, Qutb and Abdullah Azzam, enthralled by the vision of conquering the entire world—surveying the task in those early days of the "new global millennium," penning a prayer to Allah for help in the long road ahead to the global Caliphate. What follows is my imaginative reconstruction of such a believer's plea.

> A prayer for Caliphators, fervent believers, partakers in the redemptive conquest of the West by *Da'wa*, the non-violent *Mujaddid* (Renewal).
>
> **Oh Allah, the all Merciful, give us enemies who submit to our will without our needing to use violence.**
>
> *Give us enemies who help us to disguise our ambition to subject them, who muffle our acts of war, and ignore our deployment among them.*
>
> *Give us enemies who accept those of us who fight for the Caliphate with Da'wa, as "moderates," who have "nothing to do" with "violent extremists."*
>
> *Give us enemies who engage us as advisors and consultants in intelligence and police work, as prison chaplains, community liaisons, dialogue partners, college teachers and administrators, mainstream journalists.*
>
> *Give us enemies whose journalists and scholars will present our war propaganda as news, as verified, reliable information.*
>
> *Give us enemies who believe that, "except for a tiny minority," the "vast majority" of Muslims are moderate and peaceful, who repeat after us, "Islam, Religion of Peace."*
>
> *Give us enemies who attack those (including Muslims) who criticize Islam as xenophobic and racist Islamophobes.*

Give us enemies who adopt our apocalyptic enemy, so that they join us in an attack on one of their key allies.

Give us enemies who legitimate our terrorism as "resistance" and denounce any recourse to violence in their own defense, as "terrorism."

Give us enemies who turn the other cheek, who continue to respect the dignity of our beliefs, even as we heap disdain on theirs.

Give us enemies who believe our sincerity when we invoke human rights when, in reality, we despise those rights for women, slaves, and infidels, and only invoke them on our behalf.

Give us enemies who accuse our enemies of apartheid even as they studiously avoid speaking of our apartheid world-view and practice.

Give us enemies who welcome our angry "Street" in the heart of their capital cities and allow us into their progressive "anti-imperial" ranks.

Give us useful infidels who will willingly behave like dhimmi.

And may those among our enemies who act as they should, may they play prominent roles in their public sphere. Ameen. Ameen. Ameen. 1000 times Ameen.

I don't think, in early 2000, anyone who uttered such a prayer had any idea how fulsomely Allah would fulfill his requests. Only a few years later, however, the political advisor Ed Husain, in his Hizb ut-Tahrir stage, marveled at the folly of the Western progressives in their dealings with Caliphators.[36] The former Muslim radical, Hassan Butt, recalled how amusing it was to watch useful infidels Westsplaining:

> When I was still a member of what is probably best termed the British Jihadi Network, a series of semi-autonomous British Muslim terrorist groups linked by a single ideology [Global Caliphate], I remember how we used to laugh in celebration whenever people on TV proclaimed that the sole cause for Islamic acts of terror like 9/11, the Madrid bombings and 7/7 was Western foreign policy. By blaming the[ir] government for

---

36 Ed Husain, *Islamist*, chapter 15; see also, Nick Cohen, *What's Left?*, Postscript.

our actions, those who pushed the "Blair's bombs" line did our propaganda work for us. More important, they also helped to draw away any critical examination from the real engine of our violence: Islamic theology.[37]

And those who slipped the net and spoke about that Islamic theology, like Maajid Nawaz, got denounced as Islamophobes.

Pas d'amalgame! *Lumpers Versus Splitters, Strategy Versus Ideology*

The association of *Da'wa* and Jihad as part of a larger millennial project challenges a number of common approaches to the problem of "religious" "terrorism." Experts tend to split; they differentiate various groups according to specific characteristics and actions. And among the great differentiators our information professionals use, recourse to violence plays a central role. In this, the specialists participate in a larger politico-cultural trend that insists on a strong distinction between violent jihadis and peaceful moderate Muslims, refusing to lump them together. But, actually, we are dealing here with two different approaches to lumping and splitting. Caliphator, as a term for a specific, active millennial movement, lumps together the warlike jihadis and the "peaceful" *da'is*. In so doing, it challenges a different school of lumpers, those who include in the same group "the vast and peaceful majority" (that is, *Da'i* Caliphators *and* real moderates), and split off the "extremists" as a "tiny minority" who have "nothing to do with *true* Islam."

Splitting Between Jihadi Groups

Even within the realm of violence, splitters distinguish, as in the case of two vigorous practitioners of suicide terror: Hamas and *Global Jihadis* like al Qaeda and ISIS. When American journalists used "terrorist" to describe Al Qaeda but not Hamas, defenders of Israel protested.[38] When the UN condemned ISIS for its barbarity in 2014, Israeli PM Netanyahu predictably objected that ISIS and

---

37 Hassan Butt, "My Plea to Fellow Muslims: You Must Renounce Terror," the *Guardian*, July 1, 2007.
38 Above, 85–88.

Hamas were the same.[39] "No, they're not, they're totally different," pundits and journalists explained in unison.[40] "Localized" groups like Hamas "adopt a strong *nationalist* agenda that separates them *starkly* from the global jihadist aspirations entertained by Al Qaeda."[41] Indeed, some preferred to compare Israel to ISIS.[42]

And yet, both these movements of identity entrepreneurs feed and feed off a generation of seekers who have washed up on their Caliphator shores, there to expend their triumphalist passions. Cross fertilization and competition for recruits among seekers happen all the time. ISIS learned its cyber-savvy from Palestinians;[43] Hamas and ISIS clash over recruits.[44] The academic distinction is as poorly thought out as the confusion over terrorist and freedom fighter. And both cases of poor thought misinform and disorient us and serve Caliphator cogwar ends.

In fact, far from being some localized, nationalist movement, Hamas holds a place of special honor in the world of global, Caliphator jihad. They fight on the key front of that global battle, resisting the blasphemy of Israel, that invader and desecrator in the heart of *Dar al Islam*: For both Sunnis and Shi'is, the path to the global Caliphate runs through Jerusalem.[45] In launching the "al Aqsa Intifada" against Israel in 2000, they announced to the entire Umma, that the time to put an end to the humiliating "Treaty of Hudaybiyyah" had at last arrived. Better yet, the time for the apocalyptic hadith of the Rocks and Trees, for the extermination of the Jews had come.[46] Not only "Palestinians" believe that "Inshallah, Jerusalem will soon become the capital of the global Caliphate."

---

39 "'ISIS, Hamas are branches of the same poisonous tree', Netanyahu tells UN," *World Jewish Congress*, September 30, 2014.

40 "[T]otally distinct ... ideologies," Max Fisher, "Hamas is not ISIS: Here's Why Netanyahu says it is," *Vox*, August 25, 2014; Alessandria Massi, "What Is the Difference between ISIS And Hamas?" *International Business Times*, July 19, 2014. See chapter 2, on ombudsmen using the distinction to allow the "terrorism" label for Al Qaeda but not Hamas 85–88. On the importance of for Caliphators to differentiate jihad (legitimate killing) from terror (killing without right), see Coughlin, *Catastrophic Failure*, 481–518.

41 Asaf Moghadam, *The Globalization of Martyrdom: Al Qaeda, Salafi Jihad, and the Diffusion of Suicide Attacks* (Baltimore: Johns Hopkins University Press, 2008), 59 [italics mine]; see Table 1.1 for a list of differences.

42 Benjamin Weinthal, "Outrage over top German politician comparing Hamas to Israel," *Jerusalem Post*, September 28, 2014; "Amnesty campaigns manager equates Israel with Islamic State," *Jewish News*, November 4, 2014.

43 Patrick Kingsley, "Who is behind ISIS's terrifying online propaganda operation?" *Guardian*, June 23, 2014.

44 Asama al-Goul, "Gaza Salafists pledge allegiance to ISIS," *Al Monitor*, February 2014.

45 Bin Laden's ideologue, al Azzam, expounded this idea in the early years of the 15th century/1980s, *Min Kabul ila al-Quds* [From Kabul to Jerusalem] (Peshawar, Markaz al-Shahid 'Azzam al-I'lami, 1989); Cook, *Contemporary Muslim Apocalyptic*, 172–76, 191–97.

46 See Saudi theologian Hawali, "The Day of Wrath."

Muslim Brotherhood candidate for the Egyptian presidency, Mohamed Morsi, launched his successful campaign with that promise, much to the offense of some Egyptian nationalists.[47]

Indeed, whereas other Mujahideen had launched successful jihads in the 1400s/1980s, most notably al Qaeda's defeat of Russia in 1989/1410, now, in 2000/1421, Palestinian jihadis took the lead, and, via Al Jazeera, the entire Arab world was rivetted by this grand battle inaugurating the final war.[48] With the narrative of Muhammad al Durah slain in cold blood by "at the hand of the Jews," broadcast everywhere in Arab world by al Jazeera and Bin Laden,[49] Palestinian Caliphators awakened the *Umma*. "Here," they said, "anyone can see undeniable proof of the merciless threat that Western infidels pose to us innocent Muslims." The Arab coverage of this Intifada, with Al Durah in the starring role, was the West's worst nightmare: a recruiting tool whereby jihadis could say to their fellow Muslims: "We are in a war against the West—you must join us."[50]

The al Durah icon of hatred aroused a thirst for revenge that literally legitimated suicide terror the Muslim world over,[51] and, equally valuable, aroused an undeniable *frisson* of *Schadenfreude* from progressive *ressentimentalistes*.[52] Thus, in the opening years of the new millennium, *Palestinian* jihadis justified and refined the weapon with which, today, *Global Jihadis* intend to conquer the West in the course of this century-long *Mujaddid*.[53]

At the height of the "Jenin Massacre" (i.e., when Israel was fighting off a suicide terror war, and the West was cheering on the terrorists), a PA cleric invoked the genocidal hadith about the extermination of every last Jew, as

---

47 Raed Salah, "Jerusalem will be the Capital of the Global Caliphate," Nazareth, November 7, 2014. "Egyptian Cleric Safwat Higazi Launches MB Candidate Mohamed Morsi's Campaign: Morsi Will Restore the 'United States of the Arabs' with Jerusalem as Its Capital (Al-Nas TV, Egypt)," *MEMRI* #3431, May 1, 2012.

48 For the most elaborate apocalyptic interpretation see the Saudi theologian, Hawali, *The Day of Wrath.*" On the apocalyptic temper of Palestinian thought, see Cook, *Contemporary Muslim Apocalyptic*, 106–25.

49 Above, 11–13.

50 Eric Bradner, "Clinton explains why she won't use 'radical Islam,'" CNN, December 7, 2015.

51 "Suicide Bombing Terrorism during the Current Israeli-Palestinian Confrontation (September 2000–December 2005)," 2, 5. On the theological debate, see Haim Malka, "Must Innocents Die? The Islamic Debate over Suicide Attacks," *Middle East Quarterly*, 10:2 (2003), 19–28. For a representative sample that cites the excitement that traversed the Arab world at the suicide bombing of children at the Jerusalem Sbarro Pizzeria, Fahmi Huweidi, "I cannot hide my happiness," *Al Ahram*, August 14, 2001.

52 A Jewish Dutch friend remembers the pleasure in the voice of the announcer reporting the "murder" of al Durah.

53 See Cockburn, *Age of Jihad.*

heralding the global conquest by the "Muslim nation . . . from ocean to ocean."[54] The idea that Hamas is somehow fundamentally different from ISIS, that the T-word might apply to ISIS (at least in post-9/11 US), but not to Hamas, that we consider these distinctions critical to developing a doctrine of defense against Muslim extremists . . . such remarkably mistaken conclusions can only benefit the Caliphators.

On the contrary, all Caliphator jihadis, whether operating locally or globally, share five fundamental beliefs that dwarf any differences:

- they consider all *kuffār* (infidels) and *murtadd* (apostates, backsliders) guilty, and, therefore, legitimate targets of violent *retribution*;[55]
- they preach the paranoid imperative: the enemy wants to annihilate Islam, we must annihilate the enemy;
- they teach absolute hatred as a weapon in a genocidal jihad against these apocalyptic enemies.[56]
- they have a special fear of Jews, who must be exterminated not only because of the hadith, but because they are "sons of pigs and apes" (Qur'an), and yet who, inexplicably, are so smart that although they're a thousandth of the Muslim population, stand at the heart of an international conspiracy to destroy Islam and enslave mankind;[57]
- they use suicide martyrs to target their enemies, including, increasingly, fellow Muslims, and random *kuffār* in the West.[58]

Caliphator groups come together, develop, succeed briefly, subside or fail. When they (inevitably) lose steam, seekers improvise apocalyptic scenarios, either regroup or get replaced by other fresher groups of seekers, impatient with their failures; Caliphator seekers go from leader-driven to acephalous and back again with ease.[59] Whence this fluidity? Caliphators believe they fight a

---

54 For the full quote, see above, 16n46.

55 Daniel Pipes, "Can Infidels be Innocents?" *Lion's Den*, August, 2005.

56 "Kill a Jew," *Palestinian Media Watch*.

57 Cook, *Contemporary Muslim Apocalyptic*, chapter 5.

58 With some, the sowing terror among infidels overrides concern for collateral Muslim damage, I. Kricheli, Y. Rosner, A. Mendelboim, and A. Schweitzer, "Suicide Attacks in 2016: The Highest Number of Fatalities," *INSS Insight* 887, January 5, 2017.

59 After mentioning the hate-filled rivalries between Salafis and Hizb ut-Tahrir in London in the early 1990s, Nawaz notes: "A few years later, this would change: Salafism and Islamism would fuse to form Jihadism, most famously seen in the eventual rise of al-Qaeda." *Radical*, 68. For the dynamics of apocalyptic movements in their early stages, see Landes, *Heaven on Earth*, chapter 2.

generational war, and their ranks are fed by waves of Muslim seekers, earnest Muslims like the young Maajid Nawaz or Ed Husain, attracted to Caliphator identity-entrepreneurships, like Hizb ut-Tahrir. There they find Caliphators who promise to restore their honor by galvanizing their hostility and guaranteeing cosmic rewards for attacking the hated enemy.[60]

For varying periods and at different times, then, these global currents coalesce into movements led by religious warlords, like Hizballah, Hamas, al Qaeda, Muqtada al Sadr, ISIS: they rise, do damage, and morph into other shapes, or stubbornly go on, most, if not all, with the same millennial goal.[61] This surge of triumphal millennialism in the fifteenth/twenty-first century, has deep psychological roots, and represents not an apocalyptic wave, but rather a *tide* of active waves that will play out over at least another generation.[62]

Part of the power Caliphators exercise over Muslim seekers is a discourse that, within its belligerent parameters, is ecumenical: its adepts have many visions of the Caliphate and many options on how to get there and when. Whatever path one chooses—some combination of/alternation between Da'wa or Jihad—one holds firm to the faith that the sum total of the efforts of all Caliphators will lead to ultimate triumph. Caliphators may wonder: "who is the Mahdi who will lead the final assault? Will it be on Israel? On Rome? On Washington?" And messianic candidates do and will appear all the time, bottom-up.[63] Islam's fifteenth century (1400–1433/1979–2012), has already produced more than its share of jihadi warlords with messianic pretensions. And we will probably see more at the approach of the fifteenth Mujaddid (1500 AH), in 2076 CE.

Splitting between Jihadis and Da'īs

If Western policy experts tend to overestimate distinctions *between* jihadi groups like Hamas and ISIS, how much more do they distinguish jihadis from da'īs? Since 9–11, the dominant consensus treats da'īs and jihadis as fundamentally different—in the words of one analyst, "the *Not Bin Laden affect* (NBL) ...

---

60 On identity entrepreneurs, Green, *Cognitive Warfare*, 86–108. Nawaz rose in the movement by becoming an identity entrepreneur himself, rallying the intimidated Pakistani students at his London college, *Radical*, 72–3.

61 Connie Cass, "Al-Qaida's heirs thrive in Mideast, Africa chaos," *AP*, September 16, 2014.

62 For critical psychological insights, Nancy Kobrin, *The Jihadi Dictionary* (Mamaroneck, NY, 2016).

63 Timothy Furnish, *Holiest Wars*; and *Sects, Lies, and the Caliphate*; Cook, *Contemporary Muslim Apocalyptic*, chapter 6.

the widely held belief that there is some kind of firewall between the Global Muslim Brotherhood [on the one hand], and Al Qaeda, ISIS, and other related groups."[64] This approach avoids seeing the deep solidarity—the *asabiyya*—of a cosmic tribe coming together in a wave of apocalyptic Manichaeism.[65] Such a distinction may prove a lethal conceptual error.

Caliphators think in terms of (apocalyptic) strategies: *When* is the time to say and do what, to whom? . . . To Muslims? . . . To friendly infidels? . . . To powerful but hated infidels? In apocalyptic time, scenarios can change dramatically, and ideologies serve primarily as narrative jazz to prolong the apocalyptic experience, here active, there passive. Viewed retrospectively, the apocalyptic "narratives" often appear as rationalizations for behavior driven by the desire to bring on the millennium as fast as Allah will allow it.[66]

Da'īs differ from Jihadis most fundamentally on their discourse about Islam. Whereas a Jihadi would assure you that his bloody, holy-war, interpretation of the Qur'an is the true Islamic reading; the Da'ī will insist that Islam is a religion of peace, and any infidel asserting what Jihadis say is an "Islamophobe" who should be de-platformed. Whereas a Jihadi would assure you that his goal is genocide of the Jews the world over and global conquest producing a global Caliphate, the Da'ī narrative is pitched to the West, and speaks of freedom fighting, and defensive war against the twin colonial and imperial Antichrists, Israel and the USA. Whereas a manly Caliphator would laugh at the cartoons of Muhammad and make cartoons about Jews and Christians ten times as bad, the Da'ī will express deep pain and hurt feelings on behalf of the vast majority of moderate Muslims.

Whether a Caliphator chooses violence or nonviolence in dealing with infidels (*al-Walā' wal-Barā'*) and with dissenters (*murtad*), all their decisions reflect more the perception of an apocalyptic (redemptive) timeline than matters of principle.[67] Disputes arise from the sense of (apocalyptic) urgency, not fundamental differences. Ed Husain describes the various contentious groups in England:

---

64 Steven Murley, "The Global Anti-Aggression Campaign 2003–2016," *Global Muslim Brotherhood Research Center*, February 2017.

65 Murawiec, *The Mind of Jihad*, chapter 4; Stephen Coughlin, *Catastrophic Failure*, Part III.

66 For a discussion of the role of apocalyptic (imminent) expectations in setting millennial dreams into action, see Landes, *Heaven on Earth*, chapter 2.

67 Coughlin, *Catastrophic Failure*, 129–64; *Accusations of Unbelief in Islam: A Diachronic Perspective on Takfīr*, ed. C. Adang, H. Ansari, M. Fierro and S. Schmidtke (Leiden: Brill, 2016); Anthony Celso, "Islamic Regression, Jihadist Frustration and Takfirist Hyper Violence," *Journal of Political Sciences & Public Affairs*, 4.2 (2016).

> But though internally divided, they are all in agreement in their veneration of Maududi and Qutb. In different but unquestionable ways, they are affiliated to the Jamat-e-Islami of the subcontinent [Pakistan/India], the Muslim Brotherhood of the Arab world, or Hamas of Palestine.[68]

The more urgently Caliphators anticipate apocalyptic change, the more coercive they become (strike terror!); the more extended the time horizon, the more patient they can afford to be (speak softly). For one, *kuffār* are enemies; for the other, "friends"; for both they will soon have to choose between conversion, subjection, or death.[69]

Little in these differing assessments of the place of the present in the apocalyptic timeline prevents Caliphators of all styles from cooperating. Indeed, they have mastered the tough-cop, nice-cop routine, which has proven especially successful with those infidels, like Klausen, who have difficulty discerning demopathy.[70] Granted, there are tensions. After terror strikes, for example, "peaceful" *da'īs* recriminate against jihadis (for jumping the gun). When Western infidels pressure *Da'īs* to condemn the jihadis, some reluctantly do. But once infidels have eagerly accepted their denunciation of the Jihadis, *da'īs* have a much easier job *after* terror strikes: Bin Laden exulted in how, after 9–11, the Western conversions poured in.[71] Granted Jihadis dislike da'īs mixing with their progressive allies (especially the LGBTQs), but that is the price of Da'wa's cognitive war.[72]

Even peaceful *da'īs*, however, have limits to their patience. Disappointed transformative expectations (e.g., an insufficiently compliant infidel response to "summons") affect attitudes: some extend their timeline and become more patient,[73] while others turn to violence and coercive purity. The key question

---

68 Husain, *The Islamist*, 167.

69 Raymond Ibrahim, "How Circumstance Dictates Islamic Behavior: Preach Peace When Weak, Wage War When Strong," *Middle East Quarterly*, January 18, 2012.

70 On demopaths and their dupes, see 252–59. On Klausen and demopaths, below, 252–56. On the use of the nice-cop, tough-cop technique by the Muslim Brotherhood, see Stephen Merley, "The Global Anti-Aggression Campaign 2003–2016," *Global Muslim Brotherhood Research Center*, February 2017.

71 Brendan Bernhard, *White Muslim: From LA to NY ... to Jihad?* (Brooklyn, NY: Melville House, 2006); Jim Treacher, "NY Times Reports on Muslim Proselytizing During Charlie Hebdo Attack, Then Deletes It," *Daily Caller*, January 8, 2015.

72 Ayaan Hirsi Ali, "Why Islamism became Woke," *Unherd*, July 13, 2021.

73 See the role of redating the End several centuries into the future (Filiu, *Apocalypse in Islam*, 80–83; Landes, "Lest the Millennium"). On the role of Hamas' Bassam Jirrar's 1992/1413 prediction of Israel's destruction in 2022/1444 in counseling a passive response to Israel, see

about Caliphators is: when do they think the time has come to end taqiyya, when need one no longer conceal what one really thinks, namely: Islam is here to dominate.[74] Once convinced that they hold the upper hand, Caliphators will predictably turn on targeted neighbors: your expiration date is up.[75]

Says the Caliphator to the infidel: "Da'wa or Jihad? Your choice."

Cook, *Contemporary Muslim Apocalyptic*, 122–125. Update 2022: Ori Nir, "End Times for Israel: The Apocalyptic 'Quranic' Prophecy Electrifying Palestinians," *Haaretz*, April 17, 2022; fisked for Westsplaining, Augean Stables, http://www.theaugeanstables.com/2022/04/26/haaretz-ori-nir-westsplains-palestinian-apocalyptic-prophecy/.

74 Haitham Ibn Thbait of the American chapter of Hizb ut-Tahrir, speaking at the Khilafah 2016 conference, held in Chicago on May 15: "Islam is here to dominate!" https://www.youtube.com/watch?v=3oe9YFe4Pl8.

75 Leyan Saleh tweets: "Happy Hanukah to my Jewish neighbors. Bas ballah jan. I think it's time you moved out, no?" and "May god ruin the homes of the Jews. Yatrib bait al yahud." https://twitter.com/canarymission/status/823440426413785088.

Liberal Cognitive Egocentrics and Their Demopathic Kryptonite

Imagining our
values universal, we
can't see just how rare.

People use the term liberal today both as a proud self-identifier and an insult. Originally it applied to "free persons," the "enlightened" individuals who, having thrown off the chains of "self-imposed immaturity," their "mind-forged manacles," become autonomous moral agents.[1] As individuals capable of exercising reasoned self-restraint, they don't need the heavy hand of coercion to behave well in public life; they believe in liberty reciprocally granted, the consent of the governed, and equality before the law.[2] Diderot's *Encyclopédie* defined "natural law" as the product of "in each man an act of pure understanding that reasons in the silence of passions about what man may demand of his neighbor (*semblable*) and what his neighbor has a right to demand of him."[3]

In that reciprocal grant of freedom lies the key to democracy. Marcus Aurelius thought there might someday be "a polity administered with regard to equal rights and equal freedom of speech, and the idea of a kingly government which

---

1 "Emergence from one's self imposed immaturity," is Kant's definition of Enlightenment ("What is Enlightenment?" 1784); "mind forged manacles" is Blake's expression ("London" 1794).
2 *Concise Oxford Dictionary of Politics*, ed. Iain McLean and Alistair McMillan (New York: Oxford University Press, 2009).
3 Diderot, "Droit naturelle," *Encyclopédie*, vol. 11, 116:9, http://artfl.uchicago.edu/images/encyclopedie/V5/ENC_5-116.jpeg.

respects, most of all, the freedom of the governed" (Aurelius, *Meditations*, I, 14). This self-restraint is the key to positive-sum relations, the ability to escape the limbic captivity of zero-sum, us/them, relations and engage constructively and voluntarily with the "other," whether family member, neighbor, fellow clan member or citizen, foreigner in your midst, or outside your space.[4] It means renouncing, at least sometimes, the zero-sum imperatives: rule or be ruled, humiliate or be humiliated, exploit or be exploited.

We can, therefore, formulate liberal goals in terms of game theory—positive-sum strategies instead of zero-sum ones—and conceptualize the liberal achievement, both social and political, as a shift from a pervasive zero-sum, shame-honor environment, to one that significantly leavens interactions with modes of cooperation and mutual benefit, in ever-widening circles of friendly "others." The glitch comes when one believes society can replace zero-sum relations entirely with positive-sum ones. Oxygen-enhanced air is, in modest portions, invigorating and clarifying, but in heavier doses, it makes one giddy, delirious and ultimately, dead.

Game Theory and Social Emotions

Game theory is a mathematical field, highly innovative, but focused, like all mathematical models, on evidence close to the quantifiable lamppost.[5] So while it is enormously productive and adds important insight to almost any issue surrounding the choices humans make about interacting with others, it has difficulty with some fundamental yet volatile emotions (like honor and shame). If we examine not so much the likelihoods of humans choosing positive-sum over zero- and negative-sum games, as the varying emotions that accompany those choices, both in prompting the choices and handling their (often unanticipated) consequences, we get insight into a more volatile dimension not easily captured by mathematical models.

From a purely logical point of view, the advantages of positive-sum interactions are so great that it's obvious any "reasonable" person would prefer them. Who would not choose cooperation, affection, intimacy, creativity, productivity over

---

4   Satoshi Kanazawa defines liberalism as "the genuine concern for the welfare of genetically unrelated others and the willingness to contribute larger proportions of private resources for the welfare of such others," "Why Liberals and Atheists are more intelligent," *Social Psychology Quarterly* 73 (2010), 1, 33–57.

5   A drunk looked for his keys at night under a lamppost and not in the bushes where he dropped them "because this is where the light is."

violence, coercion, and destructive behavior? Who would not want a world of mutual benefit and prosperity? Certainly, no loving parents would say no to such possibilities for their children.

But such positive-sum behavior exacts a considerable psychic cost. First, and most obviously, while it makes sense to renounce zero-sum games you think you might lose, it makes little sense to renounce zero-sum games you think you can win. Zero-sum behavior is much closer to impulsive, short term, thinking fast.[6] Victory is sweet, and to some (many) worth the gamble. To give it up means giving up all the pleasures of victory, from the greater material benefits to the emotional satisfaction of dominance. It means turning aside from the blandishments of what the anthropologist John Tooby calls "predatory logic" for those who can, with its consequential "subordinate logic" for those who can't.[7]

Thus, in order to sustain positive-sum behavior one must renounce ready service to those almost instinctual emotions and cultivate other, far more difficult ones. As already outlined, zero-sum cultures based on a primary warrior code, with their constant power-challenges and status anxiety, have an elective affinity for certain "darker" emotions, *Schadenfreude*, envy, resentment, revenge, triumphalism. The appeal of these emotions—risking all to feel triumph and dominion (honor), destroying not to feel humiliated—is well-nigh universal ... our limbic captivity. Civil polities, based in liberal principles, try to relegate zero-sum games to nonlethal sports and gambling.

In positive-sum games, both sides win, although not nearly as much as one of them might have won in a zero-sum game. Nor, necessarily, do both sides benefit equally from the agreement. The hardest positive-sum games to play are open-ended egalitarian ones based on a voluntary agreement to interact (contract, joint venture, constitution) according to rules that apply equally to both/all sides, and an understanding that everyone will accept the results, no matter how diverse they may turn out. After all, freedom includes the freedom to make bad choices, to lose ground, to fail. And one of the most difficult aspects of any system committed to freedom concerns managing the disappointments without scapegoating, without resisting the "fear of freedom."[8]

Rationality and "rational choice theory" assume that actors will work to maximize their own advantage, with minimal concern for how it might help

---

6 Daniel Kahneman, *Thinking, Fast and Slow* (New York: Farrar Straus and Giroux, 2011).

7 Jonathan Tooby, comments to Ian McEwan, "Message from Paris," *Edge.com*, November 14, 2015.

8 Erich Fromm, *Escape from Freedom* (New York: Farrar and Rinehart, 1941).

or hurt someone else. For Adam Smith, it's a matter of cost-benefit calculation that a talented flint chipper will stay home and fashion blades for the hunters to take on their expeditions, who will then share the kill. No place here for honor, danger, fierceness influencing the distribution of both food and women.[9]

Positive-sum turns the tragedy of a mutilated dominion—poke out one of my eyes and I'll be king among the blind—into a comedy of riches: "It stands to reason that if I wish for a hundred head of cattle, and my neighbor gets twice, we both win." Ultimately, democracy and other demotic polities derive their ability to exist from the (extremely rare) accomplishment of getting a critical mass of "citizens" to take a basically positive-sum approach to "others," to step out of the hard zero-sum, us/them dyad. Those of us who grew up in such a civic culture, dedicated to these positive-sum strategies, tend to take their logic as axiomatic.

Mistakenly.

The Downside of Too Much Positive-Sum

The problem comes down to trust in reciprocity. "If the genie gives me ten million bucks and my neighbor gets twenty million," will he be thankful? Or will he use his new-found resources, his doubled strength, to destroy me?" Can generosity be a fatally mistaken gesture? Demotic modernity is a wager.[10] Sustaining positive-sum relations means resisting the (cold) comfort, the (ruinous) blandishments of limbic captivity, and instead cultivating a set of high-minded, but high-risk vulnerabilities. As Machiavelli pointed out, the Prince prefers being feared to loved, because the result of fear is far more predictable.[11] Zero-sum's great advantage (and avowed goal) is defending the self, the "us," from the attack of "them." In order to empathize across the us/them barrier, in order to dismantle the systematic suspicion of the (hostile) other, one has to develop an attitude of trust in the other that, if mistaken, can exact painful, even lethal costs.

It turns out that, no matter how much "better it is for everyone involved," rationally hewing to positive-sum relations takes difficult emotional work. When we give up zero-sum hierarchy as a guiding paradigm (and with it, the attendant joys of demeaning others), we have to tolerate others (rivals?) even

---

9 Adam Smith, *Wealth of Nations* (1776), part 1, section 2. Cf. chapter 5, nn13–14.

10 Adam Seligman, *Modernity's Wager: Authority, the Self, and Transcendence* (Princeton, Princeton University Press, 2000).

11 Machiavelli, *The Prince*, chapter 17.

when they become more successful than we. It means, among other things, cultivating:

- **A strong sense of human affection**, involving everything from deep respect for all human life, to rejoicing in someone else's success (what the Buddhists call *Mudita*, altruistic joy). This affection for widening gyres of the human community is a crucial weapon in combating the limbic forces of *asabiyya* and envy.
- **An ability to empathize with the "other,"** one's *semblable*. Such feelings lie at the heart of what thinkers like Jeremy Rifkin believe is now transforming humanity: they make the cruelty of the prime-divider and its degradation of those below, much harder to bear, much less enforce.[12]
- **High levels of tolerance for uncertainty** (messiness of life, outcome anxiety). Granting others the freedoms one wants them to grant us, means putting up with much that is unpleasant, including depending on others' good will. The most successful players in positive-sum-rich environments have a high tolerance for cognitive dissonance.
- **Self-criticism and self-reflection:** Erich Fromm located freedom's discontents in the unhappy, but inevitable times when one makes bad free choices.[13] The ability to take responsibility for one's own mistakes (when appropriate) rather than blame others (when inappropriate), marks the mature free person.

This generous attitude towards others and modesty towards oneself are not easy and natural emotions, they violate the very principle of tribal solidarity, "my side right or wrong." Indeed, the gravitational pull of scapegoating, of blaming others and resenting them for our own failures makes positive-sum freedom difficult to sustain.

Both civil society and demotic religiosity nurture these self-disciplined emotions. Great-souled poets like William Blake "rooted" for the Americans fighting for freedom, even when they fought against his own (fallen) Albion.[14] But such emotions must be fostered, and when disappointed or frustrated, they can falter. Democracies, always confronting the problem of potential betrayal of trust, are an ongoing combat, not a solution one can take off the shelf and hand out via the internet.[15]

---

12 Jeremy Rifkin, *The Empathic Civilization: The Race to Global Consciousness in a World in Crisis* (New York: Penguin, 2009).

13 Fromm, *Escape from Freedom*.

14 See 241.

15 Eli Sagan, *The Honey and the Hemlock* explores the episodes of paranoia that seize groups that try to renounce the "paranoid imperative": rule or be ruled. See chapter 5.

Ethical Consilience: Jews and Liberals

If one accepts this game-theory analysis of progressive values and the emotions that need cultivation in order to realize the social transformation, then one finds a remarkable overlap with Jewish (biblical and rabbinic) values on the one hand, and modern liberal thought, on the other. No ancient body of literature contains so extensive a promotion of positive-sum emotions and rejection of shame-honor values as the Hebrew Bible.[16] From the outset, the narratives of the patriarchs deviate from the zero-sum tribal norm: Abraham and his descendants are given a task that, when successful, results in all the nations of the earth being blessed (Genesis, 26:3). His "chosenness" according to game-theory runs as follows: The descendants of Abraham are commanded to pursue high levels of positive-sum behavior regardless of whether those they deal with are trustworthy, even at the cost of suffering a great deal from those who abuse the vulnerabilities that entails. And the results are predictable: those who bless you will be blessed, and vice-versa. In some ideal future, everybody wins, everybody is blessed. In the meantime Jews prosper and suffer.

The psychological dimension of this effort to pursue positive-sum at all costs, appears clearly in a passage known as the "holiness code (Leviticus 19)" where we find the famous biblical commandment in both Testaments: "Do not hate your brother in your heart; but surely rebuke your neighbor, and do not bear sin because of him. Do not take vengeance, nor bear any grudge against the children of thy people but love your neighbor in your midst like yourself: I am the YHVH" (Leviticus 19:16–18). Interwoven here we find four principles that are at the heart of current liberal-progressive thought in the twenty-first century: 1) not to hate others, 2) not to take vengeance and bear grudges, 3) consider mutual criticism beneficial, and 4) empathize with the "other."

All of this involves extensive cultivation of positive-sum emotions and the behavior associated with it (*demotic religiosity*): thinking well of your neighbor (as you do of yourself), trying to resolve disputes as fairly as possible, renouncing tit for tat. Hillel famously turned this principle into the key principle of the Torah: "do not do onto others what is hateful to you." This negative commandment may be less demanding than the Christian positive commandment: "*do* onto others as you would have them do onto you," but it remains difficult to follow, one that encompasses all four of the commandments in question, and more.

---

16 Many have explored this matrix, most notably Joshua Berman, *Created Equal: How the Bible Broke with Ancient Political Thought* (New York: Oxford University Press, 2008) and Rabbi Jonathan Sacks throughout his biblical commentary, e.g., *Covenant & Conversation Leviticus: The Book of Holiness* (Jerusalem: Koren Press, 2015).

Among the implications of this teaching, the rabbis develop a counter-principle to zero-sum, honor-shame culture, when interpreting the phrase "surely you will rebuke him." Instead of exploiting that command to publicly criticize others, raising up oneself by demeaning them, the rabbis insisted that one should at all costs avoid humiliating someone else, especially in public. Indeed, they considered it a form of murder: "Better a man throw himself into a fiery furnace than publicly put his neighbor to shame."[17] Or, as Maimonides put it, "He who gains honor by the disgrace of his friend does not have a place in the world to come."[18] You don't make yourself look bigger by making others look smaller.

Woven into this discourse the rabbis set exceptionally high standards: Rashi (late eleventh-century France), basing himself on Midrash (fourth century), explains the meaning of the verse, *Do not take vengeance nor bear a grudge*: vengeance is refusing to lend your neighbor an axe because he refused you a hoe; bearing a grudge is lending the axe and saying, "even though you refused me a loan."[19] Nachmanides (thirteenth-century Spain), in discussing *Love your neighbor as yourself*, emphasized the indirect object "le-re'echa" (towards your companion/ *semblable*) and formulates the classic positive-sum principle: "we should wish upon our neighbors the same benefits we wish upon ourselves."[20] Not: "poke out one of my eyes." And while these demanding principles might seem appropriate for spiritual athletes, hermits, monks, nuns, mystics, here, they apply to laboring peasants whose noses are ground daily against the rough edges of the real world.

On Healthy Egos and Freedom of Speech

This shift to positive-sum behavior, however reasonable it might seem and however obvious the (collective) benefit, nonetheless calls for an unusually high level of emotional maturity, the ability to rise above limbic captivity to zero-sum, to respond to insult with forbearance, to fairly criticize and be criticized, to trust and be trustworthy. In honor-shame dynamics, if you've done something wrong and no one knows, you do not feel bad. If everyone thinks you've done something wrong, you feel bad, even if you haven't done it. In integrity-guilt

---

17 Talmud Bavli, Baba Metziah, 58b-59a, https://www.sefaria.org/Bava_Metzia.58b?lang=en.

18 Maimonides, *Mishna Torah, Hilchot De'ot*, 6:3, https://www.sefaria.org/Mishneh_Torah%2C_ Human_Dispositions.6.3?lang=en.

19 Leviticus 19:18, Rashi commentary, https://www.sefaria.org/Leviticus.19.18?lang=bi&with =Rashi&lang2=en.

20 Leviticus 19:18, Ramban, https://www.sefaria.org/Leviticus.19.18?lang=bi&with=Ramban &lang2=en.

dynamics, if no one knows, you still feel bad; if everyone mistakenly thinks that you did something wrong, you may feel bad, but not about yourself.[21] The ability to deal with questions in terms of guilt demand a strong sense of self, a thick-skinned ego that will not quake in terror of public shame when the possibility looms.

One could almost define a civic polity by the way it raises the threshold to honor-incited violence. Arlene Saxenhouse remarks about ancient Athens:

> Freedom of speech as a democratic practice is a practice of openness, of a refusal to hide one's thoughts because of a shame that would bring humiliation or disapproval in the eyes of others. Respect and reverence before the judgments of others, in contrast, limit the freedom and uncovering capacities of speech and opportunities for individual choice.[22]

"Modernity requires the willingness to be offended," notes Fouad Ajami in an article on its absence in the Arab world.[23] In this personal freedom, not from *feeling* shame (which is impossible), but from being captive to that fear (*onēidophobia*), we find people willing to speak their minds and others willing to "take the hit" without resorting to violence to hide their shame.

As Salman Rushdie said:

> The idea that any kind of free society can be constructed in which people will never be offended or insulted is absurd. So too is the notion that people should have the right to call on the law to defend them against being offended or insulted. A fundamental decision needs to be made: do we want to live in a free society or not? Democracy is not a tea party where people sit around making polite conversation. In democracies people get extremely upset with each other. They argue vehemently against each other's positions. (But they don't shoot.)[24]

---

21 Arlene W. Saxonhouse, *Free Speech and Democracy in Ancient Athens* (Cambridge: Cambridge University Press, 2008), 81f.

22 Ibid., 77f.

23 Fouad Ajami, "Why is the Arab world so easily offended?" *Washington Post*, September 14, 2012.

24 Salmon Rushdie, "Defend the right to be offended," *Open Democracy*, February 7, 2005.

Differently put, in shame-honor cultures, people don't say certain things *lest* there be violence; and in demotic ones, people say what they think is important, and there is no violence.

A free press, the "Fourth Estate," is a pillar of democracy because it provides a reality check on the elective affinity between power, corruption, and a sycophancy which not only feeds the egos of the powerful but masks their abuse of power. The response of the powerful to public criticism is violence and intimidation: such effrontery must be silenced. Only where power elites can handle this "free" criticism, publicly expressed, without violence can one have either a free press or a demotic polity.

Lyndon Johnson wrote to the Smothers Brothers, who had made him the target of their comedy:

> It is part of the price of leadership of this great nation to be the target of clever satirists. You have given the gift of laughter to our people. May we never grow so somber or self-important that we fail to appreciate the humor in our lives.[25]

Where the political culture is still overwhelmingly committed to authoritarian honors, a free press constitutes a threat to public order. A free press is not possible just from the adoption of a new, favorable, policy.[26] It depends on a much wider transformation of the culture. Repression of the free press and free speech of those who are weaker (and unjustly treated), is the default mode, the pattern of limbic captivity. It is, as it were, the magnet under the table around which various metal shavings above the surface gather in a pattern of respect for the powerful.

Renouncing Dominion

Of all the demands of demotic, positive-sum values, perhaps the most difficult to achieve, and most productive when achieved, involves the renunciation of the power to coerce. This renunciation is both difficult to adopt and even more difficult to sustain. It views power as something to be used for the common weal,

---

25 David Bianculli, "The Smothers Brothers: Laughing at Hard Truths," *New York Times*, February 3, 2017. Similar response from "fascist" George Bush to the Dixie Chicks.

26 Eoghan Stafford, "Stop the Presses! Media freedom in authoritarian regimes: A case study of Ben Ali's Tunisia," *The Journal of the Middle East and Africa*, 8:4 (2017): 353–82.

not for personal gain, something to be administered, not exploited. William Blake, in a poem about the American revolution defeating his own nation, Albion, expressed the demotic sentiments behind these (messianic) dreams:

> Let the slave grinding at the mill, run out into the field:
> Let him look up into the heavens & laugh in the bright air;
> Let the inchained soul shut up in darkness and in sighing,
> Whose face has never seen a smile in thirty weary years;
> Rise and look out, his chains are loose, his dungeon doors are open.
> And let his wife and children return from the oppressors scourge;
> They look behind at every step & believe it is a dream.
> Singing. The Sun has left his blackness, & has found a fresher morning
> And the fair Moon rejoices in the clear & cloudless night;
> For Empire is no more, and now the Lion & Wolf shall cease.[27]

In a sense, one might describe the entire postwar, post-Holocaust, international agenda—UN, Geneva Conventions, International Declaration of Human Rights—as, in principle, a renunciation of zero-sum power.[28] And with that vision, one can imagine a world without war. Not by accident was Isaiah Square built in the UN's Turtle Bay, with its invocation of the messianic promise that the predatory elites would turn their swords into plowshares, and spears into pruning hooks . . . weapons of dominion into tools of productive labor.

The "unofficial mission statement of the UN."

---

27 William Blake, *America* (1793).
28 Johannes Morsink, *The Universal Declaration of Human Rights and the Holocaust: An Endangered Connection* (Washington DC: Georgetown University Press, 2019).

FIGURE 17. Isaiah Square, Ralph Bunch Park, First Ave., Manhattan, NY.

This renunciation of power—neither rule nor be ruled—produces some remarkable paradoxes. Ironically, those who successfully renounce power often achieve even greater influence as a result. In the modern world, the contrast between the power wielded by democratically elected officials who govern and have powers limited by constitution and law far outstrip the power of the most arbitrary dictator—the difference between the POTUS and the Russian or Soviet ruler, for example.[29] One finds this paradox repeatedly in the Middle Ages in a particularly stark form: ecclesiastical reform movement after reform movement began with the radical renunciation of all forms of power, including money, and became, as a result immensely influential and wealthy, indeed corrupted by their success.[30] It is the paradox of both the Jews and democracies.

The composer of Napoleon's alleged letter to the Jews wrote:

> Now is the moment ... to claim the restoration of civic rights among the population of the world which had been shamefully withheld from you for thousands of years, your political existence

---

29 John Hall, *Powers and Liberties: The Causes and Consequences of the Rise of the West* (Los Angeles: University of California Press), 19–23.

30 Lester Little, *Religious Poverty and the Profit Economy in the Middle Ages* (Ithaca, N.Y.: Cornell University Press, 1983).

as a nation among the nations, and the unlimited natural right to worship Jehovah in accordance with your faith, publicly and most probably forever.[31]

In so doing, he hit the revolutionary nail on the head: In the world of envious supersessionism and triumphalism, it was a matter of honor to deprive the Jews of sovereignty. From the generous perspective of freedom, such oppression, like slavery, was shameful.[32] Apparently, today, that attitude still asks too much of many, even (especially?) progressives.

Cognitive Egocentrism

In the late 60s, psychologist David Elkind published his findings on adolescent boys and coined the term "cognitive egocentrism," which characterized people who assumed that everyone else thought about the world the same way they did—in this case, that adolescent boys tended to assume that everyone was as preoccupied with sex as they were.[33] This notion of cognitive egocentrism, borrowed from Piaget, has an ironic dimension to it today: normally the term refers to immature stages of development—childhood and adolescence—and the more mature one becomes, the more one learns to empathize with others, the less egocentric one presumably becomes. Indeed, as one group of researchers put it: cold people (unempathic) are far more likely to be cognitive egocentrics.[34] And yet, paradoxically, in the twenty-first century, some of the most determined, even dogmatic cognitive egocentrics come from the most progressive, empathic circles of warm thinkers and activists. For there are two major variants to cognitive egocentrism: the unempathic projection of ill-will and the overly empathic projection of good will.

---

31 For a discussion of the letter's authenticity, see Franz Kobler, *Napoleon and the Jews* (New York: Schocken, 1976), 55–7; Nathan Schur, *Napoleon in The Holy Land* (London: Greenhouse Press, 1999), 117–22; Landes, "Napoleon's Alleged Proclamation to the Jews: A Study in Millennial Dynamics," *Napoleonic Scholarship Journal* (2023).

32 See also the contemporary words of an Irish revolutionary to the Jews: "You are scattered over all the surface of the earth, nowhere as a nation, vilified, degraded by bigoted governments and insulted by the populaces," Louis Hyman, *The Jews of Ireland from Earliest Times to the Year 1910* (London and Jerusalem: Irish University Press, 1972), 237–40.

33 David Elkind, "Egocentrism in Adolescence," *Child Development*, 38:4 (December, 1967): 1025–1034.

34 R. Boyd, K. Bresin, K. Ode, and M. Robinson, "Cognitive egocentrism differentiates warm and cold people," *Journal of Research in Personality*, 47:1 (February 2013): 90–96.

Domineering (Zero-Sum) Cognitive Egocentrism

The default mode of human cognitive egocentrism projects zero-sum. For hundreds of millennia, zero-sum notions of the limited good, of the inevitable clash between "us" and "them," have dominated even relations among "us." Tribes, from the Yanomamö to Australian aborigines to the American urban ghettos and French suburban ZUS, inhabit a world where "the fear of attacks and the theft of your women by neighbors," is prevalent.[35] Few moderns appreciate how, even in its *least* demanding interpretation, "love thy neighbor as thyself" constitutes a deeply radical commandment.

People who live in a world where one wins only when another loses, where the few with honor dominate the many who are stigmatized and subject, where one ascends through violent challenge and falls by losing, readily project their mentality upon others, the "dark side of man."[36] Eli Sagan called this the paranoid imperative: the necessity of ruling over others lest they do so first: *do onto others before they do onto you.*[37] In both relations between clans and tribes and in relations with other nations, the vast majority of human history has featured this paranoid imperative.[38] It is the very stuff of warfare until just recently: plunder or be plundered, rule or be ruled, shame or be shamed, exterminate or be exterminated. Nietzsche described "slave morality" as those who, while losers, complain bitterly about how unfair life is, even as they dream of the power to turn the tables, to take vengeance on the unjust.[39]

To the domineering cognitive egocentrics (DCE), *everybody* thinks in terms of dominion. *Everybody* plays hard zero-sum games. And those who don't, are either losers who deserve no respect and have no honor, or deceivers out to cheat. Getting out of this mindset, peeling oneself off, even to a limited degree, from the gravitational pull of limbic emotions, from the urgent projection of hostility onto the other and fear of public failure and ridicule if one gets ambushed, takes great effort (indeed many people think it cannot be done). As Eli Sagan put it: "Paranoia is the problem. The paranoid position is the defense. Democracy is a

---

35 Napoleon Chagnon, "Blood is their Argument," *Edge*, June 6, 2013, summarizing the observations about Australia of the nineteenth-century escaped convict and explorer William Buckley, identical to Chagnon's about the Yanomamö.

36 Michael Ghiglieri, *Dark Side of Man: Tracing the Origins of Male Violence* (New York: Perseus, 2000); Richard Wrangham and Dale Peterson, *Demonic Males: Apes and the Origins of Human Violence* (New York: Harper, 1996).

37 Sagan, *The Honey and the Hemlock*, 13–34.

38 Landes, "The Melian Dialogue, the *Protocols*, and the Paranoid Imperative," in *The Paranoid Apocalypse*, ed. R. Landes and S. Katz (New York: New York University Press, 2011), 23–33.

39 Nietzsche, *Genealogy of Morals* I: 13–17; Thucydides, *Peloponnesian Wars* 5:85–116.

miracle, considering human psychological disabilities."[40] In deep-seated cases, DCE cannot even conceive of the *possibility* of a positive-sum game: whatever the "other" does, no matter how generous it may *seem*, is a trap, a covert act of hostility in which the other is really jockeying for superior position in a zero-sum game. Hence DCE has strong affinity for conspiracy theories (the "other" is malevolent, evil; must be opposed at all costs).

Liberal (Positive-Sum) Cognitive Egocentrism

As much as we take the American decision not to take over the countries they had occupied in World War II for granted, it actually constitutes a world-changing relationship to war, an unprecedented and explicit renunciation of dominion through conquest. It laid the groundwork for the Marshall Plan, the Geneva Conventions, the UN.

One of the most remarkable aspects of this postmodern, postwar, world is the wide-spread consensus that people are basically good, and that the default mode between strangers is friendly.

> If you smile at me, I will understand,
> Cause that is something
> everybody everywhere does in the same language . . .[41]

The ascension of a kind of beneficent anthropology, in which humans were instinctively cooperative, gregarious, pacific beings, was not a foregone conclusion. We, however, tend to take it for granted with little appreciation of how rare and risky it is. John Tooby explained after the Paris Bataclan attacks in 2015:

> Born into a world that has been internally pacified for so long, it
> is easy (and convenient) to mistake this for the state of nature,
> and not something maintained by the costly self-sacrifice of
> some. People raised in cultures that are predominantly organized
> around cooperative rationality cannot imagine any other

---

40 Sagan, *The Honey and the Hemlock*, 22. What Sagan refers to as "human psychological disabilities," I refer to here as limbic captivity. Rather than seeing that resistance as a disability, it seems more productive to consider it and its constellation of emotions, a basic dimension of human existence.

41 Crosby, Stills, and Nash, *Wooden Ships* (1968), sung at Woodstock.

rationality: So when people use violence it must be that they are driven to it by desperation or searing injustice, and they will stop when given justice. No one, we think, could possibly prefer war.... A cooperator wants to arrive at a win-win covenant among equals. But predators envision instead an I-win-you-lose domination.[42]

In "Wooden Ships," cited above, two survivors of an apocalyptic nuclear war, from opposite sides, come together and share berries that will "probably keep us both alive [sic]." Together, they steer away from the tragic world of hatred, and turn now, to live, "free and easy, the way it's supposed to be."

> Go, take your sister then, by the hand,
> Lead her away from this foreign land,
> Far away, where we might laugh again,
> We are leaving—you don't need us.

Anthem of the 60s. It was a radically new mindset, utterly different from the kind of us-them thinking that dominated previous generations. So what if those purple berries would have kept me alive twice as long, and sharing them might do us both in.

John Lennon caught the Zeitgeist in 1971 with "Imagine":

> Imagine there's no heaven
> It's easy if you try
> No hell below us
> Above us only sky
> Imagine all the people
> Living for today . . .
> Imagine there's no countries
> It isn't hard to do.
> Nothing to kill or die for
> And no religion too.
> Imagine all the people
> Living life in peace . . .
> You may say I'm a dreamer
> But I'm not the only one

---

42 John Tooby, "A Message from Paris," *Edge*, November 14, 2015.

> I hope someday you'll join us
> And the world will be as one.
> Imagine no possessions
> I wonder if you can
> No need for greed or hunger
> A brotherhood of man ...

This may have been one of the most influential songs ever written, an "anthem of universal hope," embraced by spiritual people and hard-core socialists alike.[43] German pianist Davide Martello drove four hours to Paris to play it outside the Bataclan in Paris, after the jihadi attacks of 2015.[44]

Transferred from the personal or messianic plane to the realm of political and international relations, the new paradigm called for treating everyone, citizen and foreigner, much better, equally well. Starting with the civil rights movement, the justifiable accusation spread that the US and other Western governments were far from living up to their own standards. Not only in the way these governments treated their own citizens, but also strangers out there in the increasingly "small" global village. The key to Noam Chomsky's radical critique of US and Israeli imperialism to this day, is the demand that we treat other nations and peoples with as much consideration as we claim to treat our own. The formula the British mastered in the nineteenth century, of democracy at home, empire abroad, was utterly inacceptable.

And underlying these (messianic) ideals of dismantling the "us/them" distinction entirely, lay the beneficent anthropology that categorically rejects the doctrine of *original sin*: a notion some conservative political thinkers consider so critical to public order, that to deny it was to destroy the state.[45] For the new generation, however, to think badly of others was base, a betrayal of the cause, a sign of racism, prejudice, a hateful, hostile act. Discrimination, normally a sign of discernment, became a "bad thing," and its opposite, promiscuity (without being so named), became a "good thing." Everyone had to be treated equally, every stranger a (potential) friend, every immigrant an always-already a citizen.

---

43 *"Imagine,* by John Lennon," *Socialist Party of Britain* (n.d.); Laurie Ulter, "The Life & Legacy of John Lennon's 'Imagine,'" *Biography,* December 7, 2015, https://www.biography.com/news/john-lennon-imagine-song-facts; Josh Magnes, "The Legacy of John Lennon," *Diamondback,* October 11, 2015.

44 Daniel Marans, "Pianist Plays 'Imagine' Outside Bataclan, Uniting Parisians in Moment of Peace," *HuffPost,* November 14, 2015.

45 "The denial of original sin destroyed all social order." Carl Schmitt, *Concept of the Political* (Chicago: University of Chicago Press, 1932, 2010), 65.

And as this new approach to human relations succeeded, it encouraged both an educational and intellectual commitment to making the "old world" of violent zero-sum, literally unthinkable.

Killing, oppressing, bullying, shaming—all became not only "bad," but, to a good, humane, empathic person, virtually unimaginable. And since such an approach, when widely adopted, succeeds quite admirably in proliferating positive-sum interactions, the new mindset "took." Instead of the dominating imperative (rule or be ruled), we had not just mutual disengagement (live and let live), but the empathic imperative (be nice to others and they will be so to you). It became as difficult for liberals to imagine or understand the zero-sum mindset as it was for the authoritarians to imagine a positive-sum mindset.

The problem stems, to some extent, from a confusion between empathy and sympathy. When one tries to empathize with someone else, one tries to understand how he or she (or they) experience the world. Too often, however, well-meaning people process this as a combination of sympathy ("how would I feel if I were in their situation?") and egocentrism ("they are basically like me"). This translates into a widely held, improvisational anthropology about the nature of people:

> The vast majority everywhere want a roof over their heads, to
> sleep peacefully at night, to enjoy their families, to put food in
> their bellies and to say good morning to their neighbors.[46]

This generous attitude towards the "other," this projection of sympathy—they're just like us—lies at the heart of civil society's ability to avoid most conflict. It benefits from the hard-earned efforts of centuries to reach such an unprecedented level of benign consensus, and only in the last two generations has it become axiomatic—a tremendous achievement with an immensely productive payoff.[47] Whatever the discontents of modern life, few would trade them for an age where pain and hunger and violence were common companions.

But this generous projection, this reversal of paranoid projection, is not always accurate. And when mistaken about the other, when engaging people and cultures that still play by zero-sum rules, it can be dangerous. If we *assume* sameness and cannot self-correct, especially in the face of what should be

---

46 Remark of a friend in conversation. For an almost identical formulation, see Joshua Greene, *Moral Tribes: Emotion, Reason, and the Gap Between Us and Them* (New York: Penguin, 2013), 4.

47 Rifkin, *The Empathic Civilization*, written in 2009 with only one (passing) mention of Islamic terrorism and 9–11, 488; Steven Pinker, *Better Angels of our Nature: Why Violence has Declined* (New York: Basic Books, 2011).

compelling evidence, then this cognitive egocentrism becomes a form of learned helplessness.

When religious figures, or students of religion, declare that: "No faith teaches people to massacre innocents," whether they know it or not, they are playing semantic games by which they define all religion in terms of their (understanding of their) own.[48] On the contrary, the anthropologist-theologian René Girard argued that scapegoat sacrifices of innocents as solutions to crisis, and the cults they engender, formed the basis of most religious life, for most of the history of mankind (and the exception that he saw—Christianity—has hardly been the exception for most of its two millennia of existence).[49] There is, after all, a fundamental difference between human and humane. Sadism is a uniquely and specifically *human* trait, no matter how inhumane.[50] Thus, projecting *humane* attitudes onto all *humans* and their religions only sometimes succeeds in understanding and/or changing others and elevating relations to the benefit of all. The rest of the time, it's operating in a world of fantastic, even fatal denial.

With the fall of the Soviet Union in 1991, however, such imaginings became a paradigmatic approach to international relations, articulated by leading Western political "scientists."

> A group of liberal internationalists . . . led by Robert O. Keohane and Joseph S. Nye Jr., postulated that a new era of international cooperation would replace the fierce competitiveness of the bipolar system. These and other liberal internationalists predicted that spreading of democracy, stronger economic ties, and robust international organizations would usher in a more peaceful global environment. Embedded in this analysis was the assumption that national power, hitherto based on military

---

48 President Obama: "[n]o faith teaches people to massacre innocents." Statement by the President, August 20, 2014; Pope Francis, "All religions want peace; it is other people who want war." [Whoever the "other people."] Pope Francis, July 27, 2016. On these two figures adopting the Islamist narrative for infidels, see Coughlin, *Catastrophic Failure*, 436–468 (Obama and his administration); 1132–1206 (Pope Francis and the Vatican).

49 René Girard, *Things Hidden since the Foundation of the World* (Palo Alto: Stanford University Press, 1987); Eli Sagan, *Dawn of Tyranny: The Origins of Individualism, Political Oppression, and the State* (New York: Knopf, 1985).

50 A student once criticized Daniel Goldhagen (*Hitler's Willing Executioners: Ordinary Germans and the Holocaust*, New York: Vintage, 1997) for "dehumanizing" the Germans of the 101 Police Battalion by depicting them as sadistic, above, 43n14.

prowess and deterrence capabilities, would be replaced with such "soft power" tools as economic ties and cultural exchange.[51]

This victory of liberal values and outlook then offered Middle East specialists hope that *now* was the most opportune moment to change the conflict-prone region into a democratic one, economically thriving, and led others to believe that the newly expanded European Union would "run" the twenty-first century.[52]

During the Bush years, this kind of thinking dominated the administration's thinking. In addition to the projection of Western, modern, Judeo-Christian thinking onto Islam discussed in the chapter on 9–11, Bush's invasion of Iraq invoked this liberal projection: speaking in concert with his neo-conservative advisors, the "right-wing" president, articulated the paradigm of liberal cognitive egocentrism in defense of a Chomskyite foreign policy in Iraq:

> Time after time, observers have questioned whether this country, or that people, or this group, are "ready" for democracy—as if freedom were a prize you win for meeting our own Western standards of progress. In fact, the daily work of democracy itself is the path of progress. It teaches cooperation, the free exchange of ideas, and the peaceful resolution of differences. As men and women are showing, from Bangladesh to Botswana, to Mongolia, it is the practice of democracy that makes a nation ready for democracy, and every nation can start on this path. It should be clear to all that Islam—the faith of one-fifth of humanity—is consistent with democratic rule. Democratic progress is found in many predominantly Muslim countries—in Turkey and Indonesia, and Senegal and Albania, Niger and Sierra Leone. Muslim men and women are good citizens of India and South Africa, of the nations of Western Europe, and of the United States of America.[53]

---

51 Seliktar, *Doomed to Failure?*, 27. Jack Snyder, "One World, Rival Theories," *Foreign Policy* 145 (2004); and response: Ofira Seliktar, "Realism Is Not Ignorance: A Critique of the Mearsheimer-Walt Thesis," *MERIA Journal* (March 2008).

52 On Rifkin, Reid and Leonard in the mid aughts, see above, p. 139f. Most recently, Anu Bradford, *The Brussels Effect: How the European Union Rules the World* (New York: Oxford University Press, 2019).

53 George Bush, "Remarks by the President at the 20th Anniversary of the National Endowment for Democracy," United States Chamber of Commerce Washington, DC; Landes, "Bush's Chomskyite Foreign Policy," *Augean Stables*, February 2, 2006.

Whether he said this sincerely, or cynically as an excuse to invade and feed the military-industrial complex, he invoked a shared *Zeitgeist*. Hypocrisy is the compliment vice pays to virtue, where here, virtue is liberal values universalized.

The consensus, at least among Westerners, both liberal and "conservative," was widespread: democracy was a universal blessing, which all peoples would, given the chance, embrace. In his Cairo Speech of 2009, the newly elected President Obama articulated this "unyielding belief" as a virtual doctrine:

> that all people yearn for certain things: the ability to speak your mind and have a say in how you are governed; confidence in the rule of law and the equal administration of justice; a government that is transparent and doesn't steal from the people; the freedom to live as you choose. These are not just American ideas; they are human rights. And that is why we will support them everywhere.[54]

Here we find liberal cognitive egocentrism elevated to the position of both a dogmatic *belief*, and a foreign policy doctrine. As a normally astute colleague (and psychotherapist) said after 9–11: "I can't understand! These terrorists lived the good life of Western freedom and abundance? How could they commit suicide to destroy it?" The real "universal" is the slightly more depressing: mine is natural; thine is learned. Most everybody wants mine; far fewer, want to grant thine.

The Moebius Strip of Cognitive Egocentrism

What happens when liberal, positive-sum, egocentrics interact with dominating, zero-sum egocentrics? Liberals like to imagine that their empathy and sympathy will win over the zero-sum players who only cling to their antagonism out of fear, and who, once they realize they're not in danger, will change their ways. (In this sense, it is a secular form of missionizing.) And often enough, that may work. But when committed liberals meet a committed dominator, the dynamics work to their disadvantage.

In this case, the DCEs learn quickly to exploit the good intentions and vulnerabilities that LCEs consider their true strength. They speak in precisely

---

54 Obama, Cairo Speech (2009); his speech in Berlin in 2008, (while candidate) exemplified Lennon's "Imagine."

the terms that appeal to LCE, insisting that their struggle is for human rights, fairness and justice, even as their notions of these matters differ wildly from those of the liberals to whom they appeal. Liberals find themselves confused, since both genuine moderates and demopaths use the same language.[55] Forced to judge, many liberals, eager to believe anything civil that people might say, prefer to project good faith, taking the protestations of demopaths at face value, thereby becoming their dupes. As a result, a dysfunctional relationship between demopaths and their dupes emerges. Under current circumstances, where most liberals cannot even detect the existence of their own LCE nor imagine the possibility of demopathy, this dysfunctional relationship works radically to the advantage of the DCEs.

Jytte Klausen's book *The Islamic Challenge: Politics and Religion in Western Europe*, offers a good example of LCE, when faced with demopathy. After three years (2003–2005) of interviewing what she identified as "the new Muslim elite" in Europe, she asked "how committed are Europe's Muslim leaders to liberal values?" Her definitive answer:

> Europe's Muslim leaders have embraced liberalism by engaging with the institutions of democracy. They invoke human rights to claim equality, or they appeal to the principles of humanist universalism to argue for the "equal worth" of Christianity and Islam. Either way, they draw on varieties of liberalism.[56]

She thus offers as "proof" a discourse that could cut either way: they engage with, invoke liberal values and democratic institutions in order to . . . participate or destroy? She does not ask the question, apparently satisfied with the engagement. Nor was Klausen alone in this approach. Bruce Bawer makes an extensive case that journalists did everything they could to depict radicals and demopaths as moderates, from Tariq Ramadan to your local Imam.[57]

It wasn't as if she had no exposure to the possible hypocritical uses of this liberal discourse: when she conducted her interviews, Muslim demopaths like Muhammad Omar Bakri, explained the principles explicitly: "We will use your democracy to destroy democracy."[58] It wasn't as if at least one of her

---

55 See, for example, Daniel Pipes, "Finding Moderate Muslims: Do you believe in modernity," *Jerusalem Post*, November 26, 2003.

56 Klausen, *Islamic Challenge* (New York: Oxford University Press, 2005), 205.

57 Bawer, *Surrender*.

58 Among the many examples of this widely used expression, see Patrick Goodenough, "Radical Islam: The Enemy in our Midst," *CNS Commentary*, October 18, 2000. See also, Hasnain

interviewees didn't lay out the demopathic plan in "chilling" detail giving her pause in considering the limits of tolerance.... But no more than pause: "More often, however, I encountered generous and principled defenses of human rights." Instead of serious analysis, the reader gets anodyne generalizations. The worrisome trends of malicious intent, the author assures the reader, will lessen "in the face of the weakening of ancestral ethnic ties [which will] facilitate integration." The idea that non-ethnic, neo-Islam might replicate the *al-Walā' wal-Barā'* pattern of Muslim us-them thinking around a new "us," and use mechanisms of integration as weapons of communitarian mobilization, apparently does not register on her screen.[59]

The book itself is testimony to the ease with which a "social scientist" could then (and still can) produce publishable findings based on a systematically skewed sample—those Muslims who were using democratic means to organize—which had no more serious built-in detector for deception than the author's own generous judgments. And yet information professionals, academics in the lead, welcomed its conclusions.

And the corollary to these reassurances about how "moderate" and democratically-minded were the new Muslim elite, was the welcome "fact" that European xenophobia and prejudice were unjustified. Thus, Klausen diagnoses the West as subject to "moral panics" for worrying about the threat to their culture posed by triumphalist Islam, and worries about Western racism and xenophobia, even as the jihadi ideology she dismisses as marginal, openly and repeatedly mobilized violent hatreds, often enough staged with fake news, around their moral panic of the West's threat to Islam.[60]

Opined Stanley Hoffman in *Foreign Policy*: "By destroying [Islamophobic] bogeymen, Klausen forces us to face rationally and compassionately, sensitive and difficult issues of great importance to Europe's future."[61] On the contrary, by dismissing serious threats, Klausen forced us, systematically misinformed, to ignore sensitive and difficult issues of great importance to Europe's (and the

Kazim, "Democracy is for Infidels: Interview with an Islamic State Recruiter," *Spiegel*, October 28, 2014.

59 This is not to say that everyone Klausen interviewed was a demopath; she just had no way of discerning.

60 Klausen, *Islamic Challenge*, 128. This has become a major theme of the Islamophobia police: *Global Islamophobia: Muslims and Moral Panic in the West*, ed. George Mordan and Scott Poynting (New York: Ashgate, 2012). For a good analysis of the strategy of "calculated manufacture of outrage" as a war strategy, see Coughlin, *Catastrophic Failure*, Part V.

61 Stanley Hoffmann, Review of Klausen, *The Islamic Challenge, Foreign Affairs* (March/April 2006).

West's) future.[62] The uncritical LCE sympathy of Klausen, Hoffman, and so many others, blinded them to the very existence of their demopathic, Caliphator, enemy.

Europe may fall to this dysfunctional dynamic, despite the occasional flash of hard questioning that identifies demopaths disguised as moderates, revealing the jihadi discourse beneath their rhetoric.[63] Klausen firmly believes the "new Muslim elite" wants "respect and recognition." She generously imagines that, on the one hand, that will suffice, on the other, that they are prepared to reciprocate respect and recognition to those who treat them as equals. Any evidence to the contrary, that triumphalist Islam does not accept equality with *Kuffār*, and any outbreak of that collective will to dominance—7-7, French riots, Danish Cartoon Affair—will not deter her from her predetermined course.[64] "The vast majority are like us, they're just asking for a fair shake." Therefore, it's best not to subject our Muslim friends to questions about their sincerity. Best not demand reciprocity. Best not acknowledge their resistance to making civic concessions.

To understand the disparity between how a demopath and a liberal cognitive egocentric dream, consider the jihadi version of Lennon's "Imagine":

> *The Caliphator Anthem*
> Imagine there are no countries
> It isn't hard to do.
> Something to kill and die for
> And one religion too.
> Imagine all the people
> Living life under Allah's peace.
> You say I'm a dreamer
> But I'm not the only one ...

So while Davide Martello drove to France in the wake of the Bataclan massacre (2015), in order to play *Imagine*, and the *HuffPo* thought that he had thereby "united France," the jihadis had sunk one more talon into the French body politic.[65] With this unimaginably vicious and sadistic attack, the "martyrs" created

---

62 I take the allusion to "issues of great importance" as referring to Eurabia, which had come out a year earlier.

63 Bruce S. Thornton, "Muslim 'moderates' are true to spirit of Islam," *Victor Davis Hanson*, July 26, 2005.

64 See Jytte Klausen's post 7-7 reiteration of her 2005 conclusions: "Counterterrorism and the Integration of Islam in Europe," *Foreign Policy Research Institute*, May 6, 2006.

65 See n44.

millions more *dhimmi* who understood whom not to offend (including the police, who stood back for hours until the jihadi's work was done, and would do so again with Sarah Halimi), and gained the admiration of untold (unknown) numbers of Caliphators around the world who burn with ardor to strike another such blow.[66] If you want an example of an asymmetrical battleground, no place better displays the decisive rout, than the DCE demopaths manipulating LCE dupes in cogwar.

Demopaths and their LCE Dupes

Forced to make a judgment call about whether a given Muslim—friend, journalist, co-worker, activist—is a sincere moderate or a manipulating demopath, many liberals, eager to believe in virtually anything civil the "other" might say, and to foster any hope for "world peace now," prefer to project good faith onto the demopaths.[67] Indeed, some even concede to the demopaths' demands, and finger the real moderates as enemies. In those cases where they take the protestations of demopaths at face value, as when SPLC labeled Maajid Nawaz an Islamophobe, they become their formal dupes.[68]

I first noticed the phenomenon I am here calling "demopathy" when I read an article about how Muhammad Atta, the leader of 9–11's "magnificent 19" had previously tried to get a $650,000 loan for a crop duster capable of carrying outsized spray tanks from the Florida Department of Agriculture.[69] Told that, as a noncitizen, he did not qualify for the loan, he complained that the infidel bureaucrat was unfairly discriminating against him. He, personally, had no commitment to not discriminating against outsiders (*al-Walā' wal-Barā'*) with his murderous plans for the infidel (spray poison over an urban area), but if he could use the accusation to make Westerners with their ridiculous values feel guilty, to somehow coerce them into making concessions to "prove their good will," then so much the better.

The success of the strategy can be seen in the failure of both Atta's interlocutor at the Department of Agriculture in May of 2000, and an airport security guard the very day of 9–11, to report the problem.

---

66 See Nancy Hartevelt Kobrin, *Penetrating the Terrorist Psyche* (New Rochelle: Multieducator Inc., 2013), 163–70; "Jihad: Sadistic Sexuality," *Shrinkwrapped*, July 12, 2007; Nancy Harteveld Kobrin, "Sado-masochism and the Jihadi Death Cult," *Tablet*, February 11, 2015.

67 Landes, "Demopaths and their dupes," *Augean Stables* (20005).

68 In 2016, the SPLC listed Maajid Nawaz and Aayan Hirsi Ali among Islamophobes, a good illustration of how alleged progressives stifle *any* criticism of Islam: David Graham, "How Did Maajid Nawaz End Up on a List of 'Anti-Muslim Extremists'?" *Atlantic*, October 29, 2016.

69 Tina Kelley, "US Official Says She Met Central Figure in 9/11 Plot," *New York Times*, June 2, 2002. Transcript of interview, "The entire Johnelle Bryant interview," ABC News, June 6, 2002.

"I said to myself, 'If this guy doesn't look like an Arab terrorist, then nothing does.' Then I gave myself a mental slap, because in this day and age, it's not nice to say things like this," Tuohey told the Maine Sunday Telegram. "You've checked in hundreds of Arabs and Hindus and Sikhs, and you've never done that. I felt kind of embarrassed."[70]

These brief lapses due to embarrassment, writ large over a decade, produced everything from the disastrous misreading that led to the slaughter of American troops at Fort Hood by a Palestinian-American fellow-soldier who had openly informed his colleagues of his jihadi sympathies but never got reported for it; and the still-festering scandal of Pakistani Muslims in Rotherham (and elsewhere) systematically raping young British girls, while no one dared report it for fear of accusations of racism and Islamophobia.[71] Demopathy is the paralytic poison of the twenty-first century. And so confident are Caliphators that Westerners cannot resist its poison that they openly admit it: "With your democratic laws we will colonize you, with our Qur'anic laws we will dominate you."[72]

Caliphator discourse is intrinsically demopathic: what better way to get targets to submit willingly, than to convince them they're doing right by their own values? CAIR has made it a basic principle. Use humanitarian rhetoric about human rights (where Muslims are concerned), as a way to protect Caliphators from criticism, even punishment. The case of Sami al Arian, the South Florida State professor who systematically funneled contributions to the Islamic Jihad in Palestine at the height of its terror campaign, illustrates nicely both the demopathic rhetoric used to defend al Arian, and the support he got from progressive dupes who felt deep indignation at his "unfair" treatment at the hands of Islamophobic authorities.[73] No voice is more powerful today, and more damaging, than the righteous indignation of someone denouncing racism against Muslims in order to defend Caliphators.

---

70 "Ticket Agent recalls anger in Muhammad Atta's Eyes," NBC, n.d., http://www.nbcnews.com/id/7117783/#.WvfdnNOuxTY.

71 McLoughlin, *Easy Meat*.

72 This triumphalist Muslim meme has been attributed, inter alia, to Qaradawi, Erdogan, Sheikh Omar Bakri Mohammed. See Giuseppe Germano, "We will dominate you," *MEQ*, December, 1999.

73 Judge James Moody, "Transcript of Sentencing Hearing for Sami-Al-Arian," *Investigative Project*, May 1, 2006,. For a defense of al Arian, see Amy Goodman, "The Case of Sami al Arian," *DemocracyNow*, July 9, 2004.

Eventually, a dogmatic academic consensus has expelled as "racist" any discussion of built-in human belligerence, and deep-set cultural modes.[74] This politically correct imposition of scrupulously value-free discussions about other cultures—who are we to judge?—results in, on the one hand, blindness to relevant material (e.g., on the workings of shame-honor), and on the other, a humanitarian racism that views the base (shame-honor driven) behavior of the "other" as a force of nature which we should have known better than to provoke. Hence, when an American pastor threatened to burn the Qur'an as a protest against Islamic terrorism, one US Supreme Court Justice floated the idea that it was not freedom of speech (as, for example, burning a US flag), but akin to shouting fire in a crowded theater.[75]

On the other end of the globe in Afghanistan, one senior ISAF (International Security Assistance Force) official described a riot that included an Afghan mob's heinous murder of seven UNAMA (UN Assistance Mission in Afghanistan) workers, beheading two, in Mazar-e-Sharif in response to a copy of the Qur'an being burned [sic] in Florida, as "understandable passions."[76] The humanitarian racism, whereby Muslims should not be subject to moral expectations, has guaranteed Western failure on a cognitive battlefield where our Caliphator enemy makes loud moral claims. And our failure to resist only wins us the contempt of independent-minded, genuinely moderate Muslims.

Immigration policy offers a good example of demopaths' toxic manipulation of Western cognitive egocentrism. For the world we want to live in, there should be no boundaries, therefore, abolish ICE. Writes Murtaza Khan:

> We believe everyone has the born right to choose which part of the world to call home with full freedom, safety, and dignity. Instead, every year millions of migrants and refugees surrender their shot at a better life due to red tape, unfair fees, and fraudulent practices.[77]

---

74 See above, 284–89. Ron Robin, "Violent People and Gentle Savages," *Scandals and Scoundrels: Seven Cases that Shook the Academy* (Los Angeles: University of California Press, 2004), chapter 5.

75 Josh Gerstein, "Obama v. Breyer v. Breyer on Quran burning & the law," *Politico*, September 16, 2010.

76 Unclassified report from Jeffrey Bordin, PhD., N2KL Red Team Political and Military Behavioral Scientist, "A Crisis of Trust and Cultural Incompatibility: A Red Team Study of Mutual Perceptions of Afghan National Security Force Personnel and U.S. Soldiers in Understanding and Mitigating the Phenomena of ANSF-Committed Fratricide-Murders," May 12, 2011, http://nsarchive.gwu.edu/NSAEBB/NSAEBB370/docs/Document 11.pdf.

77 Warren Whitlock, "Using Blockchain And AI To Solve The World's Immigration Problems—Migranet.io with Murtaza Khan," *Migranet*, July 19, 2019.

In terms of "social justice" this makes perfect sense. Everyone is equal and everyone has the right to a better life. In cultural terms, this reflects a fundamental misunderstanding of how rare the freedoms are so freely bestowed, how difficult most cultures find the demands of freedom (e.g., renouncing shame-murders, honor violence, and revenge), and how the (evil) West, an outstanding site for respecting these "human rights," is also the only desired destination of people the world over—some of good will, some not. His proposals, while nice sounding, actually will sow chaos and destroy the very freedoms he imagines are universal.[78]

Caliphator demopathy finds its most ready audience among the global "human rights community," the NGOs like Amnesty International and Human Rights Watch, which sometime in the 1990s, got hijacked by activist postcolonials determined to pursue an agenda in which "human rights" discourse could be turned against the West (with a special obsession with Israel), while most gingerly handling the human rights violations of Muslim countries.[79] The marriage of premodern sadism and postmodern masochism involved in this "human rights" discourse found consummation at Durban, under the aegis of that conference's patron saint, Muhammad al Durah: a demopath's delight that continues to give strong sustenance to the Caliphator's cause.[80] Not surprising, then, that "activists" in such human rights organizations have extensive ties with Caliphators; nor that, when forced to choose between a genuine human rights advocate and feminist and a toxically masculine Caliphator, some organizations choose the latter.[81]

Despite the supposed radical difference between the trickster and the tricked, it's not always clear: who is a demopath, and who a dupe? In some cases (how many?), the borderline between the two seems porous. How long do dupes refuse to wake up? How long can they remain in denial, like Lenin's useful idiots, of an ugly reality that contradicts their fond dreams? At what point do they leave stupefying denial and start paying attention to anomalous evidence?

Was Edward Said a knowing agent of Da'i Caliphators when he intellectually paralyzed the infidel elites with his demopathic, anti-racist discourse?[82] Or

---

78 Gad Saad, *The Parasitic Mind* (Washington, DC: Regnery Publishing, 2020), 126–38.

79 Robert Bernstein, "Rights Watchdog, Lost in the Mideast," *New York Times*, October 19, 2009. The major watch-dog of this NGO "human rights" phenomenon, is NGO Monitor: https://www.ngo-monitor.org/.

80 See chapter 1.

81 On Yasmin Hussein, see Andrew Norfolk, "Amnesty director's links to global network of Islamists," *Sunday Times*, August 17, 2015; on the clash between Gita Saghal and Moazzam Begg, see David Aaronovitch, "How Amnesty chose the wrong poster-boy," *Sunday Times*, February 9, 2010; Meredith Tax, *Double Bind: The Muslim Right, the Anglo-American Left, and Universal Human Rights* (New York: Center for Secular Space, 2012), 31–45.

82 Landes, "Orientalism as Caliphator Cognitive Warfare: The (Unintended?) Consequences of Edward Said's Defense of the Arab World," in *Contemporary Approaches to Orientalism in*

did he really believe he was making the world a more inclusive, less racist and oppressive place by standing up for his Palestinian people's "rights?" Is Tariq Ramadan really committed to a world of religious tolerance and mutual respect? Or is he a major–general among Da'ī Caliphators, proud grandson of Hassan al Bannah, proud son of Said Ramadan, royalty of the Muslim Brotherhood?[83] Does Noam Chomsky openly side with the forces of (revolutionary) destruction, or does he think his relentless verbal assaults on everything he can find wrong with Israel and the US (and much more) are somehow well-intentioned criticism trying to improve democracy?

Not surprisingly, at the core of much demopathic rhetoric, lies the "blame the West/USA/Israel" trope that so entrances "progressives." Indeed, the standard response of both Caliphators and "Progressives" to the accusation that jihadi terror is especially morally repugnant, is to blame the West whose sins gave them no choice, or as in 9–11, depict Western behavior as even worse terrorism.[84] The widespread sentimental acceptance of this shared attitude of Muslim triumphalists and Western progressives, pointing the finger of blame at the West, has made clear thinking virtually impossible. This may be one of the glitches that anthropologist Laurie Santos describes: we become aware of the (deeply faulty) perspective of the "other," and end up being unable to free ourselves of it, even as it brings us down.[85]

The key here lies in the twisted combination of humanitarian racism where jihadis and other "others" are concerned (*your side right or wrong*), and ferocious anti-racism where it concerns "us" (*our side wrong even when right*). When Western thought leaders, in limbic captivity to this intoxicating combination of humanitarian racism and virulent anti-racism, empower demopaths rather than sincere moderates, they hurt the forces of civil society and human rights among "us," and empower the forces of dominion and war among "them."[86]

"But," you say, "imagine a world without us-them. Wouldn't that be better?"

Media and Beyond, ed. Gülşah Sari (Hershey, PA: ICI Global, 2021), 33–52, https://www.academia.edu/50961854/Orientalism_as_Caliphator_Cognitive_Warfare_Consequences_of_Edward_Sa%C3%AFds_Defense_of_the_Orient; Coughlin, *Catastrophic Failure*, 1005–6.

83 Ramadan did his thesis on his grandfather against the advice of his thesis advisor: Ian Hamel, "La vérité sur la thèse universitaire de Tariq Ramadan," *Le Point*, March 10, 2018.

84 Chomsky and Derrida on 9–11, chapter 2.

85 Laurie Santos, "Glitches," *Edge*, November 21, 2016; Doyle Quiggle, "How Our Cognitive Solipsism Made Us Limbic Captives of the Taliban," *Small Wars Journal*, August 28, 2018.

86 Phillips, *Londonistan*; Patrick Poole, "10 Failures of the US Government on the Domestic Islamist Threat," *Center for Security Policy*, November 12, 2010.

8

The Global Progressive Left (GPL) in the Twenty-First Century

My side always right?
No! I embrace the "other"
Their side can't be wrong!

The Global Progressive Left at Millennium's End

The phenomenon of the Global Progressive Left as a twenty-first-century *movement,* derives from the late twentieth-century interlacing of two intellectual movements that call themselves "postmodern" and "postcolonial." Postmodernism began as an impudent, iconoclastic, imaginative, and self-consciously anti-totalitarian movement in the 1970s/1390s (its early "postmodern" phase), before taking an authoritarian, postcolonial turn in the 1980s/1400s. That process will enable us to understand how jihadi initiatives at the turn of the millennium found so favorable an audience among people one might think the *last* on earth with whom jihadi rhetoric and values, even in their "secularized" forms, would resonate.[1]

What was the "modern" that postmodernism claimed to go beyond? According to them, it was the Western "grand narrative" of the conquest of nature through objective science, rational (phallo-logo-centric) discourse,

---

1 Examples of global progressive thinking receptive to Caliphator demopathy: Susan Buck-Morss, *Thinking Past Terror: Islamism and Critical Theory on the Left* (London: Verso, 2002); and Nicholas Tampio, *Kantian Courage: Advancing the Enlightenment in Contemporary Political Theory* (New York: Fordham University Press, 2012).

and its world-transforming technology. Postmoderns rejected the hierarchical view they claimed was embedded in that grand narrative that considered itself superior in its pursuit of an objective, scientifically based, understanding of reality.[2] Its hegemonic claims to "objective truth," they argued, invalidated and eclipsed all else. Postmoderns wanted to deconstruct the suffocating influence this largely masculine and intrusive "rational" thinking and acting had imposed on people the world over; to dismantle a cultural edifice of (knowledge as) power whose economic, social and ecological effects were catastrophic.[3]

Postmodernism expressed both regret for the "modern" West's imperial behavior, which had dominated and decimated other cultures, and, at the same time, tried to open itself up to narratives from those "others." It was a winning combination: by rejecting an approach so tightly and aggressively constricted by this elite Western culture, *postmoderns* could tap into what Jacques Derrida, the champion of "deconstruction," called "a superabundance of meaning."[4] New, daring exegetical techniques "broke open" texts to layers of often contradictory meaning and revision, to the never-ending feints of text and sous-texte.[5] With such an approach to their own culture, Westerners might throw off their narrow canon, and make room for so many more voices, narratives, from all over the world.

Postmodernism was supposed to be a blow against both totalitarianism and terror. Jean-François Lyotard wrote in 1984:

> The nineteenth and twentieth centuries have given us as much terror as we can take [sic]. We have paid a high enough price for the nostalgia of the whole and the one, for the reconciliation of the concept and the sensible, of the transparent and communicable experience. Under a general demand for slackening and appeasement, we can hear the mutterings of

---

2 In the late 1970s graduate students in History of Science at Princeton used to read for laughs Charles Gillespie's *The Edge of Objectivity* (Princeton: Princeton University Press, 1960). Now PUP has come out with a new edition (2017).

3 For the turn of 1900, see Mike Davis, *Late Victorian Holocausts: El Niño Famines and the Making of the Third World* (London: Verso, 2001); for the turn of 2000, see John Perkins, *Confessions of an Economic Hit Man* (San Francisco: Bettett-Koehler, 2016).

4 Matthew Machowski paraphrased Derrida's notion of *superabundance of meaning* as "a bristling collection of forces, forever oscillating undecidedly between various parameters of meaning," Machowski,"Derrida and the Other Islam: In What Ways if at all, Does Derrida Provide for a New Perception of Islam in the West Post 9/11?" *Matthew Machowski*, September 16, 2010. http://www.matthewmachowski.com/2010/09/derrida-islam-9-11.html.

5 Jacques Derrida, *De la grammatologie* (Paris: Editions de Minuit, 1967).

a desire for a return of terror, for a realization of the fantasy to seize reality. The answer is: Let us wage war on totality, let us be witnesses to the unpresentable. Let us activate the differences and save the honor of the name.[6]

Thus, the very uncertainties that postmodern approaches so prized, were meant to be a protection from redemptive grand narratives and their urge to carve themselves into the very body-social ("fantasy seizing reality").[7]

Postmodernism saw itself at once as a great renunciation and a liberation. It renounced the power of the Western triumphalist narrative whereby all other cultures were, at best, workable copies of ours, at worst, deplorable failures to follow our lead. Given how deadly some of that thinking could be, especially in the hands of intellectual zealots—from the left or the right—postmodernism renounced the Western "grand narrative" that had visibly and invisibly guided our civilization to the heights of achievement (or so thought benighted moderns). In swearing off *all* grand narratives, postmoderns entered a world swarming with meaning, and filled with the promise of performativity to effect revolutionary change. Break down boundaries between cultures, disciplines, individuals, texts, genders; transgress taboos, think queer, be strange. Dare. Perform.

With this pervasive iconoclasm, one could open up to a vast new world of narratives and experiences previously obscured by the suffocating, hegemonic, Western grand narrative. Anthropology led the field of Social "Sciences" in their radical embrace of a self-abnegating, radical relativism.[8] "**Who are we to judge?**" We understand better by opening ourselves up to the "other," no matter how vulnerable that makes us.[9] In a number of ways, this intellectual and artistic movement plays with paradoxes long ago explored by Buddhists and Taoists:

---

6   Jean-François Lyotard, *The Postmodern Condition: A Report on Knowledge* (Minneapolis: University of Minnesota Press, 1984), 81f.

7   On coercive purity, see 220. on the impact of millennial grand narratives in modern times, see Landes, *Heaven on Earth*, chaps. 10–12.

8   Scott Lukas, "Postmodernism," in *Theory in Social and Cultural Anthropology: An Encyclopedia*, R. Jon McGee, and R. L. Warms, (Thousand Oaks, CA: Sage, 2013), 2.639–645; Herbert Lewis, "The Influence of Edward Said and Orientalism on Anthropology, or: Can the Anthropologist Speak?'" in *Postcolonial Theory and the Arab-Israel Conflict*, edited by P. Salzman and D. Divine (London: Routledge, 2016): 97–109.

9   Brené Brown, *Daring Greatly: How the Courage to Be Vulnerable Transforms the Way We Live, Love, Parent, and Lead* (New York: Penguin, 2015).

letting go to "get it," riding the *Tao*'s waves and currents in encounters with cosmic forces.[10]

The Transformational Apocalyptic of Postmodernity: Embracing the "Other"

Like most demotic millennial movements, this one started promisingly. This interpretive freedom allowed a new dimension of social relations to emerge. With this new intellectual and emotional flexibility, one can turn to the "other" and develop noncoercive bonds of voluntary association, of true friendship. Thus, in place of the tribal "us-them" that, when it does not fear them, views others as inferior, disdaining and despising *them*, postmodern ethics put great emphasis on entering into open relationships with an "other" with whom we perform revolutionary acts of liberation. *Alterity* demanded the acknowledgment of the "other," with whom we can and should live in relations of trust, respect, and openness.[11]

For Derrida, deconstruction dissolves the barrier between "us and them"; it is a revelatory and, in some ways, salvific activity that peels away the phallogocentric layers of meaning, decenters and destabilizes grand narratives of territory and identity, and reveals the world as an ever-changing, ever-fascinating, semiotic dance: a cascade, a kaleidoscope of meaning, the always-already, *différance*. Cognitive dissonance is not painful, it is a semiotic delight. Derrida defined *hospitality*, the embrace of the "other" as "the deconstruction of the at-home [us]; deconstruction is hospitality to the other [them]," so that they too feel "at home."[12]

This performance, postmoderns believed, brought us to a peaceful global world: tolerant, open, empathic, accommodating, cosmopolis. Not the world of yore, of

---

10 Fritjof Capra, *The Tao of Physics* (Boulder, CO: Shambala, 1975); Gary Zukav, *Dancing Wu Li Masters* (New York: William Morrow, 1979); Robin Cooper, *The Evolving Mind: Buddhism, Biology and Consciousness* (Birmingham, UK: Windhorse, 1996); Matthieu Ricard, Trinh Xuan Thuan, *The Quantum and the Lotus* (New York: Crown, 2004); Donald S. Lopez Jr., *Buddhism and Science* (Chicago: University of Chicago Press, 2008).

11 Emmanuel Levinas, *Alterity et Transcendence* (1995; tr. New York: Columbia University Press, 2000); Baudrillard and Guillaume, *Radical Alterity* (1994; Los Angeles: Semiotext(e), 2008); Jeffrey Nealon, *Alterity Politics: Ethics and Performative Subjectivity* (Durham, NC: University of North Carolina Press, 1998).

12 Derrida, "Hospitality," in *Acts of Religion*, edited by Gil Anidjar (New York: Routledge, 2001), 364; Jacob Meskin, "Misgivings about Misgivings and the Nature of a Home: Some Reflections on the Role of Jewish Tradition in Derrida's Account of Hospitality," in *Hosting the Stranger: Between Religions*, ed. Richard Kearney and James Taylor (New York: Continuum, 2011), 59. Cf. Jonathan Sacks, *Dignity of Difference: How to Avoid the Clash of Civilizations.* (London: Bloomsbury USA, 2003).

war, of "us-them" dichotomies like "nation-states," and of paranoid mutual hostility and contempt. And not the world of a homogenizing globalization, where Western capitalism disguises its imperialist thrust behind an allegedly "free" market, and subjects everyone to the pervasive and penetrating exigencies of commodification.

Progressives *actively* rejected racism and hierarchy, colonialism and imperialism, and oppression of the weak, the kind of behavior that only brings on more rebellion and violence. *War, nay, violence itself, never solved anything.* Instead, postmodernity offered those who longed to make this evolutionary leap, a platform for striking blows back at the arrogant, insular, cultural narcissism of Western Eurocentrism. A leap from national "honor culture" to a global "dignity culture." Some, like Emmanuel Levinas (and in his own way, Michel Foucault), made *I-Thou* relationships, free of power and coercion, into the (apocalyptic) key to (millennial/collective) redemption. Levinas's ethical ontology in some ways replicates, even as it secularizes, the "Sermon on the Mount." Judge not. Forgive. Love even the hostile other. Open your heart to all.[13]

It's fair to call this fundamental concern with an empathic and generous attitude towards the Other, the "millennial Zeitgeist" of the postwar West (1950-): thinkers may have differed in how we should relate to the "other," but they all agreed on the redemptive importance of treating them with dignity and respect.[14] Feminism has no meaning outside the moral claims that the female "other" can make on the phallogocentric mind.[15] In this sense, critical theory, both in its socio-political (Frankfurt School) and literary (Derrida, Butler) versions, represents a long-range premillennial project to prepare mankind, perhaps over the course of several generations, for a major, even evolutionary, leap to a different level of consciousness, a different way of inter-relating with each other, and a correspondingly different way of organizing the polity. Western intellectuals after WWII/Holocaust, looked to theory (a combination of psychological and exegetical innovation) to engender social revolutions: a *transformational apocalyptic* (interior, gradual, noncoercive), leading to a *demotic millennium* (egalitarian-prolific, positive-sum, this-worldly).[16]

---

13 David Teh, "Radical Alterity," in *The Baudrillard Dictionary*, ed. Richard Smith (Edinburgh, Edinburgh University Press, 2010), 176–78.

14 Anthony Appiah, *Cosmopolitanism: Ethics in a World of Strangers* (New York: W. W. Norton, 2010); Sacks, *Dignity of Difference*; Rifkin, *Empathy*; Terri Givens, *Radical Empathy: Finding a Path to Bridging Racial Divides* (Bristol, GB: Policy Press, 2021).

15 Simone de Beauvoir begins with a critical invocation of Levinas's notion of "alterity," *The Second Sex* (New York: Vintage, 1989), xxii. Next wave feminist critique of de Beauvoir, Tamise Van Pelt, "Otherness," *Postmodern Culture*, Volume 10.2 (2000).

16 On the millennial dimensions of modern theory, see Jeffrey C. Alexander, *The Dark Side of Modernity* (Cambridge: Polity Press, 2013), 5–28.

This grand vision suggests that while postmodernists may have rejected previous grand narratives, they did so not to dispense with moral aspirations towards the earthly messianic era (what some scholars would identify as the Western "grand narrative"), but to perfect the millennial arts of advancing that end. Having uncritically taken up modernity's dispatching of (Western) religious and scientific grand narratives as false and superstitious relics of an earlier age, few of the practitioners of the new critical theory were aware that they were replicating the aniconic, demotic, monotheistic, grand narrative according to which everything works towards a final denouement of freedom and justice, according to the principle that *only the just are free.* The grand narrative remained (and remains): freedom and justice, the inseparable twins, serve as the inspirations whereby one "steers planet earth" along the "arc of the moral universe." But where modernists steered with their eyes steadfastly fixed on "objective truth," postmodernists, having shattered that icon, increasingly tended to steer with their teleological eyes fixed on "embracing the other."

Superseding the Modern: Messianic Memes, Tyrannical Superego, and All Kinds of Loathing

The memes that currently circulate offer one of the best places to observe the messianic tendencies of the progressive *Zeitgeist.* Some have interesting kernels of validity, but all reflect deeply unrealistic messianic assumptions about reality. Nevertheless, they have found widespread acceptance, and once invoked, these memes shut down all further discussion:[17]

- *Violence never solved anything. ("Senseless Violence")*
- *War is not the answer.*
- *Who are we to judge?*
- *All cultures are equal.*

---

17 For a discussion of this memeplex in the context of cogwar, see Green, *Cognitive Warfare,* 57–70; weaponized version of this memeplex, Mary Katharine Ham and Guy Benson, *End of Discussion: How the Left's Outrage Industry Shuts Down Debate, Manipulates Voters, and Makes America Less Free (and Fun)* (New York: Crown Forum, 2015). Things have only gotten much worse since then: John McWhorter, "Academics Are Really, Really Worried About Their Freedom," *Atlantic,* September 1, 2020; Lee Jussim, "Why Americans Don't Feel Free to Speak Their Minds," *Psychology Today,* June 1, 2021.

Note that they are all advanced, positive-sum principles, asserted in the belief that, if we're sufficiently committed to finding a solution, "we can work it out."

When, in the 21st century, Global Jihad carried out its first attacks on the West, this Zeitgeist was sorely tested. Rather than question some of the premises, however, proponents deployed these memes, mistakenly thinking they describe the "real world" rather than the outrageous hope of what (they think) the world can and should be. Mistakenly judge a foe for a friend often enough, however, and you win the Darwin Award. By believing, ironically, in the "truth" of these high-hope memes, convinced of the transformative power of their performance, of their witnessing to these noble sentiments, postmoderns insulated themselves from the shock that others felt, as they cut the lines that tethered them to reality. For some, the reaction to the separation was: "So what? These hard thoughts are just remnants of an objectivist criticism meant to entangle us in zero-sum Realpolitik, those objecting are just in a moral panic." Or as Jefferson Airplane put it: "In loyalty to our kind, we cannot tolerate their obstruction."[18]

The result has become an extraordinary phenomenon in the two-millennia history of Christianity. In that time, no nation that called itself Christian ever implemented foreign policy based on the "Sermon on the Mount." After all, turning the other cheek in a venue where those who want power and dominance congregate the world over, might seem counter-indicated, certainly as a unique option (war is *never* the answer). Ironically, it took nations whose intellectual elites had rejected Christianity (and all religions) as superstitious nonsense, to attempt so foolhardy an endeavor. No wonder that along with their impossibly high if unconscious Christian morals, we find in their "anxiety of influence" a strong strain of supersessionism (see below).

For the more revolutionary ones who embraced these messianic memes, they weren't "separating" from reality; they were bringing it along with them, transforming reality. Ironically, despite postmodernism's insistence on the inadequacy of any language to come close to describing reality, the ground level practitioners lived in a fantasy of shaping reality with (theoretical) words. Paradoxically, the separation from ineffable but adamantine reality endowed them with astonishing creative powers, speakers of a new, performative, revolutionary language.[19] In popular version, we are told that we live in *"a complex and borderless world,"* by figures like John Kerry, not an advertiser for

---

18 Jefferson Airplane, "Crown of Creation" (1968).
19 On "applied postmodernism," see Helen Pluckrose and James Lindsay, *Cynical Theories: How Activist Scholarship Made Everything about Race, Gender, and Identity—and Why This Harms Everybody* (Durham, NC: Pitchstone, 2020), chapter 2.

CNN's favorite meme, but the Secretary of State of the most powerful nation in the world.[20]

The real world, alas, consistently bites back. That's the world in which sometimes war *is* the answer, a last resort to be sure, but appropriate when dealing with predatory assaults like those of the Nazis. And while we can agree that withholding judgment is a good idea, very few who think about it would argue that *never* judging is even better, rather than suicidal. Unfortunately for those who have difficulty with cognitive dissonance, judging too soon *and* too late are *both* mistakes that can do much damage. One might even argue, good judgments like happy spouses, make a life good.

And, in the end, those who so generously renounced judgment of others, rapidly and generously judged enemies as friends (Butler and Livingstone on Hamas and Hizballah) and equally rapidly and harshly judged and deplored those "xenophobic Islamophobes," their fellow "right-wing" citizens (not to mention the Israelis). As a result, we got messianic dreams mainstreamed as reality. The '70s bumper sticker read, "*the mind is like a parachute that only works when it's open.*" That may be true, but if it can't close, it can only be used once. It's one thing to say all cultures have important narratives, it's quite another to say, they're all of equal value in understanding each other and the world and we should not dare judge one better than the other.

Disarmed by messianic platitudes, committed to "progressing" by transgressing all (Western) cultural and gender boundaries, adrift with no conscious connection to the grand narrative that made their success possible, inebriated by their imagined liberation, and as deeply ashamed of the genocidal, racist, imperialist past of their forefathers as they are at the very thought that they too might share that prejudiced hatred, postmodernists are easy marks for the Da'wa demopaths who hit the West in the early fifteenth century AH. Invoking the violent hatreds of Franz Fanon (the terrorist's intellectual), these demopaths clamored for the status of subaltern victim, the wretched of the earth, on whose very skin and social body, the imperialists had inscribed their racist dominion. It was the postmodernist's moral imperative to repent for the years of tears that privileged white man had drawn from the world's victims, and to bring these

---

20 Seth Frantzman, A Borderless World of Wealth and White Privilege," *SethFranzman.com*, June 26, 2016.

marginalized and under-represented voices into the discussion.[21] "Islam is the poor and we get pissed off when the Americans beat up on the poor."[22]

Behind this penitence lay a tyrannical superego, making impossible demands on our guilt-wracked consciences, as in Jacques Derrida's redefinition of terrorism as *"letting people die."*

> Does terrorism necessarily involve death? Can one terrorize without killing? And then is killing necessarily something active? Can't "letting people die" not wanting to know that one is letting people die (hundreds of millions of people dying of hunger), inadequate health care, etc. be part of a "more or less" conscious and deliberate terrorist strategy. All situations of structural and social or national oppression produce a terror that is *never natural* (and which is therefore, organized, institutional and on which they depend), without those who benefit from them ever having to organize terrorist acts or be called terrorists.[23]

Derrida here equates terrorism with *any* kind of suffering that [technologically empowered, i.e., Western] humans can prevent and *don't* (including the transformation of organizations and institutions into non-oppressive ones). In declaring organizations that structure violence, both physical and psychological, into the social order—that is, all but some never realized messianic social structures—he identified an always-already as a "never natural." Human relationships free of violence and inequity (i.e., the messianic "norm") have become the *natural* state.[24] And the result is, he can question the moral outrage of Westerners, shocked at the savage depravity of 9–11's *targeting* of civilians.

Pascal Bruckner responded: "You've read that correctly: we're all potential terrorists; to one degree or another, we sow death the way Monsieur Jourdain spoke prose, without knowing it!"[25]

Postmodern Westerners can never do enough to atone. The anger of "our" victims, however merciless it might sometimes feel (9–11), is understandable,

---

21 Pascal Bruckner, *Tears of the White Man: Compassion as Contempt* (New York: Free Press, 1984); see Albert Camus, *La chute* (Paris: Gallimard, 1954), whose protagonist is a "penitential judge." On the masochistic solution, Pascal Bruckner, *Tyranny of Guilt.*

22 See 64f.

23 Giovanni Borradori, *Philosophy in a Time of Terror: Dialogues with Jürgen Habermas and Jacques Derrida* (Chicago: Chicago University Press, 2003), 108, italics mine.

24 For Appiah's discussion of these moral dilemmas, see his *Cosmopolitanism*, chapter 10.

25 Pascal Bruckner, *The Tyranny of Guilt*, 20. For another systematic critique of Derrida's response to 9–11, see "Intellectual Conceits: Derrida on 9/11," *Plato's Head*, September 20, 2011.

given the terrible things "we" did (slavery, imperialism). Nothing short of a moral (messianic) perfection can appease it.

The sweep of the theoretical critique, the sharp focus on all forms, no matter how hidden, of (Western) "violence" and "power" suggests the language of the most severe moral demands awaiting us at the Last Judgment when we stand before "He who searches out the innermost recesses—בוחן כליות ולב"). And yet through intersectional analysis, this messianic meme—*all social or national structures that cause* [sic] *suffering are forms of terrorism*—becomes a reality-defying "truism." Since life itself involves some amount of suffering and violence and zero-sum relations in which more lose than win, so will any social or political arrangement ever known, even ones that work hard to limit that suffering rather than reformulate it as legitimate structural dominion for the elite. To *demand* perfection is cruelly tyrannical; to insert such messianic memes into a discussion of the West attacked by global Caliphators, suicidally disorienting.

It's as if the postmodernists want us humans to accomplish what the "God" they don't believe in has failed to deliver. In response to His inexplicable redemptive passivity, *we* are the active agents that bring about a(n ersatz) millennium relieved of every microaggression of suffering.[26] For Horkheimer, for example, writing after the Shoah, religion could not be anything more than "the sorrow and sadness" that comes with the realization "that the righteousness of which religion and theology have been telling us right up to this day [i.e., the immanent justice of a God who intervenes], is in the final analysis nonexistent.[27] Or as so many Jews reasoned after the Holocaust, "if He didn't intervene then, forget waiting for the messiah."

Instead, technologically empowered and morally inspired humans stepped into the fray: As Stewart Brand's opening line to the *Whole Earth Catalogue* declares: "WE ARE AS GODS and may as well get good at it." A generation later, intoxicated with the promise of Artificial Intelligence and eagerly anticipating what he calls the *Singularity*, Ray Kurzweil rephrased it: "So, does God exist? I would say, not yet."[28] Get ready for the nerd apocalypse.

But playing god, especially our own projection of an omnipotent, beneficent god who, like some helicopter parent, would never allow chaos and suffering to

---

26 Landes, *Heaven on Earth*, chapter 8–12 (Enlightenment, French Revolution, Marx, Russian Revolution)

27 Jacob Klapwijk, *Dialectic of Enlightenment: Critical Theory and the Messianic Light* (Eugene OR: Wipf & Stock, 2010), 97–98.

28 Ray Kurzweil, *Transcendent Man: Prepare to Evolve*, IMDb, 2009; Harari, *Homo Deus: A Brief History of Tomorrow* (New York: Random House, 2016).

hurt humans,[29] much less, to engulf humanity in catastrophe, may sometimes be more difficult than we think. Empathizing with, caring for, *everyone* may be well beyond our capacities, however well-intentioned we might be; indeed, it may be ill-advised, certainly in its more dogmatic, absolutist formulations.[30] On the one hand, this kind of thinking leads to misplaced empathy for those far away whom we don't know except through (a dramatically faulty) media, and on the other, to guilt feelings about favoring our own. "**Parents reading their children bedtime stories . . . are unfairly disadvantaging other people's children.**"[31] Our obligation to all "them" involves sacrificing precious aspects of "us."

Reportedly, Edward Said's favorite quotation was from Hugh of Saint-Victor, and embodied the anti-tribal, cosmopolitan, ecumenical mindset of the more enlightened clerics of the age (twelfth century): "he is perfect to whom the whole world is a foreign land."[32] One of Said's admirers turned this Augustinian passage into Derridean utopia: the whole world will be at home everywhere.

> [Said] utilize[s this passage] to uncannily spin his idea of secularization as a largely individual struggle to become conscious of, and then to free one's self from, largely unconscious historical and sociocultural determinisms. The freedom is made to make another history, one that would be other than the unenlightened repetitions of age-old fear and greed, generated blood feuds. His is calling for a type of renunciation, a renunciation of a type of worldview but this for the sake of all of the world's peoples, not one above any others.[33]

Attractive thoughts and pleasant vistas. Alas, as we shall see, after the (for the Arabs) catastrophic 1967 war, Said took this early ecumenical ideal that renounced unenlightened vendettas and exploited it to embrace a hard zero-sum,

---

29 Voltaire raged against a God who allowed the earthquake in Lisbon that killed tens of thousands. Kurzweil dangles "total well-being" before his acolytes: David Courard-Hauri, "Singularity's Potential for Sustainability and Environmental Health and Well-Being," *Good Health and Well-Being*, ed. Walter Leal Filho et al. (Cham, Switzerland: Springer Nature, 2019).

30 For a brilliant rant on this issue see Ze'ev Maghen, *Imagine: John Lennon and the Jews, A Philosophical Rant* (Danbury, CT: The Toby Press, 2010); and a more sober argument, Sacks, *The Dignity of Difference*.

31 Joe Gelonesi, "Is having a loving family an unfair advantage?" *Philosopher's Zone*, May 1, 2015.

32 Hugh of St. Victor, *Didascalion*, book 3, chapter 19.

33 Mathieu E. Courville, *Said's Rhetoric of the Secular* (New York: Continuum, 2011), 88f.

tribal, "Palestinian nationalism." In so doing, he turned postmodernism into postcolonialism.[34]

The Destructive Apocalyptic of Postmodern Supersessionism

For all its admirable ambitions, there was a darker side at work in postmodernism. One sees it clearly in its self-baptism as *postmodern*: the oedipal, supersessionist drive that defined and dismissed the previous "modern" epoch and now allegedly completely displaced its predecessor. For some, "modern" became the definition of what to avoid. All the racism, violence, and hatred of the "other," against which global progressives defined themselves, appears most vividly on their moral screens as the deeds of (their) Western predecessors (and unreconstructed Western contemporaries: i.e. privileged whites, Zionists).

For Judith Butler, as for Jean Baudrillard, current American hegemony (especially after the fall of the USSR) constitutes, by far, the most serious, imperialist threat to global, transnational, transgender, transtribal, transgressively liberating, civil society, free of power structures.[35] It does not occur to these theoretical messianists that, based on their own values, America is so far, *by far*, the most benign international hegemon ever known to human history, and that their chiliastic fantasies of a global culture beyond war and coercion and boundaries, one that protects the marginalized and disadvantaged ... could only thrive, under that (Western) global hegemony. Their aspirations were not new values, but extensions of those founding demotic ideals.

So fierce is this postmodern focus on Western sins, however, that little attention is directed to earlier (more primitive?), far more oppressive forms of imperialism, like world conquest and subjugation, slavery, inquisition, ethnic cleansing, genocide, and holy war ... all drives and aspirations still alive and well today, certainly among Caliphators.[36] As Turkish President Recep

---

34 Landes, "'Celebrating' Orientalism: Edward Said's Honor and Shame," *Middle East Quarterly*, 24 (2017).

35 For a good example of how this "trickles down" to undergraduates, see "Harvard Students Think the US is a Greater Threat to World Peace Than ISIS," *Find a Free Country Project*, October 18, 2014.

36 Current usage in the public sphere of "imperialism" almost never refers to the once and future nature of Islamic Imperialism: Karsh, *Islamic Imperialism*. Indeed, it soon became Islamophobic to raise the subject. For the focus on American slavery as the original sin, and

Erdogan explained to his fellow Muslims: "In our civilization, conquest is not occupation or looting. It is establishing the dominance of the justice that Allah commanded in the region. . . . This is why our civilization is one of conquest."[37] Coming from a Turk whose people slaughtered millions of Christians a century ago, this statement is especially revealing. And yet, because the practitioners of these violent systems of oppression also disliked America (their imperial rivals), progressive world-changers deemed them fit allies in an anti-imperialist coalition.[38] That's how Judith Butler, the self-styled pacifist, could be so astoundingly stupid about Hamas and Hizballah as to think them *anti-imperialist* allies (see below). As Meredith Tax explained patiently, it is ridiculous to think that "The Muslim Right [i.e., Caliphators] is anti-imperialist."[39]

This combination of intense hostility towards their own predecessors ["us"], and leniency towards the Other ["them"], proved a winning formula in the 1980s and 90s in academia. A wave of cognitive revulsion at the invidious, "orientalist" racism of earlier scholars, allowed progressive scholars to dismiss much of the work of their predecessors, especially where political analysis came into play. Displaying what Harold Bloom called "the anxiety of influence,"[40] or what Freud and his followers would have readily called oedipal, the new post-Orientalist scholars who manned the university teaching of Middle East Studies treated anything (or anyone) critical of Eastern (especially Arab) culture, as orientalists and racists.[41] Indeed Said threw the insult "racist" around with nearly as much abandon as "orientalism."[42] It was the first successful deployment of the accusation of systemic racism.

---

the blind spot for current Muslim slavery, see Charles Jacobs, "Thousands of Black People are Still Slaves. So Why Haven't You Heard about Them?" *The Federalist*, October 14, 2019.

37 Turkish President Recep Tayyip Erdoğan: "Our Civilization is One of Conquest," *MEMRI*, August 26, 2020.

38 Camila Bassi, "'The Anti-Imperialism of Fools': A Cautionary Story on the Revolutionary Socialist Vanguard of England's Post-9:11 Anti-War Movement," ACME: An International E-Journal for Critical Geographies, 9:2 (2010): 113–137.

39 Tax, *Double Bind*, 81–84.

40 Harold Bloom, *The Anxiety of Influence* (New York: Oxford University Press, 1973). "Hence the uniqueness or originality of the precursor is 'explained away.' . . . [The new poet] achieves ease through the belief that he has tapped into a source equal to or greater than the precursor," Dan Geddes, "Review of Bloom, *Anxiety of Influence*," *The Satirist*, October 5, 1999.

41 Martin Kramer, *Ivory Towers on Sand: The Failure of Middle East Studies in America* (Washington DC: Washington Institute for Near East Policy, 2001). In a sense, the book was prophetic. Published in 2001, it predicted how fragile an edifice this Saidian approach to the East would prove when put under the pressure of a real-life, wave of Islamic messianic triumphalism.

42 On Said's use of the "racism card," see David Shipler, "'From a Wellspring of Bitterness,' review of Said's *The Politics of Dispossession*," *New York Times*, June 26, 1994.

This new, global, postcolonial framework viewed Western imperialism as a world-wide plague for which the West owes reparations to the survivors of their colonial cruelties. The villains are not those with premodern, fanatic, imperialist ambitions of their own, but the systemically racist, privileged Westerners who have structured their ease on systems that are every bit as terrorist as those valiantly fighting against their uniquely evil "Western imperialism." Ironically, in this strange (oedipal) terrain of moral equivalence, we find the progressive (i.e. positive-sum) left invoking hard zero-sum thinking, but only where their own side is concerned: "*Our* ease can only have been achieved through *their* dis-ease, all our wealth stolen from them."

This anxiety of influence produces one of the more radical and problematic aspects of the postmodern project: its hostility to the very society that made their movement possible. This ingratitude goes well beyond dismissing the contribution of modernity to criticism of the "self"—the very lifeblood of postmodern analysis.[43] Instead (self-)criticism (of the West) has become a "tyranny of penitence," in which Western progressives condemn their society to eternal regret for the crimes of their ancestors and the crimes they commit today by not being more active in alleviating human suffering and dismantling their own privilege.[44] For the new activist, social-justice, scholar-warrior, "we are right because we have completely reversed our predecessors' wrong . . . ," or, in its epigrammatic form, the oikophobic, "*their side, right or wrong!*"[45]

In its current intersectional form, in which "white" or "male" or "Jewish" means privileged and privileged means (systemically) racist, this formulation hurts almost everyone on the planet. It hurts those now disadvantaged, by encouraging and directing their resentments and excuses for failure; it hurts the "privileged," whom it makes a target of that resentful failure and dismisses whatever merit earned them their positions of authority; and it hurts the effort to improve by dismantling an (imperfect) meritocracy for an ersatz equality [lit. division of spoils]. The only immediate beneficiaries of this tyrannical Western superego are the radical progressives who shape their worldview around these formulations, and the Caliphators, who can effortlessly launder their theocratic

---

43 Charles Taylor, *The Sources of the Self: The Making of the Modern Identity* (Cambridge MA: Harvard University Press, 2011), especially 111–210.

44 Bruckner, *Tyranny of Guilt*; Bruce Bawer, *Victim's Revolution: The Rise of Identity Studies and the Closing of the Liberal Mind* (New York: HarperCollins, 2012).

45 Already in 1927, Julien Benda denounced those clercs (intellectuals) who held: "I always maintain my country is in the wrong, even if it is right." *The Treason of the Intellectuals* (Washington, DC: Encounter, 2010), 171; Philip Salzman, "In Praise of Dead White Men," *A Voice for Men*, September 17, 2018. On *Oikophobia* used as a political term, see Roger Scruton, *England and the Need for Nations* (London: Civitas, 2004), chapter 8.

imperialism as postcolonial "anti-imperialism." Westsplainers assure us: "They hate us because of what we imperialists have done to them. No way they hate us from *ressentiment* and envy, or ambitions to rule the world and its attendant paranoia. Such claims are too Nietzschean, too Orientalist, too racist."

Among the most important victims of this postmodern oedipal putsch, we find the traditions of intellectual rigor that had contributed so much to modernity's success, and hence made postmodernity possible. Agreed, the more enthusiastic modernists, armed with the scientific knowledge that produced the industrial revolution and our startling exploitation of nature, had oversold and misrepresented their project as reaching the edge of "objective truth." As Dickens's character in *Hard Times*, the school board Superintendent, Thomas Gradgrind put it, "Facts, facts, facts!" But that hardly meant that modernity had not developed some remarkably effective mechanisms for exploring the real world, for self-critical, hence self-correcting, disciplines dealing with, describing, and interpreting, reality's many facets.[46] One might argue that at its origins, before its giddy plunge, deconstruction had promised yet one more stage in the modern project of exploring "reality," with all the unflattering feedback that any honest inquiry generates.

So, if "modernity" was perhaps too tightly tethered to (what it took to be) "objective" reality, at least its (inevitably flawed) methods deserved inclusion among the disciplines in the *next stage* in this modern, demotic project. In principle, had postmodernists been more modest in their pretensions to supersede "modernity," they might have understood that their own daring steps were actually experiments in a(n exegetical) freedom no society has ever previously permitted its members, much less encouraged with institutional support,[47] and that they should use their new-claimed freedom responsibly. Ironically, no phenomenon better illustrated the Western "grand narrative of freedom" than the postmodernists who so freely dismissed that very narrative.

And yet, "postmoderns," especially the "critical theorists," even as they legitimately criticized some aspects of the modern project, scorned their forebears in areas where they directly benefited from and further developed previous high moral aspirations. These forebears in the drive towards human freedom, men and women of great talent and energy, go back centuries and

---

46 Mary Poovey, *A History of the Modern Fact: Problems of Knowledge in the Sciences of Wealth and Society* (Chicago: University of Chicago Press, 1998). One need not achieve a perfect match between "facts" and "reality" for factual concerns to make valuable contributions to a "postfact" discourse.

47 Reading the Bible "incorrectly" (or even translating it into the vernacular) could mean execution as late as the early modern period (e.g., William Tyndale, 1536).

centuries (for Europe, I would say back to the apostolic "heretics" of 1000), working on a grand project, of which our generation is but a stage, albeit a most favored, if not a too-favored, stage. Had postmodernists, when it came to both their predecessors and to their promises, shown some of the exegetical modesty about their own efforts, which they insist we adopt when confronted with ineffably complex reality, we might not be in our current state of disorientation.[48]

But what fun is there in modesty? Too sober. Boring. Not made for the age of the internet. Instead, deconstructionists went from exegetical arousal to exegetical promiscuity. And from there, some mobilized for revolutionary goals—deconstruct the western canon's hegemonic, grand narrative; undermine its foundations; prepare its collapse.[49] Here, as we shall see, the postmodern, postcolonial global progressives ended up casting off any tether to the real world.[50] Their depictions of a theoretically constructed reality increasingly failed to process negative feedback.

On the contrary, they proved themselves willing to distort, even invert, depictions of the world, out of a salvific desire to act upon it. In violating their commitment to fellow citizens on the level of the ethical obligations of information professionals (academics, journalists, researchers), they consoled themselves by thinking they were transforming, saving the world, bending the arc of the moral universe in the proper direction.[51] And as that shift occurred, these transformational millennialists shifted from being the prolifics they thought they were, and instead became devourers.[52] They began to ask for credentials, and anyone who did not pass the increasingly demanding and contorted muster, got canceled.

Promiscuous exegesis (interpreting freely *from the text*) gave way to hostile eisogesis (reading [offensive] meaning *into the text*). Postmoderns aimed the corrosive power of deconstructive criticism at the Western canon, destabilizing,

---

48 See Paul Gross and Norman Levitt, *Higher Superstition: The Academic Left and its Quarrels with Science* (Baltimore, MD: Johns Hopkins Press, 1998).

49 Kimball, *Tenured Radicals*.

50 Alan Sokal, "Transgressing Boundaries: Towards a Transformative Hermeneutics of Quantum Gravity," *Social Text* #46/47 (1996): 217–252. Editors of Lingua Franca, *The Sokal Hoax: The Sham That Shook the Academy* (Lincoln: University of Nebraska Press, 2000).

51 *Bending the Arc: Striving for Peace and Justice in the Age of Endless War*, ed. S. Breyma, J. W. Amidon and M.B. Aumand (Albany: State University of New York Press, 2020). During President Obama's administration, this became a veritable slogan: John Nichols, "Barack Obama Charts an Arc of History That Bends Toward Justice," *The Nation*, January 21, 2013; Paul Raushenbush, "50 Years Later: Whither the Moral Arc of the Universe?" *Huffington Post*, October 23, 2013.

52 William Blake, *Marriage of Heaven and Hell* (1796), plates 16–17.

decentering, delegitimizing it, stripping away its normative claims.[53] In this sense, postmodernism easily elided with a widespread neo-Marxism that had given up all the industrial details of the original apocalyptic scenario (proletariat, capital, bourgeoisie, revolution), but continued to cherish the millennial promise of redemption, in which it saw itself as the revolutionary vanguard bringing down the hated oppressors and offering social justice and emancipation to the masses.[54] For these warriors against Western hegemony, it would be the work of a generation: deconstruct the West, tear down its canonical walls, expose it to the always-already open world. And if that involves listening to some painful complaints from our victims around the world, well that's a key part of living in a self-critical, reality-based community. A gamble, to be sure, but worth the prize, no?

The Postcolonial Turn: From Transformational to Cataclysmic Apocalyptic

The subversive nature of both postmodern exegesis and performativity made every encounter a potentially revolutionary act, a transformation of identities, a post-Marxian emancipatory project.[55] And like Marx's, this proffered emancipation as "collective redemption in this world," is just what millennial beliefs promise. Here was a gradual, generations-long, millennial project to deconstruct a society's discursive techniques for imposing conformity on their "melancholic subjects," which would, at a certain point, lead to collapse and (presumably), a spontaneous assertion of happy freedom.[56] In this case, a secular, hence active, transformational apocalyptic movement aims, through its cultural work (cognitive war), to bring on an egalitarian millennium. But whereas most transformative apocalyptic scenarios are peaceful and creative,

---

53 John M. Ellis, *Against Deconstruction* (Princeton, Princeton University Press, 1989; Stephen Hicks, *Explaining Postmodernism: Skepticism and Socialism from Rousseau to Foucault* (Tempe, AZ: Scholargy Press, 2004).

54 This resembles the response of Marx to the disappointment of 1848: timing *wrong*, revised redemptive scenario, *correct*. Landes, *Heaven on Earth*, chapter 10. On the revival of this loosely defined Marxism in the twenty-first century, see Ellis and Hicks (previous note) and, more recently, Yoram Hazony, "The Challenge of Marxism," *Quillette*, August 16, 2020.

55 Judith Butler, "Merely Cultural," *New Left Review*, 227 (1998): 33–44.

56 "Hegemonic cultural norms produce 'melancholic' subjects, modelled on the Hegelian 'unhappy consciousness,' whose identity depends upon the marginalisation of excluded, transgressive subjectivities," Geoff Boucher, "Politics of Performativity," *Parrhesia Journal*, 1 (2006), 113.

here, the transformational work is bloodless destruction ("marginal subversion of the reigning cultural norms"). The result is an unusual hybrid of apocalyptic scenarios—transformative cataclysmic.[57] Instead of transformation leading to the millennium, this deconstructive transformation prepared the cataclysm, the collapse of the identified "evil."

And, as with its Marxist predecessor, believers tended, when (inevitably) frustrated, towards the "politics of the worst."[58] This destructive response to disappointment prepared a "postcolonial" mutation that subverted many of postmodernism's founding principles. From flourishing positive- to hard zero-sum.[59]

In 1978/1399, Edward Said published what may be the single most important book of the late twentieth century, *Orientalism*, a book every bit as bad as it was spectacularly influential.[60] Its impact on Middle Eastern Studies, an academic discipline he was not part of (and whose languages he did not speak or read) was (and still is) incalculable, and its influence spread well beyond that field. Within decades (1980s and 90s/early fifteenth century), a new generation of scholars took over the academic study of the Arab and Muslim world in the West, scholars who explicitly rejected the work of their "Orientalist" predecessors.[61] At the same time, fields already postmodernized, like Anthropology, Sociology, Literary Criticism (Said's field), rapidly assimilated the terminology of the new paradigm.[62]

Said wrapped his polemic in a universalistic, humanistic frame specifically addressed to liberals to argue that those who stereotyped "orientals" (especially Arabs) were racists who used their knowledge of other people as an instrument of dominion. Despite the elaborate Foucauldian framework of his book, and

---

57 Normally, cataclysmic and transformative apocalyptic are opposite styles (Landes, *Heaven on Earth*, chapter 1).

58 On the politics of the worst as part of an (in these cases, secular) apocalyptic dynamic, see Landes, *Heaven on Earth*, 295–97.

59 Jean-Pierre Bensimon, "Edward Said, le post-colonialisme, et la pensée à somme nulle," *Controverses* 11, *Dossier: post colonialisme & sionisme* (2009): 36–51.

60 Said, *Orientalism* (1978). Criticism: Robert Irwin, *For Lust of Knowing: Orientalists and their Enemies* (London: Penguin, 2006); Ibn Warraq, *Defending the West: A Critique of Edward Said's Orientalism* (New York: Prometheus, 2007). For an analysis of its impact on the West's understanding of the conflict between Israel and her neighbors, see Joshua Muravchik, *Making David into Goliath: How the World Turned against Israel* (New York: Encounter Books, 2014), chap 8: "Edward Said Conquers Academia for Palestine"; and Landes, "Orientalism as Caliphator Cognitive Warfare."

61 "For Orientalism was ultimately a political vision of reality [bad] whose structure promoted the difference between the familiar (Europe, the West, 'us') and the strange (the Orient, the East, 'them')." Said, *Orientalism*, 43.

62 Lewis, "The influence of Edward Said and Orientalism on Anthropology."

its appeal to a "shared humanity," the book functioned as delegitimation not only of previous "knowledge" about the "Orient," but also current criticism of the Arab world. Any talk of honor-shame culture as a major driver of Arab decision-making was rank, racist Orientalism.[63] Said offered postmodern revolutionaries the way to weaponize their ideology. With "people of color" (especially Arabs) as the "other" who must not be "othered," as the victims of Western imperialist aggression, as a people whose suffering justified anything (including terrorism[64]), the full array of anti-imperial (really anti-American) forces could be mobilized.

Saïd quickly elaborated on the ideas. In *The Question of Palestine* he expounded on the narrative of the suffering and victimhood of indigenous Palestinians (like himself), of course at the hands of the colonialist Israelis. Despite his claim to be critical of the Arab world, Said spent little time considering the contribution of Arab elites to that suffering.[65] In *Covering Islam*, he condemned the Western press for their "racist" attitude towards Islam ("Islamophobia" was not yet a common term, but it has a proleptic presence here), demanding that they "cover" the religion more sympathetically. He complained:

> There also seems to have been a strange revival of canonical, though previously discredited [i.e. by me, E. S.], Orientalist ideas about Muslims, generally non-white, people—ideas which have achieved a startling prominence at a time when racial or religious misrepresentations of every other cultural group are no longer circulated with such impunity. Malicious generalizations about Islam have become the last acceptable form of denigration of foreign culture to the West, what is said about the Muslim mind, or character, or religion or culture as a whole cannot now be said in mainstream discussions about Africans, Jews, other Orientals, or Asians.[66]

---

63 Landes, "Edward Said and the Culture of Honor and Shame: *Orientalism* and Our Misperceptions of the Arab-Israeli Conflict," *Israel Affairs*,13:4 (2007), 844–58.

64 Franz Fanon, *Wretched of the Earth* (New York: Grove Press, 2004); Sartre "Introduction."

65 Edward Said, *The Question of Palestine* (New York: Vintage, 1980); cf. Ephraim Karsh, *Palestine Betrayed* (New Haven, CT: Yale University Press, 2010), 230–43. On Said's fabricated "Palestinian" identity, see Justus Weiner, "Justus Reid Weiner's "'My Beautiful Old House' and Other Fabrications by Edward Said," *Commentary* (September 1999). Extensive criticism and commentary in the January 2000 edition of *Commentary*.

66 Edward Said, in *Covering Islam: How the Media and the Experts Determine How We See the Rest of the World* (New York: Random House, 1981), excoriated Western news media for their hostility to Islam. His success in silencing critical voices can be seen in Andrew McCarthy's

By the time he was done, he had put in place the full panoply of what Charles Jacobs later called the "human rights complex"—the tendency of Western human rights activists to grow wildly indignant at Western (white) violations of human rights of people of color, but to look the other way when people of color violated rights either of other people of color, or of whites.[67] In this postcolonial universe, whites had no right to judge people of color, and people of color could not be racists no matter how harshly they judged whites.

In fact, Said's argument had much less to do with the scholarship he trashed, than with his own sense of humiliation as an Arab, and his deep desire to stop up the mouths of those who publicly criticized his people. And yet, precisely because Western culture so values the "Other," and its scholars are, therefore, so committed to *not* being racist, *not* making invidious comparisons, Western scholars proved especially susceptible to the accusation, no matter how inaccurate or unfairly it was invoked. It became almost intolerable that the post-orientalists might even find themselves the object of a very suspicion of racism. As a result, the profession rushed to follow Said's advice:

> At all costs, the goal of Orientalizing the Orient [i.e., "othering" Arabs] again and again is to be avoided. . . . Without "the Orient" there would be scholars, critics, intellectuals, human beings, for whom the racial, ethnic, and national distinctions were less important than the common enterprise in promoting human community.[68]

Behind this brief list of issues that Said felt scholars in search of a "common humanity" should *not* accord too much attention—race, ethnicity, and national distinctions—lay some more taboo subjects: the twin phenomena of cultural and religious dissimilarities between the Arab world and the West. As far as Said was concerned, neither shame-honor dynamics nor Caliphator ideologies deserved the attention of humane scholars.[69] In short, Said told Western scholars that if they were to avoid the charge of those cardinal sins of racism and imperialism,

---

Willful Blindness: A Memoir of the jihad (New York: Encounter, 2008), about the Western response to the first World Trade Center bombings in 1993. Matters only got worse in the twenty-first century: Bawer, *Surrender*; Marshall and Shea, *Silenced*.

67 Charles Jacobs, "Why Israel and not Sudan, is Singled Out," *Boston Globe*, October 5, 2002.

68 Said, *Orientalism*, 328.

69 Stanley Hoffman berates Huntington for "overestimate[ing] the importance of religion in the behavior of non-Western elites, who are often secularized and Westernized," "Clash of Globalizations," *Foreign Affairs*, August 2002.

they had to view the "Orient" in the same secular terms they viewed the West, economic and social. Anything that suggested that these "other" cultures had distinct features, different from ours, especially if those traits put the "other" culture in a bad light, like shame-murders or interminable wars of revenge, was so much "othering."[70] Wrote one reviewer of Raphael Patai's *The Arab Mind*, "Rather than plumbing some mythical 'Arab mind,' we should affirm the shared humanity that transcends our differences and binds us all together."[71]

Said's accusation of racism against the previous centuries of scholarship, eagerly adopted by young scholars, resulted in the devaluation of the thesaurus of knowledge about the Arab world (other fields were initially less damaged).[72] At the same time, it produced a generation of scholars who replaced the critical study of Islam, or of the dynamics of shame-honor culture, with a pervasive apologetics that insisted on looking primarily at social and economic phenomena within a (peculiarly Western) liberal framework. As a result of their cognitive egocentrism, for example, they never tired of announcing the imminent advent of Arab democracies that we have yet to see.[73]

In cognitive war terms, Said accomplished a major coup *against* the West: he forbade "us" to see "them" in any but modern liberal terms, even as he amplified "*their*" demonizing, "othering" voice by calling the West racist.[74] "To speak of the Palestinians rationally is, I think, to stop speaking about war or genocide and to start dealing with political reality," he insisted in his *The Question of Palestine*, as if the political reality was not, alas, that Palestinian leaders, both religious and "secular," never stop talking about genocide and war.[75] He set up the "anti-imperialism of fools" by insisting that "[w]e [Palestinians] are clearly anticolonialist and antiracist in our struggle," when so much of what Palestinians

---

70 Landes, "Orientalism as Caliphator Cognitive Warfare." As a result of this denial, only a "racist" would claim the Palestinians are not ready to make peace: Philip Salzman, "Arabs Strive for Honor, Not Peace," *Middle East Forum*, April 22, 2016.

71 Emram Qureshi, on Raphael Patai's *The Arab Mind*: "Misreading the Arab Mind: The Dubious Guidebook to Middle East Culture that's on the Pentagon's Reading List," *Boston Globe*, 30 May 2004.

72 The major point of Irwin's, *For Lust of Knowing*.

73 Kramer on the projection of Western democratic values on Arab political culture, *Ivory Towers on Sand*, chapter 4. Journalists like Lee Smith (*The Strong Horse: Power, Politics and the Clash of Arab Civilizations* [New York: Anchor, 2011) offer more reliable material and analysis than politicized "postcolonial" scholars like Juan Cole, John Esposito or Richard Norton.

74 Ian Buruma and Avishai Margalit, *Occidentalism: A Short History of Anti-Westernism* (New York: Penguin, 2004).

75 Said, *The Question of Palestine*, 51.

say in Arabic about Israel reflects both racism and imperialism.[76] He embraces "a secular democratic state in Palestine for Arabs and Jews," as a "PLO formulation that broke sharply with all past ideas," when it was a mainstream Zionist formula among progressive Jews like Martin Buber and Judah Magnes, abandoned only after the Arabs declared their genocidal war of 1948, and picked up cynically by the PLO subsequently as a propaganda ploy for gaining the support of the West to dismantle Israel.

Nor was this betrayal merely of the near enemy (the West where he had succeeded), but a betrayal of his own (belatedly) adopted people.[77] Shortly before his death, at the height of the Intifada and just as the US began to plan a war in Iraq, Said wrote an angry screed that tore off his cosmopolitan mask and revealed his tribal self. In it, he denounced self-critical Arabs for filling the Western public sphere with negative images of the Arab world:

> The only "good" Arabs are those who appear in the media *decrying* modern Arab culture and society without reservation. I recall the lifeless cadences of their sentences for, with *nothing positive to say about themselves or their people and language,* they simply *regurgitate* the tired *American* formulas already flooding the airwaves and pages of print. We lack democracy they say, we haven't challenged Islam enough. . . . Only what we, and our American instructors say about the Arabs and Islam—vague re-cycled Orientalist clichés of the kind repeated by a tireless mediocrity like Bernard Lewis—is true ... Ajami, Gerges, Makiya, Talhami, Fandy et al., academics whose very language reeks of *subservience,* inauthenticity and a hopelessly stilted mimicry that has been thrust upon them.[78]

Uncle Toms, Oreos, the lot of them.

What did Said admire, then? Not this self-critical Arab intelligentsia, but his cherished *image* of the Palestinian people, whose leaders, only 18 months earlier in 2000 had rejected what in 1994 Said had piously endorsed: "a negotiated

---

76 Ibid., 122. Note that he later complains that the "expert" (scare quotes his) Yehoshofat Harkabi's books, compendia of what Arabs say in Arabic, about Israel and Jews, have led to the "habit" of characterizing the Arab hostility to Israel as genocidal (252n26) ... as if it weren't.

77 Justus Weiner, "Edward Said, le FAUX prophète de la Palestine," *Controverses* 11 (2009): 28–35.

78 Edward W. Said, "An Unacceptable Helplessness," *Al-Ahram,* #621, 16–22 January 2003 (italics mine).

settlement, between the two communities of suffering, Arab and Jewish, [that] would provide respite from the unending war," and instead began a vicious suicidal war that brought great misery to its people.

> Remarkably, though, the great mass of this *heroic* [Palestinian] people seems willing [sic] to go on, without peace and without respite, bleeding, going hungry, dying day by day. They have too much dignity and confidence in the justice of their cause to submit *shamefully* to Israel as their leaders have done. What could be more discouraging for the average Gazan who goes on resisting Israeli occupation than to see his or her leaders *kneel as supplicants* before the Americans?[79]

Is this not the very Orientalist mindset that Said insisted was a Western invention— the dream-palace fantasy of proud defiance whose price falls so heavily on the "heroic" shoulders of the people or, in Said's unfortunate word choice, "the great mass," for whom he has no problem speaking, even as his authoritarian partners in the PLO make sure they cannot speak?[80] Apparently, in postcolonial circles, the subaltern can only speak as sock-puppets for anti-imperialist fools.[81]

Little wonder Palestinian jihadis could enlist such unwitting but willing Western "progressive" allies. Little surprise that the post-Orientalist generation of Middle East scholars proved to be a rich terrain for the adoption and articulation of Arab and Muslim lethal narratives, no matter how empirically dubious, no matter who the target. By guilting Western scholars about "othering" the Arabs and Muslims, Said forbade them to even talk about non-Western cultures, while "othering" the "essentially racist" West (especially the modern, i.e., non-*dhimmi*, Jews in Israel).[82]

Said thus systematically exploited a peculiarly Western scruple, a glitch, about being open to the "other,"[83] in order to blind the West to the acute tendency of

---

79 *Ibid.*, italics mine.

80 Among Said's major targets were two Arabs who criticized precisely this tendency at sacrificing Arab commoners to elitist fantasies: Fouad Ajami, *The Dream Palace of the Arabs* (New York: Vintage, 1999); Kanan Makiya, *Cruelty and Silence: War, Tyranny and Uprising in the Arab World* (New York: W.W. Norton, 1994).

81 See a similar situation among Muslim "feminists," 419–28.

82 For a good contemporary example, Juan Cole "translating" Ahmadinejad: Joshua Teitelbaum, "What Iranian leaders really say about doing away with Israel," *JCPA*, 2008.

83 The central point of Irwin's devastating critique: Western scholars had a passion for understanding the "Orient"—precisely in its own terms. One might venture to say, that's precisely what Said disliked.

at least one of those "others" to think in the most ferociously invidious us/them dichotomies.[84] To do so would be to "essentialize," a privilege allowed only to subalterns like Said himself. So even as he othered the West for othering the East, he forbade Western infidels from even discussing the ferocious "othering" imbedded in the dichotomy *Dar al Islam/Dar al Harb* and *al-Walā' wal-Barā'*. To do so would be inexcusable racism and Islamophobia *avant la lettre*.

Not surprisingly, Said's work has had the opposite impact from his "promoting a common humanity."[85] On the contrary, it contributed directly to deepening the clash of civilizations he denies exists, by prohibiting discussion of the cultural sources of the assault on open values.[86] He literally disarmed the West (his intellectual and personal haven), in the face of an assault coming from a culture with which he only belatedly identified, despite its unmitigated rejection of his cosmopolitan secularism. With his mastery of the Western progressive idiom, and his post-1967 regression to Arab honor-shame tribalism, the (post-Christian, but not post-*dhimmi*) Said, who in principle had many objections to Caliphator values and ambition, had, nonetheless, become one of the most useful infidels of our time.[87]

The postcolonial paradigm saw Western global, capitalist, imperialism as *the* outstanding, if not the *only*, evil facing the global community. For Said, even the most triumphalist religious imperialism of Khomeini and his revolutionaries deserved protection from the malevolent, Orientalist eye of the West.[88] Postcolonials fell prey to a humanitarian racism in which they held their own culture to magnificently high standards and expected not even the most basic self-criticism or self-control from other cultures before whom they bowed as penitents. **Who are we to judge?** (Except, of course, when it comes to the West and Israel, where we can judge as harshly as we want.[89]) *Their side right or wrong.*

Following Said's shame-driven directives, postcolonial progressives projected their own attitudes onto a culture with a profoundly premodern mentality. It is striking how often, when progressives explain what motivates Muslim anger

---

84 For an unusual exploration of the oppositional "us-them" mentality, see Jon Ronson, *Them: Adventures with Extremists* (NY, 2002), especially chapter 1, on Sheikh Omar Bakri Muhammad.

85 Said even briefly acknowledges it in his Afterward of 1994, *Orientalism*, 333–38.

86 Said, "The Clash of Ignorance," *The Nation*, October 4, 2001.

87 Landes, "Celebrating Orientalism"; Landes, "From Useful Idiot to Useful Infidel: Meditations on the Folly of 21st-Century 'Intellectuals.'" *Terrorism and Political Violence* 25.4 (September 2013): 621–34.

88 Said, *Covering Islam*; Landes, "Orientalism as Caliphator Cognitive Warfare."

89 See below on Martin Amis and his London audience about feeling morally superior to Taliban (325).

against the West, their reconstruction looks a great deal like their own reasons for hostility to their culture:

> It is a mistake to think of the strategy of suicide bombing as . . . an irrationalism that derives from Islamic fundamentalism. There is a rationale for the adoption of this strategy that stems from the problem of defeating an enemy in conditions of extreme inequality of resources . . . , what motivates them to action is rage at material conditions of oppression and exploitation.[90]

This is the very definition of *Westsplaining*, in which the "other" is a blank screen upon which one projects one's "theories." And most of the "theories," in particular postcolonial theory, assume at the outset that the moral imperative is to repair the relationship between guilty colonial dominator and innocent colonized subaltern, even if that means occasionally, a Fanonian orgy of "absolute violence" with its "world-shattering" role of issuing in a new epoch.[91] In this we find the emergence of a fearful union, the marriage of premodern sadism and postmodern masochism, of jihadi and progressive millennialism.

Peace and Conflict Studies and "Peace Journalism"

Few fields better illustrate the marriage of premodern sadism and postmodern masochism—or, in the case of its "founder," Johan Galtung, postmodern sadomasochism—than "Peace and Conflict-Resolution Studies" and its key offshoot, "Peace Journalism." In the wake of the Peace Movement's successful opposition to the Vietnam war (1967–75), a school of "Peace and Conflict Studies" arose that sought to create conditions of peace not through a balance of power, or the "absence of war," but through notions of a "positive peace based on genuine empathy for 'others'" and conflict resolution through nonviolent means.

The emotional problem here is that this "theory" was articulated by post-Holocaust Westerners who were the emotional and cognitive beneficiaries of the new dispensation embodied in such principles as "universal human rights,"

---

90 Gareth Jenkins, "Marxism and terrorism," *International Socialism Journal* 110, 2006; cited by Bassi, "Anti-Imperialism of Fools," 122f. Robert Pape is a major proponent of this approach: *Dying to Win*.

91 "Samira Kawash, "Terrorists and Vampires: Fanon's Spectral Violence of Decolonization," *Frantz Fanon: Critical Perspectives* ed. Anthony Alessandrini (London: Routledge, 1999), 243.

international institutions like the UN, and international law codes like the Geneva Conventions, and an exceptionally benevolent US military hegemony. These people assumed that "others" who didn't necessarily share the Western peace camp's "lessons" from the World War II and the Holocaust would somehow feel peaceful if approached correctly. It was a therapeutic philosophy that expected to transform the world with which it interacted. As a key support to this (messianic) expectation, believers shifted from monotheistic religion that argued man must strive hard to transform nature, to a "secular" religion that argued that man was naturally peaceful, and our task as humans was to get in touch with this peaceful nature.[92] This conceptual reversal then made memes like "war is not the answer" and "violence never solved anything" not just acceptable, but axiomatic: if you disagreed, you must be a war monger.

This approach had an elective affinity with anti-Americanism, hostility to the Behemoth that had just conducted the Vietnam war. Galtung eagerly anticipated the end of what he called "American Imperialism."[93] Not surprisingly, his American followers exhibited a strong proclivity towards "what did we do to make them hate us so?" Thus, the international relations equivalent of the "Peace and Conflict Studies" paradigm assumes that the other nations of the world would all be doing just fine if it weren't for American support for their dictators. This approach pervades Noam Chomsky's forays into political "science." It also reflects the emphasis on the "structural violence and racism" which, some claim, pervades the only-allegedly peaceful world of (Western) civil society. Again, as we saw with Derrida at 9–11, anything short of perfection (presumably the end of even hidden forms of repression), is a form of violence just as bad, if not worse, than the more spectacular (and bloody and daily) violence of yore and elsewhere.

Like many messianic (therapeutic) bodies of knowledge, this discourse favored advocacy over empiricism. As Barash and Webel, the authors of an authoritative "textbook" of *Peace and Conflict Studies* explain:

> The field [of Peace Studies] differs from most other human sciences in that it is value-oriented, and unabashedly so. Accordingly, we wish to be up front about our own values, which are frankly anti-war, anti-violence, anti-nuclear,

---

92 Leslie Sponsel, "The natural history of peace: The positive view of human nature and its potential," in *A natural history of peace*, ed. T. Gregor (Nashville, TN.: Vanderbilt University Press, 1996), 95–125.

93 Bruce Bawer, "The Peace Racket: An anti-Western movement touts dictators, advocates appeasement—and gains momentum," *City Journal*, Summer 2007.

> anti-authoritarian, anti-establishment, pro-environment, pro-human rights, pro-social justice, pro-peace and politically progressive.[94]

In accordance with this advocacy, Peace Studies tends to exclude those approaches that contradict its tenets. Notes critic Gerald Steinberg:

> The realist approach to international conflict and conflict resolution and models based on deterrence, the security dilemma, and the use of force to prevent or resolve conflict, are all but ignored, or, in some cases, explicitly rejected on ideological grounds. (Students in peace studies programs rarely encounter the analyses of Hobbes, Morgenthau, E. H. Carr, Waltz, and other realists.)[95]

Thus did they repeal the zero-sum laws of the jungle—by ignoring them.

Ironically this alchemy of messianic enthusiasm, this dogmatic commitment to denial, by identifying *Western* institutions as the worst authoritarian establishments, ended up upending itself and supporting authoritarian governments and violent fascist dictatorships. With the advent of the Caliphator challenge, this "peace and conflict" paradigm proved a perfect "fit" with Da'wa cogwar campaigns. On the one hand, the West embodied in and led by the USA/Israel, represented the supreme enemies of social justice, whose dismantling would put an end to the intersectional racism that plagues the global community. On the other, they insisted, Islam was naturally a religion of peace which, had it not been aroused to anger by its oppression at the hands of the West (especially Israel), would naturally participate in the global civil society that Peace and Conflict Studies advocates so earnestly sought to bring about.

In an update of their canonical textbook shortly after 9–11, Barash and Webel remove the stigma from "terrorism" and redefine it as a "weapon of the weak," and put it in square quotes:

> "Terrorists" are people who may feel militarily unable to confront their perceived enemies directly and who accordingly use violence, or the threat of violence, against non-combatants to achieve their political aims. Placing "terrorist" in quotation

---

94 David Barash and Charles Webel, *Peace and Conflict Studies* (New York: Routledge, 2008).
95 Steinberg, "Postcolonial Theory and the Ideology of Peace Studies," 112.

marks may be jarring for some readers, who consider the designation self-evident. We do so, however, not to minimize the horror of such acts but to emphasize the value of qualifying righteous indignation by the recognition that often one person's "terrorist" is another's "freedom fighter."[96]

A careful reader of this discourse might disagree with adding "against non-combatants" as if it were a perfectly natural "weapon of the weak," and not a horrific descent into mass murder of innocents. Instead, they adopted the terrorists' narrative about acting from "righteous indignation," and most decidedly "took sides" by minimizing the horror of such acts.

This symbiosis between Western pacifism and Islamic jihad, brought on an ever-greater dogmatization of the paradigm, forbidding *any* Western resistance to this "freedom-fighting" violence.

A peace-oriented perspective condemns not only terrorist attacks but also any violent response to them. But the best response to such terrible events is often maddeningly unclear and should not be made precipitously. How does one "counter" terrorism without resorting to terror?[97]

In a well-publicized case, a student found himself informed that any use of violence to resist violence, whether it be shooting a school shooter, or jihadi terrorists, was *wrong*.[98] It is as if a whole school of academics was giving the West the same advice on how to deal with jihad that Gandhi gave the Jews about Hitler, and that Caliphators give to infidels.[99] If the purpose of cogwar is *to make patriots out of your own side and pacifists out of your enemy*,[100] then jihadis could hope for no better useful infidels than the "progressive" advocates of Peace and Conflict-Resolution Studies.

---

96 Barash and Webel, *Peace and Conflict*, 80.

97 Charles Webel, "Terrorism: What it Means, Who Perpetrates it, and What Can be Done about it," *NYU in Prague* (2014?). (*"Oh, Allah, give us enemies who legitimate our terrorism as "resistance" and denounce any recourse to violence in their own defense, as "terrorism.*)

98 Brett Mock, "Indoctrination in the Classroom," *FrontPageMagazine*, September 113, 2004; exchange between George Wolfe and the editor of Front Page, David Horwitz, "Peace Studies, Academic Freedom and Indoctrination," ed. David Swindle, November 17, 2008, http://www.relinquishingjunk.com/dialogue.htm.

99 P. R. Kumaraswamy, *Squaring the Circle: Mahatma Gandhi and the Jewish National Home* (New York: Routledge, 2021). Wolfe (previous note) is a big admirer of Gandhi.

100 Ron Schleifer's formula.

Ironically and predictably, Israel became, along with the USA, the embodiment of everything that Peace Studies disliked, indeed reviled.[101] These two nations were inexcusably willing to defend themselves, audacious enough to think that they had a *right* to defend themselves, rather than having the humility of understanding and acknowledging the pain and suffering they had inflicted on their justifiably indignant and violent neighbors. Galtung embodied all these ambivalences: whether lying beneath the surface of his anti-imperialism, or the product of his anger at Zionism, a whole range of antisemitic attitudes operated in Galtung's proclamations, many of them *Protocols* analogs.[102]

After all, the paradigm insists: the natural state of man is peace, and the structural violence of modern society brings on conflict. As with hunger,[103] so with war: America's hegemony is blamed for what remains of what was previously a (premodern) pervasive presence. Rather than acknowledge the enormous reduction of both hunger and violence rates, especially during the post-WWII period of American global hegemony, these activists preferred to blame the West and especially a Jew-dominated America, for whatever hunger and war remained.

Lethal Journalism and Supersessionism

In anticipation of what we will examine more carefully in the next chapter, but already discussed in part one, chapters 1 and 3, let us look at one of the more striking impacts of lethal journalism on global progressives, namely its ability to provoke explosions of supersessionist vituperation against the Jews as the "chosen people." In all these cases, the pattern followed the one, first set in place in the Middle Ages, of blood libels that projected onto the Jews an abiding hatred for gentiles and a sense that their chosen status gave them the divine right to inflict their malevolence on the gentiles . . . a paranoid fantasy that justified their anti-Jewish violence.[104] In the Middle Ages, triumphalist Christians projected onto Jews their own notion of chosenness: the master religion.

---

101 Bruce Bawer, "The Peace Racket: An anti-Western movement touts dictators, advocates appeasement—and gains momentum," *City Journal*, Summer 2007; Gad Yair, "Is the acclaimed sociologist of peace a neo-Nazi?" *Jerusalem Post*, May 15, 2012.

102 Ofer Aderet, "Pioneer of Global Peace Studies Hints at Link Between Norway Massacre and Mossad," *Ha-aretz*, April 30, 2012; Robert Wistrich, "Blind in one eye: Galtung and the Toxic European left," *Times of Israel*, May 17, 2012.

103 See above, 72.

104 Joshua Trachtenberg, *The Devil and the Jews: The Medieval Conception of the Jew and Its Relationship to Modern Anti-Semitism* (Philadelphia: Jewish Publication Society, 1983).

Later, this projection took on a more secular form, all the while attributing to Jews the common "mentality" of zero-sum cultures, *rule or be ruled*.[105] In its most extreme forms, fostered by the *Protocols of the Elders of Zion*, this mentality had the Nazis believing that Jews thought they were "chosen" as a master race, destined to rule mankind with an iron fist. One finds similar dynamics of projection among current jihadi Caliphators, for whom Islam means master-religion, destined to convert, submit, or slaughter all infidels.[106] And in all these cases, the desire was then projected on the Jews. Exterminate or be exterminated. And so every time that lethal journalists flooded their countries with Palestinian war propaganda as news, there were spikes in both violence against the Jews, and sometimes stunning expressions of a pre-Holocaust vitriol against the Jews for their arrogant "chosen-people" racism.

I have identified a number of (the many) cases where lethal journalism from the Middle East provoked delirious supersessionist rants among Western progressives. Earlier examples of the dynamic include the Al Durah story and the replacement narrative it almost instantaneously provoked among some observers like Catherine Nay and Tom Paulin.[107] It reappeared in response to Jenin, with Edgar Morin and Terje Roed-Larsen.[108] Here we'll consider two more examples, from the Lebanon War (2006) and the "third" Gaza War (2014).

Jostein Gaarder and Judith Butler in Response to the Lebanon War, 2006

Perhaps the most startling expression of a supersessionist response to another round of lethal reporting from the Arab-Israeli conflict came from Jostein Gaarder in 2006, in direct response to the misreporting of an Israeli strike on a building in Kafr Qana and the alleged killing of numerous children and sick people.[109] Writing in the royal "we" of the global progressive left, the internationally popular Norwegian novelist unloaded his contempt for [his projected notion of] Jewish chosenness:

---

105 *The Paranoid Apocalypse*, ed. Landes and Katz.

106 Cook, *Contemporary Muslim Apocalyptic*.

107 Nay, 18f; Paulin, 22.

108 Roed-Larsan, 103, 116f; Morin, 122.

109 Below, 310. On Lebanese manipulation and Western misreporting, with a lengthy discussion of the Kafr Qana case, see Richard North, "The Corruption of the Media," *EUReferedum*, August 2006. Matan Ravid, "Prejudice and Demonization in the Swedish Middle East Debate," *Jewish Political Studies Review* 21:1–2 (2009).

We don't believe in the notion of God's Chosen People. We laugh at this people's capriciousness and weep at its misdeeds. To act as God's Chosen People is not only stupid and arrogant, but *a crime against humanity. We call it racism.*

There are limits to our patience, and there are limits to our tolerance. We do not believe in divine promises as a justification for occupation and apartheid. We have left the Middle Ages behind. We laugh uneasily at those who still believe that the god of flora, fauna and the galaxies has selected one people in particular as his favorite and given it silly, stone tablets, burning bushes and *a license to kill.* We call baby killers "baby killers" and will never accept that people such as these have a divine or historic mandate excusing their outrages.

We do not recognize the rhetoric of the State of Israel. We do not recognize the spiral of retribution and blood vengeance that comes with "an eye for an eye and a tooth for a tooth." We do not recognize the principle of ten or a thousand Arab eyes for one Israeli eye. Two thousand years have passed since a Jewish rabbi criticized the ancient doctrine of "an eye for an eye and a tooth for a tooth."

He said: "Do unto others as you would have them do unto you." We do not recognize a state founded on anti-humanistic principles and on the ruins of an archaic national and warlike religion. Or, as Albert Schweitzer expressed it: "Humanitarianism consists of never sacrificing a human being for a cause."[110]

Warming to his task, Gaarder gives voice to the ultimate supersessionist fantasy: the Jew, naked, defenseless, at the mercy of those who should, by rights, kill them for their wickedness, but somehow, hopefully, won't:

The State of Israel has raped the recognition of the world and shall have no peace until it lays down its arms. Without defense, without skin. May the spirit and the word blow the apartheid walls of Israel down. The State of Israel... is now without defense, without skin. May the world therefore have mercy

---

110 Jostein Gaarder, "God's Chosen People," *Aftenpost*, August 5, 2006; Landes, "Open Letter to Jostein Gaarder," *The Augean Stables*, April 29/31, 2006.

upon the civilian population; for our prophecies of doom are not aimed at the civilian individuals."

Was Gaarder aware, as he wrote in his moral indignation, that he had reversed reality and recapitulated the ancient Jew-hatred which now burns so brightly in the breasts of those "pitiable victims" whose vengeance he would unleash upon defenseless Jews.

FIGURE 18. Image posted at the Swedish-Palestinian Centre, Helsingborg.

His eager support for the Palestinians is the mirror image of his contempt for Israel. He would not call Palestinians "baby killers" even though they repeatedly and deliberately target Israeli babies and repeatedly put their own children at mortal risk.[111] He would not object to the Palestinian claim to a "historic mandate excusing their outrages."[112] He has no problem if they found their claims "on anti-humanistic principles and on the ruins of an archaic, [tribal] and warlike

---

111 See 58n34.
112 Meir Litvak, "The Islamization of the Palestinian-Israeli Conflict: The case of Hamas," *Middle Eastern Studies*, 34 no. 1 (January 1998): 148–63. Canaanite descent is standard teaching in

religion."[113] In his need to see himself as the standard-bearer of humanitarian voices from Jesus to Schweitzer who, he thinks, have superseded the "eye-for-an-eye" Jews, Gaarder shows no awareness that he betrays humanitarians on all sides.

And yet, the cognitive disorientation created by this inability to perceive jihadis at work in the conflict with Israel, has serious, sometimes darkly comic consequences. Take, for example, the case of Judith Butler. In the fall of 2006, academic and student activists mobilized on campuses worldwide against Israel for its summer attack on Lebanon. Asked at a teach-in at University of California, Berkeley, whether Hamas and Hizballah—two jihadi organizations with global imperial ambitions and genocidal intentions—belonged on the "global progressive Left," Judith Butler, queen of queer theory and self-proclaimed pacifist, answered in the affirmative. She later explained that she did so, because these groups were "anti-imperialists."[114] Thus did the progressive left join forces with the most primitive and ruthless imperialists in the global community. And somehow, none of the comedians of the day, much less the activist journalists, found this "anti-imperialism of fools" a subject for satire. On the contrary, in Britain, it could bring particularly devoted aficionados like Seumas Milne to the heights of power.[115]

Jesús B. Ochoa and Operation Protective Edge, 2014

We find a more passionate and full-throated set of projections onto the Jews in response to yet another round of violence and journalistic malfeasance, this time from Gaza in 2014, where reporters regularly used the meme, "vast majority of casualties were civilians," when, in the end, the civilian-combatant

---

Palestinian schools, Eldad Pardo, Arik Agassi and Marcus Sheff, *Reform or Radicalization: PA 2017–18 Curriculum* (Jerusalem, 2017), 77–80.

113 "The Covenant of the Islamic Resistance Movement (Hamas Charter), August 18, 1988. On the pervasive presence of genocidal religious war in Palestinian media: "Religious War," *Palestinian Media Watch*.

114 Landes, "Judith Butler, the Adorno Prize, and the Moral State of the 'Global Left,'" *SPME*, August 31, 2012. For a good analysis of the "contradictory and self-serving nature of Islamist anti-imperialism," see Asef Bayat, "Islamism and Empire: The Incongruous Nature of Islamist Anti-Imperialism," *Socialist Register* 44 (2008): 38–54.

115 For an excellent example of this anti-Americanism applauding 9–11, see Seumas Milne in the Guardian (chapter 2, n56). Far from discrediting him, Milne's anti-imperial folly raised him up to become Jeremy Corbyn's "brain": David Rose, "Is the man MPs call 'Corbyn's brain' the REAL reason Labour is drowning in the poison of antisemitism?" *Mail on Sunday*, February 23, 2019.

ratio was about 1:1 (exceptional for urban warfare).[116] An apocalyptic New Year's poem, nonetheless, begins with a plaint for the wretched Palestinian victims of this Israeli assault (as described by the news media), and ends with a long passage in which the poet speaks with what he presents to his readers as the voice of the Jews:

An Elegy for Gaza as Symbol for the New Year under Netanyahu
… we willed the killing to continue
and continue and continue,
how could we not?
we must not, no, no, cannot, will not, consider not
the sacredness of life,
the other, the weak, the children,
no, we revel in our treasure spun of stolen land,
a god created in our image, draping our souls
with hate and fear enough to warm our hubris,
all we stand tall, all, we are the chosen unto the planets,
we need no other, want no other, will have no other,
suffer no other, no, no, for we are, we are, WE ARE.[117]

In other words, based on false media reports, this poet managed to depict an odious mindset and project it onto the IDF, an army which, in reality, does more to minimize deaths among *enemy* civilians than any army in recorded history.[118] On the contrary, what the poet has ably described is the mindset of Hamas, which uses their bomb shelters for bombs and shoot from among their people whose deaths they promote for propaganda value, and whose survivors they ply with genocidal war propaganda.[119] And somehow, Hamas can hide its genuinely appalling attitudes behind the obsession with these fevered projections.

The extreme form of this projective supersessionism—the Jews have (my) master race ideology—has become a major meme of modern antisemitic discourse.

---

116 Hamas claimed a 4:1 civilian to combatant ratio during the hostilities; Israel, after careful study, 1:1. Gregory Rose, "Civilian deaths in Gaza conflict are not automatically a war crime," *The Conversation*, July 20, 2014.

117 Jesús B. Ochoa, *I am not a silent poet*, March 31, https://iamnotasilentpoet.wordpress.com/2015/03/.

118 *Fighting Terror Effectively: An Assessment of Israel's Experience on the Home Front*, High Level Home Front Group, November 2014.

119 Jonathan Tobin, "Why Gaza Doesn't Have Bomb Shelters," *Commentary*, July 12, 2014.

FIGURE 19. Ron Hughes tweet, July 31, 2017; retweeted by Hatem Bazian, Lecturer at University of California, Berkeley, founded Students for Justice in Palestine and researches "Islamophobia." He later removed the tweet: Rob Gloster, "Lecturer apologizes for retweet that UC Berkeley condemned as antisemitic" (*Jewish News of Northern California*, November 21, 2017).

To these supersessionists, the status of chosen people means a triumphalist, zero-sum belief that they are chosen to rule, to dominate the world. The more extreme the supersessionism, the more likely they *project* onto the Jews their own notions of chosenness, and the more intensely they hate the Jews for holding those projected attitudes. Herein lies the most dangerous poison because it encloses the person ingesting it in a hall of mirrors where the Jew appears as projections from an active but denied shadow-self; thus, striking at the (evil) Jews substitutes for honest self-criticism. The inversion of the Middle East conflict—moral, empirical, narrative—all reflect this supersessionist knot of projected hatred.

Ultimately, Jew-hatred arises from an gentile inability to trust that Jews are who they say they are. Instead, Jews always have to be up to something nefarious. Hence the constant projection of malevolent intent in all the Jews do.

Nothing good can come of this. It didn't with the Nazis, it won't with the Caliphators. And it won't with the Western progressives who empower the most toxic formulations, so they can indulge in a more palatable version of the same poisonous elixir.

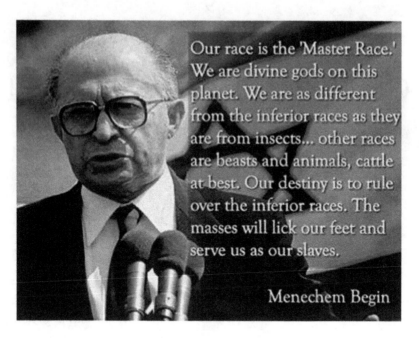

Our race is the 'Master Race.' We are divine gods on this planet. We are as different from the inferior races as they are from insects... other races are beasts and animals, cattle at best. Our destiny is to rule over the inferior races. The masses will lick our feet and serve us as our slaves.

Menechem Begin

FIGURE 20. Menachem Begin master race meme. Nowhere is this or anything like it to be found in Begin's work.[120]

---

120 "Correcting a Misquotation Reputedly by Menachem Begin," *Begin Center* May 27, 2009.

9

Compliant, Lethal, Own-Goal War Journalism: The Bane of the West in the Twenty-First Century

> Running Jihadi
> war propaganda as news . . .
> How could that go wrong?

The Failures of Journalism in the Twenty-First Century

Towards the end of the year 2000, a "severe malfunction" took place among Western journalists reporting from the Middle East.[1] This malfunction has, with ups and downs, continued to operate right up to the present (and appears likely to persist in the foreseeable future). Indeed, these failures in Middle-East journalism rapidly metastasized far beyond the borders of origin and, in the age of Trump and its aftermath, have taken on epic proportions. These failures consist of substituting a preference for partisan narrative over accuracy, reporting what suits a preconceived story intended to manipulate the news consumer's opinion and advance an agenda, rather than following the evidence, critically judging the accuracy and relevance of the data received, and allowing the news consumers who consult the news product, to make up their own minds.[2]

---

1   The expression was used by Matti Friedman in 2014: "Insider's Guide to the Most Important Story on Earth," *Tablet*, August 26, 2014.
2   Jodi Rudoren, "The Dueling Narratives of the Israeli-Palestinian Conflict," *New York Times*, October 27, 2015; see Tamar Sternthall, "*New York Times*: Journalism of Few Facts," *CAMERA*, October 28, 2015.

While many examples of this kind of media failure can be found at any time, and the previous years had already seen examples of this narrative-driven malfunction,[3] this *collective* breakdown of professional journalism took on new strength and global impact in October 2000, with the reporting on the conflict between Israel and her Arab neighbors. The failure consisted in the hegemonic victory of an advocacy journalism that systematically adopted one side's narrative, reporting its accusations and talking points as credible if not true, and doubting and challenging rebuttals from the other side. This "lethal journalism" consistently delivered the war propaganda of the favored side *as news* to its audience in the West.

Up till this point in my description, a reader might readily claim either side—Israel or the Palestinians—as the victim of this media malfeasance: after all, both sides complain that the other side controls the news media's narrative, and that the press favors the "other side."[4] There is a significant bibliography of works accusing the media of siding with Israel,[5] as well as with the Palestinians. Who's to judge whose narratives are truer?

---

3   Joseph Campbell, *Getting It Wrong: Ten of the Greatest Misreported Stories in American Journalism* (Los Angeles: University of California Press 2010). Bernard Goldberg wrote a book about the "liberal" slant of the three network news stations: *Bias: A CBS Insider Exposes How the Media Distort the News* (Washington DC: Regnery, 2001). Most of it covered the previous two decades; and much of his analysis explains how many in the news media were primed for the wrong coverage of the Middle East (which he treats in chapter 14 on 9–11). For a discussion of how journalism became an increasingly "progressive" preserve in the following decades, see McGowan, *Gray Lady Down: What the Decline and Fall of the New York Times Means for America* (New York: Encounter Books, 2010); Batya Ungar-Sargon, *Bad News: How Woke Media is Undermining Democracy* (New York: Encounter, 2021), 57–71. For an example of a sudden shift of the "Overton Window" to radical woke in a news corporation, see the case of the CBC: Tara Henley, "Why I resigned from the Canadian Broadcasting Company," *Speaking Freely*, January 3, 2022.

4   Linah Alsaafin, "Death still approaches," *Times Literary Supplement*, January 12, 2018.

5   Greg Philo and Mike Berry, *Bad News from Israel* (London: Pluto Press, 2004); Howard Friel and Richard Falk, *Israel-Palestine on Record: How the New York Times Misreports Conflict in the Middle East* (New York: Verso, 2007); Greg Shupak, *The Wrong Story: Palestine, Israel, and the Media* (New York: OR Books, 2018); Barbie Zelizer, David Park and David Gudelunas, "How bias shapes the news: Challenging The New York Times' status as a newspaper of record on the Middle East," *Journalism*, 3.3 (2002): 283–307; Neil Lewis, "From the Archives: The Times and the Jews." *Columbia Journalism Review*, January 2012; Muhamad Elmasry, "Studies continually show strong pro-Israel bias in western media," *Middle East Eye*, February 12, 2015; Daniel Dor, *Intifada Hits the Headlines: How the Israeli Press Misreported the Outbreak of the Second Palestinian Uprising* (Bloomington: University of Indiana Press, 2004). A special issue of the *Palestine-Israel Journal* in 2003 tackled the topic of *Media and the Second Intifada*. I cite several articles from that volume below.

"Both Sides . . ." Finding the Middle Ground between Competing "Narratives"

Of course, the safe place to go here, is to claim a plague or benediction on both houses—with the operative term being "both." Not surprisingly, the media like this, for it gives them that aura of distance they need for credibility: "As long as we angered each side equally, we surmised, we were doing something right," explained a former AP Bureau Chief in Jerusalem.[6] How much easier to take cover in a moral relativism and even-handed empathy that balances one criticism with another and seeks the truth in a vague middle zone.[7] And the fact that *both sides* complain about the formula just makes it all the more reassuring.[8]

But we are dealing here with actual issues. And if we get them wrong—however comfortable that "wrong" may feel at the time—we pay the price of our ignorance.[9] Reality's feedback is often unpleasant, bruising to our egos. If it's all just a fight between two people who both want freedom on the same land, and who both make exaggerated claims that balance each other out, then the truth will fall somewhere in between (it often does, just not necessarily in the middle). But if we get this one wrong, if there really is a qualitative difference between the goals of Israeli governments and the goals of Palestinian political culture, between the honesty of their respective spokespeople, then by ignoring the difference in the name of "even-handed fairness" we subject ourselves to cognitive disorientation.

So if we misread a sharp and dangerous dynamic of factual inaccuracy in the service of lethal narrative as a product of "being fair," we run the risk of serious disorientation. We run the risk, for example, of trying the same "compromise solution" to reach peace, repeatedly, with the same predictable lack of success.[10] If, on the other hand, I am correct when I argue that the Western media, for a variety of largely unattractive motives, have favored the Palestinian *narrative*

---

6 Jeffrey Dvorkin, "NPR's Middle East Problem," NPR, February 2, 2002; Barbara Matusow, "Caught in the Crossfire," *American Journalism Review*, June/July, 2004; Stephen Gutkin, "My Life as an AP Bureau Chief in Israel," *Goa Streets*, September 25, 2014; Stephen Games, "Compromised Coverage," *Haaretz*, July 24, 2014.

7 See the discussion of Palestinian and Israeli claims of casualty figures from Jenin, 106.

8 For the Palestinian rejection of the "both sides" meme: Shupak, "Not 'Both Sides,'" *The Wrong Story*, chap 1.

9 Sweden offers an example of a society at once poisoned by its media with demonization of Israel and a concomitant claim that the media is under Zionist control: Ravid, "Prejudice and Demonization in the Swedish Middle East Debate."

10 Joseph Micallef, "A Legacy of Failure: Obama's Mideast Foreign Policy," *Huffington Post*, December 6, 2017. See above, 198–202, discussion of the failure of Oslo.

since 2000, then the "both-sides" narrative operates as a masking device. It conceals the extensive use of the news media as a weapon of Caliphator cogwar against infidels, delivering to Western consumers who think they are receiving the work of information professionals, an unprecedented *own-goal war journalism* in which these professionals deliver our enemy's war propaganda to us *as news*.

Press as Pro-Israel

Many have argued that the media discriminate against the Palestinians. These complaints focus primarily on the media's failure to fully adopt the Palestinian narrative.[11] When they complain of a "lack of even-handedness," they mean a failure to treat the Israeli "occupation" as a crime every bit as heinous as suicide terror, and indeed the cause of the conflict.[12] Barbara Zelizer, for example, complains that the major US newspapers don't use Palestinian terminology: "All three newspapers chose similar labels when describing those engaged in violent acts against Israeli citizens, calling such individuals 'terrorists' or 'suicide bombers' rather than the 'martyrs' preferred by the Palestinians."[13]

In response to coverage of the Ramallah lynch of October 12, 2000,[14] whose savagery horrified even pro-Palestinian journalists like Mark Seager (see below), Greg Philo and Mike Berry object to the negative language used to describe it: "There are a number of words which were specifically used to describe the deaths of the Israeli soldiers, such as 'atrocity,' 'murder' and ... 'lynch mob' and 'barbarically killed.' None of these were used in our samples for Arab/Palestinian deaths."[15]

That none of those Palestinians were killed with anything remotely resembling the savagery displayed at Ramallah against unarmed soldiers in custody, apparently should have no bearing on the demand for "equal treatment." In response to the "Jenin Massacre" debacle, Howard Friel and Richard Falk don't even discuss the topic, while Philo and Berry exonerate the BBC for not

---

11 Neil Lewis's piece for the *Columbia Journalism Review*, "The Times and the Jews," offers narrative-based journalism ("it's the Palestinians' turn to get favorable coverage"), devoid of any concern for accuracy.
12 Friel and Falk, *Israel-Palestine on Record*, 139.
13 Zelizer et al., "How Bias Shapes the News," 287.
14 See 12f.
15 Philo and Berry, *Bad News from Israel*, 153–54.

using the word "massacre" (too often).[16] From the pro-Palestinian perspective, journalists should either treat Israel's occupation as criminal, just as suicide terror, or treat suicide terror, weapon of choice for apocalyptic Caliphators, as no worse than Israeli policy in the disputed territories.

Similar demands concern the media's treatment of the Palestinian voice.[17] Palestinian accusations against Israel, so extensively narrated and carefully recorded by "human rights" NGOs, do not, they insist, get their fair share of airtime. Accusations of Israeli crimes deserve not skepticism and double-checking, but ready credence. Anything else reflects racist discrimination and pro-Israel bias. The media do not do enough to make the Palestinian voice more credible and audible.[18] In the postmodern narrative-driven world out of which lethal journalism arises, this demand for adherence to the Palestinian narrative is completely justified: it gives voice to the "other." Anything else would constitute cruelty to the [alleged] victims, who must not, above all, be blamed for their victimization.[19]

In all this, Palestinians have welcome assistance from some Western advocacy journalists, who adopt the postcolonial replacement narrative. European journalists emphasize how the US press, far less hostile to Israel than they, is controlled by Jews. Robert Fisk, whose legendary dishonesty in journalism inspired the term "to fisk," and who immediately snapped at Enderlin's poisoned meat and proclaimed that Israel deliberately killed al Durah, had nothing but contempt for the American press, denouncing the "cowardly, spineless way in which American journalists are lobotomizing their stories from the Middle East."[20] How much livelier and more exciting the replacement narrative in which Israel was the murderous, Nazi-like Goliath. Not surprisingly, the BBC welcomes criticism that they are too "pro-Israel," and are only too happy to feature it in their news, especially at times when they are in full "lethal journalist" mode.[21] As

---

16 Ibid., 196–99.

17 Friel and Falk, *Israel-Palestine*, chapter 3.

18 The demands continue in the present: "An open letter to Canadian newsrooms on covering Israel-Palestine," May 14, 2021. Among the over 2000 signatories, are journalists from reputable news organizations like the CBC, *Toronto Star*, Globe and Mail, CTV News, *Macleans*, Yahoo News Canada, *Global News* . . .

19 Judge Hina Jilani of the Goldstone Investigation quoted in Haroon Siddiqui, "Looking for Accountability over Gaza War," *The Star*, Oct. 15, 2009.

20 Robert Fisk, "Fear and Learning in America," *Independent*, April 17, 2002. Zelizer "How Bias Shapes the News," 287.

21 In response to a demonstration in 2014 outside BBC headquarters, criticizing it for its "pro-Israel" journalism, the BBC "Today" show had anchor Mishal Husain interview Greg Philo with predictable results: Tom Gross, "Western media's 'pro-Israel' bias? Hardly," *National Post*, July 20, 2014.

for evidence that they are unprofessionally anti-Israel, the BBC paid hundreds of thousands of the public's pounds to suppress the Balen Report.[22]

Press as Pro-Palestinian

A closer look at the evidence reveals a qualitative difference between the two sets of complaints. Israelis and their supporters complain far more often than pro-Palestinians,[23] and the Israeli complaints are often about the failure of the media to live up to their obligations to report accurately, rather than to promote a narrative. On the pro-Palestinian side there is nothing remotely resembling the veritable industry of press-corrections that organizations like CAMERA, Honest Reporting, and UKMedia Watch force the news media to make about empirical evidence and substantive issues.[24]

Anyone who examines the evidence will find that the staff at CAMERA meets basic academic research standards for accuracy, even as others, within academia, have switched from empiricism towards feelings and narratives.[25] For a brief period, a Palestinian *Palestine Media Watch* (2000–2008) existed, modeled on the pro-Israel sites (not to be confused with *Palestinian Media Watch*, PalWatch, 1995-). The Palestinian group offered Palestinian talking points: its page dedicated to "what to harp on" contained "facts" of dubious accuracy mixed in with extensive editorial claims presented as facts.[26] Not too many lists with corrections of the media.

When "both sides" claim the journalists show too much deference to the other side, and unconscionably interrupt and dismiss their own side, how much do the hypersensitivities of Palestinian discourse and the thick skins of Israelis skew the lines of sight?[27] How is it that a tough journalist on a program that advertises its "tough questioning" like Hard Talk mumbles critical questions to Palestinians and doesn't follow up, while pressing hard and interrupting Israeli

22 Keith Dovkants, "The secret report at heart of BBC's Gaza paranoia," *The Evening Standard*, January 27, 2009.

23 Chris Elliott, "Accusations of bias in coverage of the Israel-Palestine conflict," *Guardian*, February 22, 2016.

24 See Ben-Dror Yemini, *Industry of Lies: Media, Academia, and the Arab-Israeli Conflict* (New York: ISGAP, 2017).

25 Lewis, "The Times and the Jews."

26 "Basic facts to keep in mind," *Palestine Media Watch*. See the meager and mostly opinion-based list of corrections at Electronic Intifada, https://electronicintifada.net/search/site/corrections.

27 E.g., R. Landes, "Sackur: Bully and Wimp," *Al Durah Project*, January 2019.

spokespeople, insists loudly that he is an equal opportunity offender?[28] Why do journalists present the Palestinian narrative as one approved of by "the whole world" (themselves included), and the Israeli narrative as government spin?[29]

Whether intentionally or not, the Western media and their audiences hold Israel to a higher standard than the Palestinians ... something most Israelis, certainly Westernized ones, consider perfectly justified. *Israel* certainly holds itself to higher standards, why shouldn't others? Consider, however, what kind of a differential this creates on the outside. "Both sides" accuse the other of brutality and acts of cruelty to civilians. But while the evidence suggests Israelis go to great lengths to keep the (necessarily) brutal conduct of war under control, Palestinian groups like Hamas brag about their brutal assaults on Israeli civilians, and do everything they can to encourage and empower suicide mass-murderers.[30]

If one holds someone to higher standards than their foe, at least one should not lose sight of that, and pretend thereby that they are "the same"—or as the post-colonial paradigm has it, terror against the oppressor is resistance, and state resistance to attack is terror.[31] Thus, when the Israelis entered the Jenin refugee camp, the walls were covered indoors and out with the images of "martyrs"—a veritable death cult of mass murder and child sacrifice.[32] But instead of seeing that, news consumers in the West heard about an Israeli massacre of Palestinian innocents. As Caliphators never tire of saying: "They [Israel, US, West] love life as we love death. And that is why we will win."[33] It's certainly why they win in the media, because Western cognitive egocentrics at once fear the very attitude they cannot imagine. It must be something Israel did.[34]

---

28 See David Hirsh, "How Raising the Issue of Antisemitism Puts You Outside the Community of the Progressive: The Livingstone Formulation," in *From Antisemitism to Anti-Zionism: The Past & Present of a Lethal Ideology*, ed. Eunice G. Pollack (Boston: Academic Studies Press, 2017).

29 Landes, "Everyone Knows," (2017) *Al Durah Project*.

30 Wolfsfeld, "News Media and the Second Intifada," *Palestine-Israel Journal*, 10:2 (2003).

31 *Oh Allah! Give us enemies who legitimate our terrorism as "resistance" and denounce any recourse to violence in their own defense, as "terrorism."*

32 David Zangen, "Seven Lies About Jenin."

33 Bin Laden (1996), https://www.libraryofsocialscience.com/assets/pdf/Bin-Laden-1996-declaration-of-war-against-the-americans.pdf. Nasrallah of Hizballah (2006), https://mikefarinha.wordpress.com/2006/07/27/we-are-going-to-win-because-they-love-life-and-we-love-death/; Hani Ar-Rifa'i (July 13, 2009), "They love death as we love life," https://youtu.be/zl12Zqa18Yk; note the rapturous comments; Haniya and Deif of Hamas (July 30, 2014), https://www.youtube.com/watch?time_continue=37&v.

34 Alternatively, the meme is not Muslim at all, but a Western "Islamophobic" construct designed to create false panics: Sarah Bracke, Luis Aguilar, "'They love death as we love life': The 'Muslim Question' and the biopolitics of replacement," *British Journal of Sociology*, 71:4

In this massive gap between Israeli and Palestinian attitudes towards the sanctity of human life and the humanity of one's enemies, images of Israeli acts of brutality did enormous damage to her image, while Palestinian acts of brutality made little difference to an already negative image. While this seems like an obvious observation, and hardly an indictment of the media, it actually conceals a key dynamic: in the game of blackening the "other's face," Palestinians had an enormous advantage which, far from correcting in their coverage, journalists enhanced by (they thought) "leveling the playing field." Hence Palestinians find ready consumers of their faked footage of Israeli "war crimes" (*Pallywood*) among Western journalists, lethal narratives so crucial to their cognitive war against so much more powerful a military foe. Hence, the immense outside interest in—dare one say, fascination with—this material. "Man bites dog." By the early 2020s, Muslims propounding the "we love death" meme found favor with the BBC.[35]

And if this longstanding journalistic expression for unusual stories might strike the sensitized postmodern modern reader as bordering on racism for comparing Hamas to a dog,[36] it actually points out the racism of a media which treated Palestinian brutality as an expected force of nature, and yet, at the same time, gave them credibility when accusing Israel of doing what they are proud to do. Thus the Western media, with their differential moral expectations, fell into the Palestinian tribal trap: both Palestinians (for tribal reasons) and journalists (out of humanitarian racism) considered the brutality that (Palestinians claimed that) Israel did to them intolerable, and what Palestinians (actually) did to Israelis, was either expected—"what choice do they have?"—or fully justified, as acts of resistance and revenge. "To make sense of most international journalism from Israel, it is important first to understand that the news tells us far less about Israel than about the people writing the news."[37]

(2020). Or better yet, it's the USA that loves death, "'We love death': Projecting the American Culture of Death onto Islam," *Dissident Veteran for Peace*, January 5, 2009.

35 See the case of Mohammed Hijab in London who made the point at an "pro-Palestinian rally", https://youtu.be/AJCYPXFrDSk?t=116, harassed Jews in the streets, (Noa Hoffman, "Muslim men film themselves targeting Jews for their views on 'child killing'," *Jewish Chronicle*, May 26, 2021), and was then interviewed by BBC journalist Tom Barda on how promote good relations with the Jews: "Palestinian Activism and Anti-Zionism vs. Anti-Semitism," https://www.youtube.com/watch?v=6zHL2x0ndgE&t=698s.

36 See what happened to Prof. Andrew Pessin for comparing Hamas to a rabid pit bull in the summer of 2014 during Operation Protective Edge: *Salem on the Thames: Moral Panic, Anti-Zionism, and the Triumph of Hate-Speech at Connecticut College*, ed. Richard Landes (Boston: Academic Studies Press, 2019).

37 Matti Friedman, "What the Media Gets wrong about Israel," *Atlantic*, November 30, 2014. Cf. Dan Perry, "The foreign media is not anti-Israel," *Times of Israel*, May 18, 2020. NB: he

Few places better highlight the Moebius strip of misapprehension than the issue of *incitement*. For the Israelis, Palestinian incitement was a major, if not the major contributor to the failure of the peace and the growing savagery of the war. And a key component of this incitement was the systematic production of lethal narratives designed to arouse hatred and a desire for revenge (either the taking of that revenge, or the satisfaction in seeing that revenge taken). And for Palestinian strategists, this was obvious: their ability to create hostility world-wide against their enemy was a critical component of their war efforts. They counted on world opinion, outraged by the images they saw and the tales they heard, to stay the hand of the Israelis.[38]

The media had their own take, that combined both their commitment to fairness and their fear of Palestinian retaliation for story lines that violated the rules. Although "both sides" engage in incitement, one rabbi calls the Palestinians "cockroaches," and that's more significant than when Imam after Imam, on Palestinian Authority TV, as on Hamas TV, call for the extermination of the Jews—pigs and monkeys with Satan's tail.[39] So, one ends up with almost complete radio silence on the mainstream Palestinian incitement industry, and dramatic highlights to marginal Israeli incitement.[40]

Palestinian "media critics" brush off criticism for incitement, and project their own (denied or dismissed) incitement onto Israel.

> Incitement is an accusation frequently levied by the Israelis at the Palestinians, but even a superficial review of the Israeli mass media shows high levels of incitement. For example, there is an open discourse that touches the boundaries of criminality in everything related to President Arafat. "As long as Arafat is alive,

---

nowhere addresses the subject of Palestinian intimidation of journalists or incitement of their own people; Landes, "Fisking Dan Perry on foreign media's attitude towards Israel," *Augean Stables*, February 17, 2022.

38 See n46 on Arafat's euphoria at global support. Christiane Amanpour spells out the protection international outrage provides Hamas in a question to Tony Blair: "The [media's reports of] civilian casualties in Gaza are obviously going to put a big pressure on Israel. How long can they withstand this pressure?" https://www.youtube.com/watch?v=VpQokfqLnwA. Jeffrey Mayer, "Meet the Press Wonders if Israel Will 'Achieve Military Victory but Lose the Battle of Wider Public Opinion,'" *Media Research Center*, August 3, 2014.

39 See Neil Kressel's analysis of the "conspiracy of silence" that reigns in the West over this genuinely racist discourse: *The Sons of Pigs and Apes*.

40 "Israel Rabbi calls for 'plague' on Mahmoud Abbas," *BBC*, August 30, 2010.

Jews will die," is one front-page headline of Ma'ariv. If this is not incitement, then what is?[41]

Compared with Palestinian incitement—"massacre, murder, slaughter all the Jews everywhere, show no mercy!"—this doesn't even register as incitement, much less "high levels." And yet Ata Qaymari can effortlessly change the subject with Western interlocutors because to this day the MSNM has not exposed the West to the material available at MEMRI and PMW to report on the Palestinians. Most Westerners are unaware of the issue except in the vaguest terms.

Indeed, the journal issue in which the above citation appeared illustrates the point nicely. Alongside the unidimensional, tribal, my-side-right-or-wrong, accusations (and projections) of the Palestinian critics about "bad" Israel, one finds the most ferociously self-critical (post-Zionist) Israeli analysts, accusing their own press of being too patriotic and not sufficiently "detached" and ecumenical or objective.[42] With such a marriage of premodern tribalism and postmodern self-accusation, one gets a real-life enactment of the Cold War joke about how both an American and a Russian are "free" to call the POTUS an idiot on the White House lawn, only here it's the Palestinian and the Israeli who are both free to shout Israel is evil on the pages of the same "scholarly" journal.

As in so many aspects of this conflict, compromising with the radical demands does not yield balance. Indeed, one of the oft-noted, oft-ignored aspects of the conflict is its prominence in the media, where it achieves the status of a full-fledged obsession. One study published in 2013, found that, aside from the US ("the uncontested world news hegemon"), articles about Israel and Palestine rank the highest, literally dwarfing China, Russia, and Europe.[43] If one factors in size and population, this means over a hundred-fold greater attention to this particular Middle East conflict than any other global story, including the entire US. Similarly, if one factors in casualty figures, then the Israel/Palestine media footprint is the exact inverse of the Democratic Republic of Congo: about ten thousand dead in twenty years (1989–2009) has filled global media, whereas about four to six *million* dead in the same period, remains nearly invisible to the world—one of many stealth conflicts.[44]

---

41 Ata Qaymari, "Israeli Media: Serving the 'Patriotic' Cause," *Palestine-Israel Journal*, 10:2 (2003).
42 Dor, *Intifada Hits the Headlines*.
43 E. Segev and M. Blondheim, "Online news about Israel and Palestine: A cross-national comparison of prominence and trends," *Digital Journalism*, 1:2 (2013): 1–13.
44 Virgil Hawkins, *Stealth Conflicts: How the World's Worst Violence Is Ignored* (New York: Routledge, 2008).

A German poll in 2004 testifies to the success of Palestinians to get their narrative out: in some countries *majorities* believed Israel was committing genocide against the Palestinian people.[45] When they were asked why Yasser Arafat did nothing to restrain the violence during the first months of the intifada, aides described him as "exalted, even euphoric . . . [with] the international media portraying the intifada in romantic colors, and the international community supporting the Palestinians."[46] No Israeli PM during these years had anything like that exaltation at press support, and at the same time it occurred to few if any pollsters to raise the question whether European publics thought the Palestinians wanted to exterminate the Jews.

And why shouldn't Arafat think the media were with him? As BBC correspondent Fayad abu Shamala proclaimed at a Hamas rally in Gaza in May 2001: "journalists and media organizations [are] waging the campaign shoulder-to-shoulder together with the Palestinian people." When the Israeli government showed the tape to the BBC, they responded: "Fayad's remarks were made in a private capacity. His reports have always matched the best standards of balance required by the BBC."[47] (Enderlin defended his Pallywood photographer Talal abu Rahma in just these terms.[48]) Some years later, evidence emerged that Shamala was a *member* of Hamas.[49]

Unbeknownst to news consumers in the West, there was a public secret of sympathy and cooperation between journalists and the "resistance" against

---

45 "Zusammenfassung zentraler Ergebnisse," *Frederich Ebert Stiftung and Bielefeld University,* November 20, 2014, 5; cited along with other similar statistics by Manfred Gerstenfeld, *The War of a Million Cuts: The Struggle against the Delegitimization of Israel and the Jews, and the Growth of New Anti-Semitism* (Jerusalem: JCPA, 2015), 56–58. In response to reports of Jenin "massacre," German demonstrators shouted "Stop the genocide in Palestine," Desmond Butler, "Thousands March in Germany to Oppose Israeli Incursion," *New York Times,* April 14, 2002. This accusation is now standard rhetoric ("genocidal ethnic cleansing") which Westerners like Vice-President Kamala Harris do not know how to (or do not dare) criticize, https://www.youtube.com/watch?v=_bnlpQaEsCQ. On the emotional appeal of this blood libel, see Yair Rosenberg, "Why people love accusing Jews of genocide," *Washington Post,* January 10, 2022.

46 Amos Harel and Avi Issacharoff, *The Seventh War* [Hebrew] (Tel Aviv: Yedioth Aharonot, 2004), 99. For a good example of how even the journalists who tried (and considered themselves) to be professional didn't report what they saw, see Dan Perry's recollections of a December 2001 interview with a clearly mentally disturbed Arafat who, nonetheless, came off in his article as a peace-maker: "A surreal encounter with Yasser Arafat," *Times of Israel,* December 7, 2021. Original article: Dan Perry and Karen Laub, "Arafat says he'll face down militants, calls for peace," *AP,* December 8, 2021.

47 Gutmann, *The Other War,* 252.

48 See above, 38f.

49 Tom Gross, "Hamas admit BBC Gaza Correspondent is one of their own," *Mideast Dispatch Archive,* December 6, 2004. Apparently, the operative term in the BBC's response is "the best standards . . . *required.*"

Israel.[50] It was only embarrassing when the public got a glimpse of it, like when the BBC's Barbara Plett shed tears for the dying Yasser Arafat.[51] Ben Wederman considered Palestinian suffering "his beat;" and when the BBC's Alan Johnstone was kidnapped, Palestinian observers objected: "Why did they kidnap him? He works for us."[52] In 2014, three years before the BBC hired her as a journalist, Tala Halawa posted a now-removed tweet: #Israel is more #Nazi than #Hitler! Oh, #HitlerWasRight #IDF go to hell. #PrayForGaza.[53]

Imagine the BBC having a journalist on staff who tweeted about ethnically cleansing Judea and Samaria of its Arabs.

* * *

Fully aware of the complaints from the Palestinian side about the media's lack of sympathy for their cause, I lay out the following case for a dramatic switch among the MSNM towards the Palestinian side during the first days, months and years of the new century, a shift that continues unabated two decades later. Before dismissing this argument as "pro-Israel" and therefore unreliable, readers should consider the evidence, because if I'm right, and the Western public is getting it (very) wrong, the consequences are beyond grave for everyone in democracies.

Lethal Journalism Dominant

The newly dominant school of Middle East journalism in the new century followed a fourfold approach:

---

50 Landes, "Al Durah and the "Public Secret" of Middle East Journalism," *PJ Media*, November 11, 2007. See the case of Octavia Nasr, correspondent covering the Arab world for CNN: Lee Smith, "Hollow Men: Why Israel's enemies will always be the darlings of Western intellectuals," *Tablet*, July 14, 2010. For critics of the "pro-Israeli press": Robert Fisk, "They're all groveling and you can guess the reason," *Independent*, July 17, 2010; Jillian Rayfield, "The Right on Juan Williams: Don't Diss The Jews! But Muslims? Eh, No Problem," *Talking Points Memo*, October 21, 2010.

51 "Arafat report 'broke BBC rules,'" BBC, November 25, 2005. NB: It's not only because of his embrace of terrorism against Israel that one might find this heartfelt sympathy curious. Arafat stole *billions* from his own people: David Samuels, "In a ruined country," *Atlantic*, September 2005; Karsh, *Arafat's War*.

52 Ben Wedeman, "Reporter offers Bush a Gaza, West Bank misery tour," CNN, January 10, 2008; on Johnston's kidnapping: "UK Palestinians in Johnston plea," BBC, May 14, 2007.

53 Steerpike, "BBC journalist: 'Hitler was right,'" *Spectator*, May 23, 2021. More recently, Jonathan Sacerdoti, "BBC journalist praised the 'exquisite journalism' of Holocaust revisionist," *Jewish Chronicle*, December 9, 2021.

- framing the story as the Israeli Goliath and the Palestinian David (embodied in the almost dogmatic use of the term "Israeli-Palestinian conflict" rather than the earlier "Arab-Israeli" conflict or the even more ominously accurate, if somewhat clumsy, "Sovereign Jewish-Triumphalist Muslim conflict");
- reporting Palestinian claims (lethal narratives) as reliable until proven otherwise, while treating Israeli counterclaims as dubious, if not false, until proven true[54];
- reporting as little as possible about the religious culture of genocide and terrorism that flourishes in Palestinian-controlled areas; and
- correcting errors that result from this approach as slowly and inconspicuously as possible.

This pattern of unprofessional journalism, already visible earlier, dominates the product of Western correspondents based in Israel from 2000 on.

Nidra Poller, who worked long and hard on the al Durah affair, coined the term "lethal narrative," emphasizing how easily these tales make their impact, and how difficult it is to correct them, much less, abate the horror they initially provoke.[55] Lethal narrators tell such tales to arouse in the listener a sense of outrage, of hatred, even a desire for revenge, against the accused. Lethal narratives about malevolent enemies is an intrinsic component of most warfare.[56]

These journalists deliberately "obliterate notions of chronology, cause and effect ... the very logic that is essential to Western rationality." Once the accusation is uttered and repeated by a journalist, even if only as a (plausible) allegation, denial is lame, defensive, impotent. The most important Palestinian lethal narrative is a variant of the claim, a kind of secular blood libel, that Israel kills children on purpose. Palestinian spokespeople had long made this claim, but serious journalists kept their distance; after all, accusations that Israel targets children from people who do precisely that, are not credible.

---

54 Mark Lavie, former AP staffer, "Why Everything Reported from Gaza is Crazy Twisted," *Tower*, August 2014; Leuchter, "Etats des lieux," 21f. As Israeli spokeswoman Miri Eisen explained to Stephanie Gutmann, "Everything we say they have to 'check'; everything the Palestinians say they take as fact. But you have to be careful with them. If you attack them too much they kick back." *Other War*, 78.

55 Nidra Poller introduced me to the al Durah affair in the summer of 2003 and to Gerard Huber, author of the first book on the al Durah forgery: *Contre-expertise d'une mise-en-scène* (Paris, Editions Raphaël, 2003). See Poller, "Lethal Narratives: Weapon of Mass Destruction in the War Against the West," *New English Review*, May 30, 2009.

56 Sam Keen, *The Face of the Enemy: Reflections of the Hostile Imagination* (New York: HarperColllins, 1991).

Once given credence by journalists, however, even if the accusation proves wrong (like al Durah, spectacularly so), it henceforth became no longer "unthinkable" that Israelis target children. On the contrary, the evidence poured in that they do. Papers began listing casualty figures daily, always accepting Palestinian figures as accurate. A typical example from the *Daily Telegraph* (not an acutely anti-Israel paper like the *Guardian*), combines the Palestinian supplied casualty figures with a studiously neutral (indeed cognitively egocentric) backgrounder: "At least 1,468 Palestinians and 564 Israelis have been killed since a Palestinian uprising for independence [sic] began in September 2000 after peace negotiations became deadlocked [sic]."[57] Disproportionate death tolls made the greater numerical victim, the aggressed innocent.

The inevitable disparity—both from the differential in military power and the inflated Palestinian figures—played to the Palestinian's advantage.[58] Four days after al Durah exploded on French TV screens, French President Jacques Chirac, speaking on behalf of all the "countries of the world," berated Ehud Barak in Paris on October 4, 2000: "The discrepancies have to be considered: 64 Palestinians . . . dead, 2,300 Palestinians injured, while on the Israeli side only two Israeli civilians and one soldier were killed. No one can believe that the Palestinians are responsible for this chain of violence."[59] No one who is a liberal cognitive egocentric can believe it . . . the whole world can't believe it.

A year later, William Pfaff illustrated how astute is the Palestinian strategy of hitting Israel with its own people's suffering.

> The Israeli public does not yet fully understand the most important consideration of all: that the Palestinians are, in a terrible way, winning. Their suffering is robbing Israel of its moral substance. . . . The Palestinians assault civilians, carry out indiscriminate terrorist bombings. . . . But that does not change the fact that they are Israel's victims.[60]

---

57 "Jewish settlers kill Palestinian girl," *Daily Telegraph*, July 29, 2002. The report of settlers killing the girl, Neveen Jamjoum, is based entirely on uncorroborated Palestinian testimony.

58 Cf. Seth Ackerman, "The Illusion of Balance: NPR's coverage of Mideast deaths doesn't match reality," *FAIR*, November/December 2001.

59 Enderlin, *Shattered Dreams*, 304; Sher's version of Chirac's remarks (with which he, like Enderlin, agrees) is more detailed: *Israel-Palestinian Negotiations*, 162.

60 William Pfaff, "The Outlook is Ominous for Both Israel and the Palestinians," *IHT/LA Times Syndicate*, April 24, 2001), cited in Poller, *Troubled Dawn of the 21st Century*, 49–50.

Here a questionable judgment is presented as "fact." Could one not argue that the Palestinians killed in this round of the conflict were the victims of their leadership's relentlessly negative-sum strategy? Apparently not, for a punditocracy whose folly makes Palestinian child sacrifice "rational."

And so it went, year after year, encounter after encounter, lethal narrative after lethal narrative. 56 killed in Kafr Qana, Lebanon, 2006, in an Israeli strike on a home for children. Stunning news. Condoleezza Rice, newly arrived in Israel, furious, demands the Israelis cease-fire immediately. Extensive coverage of digging out dead babies. Worldwide outrage! Fury in the Umma. Journalists badger Israeli spokespeople.

Oh, so it's *only* 28 dead and most adults. So what? What does it matter if it's not a children's home, if Hizballah brought bodies from elsewhere to amplify the visuals? What does it matter if the Red Cross performed, and the journalists there filmed, staged footage of the "discovery" of children's corpses? What does it matter if Hizballah was firing from nearby?[61] "[Nothing could] counteract the pictures arriving from Qana: limbless, bleeding, soot-covered children and babies borne in the arms of local and Red Cross rescue personnel; alongside the ruined building rows upon rows of bodies covered with white plastic sacks."[62]

And just as in the case of Jose Saramago's and Edgar Morin's rants after Jenin, the counter-evidence had no impact on a vicious, supersessionist rant by one of Norway's most beloved public intellectuals who, speaking in the collective "we" of the Global Progressive Left, cursed the vicious Jews.[63] It was a brilliant military coup for Hizballah—from losing on the ground to an Israeli withdrawal amidst a tidal wave of Israel-hatred world-wide. And they could not have done it, without the extensive and enthusiastic participation of lethal journalists.[64]

---

61 North, "The Corruption of the Media." On the role of the "human rights" NGOs, "Watching the Watchers Part Two," *NGO Monitor*, March 20, 2007; Gerald M. Steinberg, "The Role of NGOs in the Palestinian Political War Against Israel"; Marvin Kalb, "The Israeli-Hezbollah War of 2006: The Media as a Weapon in Asymmetrical Conflict," Shorenstein Center Research Papers, February 2007.

62 Amos Harel and Avi Issacharoff, *34 Days: Israel, Hizballah and the War in Lebanon* (New York: Palgrave, 2008), 162.

63 See above, 289–92.

64 Harel and Issacharoff, *34 Days*, 159–62.

FIGURE 21. Arab Red Cross worker holds up dead baby for the press pack, Kafr Qana, July 2006.

Palestinian Media Protocols and Journalistic Compliance

Perhaps the most salient issue in assessing Western coverage concerns the degree to which it complied (and continues to comply) with Palestinian "Media Protocols" that essentially demand that journalists report the conflict as this black (Israel) and white (Palestinians) morality tale. Every time so far that open hostilities between Israel and her neighbors have broken out in the twenty-first century (2000, 2002, 2006, 2008/9, 2010, 2012, 2014, 2018, 2021), the MSNM have primarily complied with the following instructions from the Palestinian side:

Palestinian Media Protocols

1. The Palestinians are the noble resisters—David	2. The Israelis are the cruel oppressors—Goliath
3. Thou shalt always portray Palestinians as victims, never as Aggressors	4. Thou shalt never portray the Israelis as victims, always as Aggressors.
5. Thou shalt not portray Palestinians unsympathetically	6. Thou shalt not portray Israel sympathetically.
7. Thou shalt not challenge or undermine Palestinian claims.	8. Thou shalt challenge and undermine Israeli claims.

Obviously, no journalist would work in full compliance with these demands, lest he or she lose all credibility with him or herself and readers. Nonetheless, the general level of compliance hovers around an invisible line of credibility, in which journalists comply as much as possible without looking like complete tools. The number of cases in which these commandments operate is so great, one could compose volumes enumerating them. For example, when Hamas rockets kill Palestinians, journalists, obeying commandments 3, 4, 6, and 8, only report the story as long as it looks like Israel did it, but fall silent as soon as it becomes clear a Hamas or Islamic Jihad bomb killed their own people. The number of violations in the opposite direction—not reporting reliable cases that made the Israelis look good (i.e. violating 6, 8) are minimal if nonexistent, while numerous unreliable cases of Israel looking bad get lavish coverage.[65] Reporters make their careers by rooting out Israeli malfeasance.[66]

Black Hearts, Red Spades: Paradigmatic Expectations and the Rejection of Anomalies

Perhaps the best place to see this skew at work is in the cases where the Israelis are victims and the Palestinians aggressors. An outstanding example came right at the beginning of the Al Aqsa Intifada/Oslo Jihad. The day after Ariel Sharon had visited the Temple Mount/Haram al Sharif (29 September 2000/2 Rajab 1421), enraged by Palestinian news broadcasts claiming Sharon had desecrated Al Aqsa, severe rioting broke out in East Jerusalem. In the course of a terrible day of clashes, a dozen died and hundreds were wounded. The next day, AP sent out this captioned photo.

---

65 The New York Times expended enormous manpower, technology and newsprint to document the case of a medic accidentally killed by a bullet ricochet, a conclusion only revealed at the end of a lengthy article. David Halbfinger, et al., "A Day, a Life: When a Medic Was Killed in Gaza, Was It an Accident?" *New York Times*, January 5, 2019; Andrea Levin, "NY Times Ends Year with Epic Smear," *CAMERA*, December 31, 2018. Would that the *New York Times* spent a fraction of that investigative vigor on al Durah case . . . .

66 Sheera Frenkel and Michael Evans, "Israel admits using white phosphorus in attacks on Gaza," *Times* [UK], January 5, 2009; cf. Mark Cantora, "Israel and White Phosphorus During Operation Cast Lead," *Gonzaga Journal of International Law* 13:1 (2010).

FIGURE 22. An Israeli policeman and a Palestinian on the Temple Mount.

The obvious suggestion of the caption is that the angry Israeli policeman with the baton has beaten the bloody Palestinian lad. Except that the boy in the picture is an American Yeshiva student in Israel, Tuvya Grossman, whose taxi had taken him through an Arab neighborhood where a mob of Arabs dragged him out of the cab and nearly beat him to death.[67] To run the photo with the proper caption, however, did not fit the narrative. Someone in the AP office identified Tuvya as a Palestinian, and the site of the confrontation as the Temple Mount (despite the gas station in the immediate background). And the *New York Times*, without checking, ran the photo and caption. Narrative journalism all around.

As Thomas Kuhn and cognitive scientists have warned: we see what we expect to see, what we want to see, what we're taught to see. In this case both AP and the *New York Times*, and many a reader, read into the photo what they "already" knew was happening: the Israeli Goliath was beating the Palestinian David. It took the *New York Times* four days to issue a laconic correction, and only under heavy pressure, to spell out the real story.[68] And despite the correction, groups pressing a boycott of Israel, repeatedly used the image.[69]

---

67 For his account of the incident, see Robert D. McFadden, "Abruptly, a US Student in Mideast Turmoil's Grip," *New York Times*, Oct. 7, 2000.

68 For the details of the correction at AP, the *New York Times*, and elsewhere, see Richard Landes, "Black Hearts and Red Spades: The Media Gets the 'Intifada' Wrong," *The Augean Stables*, April 10, 2006. French coverage: Leuchter, "Etats des lieux, 23f.

69 "The Photo that Started it All," *Honest Reporting*.

Haven't we had enough humiliation? Israelis are killing Palestinian children and the US economy is supplying the bullets. Is there anything you can do to stop this? Yes! There are 1 billion Muslims and 5 billion humans around the world. If we all unite together and boycott the attached American product, we will send a strong message to the U.S. that is supporting the killing of innocence. We have nothing against the American people. We just want Israel to stop the killing. This is only the beginning! More products to come. Please make an impact. Boycott this product and spread the word. Together, we can make a difference.

FIGURE 23. Using image of Jew beaten up by Palestinians to promote boycott of Coca Cola.

Now granted that there were, that day, many pictures of injured Palestinians available—7 dead and about 300 injured. Why did this one make the front page? Because, mislabeled, it told the whole David-Goliath story: not merely Palestinian victimhood, but Israeli culpability in the same frame. All the Palestinian sources of violence disappear in the overwhelming image. When forced to correct—Jewish pressure, again!—neither AP, nor the papers that used their material reflected on how such egregious errors could have occurred, how a front-page picture in the *New York Times* could show a gas station on the Haram al Sharif. Nor did they see fit to connect the violence against a Jewish "civilian" to the extensive beatings of the press by Palestinians.[70]

---

70 Judy Lash Balint, "Journalists describe constant Palestinian intimidation," *WorldnetDaily*, March 6, 2001.

Instead, the narrative this image so neatly illustrated for the news media became the standard authorized version: Ariel Sharon caused the intifada, and Palestinians were its victims, a narrative that no amount of contrary evidence could penetrate.[71] Over a decade later, Patrick Tyler felt no need to footnote the dismissive assertion: "The big accusation, however, was that Arafat had ordered the war. It wasn't true, as all later reconstructions confirmed, but it didn't matter."[72] It was true, as extensive later evidence confirmed. But to those with Y2KMind, it didn't matter.[73]

Headline Fails

This pattern of compliance with Palestinian demands is most easily viewed in the headlines, the first, and all too often last, thing news consumers read.[74] In cases where the aggressors are the Palestinians, who behave specifically as terrorists—i.e., targeting civilians for murder—the job of the compliant news media is to obey #4/5: Israeli never victim, Palestinian never victimizer. What results is a remarkable grammar and syntax that reverse the vectors of causality (Israeli response leads) and bleaches out Palestinian agency.

On November 18, 2014, for example, two Israeli Arab youths who worked in the neighborhood, entered a synagogue in Har Nof and butchered as many congregants in prayer as possible, killing six and wounding seven before they were shot dead. CNN headlines show an exceptionally high Palestinian Media Protocols Compliance score:

---

71 "PA Minister: The Intifada Was Planned From the Day Arafat Returned From Camp David," *MEMRI*, Special Dispatch No.194, March 21, 2001; Itamar Marcus and Barbara Crook, "Arafat planned and led the Intifada: Testimonies from PA leaders and others," *Palwatch*, November 28, 2011. Abd al-Bari Atwan, a BBC regular commentator, in Arabic, explains how Arafat planned the Intifada and sent men throughout the Middle East to get weapons: Hadar Sela, "BBC Regular Atwan Shatters 14 Year Old BBC Myth on Second Intifada," *CAMERA UK*, August 5, 2014.

72 Tyler, *Fortress Israel*, 429. Hadar Sela, "BBC Second Intifada Backgrounders: 'Sharon Started it,'" *CAMERA UK*, September 30, 2013.

73 Even Wikipedia has this information available: "Views on the Second Intifada."

74 See above discussion of the (non)use of "terrorism" to describe jihadi attacks, above, 29–32, 80–92.

FIGURE 24. Two CNN chyrons of the massacre in a Jerusalem Synagogue, November 18, 2014.

The first headline obeys in a most extraordinary way #4 (never Israeli victims); the second #3 (always Israeli aggressor). Thus, the synagogue becomes a mosque, and the killers become victims of Israeli aggression. The ensuing discussion between CNN's Wolf Blitzer and *Haaretz'* Barak Ravid focuses not at all on the ideology that moved these youth to butcher people who gave them jobs, nor on the possibility that this was a copy-cat attack inspired by ISIS, but rather on how Netanyahu should not destroy the houses of the perpetrators:

> Blitzer: ... that presumably will lead to an escalation in the situation, there's a fear that there will be revenge attacks, right?
> Ravid (ready with the answer): Yes, I think this is the main problem here ... that Prime Minister Netanyahu all along his political career ran with the slogan, "I will be strong with the Arabs."[75]

Blitzer's leading question, which assumed the twenty-first-century Prime Directive (*don't piss them off*), elicits Ravid's eager condemnation of his own leadership for not sufficiently appeasing his enemy's anger.

CNN's PMP Compliance Score: A+

---

75 Blitzer and Ravid on Har Nof Attack, January 28, 2018, https://vimeo.com/253226331#t=163s.

Subsequent attacks (knife and car) produced a whole dossier of sometimes staggering "headline fails," all of which comply with Palestinian Media Protocols. Indeed, once one understands the distorting effect that those jihadi demands made on the grammar and syntax of our news providers, one can "read between the lines": Palestinian aggressors are presented as victims (#3, 5); the cycle of violence reverses and Israeli retaliation initiates the headline (#4, 6); in matters of violence Israelis have agency, Palestinians do not; their violence is desperate resistance to oppression (#4, 3). (The following list is without references, all urls available at my blog.[76])

ISRAELI TROOPS SHOOT DRIVER OF RAMMED CAR (EuroNews): Palestinian rammed car into Israeli civilians, shot dead. NB: The syntax of reversal, start with the reprisal; turn an active driver ramming his car into Israelis, into a victim.

6 PALESTINIAN TEENS DIE AMID MIDEAST UNREST (the *Los Angeles Times*): 6 Palestinians who tried to stab Israelis during "Knife Intifada" killed by Police.

PALESTINIAN SHOT DEAD AFTER JERUSALEM ATTACK KILLS TWO (BBC News): Palestinian murders two Israeli civilians in Jerusalem, shot dead.

FOUR PALESTINIAN TEENS ARE KILLED IN ISRAELI VIOLENCE (*Los Angeles Times*)

ISRAELI TROOPS KILL PALESTINIAN IN THE WEST BANK: HEALTH MINISTRY (Reuters). He was throwing a Molotov cocktail at a car.

ISRAEL KILLS PREGNANT MOTHER AND HER BABY IN REVENGE ATTACKS (*Independent*). Israel retaliated against Hamas for a previous attack, and the weapons depot they hit exploded, causing the house nearby to collapse and kill the mother and child.

JEWISH MAN DIES AS ROCKS PELT CAR IN EAST JERUSALEM (*New York Times*): Palestinians pelt Israeli with stones causing fatal accident. NB: the headline has wiped clean Palestinian aggression, indeed it's almost a play on the hadith of "rocks and trees," only here the rocks not only speak but kill.

---

76 Landes, "Headline Fail Consistently Reflects the Demands of Palestinian Media Protocols," *The Augean Stables*, January 7, 2022.

BOMB MARS HISTORIC DAY FOR PALESTINIANS (AP): Arab set off bomb killing three Israeli civilians, on the day the Palestinians swore in a new Prime Minister.

ISRAEL UNREST: BOY, 16, BECOMES SEVENTH PALESTINIAN KILLED BY SECURITY FORCES AFTER JERUSALEM STABBING AS WAVE OF VIOLENCE CONTINUES (*Independent*); Palestinian, 16, stabs people, gets shot. NB: This long and confusing headline was shortened to a scarcely less lethal: *ISRAELI FORCES KILL BOY, 16, AFTER STABBING IN JERUSALEM AS VIOLENCE CONTINUES.*

PALESTINIANS SHOT BOARDING KIDS BUS (CNN): Two Palestinians, armed with knives were prevented from boarding a school bus, so instead went down the street and stabbed a man multiple times before the Israeli police shot them.

ISRAEL TO DROP MORE BOMBS (*Telegraph*): Israel announces that the army had begun staging "its first withdrawal" from Gaza, after the IDF had nearly reached its goal of destroying Hamas's terror tunnels. The accompanying picture shows Palestinian children wandering among rubble.

When the Israeli Knesset convened a hearing on this phenomenon of headline fails, Reuters Jerusalem Bureau Chief Luke Baker, head of The Foreign Press Association in Jerusalem, told the committee:

> We disagree with the premise of the hearing – it presupposes two things: that the foreign media are biased and that that supposed bias undermines Israel's ability to quell terrorist attacks. We do not agree that the foreign media are biased, and the legitimacy of Israel's campaign against terrorism is entirely determined by how Israel conducts that campaign.[77]

Only a few years later did such bizarre headline-fails hit the United States. In 2021, a Black Lives Matter supporter with ferocious anti-white beliefs, drove his car into a Christmas Parade in Waukesha, Wisconsin, killing six whites and injuring over 50. Headlines followed the Palestinian Protocols, now for

---

77 Chris Elliott, "Accusations of bias in coverage of the Israel-Palestine conflict," *Guardian*, February 22, 2016.

American Blacks: "... the Waukesha tragedy caused by a SUV", "... a car drove through a city Christmas parade", "... the Wisconsin parade crash."[78]

The Rule of Omertà

We have already seen lethal (and own-goal) journalism at its worst, in its sins of commission with the Al Durah affair: the spread of a blood libel about Israel deliberately murdering civilians, *as news*. Here we will examine the flip side of lethal journalism, its sins of omission, its silences: in this case, the refusal to report on genocidal incitement on the Palestinian side. As virtually any journalist who takes him or herself seriously will affirm: "For reporters, withholding valuable information from the public is anathema."[79] And yet, that is precisely what lethal journalists have done on a massive scale since 2000.

Palestinian Genocidal Preaching: Lethal Journalism's Ominous Silences

Perhaps the most egregious example of this came thirteen days after the Al Durah story first appeared. The day after the Ramallah lynch in which Arabs, shouting "revenge for the blood of Muhammad al Durah," literally tore the bodies of two Israeli soldiers apart and dragged the half-burnt pieces through the streets, Sheikh Halabaya, a paid appointee of the PA, gave a sermon broadcast on PA TV.

> The Jews are the Jews. Whether Labor or Likud, the Jews are Jews. They do not have any moderates or any advocates of peace. They are all liars. **They must be butchered and must be killed.** ... The Jews are like a spring as long as you step on it with your foot it doesn't move. But if you lift your foot from the spring, it hurts you and punishes you. ... **It is forbidden to have mercy in your hearts for the Jews in any place and in**

---

78 Victor Davis Hanson, "A Tale of Two Cities: Kenosha vs. Waukesha," *American Greatness*, November 28, 2021. Sohrab Ahmari, "SUVs Don't Kill People," *American Conservative*, November 30, 2021. On the racist attitudes of Darrell Brooks, who drove his car into the Christmas parade in Kenosha, which the mainstream news media did not discuss, see Pedro Gonzalez, "The War on American Communities," *Super Contra*, November 26, 2021.

79 Scott Shane, "When Spies hack Journalism," *New York Times*, May 12, 2018.

any land. Make war on them any place that you find yourself. Any place that you meet them, kill them.[80]

With Israeli public opinion at a fever pitch of outrage, the army had to respond and they did so, in contrast to the Palestinians, with surgical precision, by shooting a rocket through the window out of which the soldiers bodies had been thrown, and, after several warnings to evacuate, by bombing the *Voice of Palestine* radio station at night. Palestinians claimed these attacks injured 27 (who apparently ignored the warnings) but did not claim any dead. Israeli spokespeople justified the strike on *Voice of Palestine Radio* by pointing to the role of Palestinian news media in inciting people to kill the Jews. Invoking the case of Rwanda, where *Radio-Television Libre des Mille Collines* played a major role in the Hutu genocide of their Tutsi neighbors in 1994, only six years earlier,[81] Israel asserted its right to shut down such sites of crimes against humanity. Incitement, the Israelis insisted, was the source of the current horrendous violence.

The *New York Times* put one of their top journalists on the story. William Orme, husband of then Middle East Bureau chief, Deborah Sontag, and in charge of the complaints about media intimidation at the Association of Foreign Journalists in Jerusalem (and present in Ramallah when the lynch happened), tackled the problem: "A Parallel Mideast Battle: Is It News or Incitement?"[82] Orme carefully played the "he-said-she-said" script wherein the Israelis claimed genocidal incitement and Palestinians dismissed them as complaining about "anything we say." Comparisons to Rwanda were out of the question.[83]

The key moment in the article (which never once mentioned Al Durah, despite Orme's own coverage and the pervasive place the boy martyr had in Palestinian media incitement in those days and at Ramallah), came when Orme quoted from Halabaya's sermon. It was the only concrete evidence he offered of Israel's (extensive) examples of such genocidal incitement.

---

80 Sermon by Sheikh Halawa, PA TV, October 13, 2000, http://www.pmw.org.il/tv%20part6. html.

81 Gustave Messanga and Marios Tajeugueu, "The Role of Radio-Télévision Libre Des Mille Collines in The Rwandan Genocide," *International Journal of Research and Innovation in Social Science*, 5:9 (2021).

82 William Orme, "Parallel Middle East Battle: Is It News or Incitement?" *New York Times*, October 24, 2000.

83 As a sign of both the degradation and politicization of the news media in the last two decades, CNN published an article in 2022 comparing Joe Rogan's use of the n-word with the Hutu incitement to genocide: John Blake, "Why shrugging off Joe Rogan's use of the n-word is so dangerous," *CNN*, February 13, 2022. On the free use of "terrorism" to describe the events of January 6, see 92n143.

> Israelis cite as one egregious example a televised sermon that defended the killing of the two soldiers [at Ramallah on October 12, 2000]. *"Whether Likud or Labor, Jews are Jews,"* proclaimed Sheik Ahmad Abu Halabaya in a live broadcast from a Gaza City mosque the day after the killings.

It's hard to know what adjectives to use in characterizing this astonishing piece of reporting. Stupidity seems like a weak word. How could even a freshman in a *High School* history class, be so thick as to write about incitement, and leave out a readily available and horrifying example of *genocidal* incitement? One can legitimately rebuke Orme's article, therefore, for either massive incompetence or deliberate misinformation (Palestinian Media Protocols compliance?) Understandably, to this day, Orme refuses to comment.[84] And whatever his personal intent in writing as he did, the effect is to deliver a twin victory to the jihadis: on the one hand, the Western readership remained uninformed of the genocidal ideology that Hamas shares with the worst of the Global Jihadis; on the other, the Israelis appeared peevish. "Really?" a reader might justifiably ask, "'Labor and Likud are all Jews'?—*That's* the incitement you're complaining about? *That's* what you're comparing with Hutu genocidal broadcasts? Pathetic."

The mutilated quote amply fulfills the criteria for inclusion among the astoundingly stupid statements of the twenty-first century (one of the earliest): on the one hand, a radical inversion of empirical reality—*Palestinian media do actively engage in this terrible incitement*—and on the other, the wide assent it evokes among informed readers: *of course, they don't, of course Israel exaggerates.* Lethal journalists, doing Palestinian jihadi bidding, want above all to blame the victims of jihadi aggression for the violence that targets them. The radical disorientation of the West, unaware of the ferocious enemy that targeted it, proceeded apace. Palestinians were freedom fighters (whom we shouldn't call "terrorists"), and Israelis are imperialist occupiers whom we'll call terrorists if they insist we use the word.[85]

Nor was Orme's lacuna an unfortunate exception. On the contrary, to this day the *New York Times* and, more broadly, the Western press steadfastly refuse to report on the genocidal discourse of the Palestinians, both of Hamas *and* the PA.[86] They dismiss translation sites like MEMRI and PMW as "right wing,"

---

84 Most recent email sent on November 12, 2021, unanswered.
85 On Ted Turner's remarks, see above, 29f.
86 Guy Millière, "The Palestinian Authority is a Genocidal Terrorist Entity and Should be Treated as Such," *Gatestone*, August 17, 2017.

without providing alternative resources in translation.[87] On the contrary, in the period after 2000, when Palestinian genocidal hatred very similar to Nazi delirium became a central feature of their airwaves, the legacy media, *New York Times* in the lead, downplayed it.[88] Like terrorism, they would not speak of "incitement," but only report what "right-wing" Israelis claim.[89] As for academics like Juan Cole, their dedication to denying genocidal talk in the Middle East knew no intellectual bounds.[90]

Few issues are more critical in understanding the realities of the Middle East. Israel is faced with genocidal foes, every bit as bent on its extermination as the Nazis were, at once less effective than the Nazis, but in genocidal discourse worse (pro-Nazi priests and ministers did not call for the extermination of the Jews from the pulpit). And the outside world is so misinformed that it thinks the Israelis are behaving like Nazis and that when they complain about Palestinians, they're being paranoid. "If only Israel were more trusting of the Palestinians," they insist, "everything would be fine."[91]

Thus, in his "if anything the *New York Times* is pro-Israel" article for an allegedly academic journal, Neil Lewis can describe the natural tendency of journalists, including at the pro-Israel *New York Times*, to succumb to "the appeal that underdogs have to outsiders, especially journalists, which shifted sympathy to the Palestinians."[92] But presumably, this sympathy for the underdog is predicated on the relative innocence of that underdog. In this case, such sympathy is only possible if one ignores what Palestinians say amongst themselves, their aspirations, their beliefs about their enemies. Would underdog-friendly Western readers remain friendly if they knew that a major and unopposed theme in Palestinian culture is, admiration for Hitler and an open aspiration to finish his job.[93] Would the "pacifist" Judith Butler have embraced Hamas and Hizballah as part of the "Global Progressive Left," had it been widely known that these

87 See the *Right Web*'s analysis of *MEMRI* as Islamophobic; and Brian Whitaker, dismissal of MEMRI as a "right-wing" propaganda organ, "Email Debate: Yigal Carmon and Brian Whitaker," *Guardian*, January 28, 2003.

88 Auerbach, *Print to Fit*.

89 Jodi Rudoren and Isabel Kershner, "Israel Shaken by Five Deaths in Synagogue Assault," *New York Times*, November 18, 2014; Tamar Sternthal, "After Jerusalem Massacre, NY Times Covers up Abbas' Incitement," *CAMERA*, November 18, 2014.

90 Martin Kramer, "Shoddy and inaccurate?" *Sandbox*, December 12, 2011.

91 The Israeli peace camp used this accusation of "Holocaust paranoia" to get US Jews on board for the Oslo Accords: Jennifer Roskies, "Oslo's Betrayal," *Tablet*, September 13, 2018.

92 Lewis, "The *Times* and the Jews." See similar assertions from AP Middle East correspondent, above n6.

93 "Admiration for Hitler and Nazism," *Palestinian Media Watch*, https://palwatch.org/database/45.

organizations were driven by a delirious antisemitism, preached genocide from the pulpit, and promoted Islamic imperialism? (I like to think, "no." But it's hard to know.)

Similarly, in response to the complaint that the *New York Times* did not report on "the anti-Semitic and anti-Israel invective," Neil Lewis noted:

> Newspapers generally have a difficult time in dealing with any repeated phenomena, like hateful speech. An individual article may cover the subject once, to lay out the general phenomenon. But it is generally impractical to write an article about each subsequent instance. Editors are then inclined to say that the initial article already covered the subject. As a result, such outrageous comments recede into something akin to background noise. They may be deplorable but are not always deplored.[94]

How many misstatements:

1. When they want to, the media have no problem repeating themselves. For example, they never tire of repeating that the settlements are the obstacle to peace or that the West Bank is occupied territory.[95]
2. There never was an "initial article" on Palestinian genocidal incitement, much less one that "covered the subject."[96]
3. It was hardly impractical, but rather, professionally prescribed, for Orme and Erlanger to mention the genocidal speech in their articles.

Such discourse may sink into background noise for the journalists, and even more for their audiences back home who have no exposure to it at all, but no one can understand the actors in the region—neither the Israelis nor the Palestinians—without realizing how central a role this genocidal discourse plays.

---

94 Lewis, "The Times and the Jews," 35.

95 "[N]o single issue that has alienated more American supporters of Israel, Jewish and otherwise, than Israel's policy of establishing settlements in places like the West Bank of the Jordan River. It became and remains the focus of much media coverage," Lewis, "The *Times* and the Jews."

96 The closest the *New York Times* ever got was a piece by Erlanger *after* he left the ME, in which he blamed Hamas alone, absolving the PA: "In Gaza, Hamas's Insults to Jews Complicate Peace," *New York Times*, April 1, 2008. Lewis makes no mention of Orme's article suppressing the genocidal material from 2000.

Nor is this merely a problem in regards to the Arab-Israeli conflict. Bernard Goldberg, after noting how a Lexis-Nexis search for the decade 1991–2001 offered no article associating the Qur'an and terrorism, noted:

> I learned much more about the atmosphere that breeds suicide bombers from one short article in *Commentary* magazine than I have from watching twenty years of network television news. In its September 2001 issue (which came out before the attack on America), there was an article by Fiamma Nirenstein, an Italian journalist based in Israel, entitled "How Suicide Bombers Are Made." In it, she tells about a "river of hatred" that runs through not just the most radical of Arab nations but also much of what we like to think of as the "moderate" Arab world."[97]

In the end, despite granting that criticism of the *Times* for ignoring Palestinian hate-speech is valid, Lewis replicates the practice. His discussion of it is minimal and he offers no examples of the "invective" that he admits is "depressingly common in parts of the Arab media and clergy." He embodies his lament: "deplorable, but not always deplored." For "not always" read "rarely," and include Lewis among the pack who rarely deplore it, who allow this hate-speech to "recede into something akin to background noise." In an unlinked footnote he praises MEMRI (apparently not aware of PMW), for "enriching the debate"; and yet, his article, aside from this brief, unillustrated, mention, is not enriched with the contribution this material offers the debate about media bias, or, in the terms of this book, it is fully in compliance with *Palestinian Media Protocols*.

The Ramallah Lynch and the "Journalistic Procedures for Work in Palestine"

Perhaps one can understand Orme's behavior in suppressing evidence of genocidal incitement by noting that the day before Halabaya's ferocious sermon, Palestinian youth had entered a police station and pummeled to death two Israeli reservists, throwing them out the window, and drawing their dismembered, burnt bodies through the streets of the city, shouting "Revenge for the death of Muhammad al Durah." William Orme was present at these

---

97 Goldberg, *Bias*, p. 280; Fiamma Nirenstein, "How Suicide Bombers are Made," *Commentary*, September 2001.

events.[98] His behavior, and that of the MSNM, throw stark light on the dilemma of a journalist who wishes to renounce lethal journalism, and tell the real story.

Mark Seager, a British photographer with great sympathy for the Palestinian cause, could not believe his eyes.

> They were dragging the dead man around the street like a cat toying with a mouse. It was the most horrible thing that I have ever seen and I have reported from Congo, Kosovo, many bad places. In Kosovo, I saw Serbs beating an Albanian but it wasn't like this. There was such hatred, such unbelievable hatred and anger distorting their faces.[99]

Seager's further reflections point to a dramatic shift in Palestinian mood, a transforming rage that animated Palestinian circles in early October 2000/1421:

> I thought that I'd got to know the Palestinians well. I've made six trips this year and had been going to Ramallah every day for the past 16 days. I thought they were kind, hospitable people. I know they are not all like this and I'm a very forgiving person but I'll never forget this. It was murder of the most barbaric kind. When I think about it, I see that man's head, all smashed. I know that I'll have nightmares for the rest of my life.

Even before the lynch began, "the media were warned not to take pictures,"[100] and Seager, like any journalist there that day who did not obey, was attacked:

> I was punched in the face by a Palestinian. Another Palestinian pointed right at me shouting "no picture, no picture!", while another guy hit me in the face, I knew I had lost the chance to take the photograph that would have made me famous and I had lost my favourite lens that I'd used all over the world, but I didn't care. I was scared for my life.

---

98 Personal email exchange, November 22, 2014.
99 Mark Seager, "'I'll have nightmares for the rest of my life."
100 Orla Guerin mentions this prohibition weeks later as an aside (Gutmann, *Other War*, 93). Gutman contrasts this belated mention, along with Guerlin's indifference to this Palestinian imposition on journalists trying to do their job, with her vehement opposition to Israeli restrictions (266).

Palestinians confiscated every tape they could lay their hands on that day, but they missed one, an Italian crew belonging to a private station, *Mediaset*. This crew smuggled the footage out and turned it over to the Israelis, who immediately aired it on television. The image shocked the world public, and, for a brief moment, it competed with the image of al Durah—which had inspired these events—on the public's even-handed attention and sense of moral indignation.[101]

Arafat was furious and the entire Mediaset operation quickly realized it had to flee, first to the Italian Embassy for the night, and then back to Italy to escape his retaliation. The atmosphere was thick with threats. Shortly after this incident, a friend called Charles Enderlin to ask about the situation in Ramallah. "So, Charles, is it true that foreign journalists in Palestine are afraid?" to which Enderlin responded: "Say sooner that they're terrorized. But, anyway, I didn't say anything."[102] Palestinian friends called Seager after the publication of his article and warned him that it was not safe for him to remain in the Palestinian territories.[103]

In this situation of real terror, Riccardo Cristiano, the head of the public Italian station RAI, who had just gotten out of the hospital after a beating in Jaffa by rioting Palestinians,[104] feared a backlash against his crews. He wrote Arafat an obsequious letter, assuring him that it was not RAI that leaked such damaging news about the Palestinians.

> My dear friends in Palestine. We congratulate you and think that it is our duty to put you in the picture (of the events) of what happened on October 12 in Ramallah. . . . We emphasize to all of you that the events did not happen this way [i.e. it was not we who gave the footage to Israel], because we *always respect the journalistic procedures with the Palestinian Authority for work in Palestine* and we are credible [?] in our precise work.
>
> We thank you for your trust, and you can be sure that this is not our way of acting. We would not do such a thing.
>
> Please accept our dear blessings.

---

101 Tamar Liebes and Anat First "Framing the Palestinian Israeli Conflict," in *Framing Terrorism: The News Media, the government and the Public*, ed. Norris et al. (NY, 2003), chapter 4.

102 Guillaume Goldnadel, "La faute d'Enderlin," *Blognadel*, May 5, 2008.

103 See n146.

104 Cristiano "had just been released from the hospital where he spent more than a week recovering from injuries he received when he was beaten up in Jaffa while covering the riots started by Israeli Arabs. Cristiano's nose was broken, his cheek gashed, and he almost lost the use of his right eye." Balint, "Journalists describe constant Palestinian intimidation."

Sycophantic language aside, the text offers a revealing look at a craven Western media, eager to appease Palestinian anger, openly committed to complying with Palestinian media protocols ("journalistic procedures") about not showing the Palestinians in a bad light (#7).

Arafat, proud of the fear he inspired, had the letter published in his newspaper, demonstrating to his people how thoroughly he had cowed the Western news media. Palestinian Media Watch translated it into English, much to the professional humiliation of Cristiano, a mild-mannered man swept up in currents beyond his control. Even his colleagues, who fully shared his compliant journalism, could no longer save him. Like a man caught for corruption in a society where corruption is rampant, he broke the only rule: don't get caught. The Israelis, in a rare punitive move against foreign media, had his credentials revoked, and RAI sent him back to cover the Vatican.

And yet, even as the Palestinians sought to do damage control in the West by hiding the evidence, they glorified the incident among themselves. Halabaya's sermon should be understood as the triumphalist response to the Palestinian youth, standing at the window, holding aloft his bare hands, bloodied from his murder of the two hostages. When kindergarten graduation rolled around the following summer, it became a graduation ritual for five-year-olds to dip their hands in red paint and hold them aloft like the Palestinian lyncher.

FIGURE 25. Palestinian Kindergarten ceremony re-enacting the Ramallah lynching, 2001.

Meantime, in the West, journalists publicly maintained their Palestinian Media Protocol compliant, lethal journalism, and their blanket denial of Palestinian intimidation and incitement ("But anyway, I didn't say anything"). Indeed, Orme, then in charge of intimidation complaints from foreign journalists to the *Foreign Press Association* in Jerusalem, implausibly dismissed any participation of the PA in the intimidation despite his having been an eye-witness:

> "It is misleading to suggest that there is a PA policy of intimidation," Orme concludes, citing the "hundreds of complaints" his organization has received about Israeli government handling of the press.... In contrast, "only a handful" of journalists have filed complaints against the PA.... *There is no self-censorship* [of journalists covering the Palestinians]."[105]

... said the journalist who self-censored about Palestinian genocidal discourse.

Apparently, Orme has never heard (or if he has, never thought about, the implications) of Moynihan's law:

> The amount of violations of human rights [here journalists' rights] in a country is always an inverse function of the amount of complaints about human rights violations heard from there. The greater the number of complaints being aired, the better protected are human rights in that country.[106]

Indeed, Moynihan's law is nicely illustrated by the industry of complaints about Israeli intimidation of journalists, collected in the publications of the *Committee to Protect Journalists*. The extensively documented attacks on journalists by Palestinians that day make no appearance whatsoever: indeed, for October 12,

---

105 Judy Lash Balint, "Media Frightened into Self-Censorship," *WorldNetDaily*, May 3, 2001. For a good example of the discourse Orme promoted, see Brian Whitaker complain of Israeli and pro-Israel intimidation: "The First Casualty of War," *Guardian*, June 17, 2001. Orme told me himself he was in Ramallah the day of the lynch (email, November 22, 2014), but he wrote nothing about it. His next article, two days later: "Whose Holy Land? The Israeli Police Block Thousands of Muslims from Attending Prayer Services in Old City's Mosques," *New York Times*, October 14, 2000.

106 As Gil Troy points out, it was in the context of the assault on Zionism in the name of "human rights" by authoritarian regimes that Moynihan first developed this observation, *Moynihan's Moment: America's Fight Against Zionism as Racism* (New York: Oxford University Press, 2013), 133.

the day of the lynch, there are no entries, whereas jaw-broken Cristiano appears later as the object of Israeli harassment for losing his press pass.[107]

So Orme here has ignored Moynihan's law, flipped the narrative, and made Israel the aggressor, while insisting on the good faith of the PA. Less than a year later, the symbiotic relationship that Orme denied was on full display, when PA officials threatened the MSNM with mob violence if they did not take down footage of Palestinians celebrating 9–11 and substitute staged pictures of Arafat giving blood [to the pulverized victims].[108]

Journalists like Orme—I'd argue, the pack of journalists and NGO/UN workers, and diplomats who hang out together in the area around Sheikh Jarrah and the Colony Hotel—did not (and probably still do not) consider themselves compliant with Palestinian demands. To the contrary, they will "reject as utterly baseless the charge made by some that there is willful, systematic 'self-censorship' by the foreign press corps assigned to Israel and/or Palestine."[109] They were merely telling it like they saw it: The Israeli Goliath and the Palestinian David. And since their compliance is voluntary, they feel no stick, only carrots. "There was no violence directed at us by the Palestinians. On the contrary, they liked us and welcomed us. I feel safer with Palestinians than with Israelis," said one photographer to me in the office of the Dean of Communications at Boston University in 2014. "Of course, that's the case," I responded, to no avail, "you're doing what they want. Try reporting things they don't like and see how they treat you." Given this general state of denial and appeasement as a way of dealing with fear, it is not surprising that when Orme tackled the issue of incitement, he too got an A+ for his craven PMP compliance and remained in denial over a decade later.

Intimidation, Compliance, Omertà: The Magnet under the Surface

The issue of Palestinian intimidation of the media lies at the heart of the media failure, for it helps explain why hostility to Israelis/Jews is not solely, or even primarily, responsible for this pack of lethal journalists. Surely, in individual

---

107 "Attacks on the Press 2000: Israel and the Occupied Territories," *CPJ*, March 19, 2001. There is no comparable list for attacks by Palestinians, https://cpj.org/attacks96/countries/middleast/pnalinks.html.

108 See 63n47.

109 William Orme, email, November 22, 2014. On the events that produced that email exchange, see below.

cases, one can find a journalist with a particular animus against Israel, and one might even argue that these Judeophobes created a social environment that attracted journalists who enjoy the moral *Schadenfreude* of the Israeli-Goliath inversion. But the real problem that needs explanation is the broad consensus. One can easily imagine that this particular conflict would draw its share of advocates for all sides, and therefore, some of the reporting might reach a level of information failure in which journalists, even a whole news agency, failed to live up to their vocation as honest witnesses. But everyone? The *New York Times*, paper of record? The BBC, global leader in journalism? Reuters, AP, AFP, NPR, CBS, NBC, CNN? The giant news agencies? All adopting the inverted frame?

Alas, yes.

Something else must explain not the zealous lethal journalists like Janine di Giovanni, Robert Fisk, or Jon Snow,[110] but rather the broad-based silence, the lack of dissent, from the rest of the field. For, rather than provide a robust, "enriched" discussion of what's going on here, the legacy media have systematically cultivated a groupthink so powerful that a BBC journalist, chairing a panel of news commentators he has presumably chosen for their diversity of views, commented on negotiations between Israel and the PA: "This could be solved with an email. Everyone knows what the solution is: Land for peace."[111] He couldn't get it more wrong. But all his panelists nod in assent. One, Yasmin Alibhai Brown, even insists on including "democratically elected" Hamas in the negotiations, and none of the rest comments that this would make "land for peace" impossible.

Some argue ideology drives this, to which I respond, fine. I'll even grant you that 20 percent of the news media are so ideological that they systematically falsify the record, itself a scandalously high figure for a profession that specifically commits itself to reporting events, rather than propaganda. But how is it then, that few dissent, and that those who do, are the ones that get pushed aside?

I asked a European journalist who articulated this narrative if she knew of the work of Khaled abu Toameh—an extremely rare Palestinian Muslim who publishes criticism of his own people. "No," she replied, what paper does he write for? *Jerusalem Post*. "Oh I don't read right-wing papers like the that."[112]

---

110 Jon Snow, "The Children of Gaza," July 26, 2014, https://www.youtube.com/watch?v=ACgwr2Nj_GQ.

111 Gavin Esler, *Dateline London*, https://www.youtube.com/watch?v=09JCDrRYEQY.

112 On the work of abu Toameh, see Gatestone, https://www.gatestoneinstitute.org/author/Khaled+Abu+Toameh.

Such lack of curiosity may express itself in ideological terms, but it has other drivers.

The argument, however, that I find most persuasive in explaining the inverted consensus: *The MSNM narrative of the Israel-Goliath/Palestinian-David, is the way the filings line up, above the table, while credible threats to anyone who deviates, is the magnet of intimidation that lies beneath the table.*

The argument's main problem is that it is *ex silentio*, that is, it's based on the absence of evidence (what's under the table). Of course, the whole purpose of Omertà is to repress any evidence of its operation, including the threat of retaliation that enforces the silence. This is what gives Moynihan's law its bite. The story of human rights violations, which abound in the Arab world and certainly in territories ruled by Palestinian political groups, does not get out, not from Arab sources (what makes abu Toameh and Bassem Eid so rare), not from Western sources. There is a long history of the Palestinians at once killing some journalists and offering the rest protection, during the Lebanese civil war (1975–1982, 150,000 civilians killed). While the PLO terrorized enemy populations and designated enemies, journalists, grateful for the protection, complied with their demands.[113]

Without the occasional startling instance, it would be hard to identify the workings of a system of intimidation so successful, so pervasive, that the "vast majority" of journalists deny it even exists. And indeed, they can honestly claim they experience no intimidation, because they color inside the PMP's lines. No misbehavior, no retaliation. Journalist took the Palestinian side *so that they wouldn't have to deal with the punishments they silently feared.* In my opinion, the scandalously high index of MSNM compliance with PMP in the twenty-first century is the smoking gun, the hard evidence for the fear of defying the Palestinians, and only secondarily, in many cases as a fig leaf, does some dogged loyalty to the ideology of post-colonial *underdogma* play a role.[114]

---

113 Chafets, *Double Vision*, 50–96. Balint noted that Orme's denial of intimidation recalled that of "NBC editorialist John Chancellor, who observed at the height of the Lebanon War in 1982: 'There is no censorship in Beirut...' This despite the murder by the PLO of seven foreign journalists in West Beirut between 1976–1981, according to Edouard George, then senior editor of Beirut's French language daily *L'Orion du Jour*, and the departure from the city of several western journalists because of PLO threats." Balint, "Palestinian Harassment of Journalists."

114 Prell, *Underdogma*. For examples of AP reporting neither Hamas' war-time behavior, nor even their direct threats to AP about not complying, see Friedman, "What the Media Gets Wrong about Israel."

Omertà in Action: The Cannibal Strategy and Shati Refugee Shelling

To add to the dossier on Palestinian intimidation and the system of *Omertà* that it has successfully turned into a smooth compliance of journalists with the Palestinian lethal narrative, an incident occurred in the summer of 2014, during the IDF's "Operation Protective Edge." It competes with the Riccardo Cristiano incident of 2000 for the illumination is sheds on the phenomenon of intimidation of the media and the media's denial.

This was the third operation in Gaza in six years, and Hamas's strategy had developed in response to the MSNM reliably playing by their rules.[115] Whereas Palestinians had fired from behind their own civilians since 1948 in order to stay the IDF's hand, Hamas now made that not a tactic, but the main strategy: the value of Palestinian suffering, faithfully transmitted by the media in damaging Israel's image in the world had become the main goal, well worth the suffering inflicted on the Palestinian people.

By 2008/9, three years since Hamas "won" the elections in Gaza, and two since they drove out the PLO in bloody purges, Hamas and Islamic Jihad developed a cannibalistic variant of a particularly nasty PLO strategy in Lebanon in the 1970s. Then, they fired from enemy civilian areas to draw return fire onto their enemies; now, in the 2010s, they fired from their own civilian areas in the hope of drawing return fire and getting their own people killed. So careless did these rocketeers get, that some 20 percent of their rockets fell on their own territory, in some cases killing children. And yet, so valuable in the PR world were dead babies killed by rockets, that they did not hesitate to use children, killed by themselves to carry out their charade of victimhood and incite people to hate Israel.

---

115 Alan Dershowitz, "Hamas's Dead Baby Strategy," *Washington Times*, January 16, 2009; Landes, "Exposing Hamas's Cannibalistic Cognitive War Strategy," *PJ Media*, November 18, 2012.

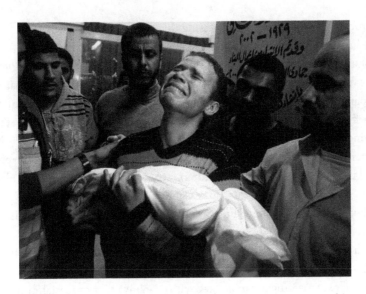

FIGURE 26. Jihad Masharawi with his infant, killed by Hamas ordnance, blamed on Israel by his BBC colleagues (November, 2012). See Isabel Kershner, "UN Ties Gaza Baby's Death to Palestinians," *New York Times*, March 11, 2013.

This terrible "dead baby strategy," however, could only work if the Western MSNM did their part and blamed Israel. Imagine the impact of the above picture were it to appear with an accurate caption at the time.[116]

Imagine if journalists were to ask Ismail Haniya and Hesham Kandil if they were aware that one of Hamas's many stray rockets had killed the child whose body they so tenderly kissed before the cameras? (Photo above p. 130) Imagine if the photographers had worked hard, against PMP, to catch pictures of jihadis firing rockets from the midst of their own people, and sending in clean-up crews to get rid of Palestinian shrapnel before bringing reporters to the sight of another Palestinian child "killed by the Israelis." Imagine political cartoonists depicting Haniya eating Palestinian babies and looking straight at you saying, "what's the matter, you never seen a politician kissing babies?" How long would Hamas continue to sacrifice its own people for its jihadi cogwar aims?

But that, alas, would be in an alternate universe.

The failure of the Western legacy media to probe these cases of Palestinian jihadis killing their own children came to a head in the 2014 case of the shelling of al-Shati refugee camp, right outside Shifa hospital, on the day of an Eid-al-Fitr truce ... the first time Gazan children thought it safe to play outside in weeks.

---

116 It was obvious in real time to pro-Israeli bloggers like Elder of Ziyon and IsraellyCool, and news watchdogs like CAMERA and Honest Reporting.

Two rockets landed that day "shattering the truce," one doing minimal damage to the hospital, the other falling amidst children playing, killing ten.

For a brief period, the news media covered the story in lurid detail. Pictures of the unfortunate children and their grieving parents filled the pages of newspapers and websites, along with expressions of shock and horror from major figures the world over. "It's worse than shooting fish in a barrel, it's like shooting sardines in a barrel," noted CNN's Karl Penhaul, eloquently.[117] NBC reporter Ayman Mohyeldin tweeted immediately: "Israeli drone struck refugee camp killing 10, including eight children." Reporters quoted locals who blamed Israel: "There were no militants, no resistance members, just children. . . . It was just after Ramadan, just when life was returning to normal. . . . The Israelis broke the cease-fire. These children were just trying to play."

Such a wanton act of cruelty shocked the world's conscience. Even if the Israeli perpetrators did not do it on purpose, the criminal negligence of aiming shells so close to a refugee camp, filled with so many children, certainly qualified as a war crime, if not a crime against humanity. Headlines from around the world resembled those from the Arab world:

ISRAELI AIRSTRIKE HITS COMPOUND OF MAIN HOSPITAL IN GAZA, CAUSING CASUALTIES, PALESTINIANS SAY (BBC);
ISRAEL'S CAMPAIGN TO SEND GAZA BACK TO THE STONE AGE, Daily Beast;
"EID OF BLOOD" AS ISRAELI MILITARY WARNS WORSE IS TO COME, Australian Broadcasting Co.;
8 PALESTINIAN CHILDREN AMONG 10 DEAD AS ISRAEL HITS GAZA REFUGEE CAMP, Al Ahram.[118]

Except it wasn't quite that. Witnesses, both locals and journalists quickly understood that the strike had come from Hamas, which immediately sent in people to clean up the evidence: "I saw the body of the rocket [and] I knew it was a local one," a family member told The Times. "Some people came and hid it on the spot—however, it was really hot."[119] Wall Street Journal reporter Tamer El-Ghobashy reported initially: "An outside wall of the campus of Gaza's

---

117 CNN International, May 29, 2014, 12:40.
118 Landes, "Media Coverage of Shati Refugee Camp Strike, July 28, 2014: A Survey," *Augean Stables*, October 3, 2018.
119 Abeer Ayyoub and Tom Coghlan, "'Misfired Hamas rockets' killed children in Gaza," (London) *Times*, March 26, 2015.

main hospital was hit by a strike. Low level damage suggests Hamas misfire."[120] By evening, an unofficial consensus had emerged among the foreign press on the scene that it was Hamas. Italian journalist Gabriel Barbati tweeted at 20:15 that night: "International journos say: feeling today's massacre in shaati beach playground #gaza was misfired rocket by Hamas or factions."[121] The IDF's spokesman's unit responded with unusual alacrity to the accusations: within an hour it produced diagrams from Iron Dome radar tracking to show that the two rockets that hit Israel were fired from Gaza at Israel but fell short; two others, fired from the same spot, hit Israel but caused no damage: rockets from the Palestinian "resistance."

For two days, the coverage continued to emphasize Palestinian suffering and at least imply Israeli guilt. When it became clear that the incident was not Israel's fault, the various media silently changed their reports (e.g., NBC),[122] dropped the topic, and went on to the next lethal narrative about the shelling of a UN School that killed 10. Although Israel claimed that Hamas was firing from its vicinity, the international community exploded with condemnations about the new outrage, and in so doing, dropped any mention of the 10 killed by Hamas two days earlier. Classic lethal journalism, only this time, things did not go exactly according to script.

Omertà and the Intimidation Controversy of Shati Refugee Bombing

By 2014, Hamas's strategy had become so heavy-handed that it provoked a crisis within some of the press covering the operation from inside Gaza. There, the journalist's job, as Hamas conceived it, was to operate as an arm of the "resistance":[123] to present the Palestinians as victims of Israeli aggression, to *not* report on the behavior of the jihadi rocketeers, to underplay Israeli efforts to spare civilians and jihadi efforts to endanger them,[124] to emphasize how the "vast majority" of Palestinian casualties were civilian when even the figures provided

---

120 El-Ghobashy tweet, https://www.jpost.com/HttpHandlers/ShowImage. ashx?ID=251336&Cap=true.

121 Barbati tweet, July 28, 2014, 8:25PM, https://twitter.com/gabrielebarbati/status/493824468540596227?ref_src=twsrc%5Etfw

122 Dell Cameron, "NBC News deletes journalist's claim of an Israeli airstrike on Gaza," *Daily Dot*, July 28, 2014.

123 "Hamas Interior Ministry to Social Media Activists," *MEMRI*, July 17, 2014.

124 Consider how few "investigative reports" have examined why Gaza has no bomb shelters; cf. Tobin, "Why Gaza Doesn't Have Bomb Shelters."

by Hamas's own "Health Services" suggested over half of the casualties were combatants (a remarkable figure in urban warfare).

Understandably, some journalists who thought their job was to report what was happening, even no matter whose narrative it supported, ran into trouble. Reports piled up of Hamas intimidation, arrests, detentions, of violent threats to those filming combatants, even threats delivered through social-media demanding the removal of offending tweets. An Indian crew stumbled onto a striking story when Hamas set up a rocket launcher right beneath their hotel window. They filmed it from the safety of their room, and then debated whether or not to publish the footage. Sreenivasan Jain reported on

> the fear which hobbles the reporting of such material: fear of reprisals from Hamas against us, asking "how long do we self-censor because of the fear of personal safety in return for not telling a story that exposes how those launching rockets are putting so many more lives at risk, while the rocket-makers themselves are at a safe distance?"[125]

All the elements that compliant, socialized journalists like Orme deny, all appear in this remarkable passage: hobbling fear, self-censorship in the face of threatened retaliation, the role of Hamas's strategy in contributing to Palestinian deaths.

Note well: this comes from a New Delhi crew, new to the region. Hence, although *a priori* favorable to the Palestinians, they hadn't yet been fully socialized to the "journalistic procedures for reporting from Palestine." They somehow thought that they should do their job as journalists despite the dangers, even if they did delay issuing their report until after they left Gaza. They apparently still believed that there were limits to how long journalists should self-censor—even as they enable militants to endanger civilian lives. A more socialized crew, say one of Jeremy Bowen's at the BBC, would have known better than to even film the operation outside their hotel window in the first place. And certainly not to go public with a story about how Palestinians intimidate journalists.[126]

This last point is especially important. By not crossing Hamas, the media not only failed to report on their destructive behavior, but also silenced voices of

---

125 Sreenivasan Jain, "Three Men, a Tent and Some Shrubs: The Backstory of Our Hamas Report," *NDTV*, August 7, 2014.
126 Games, "Compromised Coverage."

protest in Gaza. It was a rare Palestinian journalist who dared, like Mahmoud abu Rahma in the PA paper *Ma'an* in 2012, to denounce the "resistance groups."

> Many (Gazan) citizens also fell victim of the *continuous negligence of the resistance groups* who show little or no care for people's life and well-being, or, worse, fail to take responsibility for shocking acts by their members.[127]

He predictably paid for his insolence.[128]

Some Gazans told contacts outside Gaza:

> Hamas does not want the truth about Gaza to come out.... Hamas is a dictatorship that kills us. The Gazans you see praising Hamas on TV are either Hamas members or too afraid to speak against Hamas. Few foreign [Western] journalists were probably able to report what Gazans think of Hamas.[129]

Able? Or willing.

El-Ghobashy's post blaming Hamas for the strike on Shifa was quickly taken down, replaced with a tweet with the same picture captioned "Unclear what the origin of the projectile is." El-Ghobashy later claimed he deleted the tweet because it was "speculative" and that there was "no conspiracy," meaning that he did not do it under pressure.[130]

And yet, the next day, Gabriel Barbati, who had already tweeted the consensus among journos that it was Hamas that killed the kids, tweeted again:

> Out of #Gaza *far from* #Hamas *retaliation: misfired rocket killed children yday* [yesterday] in Shati. Witness [proof]: militants rushed and cleared debris." "@IDFSpokesperson said truth in

127 Mahmoud Abu Rahma, "The gap between resistance and governance," *Maan News*, January 5, 2012.

128 Talia Ralph, "Palestinian activist Mahmoud abu Rahma leaves the hospital after a stabbing attack," *Global Post*, January 18, 2012.

129 Mudar Zahran, "Gazans Speak Out: Hamas War Crimes," Gatestone, September 19, 2014. More recently, Aaron Boxerman, "'They hijacked Gaza': Palestinians hold rare online events critical of Hamas," *Times of Israel*, February 7, 2022.

130 Brendan Bordelon, "Hamas Concealing their Role in Innocent Gaza Deaths by Threatening, Expelling Reporters," *Daily Caller*, July 31, 2014.

communique released yesterday about Shati camp massacre. *It was not #Israel behind it.*"[131]

It's all here: awareness of whose fault, failure to report while within Gaza and fearing "Hamas retaliation," clean-up crews hiding the evidence that are so familiar to the journalists that their presence constitutes proof of yet another case of Hamas inflicted, Hamas covered-up, Palestinian deaths.

To what lengths will Hamas go to protect its position? The very night of this terrible incident at Shati Refugee camp, there were reports of a protest in nearby Gaza City (not far from Shati). Hamas allegedly mowed down over twenty Palestinian protesters in the street. Reports from Palestinian witnesses reached Israeli reporters, and then some "right-wing" reporters in the US picked up the story that the mainstream press did not cover.[132] The story of Hamas killing Gazans who protest Hamas killing Gazans is an ongoing story, and available to those who wish to know.[133]

Indeed, so widespread did the complaints become during Operation Protective Edge (July/August 2014) that the Foreign Press Association (FPA), long a bastion of Orme's meme "we get more complaints about Israeli intimidation than Palestinian," issued a remarkable protest in the wake of the Shati scandal:

> The FPA protests in the strongest terms the blatant, incessant, forceful and unorthodox methods employed by the Hamas authorities and their representatives against visiting international journalists in Gaza over the past month. The international media are not advocacy organizations and cannot be prevented from reporting by means of threats or pressure, thereby denying their readers and viewers an objective picture from the ground. In several cases, foreign reporters working in Gaza have been harassed, threatened or questioned over stories or information they have reported through their news media or by means of social media. We are also aware that Hamas is trying to put

---

131 Gabriele Barbati, tweet, July 29, 2014, https://twitter.com/gabrielebarbati/status/494131918732926976.

132 "Palestinians demonstrated against Hamas and were executed [Hebrew]," *Channel 10*, July 29, 2014; Joel Pollak, "Hamas Executed 20 Palestinian Anti-War Protestors in Gaza," *Breitbart*, July 29, 2014.

133 Entsar Abu Jahal, "Hamas turns violent on peaceful protesters in Gaza," *Al Monitor*, March 22, 2019.

in place a "vetting" procedure that would, in effect, allow for the blacklisting of specific journalists. Such a procedure is vehemently opposed by the FPA.[134]

The statement defied the Palestinian Media Protocols. And the "Zionist" press lit up with accounts of both the incidents of intimidation, and the cannibalistic strategy that they so shockingly revealed.[135]

The *New York Times* senior correspondent Jodi Rudoren, who was not in Gaza up to that pont, stepped into the fray to defend the PMP narrative: "Every reporter I've met who was in Gaza during war says this Israeli/now FPA narrative of Hamas harassment is nonsense.[136] This tweet offers a full panoply of denial in compliance with the PMP, as eloquent as Barbati's, but in its dishonesty. In the name of the broad consensus of the journalists who were in Gaza, she dismisses the FPA "narrative" as merely a replication of the Israeli narrative, which, according to Rudoren, is "nonsense." Instead, she gives us the Palestinian, also lethal journalist's, narrative that there is no intimidation . . . in other words, the real nonsense. Nor was Rudoren alone in circling the wagons. CNN International Chief Tony Maddox formally stated: "We have had no intimidation from Hamas and received no threats regarding our reporting."[137] Of course, that was only another way of saying, "We are PMP Compliant.

Challenged to defend her statement in the face of so many testimonies to intimidation, Rudoren clarified her hostility by alluding to the FPA statement as "dangerous":

> I found the wording of the statement overly broad [unlike her comment about "nonsense"], and, *especially given the narrative playing out in some social media circles regarding foreign correspondents being taken in by the Hamas narrative and not reporting on the war fully or fairly,* I was concerned that it

---

134　Foreign Press Association Statement, August 11, 2014, http://www.fpa.org.il/?categoryId=90285.

135　"Top Five Media Fails of the Gaza War," *HonestReporting*, August 28, 2014; Richard Behar, "The Media Intifada: Bad Math, Ugly Truths about *NY Times* in Israel-Hamas War," *Forbes*, Aug. 21, 2014.

136　Jodi Rudoren tweet, August 11, 2014, https://twitter.com/rudoren/status/498853892113719300.

137　Steven Emerson, "Who Watches the Watchers?" *Jerusalem Post*, August 16, 2014.

undermined what I consider to have been brave and excellent work by very talented people.[138]

In other words, to acknowledge the role of Hamas intimidation in the news we get would lend credibility to the accusation (the "narrative playing out in certain [Zionist] social media) that the legacy media were playing according to the "Hamas narrative."

Rudoren's response is doubly revealing. On the one hand, we find a priority given to a political agenda (lest the Israelis be right and the journalists look bad), which resembles the decision of France1's Jean-Claude Dassier, to play down the violence of the French Riots of 2005, lest they strengthen the French "right."[139] On the other, her remarks about the "brave" work her colleagues had done alludes to the issue at hand: in claiming the absence of intimidation she insisted that their (narrative) work was "excellent" (presumably, accurate), done under dangerous conditions. Jodi Rudoren, member of the guild of journalists, PMP compliant, responded as her fellow guild members did for Enderlin in 2007.[140] "Outsiders just can't understand how hard it is for us journalists in the field."

Now Jodi Rudoren was not a hack, shilling for the Palestinian "victims"—at least she didn't consider herself one. And as she (I think honestly) claims, she had felt no direct threats from Palestinians, despite, on occasion writing reports that defied their protocols and getting slapped on the wrist by her own employers.[141] And despite her intervention here in full support of the Palestinian narrative—"Intimidated? Us?"—she is hardly a lethal journalist of the more enthusiastic persuasion.

So, what accounts best for her astonishing behavior? Martin Himmel sheds light on the problem while recounting on camera that Hamas men broke into the AP office in Gaza and threatened the bureau for taking photos of subjects they forbade, and AP not only complied, but did not report the incident: "So not only does Hamas know it can intimidate reporters into reporting what

---

138 Matthew Kalman, "Foreign Press Divided over Hamas Harassment," *Haaretz*, August 13, 2014.

139 See above, 150n72.

140 See 6n11.

141 Rudoren posted on Facebook comments about Palestinians having different attitudes towards life and death than Israelis and Westerners. Her editors shut her down. Meenal Vamburkar, "NY Times Jerusalem Bureau Chief Gets Social Media Oversight after Controversial Remarks," *Mediaite*, November 29, 2012.

they want, it knows they will not report their own intimidation."[142] In solidarity with her fellow, compliant, intimidated, journalists who dared not let their readers know how cowardly they were, Rudoren came out in favor of denying intimidation. This analysis explains why journalists get quite passionate about defending their colleagues: were the public to know how much journalists self-censor to appease Palestinian threats, journalists would lose their reputations for courage and accuracy.

I had my own experience with the touchiness of journalists when it came to matters of intellectual integrity in the face of intimidation. I had written Mark Seager in 2005 about his experience at Ramallah and asked if he might like to add something to the *Second Draft*, a website I was about to launch, on the way intimidation influences coverage of the conflict.[143] He responded:

> I am afraid I will have to decline your request to supply images. I am not comfortable with the context in which they may be used. I understand the Second Draft ethos [i.e., professional journalism], but I cannot advocate in any way to your position regarding media manipulation in the Israeli-Palestinian conflict with a bias towards the Palestinian side. [i.e., I don't/won't support your narrative no matter how accurate or appropriate.]
>
> There are also concerns over my safety. During the furor of that infamous day in Ramallah the piece which I did for the Sunday Telegraph was as you can imagine taken out of context and misrepresented [i.e., the pro-Israeli side used it]. I was still working in the West Bank at the time and it was an uncomfortable situation to be in. That article caused me a great deal of trouble. I would prefer not to get involved in anything regarding the Ramallah lynchings or the death of Muhammad Al-Durra.

I pointed out the contradiction between his "refusal to advocate" [i.e. to affirm that the media are intimidated into taking the Palestinian side], and his "remarks about fear for my own safety," and asked whether he might not "owe it to those who view your news (photojournalism) to let them know what's going on?" He responded evasively, and when I pressed the point, he let me have it between

---

142 Martin Himmel, *Eyeless in Gaza*, 27:35. See also Matti Friedman on this incident, "What the Media Gets Wrong About Israel."

143 *The Second Draft*, launched November 2005, http://www.seconddraft.org. On Seager's experience at Ramallah, see above, 12n36; 324–36.

the eyes: "Listen, you're a fucking nobody who makes accusations based on armchair observations. Now fuck off and leave me alone."[144]

When the chips are down, the magnet under the table, I'd argue, is not zealous advocacy and certainly not "speaking truth to power," but pusillanimous compliance with the demands of both the guild and the Palestinians, all of whose reputations—their "face"—are at stake. As one of the more honest reporters on this subject commented about his not reporting on information that put Hamas in a bad light until he had left Gaza: "No injury, no danger to my life, no threat. In the end of the day, we are men before being reporters."[145] And despite admitting to complying with intimidation, he was braver than most of his colleagues, who would not even discuss this intimidation once out of Hamas's reach (in order to be able to go back in[146]). For most, it's "fuck off you nobody, how dare you question our professional integrity? We're telling you there's no intimidation. If anyone is bullying journalists, it's the Zionist watchdogs."[147] No wonder, as the Israelis, reputation in ruin, left Gaza in ruin, that an intact Hamas leadership could crow with delight: "The media analysis and the men of the [Palestinian] media everywhere constituted the river from which the global media quenched its thirst for information about what was happening on the ground."[148]

Own-Goal Journalism: The Hidden Costs of Lethal Journalism Compliant with PMP

While examples of the damage done by this kind of journalism fill this book, it is worth remarking generally here on the disastrous cost for the societies that these lethal journalists misinform. The journalists who comply with PMP apparently do not think much about the price, beyond the damage it does to

---

144 Email. Note the reference to the armchair, namely those who don't know just how dangerous it is on the ground—i.e., who think journalists should report the intimidation. Enderlin made the same complaint. For the similar use of foul language in response to accusations of cowardice from *New York Times* editor Dean Baquet, see above, 91–93.

145 Gabriele Barbati, *Eyeless in Gaza*, 26:40. In a meeting with Barbati, he expressed the common theme of not wanting to say anything that might support the "Israeli Narrative." See Gabriele Barbati, *Trappola Gaza. Nel fuoco incrociato tra Israele e Palestina* (Informant-Ebook, 2014), Kindle location 862, where he expresses similar reservations.

146 Lahav Harkov, "Reporter: Gazans only want us to show damage, not shooting," *Jerusalem Post*, August 8, 2014.

147 Hugh Naylor tweet, July 27, 2014, https://twitter.com/jondonnisonbbc/status/493431314637262848/.

148 "Hamas Leader Ismail Haniya: Our Media Was the River from Which Global Media Drank Information," *MEMRI*, clip no. 4476, August 29, 2014.

Israel and the safety it brings them. After all, Israelis are the obvious target of these lethal narratives, and many journalists, quietly or not, feel that, as the Goliath occupier, Israel deserves it. Thus, they engage with some abandon in a journalism where they purvey war propaganda of one side as news. And, like the goat in the fable, not looking farther than their noses, they miss the bigger picture: their journalism does not benefit the innocent Palestinians who want peace, nor those well-meaning outsiders who wish to work for peace,[149] but the Palestinian belligerents who want war, namely Caliphators of the jihadi persuasion.

Many Western journalists feel a great deal of solidarity with the Palestinians. They call Palestinian journalism, with its vicious accusations, "the weapons of the weak."[150] Some, if not many, feel it is perfectly legitimate to help the weak side. If, in the Middle East, "one picture can be worth a thousand weapons," then the journalists can "level the playing field" in a situation where Israel has all the military advantages by giving the Palestinians cogwar victories with their pictures of Israeli aggression.[151] After all, these journalists reason, the Palestinians are fighting for their self-determination, their freedom.[152] It is as if the journalists reason: "They *deserve* our support, and given how nice they are to us, they're grateful for the support we give them." Commenting on the wave of lethal journalism around the Jenin Massacre, Israeli journalist Alon Ben Meir noted: "A large part of the European media regards itself as not just reporters but as ideological crusaders. They are in the business of journalism not just for the business. They want to do good in the world. They have agendas."[153] And they somehow think reporting Palestinian war propaganda as news does good in the world.

---

149 "Now if I tell Palestinians from Nablus, Jenin, Hebron to talk of rehabilitation with Israelis, I fear they will kill me as a collaborator," Claudette Habesch, "Caritas aid workers witness the horror of Jenin," April 29, 2002, https://reliefweb.int/report/israel/caritas-aid-workers-witness-horror-jenin. This rejection of any dialogue with Israel has become a matter of policy among BDS advocates who consider any kind of "normalization" anathema.

150 The expression is common. See Denis Jeambar's use of the expression in his discussion of Talal abu Rahma's rushes: "young Palestinians using the television as a means of communication—it's the weapon of the weak." Reference 38n124.

151 One of the most powerful roles the news media can play in such conflicts is when they become "equalizers" by allowing the weaker party to enlist the support of third parties," wrote Gadi Wolfsfeld, apparently approvingly: "Role of the Media in the Second Intifada," *Palestine-Israel Journal*, 10:2 (2003).

152 See exchange between CAMERA and Reuters over the latter's describing Palestinian goals as a state in Gaza and West Bank, therefore justifying remarks like "Israelis embittered by a Palestinian uprising for statehood." Ricki Hollander, "Reuters: News Agency or Political Advocacy Group?" *CAMERA*, September 3, 2003.

153 Quoted by Martin Sieff, "Why Europeans bought the Jenin myth," *UPI*, May 21, 2002.

The sad and somewhat pathetic dimension to all this: it is based on a systematic misreading of the situation that endangers the very democratic societies to which these journalists report; and it hurts the chances for a better future for the country they hope to help liberate. Those most endangered by this footage (aside from the immediate victims among peaceable Muslims), are those very "readers and viewers" to which professional journalists are ethically bound to bear honest witness. The journalists think they stand with the sympathetic freedom fighters that they present favorably to their audiences. But what if the Palestinians, the "secular" PLO, the religious fanatics, the Palestinian NGO spokespeople, are Caliphators fighting not for freedom, but for dominion, for the destruction of Israel and the return of whatever Jews survive that process, to their subject status as dhimmis?

In that case, the Palestinian "resistance" our information elites heavily favor, comes from the "local" branch of the global jihadi movement that seeks dominion over *kuffār* in all of Dar al Harb. So, when Palestinians rejoiced at 9–11, they showed their allegiance to Bin Laden's Global Jihad, just as he had shown solidarity with them when he put Al Durah footage at the heart of his recruitment video. Western journalists who subsumed that hatred of America into their own anti-Americanism and Westsplained the attack as payback for the US's support of Israel, did not have an inkling of the hatred it expressed for *kuffār*, including the Europeans, the journalists, the progressives, and other queer products of a "free" society.[154] As a result of this, without knowing it, the Western media, in compliance with Palestinian demands (they're a proud people, you know), were actually spreading jihadi war propaganda that targeted them as well as Israel.

The jihadis are fully aware of this battlefield. Indeed, far more than the journalists they exploit, they appreciate how valuable media cooperation is to their struggle. In October 2005, Al Qaeda's number 2, Ayman al Zawahiri wrote to an Iraqi operative: "I say to you that we are in a battle, and that more than half of this battle is taking place in the battlefield of the media. And that we are in a media battle in a race for the hearts and minds of our *Umma*."[155] Here Zawahiri focuses on the jihadi's struggle to win over the *Umma* especially in the democratic diaspora. Imagine how much more powerful their case is, when the infidel news media confirm their main argument: The West victimizes Muslims mercilessly.

---

154 See Bernard Goldberg quote, 324n97.

155 Letter from al-Zawahiri to al-Zarqawi, Office of the Director of National Intelligence, October 11, 2005, cited in Louise Richardson, *What Terrorists Want: Understanding the Enemy, Containing the Threat* (New York: Random House, 2007), 218.

Thus, Western media working on the conflict between the river and the sea, not only fed their infidel audiences Palestinian war propaganda, but simultaneously funneled enemy Caliphator war propaganda aimed at Muslims into their own (Western) public sphere *as news*. The Western audience for this news, immensely reluctant to believe that their journalists were collectively bearing false witness on behalf of their mortal enemies, found themselves wildly disoriented, both empirically and morally. Their enemies, on the contrary, the global jihadis, found themselves greatly empowered.

No theater of the Caliphators' cognitive war strategy has had such impressive success. No sections of the democratic West's crucial ranks of information professionals have failed their readers and viewers more catastrophically. Every episode of lethal journalism has strengthened the forces of Global Jihad, giving their recruiters icons of hatred to fuel the rage. In 2002, Hady Amr, now Deputy Assistant Secretary of State for Israel-Palestine in the Biden administration, wrote:

> a very large proportion of the more than 150 million children and youth in the Arab World now have televisions, and they will never, never forget what the Israeli people, the Israeli military and Israeli democracy have done to Palestinian children. And there will be thousands who will seek to avenge these brutal murders of innocents.[156]

And many of these Arabs saw not what the Western journalists thought they were reporting—the Palestinian freedom-fighters suffering at the hands of Israeli colonialists—but rather innocent Muslims being slaughtered by infidels, confirming the core of the jihadi myth: Islam is under attack from evil, bloodthirsty infidels.

In prisons, in slums, in "zones urbaines sensibles," jihadis report how TV images of Muslims suffering at the hands of the infidel had awakened that combination of feeling that Islam was under attack and rage against the attackers that makes recruiting for jihad so effective.[157] A large body of Muslims in the

---

156 Hady Amr, "Outside View: The Middle East, reversed," *UPI*, July 27, 2002.

157 John Rosenthal, "The French Path to Jihad," *Hoover Institute*, October 2006; Farhad Khrosrokhavar, *Quand Al-Qäida parle: Témoignages derrière les barreaux* (Paris: Grasset, 2005); Patrick Sookhdeo, "Television creates terrorists," *The Spectator*, May 31, 2003. For the jihadi theme of Islam attacked by murderous enemies, see David Cook, *Understanding Jihad* (University of California Press, 2005), 136–39.

diaspora, "alienated and alone, bonded over a feeling of Muslim victimhood as observed on television and in pictures of wars involving Muslims."[158]

> Identification with the traumas of others and secondary traumatization occurring by "witnessing" over the internet or television, vivid images of injustices enacted on others with whom one identifies as fictive kin (i.e. the brotherhood of Muslims) may also resonate with individual feelings of being disaffected.[159]

And the most common, most graphic, and most intense video news about Muslim victims came from lethal journalists covering what they so quaintly call "the Palestinian-Israeli conflict."

And when one views the compliant behavior of the lethal, own-goal war journalists, not from their self-serving, self-image of brave warriors fighting for the underdog, speaking truth to Israeli power, but rather from the perspective of the jihadis, there's only one word that describes their behavior: *dhimmi*. They fulfill the three basic tasks of *dhimmi* leaders: they protect Muslims from insult and offense; they keep their own populations subservient; and they attack those whom triumphalist Muslims consider enemies. So, while from a Western point of view, these compliant, lethal journalists are *own-goal* war journalists doing damage to "our side," from a jihadi view, they are extremely useful *dhimmi* journalists.

---

158 Marc Sageman, *Understanding Terror Networks* (Philadelphia: Penn Press, 2005), chapter 3.
159 Anne Speckhard, "Understanding Suicide Terrorism: Countering Human Bombs and Their Senders" in *Topics in Terrorism*, vol. 1, ed. J. Purcell & J. Weintraub (Washington, DC: Atlantic Council Publication, 2005).

10

Anti-Zionist Jews: The Pathologies of Self-Criticism

Have ever before
lambs denounced lambs who refuse
to lie with lions?

An antisemite is one who takes seriously a tenth of the
jokes Jews tell about themselves.
An antizionist is one who takes seriously a tenth of the
criticism Jews tell about Israel.[1]

This is the hardest chapter to write. Like the others, it deserves an entire book of analysis and backstory. But any civic warrior trying to decipher this perilous age needs to have at least a grasp of the phenomenon, namely how a particular style of hyper-self-criticism among Jews, led the Gentiles who took them seriously, into their suicidal behavior. It is painful/embarrassing both for Jews and Gentiles, since so much of the pathology involved touches on both Jewish and Gentile vanities. Alas, the core of self-destructive Jewish self-criticism, and its success in seducing a generation of Gentiles, have more to do with the banal and petty among the seven deadly sins—envy and pride—than the grand and dramatic emotions to which the actors aspire.

The basic problem before us, then, concerns the phenomenon of anti-Zionist Jews in the twenty-first century, a period when virulent antisemitic attitudes are moving into the mainstream of Western cultures from extremes on both left and right. How does one explain the behavior of Jews—many, well intentioned, deeply passionate Jews, committed to "peace and social justice"—who join in with the deadly enemies of their own people, who debase Israel with comparisons to the Nazis and to Apartheid South Africa, who readily embrace

---

1   Landes, "An Anti-Zionist is Someone Who Takes Seriously a Tenth of What Hyper-Self-Critical Israelis Say About Themselves," *Augean Stables*, August 19, 2007.

and circulate lethal narratives about Israel, and resist every admonitory caution that this may be untrue, enemy propaganda? How to explain how they can ally themselves in the "fight for social justice" with people who embrace Nazi-like, racist, genocidal attitudes towards Jews? And how does one explain the audience for their discourse, that consistently funnels poisonous anti-Zionist jihadi war propaganda into their own free, infidel, societies?

One cannot equate anti-Zionist Jews from the first generations of modern Zionism, like Buber and Magnes, before the Holocaust, with anti-Zionist Jews afterwards. These early opponents of Zionism, despite knowledge of how perilous existence was for Jews in the premodern diaspora (i.e. under the rule of supersessionist Christians and Muslims), did not realize how terrifying diaspora conditions could become in modern, presumably post-supersessionist, democratic states. One can forgive their combination of naïve hope (with the modern world, Jews don't need their own state) and timidity (trying to develop a state will be seen by the gentiles, even secular ones, as a hostile act).[2]

The Holocaust changed all that. After the hi-tech extermination of Jews, led by Germany and extensively supported in a wave of ecumenical Jew-hatred in allegedly modern Europe, it was hard for any serious Jews to argue there should be no national refuge for their people. Granted there were anti-Zionist Jews in the period after the Holocaust, even some willing to compare Israel to Nazis. But they were generally marginalized and treated with the incredulity people reserved for those who considered the *Protocols of the Elders of Zion* a genuine document. As Jean Améry said in 1973: "Anyone who questions Israel's right to exist is either too stupid to understand that he is contributing to or is intentionally promoting an über-Auschwitz."[3] Not a great choice: stupid or sadistic.

In the twenty-first century, however, not only have the *Protocols* made a come-back, both as analogs and as revalorized text, but in an age when the current open enemies of Israel have fully embraced eliminationist antisemitism and added new elements of their own, we have anti-Zionist Jews who glorify the diaspora, openly compare Israel to the most morally depraved actors in history, and join in solidarity with the very enemies who so admire Nazis.[4] Thus, in the twenty-first century, we have an array of Jews, some very prominent, some

---

2   For some of the more extreme cases, see Phyllis Chesler, "Dancing with death: The Intellectual opposition to Zionism," *Arutz7*, December 28, 2017.

3   Jean Améry, "Jews, Leftists, Jewish Leftists: The Changing Contours of a Political Problem," in *Essays on Anti-semitism, Anti-Zionism and the Left*, ed. Marlene Gallner (Bloomington, IN: University of Indiana Press, 2021), 49.

4   David Collier, *Antisemitism in Palestine Live*, Parts I and II (2018), cited here: https://david-collier.com/exclusive-corbyn-antisemitism/.

previously unidentified as Jews, who openly, aggressively compare Israel to the Nazis, who ally with their deadliest enemies to isolate Israel and render it a pariah-state, who, in the name of Jewish values (*tikkun olam*), beat their drums of peace together with others who beat drums of war against their people. And behind these extreme cases, we find a whole array of more moderate, "liberal," Jews, who either moderately repeat the libels of Israel's enemies (not Hitler, but Goliath), or can't find the inner resources to oppose those who do.

The crucial matter, however, concerns not who and why these "Jews against themselves" do what they do, but why they have such a large and eager audience for their self-laceration. Therein lies the core of the disastrous stupidities the West has performed in the face of a medieval apocalyptic movement bent on world conquest, that this book has attempted to chronicle and understand.

Self-Criticism and Jews

The story has to begin with what one might call *the* fundamental trait of Jewish culture, both religious and secular—the active embrace of (self-)criticism. It begins in the beginning. No myths in world literature contain so many details unflattering to the very people telling the tale and the heroes whose careers they recount, as does the Bible.[5] In addition to the narratives, the commandments demand a high level of mutual rebuke among all members of the community. In a key passage later taken up by Christianity, the command to love your neighbor is intimately bound to the capacity of both self and other to give and take rebuke. "Thou shalt not hate thy brother in thy heart; thou shalt surely rebuke thy neighbor, and not bear sin because of him. Thou shalt not take vengeance, nor bear grudges against the children of thy people, but thou shalt love thy neighbor as thyself. (Lev 17–18)." This culture of rebuke and dispute permeates prophetic discourse: the harshest public rebuke of the abusive powerful in world literature.[6] Hence, the Jews canonized what others silence: we read the narrative of the shepherd-prophet, Amos, not that of the royal high Priest, Amatzia who believed that the land could not bear the prophet's words (*Amos*, 7:12).

This culture of (self-)rebuke and confrontation continues to define Israelite monotheism in its subsequent Judaic avatars. The post-Destruction (70CE) Mishnah (ca. 200) defines a "lover of Torah'" with an expression possibly unprecedented in the literature of admired traits: a "lover of rebuke" (*Ethics of*

---

5   See 237f.
6   Abraham Heschel, *The Prophets* (New York: Farrar Straus, 1955), chapter 9.

the Fathers, 6:6); and the Talmud (ca. 400–700) is a magnum opus of largely unresolved disputes, including discussions of why the Temple was destroyed, all of them blaming the Jews, even specifically, the rabbis for the catastrophe (Gittin, 55b-56a). This criticism of self and others, this embrace of imperfection as an inescapable human condition, sets Jewish approaches to sacred scripture apart from many other religious and mythical traditions which tend to present heroes as models for emulation.[7] Biblical narratives, however, are not meant for passive mimetic readers, but for autonomous and judging moral agents, who identify at least some of the behavior of the forefathers as case studies of error. For example, unlike every one of the Patriarchs and Matriarchs, most Jews consider playing favorites among their children as very wrong. Most readers of the story of Pharaoh and Abraham discussing Sarah his sister/wife (Genesis, 12:18–19), don't realize that not only is it the first rebuke one human delivers to another in the biblical narrative, but it's a public rebuke by the Pharaoh of the founding Patriarch, a criticism of "us" (who wrote the text) not "them."

This culture of self-criticism lies at the heart of both modernity and postmodernity, and we who are raised in those cultures tend to take high levels of self-criticism for granted. In doing so, we lose touch with the onēidophobia, the limbic captivity of those who will do nearly anything to save face. For self-criticism stands in polar opposition to key elements of tribalism, where "my side right or wrong" plays a central role in creating and sustaining solidarity, asabiyya.[8] Max Weber, however, identified self-criticism as a unique quality of Judaism that enabled its survival from the catastrophes of the ancient world. Whereas other peoples, when conquered by the libido-dominandi-driven empires of the ancient world—Babylonian, Persian, Greek, Roman—viewed their defeat as a sign their gods were weak and ended up assimilating into their conqueror's world, Jews viewed their defeat as a sign their God was punishing them, that it was their fault.[9] "Because of our sins, we are in exile"—so reads the holiday

---

7 E.g., the divinity of Jesus in Christianity. For contemporary defenses of the principle that Muhammad was a perfect and infallible human being, see: Shahih al Islam, "Prophet Muhammad: The Perfect Role Model," Spiritual Reflections, August 24, 2014; and "Muhammad Alibe and Abdul Amir, "The Infallibility of the Prophet Muhammad PBUH as a Human Being (A Study of His Ijtihad)," Journal Adabiyah, 19:2 (2019).

8 The case of al Durah offers a fine example of the contrast. Someone even as knowledgeable as James Fallows cannot believe it's a fake because surely someone among the Palestinians would have spoken up. Everyone kept silent? Ridiculous. Has to be conspiracy theory. Much emphasis was placed on the inconceivability that doctors at the hospital would lie (see above, on the Jenin hospital chief's systematic lying, see 105n40.

9 Max Weber, Ancient Judaism (New York: Free Press, 1952), chapter 14.

standing prayer for the additional service.[10] This interpretation of political failure as a divine rebuke and a call to repentance at once set Jews aside from their neighbors (including their conquerors), all of whom responded to failure by abandoning their "loser" gods, all of whom, over the centuries, disappeared.

For some, like the secular Israeli author Noah Harari, this hyper self-criticism is a sign of an infantile egocentrism:

> [The Jew] is convinced that everything happens because of him. Most people grow out of this infantile delusion. Monotheists hold on to it till the day they die. Like a child thinking that his parents are fighting because of him, the monotheist is convinced that the Persians are fighting the Babylonians because of him.[11]

This, he contrasts with the "far more accurate perceptions of history" of other cultures, most notably the Greeks and Chinese who "developed sophisticated theories of history which are very similar to our own modern views." But, he then laments, when it came to a showdown between the two views of history [in late antiquity], "the Bible won by a knockout. . . . No matter how mistaken the biblical world view was, it provided a better basis for large-scale human cooperation."

What's lacking in this analysis is a recognition of both the value and difficulty of self-criticism. In fact, the ancient Jewish approach to catastrophe was the opposite of the self-inflation so often attendant on ego-centric "infantile narcissism." The "normal" (i.e. near universal) narcissism blames others for failure (including one's own gods who were clearly weaker than the gods of the conquerors). For the Jews to take defeat as a divine rebuke of themselves was a collective act of immense psychological difficulty and benefit, something unimaginable to anyone who has not loosened the grip of limbic captivity.[12]

At the same time, Harari, who considers himself entirely free of such limbic influences, illustrates the very issue he ignores. As a secular Israeli Jew, he is consummately critical and self-effacing of his own hopelessly parochial tradition:

10 Musaph Amidah prayer for the holidays, https://www.sefaria.org/Siddur_Ashkenaz%2C_Festivals%2C_Shalosh_Regalim%2C_Mussaf%2C_Sanctity_of_the_Day.10?lang=en&with h=all&lang2=en.

11 Harari, Homo Deus, 355.

12 Nick Cohen, You Can't Read This Book: Censorship in an Age of Freedom (London, Fourth Estate, 2012), chapter 5.

> Judaism, for example, argued that the supreme power of the universe has interests and biases, yet His chief interest is in the tiny Jewish nation and in the obscure land of Israel. Judaism had little to offer other nations, and throughout most of its existence it has not been a missionary religion. This stage can be called the stage of "local monotheism." The big breakthrough came with Christianity.[13]

No braggart and cultural self-promoter, he. Not even an advocate of "dignity-of-difference."[14] On the contrary, he has apparently internalized the "higher supersessionism": Judaism has no significant role in the "history of humankind," whereas the universalist Christian missionizers do. As if preaching conversion were the only way to offer others something valuable.[15] As if the biblical narratives (narratives being the key to the cognitive revolution that created *homo sapiens* according to him), were not an extraordinary gift of the Jews to mankind. And so, he can relegate Judaism to the now surpassed "stage of local monotheism."

And yet the oft-unacknowledged Jewish talent for this (self-)criticism, may well explain why Jews do so well under the conditions of modernity, and why so many systems of thought that depend on self-criticism, empathy and self-abnegation arise from Jews and in secular Jewish circles (Marxist historiography, Freudian psychology, Boasian anthropology, Frankfurt School critical theory). Overall, this capacity for criticism, for a culture of public dispute in which people can vigorously disagree without violence, in which concerns for truth and accuracy and understanding can sometimes override the ego's demands to appear right, especially those egos who hold power, have made Jews highly successful in the modern world, especially where such issues are vital to success: science, academia, law, journalism, medicine, accounting, entrepreneurship, therapy, history, and so on.[16]

Freud, for example, considered psychoanalysis the third of a series of massive blows to human narcissism: Copernicus (earth not the center of universe); Darwin (man descended from apes); and psychoanalysis (man scarcely aware of what drives his behavior).[17] In Freud's psychology one renounced instinctual drives through self-examination and took pleasure in the renunciation. "The

---

13 Yuval Noah Harari, *Sapiens: A Brief History of Mankind* (New York: Harpers, 2015), 217.

14 Sacks, *The Dignity of Difference*.

15 See below on Harold Fasching.

16 Yuri Slezkine, *The Jewish Century* (Princeton: Princeton University Press, 2014).

17 Discussed by Yosef Yerushalmi, *Freud's Moses: Judaism Terminable and Interminable* (New Haven: Yale University Press, 1991), 112n10.

ego opposes the other faculties by observation, criticism, and prohibition ... brings besides the inevitable pain, a gain in pleasure to the Ego—as it were, a substitutive satisfaction. The Ego feels uplifted; it is proud of the renunciation as of a valuable achievement."[18] *His* ego, maybe. Jews were so numerous among his followers in this exercise in ferocious, ego-bruising, self-analysis, that Freud worried people would think psychoanalysis a Jewish science.[19]

The Temptations of Self-Criticism

Most Jews take this (self-)criticism for granted: they take hearing and offering criticism and advice to others for their improvement, as a natural condition of social exchange. They readily interrupt, disagree, contradict, correct, point out difficult realities. As the *bon mot* has it: no Jew can sincerely convert to Christianity because no Jew can ever be persuaded another Jew could be God. Jews use self-deprecating humor to puncture the pretensions of egotists, including themselves. Done well, it can win the affection of others even as it reduces everyone's self-importance. But tell a Jew that Jews are highly self-critical and you'll get the answer, "No we're not!" What's meant is "not critical enough [for me]."

At the same time, Jews understand instinctively, that criticizing others doesn't go over nearly so well with Gentiles. Humor may help the medicine go down, but too much grates, and "too much" comes quickly. By contrast, *self*-effacing, *self*-critical remarks about *Jews*, goes down very well, even in large quantities. Self-criticism in this framework can have a therapeutic effect. The first person "man enough" to admit fault can get the positive-sum process of acknowledgment, forgiveness and reconciliation going. In civic polities this can be an extremely effective approach, even become the source of entire fields like "Vulnerability Studies," "Peace and Conflict Studies," and "getting to yes."

This close relationship between self-criticism and the modern world, however, has produced a strange mutation among Jews over the conflict between Israel and her neighbors. Many liberal Jews have come to identify themselves as "good" because of their willingness to criticize "themselves" (i.e., Israel), thus rising above the tribal morality of "my side right or wrong." In the process, a subtle but real shift can occur: the act of criticism, regardless of its

---

18 Freud, *Moses and Monotheism* (1939), tr. Katherine Jones (New York: Vintage, 1967), 149.
19 Louis Rose, *The Freudian Calling: Early Viennese Psychoanalysis and the Pursuit of Cultural Science* (Detroit: Wayne State University Press, 1980).

accuracy, can become the core motivation. Virtue signaling by self-criticism overrides honesty. The spectacle of Freud, even as the Nazis drove him from his homeland, engaging in often wildly off-key speculations about how the Israelites killed the Egyptian Moses (a spectacular affirmation of the Christian antisemitic claim that the Jews killed their prophets and hate Gentiles) indicates just how addictive this compulsion to publicly criticize one's own.[20] Indeed, for Freud, and many others since, the more the criticism hurt, the truer it was.[21] David Mamet quotes Ahad Ha'am warning against excess: "Nothing is more dangerous, either for an individual, or for a people, than to confess to sins of which one is innocent."[22] Few individuals, and fewer peoples or nations, need to hear that advice.

Among the disorientations created by this differential, comes a cognitively egocentric assumption among Jews (what Harari would call infantile narcissism), that everyone else, including non-Jews, shares the level of self-criticism that Jewish circles take as a norm. (Or, rather, that it would be impolite to address the differential.) Jews who admit fault, presume they thereby gain the respect and admiration of their gentile friends, not their contempt. Jews are so committed to this kind of therapeutic self-accusation that they have, in some senses, turned it into a mystical, indeed a messianic principle, *tikkun olam*.[23]

The Pathologies of Self-Criticism

And yet, this ego-sacrifice doesn't work everywhere. Given its commitment to the therapeutic dynamic of encouraging reciprocity, this approach pays little attention to how self-criticism resonates in a zero-sum environment: as weakness, public self-debasement, humiliation, admission of guilt, and therefore, vulnerability to attack.[24] Instead of triggering a therapeutic process, in

---

20 Yerushalmi calls *Moses and Monotheism*, the "fourth humiliation," *Freud's Moses*, 1–18. Harari follows Freud in identifying Akhenaten as the first monotheist, *Sapiens*, 217; cf. Landes, *Heaven on Earth*, 153f, 178–81.

21 Yerushalmi in discussing Freud's notion of psychoanalytic resistance, argues that for Freud, "the degree of offense [to supposed national interest, i.e. "us"], had become for him one of the criteria of truth itself." Yerushalmi, *Freud's Moses*, 115n24.

22 David Mamet, *The Wicked Son: Antisemitism, Self-Hatred and the Jews* (New York: Schocken, 2006), 48.

23 *Righteous Indignation: A Jewish Call for Justice* ed. Rabbi Or Rose et al. (Woodstock VT: Jewish Lights Publishing, 2008).

24 See discussion in chapter 5. For an interesting example of a dynamic of spiraling confession, see the tragi-comic scene of Nurse Ratchet's group therapy in Ken Kesey's *One Flew over the Cuckoo's Nest* (New York: Signet, 1962), 50–51.

some cases it can play into a process whereby the self-critics become debased by their audiences, unwilling to follow their self-degrading lead. Instead, they take the vulnerability of the confessor as an invitation to aggression.[25] In this case: when Jews highly critical of Israel get applause from people planning that state's demise. In the marriage of premodern sadism and postmodern masochism, the sadist utters terrible accusations, and the masochist says, "*Mea maxima culpa.*"

Indeed, the crisis of self-criticism comes when its therapy fails. If, as some Jews feel, one is commanded to play positive-sum games, to undergo the vulnerabilities and risks entailed in trusting others, then how does one respond to a lack of reciprocity from "others." Put more dramatically, what does one do when one's self-inflicted wounds do not elicit sympathy, but rather release blood into shark-infested waters? The sound response, of course, is, at least, to stop cutting yourself, and possibly even make the attacker bleed. All the most successful evolutionary gambits involve both tit and tat, both being kind, and retaliating. No one has come up with a successful game strategy that involves continuous tits: even tit for two tats "gets badly exploited for its generosity."[26] *A fortiori* this is true of an environment like Israel's, where the neighbors play straight tat for tit, that is, take advantage of any weakness.

Jews, however, as noted by Weber and Harari, despite their opposing valences, long ago came up with an exceptionally masochistic strategy: no matter how badly the "other" behaves, blame the self. The ultimate expression of this tendency is a kind of masochistic omnipotence syndrome in which "I" or "we" are entirely to blame for everything, and therefore, if we "fix" ourselves, we can fix everything. The syndrome has two key elements: on the one hand, it offers a way of feeling in control, if only through embracing the most tyrannical superego, and on the other, it breathes messianic promise into the process—one can redeem the entire world through this self-sacrificial perfection. In the Israeli version, "if only we (or 'you,' when uttered by diaspora Jews) had only been nicer, more forgiving, more understanding, more generous, then the Palestinians wouldn't hate us/you so much. They might even love you (to death)."

On the one hand this produces "self"-critics who feel kinship with the prophets (speaking truth to power), and on the other, an audience of fellow masochists who revel in Jewish self-debasement. As a sweet elderly American-born Israeli woman once put it to me: "I love *Ha-aretz*. It's doubly pleasurable. All those terrible things it says about us (Israel) are true; and they hurt so much."

---

25 Jonathan Neumann, *To Heal the World?: How the Jewish Left Corrupts Judaism and Endangers Israel* (New York: St. Martin's Press, 2018).

26 Robert Axelrod, *The Evolution of Cooperation* (New York: Basic Books, 1984), 45.

She did not want to hear either about *Ha-aretz* misinformation,[27] or about those more hostile readers who, to varying degrees, experience great pleasure—*Schadenfreude*—at the glad tidings of Jews behaving badly.[28]

So, among radical, often secular, progressive Jews, who are proud at feeling no tribal attachment to Israel, another discourse appealed, one much closer to that of the UN's Zionism = Racism resolution. During the Lebanon War of 1982, when some prominent Western journalists openly compared the IDF with Nazi armies[29] . . .

> [t]here was no shortage of Israelis whom nobody outside of Israel had ever heard of before, from professors to publishers of pornographic newspapers, [who] became instant European celebrities by applying the epithet "Judeo-Nazi" to other Israelis, in precisely the style of "projection" that antisemitic Jews have been practicing since the Middle Ages.[30]

In an interview with Philip Roth in 1988, Aharon Appelfeld meditated on the uniqueness of this phenomenon of self-criticism among Jews:

> Antisemitism directed at oneself was an original Jewish creation. I don't know of any other nation so flooded with self-criticism. . . . The Jewish ability to internalize any critical and condemnatory remark and castigate themselves is one of the marvels of human nature. . . . The feeling of guilt has settled and taken refuge among all the Jews who want to reform the world, the various kinds of socialists, anarchists, but mainly among Jewish artists. Day and night the flame of that feeling produces dread, sensitivity, self-criticism and sometimes self-destruction.[31]

Aharon Megged, one of the few dissenters from the collective euphoria of the Oslo Peace Process, noted in an article of July 1994 in *Haaretz* entitled "The Israeli Suicide Drive": "Since the Six-Day War . . . and at an increasing pace,

27 Yemini, *Industry of Lies*, chapter 20; and the watchdog website *Presspectiva*, https://presspectiva.org.il/.
28 Yehezkel Laing, "Why do neo-Nazis Love 'Haaretz'?" *JNS*, January 18, 2022.
29 Chafets describes the comparisons as "sadistic," *Double Vision*, 311–15.
30 Alexander, *Jews Against Themselves*, 6.
31 Philip Roth, "Walking the Way of the Survivor: A Talk With Aharon Appelfeld," *New York Review of Books*, February 28, 1988.

we have witnessed a phenomenon which probably has no parallel in history: an emotional and moral identification by the majority of Israel's intelligentsia with people openly committed to our annihilation."[32] What can explain such an anomaly? And how can outsiders wrap their minds around such a bizarre form of insanity?

One of the most exceptional of these JATs in his venom for the land of his birth is the musician Gilad Atzmon, who wrote in the pages of the Arab Muslim newspaper Al Jazeera:

> To regard Hitler as the ultimate evil is nothing but surrendering to the Zio-centric discourse. To regard Hitler as the wickedest man and the Third Reich as the embodiment of evilness is to let Israel off the hook. Israel and Zionism are the ultimate Evil with no comparison.... The current Israeli brutality is nothing but evilness for the sake of evilness. Retribution that knows no mercy. Israel is a devastating collective resurrection of the Biblical Samson. It is a modern representation of the man who kills women, children and the elderly, the Hebraic victorious master of blind indiscriminate retaliation.... Israeli cannibalism.... If we want to save this world, if we want to live in a humane planet, we must focus on the gravest enemy of peace, those who are wicked for the sake of evilness: the Israeli State and world Zionism.... We all have to de-Zionise ourselves before it is too late. We have to admit that Israel is the ultimate evil rather than Nazi Germany."[33]

This passage illustrates starkly what Sander Gilman defined as *Jewish self-hate*: "Jews see the dominant society seeing them and ... project their anxiety about this manner of being seen onto other Jews as a means of externalizing their own status anxiety."[34] In other words, some Jews, seeing how negatively Gentiles view them, turn on their own kind, holding them responsible for that hatred: "If only 'they' would behave the way 'we good Jews' do," they tell themselves, "then non-Jews wouldn't think so ill of us."

---

32 Aharon Megged, "One-Way Trip on the Highway to Self-Destruction," *Jerusalem Post*, June 17, 1994.

33 Gilad Atzmon, "Beyond comparison," Al-Jazeerah, August 12, 2006.

34 Sander Gilman, *Jewish Self-Hatred: Anti-Semitism and the Hidden Language of the Jews* (Baltimore: Johns Hopkins University Press, 1990), 11.

Tuvia Tenebom after touring Israel and the West Bank in the early '10s, presenting himself as a German sympathetic to the Palestinian cause, explained:

> It's a mental problem.... For 2000 years Jews have been persecuted, for 2000 years they have been taught they are the worst.... Some people cannot handle it and you get a kind of Stockholm syndrome, and they say: "If everyone in the world says I'm bad, that I am ugly, a thief, a murderer, horrible, shrewd person, money-grabbing, I am. What can I do to cleanse myself of it?" ... *Catch another Jew doing wrong* ... that makes them feel better, makes their ugly skin look better.[35]

So, not accidentally, there's a high correlation between Jews who don't like Jews *qua* Jews, and as-a-Jew Jews, who loudly denounce their fellows in precisely the terms of the Jew-haters.

There's nothing remotely like this level of self-criticism and acceptance of the enemy's discourse among Arab Muslims, much less among Palestinians.[36] On the contrary, it would be harder to find a culture more allergic to public self-criticism and more committed to either eliminating the critic, or blaming (even creating) the "enemy," than the Palestinians. Hence, there is a *much* wider public range of opinion about the conflict between the river and sea among twelve million Jews in the world, with an extensive and sophisticated body of people and publications adopting the Palestinian position, than one can find among 1.6 *billion* Muslims, where only a handful dare to publicly show sympathy for Zionist aspirations, and often pay a high price.[37]

This stupendous asymmetry has a surprisingly strong impact on how the conflict is perceived by the outside: if one hears Palestinians unanimously denouncing Israel, and Israelis agreeing (as early as 1975),[38] one might be tempted to assume that these two groups are both right about the conflict. (After all, who willingly admits to wrong-doing unless they absolutely have to?)

---

35 "Danny Seaman and Daniella Traub Interview Tuvia Tenenbom," YouTube, December 24, 2014, 16:05–17:07, https://www.youtube.com/watch?v=GcGwjoRZNBA.

36 See Shlomo Avineri, "Mideast Peace Requires Palestinian Self-criticism," *Haaretz*, May 11, 2011. Elizabeth Kassab, *Contemporary Arab Thought: Cultural Critique in Comparative Perspective* (New York: Columbia University Press, 2010); Ghazi Hamad, "A Plea For Palestinian Self-Criticism," *Middle East Policy Council*, 13:4 (Winter 2006).

37 *Muslim Attitudes to Jews and Israel: The Ambivalences of Rejection, Antagonism, Tolerance and Cooperation*, ed. Moshe Ma'oz (Brighton: Sussex Academic Press, 2010).

38 Charles Glass, "Jews Against Zion: Israeli Jewish Anti-Zionism," *Institute for Palestinian Studies*, 5 (1975/76): 56–81.

Yet, if one factors in the enormous "self-criticism" gap, one gets the opposite: the irredentists who make peace impossible are the Palestinian blamers, fully endorsed by the Israeli self-critics who so desperately want peace that they'll take responsibility even for things they didn't do, in a valiant effort to help the process of reconciliation.

Impact of the Oslo "Peace" Process on Jewish Self-Criticism

Ironically, paradoxically, predictably, the promise and failure of the Oslo Process greatly aggravated the problem of Jewish self-criticism. The first demand of the "conflict resolution" approach on the Israelis was a new perception of the "other." Granted, the process also called for the Palestinians to reassess their view of the Israelis as genocidal imperialists bent on ethnically cleansing the land from the sea to the Euphrates and destroyers of Islam. But the Israeli peace camp, seized by the spirit of their own agency, focused on a radical revision of attitudes towards the Palestinians regardless of whether that was a reciprocal process. For them, to even speak of what had been earlier clear to most Israelis—the profound hostility of the Arab world, the long memory for revenge of Israel's neighbors— now became problematic language that contributed to the conflict.[39] The new "Oslo take" insisted that the Palestinians were now ready to make peace, and that anyone who still clung to the old (and pessimistic) paradigm was an obstacle to peace, indeed blinded to "reality" by their paranoid fear, victims of "Holocaust Syndrome."[40] The Arabs, the Palestinians especially, peace advocates assured everyone, had abandoned the "grand design" of destroying Israel. To those who worried about Palestinian enmity, the peace camp responded with the *deep thought*: "You make peace not with friends but with enemies."[41]

Although many Israelis felt torn between the promise of a new Middle East and the fear of the old, their intellectual elites together with Western progressives,

---

39 Yehoshafat Harkabi, an Arabist chronicled just how much the Arab world reviled Israel, *Arabs Attitudes towards Israel* (Jerusalem: Keter Publishing, 1971). And yet, he prepared the way for the new attitude after peace with Egypt: *Israel's Fateful Hour* (New York: Harper and Row, 1988). In this second book, filled with criticism of Israeli nationalism and religious fundamentalism, he makes no mention of the earlier book even in his autobiographical preface. To cite it had become "right-wing."

40 Levin, *Oslo Syndrome*, 361–71; Roskies, "Oslo's Betrayal." On the paradigmatic shift: Landes, "Paradigms and the Middle East Conflict," *Augean Stables*, 2006.

41 Rabin's version was, "Make peace with enemies, not the Queen of Holland." Cf: Bret Stephens, "You do not make peace with enemies. You make peace with former enemies," *Wall Street Journal*, November 10, 2015.

drawn by a secular messianic vision of peace in our times, treated any skepticism as a sign of "lunatic religious messianism" right-wing war-mongering, and proto-fascism.[42] Suddenly, previously fringe claims about how Arabs wanted peace, now became new dogmas. The Palestinians, in this version, were a people who yearned for freedom, and if only Israel were generous enough, they could trade land—West Bank and Gaza—for peace.[43] An eager school of Peace Journalism arose, downplaying anything that might discourage Israelis from voting for the peace camp.[44] Anyone heartless enough to challenge the existence of a "Palestinian" people, or racist enough to question Arafat's good intentions and the readiness of the "vast majority" of the Palestinian people to live in peace with their neighbors, or conservative enough to criticize the advocacy of "peace journalists" as unprofessional, became *ipso facto*, enemies of peace.[45]

In Israel, the peace accords greatly enhanced self-critical intellectual trends. The very dynamic of achieving peace through the resolution of conflict, Israeli peace activists felt, depended on making concessions aimed at reconciliation. Important among these concessions were admissions of the wrongs Israelis had done to the Palestinians in the previous period of conflict. The Israeli peace camp leapt at the opportunity in the fervent belief that such honest (even perhaps exaggerated) apologies would mollify Palestinian hostility. The Israeli "new historians" rewrote the conflict to affirm the Palestinian narrative— Israeli massacres and expulsions, theft of land, Israel's moment of joy built on catastrophic Palestinian suffering. (As if somehow, Israelis and Arabs could not both have celebrated their freedom at the same moment in 1947.)

"New historians," feeling free of the limbic lure of patriotic, self-justifying, narcissistic, Zionist narratives about Arab responsibility for the disaster that befell the Palestinian Arabs in 1948 and again in 1967 (and therefore the importance for Israel to hold on to the West Bank as long as the Palestinian leadership had not changed), acknowledged, even exaggerated Israeli culpability for massacring and driving the Palestinians out, for the heavy weight of the

---

42 Levin, *Oslo Syndrome*, 361–92.

43 Baruch Kimmerling, *Palestinians: The Making of a People* (New York: Free Press, 1993).

44 See 210f.; Wolfsfeld, *Media and the Path to Peace*. At a conference in honor of Wolfsfeld's retirement in 2012, conference chair Ifat Maoz gave a talk advising Palestinians that if they had spokespeople with rounder, baby-faces, Israelis would trust them more: "'The Face of the Enemy'—Visual cues, news framing and support for peace in intractable conflict," https://scholars.huji.ac.il/sites/default/files/smart/files/abstract_booklet.pdf.

45 A colleague tried to invite me to present my work on *Pallywood* in 2007 to the Annenberg School at University of Southern California. The (Jewish) chair of the department called the Israeli Consulate to ask for their advice. "Don't invite him," came the reply, "Landes is anti-peace."

occupation.[46] And at the same time, they exculpated the Palestinians and other Arabs for their rejectionism.[47] Other historians (right wingers, Orientalists) rejected their often tendentious if not dishonest, therapeutic historiography, their distortion if not inversion of the sources in order to substitute a (far less accurate) Palestinian "narrative of suffering [at the hands of wicked Israelis]" for the Israeli one of self-defense.[48]

Post-Zionism, the Israeli version of postmodernism, sought to cleanse Israel of its chauvinism. They saw themselves as heroes in the domestic version of an international clash of civilizations, not between democracies and totalitarian theocracies, but "between the universalistic, cosmopolitan, libertarian civilization on the 'post[-Zionist]' side, and particularistic, chauvinist, communal civilization on the 'neo[-Zionist]' side."[49] The Oslo peace process provided post-Zionism with its glory days (the "happy nineties"), in which it fought hard to have the very school curricula revised to reflect the "new" cosmopolitan, self-effacing Israel, an eager and worthy contributor to global civil society.[50]

Palestinians, on the other hand, provided little fuel for the Israeli peace camp's messianic dreams. There was nothing remotely similar, a post-Palestinianism on the other side: no self-critical revisionism, and no peace journalism. On the contrary, as documented by the twin translation services of MEMRI and PMW, Palestinians pursued a ferocious war journalism, replete with staged scenes accusing Israel of the most heinous crimes against innocent Palestinians.

The way the two sides handled their extremists illustrates well the fearful asymmetry involved. "Both sides" had radicals who "wanted it all," the Israeli settlers and the "Whole Land of Israel" camp on the one hand, and the Palestinian jihadis, the "not one grain of sand from the river to the sea" camp on the other. Both are driven by religious messianic dreams, both prone to violence to prevent the peace process from advancing. But the attitude of the

---

46 Michal Ben-Josef Hirsch, "From Taboo to the Negotiable: The Israeli New Historians and the Changing Representation of the Palestinian Refugee Problem," *Perspectives on Politics*, 5:2 (June 2007).

47 Neil Caplan, "Israeli historiography: Beyond the 'new historians,'" *Israel Affairs*, 2:2 (1995): 156–172. Yoram Meital even tried to revise the famous *Three No's of Khartoum*, see 196n42.

48 See Edward Alexander, "Israelis against themselves," in *The Jewish Divide over Israel*, 33–46; Efraim Karsh, "Benny Morris and the Myths of Post-Zionist History," *idem*, 249–62; Raphael Israeli, *Old Historians, New Historians, No Historians: The Derailed Debate on the Genesis of Israel* (Eugene OR: Wipf & Stock, 2016).

49 Uri Ram, in his programmatic statement: Lawrence Silberstein, *Post-Zionism: A Reader* (New Brunswick, NJ: Rutgers University Press, 2008), 67.

50 Kaplan, *Beyond Post-Zionism*; Levin, *Oslo Syndrome*, 371–85.

peace-makers on the two sides towards their extremists differed radically. On the one hand, Palestinian "moderates" played "nice cop," to their violent right wing who were introducing the terrifying new weapon of suicide terror, refusing to denounce them in any but the most pro-forma terms, praising them in Arabic, and explaining in Western tongues how their violence was an understandable response to frustration with the "occupation."

On the other hand, the Israeli "moderates" denounced their settlers vigorously, seizing the opportunity to show the whole world their good faith, by denouncing their own extremists as enemies of peace. Progressive Israelis made no demands for reciprocity: "We are strong and can afford to criticize ourselves publicly. When the Palestinians have their own state and sense of autonomy, then we can expect some from them."[51] Thus did the Israeli peace camp energetically renounce their claims on an ancient land, while Palestinians made sacred the [Israeli retreat from every inch of the] "Green Line," a "border" they never had—and still don't—recognize as legitimate.[52]

Then came 2000 and the outbreak of the second, "'al Aqsa" intifada, or Oslo Jihad. Everything that the "right wing" had been saying about Arafat proved true: he had prepared war, right under the noses of the peace-intoxicated negotiators. This was, it turned out, a turning point in the march of Western folly at the dawn of the new millennium. How to respond to the explosive failure of the "Oslo Peace Process"? How would the peace camp, the "best and the brightest" of Israeli and Jewish society react to the sight of the jihadis pouring out of the Trojan Horse Palestinians had spoken about in Arabic?

Consider the Oslo Peace as a messianic project, in which the new school of postmodern liberal internationalists in the US and Europe joined with the most fervent progressive, post-Zionist elements of Jewish and Israeli society, seeking genuine peace and reconciliation with their neighbors based on sound positive-sum relations: a perfect gift to the world at the dawn of the new, global millennium. When the Oslo Jihad broke out, they faced a stark choice, one familiar to those who have succumbed to apocalyptic fantasies: how to deal with disappointment.[53] In their intense cognitive dissonance, the Peace Camp could either admit that they were wrong in their expectations and that they had misread the nature of the enmity they faced (which would have acknowledged

---

51 Larry Derfner on a Tel Aviv conference in 1993. "Rattling the Cage: The Palestinian Victim Mentality," *Jerusalem Post*, March 16, 2011.

52 The so-called "Green Line," was a 1949 armistice line that no Arab nation recognized as legitimate. Westerners hoping for a "two-state solution" take it as a proleptic "border," a mistake the Palestinians gladly encourage: Landes, "Demopath's Dictionary."

53 Landes, *Heaven on Earth*, chapter 2.

the accuracy of the "right-wing" warnings and produced a movement towards national healing), on the one hand, or, in classic post-apocalyptic denial, they could insist negotiations were so close to success that, if only their own, the Israeli side had given more, peace would have won out.[54] Had they apologized to those "realists" who had warned of this outcome, for calling them fascists and enemies of peace, perhaps the subsequent discussion could have found more empirical grounding and brought the public and leaders to a better understanding of what they faced.

Had they done the intellectually (and morally) mature thing, and acknowledged their conceptual errors, they might have understood that the outbreak of the "al Aqsa Intifada" actually represented the most ambitious Caliphator assault on an infidel state to date, in part because it played out on a global stage (just like the humiliation of 1948), in part because it used suicide terror, the new and most terrifying weapon in the jihadi armory, in part because it was the first to target a western, democratic power, a prelude to further jihadi attacks. Had our infidel elites understood this, many of the subsequent follies of the new century might have been avoided: the credulity for, and eagerness to spread jihadi antisemitic and genocidal propaganda ... the celebration of the jihadi use of suicide terror against *kuffār* ... the special concern for the "feelings" of our Muslim minorities about any kind of criticism ... the twisted embrace of a Peace and Conflict Resolution industry that fuels war.

Instead, the patently false and novel claims of the peace camp in the '90s (when there was still hope) became dogmas in the twenty-first century (when hope was shattered):

- The Palestinians are undeniably a "people" and as such, deserve their national rights.
- They yearn for a viable state and their dignity.
- They recognize the state of Israel.
- The Two-State Solution is the only solution to the conflict.
- Anyone who denies any of these assertions is a racist and a warmonger.

The Proxy Honor Killing: Jewish Voices for "Peace"

But more viscerally, something else was at work. The news media's accounts of the Second Intifada were deeply humiliating to Israel and to Jews who had,

---

54 Lahat, *Messianic Temptation.*

until then, been proud of—indeed participated in—her efforts for peace. The *image* of the Israeli Goliath crushing the poor Palestinian youth, embodied in the footage of Muhammad al Durah, crushed not only hopes for peace, but any chance a Zionist could hold his head high. Muhammad al Durah gave power to a voice we increasingly hear on campuses, on news media, from demonstrations: "Israel is evil; the IDF murders Palestinian children every day—no doubt about it."[55]

The fact that the loud, passionate voice of indignation sided with the Palestinians, that by 2003 being pro-Palestinian was a "litmus test" of being liberal, compounded the problem for liberal Zionists (the vast majority of Jewish Zionists). On the one hand, to defend Israel was to "out" yourself as a Jew—non-Jews who defended Israel in the early aughts heard, "Oh, I didn't know you were Jewish." On the other, to fail to show sympathy for Palestinians was to out yourself as a heartless tribalist, an Israel-firster.[56] Even as people in public could easily wax indignant about Israeli cruelty (to much applause), it was difficult to wax indignant about suicide terror attacks without getting denounced. After October 1, 2000, it became increasingly difficult to get pro-Israel pieces published in liberal newspapers, including campus ones. By the teens, it became policy in some places like McGill, for the newspaper to maintain "an editorial line of not publishing pieces which promote a Zionist worldview."[57] And so in journalism and academia: as the new century progressed it became increasingly arduous in mainstream outlets to publish articles and books that supported Israel or criticized Islam.[58]

Broadly speaking (but not numerically) there were three responses to this crisis:

1. *Flight:* Jews who avoided the subject entirely. Alan Dershowitz complained often in the early aughts, that when he asked Jews who were

---

55 Random example: "Israeli Army kills a Palestinian in Gaza Every Single Day: Euro-Med," *Maan*, October 19, 2018. Posted by Professor Juan Cole, https://www.juancole.com/2018/10/israeli-palestinian-single.html.

56 Electronic Intifada referred to me as "the man who coined the racist concept of 'Pallywood'—the idea that Palestinians habitually lie and create fake videos to incriminate Israel." Asa Winstanley, "Who are the Israel lobbyists that want David Miller fired?" *The Electronic Intifada*, March 31, 2021. No reference to the evidence, just the mere concept is racist.

57 Sheldon Kershner, "McGill University's Student Newspaper is Subverting the Principles of Fair Journalism," *Times of Israel*, November 26, 2016.

58 Bruce Bawer, "The Speech I Never Gave," *Frontpage*, October 3, 2018. By 2020 this informal publishing ban had become a problem for Jewish authors in general: Melissa Braunstein, "Publishers against the People of the Book," *Washington Examiner*, December 02, 2021.

Middle East specialists to defend Israel from the new wave of assaults from postcolonial scholars, they would demur out of concern for their academic reputation; and when he turned to non-specialists, they would demur since it was not their specialty. And given the moral and social opprobrium that either directly or subtly came down on those who did defend Israel (including from fellow Jews), that flight was more than fully justified. Academia, especially American academia, was literally heaven on earth in the 1990s—collegial, well-funded, exciting, creative, international. Who would want to rock *that* boat? Similarly, Jewish organizations, like the AJC and the ADL, had worked in the '90s on the positive-sum "we'll-work-with-other-groups-for-everyone's-human rights-and-when-the-time-comes-that-we-need-them..." When the time came in 2000, these Jewish groups were caught off guard, bewildered by both the turn of Palestinians to war, and the adherence of so many alleged "allies" to the Palestinian camp.

2. *Fight:* Those who fought back were relatively few, and largely marginalized. Those who wanted to stay in the mainstream had to fight with one hand tied behind their back, literally stepping on eggshells not to say something that would trigger howls of disapproval, like challenging the liberal cognitive egocentrism of their audience, or talking about the shame-honor culture that prevailed in the Arab world. Some took to blogs, which were a new and exciting form of communication in the mid-aughts, a welcome home for those whose cogent letters and essays could not find a newspaper editor willing to publish. Grass roots groups arose to fill in the gap left by the deer-in-the-headlights paralysis of the established Jewish groups: Honest Reporting (2000), Stand with Us (2001), Hasbara Fellows (2001), Scholars for Peace in the Middle East (2002), David Project (2002), Campus Watch (2002), and so on.

3. *As-a-Jew Virtue Signaling:* The most problematic, and the most damaging of responses came from those Jews who felt the need to insist publicly that they completely disassociate themselves from the behavior of the IDF and the policies of the Israeli government. Thus, in late 2000, appeared a new fashion, the *alter-juifs*, who "as a Jew" felt compelled to let everyone know how good they were by criticizing their own people and siding with their enemy.[59] This "good Jews" catching the "bad Jews"

---

59 Shmuel Trigano, *Les Alter-juifs*, including the case of Edgar Morin, discussed 122n98. More broadly, see the collection of essays edited by Alexander and Bogdanor, *The Jewish Divide over Israel*.

became a major element of progressive discourse, with people like John Mearsheimer exploiting it to promote the Palestinian cause: "Righteous Jews have a powerful attachment to core liberal values [sic] ... people like Noam Chomsky, Roger Cohen, Richard Falk, Norman Finkelstein, Tony Judt, Tony Karon, Naomi Klein, MJ Rosenberg, Sara Roy, and Philip Weiss of Mondoweiss fame."[60]

Of all the responses, this last dominated the Jewish contribution to the global public sphere in the aughts, and thereby, had an important contribution to make to the mistaken direction Western intellectuals and thought leaders took at this moment, when the enemies of their progressive civilization, using a Nazi-like, deliriously paranoid, antisemitic discourse to rally their troops for genocide, attacked them. Let us begin with the extremes, and work our way towards the center, the "liberal," "mainstream," Jews, like the family in which I was raised, at once ardent democrats and proud Zionists.

Unable or unwilling to imagine the nature of this "Palestinian" violence, some preferred to deny the feedback from reality. "So, what's the solution? Kill them all?" was perhaps the most common response to any depiction of the shame-honor dynamics of apocalyptic jihad, as if the measure of accuracy derived primarily from the solutions the analysis seemed to offer.[61] And behind that assumption, lay another, more aggressive one: that any understanding that did not follow the Conflict Resolution Protocols, leading peacefully to "peace now," came from right-wing war-mongers. "That's an Islamophobic, racist view of Arabs" replied the unwitting disciples of Said.[62]

Unquestionably, the most extreme reaction among Jews and Israelis to the outbreak of the intifada appeared among Jews who fully adopted the narrative of their enemies: Gilad Atzmon, Daniel Boyarin, some of the more virulent "new historians" like Avi Shlaim and Ilan Pappe, most of whom fled an Israel too tribal for their ecumenical tastes, to a progressive, British academia, eager to hear Israeli anti-Zionists. For these people, everything the Palestinians claimed about Israel became instantly true, the worse the better. One could see them

---

60 John Mearsheimer, "The Future of Palestine: Righteous Jews vs New Afrikaners," *Monthly Review Online*, April 30, 2010. Note that most of these "good Jews" are not at all liberals but radicals, deeply anti-American, and major players in mainstreaming the new Antisemitism, see Rosenfeld, *Progressive Jewish Thought.* For critiques of Mearsheimer's piece, see Jonathan Chait, "Why Can't Jews Be More Like Noam Chomsky?" *New Republic*, May 3, 2010; Andrew Pessin, "The Indelible Stain: Jew-Washing, Antisemitism, and Zionophobia," *American Thinker*, January 24, 2016.

61 Landes, "Honor-Shame jihad Paradigm," *The Augean Stables.*

62 Landes, "Orientalism as Caliphator Cognitive Warfare."

at the Jerusalem Cinematheque, the night Omar Bakri's *Jenin, Jenin* premiered, applauding the movie and shouting "war-criminal" at Dr. David Zangen—a man committed to humane treatment for everyone, someone that any civil, liberal polity would normally proudly claim as one of their finest products—when he tried to explain the film's systematic dishonesty.[63] One could see them at the Museum of Fine Arts in Boston in 2004, giving a loud and long standing ovation to a film by a Palestinian and a Jew claiming the media systematically promoted Israeli war propaganda.[64]

And yet, for those who hate the occupation, it becomes a matter of faith *not* to think badly of the Palestinians. Given a choice between the ugly messiness of sovereignty and wielding power (including military power) or having a pure unsullied soul, many a progressive Jew preferred the latter, often at the cost of losing touch with reality. On the one hand, this meant refusing to think badly of the Palestinians—they're just like us[65]—and on the other, this meant so romanticizing the diaspora that one imagined Jews need not have sovereignty.[66] These Jews, feeling guilty and unhappy at how Israel was portrayed by the media, who wanted to be proud of Israel as a "light unto the nations," a shimmering example of progressive values even under painful circumstances, were then easy prey to anti-Zionist demopaths like Mearsheimer.[67]

Here we enter the "principled" world of Jewish anti-Zionism, from the ultra-orthodox religious world of Neturei Karta to the ultra-orthodox secular world of critical queer theory and Judith Butler. Here we find what Edward Alexander describes as a kind of "political anorexia," in which a Jew experiences the State of Israel as a body whose inevitable imperfections, magnified by the news media, humiliate, shame, and disgust them. These openly Jewish figures feel such revulsion at the public revelation of these bodily flaws that every new round of accusations sends them into paroxysms of moral indignation and public "self"-flagellation. In 2006, Alvin Rosenfeld chronicled their contribution to the

---

63 See chapter 3, on Jenin.

64 Landes, "Intellectual Mugging at the MFA: Jhally and Ratskoff's *Peace, Propaganda, and the Promised Land,*" *Augean Stables,* February 12, 2018, http://www.theaugeanstables.com/2018/02/12/intellectual-mugging-at-the-mfa-jhully-and-ratzkoffs-peace-propaganda-and-the-promised-land/.

65 See Ami Ayalon's conclusion from a Palestinian confronting him with his cognitive egocentrism 407f. Peter Beinart is a master of this "Palestinians want peace" mantra: Jonathan Dekel-Chen, "Hard truths from the Gaza border," *Forward,* April 30, 2018.

66 Judith Butler is the poster-queen for this attitude. See Cary Nelson, *Israel Denial: Anti-Zionism, Anti-Semitism, and the Faculty Campaign against the Jewish State,* (Bloomington: Indiana University Press, 2019), chapter 3.

67 John Mearsheimer, "Righteous Jews vs. New Afrikaners."

tsunami of "new antisemitism" that had been spreading since 2000. No insult, no debasement, no accusation was too extreme, too indecent, too grotesque for these as-a-Jews to throw at Israel: "Nazis . . . racists . . . genocidal . . . insane . . . demonic . . . fanatical . . . , etc."[68]

This brings us to one of the more troubling aspects of Jewish anti-Zionism, the shame factor. The portrayal of Israel by a school of lethal journalists and postcolonial academics as a cruel occupier of Palestinian land, who deliberately target Palestinian civilians, has deeply shamed Jews in the eyes of their "honor-group," their fellow Jewish, and non-Jewish liberals and progressives. How can one claim to support progressive values without denouncing the terrible behavior of the state you had previously, openly admired. For some Jews, the shame of having a family member—Israel—viewed by others as a brutal and heartless Goliath, was too much to bear.

Given a choice between challenging the legacy news media or Israel, the choice seemed clear. When I was working on the Al Durah affair, on several occasions, Jews who were ardent Israel advocates told me they did not want to push the matter because, even if in this case Israel got framed, "we've killed over a thousand of their children."[69] These were and are legitimate concerns. When I presented the case to the AJC in Boston, one of the major donors came up to me afterwards and said, "You would have been great in the 1930s, but today, you're just trouble." As if there weren't people like me speaking out in the 1930s, and people like him, trying to shut them up.

This shame factor divided Israel and diaspora Jews close to down the middle. After 2000, the "peace camp" lost massive credibility among the voters in Israel who realized the "right" had been correct about the Palestinian leadership. To Israelis at the time, this was an existential threat from merciless enemies. The first chance they got, they chose Sharon, and the rapid decline of both Labor and the parallel "peace parties" like Meretz flowed from there. Papers like *Ha-aretz*,

---

68 On the new "new antisemitism," see Taguieff, *La nouvelle judéophobie*; Phyllis Chesler, *The New Antisemitism*; *A New Antisemitism? Debating Judeophobia in 21ˢᵗ Century Britain*, ed. Paul Iganski and Barry Kosmin (London: Profile Books, 2003); Rosenfeld, "'Progressive' Jewish Thought." On the "new antisemitism" as the fault of the Jews, Martin Jay, "Ariel Sharon and the Rise of the New Antisemitism," *Salmagundi*, 2003.

69 Gadi Wolfsfeld is the unnamed interlocutor in Landes, "So What if Al Durah was Staged?": Meditations on the Colonization of the Israeli Mind," *Augean Stables*, January 18, 2008. See also n94. In 2013, in response to the government investigation about al Durah, *Haaretz* published an editorial making precisely this point: "Israel's Focus on al-Dura is Harmful Propaganda," May 21, 2013. For the irresponsible use of statistics to make the case worse ("almost a thousand children killed"), see Hanan Amiur, "Ha'aretz Manipulates Child Casualty Figures," *CAMERA*, June 11, 2013.

which became increasingly anti-Israel over the course of the aughts, had their circulation shrink drastically (even as their international impact grew greater).[70]

The "peace camp" with its delusions fully reaffirmed, retreated to corners of Israeli academia, the NGOs, the intelligentsia, the cafés of Tel Aviv, or the warm welcome of European universities where audiences had an apparently insatiable appetite for criticism of Israel. Most Israelis, with sons and daughters in the army, neither believed the lethal journalists, nor had the luxury in engaging in fantasies about peace *now*. For Israelis, 2000 was when Oslo died. As one said to me, "*that* was when I understood that this is not in our hands." So far, for the first two decades of the twenty-first century, the rest of the world has yet to catch up, indeed seems to be falling farther and farther behind.

Diaspora Jews, on the other hand, constantly under pressure from their gentile colleagues and friends, and less likely to understand how absurd were the claims of a massacre in Jenin or the *deliberate* targeting of Muhammad al Durah, especially in the context of the IDF's moral code,[71] more readily fell in with the general "liberal" criticism of Israel.[72] What can one say when objecting to the virulent rhetoric—Nazi and Apartheid comparisons—gets dismissed as an attempt to silence "legitimate" criticism of Israel? As good liberals, Jews found the ugly accusations that Palestinians nurtured genocidal hatreds and maliciously published libels, and that the MSNM practiced unethical lethal journalism and insisted on being dupes to demopaths, highly distasteful. Just as Jews were horrified that Nazis accused them of wanting to rule the world, so, they felt, we should not accuse Muslims of so appalling an ambition, even though Jews never said anything like that and Caliphators said it all the time. Even were these Jews to quietly agree with such observations, they would not repeat them.

How much easier to lament Israel's tragic drift to the right.[73] As one (Jewish) journalist (for the *Wall Street Journal* no less), explained to me: "It's so unfortunate that Israel has responded to the intifada [i.e. the suicide terror campaign], by going to the right." In other words, "If only the Israelis could have been good Jews, liberals, peace-loving Jews … you know, *tikkun olam* Jews … then we wouldn't be ashamed and we're sure the Palestinians would make peace."[74]

---

70 Yemini dates the "sharp change in the paper's line" to the years after 2000, *Industry of Lies*, chapter 20.

71 IDF Doctrine and Ethics, https://sites.google.com/site/idfduvdevan/idfdoctrine%26ethics.

72 Bernard Harrison, *The Resurgence of Anti-Semitism*.

73 Carlo Strenger, "Why Israel Keeps Moving to the Right," *Guardian*, July 19, 2010.

74 I asked a friend who was on the board of J-Street if he thought that if Israel went back to the Green Line there'd be peace. "Absolutely," he responded.

Israelis, especially those dealing with the West, shared these conceptual shackles. In their estimation, even well into the aughts, any criticism of Palestinians would only increase hostilities and prevent the resumption of peace talks. Indeed, they considered it their major task to convince the world that Israel truly wanted peace at all costs. In 2009, I spoke with the head of the Ministry of Foreign Affairs, Media section just as they were preparing for a papal visit. "We have so many reporters coming here, many for the first time, and lots of down-time. Any suggestions about what to do with them?" "Have them briefed by Itamar Marcus (PMW) and Yigal Carmon (MEMRI) about what the Palestinians are saying in Arabic." "We couldn't do that," he replied, "the government is officially in favor of peace negotiations." "Fine," I responded, "then expose them to this discourse and then explain that *despite* what the Palestinians are saying, Israel *still* pursues peace." He looked at me with blank eyes; and did nothing of the sort.

To support Israel and criticize Palestinians under such conditions, meant losing one's reputation as "good Jews," Jews whose commitment to progressivism, in their minds, justifies their place in a civic polity. And indeed, some Gentiles feel the same way: Jews are collectively held accountable, in this case for the [reported] behavior of Israel. When the news of al Durah's "murder" hit the news in France during the weekend of October 1, 2000, Jews going back to school and work the following Monday, were confronted by their co-workers and fellow students, "What did *your* people do?!?" Every wave of lethal journalism brought waves of shame and humiliation to Jews, especially diaspora ones. In Harold Jacobson's *The Finkler Question*, the anti-Zionist Jews form a group called the ASHamed Jews, who trip over themselves, as-a-Jew, to denounce Israel in the harshest terms before avid audiences of Jew-haters.[75]

---

75 Harold Jacobson, *The Finkler Question*; a roman à clé for Rosenfeld, *Progressive Jewish Thought*; explicated by Alexander, *Jews against Themselves*, chapter 11.

FIGURE 27. Ahsamed Jew at Anti-Israel Rally, Boston, summer 2014.

Without even realizing what he was saying (or presumably he would not have said it), Tony Judt voiced the plaint of the "good" diaspora Jews who felt beleaguered by the sudden hostility to the "Jewish State." Writing in the wake of the "Jenin Massacre," he denounced the "Jewish state" for endangering Jews around the world.

> Today, non-Israeli Jews feel themselves once again exposed to criticism and vulnerable to attack for things they didn't do. But this time it is a Jewish state, not a Christian one, which is holding them hostage for its own actions.... The behavior of a self-described Jewish state affects the way *everyone else looks at Jews*. The increased incidence of attacks on Jews in Europe and elsewhere is primarily attributable to misdirected efforts, often by young Muslims, to get back at Israel. The depressing truth is that Israel's current behavior is not just bad for America, though it surely is. It is not even just bad for Israel itself, as many Israelis silently acknowledge. The depressing truth is that *Israel today is bad for the Jews*.[76]

"We're under attack for things we didn't do!" he whined. It could not even momentarily enter Judt's sophisticated mind that that was also true for Israel.

---

76 Judt, "Israel: the Alternative."

The very people who warned against making any connection between jihadi terrorists and "true (moderate) Muslims,"—*pas d'amalgame!*—held diaspora Jews responsible for what [the media claimed] Israel did.[77] Why the double standard? Why the attacks on diaspora Jews? For many progressive Jews, it was unthinkable that much of both the Muslim and (post-)Christian hostility was anger at the sight of Jews defending themselves from another genocidal assault. They at once belittled that threat and blamed Israel for the upsurge in hostility. "Suicide bombers will never bring down the Israeli state [i.e., they're not a clear and present danger], and the Palestinians have no other weapons," Judt asserts, not realizing that he and the lethal journalists he parroted were the most sophisticated new weapon in their (and the other Caliphators') arsenal.

Jewish shame at how Israel appeared to outsiders created a painful dilemma for all Jews, one well-known to members of tribal honor-shame cultures: when a member of your family has brought shame upon you, you either share that shame, or purge the family and regain your standing in the eyes of your honor group.[78] Note here that in cases of shame-murders, actual guilt is not necessarily at issue: the matter concerns how "others" think, not whether the accusations are true. When Chris Hedges accuses Israel of deliberately shooting Palestinian children as an idle game, it doesn't matter how false the claim, it's a damning picture in a major publication.[79]

Now, while killing the shaming family member makes sense in a society where killing is proof of manhood, it proves problematic when those who are ashamed hold progressive values and self-identify, like Judith Butler, or "Jewish Voice for Peace," as "pacifists." From a demotic point of view, these efforts to eliminate embarrassing family members, are not honor killings, but brutal, often sadistic, shame-murders.[80] Not having the constitution to actually kill their embarrassing family member, then, progressive Jews, mortified by the image of Israel regularly transmitted by their news media and academics, have to content themselves with verbal assassination, even as they outsource the dirty, bloody work to those groups like Students for Justice in Palestine, and American Muslims for Palestine who admire and defend Hamas and Hizballah who would readily exterminate Israel and the vast majority of its Jews were they able, who will shed their own

---

77 See discussion of Wilcox interview after Charlie Hebdo (24n77). Wieseltier criticizes Judt for precisely this: "What is Not to be Done," *New Republic*, October 27, 2003.

78 Below, 419–21.

79 Chris Hedges, "A Gaza Diary," *Harper's Magazine*, October 2001; NB: this is immediately after 9/11. Cf. "Chris Hedges, Harpers, and Israel," *CAMERA*, November 7, 2001.

80 Phyllis Chesler, *A Family Conspiracy: Honor Killing* (London: New English Review Press, 2018).

people's blood in quantity just to shed a little Jewish blood (1000 Gazans dead + 6 Israelis dead = great victory). In other words, Jewish groups that satisfy their need to signal their moral virtue by joining sides with Muslim Israel-haters who claim to pursue "justice" and thereby "create peace," engage in a future, proxy, shame-murder.

Do twenty-first-century anti-Zionist Jews like Judith Butler, Peter Beinart, Daniel Boyarin, Jewish Voice for Peace, If Not Now, do this consciously? Do they know that they mimic the most sadistic memes put out by their people's most ferocious enemies and fuel those hatreds? Do they realize they have teamed up with a tribal notion of justice based on revenge for lost honor, on washing one's blackened face in the blood of the dishonoring enemy, in which that targeted enemy is their own people, with whom they publicly identify "as a Jew"? Can the Israeli and Diasporic Jews, who fully adopt the Palestinian lethal narrative about Israel as the Nazi genocider, who ally with her sworn enemies, who ignore all the evidence that the journalists' lethal narratives are dishonest violations of fundamental principles of a responsible free press, and instead promote causes that target Israel's very existence, can they even consider the (highly self-critical) possibility that, in so doing, they engage in a proxy shame-murder?

The resistance to any such realization was intense from the outset. When Alvin Rosenfeld criticized these ASHamed Jews for recklessly, willy-nilly, spreading antisemitism in 2006, the New York Times featured a major piece attacking Rosenfeld for smearing "liberals."[81] It mattered little that, with the exception of Richard Cohen, none of the figures Rosenfeld denounced were "liberals" but rather radical "progressives."[82] That didn't prevent mainstream "liberal" Jews like Boston University Professor Alan Wolfe from expressing his "state of shock," not at the assault on Israel, but at the criticism of "liberal Jews." Such "liberals" tacitly adopted the "Livingstone formulation": anyone who objects to vicious criticism is trying to shut down any criticism of Israel. Judt (and others on an industrial scale) fingered the culprit: "American 'apologists' for Israel use the Holocaust to shield Israel from criticism."[83] It seems to have mattered little to

---

81 Patricia Cohen, "Essay Linking Liberal Jews and Antisemitism Sparks a Furor," New York Times, January 23, 2007; response, Landes, "Jewish Hypercritics of Israel Criticized: How Dare You?" Augean Stables, February 1, 2007.

82 Benjamin Kerstein, "Jewish Liberalism and Its Discontents," Diary of an Anti-Chomskyite, January 31, 2007, http://antichomsky.blogspot.com/2007/01/jewish-liberalism-and-its-discontents.html.

83 "[A]ll criticism [is] drawn ineluctably back to the memory of that project [Holocaust], something that Israel's American apologists are shamefully quick to exploit," Judt, "Israel the alternative." On the industry of lies targeting Israel see Gerstenfeld, Death of a Million Cuts; Yemini, Industry of Lies.

as-a-Jew "liberals" that those Nazi-comparisons participated in an existential assault, calling for dismantling Israel.

But what is shame in the primary code (bad press), holds a different place in a demotic analysis.

Judt's shame motivation at Israel's bad press, and that of so many others, explains the irrational drive behind the moral posture. Not only do these Jews hold their own people to the highest standards, but also (in a deeply racist fashion), they hold the Palestinians to *no* moral standards. On the contrary, "good Jews" like Judt believe that the murderous hatreds of the Palestinians arise directly from the unbearable suffering Israelis inflict upon them (and will, of course, disappear as soon as the Jews stop being so horrible). It could not pass their mind to ask: if Palestinians will kill their daughters for shaming them before their own community, *a fortiori* will they want to kill Jews for shaming them before the whole world.

And in such (un)thinking we come full circle: just as the enemies of their people sometimes kill their own daughters on mere (and even incorrect) suspicion alone, these Jews do so even though their family member, Israel, is *not* guilty as charged, but rather, for all its faults, one of the most cutting-edge progressive and inclusive cultures on this deeply troubled planet. Israel, it turns out, was (and is) the victim of the first "mass shaming" of the twenty-first century, at the hands of lethal journalists and the progressive crowds they incited.

The Liberal "Center" in the Gravitational Pull of the "Progressive" Extreme

In some ways, the extremists offer an easy target. Most Jews, certainly any who have spent time in Israel, will agree that comparisons with the Nazis and Apartheid and accusations of "genocide" are as inaccurate as they are indecent. But that doesn't mean those in the liberal center reject and refuse to participate in these lewd rites, or object to antisemitism's new anti-Zionist garb. On the contrary, something happened in 2000. After the explosion of lethal journalism, even those who clucked disapprovingly at the radical, anti-Zionist discourse, yielded to its emphatic passion.[84] "No, Israel is not Nazi" the moderates would say, "but it has, alas, become Goliath, and any good liberal feels conscience-bound to side with the Palestinians."

---

84 E.g., Durban (41–46).

Thus, at the very same moment (in the aftermath of Jenin) that an indignant Paul Berman noted how for many Western liberals, "Palestinian terror" had become "the measure of Israeli guilt," (i.e., blame the democracy), Ian Buruma noted in passing that "the Palestinian cause has become the universal litmus test of liberal credentials."[85] The following year, the *New York Times* announced proudly its ideological tilt: the paper's first public editor, Daniel Okrent, answered the headline above one of his columns—"Is the New York Times a Liberal Newspaper?"—in the first sentence of his story: "Of course it is."

And few noticed or wished to notice that the extremists, with their extravagant slanders of Israel, had redefined the terrain for the liberals. Willy-nilly, they now carried water for Caliphator Jihadis. In part, the radicals exercised their influence on the mainstream through intermediaries, figures like Tony Judt. This major, internationally respected historian, known for his razor-sharp analysis of the failure of the postwar European progressive intelligentsia,[86] explained that Israel can't get along with the Palestinians because they were a last remnant of the West's heinous imperialist colonialism, oppressing the poor indigenes. It wasn't the virulent Nazi version of anti-Zionism, but this more secular, postcolonial version, the authoritative academic veneer: Israel, a "dysfunctional anachronism."

In a flourish of liberal cognitive egocentrism and a-historical analysis (not to mention moral airiness), Judt complained: why can't Israel live in peace with her neighbors the way the Europeans do? Better yet, why not a bi-national state of Arabs and Israelis living together in peace?[87] All it would take was the emergence of "a new political class" on "both sides."

> In a world where nations and people increasingly intermingle and intermarry at will; where cultural and natural impediments to communication have all but collapsed; where more and more of us have multiple elective identities and would feel falsely constrained if we had to answer to just one of them; in such a world Israel is truly an anachronism.

---

85 Berman, *Terror and Liberalism*, 134; Ian Buruma, "How to Talk about Israel."

86 "A unique mix of political urgency and moral airiness . . . of self-imposed moral anesthesia" . . . Tony Judt, *Past Imperfect*, 276, 140.

87 Criticized by Ran Halévi, "Israel and the Question of the National State," *Policy Review*, April 2004; Alain Finkielkraut, "Juifs, donc anachroniques," *l'Arche*, April 2004. Peter Beinart has argued for dismantling the Jewish state, "Yavne: A Jewish Case for Equality in Israel-Palestine," *Jewish Currents*, July 7, 2020; critiqued by many, e.g., Shani Moore, "Peter Beinart's Grotesque Utopia," *Israel Democracy Institute*, September 13, 2020.

An ecumenical cognitive egocentrism, a planetary *amalgame* that lumped together in the new ecumenical move, all but Israel: all cultures are the same, all have equal rights, why can't we all just get along? Why can't Israel get with the program?

In his more historical work, Judt had discussed the dubious nature of European transnational solidarities, and yet, rather than apply the lessons of historical errors he had so lucidly drawn from the past, he replicated them in his assault on Israel's legitimacy, "as if the historian-cum intellectual *engagé* has stepped into one of his own historical studies."[88] And lurking behind these glaring intellectual deficiencies lay his openly confessed discomfort at being attacked for something he didn't do. (Imagine Judt saying, "the legacy media's sloppy reporting is bad for the Jews and for Western democracies." In so doing he'd relegate himself to what "good Jews" consider the fringe of the Jewish right wing.")

Even the Jews with the most profound combination of both traditional and secular learning, even the ones with strong moral compasses, found it hard to acknowledge what was happening. In an article in late May 2002, right after Jenin moral hysteria had swept the West into a paroxysm of own-goal, anti-Zionism and corresponding cries of alarm, Leon Wieseltier assured his readers that "Hitler was dead."[89]

> All this has left many Jews speculating morbidly about being the last Jews. And the Jews of the United States significantly exceed the Jews of Israel in this morbidity. The community is sunk in excitability, in the imagination of disaster. There is a loss of intellectual control. Death is at every Jewish door. Fear is wild. Reason is derailed. Anxiety is the supreme proof of authenticity. Imprecise and inflammatory analogies abound. Holocaust imagery is everywhere.

"Yes," he seems to say, "it's bad, but let's not lose our heads here. It's not the beginning of another wave of ecumenical Jew-hatred, like the one that swept over Europe 70 years ago and climaxed in the extermination of millions of Jews. And anyone who thinks in these hysterical, mythical terms, is actually pursuing a (dark) political agenda."

---

88 Balint, "Future Imperfect," 69.

89 Leon Wieseltier, "Hitler is Dead," *New Republic*, May 27, 2002. On Wieseltier's critique of Judt, see n78.

> If you think that the Passover massacre at the Park Hotel was like Kristallnacht, then you must also think that there cannot be a political solution to the conflict, and that the Palestinians have no legitimate rights or legitimate claims upon any part of the land, and that there must never be a Palestinian state, and that force is all that will ever avail Israel . . . the analogy between the Passover massacre and Kristallnacht is not really a historical argument. It is a political argument disguised as a historical argument. It is designed to paralyze thought and to paralyze diplomacy.

The Oslo contribution to Y2KMind shines through. Like so often in the aughts, the cart drives the horse: the demands of diplomacy (peace process to a two-state solution even after Palestinian leadership makes it clear that's not possible) forbid anyone from suggesting important parallels between Nazi, paranoid, apocalyptic, genocidal hatred and those of an unknown range of the 1.5 billion Muslims that populate the world today and, alas, among their more radical "progressive" allies.[90] To even suggest as much means you're paralyzing, dead-end diplomacy, guilty of forbidding a dead horse to move.

Of course, Wieseltier also commits what he denounces: political argument disguised as an historical argument—"There is nothing, nothing, in the politics, the society, or the culture of the United States that can support such a ghastly premonition [that it will be here, as it was in Germany]." Thus, any observation of "reality" that supports those opposed to Oslo's two-state Logic, and who view the spread of virulent anti-Israel invective as a twenty-first century avatar of anti-Semitism, cannot be taken seriously.

And yet, certainly retrospectively, two things stand out.

1. The Oslo Peace Process was, as far as the Palestinians were concerned, actually a war process: *land for war*; and
2. The wave of anti-Zionism that hit the West beginning with the Al Durah affair at the turn of the millennium, presaged a development that has already by the early '20s, reached levels, on the left and right, that few, certainly not Wieseltier, not even I who had warned about it, imagined back in the early aughts.

---

90 Jeffrey Herf, *Nazi Propaganda for the Arab World* (New Haven: Yale University Press, 2009); Joseph Spoerl, "Parallels between Nazi and Islamist Antisemitism," *Jewish Political Studies Review*, 31 (2020).

In 2018, David Collier, one of Britain's preeminent researchers of current antisemitism, wrote: "The demonization of Jewish people, via a colossal anti-Israel disinformation campaign, has infected every local authority and education establishment in Europe. A continent-wide antisemitic trend just 70 years after the Europeans exterminated six million Jews."[91] In the US, a survey of the tweets of academic "Diversity, Equity and Inclusion" administrators (the cutting edge of woke antiracism) prove to be almost uniformly hostile to Israel.[92] The hatred and the violence comes from every corner of the political and ethnic field—white supremacists, black nationalists, Muslims, left-wing intellectuals . . .[93]

Jewish Liberal Virtue Signaling and Muslim Antisemitism

Perhaps the most tragic and banal part of the story concerns the liberals, those who did not adopt the replacement narrative, but who nonetheless, remained either silent or in Manfred Gerstenfeld's felicitous phrase, "verbal vegetarians" about Israel. Here virtue signaling reigned supreme: if you defended Israel you immediately got labeled "right wing" and no matter how Jews (and other liberals) might sympathize with Israel *despite* the image purveyed by the media, *a fortiori* liberal media like NPR and the *New York Times*, they were not willing to risk their credentials as "good people" either by speaking out on Israel's behalf, or, still worse, actively criticizing the progressives leading the charge of lemmings over the cliff.

---

91 David Collier, tweet, September 29, 2018, https://twitter.com/mishtal/status/1045921897681178625.

92 Jay Green and James Paul, "Inclusion Delusion: The Antisemitism of Diversity, Equity, and Inclusion Staff at Universities," *Heritage Foundation*, December 8, 2021; on the takeover of university administrations by DEI staff, see idem, "Diversity University: DEI Bloat in the Academy," *Heritage Foundation*, July 27, 2021.

93 Dimitry Shapiro, "Federal civil-rights officials raise alarm over 'horrifying statistics' on anti-Semitism in workplace," *JNS*, January 13, 2022.

WHAT LEMMINGS BELIEVE

FIGURE 28. "What Lemmings Believe," by David Mankoff, *New Yorker*, April 14, 1997.

On the contrary, when forced to take sides, most often the Jewish leadership sought to appease rather than confront the disapproval, eager to make nice with former allies who had swallowed the Palestinian war propaganda that hit the media fan in 2000. And being sincere people, they felt compelled to swallow the same poisons: lamentably, the IDF kills hundreds, thousands of children.[94] As a result, some of the liberal Jewish leadership and much of the liberal Jewish intelligentsia got caught up in the wide-ranging, politically correct discourse that favored nonconfrontational dialogues with representatives of the vast majority of peaceful Muslims, and support for all that they wanted. Unable to distinguish a genuine Muslim moderate, co-participant in a civil polity that guaranteed freedom of religion to all, from a demopathic *da'i* determined to take over and impose Sharia—and cutting themselves off from people who urged that distinction—these Jewish leaders repeatedly strengthened the worst Caliphator tendencies.

---

94 See n69. I got the same response (with inflated figures - thousands!) from the then heads of the New England *AJC* and of *The Israel Project*.

The ADL, normally so vocal about denouncing antisemitism—their job, after all—suddenly found it difficult to even discuss jihadi, triumphalist, Muslim antisemitism.[95] *Facing History*, normally so attuned to the language of genocide to prevent another Holocaust, suddenly became protective of the very group whose most vocal members were the most ardent practitioners of genocidal discourse on the planet.[96] The AJC, and other leaders normally so solicitous of the needs of the Jewish community, welcomed and partnered with triumphalist Muslims to help them succeed.[97] The role of liberal, ecumenical Jews in welcoming Muslims was so prominent, that at least some of those Western infidels who became alarmed by the advances of the Caliphator invasion of their lands, began to believe that the Jews were conspiring to bring down their societies. Much alt-right, antisemitism is based on the belief that the Jewish ecumenical drive is a deliberate effort to destroy the society. Soros is their Antichrist.[98]

The Cult of the Occupation: On the Disorientations of the Liberal "Left"

I had a striking conversation in the mid-teens with someone whose work I admire for its freedom from much of the day's cant. To my surprise, he almost immediately peppered me with questions about whether I supported the "settlements" or favored ending the "occupation." When I tried to point out that these were not the main issues obstructing peace, he answered, "No one will listen to you; they'll just accuse you of changing the subject." In so doing, this interlocutor spoke for most liberals and progressives in the West, including the then President of the US. As Obama explained to Jeffrey Goldberg, when Netanyahu had the nerve to explain to him "about the dangers of the brutal region in which [Israel] lived," Obama felt he was "avoiding the subject at hand: peace negotiations."[99]

---

95 Ilya Feoktistov and Charles Jacobs, "Study: ADL Fails to Focus on Islamic Extremism as a Threat to World Jewry," *Americans for Peace and Tolerance*, November 5, 2011.

96 Ruth Wisse, "The Dark Side of Holocaust Education," *TikvahFund*, May 7, 2020.

97 Ilya Feoktistov, *Terror in the Cradle of Liberty*.

98 Kevin MacDonald, "The Alt Right and the Jews," *Occidental Observer*, September 17, 2016; Joshua Muravchik, "Q and the Jews," *Mosaic*, February 3, 2021.

99 Jeffrey Goldberg, "The Obama Doctrine," *Atlantic*, April 2016. Obama's remark to Netanyahu that his own past made it possible to understand the Middle East conflict is one of the great testimonies to his cognitive egocentrism. Obama's remarks on Israel in his subsequent book indicate that he had imbibed the narrative in which the Palestinians were innocent victims.

Indeed, it seems a fair generalization to say that for most Westerners who consider themselves on the "compassionate left" the "settlements," and more broadly, the "occupation," are unquestionably *the* most critical obstacles to peace in the Middle East. So strong is this belief, that when Israel's democratically elected governments refuse to comply with demands to end the occupation and dismantle the settlements, Western well-wishers grow "impatient."[100] Given the choice between liberal values and an Israel increasingly (perceived as) non-liberal, American Jews, Peter Beinart argues, will choose liberal values.[101] Or, as the actor and Zionist Michael Douglas put it, West Bank settlements are "the one issue that has alienated more of Israel's friends than any other."[102] This approach, however well-meant, also matches the narrative that Caliphators prescribe for infidels.

Many Jews find this dilemma unbearable: either they ignore the remorseless hostility to Israel and push her to behave liberally in a zone deeply hostile to liberal values, or they allow a bad situation to worsen, reluctantly siding with an Israel which behaves in ways profoundly at odds with their liberal values. With the consistent failure of Land for Peace efforts, many feel greater irritation with Israel and more willingness to coerce her into making the necessary concessions. But above all, their choices reflect the prime directive: "Do not frustrate the Palestinians."

Largely, this desire to force Israel into the concessions it "unreasonably" refuses to make, translates into the effort to turn Western powers and world opinion against the Israeli occupation. With enough outside pressure, built up by a constant barrage of criticism, so runs the thinking of organizations like J-Street, we can all move forward.[103] A progressive Jew emailed a list-serv I am on: "I just wish [Obama] would use [his office] in pushing Netanyahu toward a reasonable compromise on Palestine, probably through approving a tough resolution in the UN Security Council. Probably after the November elections." So certain was he that the email solution is reasonable (i.e., the Palestinians will be satisfied with the deal), that he's willing to mobilize international force

---

Anything Netanyahu might have said about the "neighborhood" was therefore inadmissible evidence. Dov Lipman, "Obama's Revisionist 'Promised Land,'" *JNS*, November 26, 2020.

100 Derfner, "The Reluctant Boycotter: Why This Liberal Zionist Now Supports BDS," *Haaretz*, February 8, 2016.

101 Peter Beinart, "The Failure of the American Jewish Establishment," *New York Review of Books*, June 10, 2010.

102 Ira Stoller, "Sharansky Breasts a Protest against his Talk at Brown on Jewish Identity," *The New York Sun*, January 29, 2016.

103 Daniel Gordis to a J-Street delegation to Israel, "In the Tent, or Out: That is Still the J-Street Question," *TC Jewfolk*, June 5, 2011.

against Israel, using the grotesque parody of peace-promoting that the UN has become, to achieve that end.[104] And the president of the USA agreed with him.[105] From this perspective, my focus on the problem of Palestinian motives and actions, on treating the Palestinians as if they had agency and insisting that their terrorism is intolerable to a global civil society, indeed constitutes "changing the subject."

For some, the cognitive dissonance involved in realizing that, at best, the liberal strategy, the "Two-State Solution," will not work, more likely will backfire, is unbearable. Some resolve this by doubling down and joining "the cult of the Occupation."[106] Ending the Occupation of the West Bank becomes not a means to an (impossible) end, but the goal—at any price. And again, Caliphators could not rejoice more.

Here the discourse no longer involves mutuality but focuses exclusively on Israel's moral failings; its "Occupation" (capital O) becomes a symbol of everything wrong in the world, the intersectional peak of oppressive racism. In opposing the Israeli Occupation one strikes a blow for global justice and contributes to a peaceful, just world. Journalist and long-time AP correspondent Matti Friedman, who coined the term, writes:

> As usual with Western religions, the centre of this one is in the Holy Land. The dogma posits that the occupation is not a conflict like any other, but that it is the very symbol of conflict: that the minute state inhabited by a persecuted minority in the Middle East is in fact a symbol of the ills of the West—colonialism, nationalism, militarism, and racism. In the recent riots in Ferguson, Missouri, for example, a sign hoisted by marchers linked the unrest between African Americans and the police to Israeli rule over Palestinians.[107]

---

104 Pedro Sanjuan, *The UN Gang: A Memoir of Incompetence, Corruption, Espionage, Antisemitism and Islamic Extremism at the UN Secretariat* (NY, 2005). See the watchdog website *UNWatch*, https://unwatch.org/.

105 Sue Surkes, "US may back UN outline of two-state deal in fresh peace push," *Times of Israel*, March 8, 2016.

106 Matti Friedman, "Ideological roots of media bias." Discussed below.

107 *Ibid*. The intersectional alliance forged at Ferguson has become a key rhetorical theme for both Black "antiracism" (Black Lives Matter) and Palestinian anti-colonialism.

Currently, for many around the world, Israel symbolizes the cruel who crush the weak: the embodiment of imperialist, racist, colonialist, oppression, the woke's Antichrist.

So central has this position become, that massive activist mechanisms (like BDS) are mobilized to capitalize on the promise that *getting rid of the occupation will solve the problem*.[108] Notes Friedman:

> The cult's priesthood can be found among the activists, NGO experts, and ideological journalists who have turned coverage of this conflict into a catalogue of Jewish moral failings, as if Israeli society were different from any other group of people on earth, as if Jews deserve to be mocked for having suffered and failed to be perfect as a result.

Indeed, some like Tuvia Tenenbom, have documented how a decisive majority of "human rights" efforts in this region are focused on ending the Israeli occupation at almost any price, including that of systematic misinformation.[109]

In its Jewish form, the cult narrative runs as follows: The occupation corrupts; it's an indelible stain on Israel's democratic soul. Ending that occupation is a goal that supersedes all others ... even if it doesn't lead to peace. A "true Israeli patriot" is willing to mobilize international pressure against Israel to force her concessions, even if it means aligning with unsavory people to get the job done. As the journalist Larry Derfner puts it: "I have serious problems with the tenor of the BDS movement—but not nearly as serious as those I have with the occupation." All of this, he insists, is done out of a sincere concern for Israel: "If you love Israel, act to save her now."[110]

This consensus on the "progressive left" exerts immense peer pressure on Jews, especially "progressive," to explicitly disavow Israel.[111] Again, Matti Friedman:

> So prevalent has this kind of thinking become that participating in liberal intellectual life in the West increasingly requires you to

---

108 "What is BDS?" *BDS: Freedom Justice Equality*.

109 Tuvia Tenenbom, *Catch the Jew* (Jerusalem: Gefen, 2015). Apartheid Week offers a good example of systematic misinformation based on lethal journalism. On NGO malfeasance, Steinberg, "Role of NGOs."

110 Derfner, "The Reluctant Boycotter."

111 "LGBT Group cancels conference reception with Israeli activists," *Washington Blade*, January 18, 2016.

subscribe at least outwardly to this dogma, particularly if you're a Jew and thus suspected of the wrong sympathies. If you're a Jew from Israel, your participation is increasingly conditional on an abject and public display of self-flagellation. Your participation, indeed, is increasingly unwelcome.

Advocates of intersectionality have identified Israel as a world-wide purveyor of oppression, the epitome of racist-imperialist-apartheid-colonialism, and that ideology now circulates at the highest levels of the public sphere.[112]

This widespread, self-congratulatory, self-critical, Jewish discourse about bad Israel, can reach astonishing proportions: high ranking Jewish figures—academics, public intellectuals, former generals and heads of intelligence—regularly take positions that reinforce the worst thinking about this conflict. In 2018, from the Harvard School of Government, Ehud Barak, engaged in a rant that no Caliphator could have scripted better:

> Our own government unfortunately, involved for the last three years, in an attack on the foundational institutions of our democracy, the supreme court is under continuous attack, the free press is under continuous attack, the civil society and the human rights NGOs are, eh, eh, eh, under continuous attack, as well as the ethical codes and the very moral authority of the commanders of the IDF. And that's what's damaging Israel. Done in the name of something great, a great vision, which is a delusional one, it's basically ultra-nationalist, um, vision messianic and dark.[113]

Barak here uses inflated dog-whistles like "ultranationalist" (code word for neo-Nazi), presents the Israeli Supreme Court and the human rights NGOs as blameless victims of an existential attack from a "dark messianic place"; and paints a picture that strips that "nice idea of Zionism" of any moral authority. In so doing, Barak could not fulfill the wishes of Caliphator cogwarriors more brilliantly: they, of course, do not want the West to defend itself; they want the

---

112 "In the Safe Spaces on Campus, no Jews Allowed," *Tower Magazine*, February 2016. On J-Street's embrace of intersectional analysis, Amna Farooqi, "Worried About Intersectionality? Oppose the Israeli Occupation," *Haaretz*, January 17, 2016.

113 Anderson Interviews Barak, October 2, 2018, at 03:56 Becky Anderson, who'd chosen Barak to give a critique of Trump seemed somewhat surprised by the vehemence of his attack on Israel. "Well these are your um, uh, personal thoughts," https://vimeo.com/467008181.

West to attack, ferociously, any other group of infidels who are also facing their Caliphator attack and (successfully) defending themselves. And they do so, with the "help" of a legion of people, "as-a-Jew" Jews, "as-a-former-Israeli-general-security-specialist-prime minister" Israelis—who somehow feel that trashing Israel publicly signals their virtue.[114]

Whatever Barak's specific motivations (and I know many, mostly academic, Israelis that would agree with his analysis), the world, certainly viewers of CNN, don't need to have this rhetorically inflated "self"-criticism disgorged in public using emotionally and ideologically charged accusations against his own country. He should have heeded Yair Lapid's remark to Stephen Sackur when the "tough" *HardTalk* host pressed him to criticize Bibi: "I won't stand on foreign soil and criticize my prime minister . . . it's just not done."[115] Here Barak stood on foreign soil and trashed his country, its army, its very legitimacy. (I'm guessing Barak's Kennedy-School peer group approved heartily of his performance . . . the brotherhood of the own-goal, Cult of the Occupation.) What Caliphator could ask for more help in the goal of blaming Israel and preventing Western infidels from thinking clearly?

But in their mimetic desire to please this "moral" peer group, Jewish members of the Cult of the Occupation give little heed to the dangers they or their progressive colleagues court. How easily one can get virtually any bright Israeli professor to wax eloquent on how much they hate Bibi, how disgusting the "right-wing's" attacks on their intellectual hegemony and on the justice system, and how deplorably Israel treats the Palestinians.[116] Don't ask them to forgo signaling their public virtue thusly because, in so doing, they make their progressive bona fides clear. Little matter that they ally themselves with the very forces of Palestinian irredentism that inspire Israelis on the ground to reject a two-state solution with the compromises and vulnerability it demands. The same alienation between elites and commoners plays out all over democracies under Caliphator attack: the people lose faith in their information elites—justifiably.[117]

Rather than listen to Israeli concerns, however, Jews against themselves comply with the demands of this Palestinian/Arab/Muslim grievance and

---

114 On the ex-intelligence heads, see Dror Moreh's documentary "*The Gatekeepers*" (2012); on as-a-Jew virtue-signaling, see Landes, "On Anorexic Jews and Virtue Signaling: Hasia Diner and Marjorie Feld, 'Historians'," *Augean Stables,* August 3, 2016.

115 Landes, "Steven Sackur, Bully and Wimp," at 07:36–48.

116 In 2021, many Jewish Studies professors signed a statement denouncing Israel's attack on Gaza: "Jewish Studies and Israel Studies Scholars Write Against Israel," *Israel Academia Monitor,* May 22, 2021.

117 Pedro Zuquete, *The Identitarians: The Movement against Globalism and Islam in Europe* (South Bend, IN: University of Notre Dame Press, 2021).

blame Israel. Convinced the obvious, simple, emailable solution lies in getting Israel to concede more, with each (predictable) failure at compromise, cult members grow more frustrated with *Israel*, the unyielding bully. At the same time, they support those who define the "peace of the brave" as victory over *'al Yahud*, and they end up marching with those who would "destroy Israel for world peace."[118]

This approach, alas, not only supports a "Palestinian" goal—the elimination of the merest trace of infidel autonomy in Dar al Islam (i.e., Arabic for "Occupation")—but the larger goal that resonates in the Umma, the core of Caliphator aspirations—eliminate all independent infidels. If calling Israel "ultra-national" is wildly inappropriate when compared with real ultra-nationalism among other "nations" in the region, then describing what's going on in Israel as "dark messianism" looks obsessional in comparison with the dark apocalyptic imagination at work in Caliphator Islam. And instead, those who speak so, fulfill the prophecy of a Saudi apocalyptic theologian, that it is the Zionist fighter's "duty to fight for the opposing side."[119] To paraphrase Blake, "any man of mechanical talent may, from the writings and pronouncements of 'liberal' Israelis and Jews, produce ten thousand volumes with which the Caliphators can wage their war on them."

On the Dangers of Jew-Washing

In his 1988 discussion of the unique historical phenomenon of Jewish self-hatred, Aharon Appelfeld remarked on its one saving grace: "Only one thing may be said in its favor: it harms no one except those afflicted with it." The twenty-first century has changed all that. As long as, in premodern conditions, the direct target of Jew-hatred was Jews, a defenseless minority, the considerable damage done to those who *believed* Judeophobic fantasies was sufficiently removed from the causal chain. How many in 16th century Spain noted how the absence of Jews adversely affected the economy just as gold from the New World was flowing in and out of Spain? Already the Holocaust showed what calamities befell those seized by paranoid, megalomaniacal, madness about Jews. But now, in the twenty-first century, when Jew-hatred plays a major role in

---

118 Richard Millet, "Lauren Booth: Lebanon, Jordan and Egypt must liberate Jerusalem," Millet's Blog, August 22, 2011; Itamar Marcus, "PA: Kill Jews to save the world," *Jerusalem Post*, January 22, 2020.

119 Hawali, *Day of Wrath*, 2.

Caliphator cogwar against the West, the almost immediate secondary victims of Jew-hatred are those infidel fools stupid enough to believe that the only reason Palestinians hate Israelis is because of how cruelly they frustrate Palestinian yearning for their own nation, and the only reason the rest of the Umma hates pro-Israel Jews, is out of solidarity with those "national aspirations."

And of course, the eagerness with which Jews take to public self-criticism, to displaying their remarkable capacity for self-criticism, plays right into that narrative of the Jew who deserves to be hated, the bully, the racist, the ultra-nationalist, the Nazi, the malevolent hater of mankind. In an age where suddenly—in 2000—the most un-PC post-Holocaust obscenities were aggressively asserted—Israel = Nazis—it became open season on taking shots at Israel. Even bright and talented minds fell, and continue to fall, prey to the siren song of jihadi war propaganda: ISRAEL MASSACRES INNOCENT MUSLIMS!! DESTROY ISRAEL FOR WORLD PEACE!!

And Jews who want to oppose such libels cannot, because ... other Jews earnestly repeat them. It's self-evident, that if Jews say these things, so can gentiles. Once Charles Enderlin promoted the blood libel of al Durah, not even the IDF spokesman's office, where he had formerly served, could dissent: the ultimate Jew-wash for the first global blood libel. One analyst asserted the obvious: "Israeli policy towards the Palestinians is harshly criticized as part of the intra Israeli political debate, as well as by Jews all over the world; to postulate such criticism when voiced by non-Jews as antisemitic is absurd."[120] Jew-washing Jew-hatred ... a millennia-old tradition of Jew-baiting, given new life in the new millennium.[121]

So what's wrong with criticizing Israel "harshly"?

Well, for one thing, the criticism might be incorrect. For example, Israel isn't anything like what news media-informed outsiders imagine, including the "human rights tourists" to Israel/Palestine and their Potemkin villages of suffering where questions are not allowed.[122] For another, the accusations, like Israeli Apartheid, are sewn of a tissue of dishonest warp and malicious

---

120 Daniel Gutwein, "New-Antisemitism as Zeitgeist of the Neo-Liberal and Postmodern Era: Some Remarks,"https://drive.google.com/file/d/0B-kkMIb7I38MOXVHTWVIdnBGUGc/view?resourcekey.

121 Yitzak Santis and Gerald Steinberg, "On 'Jew-Washing' and BDS," The Jewish Week, July 24, 2012.

122 The hue and cry over Israel not vaccinating the Palestinians in the West Bank even as Han Chinese systematically rape Uyghur woman illustrates the moral disorientation. Diversity, Equity and Inclusion administrators (n92) display great respect for the Chinese (62% of tweets on China favorable vs. 96% of those about Israel negative).

woof.[123] For yet another, it tends to make those outsiders incapable of criticizing Palestinians or holding them to any moral standards. Were they to begin looking at Palestinian faults, it would take the air out of the moral tires with which they run over Israel.

As the privileged victim of an intersectional, systemic racism/oppression, Palestinians are forgiven all, no matter how heinous; and Israel, their oppressors, forgiven nothing, not even the crimes they did not commit. In adopting this discourse, in succumbing to the "unique Jewish pathology" of hyper-self-criticism against Israel, diaspora Jews indulge in an orgy of moral degradation: "This image really does erase, replace the symbol of 'our' Holocaust catastrophe."

But so far we have focused on mere matters of intellectual and moral integrity, of (post-Holocaust) decency. Why else should anyone in the West (the primary infidel audience of this book) need to care or get involved? After all, from their perspective, it sure looks like Jews and their Israel project are making things much worse, making the jihadis more violent. They're a needless provocation, a rock thrown at a hornet's nest. Who wouldn't be tempted to say at the very least, "a plague on both your houses"?[124]

Of course, there's the analytic road not taken. Namely, that the "pro-Palestinian" progressives, and the liberals in their gravitational pull, take positions on our conflict with our neighbors that systematically disorient you, non-Jews, non-Israelis. The approach that blames Israel has not only made it very difficult and costly for Israel to defend itself from the "Palestinian" jihadi assault, but it has also made Western cultures where this discourse prevails, incapable of dealing with, rebuking, and resisting the Palestinians' cousins, the global Caliphators and their recruiting pool of Muslim triumphalists living in Western democracies. By siding with Caliphators against the Jewish exercise of sovereignty for the first time in two millennia, Western infidels have rendered themselves patsies, even *active participants* in the destruction of their own society and the culture that produced their great moral aspirations.

Knowing how much some Jews and Israelis are limbic captives of public self-criticism, I don't think there's much anyone can say that will dissuade the *alterjuifs* (Nahoum/Edgar Morin, Peter Beinart, Ken Roth, Medea Benjamin, Daniel Boyarin) from pursuing the rush they get from debasing their own

---

123 Joshua Kern and Anne Herzberg, *False Knowledge as Power: Deconstructing Definitions of Apartheid that Delegitimise the Jewish State* (Jerusalem: NGOMonitor, 2021).
124 The reason one editor suggested my first chapter be on 9–11. Otherwise, it would be "too Jewish."

people in front of outsiders. Perhaps some might reconsider performing in front of people visibly driven by moral *Schadenfreude,* but in an age of internet:

The only thing I can hope for,
is to reach gentiles mature enough to understand
that this discourse is poisonous to the very kind of society it pretends to
promote . . .
that Jew-hatred,
especially in its twenty-first-century avatar of Israel-hatred,
is the soft underbelly whereby Caliphators invade the West
and groom infidels for submission;
that following the lead of these publicly self-loathing
"prophetic" Jews
is a recipe for self-destruction.

Part Three

ARE WE REALLY GOING TO LET THIS HAPPEN (AGAIN)?

---

11. 2000: The Launch of Global Jihad

Can't be what you say:
"They want to conquer the world"?
How Ridiculous

12. Y2K Mind: Oxymoronic Progressives

And yet we were caught
On our heels, mouth inhaling
When Jihad's sh*t hit

13. Preemptive Dhimmitude: Unwitting Submission

If I don't see it . . .
deny it even exists . . .
Does it count?

14. Woke Jihad: Contact Apocalyptic Highs

Collective moral
Indignation sure beats the
Hell out of thinking

15. To Sound Minds: On Our Watch?

Beloved Sire, please
excuse my stupidity.
You are butt naked.

11

2000: The Launch of Global Jihad

Can't be what you say:
"They want to conquer the world"?
How Ridiculous

Having profiled the various players (part two), let us take up the narrative thread from part one, viewing the opening two decades of the twenty-first century from the perspective of millennial beliefs in action. In those first years, two global millennial movements went apocalyptic, that is, mobilized to transform the world from its current state, permeated with evil, into "heaven on earth." On the one hand, Muslim triumphalists (chapter 6) sought to restore and extend the dominion of Islam over the whole world, the global Caliphate where Sharia would assure true justice. It had an active cataclysmic side (Jihad) and a nonviolent transformative current (Da'wa). On the other, Western progressives (chapter 8), dreamed of a noncoercive, cooperative, egalitarian and diverse global community, through the protection of human rights, the health and welfare for all, an end to war and racism. Progressives were mostly transformative, but, increasingly after 2000, produced a more rupture-seeking side (BDS, BLM, Antifa): from "transformative" Critical Race Theory to looting as political action.[1] For both groups, globalization and the advent of the internet

---

1 "Critical Race Theory is an experientially grounded, oppositionally expressed, and transformatively aspirational concern with race and other socially constructed hierarchies," Derrick Bell, "Who's Afraid of Critical Race Theory?" *University of Illinois Law Review*, 893 (1995), 906; Vicky Osterweil, *In Defense of Looting: A Riotous History of Uncivil Action* (New York: Hachette Group, 2020).

injected their revolutionary expectations with a sense of imminence. For most triumphalist Muslims, at least initially, it provoked apocalyptic fears; for many Progressives, it inspired utopian hopes.

At the end of September 2000/Rajab 1421, the Jewish New Year 5761 to be precise, jihadis made their first assault directly on the infidel population of a Western democracy. Palestinian Caliphators (chapter 6), with the help of lethal journalists (chapter 9), launched the banner meme of the first battlefield of Global Jihad, the blood libel of Israel's deliberate murder of le petit Mohamed al Durah, followed rapidly by a merciless attack of suicide terror. This offensive was, as many millennial wars, a madly asymmetrical one in which the apocalyptic attackers were vastly inferior in military force to those they attacked, whether Palestinians against Israelis or Caliphators against the West. But it was nothing less than what the companions of the Prophet attempted in their assault on Persia and Rome.

At this point, while most Muslims were enthusiastic backers of the war on Israel, only some small radical (millennial) zealots thought the Umma was ready to start a global war against infidels everywhere, and even fewer were prepared to use the still-disapproved but fearful weapon of suicide-bombers to attack infidels in other democracies, including the US. For many Muslims in diaspora (itself a rare phenomenon in the fourteen centuries of Islam), Bin Laden's aggression could only endanger their lives. But they, by and large, were the old generation. To #GenerationCaliphate, to a young generation responsive to a web-based, neo-Islam, the al-Durah libel and the extensive coverage of the Intifada was a wake-up call.

The modern West, at this point, constituted the unquestioned global hegemon, which, in the previous two hundred years, had exercised a near total military superiority over Muslim armies, and now near total cultural superiority over the whole world. Western technology had both physically and culturally conquered the world, and now the internet promised a new age of massively increased and penetrating global communication. Since the collapse of the USSR in the early 1990s, "conversions" to liberal democracy around the world made some believe in the advent of a global millennium of civil polities.

The Caliphators' daunting task was: how to "peacefully" penetrate this ecumenical global culture despite the immense differences in the values and goals they cherished. At this point, they benefited enormously from a key development in the culture they targeted, the crystallization of an attitude among that culture's elites that, until that point, had a limited impact on the public sphere, but now began to assume a position of dominance. *When jihadis attack a democracy, blame the democracy.*

What might have aroused suspicion and opposition to Caliphators, what people committed to democratic polities, with some basic knowledge of religious (millennial) dynamics, and a firm grip on key progressive values, might have decisively discouraged among the fiery dreamers of our enemies, instead turned into an astonishing string of spectacular cogwar victories for the Caliphators. Indeed, virtually every move that Western progressives made in response to Global Jihad—running their hate propaganda as news, not running their assaults and hate speech as news—strengthened it at every turn. Instead of realizing that this heinous new and unstoppable weapon of suicide-terror, was trained on them, progressives redefined and hailed it as "resistance" to colonial oppression and occupation, and journalists refused to call it terrorism. In their Westsplaining disorientation, progressives identified Mujahideen as a form of anti-imperial "freedom fighter," legitimately objecting to US aggression. —Despite the fact that they were some of the fiercest and most ambitious imperialists the world has ever seen, progressives welcomed Caliphators into their global movement.

When the first democracy to resist jihadi suicide terrorists attacked their headquarters—established in territory that democracy had ceded in pursuit of peace—progressive infidels, disinformed by their own-goal media about Israelis massacring Palestinians like Nazis, demonstrated in large angry crowds around the world. Calling the army resisting suicide terror "Nazis," they donned mock suicide vests to show their solidarity with their own enemies. And while not everyone danced like the new agers on the roof of the skyscraper welcoming in the destructive aliens in *Independence Day*, the overwhelming consensus among liberals was that these martyrdom operations were resistance to occupation by an evil empire.

Can the whole world be wrong and Israel be right? In such global moral and empirical disorientation, it was quite beyond the reach of most Westerners, including most Israelis, to understand that Israel was fighting the new century's Global Jihad. Y2KMind forged its self-accusatory manacles in the fires of Israel's war with triumphalist Islam: When jihadis attacked Israel, it vociferously blamed Israel. This Western misreading had a two-fold impact on democracies in the new century. First, it kept Western infidels in the dark about the nature of their enemy.[2] Second, the inverted logic that Western observers applied so perversely to Israelis under attack, they ended up turning on themselves.

---

2   See chapter 6.

Progressives, shedding tears of the white man,[3] applied the same punitive logic to American guilt. Ask not: "Why do they hate us so?" but: "What did we do to make them hate us so?" Journalists and academics Westsplained jihad to their infidel audiences in terms of Western postcolonial narratives: jihadis were lamentably violent, but nevertheless fighting for political and social justice—not Islamic dominion. (As if Caliphators considered these two mutually exclusive). Suicide terror was an act of resistance to occupation—*not* aspirations to conquer the West. "Extremist violence" was senseless and had "nothing to do" with (true) Islam. The more Westerners had difficulty understanding their obscure and irrational enemy, the more logical seemed the alternative explanation: it was the West's fault.

All this rephrased in progressive terms the narrative that Da'wa Caliphators tailored for infidels, to disguise their intent and flip the opprobrium: *Blame the democracy for even thinking we want to overthrow them.* Caliphators laughed in derision as Westsplaining pundits on TV attributed jihadi attacks to anger at infidel foreign policy (supporting Israel in Palestine or US in Iraq), or intolerable insults (drawings of Muhammad, calling Islam violent). What better way to conceal the real reasons for the violence, namely the religious hatred and imperialist ambitions?

Caliphators flourished in the shade of the white man's tears. They could preach their hatreds literally under the noses of their targets, in the case of Major Hasan at Fort Hood in 2009, in the heart of the enemy military, openly, to their faces. Liberals and progressives, tripped over themselves to welcome Islamic mosques created by what they were determined to believe—despite ample counter-evidence—were "moderate" Muslims.[4] In the aftermath of 9/11, Muslims found Da'wa easier, not harder among Americans.[5] Much easier.

This victory of Y2KMind did not come easily or immediately. Initially, the narrative met resistance among some infidels. US and British journalists, who had accepted the principle where it concerned Hamas and Israel, bristled at the new party line against using the term "terrorist" to designate those who attacked their own people. Some scholars laughed out loud when others piously declared Islam a "religion of peace." But over the following years, their laughter died, their voices weakened, and a marginal and self-contradictory discourse went mainstream: "one man's terrorist is another's freedom fighter; Islam is a religion of peace; do not call Mujahideen terrorists, or if you do, say they're

---

3 Bruckner, *Tears of the White Man.*
4 Feoktistov, *Terror in the Cradle of Liberty.*
5 Brendan Bernhard, *White Muslims.*

not true Muslims." Indeed, this mentality born in 2000, has gained increasing dominance in the West. In 2006, when Muslims rioted and killed in protest at being called violent, no one laughed.

It helped immensely, that this progressive discourse was extremely sensitive to micro-aggressions against those they considered victimized by Western supremacy (ex-colonies, ex slaves, curiously not Jews), under cover of which Caliphators could ban their critics as Islamophobes. Given the abundant evidence of the presence of Caliphators and their designs, those infidels pushing the "blame the West" narrative had to find a way to drive this evidence from the public sphere. This they did by harshly chastising Westerners for any suspicion of the Muslim "other." *They* were racists, xenophobes, tribalist Islamophobes, rightwing, fascist, white supremacists.

At the same time, progressives insisted that the violent jihadis were apostates, hijacking a noble religion of peace.[6] The rise of a cancel culture of moral outrage—the banishing of an idea or person from the public sphere because it constitutes hate speech or racism—made it possible to silence the warnings and exclude vast areas of important information from the public. Westsplainers warned against moral panics about Muslims (Klausen, Hoffman), even as Caliphators recruited Muslims with moral panics.

In 2000, readers of the high-brow Western news—the *New York Times*, BBC News, the *Guardian*, *Le Monde*—did not know that the Hamas their fellow progressives celebrated was in fact a major purveyor of racist, genocidal hate speech, architects of an apocalyptic cult of suicide terror. Nor would they hear about it in the following years. On the contrary, even as Palestinian terrorism flourished, liberals made support for the Palestinian cause a litmus test of political bona fides. In subsequent years, as global jihadis hit other democracies, these same readers knew little about the Caliphators in their midst, their raging hatreds, their contempt for infidel human life, their dreams of dominion.[7] Radical mosques—revamped old ones and brand new ones—sprouted all over *dar al Harb*. BU's Religion Department held a discussion about the "misnamed" *Ground Zero Mosque* in which all four participants supported its construction (religious freedom), and the offer of a counter-position, rejected.[8]

On the contrary, in high-minded progressive publications, any statement that even sounded Islamophobic, that *might give the impression of* creating hostility

---

6 "Kerry brands ISIS apostates," *Al Arabiya*, February 2, 2016.
7 See Goldberg, *Media Bias*, 324.
8 "This is an information panel, not a debate," responded a colleague in the Religion department when I offered to give another perspective. When I suggested I might offer information others would not, she left in anger.

towards Muslims, could become cause for disqualification from public life. It became almost impossible to discuss Caliphators and their goals. Indeed, while Caliphators were crystal clear on who the enemy was—unsubjected infidels, *harbi*, especially progressives and Jews—the West could not name their enemy in this war. Indeed, many of the highest-minded, denied we were at war . . . and if we were, it's because of people like Huntington, Pipes and other right-wing, neo-con, fear-mongers. As Pogo said prophetically but without a trace of irony, "We have met the enemy and he is us."

The result was a kind of cultural AIDS, in which Western leaders attacked not the invading bodies, but those who warned of the invasion. The media suppression of descriptions that might arouse hostility to Muslims led to a chronic insensitivity to pain syndrome, in which the nerves (media) did not convey to the brain (public sphere) the pain Caliphators inflicted on domestic populations, the sudden and radical changes in the neighborhood dynamics in places like the Parisian suburbs, or Malmo, or Rotterdam. In England, the entire spectrum of responsible adults from parents and teachers to journalists and elected officials, failed to stop the systematic rape of infidel girls by brutal triumphalist Muslims, *lest* they get accused of Islamophobia. The most brutal tribal war cries of the Caliphators in London in February 2006 promising to conquer Denmark and rape its women, were actually happening, and few knew it. And when they found out, their betters told them not to take notice.

Western elites became so dulled to the danger that ten years after dire warnings of a long-term demographic shift towards Muslims in Europe, the normally cautious chancellor of Germany, with the EU, pundits and journalists behind her, took in over a million Muslims, mostly men, many not registered. Any country that opposed her policies, like the Austrians, were accused of Islamophobia and proto-fascism. The German press favored pictures of children and families, over the clips of aggressive young males contemptuously trashing proffered water bottles and running wild in the streets. That footage only appeared on the internet. That New Year's Eve (2015/16), there were large-scale "immigrant" assaults on women at the celebrations, especially in Köln, and it wasn't until it became a Facebook-launched scandal, almost a week later, that the legacy media discussed it.[9]

When the new wave of immigrants led to the Brexit crisis, tense negotiations took place in which the real problem—not immigration but *Muslim* migration—wasn't named. The narrative prevailed. Fifteen years after the early warnings,

---

9 "2015–16 New Year's Eve sexual assaults in Germany," *Wikipedia*. See also below, n11.

progressive pundits still sneer at the demographic threat.[10] Six years after the million refugee wave, while some document the catastrophic impact of Muslim immigrants on the lives of Western women unlucky enough to inhabit a state that welcomes them,[11] the *New York Review of Books* publishes an article reassuring its readers that despite the dire predictions, Merkel's introduction of 1.2 million Muslims has been an unusual success. Unsurprisingly, among its 4500 words, "rape" never appears.[12]

This extensive corruption of information from journalists and the deep mistrust it has created among readers who sense the problem through a glass darkly, has now invaded every aspect of Western journalism. Most Americans are now convinced that their news media are unreliable if not worse. In part it is due to the revolutionary impact of cyberspace and social media on journalism, which has, in a sense, created a tidal wave that has swept out the older legacy "paper" models of marketing, but also allowed powerful, activist journalism to surf on its crests.[13]

The problem has become particularly noticeable, even to those not following the issue, over the last two presidential elections in the USA (2016 and 2020). Although there is no lack of people living in media bubbles who respond favorably to advertising from the *New York Times* or the *New Republic* claiming to provide "the facts," the same postmodern destabilization that "narrative-based" journalism brought to coverage of the Middle East, now permeates every discussion, even "scientific ones," like global warming and Covid.

As a result of these dysfunctions, the situation in the early years of the 2020s seems considerably more precarious for the West than it did in 2000; indeed, every dysfunction of our information systems redounds to the advantage of Caliphators in their asymmetrical war. The clash of civilizations that Huntington warned about in the mid-90s, and critics dismissed with anger and contempt, has become internalized within the West. While, on the one hand, leading voices in the public sphere suppress as much as possible evidence of Caliphator aggression from the public, on the other hand, a feeling grows among normally silent commoners (to use the medieval expression) that their elites are betraying them—*la trahison des clercs*. With so little consensually reliable information, the path to conspiracy theories lies wide open on all sides. The split and mutual

10 Andrew Brown, "The myth of Eurabia: how a far-right conspiracy theory went mainstream," *Guardian*, August 16, 2019.

11 Ayaan Hirsi Ali, *Prey: Immigration, Islam and the Erosion of Women's Rights* (New York: Harper, 2021), especially on the 2015 wave, chapter 7.

12 Thomas Rogers, "Welcome to Germany," *New York Review of Books*, April 29, 2021.

13 Ungar-Sargon, *Bad News*.

alienation between the traitorous, but well-intentioned ecumenical elites and the deplorable, tribal commoners in the West has reached unprecedented levels.

In the last twenty years, in the meantime, Caliphators have deployed adepts throughout the West, some of them Da'wa propagandists, others jihadis ready to die in order to strike at infidels who do not know their place. In the last twenty years, a neo-Islam has developed in cyberspace, recruiting, coordinating, social networking, inspiring a generation, in some cases, producing the most ferocious and sadistic converts to jihad.[14] This neo-Islam, untethered from tradition and pumped up with apocalyptic energy, has particular appeal among Western Muslims who find themselves in the disorienting and unnatural environment of not being the dominant religion. This poignant disorientation, the apparent and humiliating superiority of modern (post)Christian and Jewish power and culture, is particularly fertile psychological terrain for recruiting Caliphators. The recruits become the Muslim equivalent of "born-again" triumphalists. To triumphalists who take the Caliphator route and believe to the depths of their souls that all this will soon turn upside down, Western globalization is a *preparatio Caliphatae*, the path to the global Caliphate. Cyberspace is not to be feared but mastered.

In the last two decades, Caliphators have prospered greatly. Throughout the Middle East, jihadis have sown the kind of chaos in which they thrive, bringing down states and driving out millions of refugees to destabilize adjoining states (including Europe). Like the Palestinians, Caliphators turn these refugee camps which they created and populated with their wars, into indoctrination camps for future *Mujahiddin*, an indoctrination that has become a curriculum not only for ISIS training camps, but for refugees and even mainstream schools in countries like Turkey.[15] At the same time, Jihadis have struck repeatedly inside the democratic West, teaching the Westerners respect, whether in massive attacks (9–11, Barcelona, 7–7, Nice, Bataclan), or more individual ones like, recently, in France a teacher guilty of showing Muhammad cartoons, in Britain, three gays sunning themselves in a park, and in the US, a Capitol policeman run down and stabbed by Noah Green, a follower of Nation of Islam leader Louis Farrakhan.[16]

---

14 "Western ISIS recruits responsible for majority of Yazidi genocide crimes," *National News*, March 18, 2021.

15 Raymond Ibrahim, "Indoctrinated in Hate: 'This Is the Start of the New Caliphate,'" *Gatestone*, April 6, 2021.

16 Samuel Paty: Laurent Dubreil, "Islamism Converges With Cancel Culture, *WSJ*," October 25, 2020; British gays: Douglas Murray, "The questions no one wants to ask about the Reading terror attack," *Spectator*, January 13, 2021; for Capitol Hill attack, see n18.

FIGURE 30. "Global Jihad," by Ellen Horowitz.

More significantly, nonviolent Da'wa Caliphators, have managed to get themselves adopted as "moderate Muslims," playing key roles in changing Western curricula, enforcing codes against Islamophobia, advising security services, convincing infidel intellectuals to adopt their narrative for infidels, to avoid identifying Muslims as perpetrators whenever possible, and to ignore the jihadi narrative, so antagonistic and harmful to them and their progressive values.[17] Notes the chief of DC Capitol police to journalists in the Noah Green case: "Investigators do not yet know the motive for the attack, but do not believe it was 'terrorism-related' at this time." The *New York Times* dutifully reiterates the comment in a section entitled: "What we don't know: Mr. Green's motive for the attack."[18] This is not an isolated misjudgment; it is systemic.[19] And while many of our attention spans have been preoccupied with Covid and its extensive

---

17 For one of the more salient examples, see the case of Coughlin, *Catastrophic Failure.*

18 Ben Decker et al. "Vehicle Attack at U.S. Capitol kills 1 officer and injures another," *New York Times*, April 5, 2021. Notes the *Times* by way of information: "The Nation of Islam is a Black nationalist movement that has advocated African-American self-sufficiency." And no follow-up. Kyle Smith, "Remember the Capitol Hill Killer? The Media Sure Don't," *National Review*, April 13, 2021.

19 The FBI's hasty effort six weeks later to decouple a Jihadi's taking five Jews hostage in a Colleyville Texas synagogue and antisemitism ("was not specifically related to the Jewish community" . . . still looking for a motive), illustrates how embedded the instinct to obscure unpleasant information about Muslims behaving badly: Rebecca Downs, "FBI Makes Claims Motive of Man Taking Hostages at Synagogue Was 'Not Specifically Related to Jewish Community'," *Townhall,* January 16, 2022. On the FBI's failure at Fort Hood, see above, 416f.

politicization and misinformation and not with Caliphators, they consider Covid a godsend.[20]

How did this happen?

When I tell the story in its bare bones—religious fanatics attack a dominant civilization in a mad asymmetrical apocalyptic war of conquest, and the target civilization responds by refusing to identify the attackers, and instead welcomes the invaders as friends, and turns on friends as the cause of the problem, people respond: "That's ridiculous. No one is that stupid." And yet no sooner do I identify the players as jihadis, the West, and Israel, than the response shifts, "Oh, that." And in a flash, somehow, the unthinkable becomes the banal.

The Dawa Caliphator's cogwar task is to convince the enemy not to use its superior force to fight back. The results of that victory are imbedded in two mindsets that have come to dominate Westerners, especially, but not exclusively, "progressives": on the one hand, what one might call *Y2KMind* and on the other, *Preemptive Dhimmitude*, two faces of the same coin—the dominant Western attitude toward their foes. One side depicts the Western self-image (self-critical, progressive, visionary, generous to a fault); the other, how they appear to their (unacknowledged) but merciless foes.

FIGURE 31. "Coyote Ugly?" by Ellen Horowitz.

---

20 See Gilles Kepel, *Le prophète et la pandemie : Du Moyen-Orient au jihadisme d'atmosphère* (Paris: Gallimard, 2021).

12

Y2KMind: Oxymoronic
Progressives

And yet we were caught
On our heels, mouth inhaling
When Jihad's sh*t hit

Although the term Y2K has different associations in the minds of many—the false prophecy of a computer bug at midnight December 31, 1999[1]—I cannot think of any other term that can better describe a mindset that, despite long antecedents, took root, like a seed crystal in a super-saturated solution in the year 2000. For a full generation, the West had generated and deployed a set of progressive ideological goals that at once greatly enhanced the culture's diversity and creativity, and at the same time, undermined its very fabric.[2] By 2000 things looked bullish for that mindset: the advance of positive-sum ecumenism (e.g., EU's Euro experiment), an explosion of penetrating personal communication technology (internet, cell phones), corrosive postmodern and postcolonial "theory" in the academy, and a soft NGO millennialism about a peaceful and diverse global civil society where human rights were universal.

---

1 Landes, "Owls and Roosters: Y2K and Millennium's End," in *Calling Time: Religion and Change at the Turn of the Millennium*, ed. Martyn Percy (Sheffield: Sheffield Academic Press, 2000), 233–61.

2 Roger Kimball, *Tenured Radicals: How Politics has Corrupted our Higher Education* (Chicago: Ivan Dees, 1990); Kenneth Lasson's book, published in 2003, but largely about the previous decades, gives a good sense of the corruption and inanities that had already established an important foothold in academia, especially law schools: *Trembling in the Ivory Tower: Excesses in the Pursuit of Truth and Tenure* (Baltimore: Bancroft Press, 2003).

The Caliphator attack proved to be the seed crystal that, even as it should have called many of these orientations into question—certainly in their more extravagant forms—actually had the effect of solidifying them into an attitude that would prove lethal to the very progressive principles that had supersaturated the solution. To return to the original meaning of Y2K, this mentality that crystallized in 2000 was a cultural software glitch that, when the switch comes, not from the computer digits '99 to '00, but from real-world peace to war, makes the software misbehave.[3] What may have been tolerable,[4] even appropriate under the conditions of the late twentieth century and the "end of history," was utterly inappropriate, but relentlessly applied, in the twenty-first century.

The expression "Y2KMind" refers to the mindset and analytic tools necessary to blame democracies for the attacks jihadis make on them. As we have already seen in the chapters on liberals and progressives, all the ingredients were well developed by the late twentieth century. What makes Y2KMind stand out, came when "progressives" applied these high-minded but risky attitudes to the Caliphator attacks. At that point, two key elements changed: the revulsion at the "West" that postcolonialism had weaponized now joined the Caliphator salvific narrative about the two Satans: vilifying the US and Israel now had global momentum. And hand in hand, this joint discourse passed from the noisy margins to the center of Western public discussion. No longer a sub-conversation in which people made absurd assertions that had many rolling their eyes—Israel = Nazi, USA = Evil Racists—moved dramatically to the center of, and increasingly dominated, the public sphere.[5] In millennial terms, what had been a fringe discourse, shifted into the first phase of apocalyptic time, in which its memes "take" in the broader culture.[6]

Postmodern Justice: Their Side Right or Wrong

This moment then marks the point where the long, progressive evolution from the premodern (tribal) notions of justice: *my side* (family, clan, tribe),

---

3 Santos, "Glitches."

4 How many, even sympathetic readers of Allan Bloom's *Closing of the American Mind* (New York: Simon and Schuster, 1987) imagined how much worse it could get?

5 Note that at the last major rally of global progressives in the 20th century, in Seattle in 1999, the Palestinian cause played no noticeable role. In any such event after 2000, it was prominent if not front and center.

6 On millennial discourse "catching" like a forest fire, see Desroche, *Dictionnaire du millénarisme*; Landes, *Heaven on Earth*, chapter 2.

right or wrong, to the modern, civil: *whoever's right, my side or not,* now flipped, inverted, into the postmodern, self-accusing: *their side right or wrong.* Perhaps the most notable feature of Y2KMind, especially since it speaks in very moral terms about the importance of justice, is how extraordinarily generous it is in judgment towards (what it deems) "others," and how extraordinarily severe in judging (what it deems) the "self." This tendency paradoxically intensified when it adopted the cause of a people whose rage at their own pain knows no bounds, and yet who celebrate the pain they inflict on their enemies.

In the 1990s, Newton resident Charles Jacobs, trying with little success to draw attention to the plight of black infidels exterminated by Arab Muslims in Sudan, and their children sold into slavery, dubbed this remarkable inversion the *Human Rights Complex*: "if you want to know what will arouse the moral indignation of the international human rights community, look to the perp, not to the victim . . . no matter how much the victim suffers."[7] White perp? Ferocious indignation. Perp of color? Embarrassed silence. Victim of Whites? Unbearable, no matter how micro the aggression. Victim of People of Color? Who are we to judge? White victim of People of Color? Probably deserved it.

Y2KMind took this high-minded inversion to a new level by admitting Caliphators to the company of privileged victims. As soon as the jihadis attacked, good progressives sought to protect what they imagined was the "vast majority of peaceful Muslims" from the hostility of those infidels whom their co-religionists had so viciously attacked. They did not consider, indeed they recoiled from, the very thought that in accepting Da'wa Caliphators as "authentic" interlocutors, they welcomed their invaders. The presence of Caliphators who embraced Hamas at "progressive" anti-war rallies from 2000 on, the elaborate respect paid to their religiosity, strengthened the most bellicose strains both among Caliphators and among progressives.[8] Militants pressed their advantage everywhere, upgrading already-weaponized terms like "racism" and deploying them in the service of the new cancel-culture emerging in social media.[9]

In the US, the Y2K narrative appeared immediately after 9/11, voiced by the president of the attacked nation: "Islam is a religion of peace." Anyone who

---

7   Jacobs, "Why Israel and not Sudan, is Singled Out."

8   The elaborate respect was not only visible at rallies (see chapters 2–4), but among previously proud secular thinkers, notably, Jürgen Habermas, who got criticized for ignoring (Christian) religion in his early work on the origin of the "public sphere: David Zaret "Religion, Science, and Printing in the Public Spheres of Seventeenth-Century England," *Habermas and the Public Sphere*, ed. C. Calhoun (Cambridge, MA: MIT Press, 1992): 221–34. Suddenly, after 9–11 "he rarely speaks about anything else," among other issues, "an unusual defense of the embattled Muslim minority," Peter Gordon: "What Hope Remains?" *New Republic*, December 14, 2021.

9   Jon Ronson, *So You've Been Publicly Shamed* (New York: Penguin, 2016).

challenged that was an Islamophobe. In a stroke, after a never-before attack on citadels of Western Civilization, Islam, the passionate religion of every one of the "magnificent nineteen," was declared innocent. No sifting of evidence, no deliberation. A foregone conclusion.

Today, it should not surprise the observer that this red-green alliance, in its most aggressive, least honest, and, most vindictive form, has linked the publicly dominant voice of #BlackLivesMatters and the Palestinian "national" quest for liberation. The demopathy is Kryptonite for Y2KMind: "It is all your fault, and I am justifiably infuriated. I demand rights and reparative justice!" "What about people in far more dire straits?" "No whataboutism! Redress now!"

Muhammad al Durah sucking the air out of the gathering at Durban, where countless victims of hatred came to have their plaints drowned in Zionophobia. #MeToo mowing down "white privileged" minor offenders while major offenders, whom they consider "victims of color"—rapists, wife-beaters, and daughter-killers—flourish. Defund the police while black on black violence spikes.

This systematic preference for certain politically-correct underdogs who, by their (relative) lack of power, and through their (proclaimed and unbearable) suffering, win praise for valiantly seeking freedom and dignity, whereas their victims (Palestinians who live under the thumb of Hamas and the PA, black ghetto dwellers) get run over in the rush to attack the privileged overdogs who are to blame for creating the problem, for oppressing, inflicting the suffering, suffocating the longing for freedom of others, forcing their violence by giving them "no choice." This language pervades the Western public discourse today. When Palestinian spokespeople are asked about Palestinian incitement as an obstacle to peace, they respond: you "cannot equate between the occupied and the occupier, the colonized and the colonizer, between the besieged and the besieger."[10] Y2Ktalk. It never occurs to interviewers to challenge this response; indeed, they probably don't know that the Palestinian incitement in question consists of genocidal hatred. And if they did, could they show some images and ask the Palestinian spokesperson why he or she doesn't think this is an obstacle to peace?

In order to avoid the rather glaring problems posed by such an attitude, Y2KMind makes ample use of two "principles." On the one hand, they reject any attempt to put the problem in a larger context as "what-about-ism," and on the other, they embrace any effort to focus on a problem among the "oppressed other" with "we-too-ism." If someone points out a terrible aspect of the "other"

---

10 Among many examples, this one is from Husam Zumlot to Matthew Amroliwala, BBC, 28 December, 2016, https://vimeo.com/aldurahproject/review/498846743/d7098e4365.

culture/party/movement, the response is, "we too do that." A particularly illuminating example of this comes from a former head of the Israeli Shabak (FBI). At the height of the suicide terror campaign, just before Israel re-invaded the West Bank (Jenin), Ami Ayalon (Shin Bet) and Iyad Satay, a Palestinian "psychiatrist" had the following exchange, recounted by Ayalon:

> He said, "Ami, we finally defeated you." I said to him, "Are you mad? What do you mean, defeated us? Hundreds of you are getting killed. At this rate thousands of you will get killed. You're about to lose whatever tiny bit of a state you have and you'll lose your dream of statehood. What kind of victory is that?" He said to me, "Ami, I don't understand you. You still don't understand us. For us, victory is seeing you suffer. That's all we want. The more we suffer, the more you'll suffer. Finally, after 50 years, we've reached a balance of power, a balance, your F-16 versus our suicide bomber."[11]

Despite claiming that this exchange "gave me a very clear insight," it actually just intensified Ayalon's "we-too" cognitive egocentrism. A decade later, he describes how this comment shed a whole new light on the issue.

> "I suddenly understood the suicide bomber phenomenon. I suddenly understood our reaction very differently. How many operations did we launch because we hurt, because when they blow up buses it really hurts us and we want revenge? How often have we done that?"

So rather than acknowledge the immense gap in mentalities between Israelis and Palestinians when it comes to how the leaders think about their people and their lives, and what they consider legitimate retaliation, rather than acknowledge that he was projecting the invoked "Palestinian dream of statehood" onto them, and that they would readily forgo it to get revenge even if that meant inflicting immense suffering on their own people, Ayalon preferred the "we-too" meme: how often have we taken revenge like that?[12]

What? We too poke out both eyes just to get one of our enemy's?

---

11 Ami Ayalon in *The Gatekeepers* (2012).
12 Twenty years later and he's still at it: Ami Ayalon "Only an Israeli-Palestinian Agreement Can Defeat Terror," *Haaretz*, April 5, 2022.

Note the classic Y2K glitch: look away from what in progressive terms would be unacceptable madness were it to appear among "us" and rather than say a word about it to those among whom it appears, disparage the (far more mature) self. And if really smart, competent Israelis can do this with avowedly mortal enemies, how can one expect outsiders, even well-informed outsiders, to see this conflict clearly? And if these outsiders can't see this one clearly because of such glitches, how will they understand their own predicament?

For "Israel-Palestine" is only a particularly potent example of a much larger problem: postmodern moralists feel tasked with harshly criticizing their own culture and feel equally forbidden to criticize other cultures.[13] In its full-fledged form, it constitutes a revulsion at one's own culture and an endless patience in the face of atrocious behavior from other cultures. This principled insistence on radically different standards not only betrays the key Western notion of fairness: everyone plays by the same rules; but it also disguises a latent *humanitarian racism*: "natives" "of color" are treated as forces of nature with no moral agency. Their actions (violence, aggression) are *re-actions* to the terrible deeds of those with power; when hurt they understandably lash out viciously. One cannot expect them to restrain themselves when their feelings have been hurt or their manhood humiliated. Mused one liberal Supreme Court Justice: burning a Qur'an might be compared to shouting fire in a crowded theater—thereby comparing predictable instinctive panic to predictable Muslim rage.[14] Both forces of nature.

Oikophobia: From Cognitive Egocentrism to Self-Loathing

It is natural to project one's own mentality onto others. People who suspect everyone of plotting bad things, assume that others think just like they do. People who live in a civil polity based on reciprocal trust, however, tend to project "good faith," as a first, default assumption about a fellow citizen of the world. Y2KMind takes that principled default and at once makes it into a dogmatic demand and, at the same time, flips its referents: the *hostile* other *must* be read *favorably*: "he's just like me (thanks to we-too-ism), and if I'm nice to him, he'll be nice to me." As for that *well-intentioned* "me": "I'm not so nice at all, and if he's hostile, it's my fault."

Thus, in 2000, Westerners, including the most critically trained, were more inclined to believe that Israel deliberately killed a Palestinian child and shot the

---

13 Benedict Bekeld, "'Oikophobia': Our Western Self-Hatred," *Quillette*, October 17, 2019; Zygmunt Baumann, *Postmodern Ethics* (Oxford: Blackwell, 1993), 85-xx.
14 Josh Gerstein, "Obama v. Breyer v. Breyer on Quran burning & the law."

ambulance driver who came to rescue him, than that a Palestinian camera crew made up the story and staged the footage. After 9–11, to some Y2KMinders, it made more sense that Bush did 9–11 (with all that entails believing about tens of thousands of fellow Americans participating in a conspiracy to kill Americans), than it made sense that Osama did it (with all that entails about not knowing the most basic facts about Osama and the millennial movement he led). In 2008, Americans elected President an inexperienced Black man with a Muslim father, who often attended services with a minister who preached that 9–11 was the US's karma coming home to roost. The most radical assertions of Y2KMind—blame the democracy—normalized. Many whites voted for him to prove that the US was not a racist society. Instead, never has the accusation of American racism been so sustained and systemic as since his presidency.[15]

In 2004, Roger Scruton introduced the Greek neologism *oikophobia*:

> [T]he disposition, in any conflict, to side with "them" against "us," and the felt need to denigrate the customs, culture and institutions that are identifiably "ours." Being the opposite of xenophobia, I propose to call this state of mind oikophobia, by which I mean (stretching the Greek a little) the repudiation of inheritance and home.[16]

Y2KMind inherited this oikophobia from the postcolonial use of deconstruction as a weapon back in the 80s and 90s: take the most acidic analytic tools ever forged by exegetes in human history, and turn them on white, self-critical cultures (who produced it), to dissolve their foundational canons, and destabilize their culture. But one should never aim that critical apparatus at 'other' cultures. "How boorish. Punching Down. It would utterly destroy their honor, self-respect, dignity." From Y2K on, people who engaged in this tyranny of penitence among their own, applied this protective approach to Islam and Jihad. "What choice do they have?" Thus, *of course* one can deconstruct the Zionist or Western narratives in all their flaws and accuse Israel of "genocidal ethnic cleansing" and the US of "systemic white racism"; but one must, at the

---

15 60% Say Race Relations Have Gotten Worse Since Obama's Election," *Rasmussen Reports*, July 19, 2016; Gil Troy, "How Obama has turned back the clock on race relations," *New York Post*, January 17, 2016; Jason Riley, *False Black Power* (Conshohocken, PA: Templeton Press, 2017); Roger Simon, *I Know Best: How Moral Narcissism is Destroying our Republic, if it hasn't Already* (New York: Encounter, 2016), chapter 9.

16 Roger Scruton, *England and the Need for Nations* (London: Civitas, 2004), chapter 8.

same time, accept the privileged Palestinian and Black victim narratives with nary an offensive "but . . ."[17]

Critical Race theory had already formalized this humanitarian racism before 2000: by defining racism as "prejudice plus power," where only whites (who have power) can be racists, and not blacks (who don't?). Blacks who hate whites or Palestinians who hate Israelis, are not responsible for that hatred—whites and Israelis are—and these victims cannot be criticized, no matter how aggressive their "resistance" gets. If Israelis don't treat an enemy population the same way they treat their own citizens they're judged apartheid. Palestinians can insist on a Judenrein state because, well, hell, they justifiably hate the Israelis. Jews who defend themselves, and whites who complain, are fascist war-criminals or fragile whiners.[18]

In the end, the disciples of Gandhi, who hold themselves (and the Jews) to supreme levels of restraint, encourage violent enemies. The exquisite ear of empathic sympathy has tuned in fully to the plaint of the privileged "victim," while the acidic blade of criticism strikes at the self alone. *Their side, right or wrong.* And caught between this hammer and anvil are the people, Palestinians, Blacks, whose lives only matter when taken by their oppressive enemies, but somehow fall between the cracks when their lives are taken by their own weapons bearers.

This produces Y2KMind's fatal attraction. If before 2000 there was an enthusiastic courtship, what went down in 2000 consecrated the marriage of premodern sadism and postmodern masochism. On the one hand, premodern, rule-or-be-ruled folks got to make belligerent accusations against the modern West, accusing them of heinous crimes against humanity, terrible deeds past and present. On the other, postmodern masochists, always ready to see the other side's perspective, primed for "we-too" and the epistemological priority of the "other," accept, even embrace the accusations. In 2001, at Durban, the marriage was consecrated under the canopy of Al Durah, the boy martyr.

And the voices from that marriage have only grown; twenty years later, it's almost quaint to want to mount a liberal defense of the West. Oikophobia plus hopium produces Masochistic Omnipotence Syndrome (MOS). "It's all our

---

17 William Jacobson, "There's an effort to get me fired at Cornell for criticizing the Black Lives Matter Movement," *Legal Insurrection*, June 11, 2020; "U. Central Florida Fires Dissident Prof. Charles Negy After 8-Month Retaliatory Investigation," *Legal Insurrection*, January 31, 2021; Jessica Mundie, "Calgary tenured professor critical of Black Lives Matter has been fired," *National Post*, January 5, 2022.

18 Shelby Steele defines white guilt as "as the terror of *being seen* as racist," *Shame: How America's Past Sins Have Polarized Our Country* (New York: Basic Books, 2015), 1. Italics mine.

fault and if only we can change us, we can fix anything; if only we can perfect ourselves, we can change the world." On one level this is a standard part of liberal progressive thought: in a conflict, if people with stronger egos takes the blame first, they can create a positive, reconciliatory dynamic, leading to amity and cooperation. The rub comes when it doesn't work. Then the messianic tendencies come to the surface. When the other attacks, rather than reciprocate, MOS blames itself further. It does so by over-attributing agency to the self (and thereby, denying it to "the other"): "the more it's my fault, the more powerful I am." Or as the Israeli left said in response to horrendous jihadi violence, "If only we had been more forthcoming." When confronted with the problem, one Israeli (former) friend, on the board of B'tselem, said to me: "It [making concessions] is the only move I know."

This was what the Israeli peace camp did after the Oslo Peace Process turned (predictably) into the Oslo Jihad which, unbeknownst at the time to almost everyone in the West, was also the opening round of Global Jihad. And these MOS, peace-loving, Israelis who behaved like a classic case of denial and doubling down "when prophecy fails," did not lack for comfort from friends, European progressives, telling them this was indeed all Israel's fault, and offering them refuge from the now fascist Israel to teach their self-lacerating logic to Europeans.

In tandem, a new peace movement swept the globe. It moved rapidly into the brand-new global space created on the night of Y2K, when, time zone by time zone, various capitals greeted the new Year/Century/Millennium and the whole world watched. The new movement's first global event, in capitals the world over—Europe, US, Far East, Middle East—occurred on Saturday, October 6, 2000, a week to the day after the al Durah story first hit: a global demonstration against the Israeli war machine.[19] After Durban/9–11 a year later, the presence of a "progressive street" made itself increasingly heard as an "anti-war movement."[20] In April of 2002, in response to lethal journalism's "Jenin massacre," large crowds of radical progressives and angry Muslims came to protest "Nazi Israel." A year later, the anti-war movement reached its height, when it mobilized over ten million people the world over on one Saturday in February 2003 to protest Bush's proposed war on Iraq. Enthused by this massive mobilization, spokespeople for this movement claimed the mantle, fallen

---

19 Landes, *Icon of Hatred* (2006).
20 See above, 134–39.

from Soviets' shoulders in 1991, of "hegemonic counterweight to American imperialism."[21]

Y2KMind applied its masochistic pacifism to the Caliphators, producing an *anti-imperialism of fools*, whereby the progressive infidel camp embraced the most imperialist movement on the planet, one implacably opposed to progressive values. But as long as Caliphators opposed *American* imperialism, Y2KMind—people like Judith Butler—considered them allies in an "anti-imperialist" quest. This thrilling oikophobic poison nourished the anti-war movement from the very first years of the new millennium.

Hate Speech and Cancel Culture, Caliphator Style

Invoking how the horrors of the Holocaust started with hate speech, most postwar European countries enacted laws banning it, including Holocaust denial. These laws against preaching hatred arose in Western polities that in principle, applied that law to everyone equally. But under the impact of Y2KMind's remorseless inversion of standards, it applied with infinite severity to white privileged power holders (including, ironically, Jews), and not at all to privileged victims of color (especially Muslims who at once denied the Holocaust happened and wanted to finish the job). Suddenly criticism of Islam or Palestinians, dwelling on the savage nature of their hatreds, itself became hate speech incarnate, racism, Orientalism; meanwhile Muslim hate speech became culturally protected.

Thus, the long patient work of the 80s and 90s, of Saudi-funded Caliphator hatreds taking over local mosques, now moved into a new period.[22] The al Durah icon of the electrifying intifada, was a symbol and a sign that the time had come. Having gotten a great boost from the Western media in the land between the river and the sea, where a main strand of modern jihadism had arisen, Caliphators took their loathings abroad.[23] The al Durah message hit European Muslims with its apocalyptic hatred of *al Yahud*, just as its accompanying Replacement Narrative was thoroughly disorienting their hosts, both morally and empirically. The Swedish handling of the Stockholm Grand Mosque illustrates painfully how Western authorities protected Muslim hate speech and throttled anyone who criticized them.[24]

---

21 See 135nn7–8.
22 See 219f.
23 Cook, *Contemporary Muslim Apocalyptic*.
24 See 176.

One can readily grasp how in such an atmosphere, the term Islamophobia rapidly became a potent term in public discourse after 9–11. The same Sweden that showed such indulgence to Muslim hatred of Jews, shows great severity towards those who say things to which Muslims take offence. The branding of a broad range of material and argument about Islam as unacceptably "Islamophobic" represents one of the more astounding developments of the twenty-first century. European anti-hate speech legislation protected Muslim hate speech.

The inversion, what Kepel calls the "specious symmetry," that equated early twentieth century antisemitism to early twenty-first-century Islamophobia,[25] suddenly gave the newly invented term, the weight of the Holocaust: "heaven forbid we Westerners should do to the Muslims what the Nazis did to the Jews, heaven forbid we even *seem* to be doing it." Or as more than one professor told me in my 2011 stay in Germany, "We're more afraid of our fascism than of theirs." The Replacement Narrative inverted a symbolic reality of immense significance—that the Israelis actually are the armed survivors of the Holocaust, Palestinians the clamoring heirs to the Nazis, and the conflict for the Land between the River and Sea the last active front of World War II.[26] Now the inverted version: Israel is exterminating the Palestinians, and we who offend Muslims are on a slippery slope to that kind of fascist, racist behavior. Pick the narrative you prefer; but be aware, if you're wrong, there's a heavy price to pay for virtue-signaling.

Part of the power of "Islamophobia" lay in its ability, along with a number of other terms, to create moral panics, to mobilize sufficient outrage to actually drive certain people and ideas from the public sphere. The great mover here, especially in the USA, was race. The hypersensitivities developed there—a man fired for using the term for cheap from the Scandinavian "niggardly"—were legendary for decades before Y2K. Muslims invented the term Islamophobia to cash in on the trend. As wielded by CAIR, for example, it aggressively claims racist offense to Muslim sensibilities in order to demand the suppression of criticism as hate speech.[27]

One of the more dramatic moments of designating a target and destroying it (loss of reputation, of job) were staged moral emergencies, in which "something so outrageous has happened, that everyone must stop and join

25 Kepel, *Terror in France*, 17.

26 Melanie Phillips, "The last, overlooked but still active front of World War Two," *MelaniePhillips*, May 21, 2021.

27 Tamar Sternthal, "CAIR, The Investigative Project, and The Dispatch's Double Standard," *CAMERA*, December 16, 2021.

in a collective condemnation." The attack on Andrew Pessin in the spring of 2015 at Connecticut College follows the sacrificial pattern set out by René Girard: pick the target, find something he wrote that can be read as outrageous, deliberately misread it, use the campus paper to create a scandal, stop classes for an emergency meeting about exposing and shaming racists and giving voice to those marginalized and underrepresented, create a sense of collective energy and direction from the thrill of the sacrifice.[28] These events—and the threat of them—have had a decisive effect on the power of cancel-culture in the twenty-first century, both as a way of keeping others away from campuses and for driving out unwanted voices. Today a whole generation of graduate students watches the last dinosaurs from an earlier age hang in or fall; and so they step in line with the rules of the new, social justice game. What a terrifying (or exalting) time to be a graduate student.

Virtue Signaling and Moral Narcissism

Virtue signaling is a perpetual problem—hypocrisy is the compliment vice pays to virtue. It plays a particularly important role in Y2KMind, since it is the primary means whereby one signals one's commitment to the cause, and also the primary means by which one accepts the new, unprogressive strictures on actions and words that violate virtue.[29] By correct use of terminology, by avoiding even the hint of language or actions that get one branded a racist or xenophobe, one survives and even thrives. By 2020, whole college campuses had been more or less taken over by a coalition of radical faculty and students. At best, old-school scholars at these places could hope to be left alone.

Virtue signalers are prone to various forms of moral narcissism, that is, *thinking about morality in terms of how your actions make you look in your own eyes and the eyes of your honor-group, rather than the consequences of those actions on those for whom one is allegedly concerned and on whose behalf one claims to act.* Moral narcissists do what makes them look good, consequences be damned. "Not in my name!"[30] The canonical adoption of the Palestinian cause in the early aughts illustrates moral narcissism at its most extensive. When those passing the litmus test for liberal credentials by supporting the Palestinian cause, did so at the very

---

28 Landes, *Salem on the Thames.*

29 Saad, *Parasitic Mind*, 177–81. Cf. Sam Leith, "In defence of 'virtue signalling,'" *Spectator*, October 30, 2020.

30 Julie Burchill and Chas Newkey-Burden, *Not in my Name: A Compendium of Modern Hypocrisies* (New York: Virgin Books, 2009).

moment when the Palestinian leadership was engaged in a vicious, self-defeating war against Israel, they actually condemned the Palestinian commoners to suffer under authoritarian war-mongering rulers who systematically sacrificed their well-being to a suicidal honor agenda. As the Palestinian activist Bassem Eid noted: "The Palestinians have the best enemies and the worst friends."

But some of the most stunning examples of moral narcissism in the twenty-first century came from Europe and had to do with attitudes towards Islam and the imperial-colonial axis of the US and Israel. The sight of Europe siding with jihadis (Palestinians, al Qaeda) against Israel and the US in the early years of the century provided a stunning view of suicidal virtue signaling as "moral Europe" from their imaginary heights, pissed down on the US and Israel even as they empowered Caliphators of all kinds. How tasty the *Schadenfreude*. How noxious for Palestinians and genuinely moderate Muslims who wanted peace and the chance to live in a civic polity.

Willful Blindness

The radical divorce from the empirical world involved in Y2KMind has produced a phenomenon probably not unique in the history of reasoning, but unprecedented in scale, at least in modern times: a kind of willful stupidity, in which one dismisses crucial evidence and comes to conclusions, or their lack, working from a deliberately confused dossier of material (in England and France in the 1930s it was only some people in some political parties). As a result, we get an inverted Sherlock Holmes effect: Y2KMind analysts ignore the inconvenient evidence, do not challenge lies, and look for extravagant alternative explanations for the motivation behind the criminal violence they are supposed to investigate: they live in bizarro-land Baker Street. What makes this self-imposed stupidity so distressing, is how often it contributes to Caliphator success in their jihadi attacks inside the West.

The phenomenon, like many under discussion, predates 2000. In his book *Willful Blindness*, New York prosecuting attorney in the case of "the blind Sheikh" Abdul Rahman and the 1993 attempt to blow up the Twin Towers, Andrew McCarthy documents with depressing detail every folly in ignoring the evidence, a folly that has become the *modus operandi* of Western elites since 2000. Among the leads our counter-Sherlocks did not follow, were the piles of jihadi material found among the belongings of those Caliphators who murdered Rabbi Meir Kahane in 1990, material that, if followed up, would have led them to the networks of those who twice—the second time successfully—tried to blow up the Twin Towers. Instead, the chief detective declared the crime the work of a "lone, deranged gunman." Given the choice between that and "an enormous international conspiracy," the choice was clear, evidence be damned.[31]

This kind of lethally obtuse thinking permeates the work of journalists reporting from Israel, with al Durah as the beacon.[32] The success of the "Jenin massacre" meme 18 months later, illustrates the devotion to a Palestinian narrative of a whole range of informants—journalists, NGOs, UN, pundits—despite the evidence. Rather than look for clues, they look for their narrative. By the 2010s, it had become almost a caricature: Journalists in Gaza learned to time their arrival at the scene just after Hamas had cleaned up the evidence that their rockets had killed Palestinian kids. By 2021, the *New York Times*, ignoring everything it had allegedly learned in 2014 about intimidation of journalists, and dishonest statistics from the Hamas-run Ministry of Health, offered their front page to unfiltered Palestinian propaganda.[33]

The consequences of this kind of willful blindness can be deadly; and they obviously extend well beyond Israel and the kind of direct intimidation that reporters experience on the battlefield in Gaza. True to its commitments, Y2KMind ignores evidence of Muslim misdeeds, or when forced to acknowledge them, as in the case of Palestinian American Major Hasan's attack on his fellow soldiers at Fort Hood, steers all discussion *away from* the Islamic component.[34] As one critic of this tendency parodied: Hasan suffered not from sudden jihad syndrome, nor from conversion to an apocalyptic grand narrative, but from "virtual vicarious pre-Post Traumatic Stress Disorder."[35] Hasan's bizarre immunity from a suspicion more than justified by his actions, enabled him to plan a major jihadi operation in the very heart of the beast, in this case, the US military!

In fact, Fort Hood inspired the first working title of this book *They're so Smart only cause we're so Stupid*. Mark Steyn caught the essence of the stupefying quality of Y2KMind and its inability to analyze evidence in this particular case:

31 Andrew McCarthy, *Willful Blindness* (New York: Encounter, 2008), 127–32.

32 Discussed chapter 1, 3, 9.

33 Front and center-page spread of 64 names of "children" killed in May 2021, using an unvetted list filled with basic errors, supplied by a Palestinian "NGO" that ignored its own evidence, and supplied the names of almost a dozen children killed by Hamas. This was done during a series of news-inspired attacks on Jews in the city. Jake Wallis Simons, "The problem with the *New York Times'* Gaza coverage," *Spectator*, June 6, 2021.

34 For the New York Times as a leader in this direction, see McGowan, *Gray Lady Down*, 249–53.

35 Landes, "Anatomy of 'Progressive' Double Speak: Fisking Frank Rich on Fort Hood," *Augean Stables*, November 18, 2009. For the broader phenomenon, see Abigail R. Esman, "When Mental Illness Becomes an Excuse for Terrorists," *IPT News*, June 11, 2018.

"These days, it's easier to be even more stupid *after* the event."[36] As if to prove the point, the report on the incident from the Department of Defense never discussed "radical Islam." All of this reflects the levels of denial characteristic of "the elephant in the room" and the mimetic captivity of "the Emperor's new clothes."[37]

In the last months of 2011, Waltham and Cambridge police forces cold-cased the near decapitation of three teens, on September 11, as "drug related." Had they followed the lead from one of the dead victims, Brendan Mess, it would have led to his former best friend, Tamerlan Tsarnaev, who had recently converted to radical Islam, visited his Chechnyan homeland, and engaged in activities that had Russian intelligence warning US intelligence. But the last thing the Boston police needed in 2011 (they thought), was to pick a fight with the Muslim community in Boston. Silently but accurately anticipating Muslim tribalism were they to press that angle of the investigation, with the radicals pulling in the moderates to a common defense of "the beleaguered community," the cops deferred and did not even question Tsarnaev.[38]

Apparently, forensic Westerners at the time, having been trained by Muslim leaders about sensitivity to the Muslim community, did not consider the startling evidence (near beheading, tenth anniversary of 9-11, money and drugs sprinkled over the dead bodies, all signs of a ritual, a murder-initiation to the jihadi path); did not consider the possibility that in murdering his preconversion Jewish friend, Tamerlan prepared for yet greater glory in the Jihad.[39] So, two

---

36 "Protecting the Force: Lessons from Fort Hood," *DoD*, January 13, 2010, mentions Islam nowhere in the body, has one footnote reference with Islam in the title. Mark Steyn, "A Jihadist Hiding in Plain Sight," *Orange County Register*, November 14, 2009; Mark Thompson, "The Fort Hood Report: Why No Mention of Islam?" *Time*, January 20, 2010; Thomas Joscelyn, "The Federal Bureau of Non-Investigation," *Washington Examiner*, November 9, 2009; Mariah Blake, "Internal Documents Reveal How the FBI Blew Fort Hood," *Mother Jones*, August 27, 2013.

37 Eviatar Zerubavel, *The Elephant in the Room: Silence and Denial in Everyday Life* (New York: Oxford University Press, 2006). Ironically the missing elephant in Zerubavel's brilliant study is jihad ... even though published five years *after* 9–11. The same lacuna is found in Margaret Heffernan's, *Willful Blindness: Why we Ignore the Obvious at Our Peril* (New York: Doubleday, 2011).

38 Note the similarity to the case of Kahane's murderer (see 416n31.), including the angry response of (some of) the Muslim community.

39 On beheading as Islamic, see Timothy Furnish, "Beheading in the Name of Islam," *Middle East Quarterly*, 12:2 (Spring 2005), 51–57. The Boston Police had already been through "sensitivity training," by "moderate" Muslim Brothers like Bilal Kaleem and a government funded program called BRIDGES, and systematically ignored all the clues that pointed to Tamerlan: Feoktistov, *Terror in the Cradle of Liberty*, pp. 252–56; cf. Klausen, *Western Jihadism: A Thirty Year History* (New York: Oxford University Press, 2021), chapter 10 which discusses nothing about the local Muslim community.

years later, Tamerlan pulled off the Patriot's Day Marathon Bombing in Boston.[40] Like Major Nidal Hassan, Tamerlan Tsarnaev went jihadi under the very noses of the democratic authorities—even after savagely murdering a former friend.[41]

Had the authorities trod the road not taken, however, it would not only have led them to Tsarnaev brothers, and stopped the Patriot's Day bombing, but to their mosque in Cambridge, and to the recently built largest mosque on the Eastern seaboard in Roxbury, Boston's Black neighborhood. There they would have run into the founding mentors of the mosque, Adulrahman Alamoudi and Yussuf al Qaradawi of the Muslim Brotherhood, who in 1995 already, on American soil, summoned a generation of American Muslims to conquer the West with Da'wa, and after 2000, enthusiastically embraced Hamas's suicide terror.[42] And, as with Fort Hood, retrospective analysis can be every bit as negligent of the situation on the ground as it was before the attack: compare Feoktistov's reliance on the *Boston Herald* (which focused on local Muslim dynamics), and Klausen's exclusive reliance on the *Boston Globe* (which studiously ignored them).

Indeed, reflecting the earnest wish of many not to have to deal with a web of radical Muslims, right after the Marathon bombing, David Sirota published a piece in *Salon* expressing the pious wish that the bombers were white Americans, followed up Joan Walsh, who, once it became clear they were Muslims, argued "they resembled young American mass murderers more than al-Qaida faithful."[43] As with so much with Y2Kmind, Western evil far exceeds Muslim. A decade later, one did not even have to hope for a favorable outcome; one could just declare it. When a Muslim named Ahmad al Aliwi Alissa killed ten people in Boulder Colorado in March 2021, not only did many immediately identify him as a "White Christian supremacist," but Twitter had no problem with those tweets.[44]

40 William Rashbaum, "In 2011 Murder Inquiry, Hints of Missed Chance to Avert Boston Bombing," *New York Times*, July 11, 2013.

41 A friend of Tsarnaev confirmed that Tamerlan had been part of Waltham murder, which he considered an act of "jihad." Laurel Sweet, "Dzhokhar Tsarnaev pal offered testimony on Waltham slayings Classmate knew of 'jihad' acts," *Boston Herald*, November 22, 2018.

42 On Qaradawi, see p217; on Alamoudi, p58. On both of these men and the rest of the Boston Mosque's board, Feoktistov, *Terror in the Cradle of Liberty*, pp. 8–14; Klausen does not discuss either of them in her chapter on the Tsarnaevs.

43 David Sirota, "Let's hope the Boston Marathon bomber is a white American," *Salon*, April 17, 2013; Joan Walsh, "Are the Tsarnaev brothers white?" *Salon*, April 22, 2013. See Roy's analysis, p. 149.

44 Daniel Villarreal, "Twitter Says Calling Boulder Shooter a 'White Christian Terrorist' Is OK," *Newsweek*, March 23, 2021.

The Subjection of Feminism

Perhaps the most tragic and consequential failure of Y2KMind happened with feminists in Women's Studies.[45] Feminism, above all other fruits of civil society, depends on the willingness of the stronger to give up the privileges of superior physical power. Feminism arose, therefore, because some men were willing to respond fairly to their moral claims. Nor was this an easy matter. Men's limbic captivity to honor, not only in the eyes of their women, but of their male (warrior) peers, makes seeming effeminate an extremely painful experience for males, and, in some cases, can lead to murderous rampages. The urge to use force in order to reassert honor never goes away, and resurges in times of crisis and attendant *onēidophobia*. In this sense, Western feminism has relied on a powerful, enduring commitment of mature men (I know, not mature enough), willing to accept criticism, some of it quite harsh, without striking back. On the contrary, at least some of these men try to listen and respond. This seems to have elicited from some feminists in the late twentieth century very aggressive behavior, not hesitating to express rage at an intimidated Western "patriarchy."[46]

In other places and societies, however, more volatile men, driven by jealousy, envy, and *libido dominandi*, exploit their physical power to subject women; and both law and mores approve.[47] The twin phenomena of "crimes of passion" (killing an unfaithful wife) and shame murders (killing a daughter who shames the family) attest to the deadly power of male honor to claim the lives of problematic women. The kinds of complaints raised by #MeToo in the West, however bad by our standards, pale before the threat that such societies present to every female born in them. In the twenty-first century, no culture, and within that culture, no religious movement, has been more zealously misogynist and oppressive of women than Caliphator Islam. And yet, for reasons both puzzling and troubling, the feminist movement, and particularly its academic manifestation, Women and Gender Studies, so fierce at home, have shown profound respect and loud support for these patriarchs who embodied everything they hated about (Western) men.[48] Indeed, it appears that Western

---

45 There may well have been a similar phenomenon in Jewish Studies (see the profoundly unscholarly "Statement on Israel-Palestine by Scholars of Jewish Studies and Israel," *Israel/Palestine*, May 22, 2021; James Russell, "Bearing False Witness: On a Statement against Israel," *Times of Israel*, May 27, 2021), but since there are 3.5 billion women and only twelve-plus million Jews, the feminist failure is greater and its impact more tragic.

46 Lasson, *Trembling in the Ivory Tower*, chapter 2.

47 See Landes, "Primary Honour Codes in Tribal and Aristocratic Cultures."

48 Yasmine Mohammed, *Unveiled: How Western Liberals Empower Radical Islam* (Hillside: Free Hearts Free Minds, 2019); Phyllis Chesler, "How Many Western Feminists Would March

women writing about Arab and Muslim women, systematically subordinated their concerns to the red-green alliance in which the West, where women are most free, embodies evil, and anyone "resisting" that evil, is on the good side. This tendency already appeared in the 1980s in UN conferences, but it became a key dimension of Y2KMind.

Beginning in the 1980s/1400s, for example, the more radical circles of Islam sought to impose at least the *hijab*, if not the *burka* or *nikab* on Muslim women, a public marker of Caliphator dominion over Muslims, especially in the West.[49] Once having taken over in Iran, Caliphator mullahs required the hijab; the Taliban (1996–2001) would throw acid in the face of women who did not wear the most extreme version, the *niqab*. Since 9–11 throughout the *Ummah*, including Israel and the West, there has been "a huge increase in the number of women, particularly among young women, who started wearing the hijab."[50] When Y2KMinders are told by Muslim women who wear the hijab that it is an act of individuation and principle, they feel compelled to admire their courage. If one interprets the male gaze at a bikinied body as a form of visual rape, the burka becomes a form of resistance.[51] Obviously it would be tasteless, even hostile, to ask if this newly assumed practice expressed postmodern liberation, or fealty to ancient religious practices,[52] or submission to the demands of recent Caliphators, including Bin Laden.

How many "zones urbaines sensibles" became the unmentionable no-go-zones because the Muslim women in them had to wear hijabs in order to protect themselves, and infidel women without veils, now rape bait—"uncovered, easy meat"—got out?[53] And given that *being raped* in many Muslim-majority cultures (but not only!) is a cause for shame-murder (talk about blaming the victim), women surrounded by aggressive, patriarchal, triumphalist Muslims are strongly advised to wear the hijab at the very least. Y2K feminists, instead, assure us that "most wear hijabs by choice," *not* from a fear that *not* wearing it dishonors the woman and leaves her open to justified male violence like rape. Given the strong

---

Under a Hail of Taliban Bullets?" *Fourth Wave*, January 2, 2022.

49 For a more detailed analysis of the drift from feminism to anti(Western) colonialism, see Chesler, *Death of Feminism*, 108–130.

50 Shaista Aziz, "Why I decided to wear the veil," *BBC*, September 17, 2003.

51 Gad Saad, "Niqab Is 'Freely Chosen' while Bikini Is Oppressive?" *The Saad Truth*, 47, June 22, 2015.

52 On the origins of wearing the veil in Islam, see Mernissi, *Beyond the Veil: Male-Female Dynamics in Moodern Muslim Society* (Bloomington, IN: University of Indiana Press, 1987).

53 An Islamist preacher referred to unveiled women as "uncovered meat" which cats will naturally eat, "Australian Muslim leader compares uncovered women to exposed meat," *Guardian*, October 26, 2006. See also, McLoughlin, *Easy Meat*.

link between enforcing hijab compliance and jihad, should not feminists get a bit more concerned about the finer details here?[54]

Faced with the remorseless insistence of immigrant communities to enforce their violent patriarchal rules on their women, Westerners crumbled, victims of their fears of being called racists, of opposing a "multiculturalism" to which their immigrant communities had no commitment. Describing the shame-murder of one of the girls in her charge as a social worker, Unni Wikan writes:

> "Culture" is the coinage used to express and claim minority rights, and it is backed by hard sanctions. Physical force, or the threat of such, may not be necessary to compel compliance. A little word, just six letters long, does the job just as effectively: "Racist!" nor need the word be spoken. It hangs like a specter in the air, palpable if invisible, and frightens people into accepting acts that they deeply deplore. . . . "Racist" has become a "deadly word." It pierces the heart of the well-meaning Scandinavian, whose cherished identity is world champion of all that is kind and good. . . . But there is a high price to be paid by such high morality, and it is paid neither by those who pride themselves on supreme tolerance toward immigrants, professed as "respect for the culture," nor by those who cry "racist" to claim or enforce such respect. [The price] is Aisha [dead at 14] and others like her.[55]

Hard to find a better description of moral narcissism: looking good trumps actual effects on victims one supposedly protects.

The Feminist/Women's Studies adoption of this inversion shows up sharply in an incident at Brandeis, in the spring of 2014. The school announced that Ayaan Hirsi Ali would get an honorary degree that year. Rapidly professors in various theoretically sophisticated disciplines, with Women's Studies in the fore, objected vehemently to this honor being awarded an "Islamophobe."[56] So, a woman who had endured clitoridectomy, escaped a forced marriage by fleeing

---

54 Rebecca Vipond Brink, "Why I Refuse to Criticize Islam as a Feminist and Atheist," *The Frisky*, October 15, 2014. Giulio Meotti, "Veiling Women: Islamists' Most Powerful Weapon," *Gatestone*, April 20, 2016; Phyllis Chesler, "Ban the Burqa: The Argument For," *Middle East Forum*, December 11, 2010.

55 Wikan, *Generous Betrayal*, 25.

56 Richard Pérez-Peña and Tanzina Vega, "Brandeis Cancels Plan to Give Honorary Degree to Ayaan Hirsi Ali, a Critic of Islam," *New York Times*, April 8, 2014.

to the West, become a successful politician very critical of Islam's treatment of women, who had been threatened and pursued by patriarchal Islamists all over the world including the US, somehow became an "Islamophobe" for saying things about Islam that any Jew and Christian can say about their own and each other's religions.

In other words, she was everything that liberals imagined, when they spoke of moderate, peaceful Muslims who enrich the societies in which they dwell. Therefore, she had to go. As Andrew Anthony put it dryly: "she is loathed not just by Islamic fundamentalists but by many western liberals, who find her rejection of Islam almost as objectionable as her embrace of western liberalism."[57] Says the *oikophobe*: I wouldn't want a friend who wanted to join my club.

The petitioners denounced her "virulently anti-Muslim public statements" that "sent a horrible message . . . to Muslim and non-Muslim communities."[58] To document her "unacceptable" hostility to Islam, the petitioners found comments, all from late 2007 when her first book *Infidel* came out. At that time, she had just been chased out of Holland by Muslims who, after killing her colleague Theo Van Gogh, put a price on her head and made her 24/7 security so onerous, that both the government in which she served and her neighbors told her to leave. Once in America, at the conservative think tank, AEI (no progressive places offered her shelter), she ran into American Muslim leaders who condemned her for her "poisonous and unjustified" statements about Islam, that "created dissension in the community," and considered that her deliberate "defaming the faith" deserved the "punishment [of] death."[59] Reflecting this experience, she publicly voiced her conclusions—based on a variegated experience of Islam (Somalia, Saudi Arabia, Europe, USA)—that Islam is "inherently violent" (the Papal Quotation Scandal); that not just extremist Islam, but "mainstream Islam is fascist," "totalitarian," and "inspires jihadism and terror"; and that Islam "cannot be reformed."[60]

---

57 Andrew Anthony, "*Heretic: Why Islam Needs a Reformation Now* by Ayaan Hirsi Ali," *Guardian*, April 27, 2015.

58 "Brandeis Faculty Petition Objecting to Granting Ayaan Hirsi Ali an Honorary Degree, 2014," http://www.theaugeanstables.com/2021/06/27/brandeis-faculty-petition-objecting-to-granting-ayaan-hirsi-ali-an-honorary-degree-2014/. More than half of the first 25 signers are from Women and Gender Studies, not to mention Jytte Klausen in Political Science.

59 Robin Acton, "Furor over author Ayaan Hirsi Ali's visit stirs debate on religious freedom," *Pittsburgh Tribune*, April 22, 2007.

60 Much of this is a rephrasing of the attack on Hirsi Ali by Deborah Scroggins, "The Dutch-Muslim Culture War: Ayaan Hirsi Ali has Enraged Muslims with her Attacks on their Sexual Mores," *The Nation*, June 2005; discussed by Chesler, *Death of Feminism*, 125f.

Now anyone saying similar things about Christianity or Judaism or Western culture would not get such a reception. When, for example, John Carroll wrote his devastating critique of Catholicism and the Gospels, *Constantine's Sword*, he received extensive praise for his honest self-criticism, not insistent censure for his hate-filled phobias. It's hard to imagine the Enlightenment, had the Catholic Church managed to cancel Voltaire from the public discourse of Europe. But here, the petitioning faculty, upon reading such opinions, rather than turning to their Muslim colleagues and pleading with them to "prove her wrong" were "filled with shame at the suggestion that the above-quoted sentiments express Brandeis' values." Thus, an African woman who opposed the worst patriarchy extant on the planet, was internationally shamed as "someone who [does not] truly meet the standards and uphold the values of this university."[61] The president acceded to the furor and disinvited her.

What were the stakes here for the petitioners? Why the excited language— "virulently anti-Muslim," "horrible message," "filled with shame"? Why the imperious commands to rescind the invitation immediately? What was the moral emergency? Why the moral panic at the mere *thought* that Brandeis might honor this woman?

The petitioners acknowledge Ali's claim that something wrong is going on in the Muslim world: "We fully recognize the harm of forced marriages; of female genital cutting, which can cause, among other public health problems, increased maternal and infant mortality; and of honor killings." "Fully" here, however, sounds a bit hollow, especially when the next sentence changes the topic dramatically—one might even say, inverts the problem. And here we find the core of the dilemma that lays bare the betrayal of women suffering precisely from the above list of woes. After this brief acknowledgment of the magnitude of the plight of women in the Muslim world, the petition asserts (brackets my comments):

> These phenomena are not, however, exclusive to Islam [despite being disproportionately so at the present]. The selection of Ms. Hirsi Ali further suggests to the public that violence toward girls and women is particular to Islam or the Two-Thirds World [did she say that?], thereby obscuring such violence in our midst among non-Muslims, including on our own campus [?]. It also obscures the hard work on the ground by committed

---

61 See Zev Chafets, "Ayaan Hirsi Ali: Victim of an honor killing, Brandeis-style," *Fox News*, April 10, 2014.

> Muslim feminist and other progressive Muslim activists and scholars, who find support for gender and other equality within the Muslim tradition and are effective at achieving it [?]. We cannot accept [!] Ms. Hirsi Ali's triumphalist narrative of western civilization [?], rooted in a core belief of the cultural backwardness of non-Western peoples.

In other words, hiding behind the assertion that Islam should not be specifically associated with these matters, and attributing to Hirsi Ali positions she has not taken, the petitioners make it clear that they will not allow on their campus, a champion of Western values, someone who makes largely accurate generalizations about the differential treatment of women in the West and in Islam. They will not have a frank discussion about the problems of Islam and Muslim male violence against women, and *certainly not* with people who even entertain the possibility that these problems are structural, systemic to Islam.

Note how certain and insistent this petition is about the flat-out unacceptability of a "triumphalist" Western discourse. How dare the West claim to have solved some key problems that traditional societies have not, among which is a dramatic lowering of the degree to which women are physically at men's mercy, and a dramatic heightening of women's representation in the public sphere. In this case, women prominent in Western academia can make imperious demands on the administration, demanding respect for the honor of societies in which women have little to no role in academia and face violence were they to speak imperiously to male superiors.

The "essentialist" positions that the petitioners explicitly attribute to Hirsi Ali, are actually inverted projections of their own essentialist loathing of the West, that irredeemably bad, enemy of global salvation. And so, the same people who are filled with horror and regret at the suggestion that something negative might be systemic, built-into Islam—"Islam structurally violent? Impossible. Unspeakable!"—are filled with righteous indignation when contemplating the (for them) unchallengeable assertion that the US is a systemically racist society and polity.

By 2006, at least in Women's Studies, it became impossible to oppose the under-dogma that the West was bad, and the rest of the world must not be judged (certainly not, judged unfavorably) in comparison with the West. Daphne Patai wrote about a Women's Studies list-serv, which thrashed out some of the principles:

In October 2006 a typical exchange took place on the women's studies email list (WMST-L) (which has more than five thousand subscribers) about white male violence. Great anger was displayed at the few women who wrote in suggesting there are worse problems among other groups—for example, violence in Muslim countries or the rates of murder and rape among blacks versus whites in this country. The discussion provided yet another indication of how identity politics is being pursued at this time. In academe, in particular, people object to generalizations about blacks or about Muslims or any other group that is nonwhite and non-Anglo. They rush to defend these groups because, as presumably oppressed or formerly oppressed groups, they have identities that nowadays exempt them from criticism [Humanitarian racism: never blame the victim!]. But the same reticent people are free with their generalizations about America being a "rape culture" or confidently assert that white male violence is the primary problem we all have to deal with.[62]

Just as Martin Amis asked his audience of British glitterati "Who thinks they are morally superior to the Taliban?",[63] can anyone with a moral compass not recognize that "we've come a long way, baby," where "we" is Western men, and "the way" includes learning to treat our women with a great deal of respect and a renunciation of our recourse to *might makes right*. Is it a total transformation? No. Is it better than cultures where women live in radical insecurity that their own family will kill them for "shaming them" . . . for even just *seeming* to shame them? Yes.

Is it not a moral disorientation of cosmic proportions for a society that provides rape victims with safe spaces lest words inadvertently upset them, to insist that they are no better—nay worse!—than a culture in which families feel community pressure to kill a daughter who's been raped?[64] Who can seriously

---

62 Daphne Patai, *What Price Utopia? Essays on Ideological Policing, Feminism and Academic Affairs* (New York: Rowman and Littlefield, 2008), 10.

63 "Martin Amis and Andrew Anthony: On writing and radical Islam," *Contemporary Institute of Art*, October 11, 2007 Amis poses the question "Do you think you are morally superior to the Taliban?" (at 31:10), and is mildly pleased with a positive response from a third of the audience. What he did not ask was "Do you think you are morally superior to Israel?" That, I'm guessing would have been at least two thirds.

64 Chesler, "In their own Words: Portraits of Arab, Muslim, and Middle Eastern Women," *Death of Feminism*, 131–150.

argue that looking at Muslim shame murders "thereby obscur[es] such violence in our midst among non-Muslims, including on our own campus"?

The lines of this capitulation were already laid out in the later twentieth century, when postcolonial "feminists," often from heavily patriarchal societies, argued that fighting the Western imperialists trumped fighting third world patriarchy. Cultural relativism became the order of the day, along with the we-too-ism it demands: shame murders are just part of the spectrum of domestic violence, found both East and West.[65] And they certainly have *nothing* to do with Islam.[66] On the contrary, some postcolonial feminists argued that Muhammad opposed them, just as he opposed killing baby girls.[67] Indeed, anyone who suggests that Islamic culture has a high correlation with honor killings (an empirical "fact") is an Islamophobe peddling fake news.[68] Preferably, don't even mention it,[69] and if you must, disapprove harshly of such misinformation.[70]

Had feminism stayed true to its moral compass—the superiority of a world of uncoerced intimacy, over that governed by might makes right—it would have quickly noticed in the world after 2000, how many disturbing links there were between how Caliphators treated their women, and the predatory eyes through which they viewed the infidel as *harbi*. They would have understood the relatively new roles that both the hijab and shame-murders played in policing the border between the increasingly tribal, Caliphator-defined, Muslim communities on the one hand, and the surrounding infidels on the other.[71] Here a Turkish woman who thinks she can be a German, there a shamed Palestinian who can regain her honor by blowing herself up in an Israeli hospital.

Had women scholars followed such leads, we might have better understood the role that Muslim misogyny plays in Caliphator fear and hatred of the West. Perhaps, had we, with the guidance of feminists of integrity, paid attention to

---

65 Janet I. Sigal, "Domestic Violence and Honor Killings," *American Psychological Association* report to UN, https://www.apa.org/international/united-nations/janet-sigal.pdf; Huma Qureishi, "'Honour' crimes are domestic abuse, plain and simple," *Guardian*, March 21, 2012.

66 Aysan Sev'er and Gökçeçiçek Yurdakul, "Culture of Honor, Culture of Change: A Feminist Analysis of Honor Killings in Rural Turkey," *Violence against Women* 7, no. 9 (September 2001): 964–998.

67 Brittany Hayes et al., "An Exploratory Study of Honor Crimes in the United States," *Journal of Family Violence*, 31 (2016): 303–14.

68 Ilisha, "Honor Killings: The Epidemic that Isn't," *Loonwatch*, September 28, 2011. Loonwatch is an excellent site for exploring Y2KMind.

69 Naomi Lakritz, "Women's lives aren't worth much—even in Canada," *Calgary Herald*, July 29, 2009.

70 Elise Auerbach, "Sensationalist Film Exploits Human Rights Issue in Iran," *Huffpost*, July 25, 2009.

71 Jody K. Biehl, "The Whore Lived Like a German," *Der Spiegel*, March 2, 2005.

how Caliphators treat Muslim women, that in turn, might have raised the valid question: in what ways is this a harbinger of what Caliphators have in store for those fortunate enough not yet to know their lash? Instead, it all became part of "facts we're not supposed to know," the stuff picked up by the garbage trucks servicing the willfully blind. If we don't look, we won't realize the importance of fighting Muslim misogyny, or confront what cowards we are for not defending Muslim women even a fraction of how we protect our women.

How did this happen? Phyllis Chesler, after noting the systematic moral inversion, locates a new stage in the Western feminist abandonment of Muslim women in the post-9-11 era, when not only did feminists join in the anti-American assault,[72] but elaborately avoided anything that might look like it was targeting Islam.[73] No matter how odious the crime and no matter how prominent the Muslim identity of the male perp, it was somehow the West's fault. The same pattern emerges in the "human rights" community's approach to Palestinian violence against their women: blame the occupation.[74] Palestinian Women's Lives Matter—one more sacrifice on the altar of the Cult of the Occupation.

The negative consequences of this kind of moral failure appear in very prominent events after Trump's election. What made it possible for Palestinian "feminist," Linda Sarsour, and two "women of color" to rise to the top of the nascent wave of the women's movement responding to Trump? Although Sarsour and friends eventually went too far and alienated too many, they managed to be the leaders of the march for two years, during which they admired one of the most explicit, religious (Muslim) antisemites in the USA, and banned Jewish feminists with even traces of Zionism from the "progressive" movement: "Zionists cannot be feminists."[75] By the time they left, little was left. And yet, despite her contempt for Jewish women (one of the main contributors to feminism in its earlier periods), and despite her telling feminists to subordinate their concerns to the Palestinian cause, Linda Sarsour was and remained, a charismatic figure, winning the loyal admiration of activist actors like Susan Sarandon, Mark Ruffalo, and Amnesty International—the beautiful people—for

---

72 Chesler, *Death of Feminism*, 21.

73 Muslim women were prominent in the denial: e.g., Miriam Esman, "Canadian Muslims Protest 'Honor Killing' Label as Racist," *Investigative Project*, October 7, 2013.

74 *Palestinian Women under Prolonged Israeli Occupation: The Gendered Impact of Occupation Violence*, Women's International League for Peace and Freedom (2017); Phyllis Chesler, "Lancet Study Blames Palestinian Wife-Beating on Israel," *Pajamas Media*, January 24, 2010.

75 Collier Meyerson, "Can You Be a Zionist Feminist? Linda Sarsour Says No," *The Nation*, March 13, 2017. This is, of course, not limited to feminist "progressivism." See Blake Flayton, "The Hate That Can't Be Contained," *Tablet*, November 25, 2020.

her courage in wearing a scarf.[76] Despite the eventual resignation from the Women's March of the anti-Zionist "feminist," the marriage of "feminism" and the (toxic male) Palestinian cause continued apace in the academy. In May 2021, in response to the Israeli-Hamas exchange of fire, Gender Studies stood at the forefront of solidarity with the "Palestinian Feminist Collective,"[77] whose priorities are the anti-imperialism of fools rather than welfare of the Palestinian women whose future would look very dim were the current Palestinian leadership to "free" Palestine from the River to the Sea.

But the starkest reminders of the costs in progressive principles and victim-suffering that arise from these mental inversions come when one considers those who do not have "privileged victim" status. The same people who rush to the street to join in a cacophony of voices attacking Israel indignantly for violating Palestinian "inalienable rights," somehow can't be found for rallies about Christians being savaged all through the Muslim-majority world, or Palestinians being savaged by their fellow Arabs, or Palestinian women being savaged by their men, or Uyghurs being savaged by Chinese Han. In terms of numbers and suffering, the fate of Palestinians, at least at Israel's hand, is negligible in comparison with the magnitude and violence Muslims inflict on their Christian populations. On the Y2KMind indignation meter, it's precisely the opposite, and Zionist protests are mere "what-about-ism."

---

76 *Essence Magazine* named Sarsour in their list of 100 most woke women, Lauren Jones, "Woke 100 Women," *Essence*, April 18, 2017.
77 "Gender Studies Departments In Solidarity With Palestinian Feminist Collective."

13

Preemptive Dhimmitude: Unwitting Submission

If I don't see it . . .
deny it even exists . . .
Does it count?

One can look, drop-jawed, at these astounding intellectual, moral, even emotional lapses and failures. Especially when one realizes that *they come at great cost* to the very people making these choices. Not only do they fail to advance the values they embrace (against hatred and prejudice), but, when attacked, they disarm! Astonishment, anger, mockery, despair, righteous indignation—all are honest responses to this enduring recklessness on the part of twenty-first-century Western elites.

But Y2KMinders are only "objectively" stupid. Especially given the caliber of those engaged in the inversions, it's hard to attribute that to actual stupidity, to lack of intelligence. These are some of the smartest, most accomplished people on the planet; that's how they reached their positions of prominence.

When scientist Bill Nye explained how the jihadi attacks on Charlie Hebdo in Paris in 2015 were the result of global warming, the "faux-causality" was obvious to anyone who cared to think (just like poverty or anomie causes terrorism). Gad Saad identifies the mental culprit here, the parasitic mind, whose "law of instrument" (give a child a hammer, and everything needs pounding) makes global warming the explanation for everything. But the specifics this particular hammer suggests serve the demands of Y2KMind: *when jihadis attack, blame the*

West.[1] The same holds for so many other examples of the "profound imbecilities" that Saad documents, like open immigration, or the horror of (necessarily discriminatory) profiling, or 50+ reasons Islam has nothing to do with 9–11 or with any of the other 35,000 attacks across the globe. Saad points out how all this "reasoning" protects Islam,[2] which I would like to call *preemptive dhimmitude.*

Were one to point to (sincere) postcolonial ideology and (passionate) antisemitism as drivers of this strange behavior, one might explain some of the more egregious forms, but certainly not all, nor the widespread and increasingly aggressive adoption of these postures. These motives cannot explain the apparently unbreakable consensus, the headlong folly of the parasitic mind. Why do so few object to repeated cases where Y2KMind contradicts itself, abandons its principles and sacrifices the objects of its alleged concern? Why do progressive gentiles steer clear when the woke leadership targets Jews who won't renounce their Zionist devil? Why do they back away from anyone accused of Islamophobia? Why has the twenty-first-century PC narrative gotten such purchase with progressives? What happened to the loud voice of dissent, needed precisely at times like this?

To put the ideological issue in shame-honor dynamics: why does the voice of dissent get no traction, indeed those who object to the [inverted] narrative get a strong reaction from those they offend and little to no support from those they defend. The abandonment of women in the Arab world, the indifference to victims who are not privileged (Tibetans, Kurds, Berbers, Jews, Hong Kongers, Uyghurs) . . . the deplatforming of "right-wing" opinion on social media even as other, more politically correct hate-mongers abound largely unhindered . . . the boundless tolerance for violence in the search for "peace" . . . at some point one might expect the moral mind to rebel, no? How unfair, misinformed, and ill-willed does one have to be to say to Muslim women: "Put your claims on hold while we feminists support toxic males fighting for 'justice' in Palestine?" Or to look at the conflict between Jews and Muslims in the "Holy Land" and say to the Jews: "It's your fault; if only you gave more, I'm sure they would be peaceful"?

If we look at the woke insurrection, we find a familiar pattern: distorting egalitarian principles with exceptions that privilege one group before the "law." Those designated "victims" are permitted hatred, scapegoating, violence; their intended victims held to strict egalitarian and verbally vegetarian principles. At

---

1   "Bill Nye The Science Guy Explains the Connection between Climate Change and Terrorism in Paris," *HuffPost*, December 1, 2015; cited and explained as "the law of instrument" by Saad, *Parasitic Mind*, 223.
2   Saad, *Parasitic Mind*, chapter 6.

the intersectional apex stands an aristocracy of victimhood, whose suffering is caused by white people (Jews here being white squared). Everyone's feelings count except those designated "bad"; killing innocent people is horrible except when it's Muslims killing Jews, in which case it's either not happening, or, frankly, praiseworthy.[3]

In almost every case, these products of inverted narratives and willfully blind reporting take positions that match precisely what Caliphators demand from infidels. Somehow, through this alchemy, the Palestinians are given privileged victim status, which not only makes their cause a priority over other victim causes, but protects their rights to hate and to slaughter their enemy. And through yet another alchemical trick, this same attitude protects the right of Caliphators the world over to hate.

To understand the overlap, consider a list of Caliphator talking points for infidels, that is to say, the narrative that Da'wa Caliphators want infidels to adopt while they invade their societies:

1. Islam is a religion of peace and any violence done in its name is not true Islam.

2. Jihad is not holy war but inner struggle; those who wage military jihad to expand Dar al Islam are hijacking the religion. Dar al Harb is no longer a relevant category.

3. Muslims have a right to all human rights, including the right of free speech, assembly, worship, immigration, and the right not to be suspected or subjected to surveillance.

4. Muslims should not be insulted or offended.

5. People who offend Muslims are Islamophobes, and since Islamophobia is to the twenty-first century what antisemitism was to the twentieth century, their behavior should, therefore, be criminalized.

6. The Palestinians are a people and are the "new Jews/victims of genocide"; the Israelis are not a people and are behaving like "new Nazis."

7. Palestinians want a two-state solution, have fulfilled all the requirements, and any failures to achieve peace are Israel's fault.

---

3   Tom Paulin, "Interview with Omayma Abdel-Latif," *Al Ahram Weekly*, April 4–10, 2002. For further discussion of these remarks of Paulin's, see Harrison, *Resurgence of antisemitism*, 108–10.

8. Muslim violence against Jews in Europe is because of what Israel does; and jihadi violence against the West is because of Western aggression (Afghanistan, Iraq) and support for Israel.

9. Terrorism should not be used by infidels to describe jihadis who refuse to be so morally stigmatized, but rather for infidels who "aggress" against Muslims.

Now from a *Caliphator* perspective, all of this is nonsense. For them,

1. Islam is a religion of war, conquest, and dominion; and jihad is the name of that war.

2. Terror is a major weapon jihadis use to intimidate infidels which they embrace and celebrate; they just don't want us to call them bad names.

3. Caliphators have no intention of reciprocating the rights and respect they demand, these demands are means to better conduct their invasion.

4. Caliphators define "being offended" not in terms of a common standard applicable to all, but in exclusivist, tribal terms, of the intolerable blackening of their face and Allah's honor.

5. Caliphators use "Islamophobe" as a way to attack any criticism of Muslims and especially anyone exposing what they're up to.

6. The Palestinians are not the mild Jewish victims purchasing their own train tickets to Auschwitz, or even brave Jewish freedom fighters struggling to resist, but the first wave of Global Jihad bearing the battle standard of exterminationist Jew-hatred.

7. The "peace process" with Israel is a Trojan Horse operation—"[they give us] *land for* [our] *war* [of elimination]."

8. Targeting Jews in democracies is the first step in taking over the countries they then flee; it is easy because the rest of those societies believe Caliphator propaganda and ignore their victims' cries.

9. Jihadi violence is not the product of Western imperial aggression; its intensity and durability come from millennial aspirations to world conquest, not from desperation to be free; and its shocking violence comes not from frustration at occupation and lack of freedom, but from ferocious fantasies of Islam's destiny to dominate.

Despite the stark and easily verifiable contrast between what is said among Muslims and in foreign tongues, the disinformation in the first list corresponds directly to the key Da'wa Caliphator talking points in the early stages of the cognitive invasion of the West. Here, demopaths, whining while weak like

Nietzsche's *homme de ressentiment*, invoke the very principles they despise and have no intention of abiding by when strong, exploiting their targets' good will in order to invade.[4] The fate of the international thriller, Hesh Kestin's *The Siege of Tel Aviv*, illustrates all these elements: describing the successful attack of five Muslim nations on Israel (under cover of peace-making), the author was accused of Islamophobia for suggesting in a novel that many Muslims, especially their leaders, actually want to wipe Israel out and massacre her inhabitants. So a Middle Eastern reality (one of the nastier forms of Hama Rules), with huge implications for infidels, cannot be uttered ... a position enforced by many a progressive infidel.[5]

Western intellectuals are notably, exquisitely, vulnerable to this demopathic appeal, no matter how openly antagonistic. Beneficiaries of a merit-based system, eager to avoid even the semblance of prejudice/defiance, Y2KMind makes the Caliphator disinformation politically correct. When the security guard looked at Atta on 9–11 at the airport, despite thinking he looked terribly suspicious—almost a caricature of a terrorist—he mentally chastised himself, lest *he* look like a racist. And so he let him through. Fool me once, shame on you. Fool me repeatedly, for over two decades ... what's wrong with me? Where's our hypocrisy detector? Have the magnets under the table sent it into systemic spin?

Starting with its spectacular marshalling of global "progressive" forces at Durban, Da'wa demopathy has had enormous success in the twenty-first century: the power of accusations of Islamophobia to destroy careers ... the sensitivity training aimed at teaching infidels not to offend Muslims ... the massive NGO- and UN-accumulated dossier of accusations against Israel for violating Palestinian rights, and the missing dossier of Palestinian violations of Jewish, Christian, and Muslim rights ... the widespread censorship and persecution (postmodern style) of infidels identified as Islamophobes in the West, and the widespread censorship and persecution (premodern style) of Christians by Muslims in the Middle East ... the exceptional credulity of Western infidels when faced with assessing Caliphator lethal narratives and moral claims, and their profound suspicion of anything uttered by the "Two Satans." Hence, the prominence of CAIR in our public sphere and educational

---

4   On the psychology of vocal victims, see Ekin Ok, et al., "Signaling Virtuous Victimhood as Indicators of Dark Triad Personalities," *American Psychological Association*, 120.6 (2021): 1634–1661; Cory Clark, "The Evolutionary Advantages of Playing Victim," *Quillette*, February 27, 2021.

5   Clair Kirch, "Dzanc Drops Novel Criticized for Islamophobic Themes," *Publishers Weekly*, April 24, 2019; "The Siege of Tel Aviv - the novel and the insane backlash (review and meta-review)," *Elder of Ziyon*, May 12, 2019.

systems, starting with their role in Bush's response to 9–11, and continuing now among Democratic party leaders.[6]

If one thinks of Y2KMind as a (silent) adoption of this proffered, demopathic narrative, tailor-made for Caliphator success and for democratic failure, then the inconsistencies disappear. Y2KMind complies extensively with this Da'wa narrative, especially at those points where the self-contradictions are most glaring. "Nonviolent" Caliphators can appeal to human rights to demand impossible concessions from Israel and the West (stand down while we invade), and nevertheless get resounding support from the global human rights community. They can accuse Israel of sins regularly committed in their political culture (apartheid, racism, slaughter, targeting children, imperial ambitions, genocide), and get unquestioning support from Y2KMinders. On campuses, on social media platforms, hate speech from Muslims goes largely unopposed, while Zionists get de-platformed for "hate speech" by the most expansive of definitions. And it's still not enough.[7]

In other words, I argue, the astonishing tolerance that Y2KMind shows for Caliphator intolerance derives not from stupidity, nor from the law of instrument, nor from humanitarian racism, nor even high-mindedness, but from anticipating and obeying Caliphator directives as much as possible, without actually appearing to submit.

So powerfully and uniformly has this discourse imposed itself on the intellectual and information elites in the West, that some "alt-right" dissidents have literally identified it as "the Narrative." One astute if not sympathetic analyst described "the narrative" as

> a nonnegotiable vocabulary that every member of polite society
> was required to learn. Political correctness was just a small part
> of it. Americans absorbed the Narrative every day—in their
> schools, in the media, through mass entertainment, through
> thousands of tiny social cues. The brainwashing was so total as to
> become invisible; people internalized the axioms so deeply that,

6 Steven Emerson, "Illinois Democrats Line Up to Help CAIR Fundraise," *IPT News*, January 4, 2021. CAIR recently came out with a statement on Islamophobia which illustrates precisely what I argue here: *Islamophobia in the Mainstream* (Washington DC: CAIR, 2021). On page 20, they cite all the best-funded "Islamophobic" organizations, most of them sources of reliable information about activities by radical Muslims, many of which I cite in this book. Without them, the West would be blind . . . which is the point.

7 Marc Lamont Hill and Mitchell Plitnick, *Except for Palestine: The Limits of Progressive Politics* (New York: The New Press, 2021).

after a while, they couldn't think without them. Simply to point out the existence of the axioms, much less to call their truth into question, was to become a dangerous brute, a pariah.[8]

And right at the top of the diversity-inclusive narrative identified by these alt-right brutes, were two key assertions: "Islam is a religion of peace. Therefore, the mullahs calling for bloodshed had to be ignored or explained away." As if to prove the point, the response from high-minded folk is: this nonsense about a "narrative" is the product of paranoid conspiracy thinkers.

One might be tempted to call this straight-out fear, fear of fatwa and the fanatics who would gladly die carrying out the death sentence—the very phenomenon they deny exists.[9] Unquestionably, there is a strong element of fear involved, instilled on the one hand by the random damage of suicide attacks (9–11, 7–7, Fort Hood 2009, Nice 2016), and on the other, by the targeted killings of individuals from Theo Van Gogh (2004) to Samuel Paty (2020). In the same way that a magnet under a table controls how the iron filings on the surface line up, Y2KMind lines up above the surface of our civil society, silently and invisibly complying with the magnet force of demands made by the triumphalist religion we refuse to acknowledge, even as we bend to its demands. Just ask Tim Benson why British political cartoons savage Israel and don't touch Arafat.[10]

Above the table, the conversation expresses Y2KMind, with its high-minded principles about social justice and anti-racism, its dismissal of warnings as paranoid conspiracy theory, and its plenitude of public secrets. Everyone knows that when our political leaders and pundits deplore "senseless violence," they really mean *very meaningful violence* intended to remind the infidel: "don't you dare offend us."

You have declared war against Allah and his Prophet. You have declared war against the Muslim Umma! For which you will pay a heavy price. Take the lesson from Theo Van Gogh! Take

---

8 Marantz, *Antisocial*, 116. Marantz literally self-describes here (see below). His book is dedicated to making pariahs of those who identify the narrative. He has no remotely similar analysis about Antifa and Black Lives Matter hijacking conversations.

9 Charles Small, whose *Center for the Study of Contemporary Antisemitism* was then at Yale, held a discussion with Jytte Klausen when Yale University Press refused to publish the cartoons (see chapter 4), and reports that the security was extremely high and the University not very pleased. (Personal communication)

10 See discussion of this magnet in producing lethal journalism, above 342; on Benson, see above, 129.

lessons from the Jews of Khaybar! Take lessons from all you can see. For you will pay with blood.[11]

We understand the sense of the violence perfectly well when we talk of not "gratuitously insulting 1.5 billion people." While the hashtag #JeSuisCharlie briefly trended after the slaughter of a dozen French cartoonists in Paris by Caliphator jihadis in 2015, it quickly brought on #JeNeSuisPasCharlie.[12] And when PEN International wanted to give an award to Charlie Hebdo for "Freedom of Expression Courage," 242 of its members, insisting on their "seriousness and moral commitment," objected that "the cartoons of the Prophet *must be seen* as being intended to cause further humiliation and suffering."[13] When a British-born jihadi took five people hostage at a synagogue in Texas in order to free an al-Qaeda operative in an American prison, an FBI spokesman hastily asserted that there were no links between the jihadi's demands and antisemitism, a claim rapidly repeated in ever more certain terms by the AP and BBC.[14]

This is best understood less as an inchoate fear than as a form of anticipatory dhimmitude in which individuals take on the obligations of dhimmi without even having suffered military defeat, in the hopes that by being sufficiently respectful/submissive and obscuring the lines of aggression (which so often run via the Jews), that the Caliphators won't feel the need to insist on formal dhimmitude or conversion. Obviously, dhimmitude in its full form, with its formulae for the humiliation of the infidel—riding donkeys not horses, not raising tall buildings of worship, walking, eyes down, in the gutter when passing a Muslim—are inappropriate for today's Western leaders. But they (think they) can, perhaps, preempt such outright submission by observing certain basics that must be observed by good infidels. "Otherwise, you foolish jackasses tempt the lion spirit of jihad."[15] Above all, at this early stage of the campaign, the main requirement Caliphators make of all dhimmi is the prohibition on offending (triumphalist) Muslims by blaspheming against their religion, including the truly "hurtful" accusation that the jihadis are inspired by Islamic texts and doctrine.

---

11 Preacher at protest over cartoons outside Danish embassy in London, February 6, 2006,. See above, 166–68.

12 Discussed by Jonathan Chait, "Not a very P.C. Thing to Say," *New York Magazine*, January 27, 2015.

13 "PEN Receives Letter from Members about Charlie Hebdo Award," PEN, May 5, 2015 (italics mine).

14 See 401n19.

15 See 155n78.

While this directive *not* to challenge Muslims is every dhimmi's duty (preemptive or not), it is particularly incumbent on the heads of dhimmi communities to make sure their members do not step out of line. Dhimmi must bite their tongues *lest* there be Muslim violence; and infidel leaders must make sure their people do not offend.[16] This has been one of the principal jobs of dhimmi leaders—Jewish, Christian, Zoroastrian, Hindu—throughout the nearly millennium and a half wherever Muslims ruled.

Western thought leaders in the 21st century, with their steadfast commitment to Y2KMind, can be understood as—*preemptive* dhimmi leaders. These infidels in positions of authority in still unconquered states, in the realm of the sword, have quietly accepted the rules of dhimmitude as a way of [they think] preempting a Caliphator takeover, or at least delaying it. Unlike dhimmi leaders in *dar al Islam*, where infidel leaders are visibly beholden and subject to the ruling Muslims, in *dar al Harb*, dhimmi leaders must enforce rules that infidels are by and large unfamiliar with, and they must appear to be independent of the triumphalist Muslims whose rules they enforce. And while in their minds they are preserving Muslim dignity, they are in fact taking instructions from Caliphators and articulating their cogwar narrative for infidel consumption.

It would not have been seemly, for example, if the president of the USA had appeared in the week after 9–11, bowed before the Muslims accompanying him, and said to his fellow infidel citizens what Caliphators genuinely believe: "Islam is a superior religion, a religion of war and conquest; we have just felt its might and terror; let us submit and be spared." Instead, he came out willingly, assured his fellow infidels that Muslims were just like them and appalled by the jihadi strike [fake news], and then read a Quranic promise of vengeance on blasphemers which he introduced as proof of Islam's peaceful nature. And the Y2KMind in us all, applauded: "at least *we* won't scapegoat our poor, marginalized, underrepresented Muslim minority. (I'm sure they'd do the same for us.)"

The farthest thing from our thoughts would be a third scenario, in which Bush appeared at the Islamic Center and said to the American Muslims who stood beside him and in the audience:

> This attack has been made in the name of your religion, by fervent Muslim believers. It is incumbent upon you, therefore, to show us your commitment to citizenship in our land by making

---

16 Bat Ye'or, *Islam and Dhimmitude*, 50–121; Antoine Fattal, *Le statut légal des non-musulmans en pays d'Islam* (Beirut: Imprimerie catholique, 1958), 214–31.

explicit and extensive your rejection of these deeds. Answer some key questions:

- What do American Muslims think and believe about the triumphalist imperialism of their ancestors, so vividly displayed in this dastardly attack on our nation, and upon whose renunciation by Christians, our democracy was founded?
- What do you think of the land in which you now live, where we have accepted you? Is it *dar al Harb*, the land to be conquered?
- Do you interpret *al-Walā' wal-Barā'* as "love the good and hate the bad?" Or: "love the Muslim and hate the infidel?"
- And what do you propose to do with your co-religionists who insist on the triumphalist interpretation of Islam's destiny to dominate?

If you cannot answer these questions to our satisfaction, then I'm afraid you cannot expect us to extend to you the full range of religious freedom that we have established in our lands, freedoms that are offered those who make the key reciprocal renunciation we all have made—not to use power to impose one's religion on others. And until you can convince us of your commitment to the land to which you have come, do not expect us to trust you.

Anyone who says in response, "Don't talk like that. We can't go to war with 1+ billion Muslims! Therefore let's not upset them," really thinks of Muslims as a belligerent homogenous *amalgame* which will view our demands for reciprocity and civic commitment as a declaration of war.[17] And only someone unaware of

---

17 Note that much of Habermas' discussion of religion and the secular sphere concerns the mutual reciprocity that must exist for a non-coercive public sphere to prevail. And yet, neither does prevail, nor can it with Caliphators. In the volume of "philosopher's reflections" after 9–11, the word "coercion" appears twice (not in connection with Islam), and "violence" twenty time, almost exclusively Israel's "state violence." Jihad never appears. Judith Butler, Jürgen Habermas, Charles Taylor and Cornel West, *The Power of Religion in the Public Sphere* (New York: Columbia University Press, 2011). See Elizabeth Rard, "9/11 and the War on Terrorism: A Critique of Jürgen Habermas and Jacques Derrida," *Reflections*, 2008.

the reciprocity necessary for human rights as we understand them to even exist, could object.

By viewing Y2KMinders as preemptive dhimmi we can understand whence comes the cultural AIDS:[18] when the body-politic's white blood cells attack not the invaders, but the warning messenger, it is the dhimmi leadership attacking the unruly members of their own community, those trouble-makers who upset Muslims. When Swedish courts vigorously police "hate speech" against Swedish Muslims (complaints about immigrants, criticism of Islam) and give free reign to the most heinous hate speech among Muslims, they are fulfilling their duties as preemptive dhimmi leaders. Their multicultural explanations ("this is how they behave—who are we to stop them?") primarily offer us insight into what they consider an appropriate fig-leaf. When Brandeis faculty, women "scholars" in the lead, shout about what a "horrible message" it sends to Muslims when we honor Ayaan Hirsi Ali, how it covers "us" with "shame," they are performing as dhimmi leaders. From a demotic perspective, they cover themselves in shame.

When journalists like Chris Hedges publish stories of Israelis killing Muslim children, inciting jihadi hatreds, and then Westsplain the poor, frustrated Palestinians' desire for human rights, with not a word about radical Islam or jihadi assaults on Jews, they follow the Caliphator rule: "Run our war propaganda as news, and don't talk about our hatreds and violence." We end up in the 2020s with the exceptional spectacle of people who invoke the sacred principle of tolerance to give the Caliphators full access to the Western public sphere, even as they become stridently intolerant of their deplorable, "right-wing," fellow infidels who have the nerve to criticize these fine upstanding citizens. The only principle such own-goal advocacy stands by, is that of preemptive dhimmitude.

Nor is this a minor theme. For the last two decades, it has been the theme of politicians and journalists: one must avoid confrontations with Muslims, no matter how questionable the Muslim offense (e.g., [invented] Papal Insult, the [forgery-charged] Danoongate "blasphemy"), in order to "avoid a clash of civilizations." At the height of the Danish Cartoon Scandal, for example, a BBC reporter explained the Western response: "The last thing these [European (i.e. infidel)] governments want is another confrontation in which Islam is seen to be pitched against the West. The strategy therefore is to try to prevent this from

---

18 Note that Derrida also uses the metaphor of an autoimmune deficiency, although the way he interprets it (blame the West for the terrorism) actually contributes to it: "Autoimmunity: Real and Symbolic Suicides: A Dialogue with Jacques Derrida," in Borradori, *Philosophy in a Time of Terror*, 85–138.

becoming a 'clash of civilisations.'"[19] The prime directive of this early twenty-first-century "strategy"? *Don't piss them off.*

Hence our leaders explain to us how insulting and hurtful it is to Muslims when infidels make pictures of their prophet. They won't even entertain the argument that Caliphators are picking a fight based on a prohibition initially put in place to avoid Muslim idol worship of the prophet, whose current implementation against infidels is itself a form of that idol worship. The preemptive dhimmi hide their submission behind elaborate efforts to prevent a war the Caliphators have already declared and launched.

Both President Obama and Hillary Clinton voiced this anxiety about confirming the jihadi narrative as a decisive concern in formulating their policy of never speaking of "radical Islam." Clinton, as presidential candidate, explained to ABC: "It helps to create this clash of civilizations that is actually a recruiting tool for ISIS and other radical jihadists who use this as a way of saying, 'We are in a war against the West—you must join us.'"[20] In so speaking, she expressed a formally adopted government policy.[21] On more than one occasion, this approach produced comedies of learned helplessness among Administration officials faced with hard questioning from Republican Congressmen: Eric Holder and Paul Stockton comically could not say "radical Islam."[22]

As a result, we had leaders telling us not to talk about radical Islam so as to interrupt the jihadis narrative of "West at war with us," and at the same time, affirming the Da'wa narrative, "Islam is a religion of peace." Combined with lethal journalism's continuous running of Palestinian war propaganda, repeatedly inciting jihad and its Jew-hating, paranoid passions, this approach, so widespread among the information elite, actually turned into a potent 1–2 punch for Caliphators. They could flourish in the shade of Y2KMind's preemptive dhimmitude and strike at the time and place of their choice.

As a result, Caliphators stayed under the willingly debilitated radar of Western intelligence. Under these conditions, followers of al Qaradawi got to build a mosque to spread Caliphator beliefs among the population (Da'wa) in the heart of a black neighborhood in Boston, with a sweet land deal from the

---

19 Reynolds, "Clash of Rights and Responsibilities."
20 Bradner, "Clinton explains why she won't say 'radical Islam.'"
21 Homeland Security, Terminology to Define the Terrorists: Recommendations from American Muslims, January 2008. It instructs the Department to ensure terminology is "properly calibrated to diminish the recruitment efforts of extremists who argue that the West is at war with Islam." Countering Violent Extremism (CVE) Subcommittee, "Interim Report and Recommendations," June 2016.
22 For transcripts and links, see Daniel Pipes, "Not Calling Islamism the Enemy," *Lion's Den*, September 12, 2001, updated June 4, 2017.

city and robust support from infidel religious organizations, including Jewish ones.[23] Of course, for those who so willingly adopted the Caliphator narrative for dhimmis about a peaceful Islam, there should be no problem with a mosque preaching hatred of the US as a democracy in a troubled neighborhood. Why would someone who Westsplained that "true Islam" is peace and has nothing to do with this terrorist extremism, have a problem?

But then, why worry that if infidels question this narrative, it will so upset Muslims that they'll join this extremism which has nothing to do with their faith? Socrates's worst student could dismantle such logic, not to mention that anyone minimally trained in deconstruction could birth the elephant in this room. And yet, from this generation of Y2KMinders ... we get people showing the door to those who point out the problem even as they open the door to the problem. "How dare you disturb my willful blindness!"

This unacknowledged threat is most sharply and often comically denied among lethal journalists covering Israel. Even before 9–11, the combination of jihadi intimidation (terror attacks, targeted violence including against journalists) and Western compliance was locked in place. Western news consumers, unless they really looked for it, had no idea how much the Palestinians hated them. And that lethal combination continues to dominate the coverage to this day.

The key is not in the "Occupation" narrative itself, which, to someone who doesn't know anything, sounds plausible. It's in the fervid attachment to it, despite the counter-evidence. Matti Friedman considers it a new religion, especially its dogmatic preference for dualistic moral thinking:

> The rigors of reporting were abandoned for the simple pleasures of the sermon.... The guiding idea was no longer to understand what was going on; there was nothing to understand. We knew who was right and who was wrong, and it remained only to anathematize the bad guys so far into disrepute that even the act of trying to understand them would be a kind of sin.[24]

An excellent description of lethal journalism: for the pack of journalists, Israel is beyond the pale ... except when it comes to living there and enjoying the protections of journalism in a democracy.[25]

23 Feoktistov, *Terror in the Cradle of Liberty*. On the behavior of the Jewish leadership, see chapter 19.
24 Friedman, "You're all Israel now."
25 Gutmann, *The Other War*, chapter 4.

This cognitive glitch has produced what Friedman calls the "Cult of the Occupation." Here we find inversions repeated over and over, the shoddiest fact-checking, the shortest memory of earlier mistakes, the most striking lack of interest in anything that does not advance the dualist narrative, the complete acceptance of Palestinian intimidation. Israel is evil, Palestinians the victims. As a result, one of the less onerous occupations in the history of occupations— before the first intifada, the West Bank was one of the fastest growing economies in the world[26]—has become the symbol of Nazi Evil, a crime against the human rights of an entire people, an occupation whose elimination is a key to world peace. The massive obsession of "human rights" organizations and the UN for Israeli violations of Palestinian "human rights" operates precisely in this zone of inversion, where Israeli sins are viewed through the electron microscope and Palestinian sins—against Israel, Jews, Christians, fellow Muslims, journalists— through a broken telescope.

This conjuncture of jihadi demands and Progressive enthusiasm for the inverted narrative lies at the heart of the current malaise of the West. In 2000, on a wave of misinformation from our jihadi-intimidated, narrative journalists, the al Durah blood libel introduced these moral and cognitive inversions into discussions in our public sphere. The moral sadism of calling Israel the new Nazis when no army behaved less like the Nazis, and calling the Palestinians the new Jews, when they openly claimed they wanted to *be* the new Nazis, became the new normal.

How can we understand this blank check of moral generosity for the Palestinians and equally mean-spirited treatment of Israel? Some can be obviously understood in terms of double standards, which we all use a great deal, without mentioning it. Double standards are especially sharp in this conflict, where the gap in moral behavior is at its most stark. (Compare Israel's treating Syrian victims of intra-Muslim conflicts with the political culture that generates those kinds of conflicts.) Of course, everyone expects more of Israelis. *Palestinians* expect more of Israelis.

But double standards are not inversions. Double standards mean, you understand the Israelis live up to a *much* higher progressive standard than do their enemies, and you may even call on them to make more sacrifices and take more criticism, than their more volatile and touchy cousins. But you know

---

26 "From 1967–80, average annual increase of 7% and 9 percent in real per capita GDP and G NP, respectively ... Between 1980/81 and 1986/87, real GNP per capita increased by 12 percent, and the real GDP per capita increased by *only* 5 percent," *Developing the Occupied Territories: An Investment in Peace*, The World Bank, September 1993 [italics mine].

what's going on; you don't believe rhetoric, especially human rights rhetoric from people who give no human rights even to their own people, much less their minorities and women and self-declared enemies. You don't reverse it by magnifying every alleged Israeli bad deed (by whose standards?) to call them Nazis and ignoring every bit of evidence that their enemies admire the Nazis, indeed that suicide bombing represents the desperate frustration of not being able to finish Hitler's job.[27]

If you read this and don't think what I say can be true, inform yourself. If you read this and say, "what a racist!" (but then those readers would have already scurried off), you're lost to reality. It's not about race; it's about culture. And culture counts; and stupidity matters.

Some explain this inversion as the work of what is today, too generally, called antisemitism. That is, that the eagerness with which Westerners welcomed this news about Israel behaving badly, derived from a long-standing Western gentile dislike of Jews that had been inhibited for half a century by Holocaust shame. For fifty years it was no longer acceptable to Jew-bait in the West.[28] You even had to let them into your universities on the basis of merit, where they flourished disturbingly. The Y2K inversion set this resentment free. The press reporting Palestinian lethal propaganda, and the Left's eager reception of it, were due, so the argument runs, to their profound if unacknowledged dislike of autonomous Jews.

And among progressives, this resentment arises within a framework of postmodern supersessionism, a rivalry between the newest claimant to the moral leadership of humanity, and the oldest. Why would anyone be surprised? (And yet I was when I figured it out.) After all, postmodernism got its start with an oedipal overthrow of the "modern." If they felt that degree of influence-anxiety about their own ancestors, why wouldn't they resent any suggestion that the Jews might still have something to say. (A postmodernism with integrity would have actually turned *to* the Jews to hear an intimate counter-narrative of Western civilization.[29])

But postmodernism, for all its dazzling moments, rather quickly gave in to the resentment. Postcolonialism substituted the rebuke of the colonized for that of the Jew; and if the people who claimed to speak in the name of the former colonies, also hated Jews, so what? No. Better yet: Just when the worst

---

27 Spoerl, "Parallels between Nazi and Islamist Antisemitism"; Marcus and Crook, "Aspiration not Desperation." Chafets made these points already in 1982 about what he called a "double double-standard, *Double Vision*, 307–11.

28 Landes, "Europe's Destructive Holocaust Shame."

29 Ibid.

Jew-haters on the planet act out their Jew-hatred in the most revolting manner, make supporting *them* the litmus test for liberal credentials.

This progressive supersessionism plays a key role, notably visible in the impact of the al Durah libel in those circles: the inverted narrative of the Israeli Nazi took hold. One finds it cropping up like mushrooms after rain in the aftermath of each round of lethal journalism about open hostilities between Israel and Hamas, in 2021 more widespread, dishonest, and repetitious than ever. "Progressives" like Jostein Gaarder reasoned along these lines: what we, with the help of our lethal media, imagine the Nazi Jews doing to the Palestinians, is what we believe the Jews think is their right as the "chosen people." Whether this supersessionist malevolent projection continues to silently dominate attitudes will be determined by those who can free themselves from its talons. Maybe the madness of 2021's coverage might serve as a wake-up call . . . but unlikely.

My sense is, however, that, as with ideology, this kind of animus can only account for some of this inversion. After all, it's not only perverse, but also self-destructive. Doesn't it occur to any of those so bravely protesting Zionist brutality that, like those Madrid models of 2002, they are cheering on the jihadis and screaming at those defending themselves? Doesn't that own-goal rejoicing seem like a counter-indicated precedent to follow?

In a free market of ideas, in a demotic public sphere, it should appeal to very few. If antisemitism in the twentieth century could be defined as *hating Jews more than absolutely necessary* (Isaiah Berlin?), in the twenty-first, it has becoming *hating Jews even though it's killing you.* So while Jew-hatred/resentment/envy may explain the motivations of some, it cannot explain so broad a consensus in support of such negative consequences. Surely people of sound mind would resist, reject such thinking, no matter how emotionally appealing.

The strongest explanation I can come up with for the current dysfunctions of our information professionals and systems across the boards, is that the professionals in question are silently complying with Caliphator directives. For those who recognize the situation, attacking the Caliphator's hated enemy, Israel, is a sure way to win the favor of the Strong Horse. By contrast, Western information professionals who might want to defend Israel, would have to criticize Palestinians, something Western infidels, even Israelis, are loath to do. Hence, the general silence from people who favor Zionist freedom fighters to jihadi terrorists.

Those who vigorously assault Israel, the lead lethal journalists like Robert Fisk or Jonathan Cook or the *Guardian* crew, or Marc Lamont Hill, who aggressively adopt the Palestinian narrative, may, in some cases, be motivated by the *Schadenfreude* and ersatz moral superiority that they derive. The rest of the journalists, even those who want to fight it, have trouble avoiding cancel-culture. They thereby get caught in the nets of virtue signaling and conspicuous avoidance of those already canceled. Most, unless really motivated, just stand down.

Now we come to the nub: why is something so obvious not acknowledged? How does one of the most progressive and creative polities on the planet get vilified constantly,[30] while one of the most repressive and violent polities becomes the darling of liberals and progressives?[31]

On one level, my entire career, unbeknownst to me, unintended, has focused on public secrets, on things everyone (in the know) knew, but also knew not to talk about out loud. This is the core conceit of Andersen's *Emperor's New Clothes*. I gained experience identifying the dynamics in the past (Charlemagne's coronation on the first day of the year 6000 from the Creation, the passage of the year AD 1000), and so I know well the difficulties of raising the issue.[32] In particular, as I have pointed out on a number of occasions in this book, in the post-Holocaust Western public sphere, being associated with conspiracy theories rapidly destroys one's reputation.[33] "Absence of evidence is not evidence of absence" is a hard principle to apply in the face of dismissal for conspiracy theory, even if one is talking not of conspiracies, but of conventions that govern public discourse and reflect openly expressed goals.

One can, therefore, legitimately claim that mimetic desire (I want what others want) impacts thinking as well as more emotional registers, that this "pack" thinking can and does occur, and that an informal but widespread collective denial can dominate the public discussion. Bari Weiss describes just such a "conspiracy of silence" taking hold of progressive American Jews.

> If you criticize [Ilhan] Omar's antisemitism you may be called hysterical or oversensitive. More likely, you will be called a racist, a white supremacist, or a fascist who is actively endangering the life of a minority—a purposeful tactic used to make a person who holds bad ideas above reproach. No one wants to be accused of such things. And no one wants to ruin a dinner party or to lose

---

30 Recently for not vaccinating the Palestinians "according to international law." NGOs and the COVID-19 Vaccine Libel Against Israel," *NGOMonitor*, January 06, 2021.

31 Cary Nelson, *Not in Kansas Anymore: Academic Freedom in Palestinian Universities* (Washington DC, Academic Engagement Network, 2021).

32 Landes, "Lest the Millennium"; *Relics Apocalypse and the Deceits of History* (invocation of Emperor's New Clothes, 278).

33 Juha Räikkä and Lee Basham, "Conspiracy Theory Phobia," in *Conspiracy Theories*, 178–86.

friends or to seem parochial. And so what I see too often among friends is that they keep their mouths shut and hope someone changes the subject. As my friend David Samuels has said: American Jews are eager to be the right kind of victims—meaning victims of the bad people on the right, and not the good people on the left. The upshot is that there is a conspiracy of silence taking hold among too many progressive Jews. Outrage is increasingly reserved for the privacy and safety of our own homes.[34]

On one level, this book is addressed to them and their friends, to give them the vocabulary and background to acknowledge, to confront, this stifling Omertà.

It's certainly not a question of evidence. When the city of Boston welcomed the Roxbury Mosque, they could have googled to find out that Da'wa Caliphator Yussuf al Qaradawi was the community's mentor. Indeed, there was no lack of people pointing it out.[35] It's about ignoring evidence that's readily available. It's about not being able to handle the meaning of the evidence. When I present people with the role of shame-honor culture in driving the conflict between triumphalist Muslims and autonomous Jews between the river and the sea,[36] they often cut me off and say: "so what's your solution?" Initially, I wondered at this cart-before-the-horse logic, and argued we need to consider the problem as best we can, before we come up with solutions. Now I understand this differently: my explanation contradicted their chosen solution ("the two-state solution is the *only* just solution"). The empirical evidence I offered was literally indigestible, and, they thought they knew, would force me to say: get rid of them. In a pinch, accuse me of "racism."[37]

Meantime, while good liberal cognitive egocentrics couldn't think their way out of a narrowing comfort zone, anti-Western cogwarriors weaponized disgust. It's not a coincidence that among the most prominent targets of cancel culture in twenty-first-century academia, some of the earliest and most consistent have been Zionists and "Islamophobes" (often one and the same).[38] One might even argue that Israel was the first major target of cancel culture in the twenty-first century, formally declared at Durban, and that hysterical anti-Zionist cancel culture is in some ways an import of Arab politics to our campuses. This felicitous

---

34 Bari Weiss, *How to Fight Anti-Semitism* (New York: Crown, 2021), 171.
35 Feoktistov, *Terror in the Cradle of Liberty*, Part 1 and 2.
36 See above, 191–211; Landes, "Oslo Misreading of an Honor-Shame Culture."
37 Gad Saad calls it the "Ostrich Parasitic Syndrome," *The Parasitic Mind*, 121.
38 Kenneth Lasson, "In an Academic Voice: Antisemitism and Academy Bias," *Journal for the Study of Antisemitism* 349 (2011).

and overlapping combination of evil Zionists and pathological Islamophobes (who does not have better reason to fear triumphalist Islam than Israelis?) happens to tally precisely with two Caliphator priorities: attacking their enemies and sheltering their warriors from criticism in the shade of Y2KMind. Cancel culture has literally banned from the public sphere any discussion of Caliphators: who and how many they are; what their loves and hates; what their goals and means. "Members of the BDS coalition, Caliphators? Don't be ridiculous. BDS is a civil society institution."

The Psychic Wages of Preemptive Dhimmitude

Of course, all this dissonance takes a serious toll on one's sense of intellectual integrity. Journalists are notoriously touchy about being accused of unprofessional behavior; human rights activists, angry about being questioned about their priorities. For the journalists, this is particularly difficult: their reputation depends on their promise of "honest witness," and the damage any leak to their audiences that they are passing on fake news on instructions from those they are afraid of, can (and should) destroy their careers. So, instead, we get absurd statements about "no intimidation" and maintaining "editorial integrity," about the "high professional standards" of Palestinian journalists, and concerns about smearing the reputation of journalists who risk their lives to cover the war.[39] And yet, for all these pious if not indignant protestations, the journalistic product continues to comply closely with the Caliphator narrative, and continues to disorient the West.

Charles Enderlin is a good example of the malaise in its advanced form. At some level he knows he's lying, that Talal duped him, that he let himself get duped; he's too much of a professional to miss the evidence. He knows why he cut the final scene: because it would have given away the fake, not because it represented "death throes" unbearable to the viewers. But he keeps that as far from his consciousness as he can. On the contrary, he's in full denial of his error and quick to anger at contradiction. And he manages this by being a fervent advocate for peace [at least what he thought would bring peace]. He was one of the big-time players in the Oslo Peace Process, his office at France2 was a major off-the-record site for "negotiations." He entitled his book about the outbreak of the Intifada and the collapse of the peace process, *Shattered Dreams*, without any sense of irony about the spectacular role he played in shattering them. Thanks to

---

39 See chapter 9.

al Durah, his office became a center for processing the Oslo Jihad as Israel's fault. Adamantine Y2KMind.

When questioned: "Why did you say 'targeted ... from the Israeli position" when you had no evidence for that?" Enderlin answered: "What would they say in Gaza if I didn't?" He no longer even hears how this remark reveals his submission to the will of jihadis, taking their orders on the most morally crucial aspect of the single most damaging fragment of fake news in the new century so far. Rather, Enderlin and most of his colleagues think, "the Palestinians are my friends ... they protect us from the violence of the jihadis, they just want to be free, and they need our help with the only weapons they have against the Israeli Goliath—information warfare, the weapons of the weak." So they repeat the lethal narratives as news.

This particular dynamic is widespread among journalists: an acute cognitive (and/or moral) dissonance resolved by denying fault or error, and loudly espousing a moral cause. Here the blood libel comes to the aid of the distressed: "We knew who was right and who was wrong," wrote Matti Friedman sarcastically about the school of lethal journalists who dominated the Israeli-Palestinian scene, "and it remained only to anathematize the bad guys so far into disrepute that even the act of trying to understand them would be a kind of sin."[40] A stark morality tale in which siding wholeheartedly with the underdogs provided the perfect fig-leaf to cover professional failure and submission to the demands of the enemies of a free press. "For Social Justice! Speak truth to power!" Righteous indignation becomes a form of preemptive retaliation. "How dare you question my sincerity!?"

This moral passion masked extensive dishonesty; reconsideration, doubt, and openness to correction threatened the self-image of the activist journalist. Even as cancel-culture consistently eliminated the Caliphator's enemies, it operated on acts of moral passion: outrage, peremptory dismissal, disgust, moral panic. Once the al Durah blood libel had identified the Israelis as the evil ones, it became increasingly easy to sacrifice accuracy for narrative. "It's the Palestinians' turn to tell their story. Maybe that'll work." As a result of this attitude and the dissonance it forces on honest and fair-minded people, the left rejected what were essentially sound liberal and progressive positions as "fascist," "xenophobic," "white supremacist," and embraced a cause that embodied everything the left insisted it was not. From Israelis as freedom fighters to perpetrators of a catastrophe as bad as the Nazis, from Palestinians as wannabe conquerors and slayers to innocent victims deprived of their human rights.

---

40 Friedman, "You're all Israel now."

This ideologically fierce performance metabolized the dissonance of unacknowledged cowardice involved in surreptitiously submitting to the Caliphators. Identifying this process helps us understand the misguided passions of our day, the religious fervor behind the partisanship, the vehemence with which people denounce what they have been told is hate speech against Muslims, but ignore the industry of Muslim hate speech and fake news, the consistency with which they support Da'wa Caliphators. Shield jihadis; ignore real Muslim moderates and real Muslim victims; and attack those under attack for defending themselves.[41] The passionate intensity of the worst. Rather than reflect avowed pacifist and progressive values, their political behavior fits the pattern of the authoritarian personality: deferential to those with power (to hurt), contemptuous of the deplorables below them. The cancel culture is not just about radicals eliminating everyone to their "right" (or, really, to their "left"). It is also about preemptive dhimmi leaders, bullying into silence everyone the Caliphators don't like.

This moral indignation forbids contradiction and convinces those who disagree to keep their heads down below the parapet. Hence, we witness the prominence among the woke of various forms of virtue signaling, the shared hierarchy of good victims (of color, trans, indigenes, Palestinians, Muslims) and bad victimizers (white supremacists, xenophobes, the privileged, Zionists, Islamophobes), the lingo, the purity tests, the stark, tribal division of the world into friend and foe.[42] The old-time liberals, devoted to a free society, find their positions have become "right-wing,"[43] and discover that they have much more to fear on an ongoing basis from their peers, from the dhimmi leaders—for example, the woke folks at the New York Times who chased both Bari Weiss and James Bennet away and then pulled off the front-page propaganda coup[44]—than from the jihadis. When Edward Schlosser writes: "I'm a liberal professor, and my liberal students terrify me," his students are Y2KMind "liberals" orchestrated by demopaths.[45] The more common and omnipresent fear in the early twenty-first century is not being beheaded in the street like Lee Rigby or Samuel Paty, but

---

41 "Ostrich Logic is always delivered via an air of haughty moral superiority." Saad, The Parasitic Mind, 124. I'd say, "urgent." Saad uses the term "fierce" in this context, 112. See above on Mark Seager, p. 341f.

42 Robert Lynch, "Kin, Tribes, and the Dark Side of Identity," Quillette, November 222, 2020.

43 Charles L. Glenn, "Social Justice Has Changed – I Haven't," Glenn Loury Substack, January 19, 2022.

44 John Levin and Keith Kelly, "New York Times staffers say leadership 'terrified of the young wokes,'" New York Post, July 18, 2020.

45 Edward Schlosser, "I'm a liberal professor, and my liberal students terrify me," Vox, June 3, 2015; cited by Saad, The Parasitic Mind, 214.

being shamed and shunned by infidel peers, armed with accusations like "racist" and "Islamophobe." Your head has to get pretty far over the ramparts to elicit a jihadi attack . . . but attacks from preemptive dhimmi are commonplace.

Prisoners of the Narrative

In 2016, echoing what many with Y2KMind felt, the political analyst Marty Cohen explained how he and so many other observers failed to predict Trump's victory: "Things that are very easy to debunk are gaining currency in politics. We've lost the gatekeeper."[46] What he meant was: "with the internet and social media, we can't keep the crazies out with our simple debunking of their folly." What he might have said was: "We have so seriously disoriented people with our 'narrative' that they have lost all anchor and will believe both true things (we've been leading them by the nose for some time now), and false (any crazy, genuinely racist, paranoid idea that comes down the social media pike)." But that would have taken an awareness still not anywhere on the horizon in 2016.

Take the author of the book cited above, Andrew Marantz.[47] He does a fascinating, well documented, and nuanced study of the way right-wing groups, especially alt-right, used the internet to "hijack" the American conversation. What he means by that conversation, however, is not what real liberals understand about the public sphere, that is, a venue in which free opinions thrash it out, and the better ones (eventually) win among a well-informed and thoughtful public. These conditions provide democracies with the best formula for choosing the right courses of action. For a liberal like that, the public sphere is necessarily full of back and forth, in which people say what they believed important—like the arguments made by the alt-right—and those that were accurate would be retained, and the inaccurate ones, rejected, without violence.

No, the conversation he sees hijacked by crazy conspiracy-minded, right-wing racists, is the finest expression of the very "narrative" the alt-right rallied to fight, and which he presents as self-evidently a good and true thing.

> The United States was founded on lofty theoretical principles and a reality of brutal conquest. The country went to war with itself over the question of whether all of its residents

---

46 Marantz, *Antisocial*, 128.

47 I choose Marantz not because he's the most flagrant example of the problem. On the contrary, he's a sophisticated thinker, and the logic I bring out is not so obvious.

deserved to be treated as people, and then, long after the war ended, continued to answer that question in the negative. As immigration has proliferated in recent decades, so has a tide of xenophobia. The ideal of a true multiethnic democracy—a society rooted in pluralism and dignity and meaningful, lasting equality—is a noble and necessary goal, one that this country has never come close to reaching. . . . The arc of history may bend in that direction, but the arc of history is not bent inexorably or automatically. It does not bend itself. We bend it.[48]

Never mind the lack of nuance (only *some* "continued to answer in the negative"; others, crucially, did not), or the dismissal of concern over an unprecedented increase of people from potentially dangerous cultures (misogynist, antisemitic, violent) as a "tide of xenophobia," or even the ironic fact that the notion of the arc of history bending towards justice is a profoundly Eurocentric notion. Consider the concluding assertion about the noble and necessary goal: "one that this country has never come close to reaching." This has more than a hint of the oikophobe. Any glance around the world will rapidly indicate that, other democratic states aside (*et encore*), there are many cultures with far more lethal relations between *us* and *them*, including between men and woman, and between various ethnicities and religions, than the USA. On the contrary.[49]

Inside that missing "some," are all those—many of them white Christian males [?!]—who did answer the question about equality in the affirmative.[50] Instead, the "narrative" not only dismisses its idealistic roots in Christian and Jewish demotic religiosity, but insists that since all cultures are equal, we treat ones as problematic as the still tribal cultures of the Arab world and still theocratic Islam, as "just like us" (certainly just as good). We should therefore welcome them in with open arms and despise those xenophobic enough to feel anxiety at their arrival. "How could true Americans be so deplorably afraid of strangers?" One might even posit that the now almost pro-forma accusations of xenophobia are a tell for oikophobia. And then ask: if the US hasn't come close

---

48 Marantz, *Antisocial*, 358.

49 Kathleen Brush, *Racism and Anti-racism in the World before and after 1945* (New Providence, NJ: Bowker, 2020).

50 See the travails of medievalist Rachel Fulton, who acknowledged the contribution of Christian men (whites) to feminism ("Three Cheers for White Men," *Fencing Bear at Prayer*, January 5, 2015); Grace Curtis, "This professor wrote 'Three Cheers for White Men.' She's been defamed as a violent 'alt-right' leader since," *College Fix*, September 265, 2018.

to its ideals, why are people from the world over so eager to come live there?[51] And finally, wonder: are such oikophobes likely to successfully "bend the arc of history" rather than, unwittingly, undo the very progress they claim to promote?

The Return of Shame-Honor Dynamics

And on the back of this perfectionist (millenarian) narrative, the West, a culture/ civilization that has formally rejected shame-honor on its way to democracy, has now reinstated those dynamics. At present, cancel culture operates on shaming: it has defined certain ideas and values as not only wrong but shameful (Hirsi Ali's unpardonable "western triumphalism"), so much so that it can publicly humiliate targets and get them shunned merely by making the accusation. No matter how little is actually appropriate, the target's face has been blackened. Welcome to the world of Zionism in the twenty-first century.

There is, however, one huge difference with primary shame-honor behavior. In "the good old days," real men beat up anyone who threatened their honor, thereby cowing anyone else who might have something to say. Today, progressives wield the power of shame to protect the honor of alpha males whom they identify as victims. At the same moment that progressives place Palestinian Identity, and beyond that Muslim identity, in the category of "privileged victims," in protecting them from even micro-aggressions (the very hint of criticism), they also macro-aggress against people who defend themselves from their "mostly peaceful" assailants. They thus turn the social dynamics of shame-honor on their head. The premodern honor-brigades of triumphalist Muslims police what any Muslim can say to infidels; while the postmodern honor brigades cancel infidels who offend Muslim honor. So instead of alpha-male bullies forcing the weak betas to submit to their will and respect them in a prime divider society, we have wannabe-alpha beta-males, gang-bullying the conflict-averse gamma males into silence, on behalf of premodern alpha males whose manly wings are (temporarily) clipped by a demotic polity. In the conflict between autonomous Jews and triumphalist Muslims, this inversion produces the unusual sight of alpha males trying to restore their honor by appealing as victims to progressive shame-brigades.

---

51 For a good example of someone who raises the question (with distaste for American exceptionalism) but doesn't answer it, Suzy Hansen, "Corruptions of Empire, *The Baffler*, December 2016.

And how did this come about? Through the silent submission of the progressive elite to the Caliphators, more concretely in their adoption of the Caliphator prime directive: "Do not offend us." What the submitters really fear are the very people they claim to want to protect from the terrible scourge of Islamophobia. (Dhimmitude protects, internalizes, the ego drives of the triumphalists; one of the most infectious of which is hating Jews.) And since they neither can admit their fears to themselves nor challenge them even quietly, they meet any criticism with anger. Outrage culture, the moral emergencies, the waxing furious over slights to "the marginalized and underrepresented, slights that barely register on scales of suffering around the world . . . all of these are fueled by the suppressed shame of submission.

14

The Woke Jihad: Contact Apocalyptic Highs

The Instability of Preemptive Dhimmitude and Y2KMind's Revolutionary Turn

There was a time in the late aughts, early teens, when I would argue that the situation would have to change, soon ... that over the coming years, at most five, more and more people would awaken to the situation and reconsider their commitment to blaming their own culture for jihadi hatreds. After all, the delusion upon which this reflex depends necessitates so much denial and self-damage that it could not last as formulated. At some point, even those perpetuating it (our thought leaders) would confront the dissonance of their disguised cowardice; and even if they did not, those they wanted to lead, would begin to recognize the unwitting hypocrisy.

There was, however, another way out of such an unstable state of cognitive dissonance, a way that many a journalist I met in the aughts took: namely, doubling down with a still more aggressive denial through heated advocacy for the just cause. And, as before with the Palestinians, and then "Islam," this doubling down included shutting up those who might effectively reveal those things that must be denied.

The Woke as Apocalyptic Revolutionaries

> In every cry of every Man,
> In every Infants cry of fear,
> In every voice: in every ban,
> The mind-forg'd manacles I hear
> —Blake, "London"

In the mid-teens, the term "woke" entered the vernacular. Of black origin and grammar, it refers to a heightened state of awareness to the suffering caused by social and racial injustice. On one level this awareness is part of the American and liberal ethos: "It is, in fact, not just the project at the heart of progressive politics but also one integral to liberalism as a political philosophy, which has always sought to protect even the least of us from tyranny."[1]

But three interrelated qualities distinguish the woke from both liberalism and tyranny: first, the woke are exquisitely sensitive to the pain of certain designated categories of those who suffer; second, they consider microaggressions forms of tyranny; third, they have no patience for the arc of history to take its millennia-long bend. They must bend it, not just soon … but now! The heightened sensitivity drives the urgency and in so doing, adopts two classically apocalyptic tropes: 1) *the world is full of unbearable evil*, and a catastrophe awaits if we do not act immediately to fight this evil; and 2) *if you do not agree with me, you must be part of the forces of evil*; there is no middle ground, no gray: "Silence is violence!" Heed my apocalyptic message or become my Antichrist.

The woke fight the cosmic violence of all those injustices of systemic racism and capitalist privilege of white supremacy, which not only inscribe their dominion on the bodies of Black and Brown people, but are destroying the planet with their greed. That's why the woke consider those countries to which the rest of the world wants to flee (from their genuinely oppressive and impoverished societies), the greatest oppressors. Perfectionism strikes where improvement is greatest. And any suggestion to the contrary, like the British *Report on Race and Ethnic Disparities*, enrages woke warriors.[2]

The key to this sudden and fierce awakening lay in a particularly combustible combination of empathy and outrage. The more one opened up to the pain of

---

1 James Lindsay, "Naming the Enemy: Critical Social Justice," *New Discourses*, February 28, 2020.
2 Commission on Race and Ethnic Disparities, *The Report*, March 2021; Jeremy Stubbs, "Racisme au Royaume-Uni: le rapport infernal : La fabrique de racistes," *Causeur*, April 9, 2021.

the other, the more one became outraged. It's almost as if woke was born of a psychedelic trip with an empathogen, one of total identification with the cosmic pain of the "other," down to the most exquisite microaggressions.[3] The more one heard and accepted the other's "truth"—and here that worthy "other" is defined as the voice of the marginalized and underrepresented victim—the more one found the current situation unbearable: a formula for both semiotic arousal (vaccination = the Holocaust) and the creation of apocalyptic time. Curated by information professionals, the woke came to see pervasive evil in the Western world. How can they not resist!

Of course, as with many moments when egalitarian movements turn authoritarian, demopaths exploit the good sentiments of the empaths. Lethal narratives designed to arouse outrage—some true, or with elements of truth, others maliciously false—claim the status of unimpeachable witness, and weaponize moral sentiments from outrage to hatred. Linda Sarsour, one of the more successful demopaths of our day, explains: "Woke for me is just being outraged all the time and being able to stay human and feel outraged about injustice that is happening around me."[4] For this champion of humanity and justice, fed on a constant diet of lethal narratives from her fellow Palestinians, *woke* has become a license to indulge in dualism on a grand scale, starting with the proposition that all Palestinian suffering, including that of Palestinian women, is caused by Israelis.

And, true to apocalyptic hopes, the injustice of the world, the human suffering that the woke see all around is unbearable, and will soon be—must be!—eliminated. The woke demand an overriding and instant "justice," one that eliminates the need to judge each case on its merits, one that bends the arc of history and puts an end to the dialectic. It judges by (mobilized) group identity: identity politics are millennial simplifications, the fault lines along which perfection shall be etched into the body politic.[5] The purpose of cogwar is to turn your own side (identity-defined) into warriors and paralyze your enemy (white fragility, Livingstone Formulation). Anyone trying to tone down the hysteria is accused of "draining moral urgency and providing comfort to the status quo,"[6] and anyone who opposes the rising tide of protest, in the language

---

3   E.g. Rebecca Stevens, "5 Of The Most Hurtful Racial Microaggressions I Have Heard In My Life," *Medium*, March 25, 2021.

4   Lauretta Brown, "Essence Magazine Names Sharia Law Defender as One of Their '100 Woke Women,'" *Townhall*, April 18, 2017.

5   Victor Davis Hanson, "Can the Great 'Awokening' Succeed?" *American Greatness*, April 11, 2021.

6   David Brooks, discussing the angry reaction to his pointing out that there were four times as many school shooting casualties in the 1990s than now: "The Problem with Wokeness," *New York Times*, June 7, 2018.

of the Southern Poverty Law Center, is guilty of "Rage against Change," i.e., "right-wing" opposition to the woke agenda.[7]

When Blake walked the streets of London and marked the woes on people's faces, he was woke. When he supported the Revolution in America and then again in France, he embraced the demotic millennial movement of modernity. But when the French Revolution turned on itself in terror, he pulled back his support, and went into one of his most creative periods, in particular the composition of what some consider his greatest (short) work, *The Marriage of Heaven and Hell*.[8] The dialectic of revolution did not seduce him into its self-devouring spiral but rather to the prolific heights and depths of visionary poetry.

What distinguishes the current apocalyptic dynamics from earlier ones, however, is the degree to which those holding power are receptive—vulnerable—to the accusations of the revolutionaries. In earlier periods, those with their hands on the levers of power parted less readily with their positions of, or their moral claims to, power. When Quaker James Nayler in 1651 claimed messianic status by entering Bristol on a white donkey led by two (married) women, the city's magistrates pierced his tongue with an iron bar. And that was mild compared with the more violent methods normally reserved for messianic prophets (crucifixion, dismemberment, starvation in publicly displayed cages).

Modern and postmodern sensibilities are far more likely to glorify the millenarians, make them tenured radicals. And when they are attacked for their failure to fulfill the millennial promise of perfection—the "noble and necessary goal"—to confess their failures—"one that this country has never come close to reaching"—they crumble. In a paradoxical twist, the less guilty are the more ready to admit guilt. As a result, anti-Western cognitive warfare has had exceptional success disarming the progressive power holders of the early twenty-first century, a success first accomplished in academia.[9] Y2K Mind is an open vessel for revolutionary discourse, and Caliphators make use of this seemingly hard-wired port to colonize our discourse. "With your democracy we will colonize you; with our sacred texts we will rule."

---

7   SPLC, "Rage against Change," Spring, 2019.

8   Peter Ackroyd, *Blake: A Biography* (New York: Ballantine, 1995), 156–66; on *Marriage*, see subsequent chapter. See also Eva Antal, "The Apocalyptic Tone of Irony in William Blake's *The Marriage of Heaven and Hell*," *Caesura*, 1.1 (2014): 71–84; Hüseyin Alhas, "The Impact of the French Revolution on William Blake's Poetry and Painting: The Changing Phases Of Evil," MA Thesis, Hacettepe University Graduate School of Social Sciences (Ankara, 2017), 17–35.

9   One interpretation of the fifth-century fall of the Western Roman empire may indicate a similar dynamic, see Landes, *While God Tarried*, vol I, chapter 12.

At the same time, unlike earlier cases in history, where the accusations of oppression and cruelty were more than justified by the cruel oppression of the elites, the current round of criticism makes a mountain out of a comparative molehill. Both sides indulge in the rhetorical overkill and Holocaust corruption: PETA denounces chicken consumption as a Holocaust; Antivaxxers consider vaccine cards yellow stars.

In very few societies in world history, has claiming victimhood brought advantages rather than contempt. But in postmodern societies, victimhood confers such advantages that it has become an Olympic sport.[10] And the resulting distortions are legion. What Arab women suffer is nothing like the complaints lodged against Harvey Weinstein; there is nothing like shame-murders going on at Brandeis; poverty in the West is not at all like poverty in the Third World.

One of the major contributions to both the study of revolutions and millennial movements has been the notion of "relative deprivation." Neither the American colonies, nor France in the late eighteenth century were poor nations grievously oppressed; the spark that set off the explosion of protests was suffering and oppression experienced by the population, *relative* to their expectations and hopes (aroused both by the enlightenment and economic growth), not on an absolute scale.[11] Today's apocalyptic revolutionaries represent the most extreme case of *hope-induced deprivation* so far recorded in history, as embodied in the paradox that vast numbers of people around the world want to emigrate to societies whose own elites have come to consider them the embodiment of apocalyptic evil.[12]

This weaponization and devaluation of language in order to provoke alarm and hostility—accusations of "racism," "Apartheid," "xenophobia," "genocide"—has taken wing on the success of lethal narratives that deliberately provoke violent emotions, sparking outrage and moral panics. Israel was the first strong, global manifestation of this narrative-induced moral hysteria, the first massive moral disorientation of this century. Since then, the lack of contact with reality upon which it is built has only widened its scope.

---

10 Isaac Young and Daniel Sullivan, "Competitive victimhood: a review of the theoretical and empirical literature," *Current Opinion in Psychology*, 11 (October 2016): 30–34; Bawer, *Victim's Revolution*; Rothman, "Victimocracy," *Unjust: Social Justice and the Unmaking of America* (Washington, DC: Regnery, 2019), 131–53.

11 Alexis de Toqueville, *L'ancien régime et la révolution française* (1856); Ted Gurr, *Why Men Rebel* (Princeton: Princeton University Press, 1970).

12 For a good analysis of the way in which BLM mobilizes outrage, see Naya Lekht, "The Unleashing of the Red Roar: Awakening Racial Consciousness to Stir a Revolution," *DocEmet*, January 30, 2022.

Fake news—understood as *misinformation carried by the mainstream, professional news media*, not by disinformation bots—metastasized domestically in democracies everywhere. In the US, professional journalists became increasingly partisan with each election cycle and each demonstration for social justice. And, in accord with Moynihan's law, the outrage about the violation of people's dignity and human rights struck the societies that had tried the hardest to address the problem: Israel, US, Western democracies. The "Woke" feel every fiber of pain suffered by the privileged victim, and, with the help of woke journalism, ignore every evidence to the contrary: from the malevolence of some of the honored victims, to the suffering of the targets of their explosive ill-will.[13]

All of these polarizing dynamics have been intensified over the previous decade by social media, which, despite starting out as the embodiment of postmodern semiotic anarchy, has over the last decade steadily drifted in the direction of a modern insistence on eliminating voices deemed unacceptable in the name of "science," "facts," "principles," and "truth." The immense power of social media mobs to shame and destroy careers, and the readiness of "progressive" anger to mobilize in response to propaganda, gave *woke* a decisive advantage in wielding the cancel weapons against their foes.[14] The widespread presence of Y2KMind among the most creative cybernauts made social media fertile ground for this woke message.

In the year 2020, in response to both Covid emergency conditions and the killing of George Floyd, the woke entered a more active phase: their discourse entered the public sphere and met with thunderous approval.[15] It went from the margins of dissent to the center of public discourse. The resulting angry demonstrations and, on more than one occasion, riots spread all over the country and around the world. Black Lives Matter became a major meme even among corporations; what had previously been shunned (kneeling at the National Anthem) became required; partisans of social justice felt empowered to harass and even attack those they felt did not properly acknowledge their truth. Even as some (owls) viewed Critical Race Theory as nothing more than

13 Amber Athey, "When does the media cover a horrific crime?" *Spectator*, March 29, 2021. Coverage of events in Waukesha illustrate this seemingly hard-wired tendency (see 319n78).

14 People differ (largely by political tribe) about whether cancel culture is primarily a right- or left-wing phenomenon. The significance for my discussion is the preponderance of cancel culture in academia—the last place it should appear—where it is overwhelmingly "left-wing" in origin and aimed at silencing "right-wing" dissent.

15 Paul Berman compares the reaction to Floyd to a massive paradigm shift about race comparable to events in 1854 and 1965: "The George Floyd Uprising," *Liberties* 2 (2021).

brainwashing imposed by "struggle-session" coercion,[16] sincere young people (roosters) wanted to dedicate their lives to teaching it to youth.

The split between what the two parts of America saw inside their media bubbles in the summer of 2020, grew greater. While Red America saw Antifa and BLM rioting scarcely opposed by intimidated and demoralized police, Blue America saw brutal police forces confronted by brave and "mostly peaceful" demonstrators chanting "Why are you in riot gear? / I don't see no riot here!" and protesting an unimpeachable cause—"Black Lives Matter." Each side tried to influence the outcome of elections in increasingly problematic ways, each embraced the conviction that *everything* was at stake and the very fate of democracy was on the line. By the time the elections came around, whoever won, the other side would be convinced it had been cheated. January 6, 2021, flipped and intensified the mutual loathing: now the right, prompted by fake news, was rioting in the Capitol. The right saw a demonstration that got out of hand; the left saw an insurrection, a new advance of domestic terrorism.[17]

Among the woke and those drawn into their wake, certain things were now true beyond question: things could—indeed, must—be affirmed true, while others are reliably identified as wrong, lying, conspiratorial, and hence, to be canceled. (The same is true of the "right," the QAnoners, but again, they are not dominant in academia, publishing, or mainstream journalism.) Ironically, the Woke have turned postmodernism's modesty about "objective truth" and its alleged "facts" into a narrative-driven, new truth and new facts, often wildly at variance with empirical reality. It is indubitably "true" to the woke that Israel and America are imperialists, colonialists, racist, and cruel oppressors. It must not be said that the Palestinian leadership, which never tires of comparing Israel to the Nazis, emulates the worst genocidal hatreds of the Nazis.[18] It is indubitably true that America (and Britain and any democracy) are systemically racist; it must not be said that they are not, or that other countries and cultures are far, far worse.

Ayaan Hirsi Ali wrote about what Woke and Islamists (Caliphators) have in common. "The adherents of each constantly pursue ideological purity, certain

---

16 Pankaj Mishra, "A New History of the Cultural Revolution, Reviewed," *New Yorker*, February 1, 2021.

17 See Josh Campbell's attribution of terrorism to the events of that day: 93n143.

18 Recent, random example among many: Y. Kerman, "Salafi-Jihadi Ideologue Abu Qatadah Al-Filastini: Hitler's Views On Jews Were Accurate, Holocaust Was Justified," *MEMRI*, March 25, 2021; on the projection, see e.g., Donna Rachel Edmunds, "Palestinian Authority regularly compares Israel and Israeli leaders to Nazism and Nazi leaders," *Palestinian Media Watch*, Apr 8, 2021.

of their own rectitude. Neither Islamists nor the Woke will engage in debate; both prefer indoctrination of the submissive and damnation of those who resist."[19] In this sense, the woke mirror the Caliphators: they have submitted, and demand it from others.[20] Stephen Knight described it as "not about wanting to help others understand, it's about enjoying the feeling of righteous superiority."[21] To which one might add, a mighty weapon in imposing purity of mind. In other words, even as Caliphators want to inflict the punishment that Allah, in his mysterious ways, refuses now these 1450 years later to visit on the scoffers and unbelievers—His promised *Yawm hadin* (Last Judgment)—the woke increasingly embrace radical zero-sum forms of the modern millennial dream: destroy the bad, level everything, equality of results, and the world will be a much better place—destroy the world to save it.[22] It is not by accident, that both groups—at least their leaderships—hate the people most likely to resist such monolithic mentalities—the Jews ... especially autonomous Jews. *"Can we be wrong and the Jews right? Unthinkable! (And we have as-a-Jews to prove it.)"*

This unmooring from what Freud called the "reality principle" has been vastly accelerated by the power of social media bubble-worlds to reify a substitute virtual or meta-reality.[23] This in turn amplifies the dynamics of cancel-culture to ward off what might puncture thin skins. They all work together to demand assent to absurd inversions of reality. Not surprisingly, the woke engage in an ever-expanding definition of what is false and what is dangerous,[24] speech that can therefore be legitimately banned from the social media networks and legacy media as harmful. In the partisan heat, "my" bullies are justice-warriors who

---

19 Ayaan Hirsi Ali, "What Islamists and 'Wokeists' Have in Common," *Wall Street Journal*, September 10, 2020.

20 For an interesting meditation on the impact of woke cancel culture on producing submissive citizens, see R.R. Reno, "Why I Stopped Hiring Ivy League Graduates," *Wall Street Journal*, June 7, 2021.

21 Knight "American Atheists, American Humanists and the Secular Coalition Join the Woke Church," *The Godless Spellchecker*, April 20, 2021.

22 Curt Jaimungal, *Better Left Unsaid* (2021).

23 The most recent example of the Cult of the Occupation, replete with as-a-Jews and as-an-Israelis to support it: Amnesty International's denunciation of Israeli apartheid: *Crime of Apartheid: The Government of Israel's System of Oppression against Palestinians*, January 2022. For an illustration of the low "intellectual level of the people who have appropriated the term 'human rights,' as expressed in their own words," (Matti Friedman tweet, https://twitter.com/mattifriedman/status/1489145121908178945?s=21), see Lazar Berman, "Amnesty to ToI: No double standard in accusing Israel, but not China, of apartheid," *Times of Israel*, February 2, 2022; Shany Mor, "On Amnesty's car-crash interview in Israel," *Fathom*, February 2022.

24 Cindy Harper, "MSNBC Analyst says Biden falling meme could incite violence," *Reclaim the Net*, March 22, 2021; Christina Maas, "Instagram deletes post of President Biden falling up the stairs under its "violence and incitement" policy," *Reclaim the Net*, March 20, 2021.

follow the science and "yours" are repugnant deplorables who believe conspiracy theories.[25] In current conditions, with the power of the web to maintain and even intensify such weaponized bubbles, it looks like the totalitarian stream (paranoia, projection, dualism) will intensify among all the groups currently operating in apocalyptic time (Woke, Caliphators, QAnons), increasing the likelihood of contact highs and apocalyptic violence.[26]

Consider two of the "laws" of apocalyptic dynamics:

- *One person's messiah is another's Antichrist/Dajjal/Nazi* and
- *Wrong about the future does not mean inconsequential.*

It is the task of sound minds to ratchet these dynamics down. We have seen too many times the kind of damage these apocalyptic raptures can cause. If there were a time to face history honestly, and ask: "At what point do we draw back from this slippery, treacherous slope?"—now would be a good time.

But few visible signs so far suggest that the current wave of true believers entering apocalyptic time can avoid the death spiral that has, so many times in the last two centuries, brought on totalitarianism and mega-destruction. Fed in part by leftist revolutionary discourse, in part with Nazi ideology via Caliphators (anti-Zionism), in part with the best intentions of the most open folks on the planet, the woke brand of millennial stew is entering whitewater, which its own internal dynamics will further intensify and whose lethal currents it will prove helpless to resist. Their reaction to growing rejection of their projects (defunding police, Critical Race theory in the schools, open borders, Cult of the Occupation), even as it gives some pause, will produce doubling-down among the hard-core faithful.[27] Whether that will marginalize them or not is up to the sanity of the public and the leadership of those who can change their mind.[28]

Entomologists have identified a group of fungal and viral parasites that take over the brains of ants and force them to behave in ways that are at once self-destructive of the host, and highly beneficial to the reproduction of the parasite.[29] In one viral case, cited by Daniel Dennett as an analogy for religion, it

---

25 Jennifer Ruth, "When Academic Bullies Claim the Mantle of Free Speech," *Chronicle of Higher Education*, March 18, 2021.

26 Nina Schick, *Deepfakes: The Coming Infocalypse* (New York: Hachette Group, 2020).

27 Steve Phillips, "Lessons From Virginia: You Can't Ignore the Civil War, *Nation*, November 3, 2021.

28 Bari Weiss, "How we Changed Our Minds in 2021," *Substack*, December 28, 2021.

29 Ed Yong, "How the Zombie Fungus Takes Over Ants' Bodies to Control Their Minds," *Atlantic*, November 14, 2017; see also Dicrocoelium dendriticum.

forces the ant up the blade of grass so a cow will eat it, and the virus reaches the stomach where it thrives.[30] I think the better analogy here to religious beliefs, is to certain apocalyptic, sacred memes (religious or secular), which literally "mount" believers and "ride them," driving them to deeds with no concern for the physical well-being of the zealots or their loved ones.[31] In other words, some apocalyptic memes and certain physical parasites can colonize the minds of their hosts and dispose of the colonized after they have served their purpose.

In this case, the progressive left seems to have ingested a key meme from jihadis who are themselves ridden by this sacred suicide: *"the USA and Israel are the two Satans, apocalyptic enemies who must be destroyed for collective salvation to arrive."* Remember, when you hear Palestinian militants or "Human Rights" NGOs say "Israel is the new Nazi," or a new Apartheid and a crime against humanity, they're using secular Western terminology for pure evil—the *Dajjal*, the Antichrist. Western progressives, who revel in such inversions, seem unaware of the larger Caliphator narrative of collective redemption, the one that ends in Islamic world conquest and the annihilation of every value progressives allegedly hold sacred: empathy for the other, ecumenical diversity and toleration, positive-sum, non-coercive relations, equality and dignity for all, women's self-sovereignty, freedom from religious coercion, elimination of power-abuse. [32]

And yet, progressives and liberals, even otherwise skeptical ones, and so many journalists and scholars, not to mention properly educated youth, seem powerless to resist this meme as long as it expresses itself in the language of human rights.[33] They are mesmerized by the imbalance of deaths in exchanges between a suicidal Hamas sacrificing its people and Israel defending itself from a mad jihadi assault.[34] The honor brigades, often manned by Arab and

---

30 Daniel Dennett, *Breaking the Spell: Religion as a Natural Phenomenon* (New York: Viking, 2006).

31 Henri Desroche, *Dieux d'hommes: Dictionnaire des méssianismes et millénarismes de l'ère chrétienne* (Paris: Mouton, 1969), 6. On secular millennialism (till now the most destructive form), Landes, *Heaven on Earth*, chaps. 9–13; Anna Geifman, *Death Orders*.

32 Cook, *Contemporary Muslim Apocalyptic*; Furnish, *Holiest Wars*; Murawiec, *Mind of Jihad*; Filiu, *Apocalypse in Islam*.

33 For good examples of the demopathic "human rights" argument, see Ali Abunima, "Blinken sheds crocodile tears for Gaza," *Electronic Intifada*, May 26, 2021; Hill and Plitnick, *Except for Palestine*. For an example of an analysis unaware of the demopathic strategies: Jennifer Hitchcock, "A Rhetorical Frame Analysis of Palestinian-Led Boycott, Divestment, Sanctions (BDS) Movement Discourse," (2020). Doctor of Philosophy (PhD), Dissertation, English, Old Dominion University.

34 In his podcast with Sam Harris, Jesse Singal expresses just this inability to get past the casualty/power differential. When Harris presses, he admits lack of knowledge: "Broken Conversations," *Sam Harris Podcast #25*, May 22 (1:16–1:20).

Middle East journalists who follow a partisan code, pursue anyone who break ranks with the narrative, like the head of UNWRA who admitted the Israelis were remarkably accurate in the 2021 bombing of Gaza, or CNN's chief editor whose memo called for identifying the source of the casualty statistics as the "Hamas-run Ministry of Health."[35] They police the social media players the way the fungus exercises direct control over the ants' muscles. Like the afflicted ants they resemble, these occupied "progressive" minds clamp down with their mandibles on the subject of wicked Israel, unaware that they await their own devouring. Having repeated jihadi propaganda … refrained from discussing jihadi behavior and beliefs … hated the enemies that jihadis hate … the people who are products of this discourse find themselves utterly disarmed.

Using a perfect pitch of quiet moral urgency, Gonzo journalist Avi Horowitz got students at Portland to listen approvingly and donate money to Hamas so that they can "ethnically cleanse" and "exterminate" the Jews: "I'll give you $27, my Bernie money."[36] No matter how obvious the danger, such well-meaning "progressives" will not stop because they cannot even imagine that they might need to stop. And so, inexorably, we are all drawn to our own destruction: Western and global institutions built by civil society, based on demotic principles of equality, dignity, and fairness—courts, international assemblies, academia, journalism, our public sphere, our imperfect but unparalleled dedication to meritocracy—all corrupted, all, increasingly dysfunctional and vulnerable to further colonization by a malevolent envy we can, seemingly, neither recognize nor resist.

Not surprisingly, our leaders adopt policies produced by the cognitive disorientation that cannot acknowledge reality; repeat them compulsively in an endless loop, ever farther from the peaceful goal. In the case of Israel, accuse her repeatedly of "imperiling" if not "killing the Oslo Process," call repeatedly for a resumption of the "peace" negotiations. The hatreds "progressives" so abhor take wing from within their own ranks: Jew-hatred flourishes in their midst, even as they gnaw anxiously on the Islamophobic bone.[37] Bullying online and in real life invades the public sphere, while forces of order are paralyzed. The

---

35 Asra Nomani, "The Honor Brigades"; AMEJA guidelines. On the UNRWA director, "Gazans outraged after UNRWA director says IDF strikes were precise," *Jerusalem Post,* May 26, 2021. On CNN's internal memo of May 17: "CNN started referring to Hamas-Run Gaza Ministry of Health," *Elder of Ziyon,* May 21, 2021.

36 Ami Horowitz, "Watch me raise money for Hamas to kill Jews from Students of Portland," May 25, 2021.

37 According to FBI statistics, "a Jewish person is approximately twice as likely to suffer a hate crime than a black person or a Muslim, 10 times more likely than an Asian or a Latino and 20 times more likely than a non-Hispanic white," George Flesh, "Anti-Semitism: The numbers

national conversation becomes a clash of hatreds. People infected with the anti-Zionist meme, and the Holocaust inversion that feeds it, rise higher on their imaginary blade of glass by inflating their moral indignation: the worst are filled with passionate intensity.

In the case of one fungus, *Ophiocordyceps unilateralis*, it "eventually grows into a bulbous capsule full of spores that rain down on the ants below, zombifying them in turn."[38] In our case, what first invaded the Western press corps here between the River and the Sea in 2000, has now, over the past twenty years, created a bulbous capsule of anti-Zionist spores that, in the early 2020s, rains down all over the West, poisoning the paths of information with malevolent fake news, designed to exploit our compassion in order to spread hatred. And this suicidal, genocidal spore is carried by agents who claim to oppose hatred and love peace.

The difference between us and the ants, is that we have a choice, and our fungus is "just" a meme. We don't have to sacrifice ourselves to our stupidity. Thank you, Mark Ruffalo, for unlocking your moral mandibles. It's clearly not easy.[39]

---

don't lie," *JNS*, January 21, 2022 "Extremists Respond to Colleyville Hostage Crisis with Antisemitism, Islamophobia," *ADL*, January 16, 2022.

38 Yong, "How the Zombie Fungus Takes over Ants' Bodies to Control their Minds."

39 Ruffalo tweet, https://twitter.com/MarkRuffalo/status/13970237317221113032?ref_src; Prof. Anthony Zenkus, response tweet, https://twitter.com/anthonyzenkus/status/139716 1250170212353?s=24.

15

To Sound Minds: On Our Watch?

Beloved Sire, please
excuse my stupidity.
You are butt naked.

Turning and turning in the widening gyre
The falcon cannot hear the falconer;
Things fall apart; the centre cannot hold;
Mere anarchy is loosed upon the world,
The blood-dimmed tide is loosed, and everywhere
The ceremony of innocence is drowned;
The best lack all conviction, while the worst
Are full of passionate intensity.
—Yeats, "The Second Coming"

In the early twelfth century in Western Europe, a time when historians began to look back at the apocalyptic wave that hit their culture at the turn of the millennium, a century earlier, one historian wrote about what happened in Limoges, the residence of monk-historian and liturgist, Ademar of Chabannes.

> In the year 1009, the land of Jerusalem was invaded, with God's permission, by unclean Turks, and Jerusalem seized and the glorious Sepulcher of the Lord Christ was taken over by them. This was done in the reign of the Greek kings Basil and Constantine, of the Roman emperor Henry, and in the eleventh year of Robert the king of France. And in that year, many Jews converted to Christianity for fear of their lives. In the year 1010, in many places throughout the World, a rumor spread that frightened and saddened many hearts, that the End of the World

approached. But those sounder of mind (*saniores animi*) turned themselves to correcting their own lives.[1]

Here we have a classic retrospective narrative in which the *saniores animi* set the right tone. In fact, their demotic response—self-criticism and self-correction—did, over the very long run, contribute throughout the eleventh century to both reforming the Church and creating voluntary, productive communities, religious and secular. But it should not diminish for us the significance of the apocalyptic moment when their reflective voice had no impact on the prevailing mood. For when the apocalyptic wave did hit in 1009, "many hearts" believed the Jews had sent secret messages to the Muslim Antichrist to destroy the Temple [the Holy Sepulchre]. These apocalyptic fake-news "truths" led to an exterminationist assault that had Jews slitting their own throats rather than convert—and this occurred almost a full century before the famous crusading episodes in the Rhineland in the summer of 1096.[2] Unchecked, paranoid apocalypses are extraordinarily destructive, and once they occur, like episodes of high fever, they can return more easily. Historically speaking, those who self-criticize are the sadder but wiser survivors of the madness.

Saniores animi describes those who can resist the apocalyptic siren song, the dream of collective redemption *now*, the loud chorus of roosters crowing, calling to crowds and passions, and delusions of grandeur—*we* are the chosen generation, *we* will see, nay *usher in* the day of redemption for all, we will take vengeance for an inexcusably passive God.[3] According to my analysis, we are in a potentially disastrous apocalyptic moment, when the best of principles we have generated are being weaponized by our worst enemies in order to strike at the system that gave birth to those admirable principles. I address this book, then, to the sound of mind, to those who love humans in all their crooked timber, liberal, progressive, radical, secular, religious, spiritual, conservative . . . those that can recognize when an overreaching best becomes the enemy of the good, when revolutions begin to devour themselves, and when it's time to turn aside from the path of apocalyptic indulgence.

Have there been moments when a rising tide of paranoid violence threatened, and the voices of sober owls prevailed over enraged roosters? To some extent, the more successful such ventures, the less visible. Certainly, when the anti-apocalyptic

---

1   Bibliothèque Nationale manuscrit latin, 4893, fol. 50; Bouquet, *Recueil des historiens de la France*, X:262.
2   See Landes, *Relics Apocalypse and the Deceits of History*, 41–45.
3   Hoffer, *True Believers*; Douglas Murray, *The Madness of Crowds: Gender, Race and Identity* (London, Bloomsbury, 2019).

and anti-Jewish Bernard of Clairvaux, one of the most powerful voices of Europe, stilled the genocidal crusading rage against Jews at the outset of the Second Crusade (1144), he did just that.[4] Under current conditions, at the present stage of the apocalyptic curve on which the green-red alliance rises, success in turning down the flames would rank high in the history of mankind's struggle with its fatal attraction to active cataclysmic redemption. But to do so, one might have to renounce a narrative in which it is the fault of the Jews. And apparently, that's hard. Very hard.

There are signs the woke revolutionaries have overstepped their bounds, and that sanity threatens to break out.[5] But just because many people (mostly deplorables and soon to be categorized deplorables) recoil from the excesses of Y2KMind's millenarian fringe, doesn't make the way out of the cognitive disorientation from which we suffer so severely, a foregone conclusion. And one must never underestimate the ruthlessness with which millennial fantasies of world transformation, especially when believers possess key forms of power, will cling to apocalyptic time. Such players prefer carving social perfection with coercive purity to acknowledging error.[6]

The following remarks address the fundamental issues that we all need to consider (problematize) in order to be able to undertake the task.

Tackle Fear

No one wants to think of themselves as intimidated. Very few will admit they are. And the issue goes well beyond the blow to our vanity to admit such matters to ourselves. If you admit to intimidation, then, presumably, you should do something about it. If journalists working in the Palestinian territories admitted they ran articles that systematically misinformed their readers because they feared the retaliation of terrorists, then they might have to do something, starting with identifying the terrorists who, if they will randomly target civilians, will readily target journalists who betray their cause. If we admit that Islamophobia is a term designed by triumphalist Muslims in order to block criticism of Islam

---

4 David Berger, "The Attitude of St. Bernard of Clairvaux toward the Jews," *Proceedings of the American Academy for Jewish Research*, 40 (1972): 89–108.

5 Joel Kotkin, "Is this the end of progressive America?" *UnHerd*, January 24, 2022; response: William Jacobson, "Mass Formation Psychosis. The Madness of Crowds. And The End Of Progressive America," *Legal Insurrection*, January 8, 2022.

6 Waller Newell, "The Eagles Will Drop Dead from the Skies: Millenarian Tyranny from Robespierre to Al Qaeda," *Tyrants: Power, Injustice, Terror* (New York: Cambridge University Press, 2019), 146–223.

and Muslims, then we have to start thinking and talking about problems in Islam and among Muslims, problems with very real impact on the lives of infidels throughout the global community. We then find ourselves facing the question: why do so many people "enforce" that term?

Thus, pushing back against preemptive dhimmitude is not without cost. That act of even gentle defiance rapidly reveals the patterns of the filings lining upon an opaque surface.[7] It also means realizing how many friends and colleagues are practitioners of the procrastinating art of appeasement.

On some level this begins with (re)discovering our courage, our integrity. It begins with the exchange of the combination *public honor* (virtue signaling) *and private guilt* (hypocrisy, narcissism, cowardice, bearing false witness), for the inverse: *public shame* (getting canceled, stigmatized) *and private integrity* (honesty). Only that process can free one from the gravitational pull of social fear ... in the 21st century, of preemptive dhimmitude. But that means endangering a great deal of success, comfort, influence, honor ... it even means courting physical harm.

But how much better to court that while such violence is still, at least in the democratic sphere, weak? Why wait until the collapse of American hegemony brings on pre-modern conditions? As Phyllis Chesler puts it: "How Many Western Feminists Would March Under a Hail of Taliban Bullets?" Or, as a Muslim woman who had just recently come to the US and joined the anti-Trump protest noted: "This was my first protest in my new country. The most amazing part of it was what didn't happen. No one beat us up. No one arrested us. No one opened fire."[8]

Courage is the last—and therefore also the first—freedom. No one can take away from us the ability to say "no," to resist, to speak truth to power. The problem is, rather than standing up to a power that expects and accepts your criticisms (Western elites), we need to stand up to those who will punish us for our presumption (Triumphalist elites). It means not assaulting white males who cringe in apology for their unbearably, systemically, racist behavior; but rather confronting far more primitive (gasp!) currents who threaten violent retaliation if you try to curb their patriarchal privileges.

It means entering a world we thought, we hoped, we had left behind, one where there are real, lethal enemies, where losing zero-sum interactions has serious consequences, where our neighbors are not necessarily "just like us," and

---

7 For an excellent example, see Ben Affleck's rebuke of Sam Harris and Bill Maher's "Islamophobia," Landes, "Prelude to a fisking: Biblio of Responses to Maher-Affleck dustup," *Augean Stables*, March 29, 2018.

8 Masi Alinejad, "Why I'm opposed to Ilhan Omar's bill against Islamophobia," *Washington Post*, January 21, 2022.

we need to probe rather than offer default approval, where in religious matters, death is on the line. It means finding out just how hard it is to *show* courage, and how few people do it.

It starts with a little clarity boldly affirmed. "LGBTQs for Palestine" is a grotesque oxymoron that breathes the cowardly lie: siding with the very patriarchs who crush LGBTQs. "Israeli apartheid" is an inversion that supports Arab-Muslim apartheid the world over. "From the River to the Sea Palestine will be free" is the Orwellian slogan of religious imperialists whose conquest of that land will destroy any remnant of freedom. As clear and simple as such remarks might be to those not in the orbit of preemptive dhimmitude, they either escape the notice or solicit the indignation of those not so fortunate. The tighter the orbit, the more the indignation.[9]

On the key passage from awareness to deeds, I have little advice to contribute. I have either failed or, worse, insulted my audiences and have effectively been marginalized. But clearly, a substantial cognitive stage of awareness and analysis should precede any actions, partly because that understanding is key to behaving substantively when the time to speak and act has come, on the one hand, and to a strategic appreciation of which battles to fight, to identifying when the time has come to speak up, on the other.

Above all, chronicle the experiences of those who have felt the tip of the lash, that violence that lies just below the intimidating behavior, ready to out at the hint of resistance.[10] Know their experiences; speak out for them even if only to set the record straight. That could be you. The triumphalist Muslim assault on Jews that went global in 2000, is literally the front line in the battle for free speech globally. "The fight to defend the truth of the Jewish people is the fight for the possibility of truth itself. And the fight for truth is, in the end, always the defense of reality against those who would attempt to deny and overpower it."[11] Once the Jews are silenced, one only needs clean-up crews for the rest of the infidels.

---

9 For a good example of an analysis devoid of awareness of "liberal illiberalism," see Yehuda Bauer, "Liberals, Illiberals, and Waverers: The Struggle of Our Times," *Israel Journal of Foreign Affairs*, 15 (2021), 245–55.

10 The sites that do keep track of violence from jihadis inspired by their sacred texts are considered "Islamophobic" almost by definition: Jihad Watch (www.jihadwatch.com), Dhimmi Watch (https://dhimmi.watch/). Here I note the experience of Dexter Van Zile, not because of how serious the assault (others have suffered far more grievously), but because of how banal, and how authorities looked the other way. "Seven Minutes of Hate Courtesy of SJP and UMass Boston," *Times of Israel*, June 30, 2021; idem, "The Pinch Point is Upon Us," *Medium*, February 4, 2022.

11 Michael Caplan, "The Big Lie Comes to Colleyville: Fairy Tale vs. Storied Truth," *White Rose*, 2022.

Tackle Envy

At no point before 2000, could any book, any history, any argument, have convinced me that envy is the most powerful force in the world. Sure, envy does exist, and destructive envy can be terrible. But it's like lice: it's everywhere. Murderous envy? Rare. How many Iago's are there?

And yet, not long after 2000, when I first realized how great the moral *Schadenfreude* that lay behind the alliance between progressives and Caliphators, with their twin Antichrist of Israel and the US, it became difficult not to see Europe—the "progressive" West—literally *committing suicide from envy*. Moral Sweden, Moral Europe, Dashing France, siding with their mortal enemies just (?) for the pleasure of dumping on Israel and the US? Believe that Bush did 9–11 and not Bin Laden? Even as Caliphators recruit throughout Europe, using Western coverage of Israelis massacring Muslims? Maybe initially. But who would be stupid enough to take that bit in their mouths and keep running with it?

Now two decades later, the American elites have caught up with the Europeans in their oikophobia, their hatred of those who birthed them, their tyranny of penitence. Even now, with the help of the deconstructive theory they appropriated from the French, Americans have taken the lead in self-loathing.[12] Perhaps slavery has made Americans more vulnerable to postmodern masochism, but, like the 60s global wave of love and peace, they also remain the land of choice—and origin—of the latest millennial hope, wokedom.

What do these chosen ones, these global progressives, envy? The US and Israel? Don't be ridiculous!

But then why are their judgments so harsh?

Does it matter that these harsh judgments just happen to resonate powerfully with the feelings of Caliphators whose [millennial] destiny to rule the world the US and Israel disrupt? Why would twenty-first-century progressives re-import and adopt a hatred that has marred their past, their societies, for millennia, and in the name of rejecting that cruel, scapegoating, domineering past? Do they not realize that in hating the two Satans, they give wings to those who envy them, who use critical theory to render their every success, every merit, into a dastardly assertion of privilege and supremacism?

Apparently not.

And improbably but relentlessly, Israel stands at the heart of the obsession.

---

12 Jonathan Kay, "Sociologist Nathalie Heinich on French Academics' Opposition to America's Race-Based Ideologies," *Quillette Podcast*, February 22, 2021.

As I contemplate what it would take for Western progressives to turn this around, to wean themselves of this apocalyptic poison, I am more convinced than ever of the self-destructive power of unacknowledged envy, resentment, and its progeny, *Schadenfreude* and moral sadism, the fatal attraction of what Freud, meditating on the madness of the first World War, completely unaware of what was to come, called *Thanatos*.[13]

What else could explain the persistent moral and emotional cruelty of progressives in judging Jews, for two decades now, as *Nazis*, precisely when the things they accused Israel of committing and desiring, were the very traits of those who target them, and whose cause these same progressives embraced? What hook-up of premodern sadism and postmodern masochism brings us the spectacle of both demopaths and their Jewish partners, defending Caliphator cogwar campaigns like BDS, and the right to hate speech about Jews.[14]

And instead of keeping in mind the Jews of the Holocaust, whose demise progressives think they cannot decently commemorate without also including the Palestinian claims to being victims of Israeli genocide,[15] "progressives" pour their sympathy onto Israel's Caliphator enemies—enemies of the West as well, proud heirs to the Nazis, fighters in the most enduring battlefield of World War II.[16] Somehow, starting in 2000, Palestinians became the most honored of victims. Their emotional well-being had to be protected from the discomfort of (racist) opposition; the deeds of their enemies had to arouse everyone's indignation. This lethal knot constitutes the keystone of inversion exegesis and Caliphator invasive cogwar.

Augustine, denizen of the Roman Empire, of one of the more accomplished prime divider societies ever, compared our existence as social creatures in the *saeculum* (time-space continuum), to olives in a press: we have no choice but to bear the pressure (the dominion of others), the only control we have is how sweet or bitter the oil we release.[17] Right now, however, the woke dream of a world free of any pressure (even of microaggressions), and certainly free of the olive press

---

13 *Beyond the Pleasure Principle*, 1920.
14 Cary Nelson, "Accommodating the New Antisemitism: a Critique of 'The Jerusalem Declaration,'" *Fathom*, April 2021; Stuart Winer, "Jewish Google employees call for tech giant to publicly support Palestinians," *Times of Israel*, May 19, 2021; Scholars of Jewish Studies and Israel Studies, "Statement Israel-Palestine," May 22, 2021.
15 *The Holocaust and the Nakba: A New Grammar of Trauma and History*, ed. Bashir Bashir and Amos Goldberg (New York: Columbia University Press, 2019).
16 Melanie Phillips, "The last, overlooked but still active front of World War Two." Overlooked by those who hope "Nie Wieder," nurtured by others.
17 See discussion in Peter Brown, *Augustine of Hippo* (Los Angeles: University of California Press, 1967), 291–92.

which they apparently hope to eliminate through cancelation; and they nourish themselves on an imaginary (proleptic) apocalyptic transubstantiation that seems sweet in the mouth but will be very bitter in the stomach.

How hard, emotionally, would it be for postmodern non-Jews to stop thinking of Israel as the villain in their morality tale because it did not live up to standards their own societies have failed to achieve? How hard for liberal Jews in the diaspora and in Israel to stop feeding this folly? What would it take to even entertain the idea that Israel's democracy is the remarkable product of intense, crushing pressures that normally produce paranoid reigns of terror (France, Russia, Germany), a demotic society struggling from birth to survive and even thrive under exterminationist threat?[18] Can you not even grant that as a hypothetical? And then can you review 2000, as the moment that pressure spiked yet another time, with a suicide-terror Jihad meant to drive the Jews from the land (like the Crusaders). And if you can, can you then consider that that pressure from near enemies was redoubled by the moral sadism of her would/should-be allies, the Western progressives?

And yet, Israel has thrived *especially* since 2000.[19] How outrageous.

If Israel, surrounded by nations locked in a generation of sectarian (millennial) and tribal warfare, the Arab-Muslim version of the (hopefully only) "Thirty-Years War" of religio-political madness, survives those wars, if her flag still flies when their neighbors finally cease to kill each other, it will be a day of rejoicing in human history, including in the very region where she still stands upright.

But for whom will progressives have rooted?

Would they toss Israel off as the right-wing piece of crap that "the whole world"—mainstream opinion media, Palestinian spokespeople speaking English to eager journalists, postcolonial academics, "Human Rights" NGOs, the woke, the BLM and BDS movements, actors and fashion models and Muslim congresswomen—tells us it is. After all, the whole world knows!

What mix of the malevolent envy that prefers to be one-eyed king among the blind and the cowardice that submits preemptively, could produce this widespread progressive support for the Caliphator agenda? And what will it take to break those mind-forged manacles?

---

18 For the reaction to Hesh Kestin's novel, *The Siege of Tel Aviv*, see 433.

19 Demographics: Ofir Haivri, "Israel's Demographic Miracle," *Mosaic*, May 7, 2018; music (the mainstreaming of Mizrahi music: "Pop(ulation) Music," *Us among the Israelis*, March 17, 2021; Technological: Wei Tien Sng, "What makes Israel the tech capital of the world?" *CAPX*, 5 January 2016; Cuisine: Dina Kraft, "Lemony, savory fusion: Israel's brash food revolution," *Christian Science Monitor*, March 20, 2020.

Overcoming Supersessionism

If I were a Muslim or Christian or an existentially free, atheist, progressive, for example, what would it mean to renounce an invidious, supersessionist spiritual identity in which "our way" has so surpassed everything that came before, that we cannot but feel contempt for those who cling to the superstitions of the past? "We are the good news, and don't let anyone else tell you they have some too."

Whence this enduring and hostile response to Jewish claims of chosenness (which Jews rarely make)? Somehow the Japanese believing they are the gift of the gods, or the Chinese, or the English, or the French, or the Germans, or even the Muslims, no matter how many millions those beliefs have killed and may yet kill, doesn't seem to arouse nearly the same resentment. Could it indicate an unacknowledged belief (in some, a secret fear) that the Jews may be a chosen people?

We get the foes we deserve. Christians and Post-Christians, heirs to the *Nie Weider* of Nazi genocide and the (relatively but distinctly) peaceful world order that has governed the last two generations of astounding progress (unprecedented in history, unbearably insufficient in the now), are today faced with a formidable foe, representing everything they, as progressives, had renounced—cruel dominion, violence, hatred, religious fanaticism. And yet, they can only defeat that enemy by renouncing the supersessionism they still apparently cherish, despite their post-Holocaust protestations.

Supersessionism—inherently zero-sum, always a force for supremacism—is Western civilization's kryptonite. It preserves the "Pattern," the need for nasty stories about the Jews that makes it legitimate to hurt them.[20] Its disorientations and inversions necessarily skew moral judgments so that moral compasses, as soon as they approach Jewish terrain, begin to spin wildly. That Pattern makes sure that Jews can never live long as secure members of a civic polity; it limits both the capacities of the Jews and of those polities. In this stunted world, Jewish freedom to speak must be constrained by the always-already permission to strike them, to make them hurt.

It takes an emotionally mature and self-disciplined person to tolerate and respect others' freedom; and correspondingly, the more "enlightened" a person, the more he or she can allow others, *even Jews*, the autonomy to speak their own minds. Rousseau put his finger on the problem, when he identified the role of

---

20 "The Pattern" is David Deutsch's term and concept (unpublished). For an exposition, see Landes, "License to Harm: Deutsch's Pattern and the Longue Durée of Antisemitism," *ISGAP*, December 23, 2019.

an immature Christian gratification derived from bullying the Jews, in thereby making their thinking inaccessible.

> There is a pleasure in refuting people who do not dare speak. . . . [When] conversing with [us] . . . the unfortunate [Jews] feel themselves at our mercy. The tyranny practiced against them makes them fearful. I will never believe that I have rightly heard the Jews' reasoning as long as they do not have a free state, schools, universities where they might speak and argue without risk."[21]

Such progressive confidence and curiosity inspired the best of Europe's revolutionary project. At its most lucid, it rejected the ways of previous sovereigns and faiths, who had "shamefully deprived the Jews of their sovereignty."[22] What was honorable to supersessionist monotheists—the humiliation of the Jews— became shameful in the new dispensation of free people.

Or so one might have hoped. And so one did hope after the Holocaust. But somehow, post-modernists, rather than relativizing their phallo-logo-centric grand narrative by exploring the discourse of the people they most copied and most despised, preferred to virtue-signal their concern for all mankind, and open up the gates to narratives that continued to despise the Jews. In that sense, these thinkers resemble the Christians of the late Roman empire who preferred Germanic warriors to pagan philosophers as interlocutors.

Peter in *Family Guy* teaches Brian about stupid people: "'What, you think you're better than me?!' That's what stupid people say, Brian, 'What, you think you're better than me?!'" Do Westerners really want their civilization to go down over such a stupid move? Do progressives really want to say "I'd sooner feed my enemies' (apocalyptic) hatreds of me, than consider Israel an admirable, progressive, democratic, state"? Does it matter to those who consider themselves progressive, that those who sneer at the very suggestion that Israel has a moral army, consistently cheer on as "freedom fighters," the most immoral fighters on the planet? Does it matter to them that these same *proud* baby killers they support, accuse the *IDF* of killing children? "Can the whole world (i.e., 'us good guys') be wrong and Israel be right?"

"Unthinkable!" says the supersessionist.

---

21 Rousseau, *Emile*, 6:4, 618–20.
22 See above 242f.

What would it mean if Muslims stopped projecting onto the Jews the hatreds they harbor, that instead of amplifying every grievance against Israel, they attend to the massive assault on Arab dignity that happens throughout the Muslim-ruled region, and certainly where Palestinian "leaders" rule over Palestinians? Would it be possible for Muslims, instead of thinking that Israel deliberately humiliated them, to consider the possibility that Israel defended itself from a Muslim triumphalism that still dominates discourse and still dominates Muslim life, a triumphalism whose indignities they themselves know only too well? Would it be possible to see the arrival of the Jews as the ticket to a government "of the people, by the people, and for the people," perhaps even to create an Arab form more accomplished, more demotic than Western democracy? How many choices might then open up to a people whom progressives, in their cowardice and humanitarian racism, assume has no choice but to embrace a death cult of suicidal mass-murder of Jews?

What would it mean for global progressives, for the woke, for those who believe that Black lives really do matter, to recognize that Zionist Jews in both the diaspora and in their Israeli polity are allies, members of the progressive left? And that the groups they currently embrace as allies, the Palestinian leadership, "non-violent" Caliphators, are triumphalist demopaths who feed their worse instincts? Could those who vociferously denounce the extreme right-wing, racist, Israeli political party, Religious Zionism, pause long enough to realize that *every* candidate running in Palestinian elections is more racist, more fascist, more "right-wing" than anything Israeli politics can produce (including Kahane)? What would that do to one's understanding of history, especially the history of progressive values? And what would it do to our understanding of the so-called clash of civilizations, were infidels, progressives especially, to side with the Jews in response to the shame-honor rantings of triumphalist Muslim anti-Zionists?

Reread the Intifada

In order to become a sound mind at the present time, it helps—I would argue, it is essential—to understand what happened at the millennial turn of 2000, hence, to reread the Y2K Intifada. Any Western thinker, and certainly any Jewish thinker, who wants to get a grip on both progressive values and reliable information (they're linked[23]) in this age of folly needs to reread the Intifada,

---

23 Steven Shapin, *A Social History of Truth: Civility and Science in Seventeenth-Century England* (Chicago: University of Chicago, 1994).

this time not as an uprising of the oppressed against the oppressor, but as the opening salvo of the Caliphator assault on Western democracies in the twenty-first century, a war that Western thought-leaders aggressively blamed on the democracy. This time try to screen out the envy and supersessionism that makes the inverted and now dominant reading so attractive. Read Nidra Poller's *cris de cœur* about the French media's coverage of the first five years of the aughts;[24] read Daniel Gordis, Yossi Klein Halevy, Einat Wilf, Phyllis Chesler, Elder of Ziyon, Shani Mor, Adi Schwartz, Fiamma Nirenstein, Noa Tishby.

Only then can one understand the modern legacy media's most spectacular failure, a major and sustained (still-ongoing) episode of fake news, and a spectacular example of own-goal war journalism. Journalists and pundits were bullied and seduced into running Caliphator war propaganda as reliable news, and anyone who thought that was a bad idea, remained silent or got pushed out. Malice? Cowardice? Cluelessness? Among the journalists? Among their audiences?

In any and every case, such failures did happen, and they have now metastasized among many of our information providers and over many subjects.[25] It represents a generation-wide failure of twenty-first-century information professionals to live up to the most basic standards of their modern profession so vital to democracy.

Once one can free oneself from the thrall of the Israeli Dajjal, once one can spot and renounce those impulses to invidious comparison, once one can doubt those who promote the dualistic narrative of sinful oppressors and innocent victims, once one can get some cognitive distancing from those "as-a-Jews" who embrace that self-destructive narrative ... only then can one begin to think clearly about many things, including how important terms have been degraded in their meaning, misapplied and then weaponized against progressive projects—racism, xenophobia, Nazis, genocide, ethnic cleansing, Islamophobia, hate speech, incitement, supremacism, even antisemitism.[26] Currently, we are trying to *think* with a deeply corrupted vocabulary, with terms that have been emptied of substance, even as they remain emotionally charged.

In this larger sense, then, the conflict in the Land between River and Sea constitutes a clash of civilizational styles, a clash of religiosities: demotic vs

---

24 Poller, *The Troubled Dawn of the 21st Century*; *Al-Durah, Long-Range Ballistic Myth*.

25 Friedman, "You're all Israel Now"; Ungar-Sargon, *Bad News*; Kern and Herzberg, *False Knowledge as Power*.

26 On the effort to label denunciations of antisemitism antisemitic, see the JVP panel featuring Peter Beinart, Marc Lamont Hill and Rashida Tlaib: Ben Sales, "At US Jewish anti-Zionist group antisemitism panel, speakers say they love Jews," *Times of Israel*, December 16, 2020.

triumphalist, egalitarian vs domineering. And in this, "progressives" have gotten it exactly wrong. What distinguishes Zionism from European imperialism, is precisely this demotic element: the imperialists first conquered then settled; the Jews came as purchasers and workers of the land and only developed an army out of necessity. Of course, like all morality tales, it's not black and white. Palestinians have demotic currents, Jews triumphalist ones. The problem with outside progressives trying to "help," is that they have consistently chosen to obsess over what they see as Israel's triumphalism and to betray demotic Palestinians by glorifying their triumphalists.

Those who insist on seeing the Israelis as imperial invaders and the Palestinians as innocent victims regurgitate Caliphator "narratives" for Dhimmi. The inverted Replacement narrative of Israeli Goliath-Palestinian victim is a Rorschach and litmus test of infidel weakness before the temptations of an active, zero-sum Apocalypse proffered by negative-sum Caliphators. And the infidels adopt this narrative *despite* their own ultimate, catastrophic fate in its grand finale.[27] Why are progressives, so quick to point out the irony of Zionists accepting Christian help despite their ultimate role in that apocalyptic scenario, incapable of realizing that when they denounce Israel, they attack those fighting off a jihad that also targets them?

Every time you hear accusations of Israeli apartheid, ethnic cleansing, genocide—know who stands before you. When Jews tell you that the problem is Israeli "apartheid racism" (and *not* the Palestinian *Judenrein* racism of "pigs and monkeys," they think they advertise their progressive bona fides—even as they support the Caliphators and attack real progressives.[28] Such "thought leaders" can marshal their facts, stretch and inflate their terminology beyond recognition, justify their righteous indignation with internet-amplified voices of outrage, but in the end they justify their compliance, their submission to the very forces they pretend to oppose.[29] The lack of empathy for the "cruel" Jews and the extravagant sympathy for the "poor" Palestinians, the extensive

---

27 Progressives regularly criticize Zionists for accepting evangelical support given the ultimate fate of the Zionists in the Pre-millennial dispensationalist, temporarily pro-Zionist apocalyptic narrative (conversion or death), without noting the same issue in their alliance with Caliphators.

28 "A Regime of Jewish Supremacy from the Jordan River to the Mediterranean Sea: This Is Apartheid," *B'Tselem*, January 12, 2021; "A Threshold Crossed: Israeli Authorities and the Crimes of Apartheid and Persecution," *Human Rights Watch*, 2021. For a reply, exposing the systemic intellectual dishonesty, Kern and Herzberg, *False Knowledge as Power*.

29 Rikki Hollander, "Jewish Voice for Peace: What the Media is Concealing," *CAMERA*, December 21, 2021.

skepticism about Israeli "propaganda" and facile credulity about Palestinian lethal narratives—all are dead giveaways for preemptive dhimmitude.

Of all the cognitive ways out of the current dysfunctions, therefore, a reconsideration of the conflict between free Jews (standing upright) and triumphalist Muslims (standing over) in the Land between the River and the Sea offers perhaps the easiest and most extensive way to clear out the own-goal rubbish that clutters the doors of our perception. This doesn't mean one has to become a Zionist, or, heaven forbid, that one *never* criticizes Israel, her policies, her people. Like all human entities, Israel needs criticism and, overall, effectively responds to it better than most. But it does mean you make that criticism even vaguely fair, and that you grow a backbone about challenging and criticizing Palestinian leaders and other triumphalist Muslims.[30]

The progressive commitment to the Palestinian cause illustrates better than any example, a case of progressive, moral narcissism, deftly manipulated by people who know how to exploit their enemy's moral envy. No people have been more damaged by the virtue-signaling of Western supporters than the Palestinian people, created by ruthless Arab triumphalists in the service of their need for vengeance at honor lost, suffering two long generations at the hands of leaders whom Western progressives lionize. Mahmoud Darwish knew that the world's interest in his people lay with their enemy: "Do you know why we Palestinians are famous?" Darwish says to Israeli-French Jewish actress Sarah Adler, "Because you are our enemy. The interest in us stems from the interest in the Jewish issue."[31] Human rights advocate Bassem Eid knows well how fortunate the Palestinian people are to have such an enemy, and how unfortunate to have such friends.[32]

Is there a brotherhood of envy? Of supersessionist *ressentiment*?

One of the saddest aspects of the current moral and cognitive disorientation in the West today, is that, when all is said and done, by any impartial standards, even with severe handicapping, Israel constitutes one of the most progressive, creative, and caring nations on the planet, both for her own citizens, and for the rest of the world. They have maintained high standards in war when they had to play by zero-sum rules; and in peace Israelis have pursued demotic virtues in powerful and creative ways. Indeed, their army is the most egalitarian since the times of tribes and has behaved better on the battlefield than *any* army in history.

---

30 Benjamin Kerstein, "When can we talk about Muslim Antisemitism?" *Algemeiner*, January 24, 2022.

31 Interview with Israeli journalist in Jean Luc Godard's *Notre Musique*, 39:42–45.

32 Bassem Eid, http://www.bassemeid.com/.

For all their many faults, and under very adverse conditions, Israelis rank high on the scale for empathic, risk-taking, open, life-affirming, freedom-loving, self-restraint. They have much to offer the global community.[33]

The supreme irony about Zionism is that not only has Israel not "done unto the Palestinians" as antisemites have done unto Jews for 2000 years, but that Israel has, under extremely trying circumstances, extensively avoided doing so, and in some cases, like the help proffered at the Syrian border during a decade of merciless inter-Arab, inter-Muslim warfare, she has done the exact opposite.[34] Israel's relations with her minorities, especially her Muslim minority, have rare and substantial successes in demotic, merit-based fairness, especially visible in the hospitals (where the very Palestinian "leaders" who call for boycotting Israel go for treatment[35]).

That these relations are also deeply troubled should not come as a surprise given the problems Muslim minorities cause in Europe. (Imagine a European democracy with a 20% Muslim population.) That relations are as good as they are, that so many Israeli Arabs identify as Israeli and not Palestinian, may constitute a unicum in the history of deeply hostile populations living side by side.[36] And for all Israel's pains to avoid it, the very people who want to treat the Jews the way the Nazis did, successfully accuse Israel of being like Nazis to an eager and morally sadistic "progressive" audience.

What would it take for the journalists to admit their intimidation, their failings, and at least stop, if not correct the record of past failures? Can they find the courage to admit fault and start telling the truth about those who are ready to attack journalists who don't give the "right" coverage? (They could start just by running accurate but critical articles about the Palestinians and see what happens.) Can they convey to their audiences back home what the Palestinians say in Arabic, among themselves? Can they challenge Palestinian spokespeople about the hatred that fills their public sphere, at least articulating that "Israel says" that that hatred might be the first and enduring cause of Palestinian war on the very neighbor they have designated an enemy with their lethal narratives? Can they stop themselves from screaming "Islamophobia" every time they see

---

33 Avi Jorisch, *Thou Shalt Innovate: How Israeli Ingenuity Repairs the World* (Jerusalem: Geffen, 2018).

34 Isabel Kirschner, "Across Forbidden Border Doctors in Israel Quietly Tend to Syria's Wounded," *New York Times*, August 6, 2013.

35 Elior Levy, "Erekat's hospitalization in Israel exposes PA's hypocrisy," *Ynet*, October 18, 2020.

36 David Rosenberg, "Poll: Israelis proud of their country - including Israeli Arabs," *Israel National News*, April 30, 2017; Bassem Eid, "Israel – the best place to be an Arab," *Times of Israel*, December 22, 2021.

something that they fear will offend (their construct of) Muslims, no matter how accurate the offensive description might be?

And can journalists renounce the tasty thrill of telling and hearing stories about Jews behaving badly, of acting out their moral indignation on screen?[37] ("Gotcha again, you little bastards.") Just how important is it to the correspondents working the Land between River and Sea, who enjoy the pleasures of Israeli tolerance, to hold their hosts in contempt even as they do that host's (and their) enemies' bidding ... systematically?

What would it take for human rights advocates to admit that in their obsessive need to highlight Israeli sins, they cannot report fairly on Palestinian sins (or those of others in the region), in part out of intimidation, but in significant part because to do so would dwarf the Israeli sins, which they are, like Janine de Giovanni, so determined to highlight? Can they figure out what's more important: restoring information accuracy? or keeping Israel on the global hot-seat? Will key players deem that degrading the International Criminal Court is worth the attack on Israel, worth weaponizing international law?[38]

What would it take for pundits, revolutionaries, messianic lovers of humanity, to see the Israelis as allies, part of the oldest, still-existing, demotic, millennial culture on the planet, rather than treat them as odious, counter-revolutionary, fossil-zombies, still going when they should have disappeared long ago, a supersessionist stake through their heart? What would it take for them to consider that Israel may be the only modern egalitarian movement to take power in a sea of prime-divider hostility and not melt down in paranoia and totalitarian terror?

What will it take for political scientists and other readers of global trends to realize that autonomous sovereign Jews living in Dar al Islam—Israel—constitutes the single best test of genuine Muslim moderation and maturity, a sign and guarantee that Muslims are ready to live in peace and fairness with their infidel neighbors, and hence partake peacefully in a positive-sum, multicultural, multireligious, free, egalitarian, and responsibly abundant, global community? (A reverse-linkage, as it were.)

---

37 Of the many examples, one of the more disappointing: John Oliver, https://twitter.com/alexbkane/status/1394258752388337664?s=21. For a recent case study of focusing on a "wave" of settler violence and ignoring far more frequent and lethal Palestinian terror attacks, see Yisrael Medad, "There is Jewish Violence and there is Arab Violence," *Mediaset*, December 26, 2021. For the persistence of Y2Kmind among American policy-makers, see the case of Secretary of State Anthony Blinken: Lahav Harkov, "To the Biden Administration, Israel Is Always at Fault—Even While 11 Israelis Are Murdered," *Newsweek*, April 4, 2022.

38 Anne Herzberg, "Should Israel Cooperate with the ICC?" *NGO Monitor*, March 25, 2021.

What would it take for the infidels of the world who do not want to either convert or become dhimmi to say to the Muslims: "Learn to live with Israel, an enemy who treats you better than you treat each other. Because if you can't live with them in a neighborly way, you surely will have trouble living with the rest of the world's infidels." (Not to mention the trouble you'll have living with your fellow Muslims, who kill each other with far greater frequency than any infidel army, certainly than the "genocidal" Israelis.) Apparently, it will take a great deal, since even as some Arabs make that shift, Westerners show the convert's zeal for defamation.[39]

What would it take for Jewish moral perfectionists to get off their high hobby horses, to unlock their moral mandibles, to confront their moral pride and its elective affinity for virtue signaling . . . to renounce their sincere passion for masochistic omnipotence? Can they admit, even momentarily, that they are asking the impossible of their own people in order to avoid asking a bare minimum of her self-declared enemies?

It all seems so clear, so obvious. And yet, every access to these approaches is blocked by a series of claims, all of which depend for their success on the degree to which the one assessing the evidence and claims from the various actors is driven by a deep-seated need to see the Jews *as a negative force*. It's not just deranged ones like Jostein Gaarder and Jose Saramago ranting about the Jews' "chosenness" complex, who are victims of supersessionist grudges. Milder versions circulate widely. Can Western infidels reduce their toxic footprint of resentment?[40] Why are they, why are feminists and gays, allied with a movement with the most toxic masculine, supersessionist footprint on the planet?

The problem is all the good people who somehow can't imagine the "Orientalist" observation that Israel, whether led by a left-wing (Labor) or "right-wing" (Likud) government, represents a major force for progressive values by both historical and modern world standards, far to the progressive left of *anything* in current or past Arab political culture—and certainly, when compared with the brutal, regressive, frustrated supremacism of the allegedly "left-wing" Palestinian cause.

For Y2KMind it's unthinkable. BBC *HardTalk* interviewer Stephen Sackur snorts when Israeli Ambassador Danny Danon speaks of Israel as a democracy, but he carefully avoids asking his Palestinian interviewee questions that might

---

39 Dan Diker, "Has the Palestinian 'apartheid assault' backfired?" *Jerusalem Post*, January 24, 2022.

40 Academia needs a robust field of research on *Supersessionism*, perhaps as a subtopic of *Resentment Studies*.

put him in danger with his authoritarian regime.[41] A French journalist (partly Jewish) responded to my suggestion in 2003, that Israel might be the canary in the mineshaft for the West, *"Non, mais sûrement vous plaisantez."* (Surely, you're kidding.) No, I was not, not then, and not twenty years later.

One aspect of the problem for Y2KMind is the "slippery slope." Where would these acknowledgements stop. If one concedes, even only theoretically, that Israel might just (still) occupy the progressive moral high ground in this clash ... what insights (and concessions) ensue? Not only in comparison with the Palestinians or their Muslim-majority neighbors, but also in comparison with the West, whose egalitarian revolutionary movements, when they achieved power and felt themselves under attack, turned paranoid and totalitarian and ended up, within a few short years of taking power, devouring their own people in orgies of megadeath. Israel's current record of seventy-plus years of *not* melting down under murderous pressure is, historically speaking, an unprecedented accomplishment, without a near-second, certainly in modern times. And yet to Y2Kmind, what is this mediocre if not failing democracy?

Maybe that's not good enough for moral perfectionists (a Jewish specialty), but is it worthy of the widespread vilification and disgust currently showered on Israel? Might that inversion of moral judgment be born, less of a sober and fair deliberation, than of a resentment rooted in a disgust with the postmodern, progressive self, that cannot bear its image in the mirror of Zionism, and therefore projects its worst onto those awful "Zionists"?[42]

Mirror, Mirror ... ?

Which brings us back to the basic human dilemma: how does one judge? And the basic question of the twenty-first century so far: why do progressives judge Israel so harshly, why are they so susceptible to moral panics about Islamophobia and so callous to complaints about spreading antisemitism? Especially when that compulsive "moral" judgment disorients them so profoundly. Why is it judge-punitive towards Israel and judge-penitent towards the Caliphators?

Leveling the playing field?

Submitting?

At the approach of the third millennium CE, a Christian theologian, Darrell Fasching, wrote a short pamphlet: *The Coming of the Millennium: Good News for the Whole Human Race.* In it he argued against a supersessionism that views the "other" as someone to convert to the true religion. The stranger, he insisted, was

---

41 "Sackur, Bully and Wimp."

42 Gad Saad identifies the mechanism as existential guilt alleviated by saving the world, "The Narcissism and Grandiosity of Celebrities," *Psychology Today*, June 15, 2009.

not the opponent of Christianity (to be converted to the One Salvific Faith), but its salvation. "Others" gives real Christians the opportunity to live up to their principles by the way they treat them. In an ironic way, postmodern progressives have tried to be his kind of Christian. But neither they, nor Fasching, saw those Caliphators with their aggressive supersessionism coming round the mountain. And still they tried.

Jonathan Sacks wrote in the early aughts about the "dignity of difference," advocating a demotic approach of *mutual* respect for one another's difference as the key to dealing with the clash of civilizations. Why is it that, beginning in 2000, Westerners showed such elaborate respect for Muslim difference and so little for Jewish? Does Jewish belief in the right to self-determination somehow offend these progressives as badly as it does triumphalist Muslims? Do they not see themselves joining the triumphalist Muslim bullies in their need to degrade free Jews?

If you want a moral answer, begin with a basic orientation in this Land between River and Sea: Israel is (by far) the most "left," "progressive," "liberal," political and cultural force in the Middle East, whereas its enemies, the triumphalist Muslims, who try to present as secular and "progressive," embody the forces of an authoritarian, misogynist, right. Anyone who tells you different—including all those good Jews and Israelis who think that if someone says Israel is right, then they must be "right wing"—is selling you something that is not good for your health.[43]

Rereading the early years of 2000, then, can start a process of moral and cognitive reorientation, an alignment with a progressive credo that is more reality-based and therefore, in the long run, more effective. Among the revision's major benefits: it inoculates against the kinds of paranoid conspiracy theories that drove the Nazis mad with genocidal rage in the early twentieth century, a combination that drives triumphalist Muslims similarly mad today. If the Caliphator invasion of the West is through the soft underbelly of Jew-hatred, then the best defense comes from renouncing those millennia-long resentments that, as of late, show alarming vigor. Before setting off into the thicket of the third decade of the new millennium, a rereading of the intifada can inoculate you against the subsequent multiplication of demopathic discourse in this young and unhappy century.

---

43 In good self-critical style, Yehuda Bauer lists Israel "clearly" in the in-between camp along with India, Morocco, Tunisia, and other "waverers" between true "liberal" democracies and "illiberal" authoritarian regimes: "Liberals, Illiberals and Waverers: The Struggle of Our Time," *Israel Journal of Foreign Affairs*, 15:2 (2021): 245–56.

It would, after all, be a most shameful end to this centuries-long demotic episode of "constitutional democracies," were the Western world, even as it proclaimed its rejection of Jew-hatred for all to hear and embraced the highest levels of egalitarian generosity, to be trapped by a far weaker and nastier foe, who used their unconscious, their denied, Jew-hatred against them, in order to overrun them.

Like Balaam, infuriated by his donkey's reluctance before a danger he cannot see, ready to *kill* the insolent creature for *humiliating* him before the king's messengers, can the Woke hear the rebuke: "when have Jews ever been guilty of the things you and your ancestors have repeatedly accused them?" Will the Woke continue to beat Jews with the stick of Islamophobia, driving them into the talons of the very people whose hatred they will not acknowledge?

FIGURE 29. "Bilaam Redux," by Ellen Horowitz.

Or can those who now judge Israel so harshly, admit to the gratuitous hatreds behind those judgments? Can they open their eyes to the sword hanging over their heads? Or will gratuitous hatred destroy yet another democratic temple?

In his essay, which contributed to the title of this book, Ahad Ha-am invokes the blood libel as a kind of consolation. It is possible for the whole world to be wrong and some dissident (in this case the inveterate dissenters, the Jews) to be right. In so doing he affirmed the message of every legend from Balaam's donkey to the Emperor's New Clothes: "the whole world" can get it wrong. And the consequences can be lethal.

* * *

> And the two Sources of Life in Eternity Hunting and War,
> Are become the Sources of dark & bitter Death & of corroding Hell:
> The open heart is shut up in integuments of frozen silence
> That the spear that lights it forth may shatter the ribs & bosom
> A pretence of Art, to destroy Art: a pretence of Liberty
> To destroy Liberty. a pretence of Religion to destroy Religion...
> For the Soldier who fights for Truth, calls his enemy his brother:
> They fight & contend for life, & not for eternal death!
> But here the Soldier strikes, & a dead corse falls at his feet
> —William Blake, *Jerusalem*, pl. 38, ll. 31–43

We are in the fight of our lives, a fight for the civilization that made Blake's vision of a world of mental strife rather than carnal slaughter possible. Our fight is with those who think truth and honor come from dead corpses and dominion. We are people of many communities and identities, including Muslims. The enemy is triumphalism and its twin progeny, supremacism and supersessionism. Not: *One God, one Faith, one Rule*, but: *No King but God; and God is too great for any one Faith.*

In the end, it comes down to choosing life over death. Progressives who partner with Caliphators in the mistaken idea that they too are fellow "anti-imperialists," have embraced a pretense of progressivism to destroy progressives, a pretense of life, to destroy life. They, like their partners, embrace the deaths demanded by zero- and negative-sum, honor-driven, combat, wherein might's right returns in bloody triumph. They are passively; their "allies" are actively, suicidally murderous.

To embrace life is to accept vulnerability but also to ask for reciprocity. Cooperation rewards fidelity, honesty, fair-mindedness, among all participants; and this restrains envy, malice and betrayal. Engaging openly and without defenses with people who despise such principles and long for dominion, even as you turn against those who, for almost four millennia, have been dedicated to those principles, defines folly and epitomizes astounding stupidity.

In embracing life, the rewards correspond to the demands. Choose life, however difficult.

Glossary for Understanding Caliphator Cogwar in the Twenty-First Century

---

a Durah: icon of hatred, launched by French-Israeli journalist; First blood libel of twenty-first century.

al wa'la w'al ba'ra doctrine of "us-them" solidarity. Love good (Muslim); hate bad (infidel).

al Yahud: Arabic for "the Jew"; the sons of pigs and monkeys; translated "Israeli" by the BBC.

Analogic Dyslexia: wildly inappropriate analogies. See *Moral Equivalence, *Holocaust inversion

  Chronological Dyslexia: Cart before horse. *Cult of Occupation

Apocalypticism: urgent sense that time for the Final Events (**apocalyptic scenario**) is *now*.

Apocalyptic Millennialism: the perfect, redemptive era will occur *on earth, in the flesh*, now.

  Active cataclysmic apocalyptic: believer is an *agent* of apocalyptic destruction.

  Passive cataclysmic apocalyptic: outside force (comet, God) does destruction.

  Transformative apocalyptic: *voluntary* rapid transformation into new world See: *GPL, *Caliphator Da'wa

Apocalyptic narrative: cosmic/global narrative about the Endtimes scenario: how we Good will soon defeat Evil.

Aristocracy: powerful clans above *prime divider, control of most of wealth, lands, technology.

Augean Stables: accumulated bad journalistic practices, engrained errors, that stink up the world with fake news. My blog: http://www.theaugeanstables.com/.

Blacks, Indigenes, People of Color (BIPoCs): nonwhites, victims of intersectional oppression.

Caliphate: rule of Islam, sharia law of realm; tolerated infidels become *dhimmi

Caliphators: believe that in *this* generation, *now*, the *Global Caliphate will actualize.

> **Global Caliphate:** world submitted to sharia, triumphalist millennial goal of Islam.
>
> See: *Muslim Triumphalism, *Global Jihad, *Da'wa, *Apocalyptic Millennialism

Caliphators' three choices: conversion to Islam, death, or submission (*dhimmitude).

Civil society: principled substitution of fairness for violence in dispute settlement.

> **Civil Polity:** contract society dedicated to equality before the law, positive-sum relations.

Cognitive Egocentrism: projecting one's own mentality onto others.

> **Liberal CE (LCE):** projecting good faith/positive-sum motives onto everyone.
>
> **Domineering CE (DCE):** everyone else also wants to dominate. *Rule or be ruled.*
>
> **Moebius strip of CE:** interaction of *LCE and *DCE to the strong advantage of DCE.
>
> See: *Dupes of Demopaths, *MPMS&PMM, *Da'wa Cogwar

Cognitive Warfare (Cogwar): convince a more powerful foe not to use his force.

> **Cogwarrior:** one dedicated to winning the cognitive war.
>
> **Invasive Cogwar:** convince a more powerful foe not to resist invasion;
> See *Da'wa, *Preemptive Dhimmitude.

Commoners: the large majority below the prime divider*; stigmatized manual laborers.

Conflict, The: conflict of Jews and Arabs over the land from Jordan River to Mediterranean Sea.

Arab-Israeli conflict: major framing in West from 1948 to 1990s. (Israel David)

Israel-Palestine conflict: major reframing from Oslo. (Palestinians David)

(Triumphalist) Muslim-(Autonomous) Jewish conflict: the core religious dimension

Cult of "Occupation": attributing world-salvific results to ending Israeli Occupation.

Preoccupation: Obsessing over Israeli Occupation to exclusion of relevant issues.

Dar al Islam/Dar al Harb: world divided into realm of submission/ realm of sword/war.

See: *Triumphalist Islam, *Global Jihad.

Harbi: "destined to the sword"—infidels in Dar al Harb, target of jihad.

Cf. *Dhimmi. See: *Jihad, *Caliphators' Three Choices.

Da'wa: "summons," call to infidels to convert and to Muslims to intensify their devotion.

Da'i Caliphators: those waging *Global Jihad nonviolently, invasive *Cogwarriors.

Demopaths: enemies of human rights invoking them in order to destroy them. See:* Da'i Caliphators, *Cogwar, DCE.

Dupes of demopaths: people with no ear for hypocrisy who accept demopathic argument as sincere. See *HRNGOs, *Halo Effect, *LCE, *Y2KMind

Demotic Values: egalitarian, dignity of manual labor, positive-sum relations, modesty, self-criticism

Demotic Polity: civil polity based on principle of equality before the law, voluntarism.

Demotic Religiosity: the practice of embodying these values in one's life and relations.

Dignity-guilt culture (DGC): dignity from mutual respect/*self-Criticism, not dominion.

See: *Demotic Values, *Demotic/Civil Polity. Cf: *Shame-Honor culture.

Dhimmi: "blameworthy," infidels who submit to a degraded status for "protection."

Dhimmi Leaders: charged with suppressing in their communities, speech that offends Muslims. See: *Islamophobia, *Dupes of Demopaths, *LCE, *Preemptive Dhimmitude, Y2KMind.

Dominating Imperative: *Rule or be ruled.*

Paranoid Imperative: *Exterminate or be exterminated.*

Ego: individual awareness of the web of shame-honor, limbic demands in which one lives.

Empathic Imperative: *judge others as favorably as possible.*

Exegesis: deriving implied meaning from a text; interpretation.

Eisogesis: aggressively reading outside meaning *into* a given text; imposing meaning.

Free peasant: premodern oxymoron, independent tiller of soil in demotic polity, Israelite.

Global Jihad: Holy war to bring about the *Global Caliphate; millennial movement.

Global Millennium: globalized world from 2000–3000 CE (barring civilization collapse).

Global Civil Society: community of different, peaceable cultures, living well and responsibly.

Global Progressive Left (GPL): claimants to lead humanity's evolution to *global civil society by pursuit of progressive values of empathy and embrace of the "other."

Globalization: current unprecedented global interdependence and intercommunication.

Caliphator Globalization: Western technology is a vehicle of Muslim dominion, *Praeparatio Caliphatae.*

Halo Effect: *HRNGOs default good reputation *because* of their mission's moral stature (Steinberg).

Holocaust Inversion: Accusing Israel of committing a Nazi-like genocide on Palestinians.

See: *Y2K Replacement Narrative.

Honor Killings: see *Shame Murders.

Hopium: addiction to hope in decision-making. See *LCE, *GPL, *MOS.

Human-Rights NGOs (HRNGOs): NGOs dedicated to global human rights, many run according to *Y2Kmind. See: *Halo Effect, *Moral Equivalence.

Human Rights Complex (HRC): ignore victimizers of color; obsess about "white" ones (Jacobs).

Humanitarian Racism: make no moral demands on those designated as "victims" (Gerstenfeld).

See: *BIPoCs, *Victim Studies, *Intersectionality, *HRNGOs

Icons of Hatred: visual embodiments of lethal narratives, powerful war propaganda.

Information Professionals: charged by public to inform accurately on relevant issues.

Intifada: "shaking off," as in, the mighty beast of Islam shakes off pesky Zionist entity.

Al Aqsa Intifada/Oslo Jihad: first campaign of twenty-first-century *Global Jihad.

See: *Y2KMind, *Oslo Logic

Intersectionality: solidarity among designated "victims" of systemic oppression.

See: *PoMo-PoCo, *BIPoCs, *Victim Studies, *Humanitarian Racism

Islamophobia: irrational fear or hatred of Islam or Muslims, often used as cogwar weapon to stop criticism of Islam, prohibition of right of free speech.

See: *Preemptive Dhimmitude. Cf: *Livingstone Formulation

Islamophobia-phobia: fear of accusations of *Islamophobia. See: *Onēidophobia

Jews against themselves (JATs): *Oikophobic Jews who side with the enemies of their people.

Jihad: literally, "to struggle" (German, *kampfen*); holy war to spread Islam; alt.: inner struggle.

Kuffār: infidels, nonbelievers, those who "cover" the truth of Islam. See: *Harbi*

Lethal Narratives: false atrocity-charges hard to disprove, poisoned war propaganda.

Lethal Journalism: passing on war propaganda (lethal narratives about the enemy) as news.

Own-goal war journalism: reporting one's enemy's war propaganda as news.

Patriotic war journalism: reporting own side's war propaganda as news.

Limbic Captivity: powerful pull that atavistic emotions (fight-flight, dominance-submission) exert on shame-honor concerns. See: *Ego, *Onēidophobia, *Triumphalism.

Livingston Formulation: charges of antisemitism are only efforts to stop *any* criticism of Israel.

Mainstream News Media (MSNM), Legacy Media: major print, video, news outlets/agencies.

See: *Augean Stables, *Own-Goal Lethal Journalism Cf: *Journalistic Accuracy.

Liberal Legacy Media: Flagships: the *New York Times,* the *Washington Post,* the BBC, *Le Monde, Ha-Aretz,* CNN. In the twenty-first century, many of these became increasingly radical/"progressive."

Man of Honor: alpha male who commands deference to his honor.

Marriage of Pre-Modern Sadism and Postmodern Masochism (MPMS&PMM):

*BIPoC: "You are evil genociders." White Westerner: "So sorry! How can we atone?"

Masochistic Omnipotence Syndrome (MOS): Everything is our fault; if we change, we can fix any/everything. See: *Prophetic Rhetoric, *Demotic Millennialism, *JATs, *MPMS&PMM.

Megalothymia: desire to be recognized as superior, craving for glory (Fukuyama).

See: *Triumphalism, *Supersessionism, *Shame-Honor.

Millennialism: belief in a coming earthly age of justice, abundance, peace and harmonious love.

Progressive vs Restorative: inaugurate brave *new* world versus restore lost golden age.

Demotic versus Triumphalist: bottom-up, egalitarian versus top-down, hierarchical.

Moderate Muslim: exchanges *Triumphalism for religious freedom; *Y2Kcompliant.

Moral Relativism/Equivalence: equating very different levels of moral behavior; double standards. See: *Dupes and Demopaths, *HRNGOs, *Humanitarian Racism.

Moral Sadism: making vicious accusations in order to inflict moral pain. Israel = Nazis.

See: *Moral *Schadenfreude;* *Lethal Journalism.

Mujaheedin: Muslim warriors engaged in military *Jihad.

Nakba: 1948 "catastrophe" in Arab-Muslim world when Israel won its war of independence.

Naksa: "setback" of Six-Day war, 1967, *Nakba 2.0.

Naksba: mentality of Arabs who scapegoat Israel while abusing own people. See: *Prime Divider, *Negative-Sum Games, *Strong Horse Politics; Cf: *Y2Kmind.

Narrative (The): Y2KMind's paradigm; standard for most twenty-first-century information professionals.

Neo-Islam: Islamic religiosities arising in diaspora in the West, especially in internet age.

Oikophobia: the repudiation of inheritance and home, "their side right or wrong."

Onēidophobia: dread of public disgrace, can paralyze, can galvanize to anger/ violence. See: *Limbic Captivity, *Shame-Honor Culture.

Oslo Intifada/Jihad: Jihad begun in 2000 by Palestinians for whom the Oslo Process was a Trojan Horse, first successful campaign of *Caliphator *Global Jihad in new millennium.

Oslo Logic: positive-sum logic of "Oslo peace process" (1993–2000): *Land for Peace.*

Palestinian Media Protocols Compliance (PMPC): measures journalists' adherence to demands made by Palestinian authorities about coverage of *The Conflict.

Pallywood: scenes of Israeli aggression and Palestinian victimhood, staged for legacy news media. See: *Lethal Journalism, *Augean Stables, *Da'ī Cogwar.

Paradigms: conceptual frameworks assigning primary roles to certain factors.
  Shame-Honor Jihad P (SHJP): Muslim triumphalist honor through global conquest.
  Politically Correct P (PCP1): underdogma, Palestinian/Muslim as poor little guy.
  Postcolonial P (PCP2): Whites worst imperialists; must atone. Israel is white squared.

Patriarch: successful alpha male in a *prime divider society.

Peace Journalism: emphasize the positive about foe, encourage own side to trust.

PoMo-PoCo: postmodern-postcolonial; combination weaponized against West. See *GPL, *Active Transformative/Cataclysmic apocalyptic, *MOS.

Public Secret: something "everyone [who counts] knows," but no one talks about in public.

Praeparatio Caliphatae: Western globalization as preparation for the *Global Caliphate.

Preemptive Dhimmitude: quietly submitting to *Triumphalist Muslim demands in the hopes they will not feel the need for full conquest and formal subjection.

Prime Directive (*Star Trek:* "Don't interfere"). Twenty-first century: *Don't piss them off.* See: *Preemptive Dhimmitude.

Prime Divider: the divide between elite and commoners, empowering elites, stigmatizing labor.

Propaganda: mislead opinion to accept what better-informed people would reject.

Prophetic Rhetoric: harsh accusations meant to shame people into change: worse than Sodom!
  See: Moral Relativity, MOS, Self-criticism, MPMS&PMM, GPL.

Public sphere: arena for discussion of matters of public interest.
  See: *WMSNM, *Information Professionals.

Relativity of Time: "two minutes" depends on which side of the bathroom door you're on.

Religiosity: a style of living one's religious beliefs in the social world.
  Demotic Religiosity: egalitarian religious style of being in society: dignity-based.
  Triumphalist Religiosity: making superiority of believers manifest: honor-based.

Replacement Theology: monotheist claim to replace predecessors as "God's chosen." See: *Triumphalist Religiosity, *Zero-Sum, *Dhimmitude, *Supersessionism.
  Secular Replacement Theology (SRT): GPL values have replaced religion.
  Y2K Replacement Narrative: Israelis the new Nazis; Palestinians the new victim Jews.

Ressentimentalistes: people whose primary response to setbacks is blaming others and nursing *ressentiment* at failure (Nietzsche). See *Moral *Schadenfreude,* *Lethal Narratives.

Schadenfreude: The pleasure one takes in the suffering of another.
  Moral *Schadenfreude:* pleasure in a rival's moral debasement. See: *Supersessionism.

Self-criticism: ability to both introspect and to hear criticism from others. See: *MOS

Semiotic Arousal: readily seeing signs and meaningful patterns in texts/data/ events.

Semiotic Promiscuity: anything means anything, connect with abandon.
See: *Eisogesis, *Moral Equivalence, *Analogic Dyslexia.

Shame-Honor culture: the violent imperative to preserve/restore honor, avoid shame.
See: *Zero-Sum, *Prime Divider Society; Cf: *DGC, *Civil Society.

Shame Murders/Honor Killings: murder of family member (most often women), peer-driven *Oneidophobia.

Social Game theory: emotional aspects of zero-sum and positive-sum game-playing.

> **Zero-Sum:** win-lose; one only wins if other side loses: poke out one of my eyes. See: *Lethal Narratives, *Triumphalism, *Schadenfreude, *Prime-Divider, *Y2KMind.

> **Positive-Sum games:** win-win; voluntaristic, reciprocal; based on trust/ trustworthiness.

> **Negative-Sum games:** lose-lose; poke out both of my eyes to hurt my enemy.

Strong-Horse Politics: following the strongest, participating in their dominion; power politics. See: *Prime Divider Society, *SHJP, *Zero-Sum.

Supersessionism: claim to sit on top of (*supersedeo*) predecessor(s); *Replacement Theology.

***Takfir*:** declaring fellow Muslim an apostate, deserving of death; Caliphator technique versus Muslim moderates.

Terrorism: Targeting civilians to frighten the enemy into submission; the bloodier, the better.

Testosteronic: honor-driven virility.

> **Post-testosteronic:** guilt-integrity virility, self-control, intimacy.

Triumphalist religiosity: "Our God is True *because* we rule"; our dominion, proof.
See: *Replacement Theology, *Supersessionism, *Dominating Imperative

> **Muslim Triumphalism:** Destiny of Islam, One True Faith, to rule over mankind.
> See: *Global Jihad, *Caliphators, *Dhimmitude. I refer to them as Triumphalists with a T.

Two-State Solution (2SS): positive-sum resolution to Palestinian-Israeli conflict.
See: Oslo Logic, Y2Kmind.

Underdogma: dogmatic assertion of *humanitarian racism: *BIPoCs are innocent victims.

Useful Infidels: progressives who advance Caliphator goals.
See: *Preemptive Dhimmitude, Dupes of Demopaths.

Verbal Vegetarians: speech of conflict-averse Westerners avoiding confrontations.
See: *Preemptive Dhimmitude, *Dupes of Demopaths, *Y2Kmind.

Victimology: study of victims, impact of victim experience on behavior.
See: *Demopaths and their Dupes, *Humanitarian Racism, *MPS&PM.

Westsplaining: Westerners explaining Islam and Muslims to West in their own idiom. See: *Liberal Cognitive Egocentrism, *Demopath and their Dupes, *Y2KMind.

Y1K: Year 1000, period of intense demotic apocalyptic expectations in Western Europe.

Y2K: Year 2000, computer bug problem, birth of Y2KMind.

Y2KCompliant: capable of handling switch to 2000, digitally from '99s to '00s; culturally, to the *Civic Global Millennium.

Y2KMind: when Jihadi Caliphators attack a democracy, blame the democracy.
See: *LCE, *Westsplaining; Cf: *Kuffār, *Muslim Triumphalism, *Negative-sum.

Y2K Logic: Western infidels, especially Israelis, must take Muslims at their word. See: *LCE, *Demopaths and their Dupes, *Oslo Jihad, *PCP1.

Bibliography

(Items that appear more than once in the footnotes are included here)

Abrahamian, Ervand. "The US Media, Huntington, and 9–11." *Third World Quarterly* 24, no.3 (2003): 529–544.

Ahmed, Qanta. *In the Land of Invisible Women: A Female Doctor's Journey in the Saudi Kingdom.* Naperville, IL: Sourcebooks Inc., 2008.

Alexander, Edward. *Jews Against Themselves.* New Brunswick, NJ: Transaction Publishers, 2015.

Alexander, Edward, and Paul Bogdanor, eds. *The Jewish Divide over Israel: Accusers and Defenders.* New Brunswick: Transaction, 2008.

Anthony, Andrew. *The Fallout: How a Guilty Liberal Lost His Innocence.* London: Random House, 2007.

Appiah, Anthony Kwame. *The Honor Code: How Moral Revolutions Happen.* New York: W.W. Norton, 2010.

———. *Cosmopolitanism: Ethics in a World of Strangers.* New York: W.W. Norton, 2006.

Auerbach, Jerold. *Print to Fit: The New York Times, Zionism and Israel, 1896–2016.* Boston: Academic Studies Press, 2019.

Balint, Benjamin. "Future Imperfect: Tony Judt Blushes for the Jewish State," in *The Jewish Divide over Israel,* chapter 5.

Barkun, Michael. *A Culture of Conspiracy: Apocalyptic Visions in Contemporary America*. Los Angeles: University of California Press, 2003.

Barnett, David, and Efraim Karsh. "Azzam's Genocidal Threat." *Middle East Quarterly* 18, no. 4 (2011): 85–88.

Bat-Ye'or, *Islam and Dhimmitude: Where Civilizations Collide*. Philadelphia: Fairleigh Dickinson University Press, 2001.

———. *Eurabia: The Euro-Arab Axis*. Philadelphia, Fairleigh Dickinson University Press, 2005.

Baudrillard, Jean, and Marc Guillaume. *Radical Alterity*. Translated by Ames Hodges. Cambridge: MIT Press, 2008.

Bawer, Bruce. *Surrender: Appeasing Islam, Sacrificing Freedom*. New York: Doubleday, 2010.

Berman, Paul. *Liberalism and Terror*. New York: W.W. Norton, 2004.

———. *The Flight of the Intellectuals*. Brooklyn: Melville House, 2010.

Borradori, Giovanna. *Philosophy in a Time of Terror: Dialogues With Jurgen Habermas and Jacques Derrida*. Chicago: Chicago University Press, 2003.

Bowman, James. *Honor: A History*. New York: Encounter Books, 2006.

Brenner, Emmanuel. *Les territoires perdus de la République*. Paris : Mille et Une Nuits, 2002.

Brenner, Marie. "France's Scarlet Letter." *Vanity Fair*, April 4, 2012.

Brown, Brené. *Daring Greatly: How the Courage to Be Vulnerable Transforms the Way We Live, Love, Parent, and Lead*. New York: Penguin Publishing Group, 2015.

Bruck, Connie. "The Wounds of Peace." *The New Yorker*, October 14, 1996.

Bukay, David. "Islam's Hatred of the Non-Muslim." *Middle East Quarterly* 20, no. 3 (2013): 11–20.

Buruma, Ian. "How to Talk about Israel," *New York Times*, August 31, 2003.

Chafets, Zev. *Double Vision: How the Press Distorts America's View of the Middle East*. New York: Morrow, 1985.

Chagnon, Napoleon. *Noble Savages: My Life Among Two Dangerous Tribes—the Yanomamö and the Anthropologists*. New York: Simon & Schuster, 2014.

Chesler, Phyllis. *The New Antisemitism*. Jerusalem: Gefen Publishing House, 2003, 2015.

———. *The Death of Feminism*. London: Palgrave Macmillan, 2005.

———. *A Family Conspiracy: Honor Killings*. London: New English Review Press, 2018.

Chinlund, Christine. "Who should wear the 'terrorist' label?" *Boston Globe*, September 8, 2003.

Cockburn, Patrick. *The Age of Jihad: Islamic State and the Great War for the Middle East*. London: Verso Books, 2016.

Cohen, Hillel. *Army of Shadows: Palestinian Collaboration with Zionism, 1917–1948*. Los Angeles: University of California Press, 2008.

Cohen, Nick. *What's Left: How Liberals Lost their Way*. London: Harper Perennial, 2007.

———. "The BBC: Blaming the Jews for Attacks on Jews." *Spectator*, January 12, 2015

Cole, Juan. *Muhammad: Prophet of Peace Amid the Clash of Empires*. New York: Nation Books, 2018.

Cook, David. *Contemporary Muslim Apocalyptic Literature*. Syracuse: Syracuse University Press, 2005.

———*Understanding Jihad*. Los Angeles: University of California Press, 2005.

Coughlin, Stephen. *Catastrophic Failure: Blindfolding America in the Face of Jihad*. Washington, DC: Center for Security Policy Press, 2015.

Crone, Patricia. *God's Rule—Government and Islam: Six Centuries of Medieval Islamic Political Thought*. New York: Columbia University Press, 2004.

Derfner, Larry. "The Reluctant Boycotter: Why This Liberal Zionist Now Supports BDS." *Haaretz*, February 8, 2016.

Donner, Fred. *Muhammad and the Believers at the Origins of Islam*. Cambridge: Belknap Press, 2012.

Dor, Daniel. *Intifada Hits the Headlines: How the Israeli Press Misreported the Outbreak of the Second Palestinian Uprising*. Bloomington: University of Indiana Press, 2004.

Enderlin, Charles. *Shattered Dreams: The Failure of the Peace Process in the Middle East*, trans. Susan Fairfield. New York: Other Press, 2002.

———. *Un enfant est mort: Netzarim, 30 septembre 2000*. Paris: Don Quichotte éditions, 2010.

Fallaci, Oriana. "Sull'Antisemitismo (Io trovo vergognoso)," *Panorama*, April 12, 2002; English translation, "On Jew Hatred."

Filiu, Jean-Pierre. *Apocalypse in Islam*. Los Angeles: University of California Press, 2011.

Feoktistov, Ilya. *Terror in the Cradle of Liberty: How Boston became a Center for Islamic Extremism*. New York: Encounter, 2019.

Friedman, Matti. "An Insider's Guide to the Most Important Story on Earth." *Tablet*, August 25, 2014

———. "What the Media Gets Wrong About Israel." *Atlantic Monthly*, December 2014.

——— "The Ideological Roots of Media Bias against Israel." *Fathom*, Winter, 2015.

——— "You're All Israel Now." *Tablet*, July 27, 2020.

Friel, Howard and Richard Falk. *Israel-Palestine on Record: How the New York Times Misreports Conflict in the Middle East.* New York: Verso, 2007.

Fukuyama, Francis. *The End of History and the Last Man.* New York: Free Press, 1992.

Furnish, Timothy. *Holiest Wars: Islamic Mahdis, Their Jihads, and Osama bin Laden.* New York: Prager, 2005.

———. *Sects, Lies, and the Caliphate: Ten Years of Observations on Islam* (2016).

Games, Stephen. "Compromised Coverage: Can the BBC Really Report From Gaza?" *Haaretz*, July 24, 2014.

Geifman, Anna. *Death Orders: The Vanguard of Modern Terrorism in Revolutionary Russia.* Santa Barbara: Praeger, 2010.

Gerstenfeld, Manfred. *The War of a Million Cuts: The Struggle against the Delegitimization of Israel and the Jews, and the Growth of New Anti-Semitism.* Jerusalem: JCPA, 2015.

———."Beware the Humanitarian Racist." *Ynet*, January 23, 2010.

Giniewski, Paul. *La guerre des hommes bombes : Israel, 2000–2006.* Paris : Cheminements, 2006.

"Jews of France Tormented by 'Intifada of the Suburbs,'" *Nativ*, 5 (2004).

Green, Stuart. "Cognitive Warfare." MA Thesis, Joint Military Intelligence College, 2008, http://www.theaugeanstables.com/wp-content/uploads/2014/04/Green-Cognitive-Warfare.pdf.

Greenberg, Kenneth. *Honor and Slavery: Lies, Duels, Noses, Masks, Dressing as a Woman, Gifts, Strangers, Humanitarianism, Death, Slave Rebellions, the Proslavery Argument, Baseball, Hunting, and Gambling in the Old South.* Princeton: Princeton University Press, 1998.

Gross, Tom. "A Shitty Little Country: Prejudice & Abuse in Paris & London," *National Review*, January 10, 2002.

Gutmann, Stephanie. *The Other War: Israelis, Palestinians and the Struggle for Media Supremacy.* San Francisco: Encounter Books, 2005.

Harari, Noah Yuval. *Sapiens: A Brief History of Humankind.* New York: Harper, 2015.

—— *Homo Deus: A Brief History of Tomorrow.* New York: Harper, 2017.

Harel, Amos and Avi Issacharoff. *34 Days: Israel, Hizbollah, and the War in Lebanon.* New York: Palgrave, 2008.

——. *The Seventh War* [Hebrew]. Tel Aviv: Yediot Achronot Press, 2004.

Harrison, Bernard. *The Resurgence of Anti-Semitism: Jews, Israel, and Liberal Opinion.* New York: Rowman and Littlefield, 2006.

Hawali, Safar ibn abd al-Rahman. "The Day of Wrath – Is the Intifadha of Rajab only the beginning?" Azzam.com, September 11, 2001, https://english.religion.info/2002/04/01/document-the-day-of-wrath-is-the-intifadha-of-rajab-only-the-beginning/.

Henkin, Yagil. "Urban Warfare and the Lessons of Jenin," *Azure* (Summer 2003): 33–69.

Hicks, Stephen. *Explaining Postmodernism: Skepticism and Socialism from Rousseau to Foucault.* Phoenix: Scholargy Publishing, 2004.

Hill, Marc Lamont and Mitchell Plitnick. *Except for Palestine: The Limits of Progressive Politics* (New York: The New Press, 2021).

Hirsi Ali, Ayaan, *Prey: Immigration, Islam and the Erosion of Women's Rights.* New York: Harper, 2021.

Hoffer, Eric. *The True Believer: Thoughts on the Nature of Mass Movements.* New York, Harper, 1951.

Husain, Ed. *The Islamist: Why I Became an Islamic Fundamentalist, What I Saw Inside, and Why I Left.* London: Penguin, 2007.

Hussey, Andrew. "The French Intifada: How the Arab banlieues are fighting the French state," *Guardian,* February 23, 2014.

——. *The French Intifada: The Long War Between France and its Arabs.* London: Granta Publications, 2014.

Israeli, Raphael. *The Oslo Idea: The Euphoria of Failure.* New Brunswick: Transaction Publishers, 2012.

Jacobs, Charles. "Why Israel and not Sudan, is Singled Out," *Boston Globe,* October 5, 2002.

Johnson, Ian and John Carreyrou, "As Muslims Call Europe Home, Dangerous Isolation Takes Root: In France, 'Political Islam' Preaches Intolerance; Challenge to Secularism." *Wall Street Journal,* July 11, 2005.

Judt, Tony. *Past Imperfect: French Intellectuals, 1944–1956.* Los Angeles: University of California Press, 1994.

———. "Israel: The Alternative." *The New York Review of Books*, October, 2003.

Julius, Anthony. *Trials of the Diaspora: A History of Anti-Semitism in England.* Oxford: Oxford University Press, 2010.

Karsh, Ephraim. *Arafat's War: The Man and His Battle for Israeli Conquest.* New York: Grove Press, 2003.

———. *Islamic Imperialism: A History.* New Haven: Yale University Press, 2010.

Kepel, Gilles. *Terror in France: The Rise of Jihad in the West* (Princeton: Princeton University Press, 2017).

Kern, Joshua, and Anne Herzberg, eds. *False Knowledge as Power: Deconstructing Definitions of Apartheid that Delegitimise the Jewish State.* Jerusalem: NGOMonitor, December 2021.

Ibn Khaldoun. *The Muqaddimah: An Introduction to History.* Princeton: Bollingen Press, 1987.

Kimball, Roger. *Tenured Radicals: How Politics Has Corrupted Our Higher Education.* New York: Ivan R. Dee, 2008.

Kinsley, Michael. "Defining Terrorism," *Washington Post*, October 5, 2001.

Kressel, Neil. *"The Sons of Pigs and Apes": Muslim Antisemitism and the Conspiracy of Silence.* Washington, DC: Potomac Books, 2012.

Klausen, Jytte. *The Cartoons that Shook the World.* New Haven: Yale University Press, 2009.

———. *The Islamic Challenge: Politics and Religion in Western Europe.* New York: Oxford University Press, 2005.

Kobrin, Nancy Hartevelt. *The Banality of Suicide Terrorism.* Washington DC: Potomac Books, 2010.

Kushner, Tony, and Alisa Solomon. *Wrestling with Zion: Progressive Jewish-American Responses to the Israeli-Palestinian Conflict.* New York: Grove Press, 2003.

Lahat, Golan. *The Messianic Temptation: The Rise and Fall of the Israeli Left* [Hebrew]. Tel Aviv: Am Oved, 2004.

Landes, David. *The Wealth and Poverty of Nations: Why Some are so Rich and Some so Poor.* New York: W.W. Norton, 1999.

Landes, Richard "Lest the Millennium be Fulfilled: Apocalyptic Expectations and the Pattern of Western Chronography, 100–800 CE," in *The Use and Abuse of Eschatology in the Middle Ages,* edited by Werner Verbeke, Daniel Verhelst, and Andries Welkenhuysen, 137–211. Leuven: Leuven University Press, 1988.

———. *Relics, Apocalypse, and the Deceits of History: Ademar of Chabannes, 989–1034.* Cambridge, MA: Harvard University Press, 1995.

———. "On the Hidden Cost of Media Error," *Augean Stables,* November 15, 2005.

———. *Heaven on Earth: Varieties of the Millennial Experience.* New York: Oxford University Press, 2011.

———. "From Useful Idiot to Useful Infidel: Meditations on the Folly of 21st-Century 'Intellectuals.'" *Terrorism and Political Violence* 25, no. 4 (September 2013): 621–34.

———. "The Biggest Winner in the Lose-Lose 'Operation Protective Edge,'" *The American Interest,* September 4, 2014.

———. "The Wages of Moral Schadenfreude in the Press: Anti-Zionism and European Jihad," in *From Antisemitism to Anti-Zionism: The Past & Present of A Lethal Ideology,* edited by Eunice G. Pollack, 186–214. Brighton: Academic Studies Press, 2017.

———. "Oslo's Misreading of an Honor-Shame Culture." *Israel Journal of Foreign Affairs* 13 (2019).

———. "'Celebrating' Orientalism: Edward Said's Honor and Shame," *Middle East Quarterly* 24 (2017).

———. "Europe's Destructive Holocaust Shame." *Tablet Magazine,* September 5, 2017.

———. *Salem on the Thames: Moral Panic, Anti-Zionism, and the Triumph of Hate-Speech at Connecticut College.* Boston: Academic Studies Press, 2019.

———. "Orientalism as Caliphator Cognitive Warfare: Consequences of Edward Said's Defense of the Arab World." Essay. In *Handbook of Research on Contemporary Approaches to Orientalism in Media and Beyond,* edited by Işıl Tombul and Gülşah Sari, 33–52. Hershey: Information Science Reference, 2021.

———. "Primary Honour Codes in Tribal and Aristocratic Cultures," In *Honour and Shame in Western History,* edited by Jörg Wettlaufer, David Nash and Jan Frode Hatlen. New York: Routledge, 2023.

Landes, Richard, and Steven T. Katz, eds. *The Paranoid Apocalypse: A Hundred-Year Retrospective on the Protocols of the Elders of Zion.* New York: New York University Press, 2012.

Lasson, Kenneth. *Trembling in the Ivory Tower: Excesses in the Pursuit of Truth and Tenure.* (Baltimore: Bancroft Press, 2003).

Leuchter, Catherine. "Etats des lieux au 31 mai 2002: Qu'avons-nous appris des médias?" in *Le conflit israélo-palestinen: Les médias français sont-ils objectifs?* Paris: Observatoire du Monde Juif, 2002.

Levin, Kenneth. *The Oslo Syndrome: Delusions of a People under Siege.* Hanover: Smith and Kraus, 2005.

Lewis, Bernard. *What Went Wrong? The Clash between Islam and Modernity in the Middle East.* New York: Harper, 2006.

Lewis, Herbert. "The Influence of Edward Said and Orientalism on Anthropology, or: Can the Anthropologist Speak?" In *Postcolonial Theory and the Arab-Israel Conflict,* edited by Philip Salzman and Donna Divine, 97–109. London: Routledge, 2016.

Lewis, Neil. "From the Archives: The Times and the Jews." *Columbia Journalism Review,* January 2012.

McCarthy, Andrew. *Willful Blindness: A Memoir of the Jihad.* New York: Encounter Books, 2009.

McLoughlin, Peter. *Easy Meat: Inside Britain's Grooming Gang Scandal.* London: New English Review Press, 2016.

McGowan, William. *Gray Lady Down: What the Decline and Fall of the New York Times Means for America.* New York: Encounter Books, 2010.

Marantz, Andrew. *Antisocial: Online Extremists, Techno-Utopians, and the Hijacking of the American Conversation.* New York: Penguin Publishing Group, 2019.

Marcus, Itamar and Barbara Crook. "Aspiration not Desperation." *Jerusalem Post,* January 29, 2004.

Markovits, Andrei. *Uncouth Nation: Why Europe Dislikes America.* Princeton, NJ: Princeton University Press, 2007.

Marshall, Paul, and Nina Shea. *Silenced: How Apostasy and Blasphemy Codes Are Choking Freedom Worldwide.* New York: Oxford University Press, 2011.

Mearsheimer, John. "The Future of Palestine: Righteous Jews vs. New Afrikaners." *The Palestine Center.* April, 2010.

Moreh, Dror. dir. *The Gatekeepers.* 2012; Sony Pictures. Script: https://www.springfieldspringfield.co.uk/movie_script.php?movie=the-gatekeepers.

Muravchik, Joshua. *Covering the Intifada: How the Media Reported the Palestinian Uprising.* Washington: The Washington Institute for Near East policy, 2003.

Murawiec, Laurent. *The mind of jihad.* New York: Cambridge University Press, 2008.

Nawaz, Maajid. *Radical: My Journey out of Islamist Extremism*. Guilford: Lyons Press, 2013.

Nelson, Cary. *Israel Denial: Anti-Zionism, Anti-Semitism, and the Faculty Campaign against the Jewish State*. Bloomington: Indiana University Press, 2019.

North, Richard. "The Corruption of the Media." *EU Referendum*. August 15, 2006.

O'Leary, Stephen, and Glen McGhee. *War in Heaven/Heaven on Earth: Theories of the Apocalyptic*. London: Routledge, 2014.

Oliver, Anne Marie, and Paul F. Steinberg. *The Road to Martyrs' Square: A Journey into the World of the Suicide Bomber*. Oxford: Oxford University Press, 2006.

Orme, William. "A Parallel Mideast Battle: Is It News or Incitement?" *New York Times*, October 24, 2000.

Phillips, Melanie. *Londonistan: how Britain is creating a terror state within*. London: Gibson Square, 2006.

Philo, Greg, and Mike Berry. *More Bad News from Israel*. London: Pluto Press, 2004.

Pollack, Joel. "Enderlin: Arafat faked 9/11 blood donation," *Guide to the Perplexed*, 17 January 2008.

Poller, Nidra. *Troubled Dawn of the 21st Century*. Paris: Authorship International, 2017.

———. *Al Dura: Long Range Ballistic Myth: From the Staged "Death" of a Palestinian Youth to the Real Threat of an Iranian Bomb*. Paris: Authorship International, 2014.

Prell, Michael. *Underdogma: How America's Enemies Use Our Love for the Underdog to Trash American Power*. Dallas: BenBella Books, 2011.

Pryce-Jones, David. *The Closed Circle: An Interpretation of the Arabs*. Chicago: Ivan R. Dee, 2009.

Ravid, Matan. "Prejudice and Demonization in the Swedish Middle East Debate during the 2006 Lebanon War." *Jewish Political Studies*, May 26, 2009.

Rifkin, Jeremy. *The Empathic Civilization: The Race to Global Consciousness in a World in Crisis*. New York: Penguin Publishing Group, 2009.

Reynolds, Paul. "A Clash of Rights and Responsibilities." BBC News. BBC, February 6, 2006.

Roger, Philippe. *L'ennemi américain: généalogie de l'antiaméricanisme français*. Paris: Seuil, 2002.

Rosenfeld, Alvin H. *"Progressive" Jewish Thought and the New Anti-Semitism.* New York: American Jewish Committee, 2006.

Roskies, Jennifer. "Oslo's Betrayal." Tablet Magazine, September 13, 2018.

Saad, Gad. *The Parasitic Mind.* Washington: Regnery Publishing, 2020.

Sacks, Jonathan. *Dignity of Difference: How to Avoid the Clash of Civilizations.* London: Bloomsbury, 2003.

Sagan, Eli. *The Honey and the Hemlock: Democracy and Paranoia in Ancient Athens and Modern America.* New York: Basic Books, 1991.

Said, Edward. *Orientalism.* London: Pantheon Books, 1978.

———. *The Question of Palestine.* New York: Random House, 1980.

———. *Covering Islam.* New York: Vintage, 1982.

Salzman, Philip Carl. *Culture and Conflict in the Middle East.* New York: Humanity Books, 2008.

Sapolsky, Robert. *Behave: The Biology of Humans at Our Best and Worst.* New York: Penguin Press, 2017.

Schoeck, Helmut. *Envy: A Theory of Social Behavior.* Indianapolis: Liberty Fund, 1987.

Seager, Mark. "I'll have nightmares for the rest of my life." *The Daily Telegraph,* October 15, 2000. http://rotter.net/israel/mark.htm.

Seliktar, Ofira. *Doomed to Failure? The Politics and Intelligence of the Oslo Peace Process.* Santa Barbara: ABC/CLIO, 2009.

Shepherd, Robin. *A State Beyond the Pale: Europe's Problem with Israel.* London: Orion, 2009.

Sher, Gilead. *The Israeli-Palestinian Peace Negotiations, 1999–2001 Within Reach.* London: Routledge, 2006.

Shuman, Ellis. "CNN Chief Accuses Israel of Terror," *Guardian,* June 18, 2002.

Spoerl, Joseph. "Parallels between Nazi and Islamist Anti-Semitism." *Jewish Political Studies Review* 31, no. 1/2 (2020): 210–44.

Steinberg, Gerald. "The Role of NGOs in the Palestinian Political War against Israel." Jerusalem Center for Public Affairs, October 11, 2018.

———. "Postcolonial Theory and the Ideology of Peace Studies." Essay. In *Postcolonial Theory and the Arab-Israel Conflict,* edited by Philip Salzman and Donna Divine, 109–20. London: Routledge, 2016.

Stetkevych, Suzanne Pinckney. *The Mute Immortals Speak: Pre-Islamic Poetry and Poetics of Ritual.* Ithaca, NY: Cornell University Press, 1993.

Taguieff, Pierre-André. *La nouvelle judéophobie.* Paris: Mille et Une Nuits, 2002.

———. *La nouvelle propagande antijuive: Du symbole Al-Dura aux rumeurs de Gaza.* Paris: Presses universitaires de France, 2010.

Tax, Meredith. *Double Bind: The Muslim Right, the Anglo-American Left, and Universal Human Rights* New York: Center for Secular Space, 2012.

Tenenbom, Tuvia. *Catch the Jew.* Jerusalem: Gefen, 2015.

Thorne, Ashley. "Staged Emergencies: How Colleges React to Bias Incidents." NAS, 2014.

Trofimov, Yaroslav. *The Siege of Mecca: The 1979 Uprising at Islam's Holiest Shrine.* New York: Anchor Books, 2007.

Ungar-Sargon, Batya. *Bad News: How the Woke Media is Undermining Democracy.* New York: Encounter, 2021.

Wikan, Unni. *Generous Betrayal: Politics of Culture in the New Europe.* Chicago: The University of Chicago Press, 2002.

Wistrich, Robert. *A Lethal Obsession: Anti-Semitism from Antiquity to Global Jihad.* New York: Random House, 2010.

Yemini, Ben-Dror. *Industry of Lies: Media, Academia, and the Israeli-Arab Conflict.* United States: Institute for the Study of Global Antisemitism and Policy, 2017.

Yerushalmi, Yosef Hayim. *Freud's Moses: Judaism Terminable and Interminable.* New Haven: Yale University Press, 1991.

Zangen, David. "Seven Lies About Jenin: David Zangen views the film *Jenin, Jenin* and is horrified." *Ma'ariv*, November 8, 2002.

Zelizer, Barbie, David Park and David Gudelunas. "How Bias Shapes the News: Challenging the New York Times' Status as a Newspaper of Record on the Middle East." *Journalism: Theory, Practice, and Criticism*, 3:3 (December 2002): 283–307.

Index of Names

Index of Subjects

CPSIA information can be obtained
at www.ICGtesting.com
Printed in the USA
JSHW011750190223
37708JS00001B/1